289.4
Sw3m

MISCELLANEOUS
THEOLOGICAL WORKS
OF
EMANUEL SWEDENBORG

MISCELLANEOUS
THEOLOGICAL
WORKS

OF

EMANUEL SWEDENBORG

THE NEW JERUSALEM AND ITS HEAVENLY DOCTRINE
BRIEF EXPOSITION
THE INTERCOURSE BETWEEN THE SOUL AND THE BODY
THE WHITE HORSE MENTIONED IN THE APOCALYPSE, CHAPTER XIX
APPENDIX TO THE TREATISE ON THE WHITE HORSE
THE EARTHS IN THE UNIVERSE
THE LAST JUDGMENT
CONTINUATION CONCERNING THE LAST JUDGMENT

TRANSLATION BY
JOHN WHITEHEAD

Standard Edition

SWEDENBORG FOUNDATION
INCORPORATED
NEW YORK

Established in 1850

First published in Latin, London, 1758-1769
First English translation published in U.S.A., 1857
16th Printing, 1976
ISBN 0-87785-070-4 (Student)
0-87785-071-2 (Trade)

Library of Congress Catalog Card Number 76-46143

Manufactured in the United States of America

CRITICAL NOTES OF THE REVISER.

Page	Line		Page	Line	
91	31	Swedenborg has "*tertio,*" *third*, the Greek is *second*, see *Mark* xiv. 30, 72. In *A. C.* 10134 Swedenborg has "*bis,*" *twice.*	236	18	The original Latin has "*anno* 318," *in the year* 318. There were 318 bishops in attendance; the Council met in the year 325.
93	16	In the original edition the following words were omitted by the printer, which Swedenborg afterward in a letter supplied to the publisher, "*et præcipue consistit in eo, quod homo ponat omnem cultum Divinum in sancto cum est in templis;*" *and especially consists in this, that man places all Divine worship in sanctity when he is in temples.*	422	31	The original Latin has "*immaterialium,*" *immaterial*; but in number 107, referring to this passage, it gives "*materialium,*" *material*, which is also found in *A. C.* 7253.
			484	15	The original Latin has "*infra,*" *below;* some translators think this is a misprint for "*intra,*" *within*; but *A. C.* n. 10516 has "*infra,*" in which the same account occurs.
131	18	In the original Latin "*non*" occurs twice in the sentence.	546	13	The original Latin has "*tertio,*" *thrice.* In *A. C.* 10134 we read "*bis,*" *twice*. See note above, page 91.
194	21	The original Latin has "*inductis*" for "*induitio.*"			

For other corrections see the Critical Notes of the Latin edition of the American Swedenborg Printing and Publishing Society, with the corrections of the editor, the Rev. Samuel H. Worcester. The above omissions and errors are evidently made by the printer, but as the original manuscript was not preserved, the errors are noted for the information of the reader.

GENERAL INDEX.

	Pages.
THE NEW JERUSALEM AND ITS HEAVENLY DOCTRINE........	3–205
A BRIEF EXPOSITION OF THE DOCTRINE OF THE NEW CHURCH.	207–313
THE INTERCOURSE BETWEEN THE SOUL AND THE BODY.......	315–353
THE WHITE HORSE MENTIONED IN THE APOCALYPSE, CHAP. XIX.	355–384
APPENDIX TO THE TREATISE ON THE WHITE HORSE..........	385–393
THE EARTHS IN THE UNIVERSE.............................	395–504
THE LAST JUDGMENT.....................................	505–588
CONTINUATION CONCERNING THE LAST JUDGMENT.............	589–634

☞ The figures in brackets at top of pages refer to the *section* numbers on each treatise.

The New Jerusalem

AND ITS

Heavenly Doctrine

The New Jerusalem

AND ITS

Heavenly Doctrine

FROM

WHAT HAS BEEN HEARD FROM HEAVEN

TO WHICH IS PREFIXED

SOMETHING CONCERNING THE NEW HEAVEN AND THE NEW EARTH

FROM THE LATIN OF
EMANUEL SWEDENBORG
SERVANT OF THE LORD JESUS CHRIST

BEING A TRANSLATION OF HIS WORK ENTITLED

"DE NOVA HIEROSOLYMA et ejus Doctrina Cœlesti: ex auditis e Cœlo. Quibus præmittitur aliquid de Novo Cœlo et Nova Terra." Londini, 1758.

MATTHEW vi. 33

*Seek ye first the Kingdom of GOD, and all things shall be
added unto you*

CONTENTS.

	Sections.
THE NEW HEAVEN AND NEW EARTH, AND WHAT IS MEANT BY THE NEW JERUSALEM	1–7
INTRODUCTION TO THE DOCTRINE	8–10
GOOD AND TRUTH	11–27
THE WILL AND THE UNDERSTANDING	28–35
THE INTERNAL AND EXTERNAL MAN	36–53
LOVE IN GENERAL	54–64
THE LOVES OF SELF AND THE WORLD	65–83
LOVE TOWARDS THE NEIGHBOR, OR CHARITY	84–107
FAITH	108–122
PIETY	123–129
CONSCIENCE	130–140
LIBERTY	141–149
MERIT	150–158
REPENTANCE AND THE REMISSION OF SINS	159–172
REGENERATION	173–186
TEMPTATION	187–201
BAPTISM	202–209
THE HOLY SUPPER	210–222
THE RESURRECTION	223–229
HEAVEN AND HELL	230–240
THE CHURCH	241–248
THE SACRED SCRIPTURE, OR THE WORD	249–266
PROVIDENCE	267–279
THE LORD	280–310
ECCLESIASTICAL AND CIVIL GOVERNMENT	311–325

THE NEW JERUSALEM

AND ITS

HEAVENLY DOCTRINE.

THE NEW HEAVEN AND THE NEW EARTH, AND WHAT IS MEANT BY THE NEW JERUSALEM.

1. It is written in the *Apocalypse*:—

I saw a New Heaven and a New Earth; for the first heaven and the first earth were passed away. And I saw the holy city, New Jerusalem, coming down from God out of heaven, prepared as a bride before her husband. The city had a wall, great and high, which had twelve gates, and at the gates twelve angels, and names written thereon, which are the names of the twelve tribes of Israel. And the wall of the city had twelve foundations, in which were the names of the twelve apostles of the Lamb. The city itself lieth four-square, and the length is as great as the breadth. And he measured the city with the reed, twelve thousand stadia; the length and the breadth and the height of it were equal. And he measured the wall thereof, a hundred forty-four cubits, the measure of a man, which is, of an angel. And the wall of it was of jasper; and the city itself was pure gold, like unto pure glass; and the foundations of the wall of the city were of every precious stone. The twelve gates were twelve pearls. And the street of the city was pure gold, as it were pellucid glass. The glory of God did lighten it, and the lamp of it was the Lamb. The nations which were saved shall walk in the light of it; and the kings of the earth shall bring their glory and honor into it. (xxi. 1, 2, 12–24.)

The man who reads these things, understands them only according to the sense of the letter; namely, that the visible heaven and earth will perish, and a new heaven will exist, and that the holy city Jerusalem, answering to the measures above described, will descend upon the new earth; but the angels understand these things altogether differently; namely, what man understands naturally, they understand spiritually; and as the angels understand, so they signify; and this is the internal or spiritual sense of the Word. In the internal or spiritual sense, "a New Heaven and a New Earth" means a New Church, both in the heavens and on the earth, which will be more particularly spoken of hereafter. "The city Jerusalem coming down from God out of heaven" signifies its heavenly doctrine; "the length," "the breadth," and "the height," which are equal, signify all the goods and truths of that doctrine in the aggregate. By "the wall" of it is meant the truths which protect it; "the measure of the wall," which is "a hundred forty-four cubits, which is the measure of a man, that is, of an angel," signifies all those protecting truths in the aggregate, and their quality. "The twelve gates" of pearl mean introductory truths; "the twelve angels at the gates" signify the same. "The foundations of the wall" which are "of every precious stone," mean the knowledges on which that doctrine is founded. "The twelve tribes of Israel," and "the twelve apostles," mean all things of the church in general and in particular. The city and its streets being of "gold like unto pure glass," signifies the good of love from which the doctrine and its truths are pellucid. "The nations" who are saved, and "the kings of the earth" who bring glory and honor into it, mean all of the church who are in goods and truths. "God" and "the Lamb" mean the Lord as to the Divine itself and the Divine Human. Such is the spiritual sense of the Word, to which the natural sense, which is that of the letter, serves as a basis; but still these two senses, the spiritual and the natural, form a one by correspondences. It is not the design of the present work to show that there is such a spiritual meaning in the afore-mentioned passages, but the proof of it may be seen in the *Arcana Cœlestia*, in the following places: In the Word by "land" (earth) the church is signified, particularly when it is applied to the land of Canaan (n. 662, 1066, 1067, 1262, 1413, 1607, 2928, 3355, 4447, 4535, 5577, 8011, 9325, 9643). Because by "land" in the spiritual sense is meant the nation dwelling therein, and its worship (n. 1262), "the people of the land" signify those who are of the spiritual church (n. 2928). "A New Heaven and a New Earth" signify something new in the heavens and on earth, as to goods and truths, thus as to those things that relate to the church in each (n. 1733, 1850, 2117, 2118, 3355, 4535, 10,373). What is meant by "the first heaven and the first earth" which passed away, may be seen in the work on *The Last Judgment and Babylon Destroyed*, from beginning to end, but particularly (n. 65 to 72).

"Jerusalem" signifies the church as to doctrine (n. 402, 3654, 9166). "Cities" signify doctrines which are of the church and religion (n. 402, 2449, 2712, 2943, 3216, 4492, 4493). "The wall of a city" signifies the truth of doctrine defending (n. 6419). "The gates of a city" signify truths introducing to doctrine, and through doctrine to the church (n. 2943, 4477, 4492, 4493). "The twelve tribes of Israel" represented, and thence signified, all the truths and goods of the church in general and in particular, thus all things of faith and love (n. 3858, 3926, 4060, 6335). The same is signified by "the Lord's twelve apostles" (n. 2129, 3272, 3354, 3488, 3858, 6397). When it is said of the apostles, that "they shall sit upon twelve thrones, and judge the twelve tribes of Israel," it signifies that all are to be judged according to the goods and truths of the church, thus by the Lord from whom they are (n. 2129, 6397). "Twelve" signifies all things in the aggregate (n. 577, 2089, 2129, 2130, 3272, 3858, 3913). Also "a hundred forty-four" signifies the same because that number is the product of twelve multiplied by twelve (n. 7973); "twelve thousand" has also the same signification (n. 7973). All numbers in the Word signify things (n. 482, 487, 647, 648, 755, 813, 1963, 1988, 2075, 2252, 3252, 4264, 6175, 9488, 9659, 10,217, 10,253). Numbers multiplied into each other have the same signification as the simple numbers from which they arise by multiplication (n. 5291, 5335, 5708, 7973). "Measure" signifies the quality of a thing as to truth and good (n. 3104, 9603, 10,262). "The foundations of a wall" signify the knowledges of truth on which doctrinals are founded (n. 9643). "Quadrangular" or "square" signifies what is perfect (n. 9717, 9861). "Length" signifies good and its extension, and "breadth" truth and its extension (n. 1613, 9487). "Precious stones" signify truths from good (n. 114, 9863, 9865). What "the precious stones" in the Urim and Thummim signify, both in general and in particular (n. 3862, 9864, 9866, 9891, 9895, 9905). What the "jasper" of which the wall was built signifies (n. 9872). "The street of the city" signifies the truth of doctrine from good

(n. 2336). "Gold" signifies the good of love (n. 113, 1551, 1552, 5658, 6914, 6917, 9510, 9874, 9881). "Glory" signifies the Divine truth, such as it is in heaven, and the intelligence and wisdom thence (n. 4809, 5068, 5922, 8267, 8427, 9429, 10,574). "Nations" signify those in the church who are in good, and, in the abstract sense, the good of the church (n. 1059, 1159, 1258, 1261, 1285, 1416, 1849, 4574, 7830, 9255, 9256). "Kings" signify those in the church who are in truths, and thence abstractly the truth of the church (n. 1672, 2015, 2069, 4575, 5044). The rites at the coronation of kings, involve such things as are of the Divine truth, but the knowledge of these things is at this day lost (n. 4581, 4966).

2. Before the New Jerusalem and its doctrine are treated of, something shall be said of the New Heaven and the New Earth. What is meant by "the first heaven and the first earth," which passed away, is shown in the small work on *The Last Judgment and Babylon Destroyed*. Immediately after that event, that is, after the Last Judgment was completed, a New Heaven was created or formed by the Lord. This heaven was formed of all those who, from the coming of the Lord to the present time, had lived the life of faith and charity, since these alone were forms of heaven. For the form of heaven, according to which all consociations and communications therein are effected, is the form of the Divine truth from the Divine good proceeding from the Lord; and this form man as to his spirit acquires by a life according to the Divine truth. That the form of heaven is thence may be seen in the work on *Heaven and Hell* (n. 200–212), and that all the angels are forms of heaven (n. 51–58, and 73–77). From these things it may be known, who they are of whom the New Heaven consists; and thereby what its quality is, namely, that it is altogether unanimous. For he who lives the life of faith and charity, loves another as himself, and by love conjoins him to himself, and thus reciprocally and mutually; for in the spiritual world, love is conjunction. Wherefore, when all act thus, then from many, yea from innumerable individuals consociated according to the form of heaven, unanimity exists, and they become as one; for then nothing separates and divides, but everything conjoins and unites.

3. Since this heaven was formed of all those who had been such from the coming of the Lord until the present time, it follows that it is composed both of Christians and of Gentiles; but chiefly of all infants from the whole world, who have died since the Lord's coming; for all these were received by the Lord, and educated in heaven, and instructed by the angels, and reserved, that they, together with the others, might constitute the New Heaven; whence it may be concluded how great that heaven is. That all who die in infancy are educated in heaven, and become angels, may be seen in the work on *Heaven and Hell* (n. 329–345). And that heaven is formed of Gentiles as well as of Christians (n. 318–328).

4. Moreover, with respect to this New Heaven, it is to be known, that it is distinct from the ancient heavens which were formed before the coming of the Lord; but still they together with this are so arranged that they form one heaven. The reason why this New Heaven is distinct from the ancient heavens, is because in the ancient churches there was no other doctrine than the doctrine of love and charity; and then they did not know of any doctrine of faith separated from love and charity. Hence also it is that the ancient heavens constitute higher expanses, while the New Heaven constitutes an expanse beneath them; for the heavens are expanses one above another. In the highest expanse those dwell who are called celestial angels, many of whom were of the Most Ancient Church; they who are there are called celestial angels from celestial love, which is love to the Lord. In the expanse beneath them are those who are called spiritual angels, most of whom were of the Ancient Church; they are called spiritual angels from spiritual love, which is charity towards the neighbor. Below these are the angels who are in the good of faith; these are they who have lived the life of faith. To live the life of faith, is to live according to the doctrine of their church; and to live is to will and to do. All these heavens, however, form a one, by mediate and immediate influx from the Lord. But a more full idea of these heavens may be obtained from what is said of them in the work on *Heaven and Hell*, and particularly in the article which treats of the Two Kingdoms into which the heavens in general are distinguished (n. 20–28);

and in the article concerning the Three Heavens (n. 29–40); concerning mediate and immediate influx, in the extracts from the *Arcana Cœlestia*, after (n. 603); and concerning the Most Ancient and Ancient Churches in the small work on *The Last Judgment and Babylon Destroyed* (n. 46).

5. These things are concerning the New Heaven; something shall now be said concerning "the New Earth." By "the New Earth" is meant the New Church on the earth; for when a former church ceases to exist, then a new one is established by the Lord. For it is provided by the Lord that there should always be a church on earth, since by means of the church there is a conjunction of the Lord with the human race, and of heaven with the world; for there the Lord is known, and there are the Divine truths by which man is conjoined to Him. That a New Church is at this time being established, may be seen in the small work on *The Last Judgment* (n. 74). The reason why a New Church is signified by "the New Earth" arises from the spiritual sense of the Word; for in that sense, by the "earth" no particular country is meant, but the nation dwelling there, and its Divine worship; this, in the spiritual sense, being what answers to earth in the natural sense. Moreover, by "earth" in the Word, when there is no name of any particular country affixed to the term, is signified the land of Canaan; and in the land of Canaan a church had existed from the most ancient times; in consequence of which, all the places therein, and in the adjacent countries, with the mountains and rivers, which are mentioned in the Word, became representative and significative of the things which are the internals of the church, and which are called its spiritual things. Hence it is, as was said, that "earth" in the Word, because it means the land of Canaan, signifies the church; in like manner here by "the New Earth"; from this comes the custom in the church to speak of the heavenly Canaan, by which is meant heaven.

That "the land of Canaan," in the spiritual sense of the Word, signifies the church, is shown in the *Arcana Cœlestia*, in various places, of which the following are here adduced:—

The Most Ancient Church, which was before the flood, and the Ancient Church, which was after the flood, were in the land of Canaan (n. 567, 3686, 4447, 4454, 4516, 4517, 5136,

6516, 9325). Then all places in that land became representative of such things as are in the kingdom of the Lord, and in the church (n. 1585, 3686, 4447, 5136). Therefore Abraham was commanded to go thither, since with his posterity from Jacob, a representative church might be established, and that the Word might be written, the ultimate of which should consist of representatives and significatives which are there (n. 3686, 4447, 5136, 6516). Hence it is that "earth" and "the land of Canaan," when they are mentioned in the Word, signify the church (n. 3038, 3481, 3705, 4447, 4517, 5757, 10,568).

6. What is meant by "Jerusalem" in the spiritual sense of the Word, shall also be briefly stated. "Jerusalem" means the church itself as to doctrine, because there in the land of Canaan, and in no other place, were the temple, the altar, the sacrifices, and thus Divine worship itself. On this account, also, three festivals were celebrated there every year, to which every male throughout the whole land was commanded to go. This, then, is the reason why "Jerusalem," in the spiritual sense, signifies the church as to to worship, or, what is the same, as to doctrine; for worship is prescribed in doctrine, and is performed according to it. The reason why it is said, "The holy city, New Jerusalem, descending from God out of heaven," is because, in the spiritual sense of the Word, "a city" (*civitas*) and "a town" (*urbs*), signifies doctrine, and "the holy city" the doctrine of Divine truth, since Divine truth is what is called "holy" in the Word. It is called "the New Jerusalem" for the same reason that "the earth" is called "new"; because, as was observed above, "the earth" signifies the church, and "Jerusalem," the church as to doctrine; which is said "to descend from God out of heaven," because all Divine truth, whence doctrine is derived, descends out of heaven from the Lord. That "Jerusalem" does not mean a city, although it was seen as a city, manifestly appears from its being said that:—

Its height was, as its length and breadth, twelve thousand stadia (*Apoc.* xxi. 16).

And that the measure of its wall, which was a hundred forty-four cubits, was the measure of a man, that is, of the angel (ver. 17).

Also from its being said that:—

It was prepared as a Bride adorned for her Husband (ver. 2).

And afterwards the angel said:—

Come, I will show thee the Bride, the Lamb's Wife: and he showed me that great city, the holy Jerusalem (vers. 9, 10).

The church is called in the Word "the Bride" and "the Wife" of the Lord; she is called "the Bride" before conjunction, and "the Wife" after conjunction. As may be seen in the *Arcana Cœlestia* (n. 3103, 3105, 3164, 3165, 3207, 7022, 9182).

7. To add a few words respecting the doctrine which is delivered in the following pages. This, also, is from heaven, because it is from the spiritual sense of the Word, and the spiritual sense of the Word is the same with the doctrine that is in heaven; for there is a church in heaven as well as on earth. In heaven there are the Word, doctrine from the Word, there are temples there, and preaching in them; there are also both ecclesiastical and civil governments there: in a word, the only difference between the things which are in heaven, and those which are on earth, is, that in heaven all things exist in a state of greater perfection, since those who are there are spiritual, and spiritual things immensely exceed in perfection those that are natural. That such things exist in heaven may be seen in the work concerning *Heaven and Hell* throughout, particularly in the article concerning Governments in Heaven (n. 213–220); and also in the article on Divine Worship in Heaven (n. 221–227). From these things it may be evident what is meant by "the holy city, New Jerusalem, was seen to descend from God out of heaven." But I proceed to the *doctrine* itself, which is for the New Church, and which is called *Heavenly Doctrine*, because it was revealed to me out of heaven; to deliver this doctrine is the design of the present book.

INTRODUCTION TO THE DOCTRINE.

8. The end of the church is when there is no faith because there is no charity. This is shown in the small work on *The Last Judgment and Babylon Destroyed* (n. 33–39, *seq.*). Because the churches in the Christian world have separated themselves from each other solely by such things as are of faith, when yet there is no faith where there is no charity, I will, by way of introduction to the doctrine which follows, make some observations concerning the doctrine of charity with the ancients. It is said *the churches in the Christian world*, and by them is meant the churches with the Reformed or Evangelical and not the Papists, since the Christian church is not there; for where the church exists the Lord is adored and the Word is read; whereas, with the Papists, they adore themselves instead of the Lord; they forbid the Word to be read by the people; and affirm the Pope's decree to be equal, yea, even above it.

9. The doctrine of charity, which is the doctrine of life, was the doctrine itself in the ancient churches. Concerning these churches see in the *Arcana Cœlestia* (n. 1238, 2385). And that doctrine conjoined all churches, and thereby formed one church out of many. For they acknowledged all those as men of the church who lived in the good of charity, and called them brethren, however they might differ respecting truths, which at this day are called matters of faith. In these they instructed one another, which was among their works of charity; nor were they indignant if one did not accede to the opinion of another, knowing that every one receives truth so far as he is in good. Because the ancient churches were such, therefore they were interior men; and because they were interior men they excelled in wisdom. For they who are in the good of love and charity, as to the internal man, are in heaven, and as to that are in an angelic society which is in similar good. Hence they enjoy an elevation of mind towards interior things, and, consequently, they are in wisdom; for wisdom can come from no other source than from heaven, that is, through heaven from the Lord; and in heaven there is wisdom, because there they are in good. Wisdom consists in seeing truth from the light of truth; and the light of truth is the light which is in heaven. But in process of time that ancient wisdom decreased; for as mankind removed themselves from the good of love to the Lord, and of love towards the neighbor, which love is called charity, they removed themselves in the same proportion from wisdom, because, in the same proportion, they removed themselves from heaven. Hence it was that man, from being internal, became external, and this successively; and when he became external, he became also worldly and corporeal. When such is his quality, he cares but little for the things of heaven; for the delights of earthly loves, and the evils which, from those loves, are delightful to him, then possess him entirely. And then the things which he hears concerning the life after death, concerning heaven and hell, in a word, concerning spiritual things, are as it were out of him, and not within him, as nevertheless they ought to be. Hence also it is, that the doctrine of charity, which with the ancients was held in such high estimation, is at this day among the things that are lost. For who, at this day, knows what charity is, in the genuine sense of the term, and what, in the same sense, is meant by our neighbor? whereas, that doctrine not only teaches this, but innumerable things besides, of which not a thousandth part is known at this day. The whole Sacred Scripture is nothing else than the doctrine of love and charity, which the Lord also teaches, when He says:—

Thou shalt love the Lord thy God with all thy heart, and with all thy soul, and with all thy mind; this is the first and great commandment; the second is like unto it, thou shalt love thy neighbor as thyself: on these two commandments hang all the law and the prophets (*Matt.* xxii. 37, 38, 39).

"The law and the prophets" in each and all things are the Word.

10. In the following doctrine we will annex to each section extracts from the *Arcana Cœlestia*, because in these the same things are more fully explained.

I.

GOOD AND TRUTH.

11. All things in the universe, which are according to Divine order, have relation to good and truth. There is nothing in heaven, and nothing in the world, which has not relation to these two; the reason is, because both good and truth proceed from the Divine from Whom all things are.

12. Hence it appears that there is nothing more necessary for man to know than what good and truth are; how the one has respect to the other; and how one is conjoined to the other. But such knowledge is especially necessary for the man of the church; for as all things of heaven have relation to good and truth, so also have all things of the church, because the good and truth of heaven are also the good and truth of the church. It is on this account that a beginning is made from good and truth.

13. It is according to Divine order that good and truth should be conjoined, and not separated; thus, that they should be one, and not two; for they proceed in conjunction from the Divine, and are conjoined in heaven, and therefore they should be conjoined in the church. The conjunction of good and truth is called, in heaven, the heavenly marriage, for all there are in this marriage. Hence it is that in the Word heaven is compared to a marriage, and that the Lord is called the Bridegroom and Husband, but heaven, and also the church, are called the Bride and Wife. That heaven and the church are so called, is because they who are therein receive Divine good in truths.

14. All the intelligence and wisdom which the angels have is from that marriage, and not any of it from good separate from truth, nor from truth separate from good. It is the same with the men of the church.

15. Because the conjunction of good and truth is an image of marriage, it is plain that good loves truth, and truth, in its turn, loves good, and that one desires to be conjoined with the other. The man of the church, who has not such love and such desire, is not in the heavenly marriage, consequently the church as yet is not in him; for the conjunction of good and truth constitutes the church.

16. Goods are manifold; in general there is spiritual good and natural good, and both are conjoined in genuine moral good. As goods are manifold, so also are truths, because truths are of good, and are the forms of good.

17. As it is with good and truth, so it is in the opposite with evil and falsity; namely, as all things in the universe, which are according to Divine order, have relation to good and truth, so all things which are contrary to Divine order have relation to evil and falsity. Again, as good loves to be conjoined to truth, and *vice versa,* so evil loves to be conjoined to falsity, and *vice versa.* And again, as all intelligence and wisdom are born from the conjunction of good and truth, so all insanity and folly are born from the conjunction of evil and falsity. The conjunction of evil and falsity is called the infernal marriage.

18. Since evil and falsity are opposite to good and truth, it is plain that truth cannot be conjoined to evil, nor good to the falsity of evil; if truth be adjoined to evil, it is truth no longer, but falsity, because it is falsified; and if good be adjoined to the falsity of evil, it is good no longer, but evil, because it is adulterated. But falsity which is not of evil may be conjoined to good.

19. No one who is in evil, and thence in falsity from confirmation and life, can know what good and truth is, for he believes his own evil to be good, and thence he believes his falsity to be truth; but every one who is in good and thence in truth from confirmation and life may know what evil and falsity are. The reason of this is, because all good and its truth is, in its essence, heavenly, and what is not heavenly in its essence is still from a heavenly origin; but all evil and its falsity is in its essence infernal, and what is not infernal in its essence has nevertheless its origin from thence; and all that is heavenly is in light, but all that is infernal is in darkness.

FROM THE ARCANA CŒLESTIA.

20. Each and all things in the universe have relation to good and truth, and to evil and falsity; those things which are and are done according to Divine order, to good and truth; but those which are opposite to Divine order, to evil and falsity (n. 2452, 3166, 4390, 4409, 5232, 7256, 10,122). Consequently everything in man has reference to the understanding and will, since the understanding is the recipient of truth, or of falsity; and the will the recipient of good, or of evil (n. 10,122). At this day it is little known what truth in its genuine essence is, because it is little known what good is, when nevertheless all truth is from good, and all good is by truths (n. 2507, 3603, 4136, 9186, 9995).

There are four kinds of men:—
1. *Those who are in falsities from evil; and those who are in falsities not from evil.*
2. *Those who are in truths without good.*
3. *Those who are in truths, and by them look and tend to good.*
4. *Those who are in truths from good. But each of these shall be spoken of in particular.*

21. [1]. *Of those who are in falsities from evil, and of those who are in falsities not from evil: thus of falsities from evil, and of falsities not from evil.*

There are innumerable kinds of falsities, namely, as many as there are evils; and the origins of evils, and thence of falsities, are many (n. 1188, 1212, 4729, 4822, 7574). There is falsity from evil, or falsity of evil; and there is evil from falsity, or evil of falsity, and again falsity thence, thus derivative (n. 1679, 2243). From one falsity, especially if it is in the place of a principle, there flow falsities in a continual series (n. 1510, 1511, 4717, 4721). There is falsity from the cupidities of the love of self and of the world; and there is falsity from the fallacies of the senses (n. 1295, 4729). There are falsities of religion, and there are falsities of ignorance (n. 4729, 8318, 9258). There is falsity in which there is good, and falsity in which there is not good (n. 2863, 9304, 10,109, 10,302). There is what is falsified (n. 7318, 7319, 10,648). All evil has falsity with it (n. 7577, 8094). Falsity from the cupidities of the love of self is the very falsity of evil; and the worst kinds of falsities are thence (n. 4729).

Evil is heavy, and has in itself a tendency to fall into hell, but not so falsity, unless derived from evil (n. 8279, 8298). Good is turned into evil, and truth into falsity, when it descends from heaven into hell, because as it were into a gross and impure atmosphere (n. 3607). Falsities from evil appear as mists and foul waters over the hells (n. 8137, 8138, 8146). They who are in the hells speak falsities from evil (n. 1695, 7351, 7352, 7357, 7392, 7699). They who are in evil cannot but think falsities, when they think from themselves (n. 7437). More is said concerning evil of falsity (n. 2408, 4818, 7272, 8265, 8279); and concerning falsities of evil (n. 6359, 7272, 9304, 10,302).

Every falsity may be confirmed, and when confirmed appears as truth (n. 5033, 6865, 8521, 8780). Therefore everything should be examined to see whether it is true before it is confirmed (n. 4741, 7012, 7680, 7950, 8521). Care should be taken that the falsities of religion be not confirmed, because the persuasion of falsity arises thence, which adheres to man after death (n. 845, 8780). How hurtful the persuasion of falsity is (n. 794, 806, 5096, 7686).

Good cannot flow into truths so long as man is in evil (n. 2434). Goods and truths are so far removed from man as he is in evil, and thereby in falsities (n. 3402). The greatest care is taken by the Lord lest truth be conjoined to evil, and the falsity of evil to good (n. 3110, 3116, 4416, 5217). Profanation arises from such mixture (n. 6348). Truths exterminate falsities, and falsities truths (n. 5207). Truths cannot be deeply received so long as incredulity reigns (n. 3399).

How truths may be falsified, from examples (n. 7318). The evil are permitted to falsify truths, the reason (n. 7332). Truths are falsified by the evil, by being applied and thus turned aside to evil (n. 8094, 8149). Truth is said to be falsified when it is applied to evil, which is done especially by fallacies and appearances in externals (n. 7334, 8062). The evil are allowed to assault truth, but not good, because they can falsify truth by various interpretations and applications (n. 6677). Truth falsified from evil, is contrary to truth and good (n. 8062). Truth falsified from evil has a grievous stench in the other life (n. 7319). More is said concerning the falsification of truth (n. 7318, 7319, 10,648).

There are falsities of religion which agree with good, and others which disagree (n. 9258, 9259). Falsities of religion, if they do not disagree with good, do not produce evil, except with those who are in evil (n. 8318). Falsities of religion are not imputed to those who are in good, but to those who are in evil (n. 8051, 8149). Truths not genuine, and also falsities, may be consociated with genuine truths with those who are in good, but not with those who are in evil (n. 3470, 3471, 4551, 4552, 7344, 8149, 9298). Falsities and truths are consociated by appearances from the sense of the letter of the Word (n. 7344). Falsities are made true by good, and grow soft when they are applied and turned to good, and evil is removed (n. 8149). Falsities of religion with those who are in good, are received by the Lord as truths (n. 4736, 8149). Good whose quality is from the falsity of religion, is accepted by the Lord, if there is ignorance, and therein innocence, and a good end (n. 7887). Truths with man are appearances of truth and good imbued with fallacies; but nevertheless the Lord adapts them to genuine truths with the man who lives in good (n. 2053). Falsities in which is good are given with those who are out of the church, and thence in ignorance of truth; also with those who are within the church where are falsities of doctrine (n. 2589–2604, 2861, 2863, 3263, 3778, 4189, 4190, 4197, 6700, 9256). Falsities in which there is not good are more grievous with those who are within the church, than with those who are out of the church (n. 7688). Truths and goods are taken away from the evil in the other life, and given to the good, according to the words of the Lord:—

To him that hath shall be given that he may abound; and from him who hath not shall be taken away that which he hath (*Matt.* xxv. 29, n. 7770).

22. [2]. *Of those who are in truths, and not in good; consequently of truths without good.*

Truths without good are not in themselves truths because they have no life, for all the life of truths is from good (n. 3603.) Thus they are as a body without a soul (n. 8530, 9154). The knowledges of truth and good which are only in the memory and not in the life, are believed by them to be truths (n. 5276). The truths are not appropriated to man, nor become his own, which he only knows and acknowledges from causes which proceed from the love of self and the world (n. 3402, 3834). But those are appropriated, which he acknowledges for the sake of truth itself and good (n. 3849). Truths without good are not accepted by the Lord (n. 4368); neither do they save (n. 2261). They who are in truths without good, are not of the church (n. 3963). Neither can they be regenerated (n. 10,367). The Lord does not flow into truths except through good (n. 10,367).

Of the separation of truth from good (n. 5008, 5009, 5022, 5028). The quality of truth without good, and its quality from good (n. 1949, 1950, 1964, 5951); from comparisons (n. 5830). Truth without good is morose (n. 1949–1951, 1964). In the spiritual world it appears hard (n. 6359, 7068); and pointed (n. 2799). Truth without good is as the light of winter, in which all things of the earth are torpid, and nothing is produced; but truth from good is as the light of spring and summer, in which all things flourish and are produced (n. 2231, 3146, 3412, 3413). Such a wintry light is turned into dense darkness when light flows in from heaven; and that then they who are in those truths come into blindness and stupidity (n. 3412, 3413).

They who separate truths from good are in darkness, and in ignorance of truth and in falsities (n. 9186). From falsities they cast themselves into evils (n. 3325, 8094). The errors and falsities into which they cast themselves (n. 4721, 4730, 4776, 4783, 4925, 7779, 8313, 8765, 9222). The Word is shut to them (n. 3773, 4783, 8780). They do not see and attend to all those things which the Lord spake concerning love and charity, thus concerning good (n. 2051, 3416). They know not what good is, nor what heavenly love and charity are (n. 2471, 3603, 4136, 9995). They who know the truths of faith, and live in evil, in the other life abuse truths to domineer thereby; concerning their quality and lot there (n. 4802).

Divine truth condemns to hell, but Divine good elevates to heaven (n. 2258). Divine truth terrifies, not so Divine good (n. 4180). What it is to be judged from truth, and to be judged from good (n. 2335).

23. [3]. *Of those who are in truths, and by them look and tend to good; thus of truths by which there is good.*

What man loves, this he wills, and what man loves or wills this he thinks, and confirms in various ways: what man loves or wills, this he calls good, and what man thence thinks and confirms in various ways, this he calls truth (n. 4070). Hence it is, that truth becomes good, when it becomes of the love or will, or when man loves and wills it (n. 5526, 7835, 10,367). And because the love or the will is the very life of man, truth does not live with man when he only knows it, and thinks it, but when he loves and wills it, and from love and will does it (n. 5595, 9282). Thence truths receive life, consequently from good (n. 2434, 3111, 3607, 6077). Thence the life of truths is from good, and they have no life without good (n. 1589, 1947, 1997, 3180, 3579, 4070, 4096, 4097, 4736, 4757, 4884, 5147, 5928, 9154, 9667, 9841, 10,729); illustrated (n. 9154). When truths may be said to have acquired life (n. 1928). Truth when it is conjoined to good, is appropriated to man because it becomes of his life (n. 3108, 3161). That truth may be conjoined to good, there must be consent from the understanding and will; when the will also consents, then there is conjunction (n. 3157, 3158, 3161).

When man is regenerated, truths enter with the delight of affection, because he loves to do them, and they are reproduced with the same affection because the two cohere (n. 2474, 2487, 3040, 3066, 3074, 3336, 4018, 5893, 7967). The affection which is of love always adjoins itself to truths according to the uses of life, and that affection is reproduced with the truths, and the truths are reproduced with the affection (n. 3336, 3824, 3849, 4205, 5893, 7967). Good acknowledges nothing else for truth than what agrees with the affection which is of the love (n. 3161). Truths are introduced by delights and pleasantnesses that agree therewith (n. 3502, 3512). All genuine affection of truth is from good, and according to it (n. 4373, 8349, 8356). Thus there is an insinuation and an influx of good into truths, and conjunction (n. 4301). And thus truths have life (n. 7917, 7967).

Because the affection which is of love always adjoins itself to truths according to the uses of life, good acknowledges its own truth, and truth its own good (n. 2429, 3101, 3102, 3161, 3179, 3180, 4358, 5407, 5835, 9637). Thence is the conjunction of truth and good, concerning which (n. 3834, 4096, 4097, 4301, 4345, 4353, 4364, 4368, 5365, 7623–7627, 7752–7762, 8530, 9258, 10,555). Truths also acknowledge each other, and are mutually consociated (n. 9079). This is from the influx of heaven (n. 9079).

Good is the *esse* of life, and truth the *existere* of life thence; and thus good has its *existere* of life in truth, and truth its *esse* of life in good (n. 3049, 3180, 4574, 5002, 9154). Hence every good has its own truth, and every truth its own good, because good without truth does not exist, and truth without good is not (n. 9637). Good has also its form and quality from truths, and that truth is the form and quality of good (n. 3049, 4574, 6916, 9154). And thus truth and good ought to be conjoined that they may be something (n. 10,555). Hence good is in the perpetual endeavor and desire of conjoining truths to itself (n. 9206, 9495); illustrated (n. 9207). And truths in like manner with good (n. 9206). The conjunction is reciprocal, of good with truth, and of truth with good (n. 5365, 8516). Good acts, and truth re-acts, but from good (n. 3155, 4380, 4757, 5928, 10,729). Truths regard their own good, as the beginning and end (n. 4353).

The conjunction of truth with good is as the progression of man's life from infancy, as he first imbibes truths scientifically, then rationally, and at length makes them of his life (n. 3203, 3665, 3690). It is also as with offspring that is conceived, is in the womb, is born, grows up, and becomes wise (n. 3298, 3299, 3308, 3665, 3690). It is also like seeds and soil (n. 3671). And as with water and bread (n. 4976). The first affection of truth is not genuine, but as man is perfected it is purified (n. 3040, 3089). Nevertheless goods and truths, not genuine, serve for introducing goods and truths that are genuine, and afterwards the former are left behind (n. 3665, 3690, 3974, 3982, 3986, 4145).

Moreover man is led to good by truths, and not without truths (n. 10,124, 10,367). If man does not learn or receive truths, good cannot flow in, thus man cannot become spiritual (n. 3387). The conjunction of good and truth takes place according to the increase of knowledge (n. 3141). Truths are received by every one according to his capacity (n. 3385).

The truths of the natural man are scientifics (n. 3293, 3309, 3310). Scientifics and knowledges are as vessels (n. 6004, 6023, 6052, 6071, 6077). Truths are vessels of good, because they are recipients (n. 1496, 1900, 2063, 2261, 2269, 3318, 3365, 3368).

Good flows into man by an internal way, or that of the soul, but truths by an external way, or that of hearing and sight; and they are conjoined in his interiors by the Lord (n. 3030, 3098). Truths are elevated out of the natural man, and implanted in good in the spiritual man; and thus truths become spiritual (n. 3085, 3086). And afterwards they flow thence into the natural man, spiritual good flowing immediately into the good of the natural, but mediately into the truth of the natural (n. 3314, 3573, 4563); illustrated (n. 3314, 3576, 3616, 3969, 3995). In a word, truths are conjoined to good with man, so far and in such manner as man is in good as to life (n. 3834, 3843). Conjunction is effected in one manner with the celestial, and in another with the spiritual (n. 10,124). More concerning the conjunction of good and truth, and how it is effected (n. 3090, 3203, 3308, 4096, 4097, 4345, 4353, 5365, 7623-7627). And how spiritual good is formed by truths (n. 3470, 3570).

24. [4]. *Of those who are in truths from good, consequently of truths from good.*

Of the difference between truth that leads to good, and truth which proceeds from good (n. 2063). Truth is not essentially truth, any further than as it proceeds from good (n. 4736, 10,619); because truth has its *esse* from good (n. 3049, 3180, 4574, 5002, 9144); and its life (n. 2434, 3111, 6077); and because truth is the form or quality of good (n. 3049, 4574, 5951, 9154). Truth is altogether as good with man, in the same ratio and degree (n. 2429). In order that truth may be truth, it must derive its essence from the good of charity and innocence (n. 3111, 6013). The truths which are from good are spiritual truths (n. 5951).

Truth makes one with good when it proceeds from good, even so that both together are one good (n. 4301, 4337, 7835, 10,252, 10,266). The understanding and will make one mind and one life, when the understanding proceeds from the will, because the understanding is the recipient of truth, and the will, of good, but not when man thinks and speaks otherwise than he wills (n. 3623). Truth from good is truth in will and act (n. 4337, 4353, 4385, 4390). When truth proceeds from good, good has its image in truth (n. 3180).

In the whole heaven and world, and in the single things thereof, there is an image of marriage (n. 54, 718, 747, 917, 1432, 2173, 2516, 5194). Particularly between truth and good (n. 1904, 2173, 2508). Because all things in the universe have relation to truth and good, in order that they may be anything, and to their conjunction, in order that anything may be produced (n. 2452, 3166, 4390, 4409, 5232, 7256, 10,122, 10,555).

The ancients also instituted a marriage between truth and good (n. 1904). The law of marriage is, that two be one, according to the words of the Lord (n. 10,130, 10,168, 10,169). Love truly conjugial descends and exists from heaven, from the marriage of truth and good (n. 2728, 2729).

Man is so far wise, as he is in good and thence in truths, but not so far as he knows truths and is not in good (n. 3182, 3190, 4884). The man who is in truths from good, is actually elevated from the light of the world into the light of heaven, consequently from what is obscure into what is clear; but on the other hand, he is in the light of the world, and what is obscure, so long as he knows truths and is not in good (n. 3190, 3192). Man does not know what good is, before he is in it, and knows from it (n. 3325, 3330, 3336). Truths increase immensely when they proceed from good (n. 2846, 2847, 5345). Of which increase (n. 5355). This increase is as fructification from a tree, and multiplication from seeds from which whole gardens are produced (n. 1873, 2846, 2847). Wisdom increases in a like degree, and this to eternity (n. 3200, 3314, 4220, 4221, 5527, 5859, 10,303). The man also who is in truths from good is in a like degree enlightened, and he is so far in enlightenment when he reads the Word (n. 9382, 10,548–10,550, 10,691, 10,694). The good of love is as fire, and truth thence as light from that fire (n. 3195, 3222, 5400, 8644, 9399, 9548, 9684). In heaven truths from good shine (n. 5219). Truths from good, by which is wisdom, increase according to the quality and quantity of the love of good; and on the other hand, falsities from evil, according to the quality and quantity of the love of evil (n. 4099). The man who is in truths from good comes into angelic intelligence and wisdom, and they lie hid in his interiors so long as he lives in the world, but they are opened in the other life (n. 2494). The man, who is in truths from good, becomes an angel after death (n. 8747).

Truths from good are like generations (n. 9079). They are disposed in series (n. 5339, 5343, 5530, 7408, 10,303, 10,308). The arrangement of truths from good compared with the fibres and blood-vessels in the body; and thence with their textures and forms, according to the uses of life (n. 3470, 3570, 3579, 9154). Truths from good form as it were a city, and this from the influx of heaven (n. 3584). The truths which are of the principal love are in the midst; and the rest are more or less remote from thence according to their degrees of disagreement (n. 3993, 4551, 4552, 5530, 6028). Conversely with the evil (n. 4551, 4552).

Truths when they proceed from good are arranged in the form of heaven (n. 4302, 4904, 5339, 5343, 5704, 6028, 10,303). And this according to the order in which are the angelic societies (n. 10,303). All truths when they proceed from good are conjoined to one another by a certain affinity, and they are as derivations of families from one father (n. 2863). All truth has a sphere of extension into heaven, according to the quality and quantity of the good from which it is (n. 8063). The marriage of good and truth is the church and heaven with man (n. 2731, 7752, 7753, 9224, 9995, 10,122). Of the delight and happiness of those with whom good is in truths (n. 1470). Truths from good, in conjunction, present an image of man (n. 8370). Man is nothing but his own good, and truth thence derived; or evil, and falsity thence derived (n. 10,298).

A summary:—Faith is by truths (n. 4353, 4997, 7178, 10,367). Charity towards the neighbor is by truths (n. 4368, 7623, 7624, 8034). Love to the Lord is by truths (n. 10,143, 10,153, 10,310, 10,578, 10,645). Conscience is by truths (n. 1077, 2053, 9113). Innocence is by truths (n. 3183, 3494, 6013). Purification from evils is by truths (n. 2799, 5954, 7044, 7918, 9088, 10,229, 10,237). Regeneration is by truths (n. 1555, 1904, 2046, 2189, 9088, 9959, 10,028). Intelligence and wisdom are by truths (n. 3182, 3190, 3387, 10,064). The beauty of angels, and also of men, as to the interiors which are their spirits, is by truths (n. 553, 3080, 4985, 5199). Power against evils and falsities is by truths (n. 3091, 4015, 10,488). Order, such as it is in heaven, is by truths (n. 3316, 3417, 3570, 4104, 5339, 5343, 6028, 10,303). The church is by truths (n. 1798, 1799, 3963, 4468, 4672). Heaven is with man by truths (n. 3690, 9832, 9931, 10,303). Man becomes man by truths (n. 3175, 3387, 8370, 10,298). Nevertheless all these things are by truths from good, and not by truths without good; and good is from the Lord (n. 2434, 4070, 4736, 5147). All good is from the Lord (n. 1614, 2016, 2904, 4151, 9981).

25. *All good and truth is from the Lord.* The Lord is good itself and truth itself (n. 2011, 4151, 10,336, 10,619).

The Lord, as to both the Divine and the Human, is the Divine good of the Divine love; and from Him proceeds Divine truth (n. 3704, 3712, 4180, 4577). The Divine truth proceeds from the Divine good of the Lord, comparatively as light from the sun (n. 3704, 3712, 4180, 4577). The Divine truth proceeding from the Lord appears in the heavens as light, and forms all the light of heaven (n. 3195, 3223, 5400, 8694, 9399, 9548, 9684). The light of heaven, which is the Divine truth united to the Divine good, enlightens both the sight and the understanding of angels and spirits (n. 2776, 3138). Heaven is in light and heat, because it is in truth and good, for the Divine truth is light there, and the Divine good is heat there (n. 3643, 9399, 9400); and in the work on *Heaven and Hell* (n. 126–140). The Divine truth proceeding from the Divine good of the Lord, forms the angelic heaven and arranges it in order (n. 3038, 9408, 9613, 10,716, 10,717). The Divine good united to the Divine truth, which is in the heavens, is called the Divine truth (n. 10,196).

The Divine truth proceeding from the Lord is the only reality (n. 6880, 7004, 8200). By Divine truth all things were made and created (n. 2803, 2894, 5272, 7678). All power belongs to the Divine truth (n. 8200).

Man from himself can do nothing of good, and think nothing of truth (n. 874–876). The rational of man cannot perceive Divine truth from itself (n. 2196, 2203, 2209). Truths which are not from the Lord, are from the proprium of man, and they are not truths, but only appear as truths (n. 8868).

All good and truth is from the Lord, and nothing from man (n. 1614, 2016, 2904, 4151, 9981). Goods and truths are so far goods and truths, as they have the Lord in them (n. 2904, 3061, 8480). Of the Divine truth proceeding immediately from the Lord, and of the Divine truth proceeding mediately through the angels, and of their influx with man (n. 7055, 7056, 7058). The Lord flows into good with man, and by good into truths (n. 10,153). He flows in by good into truths of every kind, and particularly into genuine truths (n. 2531, 2554). The Lord does not flow into truths separate from good, and no parallelism exists between the Lord and man, with respect to them, but with respect to good (n. 1831, 1832, 3514, 3564).

To do good and truth for the sake of good and truth is to love the Lord, and to love the neighbor (n. 10,336). They who are in the internal of the Word, of the church, and of worship, love to do good and truth for the sake of good and truth; but they who are in the external of these, without the internal, love to do good and truth for the sake of themselves and the world (n. 10,683). What it is to do good and truth for the sake of good and truth, illustrated by examples (n. 10,683).

26. *Of the various kinds of goods and truths.*

There is an infinite variety, and one thing is never exactly the same as another (n. 7236, 9002). There is also an infinite variety in the heavens (n. 684, 690, 3744, 5598, 7236). Varieties in the heavens are varieties of good, and thence is the distinction of all therein (n. 3519, 3744, 3804, 3986, 4005, 4067, 4149, 4263, 7236, 7833, 7836, 9002). These varieties are from truths, which are manifold, by which every one has good (n. 3470, 3519, 3804, 4149, 6917, 7236). Thence all the angelic societies in the heavens, and every angel in a society are distinguished from each other (n. 690, 3241, 3519, 3804, 3986, 4067, 4149, 4263, 7236, 7833, 7836). But they all act in unity by love from the Lord, and thereby regard one end (n. 457, 3986).

In general, goods and truths are distinguished according to degrees, into natural, spiritual, and celestial (n. 2069, 3240). In general, there are three degrees of good, and consequently of truth, according to the three heavens (n. 4154, 9873, 10,270). The goods and thence the truths in the internal man, are of a threefold kind, and so also in the external (n. 4154). There is natural good, civil good, and moral good (n. 3768). Natural good, into which some are born, is not good in the other life, unless made spiritual good (n. 2463, 2464, 2468, 3408, 3469, 3470, 3508, 3518, 7761). Of natural spiritual good; and of that which is not spiritual (n. 4988, 4992, 5032). There is intellectual truth, and scientific truth (n. 1904, 1911, 2503).

27. *That wisdom is from good by truths.*

In what manner the rational is conceived and born with man (n. 2094, 2524, 2557, 3030, 5126). This is effected by an influx of the Lord through heaven into the knowledges and sciences which are with man, and thence is elevation (n. 1895, 1899–1901). Elevation is according to uses, and the love of them (n. 3074, 3085, 3086). The rational is born through truths, hence such as they are, such is the rational (n. 2094, 2524, 2557). The rational is opened and formed by truths from good; and it is shut and destroyed by falsities from evil (n. 3108, 5126). Man is not rational by this that he can reason on any subject, but that he can see and perceive whether a thing be true or not (n. 1944). Man is not born into any truth, because not born into good; but he is to learn and imbibe both (n. 3175). It is with difficulty that man can receive genuine truths, and thence become wise, on account of the fallacies of the senses, the persuasions of falsity, and the reasonings and doubts thence (n. 3175). Man first begins to be wise, when he begins to be averse to reasonings against truths, and to reject doubts (n. 3175). The unenlightened human rational laughs at interior truths, from examples (n. 2654). Truths with man are called interior when they are implanted in his life, and not in consequence of his knowing them, although they may be truths which are called interior (n. 10,199).

In good there is the faculty of becoming wise, whence those who have lived in good in the world come into angelic wisdom after their departure out of the world (n. 5527, 5859, 8321). There are innumerable things in every good (n. 4005). Innumerable things may be known from good (n. 3612). Concerning the multiplication of truth from good (n. 5345, 5355, 5912). The good of infancy by truths, and by a life according to them, becomes the good of wisdom (n. 3504).

There is the affection of truth and the affection of good (n. 1904, 1997). What is the quality of those who are in the affection of truth, and what is the quality of those who are in the affection of good (n. 2422, 2429). Who are able to come into the affection of truth, and who are not able (n. 2689). All truths are arranged in order under a general affection (n. 9094). The affection of truth and the affection of good in the natural man are as brother and sister; but in the spiritual man, as husband and wife (n. 3160). Pure truths are not given with man, nor even with an angel, but only with the Lord (n. 3207, 7902).

Truths with man are appearances of truth (n. 2053, 2519). The first truths with man are appearances of truth from the fallacies of the senses, which nevertheless are successively put off, as he is perfected as to wisdom (n. 3131). Appearances of truth with the man who is in good are received by the Lord for truths (n. 2053, 3207). What, and of what quality the appearances of truth are (n. 3207, 3357–3362, 3368, 3404, 3405, 3417). The sense of the letter of the Word in many places is according to appearances (n. 1838). The same truths with one man are more true, with another less so, and with another false, because falsified (n. 2439). Truths are also truths according to the correspondence between the natural and the spiritual man (n. 3128, 3138). Truths differ according to the various ideas and perceptions concerning them (n. 3470, 3804, 6917).

Truth when it is conjoined to good, vanishes out of the memory because it then becomes of the life (n. 3108). Truths cannot be conjoined to good except in a free state (n. 3158). Truths are conjoined to good by temptations (n. 3318, 4572, 7122). There is in good a continual endeavor of arranging truths in order, and of restoring its state thereby (n. 3610). Truths appear undelightful when the communication with good is intercepted (n. 8352). Man can scarcely distinguish between truth and good, because he can scarcely distinguish between thinking and willing (n. 9995). Good is called in the Word the "brother" of truth (n. 4267). Also in a certain respect good is called "lord," and truth, "servant" (n. 3409, 4267).

II.

THE WILL AND THE UNDERSTANDING.

28. Man has two faculties which make his life; one is called the *Will*, and the other the *Understanding*. These faculties are distinct from each other, but are so created that they may be one; and when they are one they are called the *Mind*. Of these, then, the human mind consists; and the whole life of man is there.

29. As all things in the universe, which are according to Divine order, have relation to good and truth, so all things with man have relation to the will and the understanding; for good with man is of his will, and truth with him is of his understanding; for these two faculties, or these two lives of man, are their receptacles and subjects. The will is the receptacle and subject of all things of good, and the understanding the receptacle and subject of all things of truth. Goods and truths with man are nowhere else; and because goods and truths with man are nowhere else, so neither are love and faith elsewhere; for love is of good, and good is of love; and faith is of truth, and truth is of faith.

30. Since, then, all things in the universe have relation to good and truth, and all things of the church to the good of love and the truth of faith; and since man is man from those two faculties, therefore they also are treated of in this doctrine; otherwise man could have no distinct idea of them, on which to found his thought.

31. The will and the understanding also constitute the spirit of man; for his wisdom and intelligence, and his life in general, reside in them; the body is only obedience.

32. Nothing is more important to know than how the will and the understanding make one mind. They make one mind as good and truth make one; for there is a similar marriage between the will and the understanding as there is between good and truth. What is the quality of that marriage may fully appear from what has been quoted above, concerning good and truth, namely, as good is the very *esse* of a thing, and truth the *existere* of a thing thence derived, so the will with man is the very *esse* of his life, and the understanding the *existere* of life thence; for good, which is of the will, forms and renders itself visible in the understanding.

33. They who are in good and truth have will and understanding, but they who are in evil and in falsity have not will and understanding; but instead of will they have cupidity, and instead of understanding they have science. For the truly human will is the receptacle of good, and the understanding is the receptacle of truth; for which reason will cannot be predicated of evil, nor can understanding be predicated of falsity, because they are opposites, and opposites destroy each other. Hence it is, that the man who is in evil and thence in falsity, cannot be called rational, wise, and intelligent. With the evil, also, the interiors of the mind, in which the will and the understanding principally reside, are closed. It is believed that the evil also have will and understanding, because they say that they will, and that they understand; but their willing is only cupidity, and their understanding is only knowing.

FROM THE ARCANA CŒLESTIA.

34. *Spiritual* truths cannot be comprehended, unless the following *universals* are known:—

I. All things in the universe have relation to good and truth, and to the conjunction of both, in order that they may be anything; consequently to love and faith, and their conjunction.

II. With man there is will and understanding, and the will is the receptacle of good, and the understanding the receptacle of truth, and all things with man have relation to those two, and to their conjunction, as all things relate to good and truth, and their conjunction.

III. There is an internal man and an external, and they are distinct one from the other like heaven and the world, and nevertheless that they ought to make one, in order that man may be truly man.

IV. The light of heaven is that in which the internal man is, and the light of the world that in which the external is; and the light of heaven is the Divine truth itself, from which is all intelligence.

V. There is a correspondence between the things which are in the internal, and those which are in the external man; and consequently they appear in each under a different form, so that they can only be discerned by the science of correspondences.

Unless these and many other things are known, it is impossible to form any ideas concerning spiritual and celestial things, but such as are incongruous; and thus the scientifics and knowledges, which are of the external man, without these universals, can be of little service to the rational man for understanding and growth. Hence it appears, how necessary scientifics are. Concerning those universals, much is said in the *Arcana Cœlestia*.

35. Man has two faculties, one which is called the will, and the other the understanding (n. 35, 641, 3539, 3623, 5969, 10,122). Those two faculties constitute the very man (n. 10,076, 10,109, 10,110, 10,264, 10,284). The quality of man is according to those two faculties with him (n. 7342, 8885, 9282, 10,264, 10,284). By them also man is distinguished from beasts, by reason that the understanding of man may be elevated by the Lord, and see Divine truths, and in like manner his will may be elevated and perceive Divine goods; and thus man may be conjoined to the Lord by those two faculties, which make him; but that the case is otherwise with beasts (n. 4525, 5114, 5302, 6323, 9231). And since man may thus be conjoined to the Lord, he cannot die as to his interiors, which are his spirit, but he lives for ever (n. 5302). Man is not man from his form, but from good and truth, which are of his will and understanding (n. 4051, 5302).

As all things in the universe relate to good and truth, so do all things in man to the will and the understanding (n. 803, 10,122). For the will is the receptacle of good, and the understanding is the receptacle of truth (n. 3332, 3623, 5835, 6065, 6125, 7503, 9300, 9930). It amounts to the same, whether you say truth or faith, for faith is of truth, and truth is of faith; and it amounts to the same whether you say good or love, for love is of good, and good is of love; for what a man believes, that he calls true; and what he loves, that he calls good (n. 4353, 4997, 7178, 10,122, 10,367). Hence it follows that the understanding is the recipient of faith, and the will the recipient of love; and that faith and love are in man, when they are in his understanding and will, for the life of man is nowhere else (n. 7179, 10,122, 10,367). And since the understanding of man is capable of receiving faith in the Lord, and the will of receiving love to the Lord, that by faith and love he may be conjoined to the Lord, and whoever is capable of conjunction with the Lord by faith and love, cannot die to eternity (n. 4525, 6323, 9231). Love is conjunction in the spiritual world (n. 1594, 2057, 3939, 4018, 5807, 6195, 6196, 7081, 7086, 7501, 10,130).

The will of man is the very *esse* of his life, because it is the receptacle of good, and the understanding is the *existere* of life thence derived, because it is the receptacle of truth (n. 3619, 5002, 9282). Thus the life of the will is the principal life of man, and the life of the understanding proceeds therefrom (n. 585, 590, 3619, 7342, 8885, 9282, 10,076, 10,109, 10,110); comparatively as light proceeds from fire or flame (n. 6032, 6314). Whatever things enter into the understanding, and at the same time into the will, are appropriated to man, but not those which are received in the understanding alone (n. 9009, 9069, 9071, 9133, 9182, 9386, 9393, 10,076, 10,109, 10,110). Those things become of the life of man, which are received in the will, and thence in the understanding (n. 8911, 9069, 9071, 10,076, 10,109, 10,110). Every man also is loved and esteemed by others according to the good of his will and thence of his understanding; for he who wills well and understands well, is loved and esteemed, and he who understands well and does not will well, is rejected and is held in low estimation (n. 8911, 10,076).

Man also after death remains such as his will and the understanding are (n. 9069, 9071, 9386, 10,153); and those things which are of the understanding, and not at the same time of the will, then vanish, because they are not in man's spirit (n. 9282). Or, what amounts to the same, man after death remains as his love and its faith are, or as his good and its truth are; and the things which are of the faith and not at the same time of the love, or the things which are of truth and not at the same time of good, vanish, because they are not in the man, thus not man's (n. 553, 2363, 10,153). Man is capable of comprehending with the understanding what he does not do from the will, or he may understand what he does not will, because it is against his love (n. 3539).

The will and the understanding constitute one mind (n. 35, 3623, 5835, 10,122). Those two faculties of life ought to act as one, that man may be man (n. 3623, 5835, 5969, 9300). How perverted a state they are in, whose understanding and will do not act as one (n. 9075). Such is the state of hypocrites, the deceitful, flatterers, and simulators (n. 2426, 3573, 4799, 8250). The will and the understanding are reduced to one in another life, and there it is not allowable to have a divided mind (n. 8250).

Every doctrinal of the church has its own ideas by which its quality is perceived (n. 3310). The understanding of the doctrinal is according to those ideas, and without an intellectual idea, man would only have an idea of words, and none of things (n. 3825). The ideas of the understanding extend themselves widely into the societies of spirits and angels round about (n. 6599, 6600–6605, 6609, 6613). The ideas of man's understanding are opened in another life, and appear to the life as to their quality (n. 1869, 3310, 5510). Of what quality the ideas of some appear (n. 6200, 8885).

All the will of good and the understanding of truth is from the Lord, but not so the understanding of truth separate from the will of good (n. 1831, 3514, 5482, 5649, 6027, 8685, 8701, 10,153). It is the understanding which is enlightened by the Lord (n. 6222, 6608, 10,659). The Lord grants to those who are enlightened, to see and understand truth (n. 9382, 10,659). The enlightening of the understanding is various, according to the states of man's life (n. 5221, 7012, 7233). The understanding is enlightened as far as man receives truth in the will, that is, as far as he wills to act according thereto (n. 3619). They have their understanding enlightened who read the Word from the love of truth and from the love of the uses of life; but not they who read it from the love of fame, honor, and gain (n. 9382, 10,548, 10,549, 10,551). Enlightenment is an actual elevation of the mind into the light of heaven (n. 10,330); from experience (n. 1526, 6608). Light from heaven is the enlightenment of the understanding, as light from the world is to the sight (n. 1524, 5114, 6608, 9128). The light of heaven is the Divine truth, from which is all wisdom and intelligence (n. 3195, 3222, 5400, 8644, 9399, 9548, 9684). It is the understanding of man which is enlightened by that light (n. 1524, 3138, 3167, 4408, 6608, 8707, 9128, 9399, 10,569).

The understanding is such as are the truths from good, of which it is formed (n. 10,064). The understanding is that which is formed by truths from good, but not what is formed by falsities from evil (n. 10,675). The understanding consists in seeing truths, the causes of things, their connections, and consequences in regular order, from those things which are of experience and science (n. 6125). The understanding consists in seeing and perceiving whether a thing be true, before it is confirmed, but not in being able to confirm every thing (n. 4741, 7012, 7680, 7950, 8521, 8780). The light of confirmation without a previous perception of truth, is natural light, and may be possessed even by those who are not wise (n. 8780). To see and perceive whether a thing be true before it is confirmed, is only given with those who are affected with truth for the sake of truth, consequently who are in spiritual light (n. 8780). Every dogma even what is false may be confirmed, even so as to appear true (n. 2243, 2385, 4677, 4741, 5033, 6865, 7950).

How the rational is conceived and born with man (n. 2094, 2524, 2557, 3030, 5126). It is from the influx of the light of heaven from the Lord through the internal man into the knowledges and sciences, which are in the external, and an elevation thence (n. 1895, 1899, 1902). The rational is born by truths, and not by falsities; consequently according to the quality of the truths, such is the rational (n. 2094, 2524, 2557). The rational is opened and formed by truths from good, and it is shut and destroyed by falsities from evil (n. 3108, 5126). A man is not rational who is in falsities from evil; and consequently a man is not rational from being able to reason upon every subject (n. 1944).

Man scarcely knows how to distinguish between the understanding and the will, because he scarcely knows how to distinguish between thinking and willing (n. 9995).

Many more things concerning the will and the understanding may be known and concluded from what has been just adduced concerning good and truth, provided the will be perceived instead of good, and the understanding instead of truth, for the will is of good, and the understanding is of truth.

III.

THE INTERNAL AND THE EXTERNAL MAN.

36. Man is so created as to be in the spiritual world and in the natural world at the same time. The spiritual world is where the angels are, and the natural world where men are. As man is so created, there has been given to him an internal and an external; an internal by which he is in the spiritual world, and an external by which he is in the natural world. His internal is what is called the internal man, and his external is what is called the external man.

37. Every man has an internal and an external; but they differ with the good and the evil. With the good, the internal is in heaven, and in its light, and the external is in the world, and in its light, which light with them is illumined by the light of heaven, so that the internal and the external act as one, like the efficient cause and the effect, or like what is prior and what is posterior. But, with the evil, the internal is in the world, and in its light; as is also the external; for which reason they see nothing from the light of heaven, but only from the light of the world, which they call the light of nature. Hence it is that to them the things of heaven are in thick darkness, whilst the things of the world are in light. From this it is manifest that the good have both an internal and an external man, but that the evil have not an internal man, but only an external.

38. The internal man is called the spiritual man, because it is in the light of heaven, which light is spiritual; and the external man is called the natural man, because it is in the light of the world, which light is natural. The man whose internal is in the light of heaven, and whose external is in the light of the world, is a spiritual man as to both; but the man whose internal is not in the light of heaven, but only in the light of the world, in which is his external also, is a natural man as to both. The spiritual man is called in the Word "living," but the natural man is called "dead."

39. The man whose internal is in the light of heaven, and his external in the light of the world, thinks both spiritually and naturally; but then his spiritual thought flows into his natural thought, and is there perceived. But the man whose internal and external are in the light of the world, does not think spiritually, but materially; for he thinks from such things as are in the nature of the world, all which are material. To think spiritually is to think of things themselves as they are in themselves, to see truths in the light of truth, and to perceive goods from the love of good; also, to see the qualities of things, and to perceive their affections, abstractly from matter. But to think materially is to think, see, and perceive them together with matter, and in matter, thus in a gross and obscure manner respectively.

40. The internal spiritual man, regarded in himself, is an angel of heaven; and, also, during his life in the body, is in society with angels, although he does not then know it; and after his separation from the body, he comes among the angels. But the merely natural internal man, regarded in himself, is a spirit, and not an angel; and, also, during his life in the body, is in society with spirits, but with those who are in hell, among whom he also comes after his separation from the body.

41. The interiors, with those who are spiritual men, are also actually elevated towards heaven, for that is what they primarily regard; but the interiors which are of the mind with those who are merely natural, are actually turned to the world, because that is what they primarily regard. The interiors, which are of the mind [*mens*], are turned with every one to that which he loves above all things; and the exteriors which are of the mind [*animus*], are turned the same way as the interiors.

42. They who have only a general idea concerning the internal and the external man, believe that it is the internal man which thinks and wills, and the external which speaks and acts; because to think and to will is internal, and to speak and to act thence is external. But it is to be known that when man thinks intelligently and wills wisely, he then thinks and wills from a spiritual internal; but when man does not think intelligently, and will wisely, he thinks and wills from a natural internal. Consequently, when a man thinks well concerning the Lord and those things which are of the Lord, and well concerning the neighbor, and those things which are of the neighbor, and wills well to them, he then thinks and wills from a spiritual internal, because he then thinks from the faith of truth and from the love of good, thus from heaven. But when man thinks and wills wickedly concerning them, he then thinks and wills from a natural internal, because he thinks and wills from the faith of falsity and from the love of evil, thus from hell. In a word, so far as man is in love to the Lord, and in love towards the neighbor, so far he is in a spiritual internal, from which he thinks and wills, and from which also he speaks and acts; but so far as man is in the love of self, and in the love of the world, so far he is in a natural internal, from which he thinks and wills, and from which also he speaks and acts.

43. It is so provided and ordered by the Lord, that so far as man thinks and wills from heaven, so far the internal spiritual man is opened and formed. It is opened into heaven even to the Lord, and the formation is according to those things which are of heaven. But, on the contrary, so far as man does not think and will from heaven, but from the world, so far the internal spiritual man is closed, and the external is opened. The opening is into the world, and the formation is to those things which are of the world.

44. They with whom the internal spiritual man is opened into heaven to the Lord, are in the light of heaven, and in enlightenment from the Lord, and thence in intelligence and wisdom; these see truth because it is truth, and perceive good because it is good. But they with whom the internal spiritual man is closed, do not know that there is an internal man, and much less what the internal man is; neither do they believe that there is the Divine, nor that there is a life after death; consequently they do not believe the things which are of heaven and of the church. And because they are only in the light of the world and in the enlightenment thence, they believe in nature as the Divine, they see falsity as truth, and they perceive evil as good.

45. He whose internal is so far external, that he believes nothing but what he can see with his eyes and touch with his hands, is called a sensual man; this is the lowest natural man, and is in fallacies concerning all the things which are of the faith of the church.

46. The internal and the external, which have been treated of, are the internal and the external of the spirit of man; his body is only a superadded external, within which they exist; for the body does nothing from itself, but from its spirit which is in it. It is to be known that the spirit of man, after its separation from the body, thinks and wills, speaks and acts, the same as before; to think and to will is its internal, and to speak and to act is its external; concerning which, see in the work on *Heaven* (n. 234-245, 265-275, 432-444, 453-484).

FROM THE ARCANA CŒLESTIA.

47. *Of the internal and the external with man.*

It is known in the Christian world, that man has an internal and an external, or an internal man and an external man; but it is little known what is the quality of the one and of the other (n. 1889, 1940). The internal man is spiritual, and the external is natural (n. 978, 1015, 4459, 6309, 9701-9709). How the internal man which is spiritual is formed to the image of heaven; and the external which is natural to the image of the the world; and man was therefore called by the ancients a microcosm (n. 3628, 4523, 4524, 6057, 6314, 9706, 10,156, 10,472). Thus in man the spiritual world and natural world are conjoined (n. 6057, 10,472). Thence man is such that he can look up towards heaven, and down towards the world (n. 7601, 7604, 7607). When he looks upwards, he is in the light of heaven and sees thence; but when he looks downwards, he is in the light of the world and sees thence (n. 3167, 10,134). There is given with man a descent from the spiritual world into the natural (n. 3702, 4042).

The internal man which is spiritual, and the external man which is natural, are altogether distinct (n. 1999, 2018, 3691, 4459). The distinction is such as exists between cause and effect, and between prior and posterior, and there is no continuity (n. 3691, 4154, 5145, 5146, 5711, 6275, 6284, 6299, 6326, 6465, 8603, 10,076, 10,099, 10,181). Consequently that the distinction is like that between heaven and the world, or between the spiritual and the natural (n. 4292, 5032, 5620, 5639). The interiors and exteriors of man are not continuous, but distinct according to degrees, and each degree is terminated (n.

3691, 4145, 5114, 6326, 6465, 8603, 10,099). He who does not perceive the distinctions of the interiors and the exteriors of man according to degrees, and does not understand the quality of those degrees, cannot comprehend the internal and the external of man (n. 5146, 6465, 10,099, 10,181). The things of a higher degree are more perfect than those of a lower degree (n. 3405). There are three degrees in man answering to the three heavens (n. 4154). The exteriors are more remote from the Divine with man, and therefore they are respectively obscure, and of a general nature (n. 6451). And they are also respectively not in order (n. 996, 3855). The interiors are more perfect, because nearer to the Divine (n. 5146, 5147). In the internal there are thousands and thousands of things, which in the external appear as one general thing (n. 5707). Thence thought and perception is clearer in proportion as it is interior (n. 5920). Hence it follows that man ought to be in internals (n. 1175, 4464).

The interiors of the mind, with the man who is in love and charity, are actually elevated by the Lord, and otherwise they would look downwards (n. 6952, 6954, 10,330). Influx and enlightenment from heaven with man, is an actual elevation of the interiors by the Lord (n. 7816, 10,330). Man is elevated when he advances to spiritual things (n. 9922). As far as man is elevated from externals towards interiors, so far he comes into light, consequently into intelligence; and this is what is meant by being withdrawn from sensual things, according to the saying of the ancients (n. 6183, 6313). Elevation from the external to the interiors, is like that from mist into light (n. 4598).

Influx from the Lord is through the internal man into the external (n. 1940, 5119). Interiors can flow into exteriors, but not the contrary; consequently that influx is spiritual and not physical, namely, from the spiritual man into the natural, and not from the natural man into the spiritual (n. 3219, 5119, 5259, 5427, 5428, 5477, 6322, 9109, 9110). The Lord from the internal, where there is peace, governs the external, where there is turbulence (n. 5396).

The internal can see all things in the external, but not the reverse (n. 1914, 1953, 5427, 5428, 5477). When man lives in the world, he thinks from the internal in the external, consequently his spiritual thought flows into his natural, and there presents itself naturally (n. 3679). When man thinks well, it is from the internal or spiritual in the external or natural (n. 9704, 9705, 9707). The external man thinks and wills according to conjunction with the internal (n. 9702, 9703). There is an interior and an exterior thought; the quality of the one and the other (n. 2515, 2552, 5127, 5141, 5168, 6007). The thought and affection in the internal is not perceived by man during his life in the world, but only that which is in the external therefrom (n. 10,236, 10,240). But in the other life externals are taken away, and man is then let into his own internals (n. 8870). It then becomes manifest what is the quality of his internals (n. 1806, 1807).

The internal produces the external (n. 994, 995). And the internal then invests itself with such things as enable it to produce its effects in the external (n. 6275, 6284, 6299); and by which it may live in the external (n. 1175, 6275). The Lord conjoins the internal or spiritual man to the external or natural man, when He regenerates him (n. 1577, 1594, 1904, 1999). The external or natural man is then reduced into order through the internal or spiritual man, and is subordinated (n. 9708).

The external must be subordinate and subject to the internal (n. 5077, 5125, 5128, 5786, 5947, 10,272). The external is so created, that it may serve the internal (n. 5947). The internal must be lord, and the external its minister, and in a certain respect its servant (n. 10,471).

The external ought to be in correspondence with the internal, that there may be conjunction (n. 5427, 5428, 5477). What the quality of the external is when it corresponds with the internal, and what when it does not correspond (n. 3493, 5422, 5423, 5427, 5428, 5477, 5511). In the external man there are things which correspond and agree with the internal, and there are things which do not correspond and agree (n. 1563, 1568).

The external has its quality from the internal (n. 9912, 9921, 9922). How great the beauty of the external man is, when it is conjoined with the internal (n. 1590). And how great its foulness when not conjoined (n. 1598). Love to the Lord and charity towards the neighbor conjoin the external man with the internal (n. 1594). Unless the internal man be conjoined with the external, there is no fructification (n. 3987).

The interiors successively flow into the exteriors, even into the extreme or ultimate, and they there exist and subsist together (n. 634, 6239, 9215, 9216). They not only flow in successively, but also form in the ultimate what is simultaneous, in what order (n. 5897, 6451, 8603, 10,099). All the interiors are held in connection from the first, through the ultimate (n. 9828). Thence also in the ultimates are strength and power (n. 9836). And therefore responses and revelations were made from the ultimates (n. 9905, 10,548). Thence also the ultimate is more holy than the interiors (n. 9824). Hence also in the Word, "first and last" signify all and every particular, thus the whole (n. 10,044, 10,329, 10,335).

The internal man is open to him who is in Divine order, but shut to him who is not in Divine order (n. 8513). There is no conjunction of heaven with the external man without the internal (n. 9380). Evils and the falsities of evil shut the internal man, and cause man to be only in externals (n. 1587, 10,492). Especially evils from the love of self (n. 1594). The interiors are shut even to the sensual, which is the ultimate, if the Divine is denied (n. 6564). With the intelligent and learned of the world, who from the sciences confirm themselves against the things of heaven and the church, the internal is shut more than with the simple (n. 10,492).

Because the internal man is in the light of heaven, and the external in the light of the world, therefore they who are in the external without the internal, that is, they with whom the internal is shut, do not care for the internal things of heaven and the church (n. 4464, 4946). In the other life they cannot at all endure internal things (n. 10,694, 10 701, 10,707). They believe nothing (n. 10,396, 10,400, 10,411, 10,429). They love themselves and the world above all things (n. 10,407, 10,412, 10,420). Their interiors, or the things which are of their thought and affection, are vile, filthy, and profane, howsoever they may appear in externals (n. 1182, 7046, 9705, 9707). The ideas of their thought are material, and not at all spiritual (n.

10,582). The quality further described of those whose internal that looks heavenward, is shut (n. 4459, 9709, 10,284, 10,286, 10,429, 10,472, 10,492, 10,602, 10,683).

So far as the internal, which is spiritual, is opened, so far truths and goods are multiplied; and so far as the internal, which is spiritual, is shut, so far truths and goods vanish (n. 4099). The church is in the internal spiritual man, because that is in heaven, and not in the external without it (n. 10,698). Hence the external church with man is nothing without the internal (n. 1795). External worship without internal worship is no worship (n. 1094, 1175). Concerning those who are in the internal of the church, of worship, and of the Word; of those who are in the external in which is the internal; and of those who are in the external without the internal (n. 10,683). The external without the internal is hard (n. 10,683).

The merely natural man is in hell, unless he be made spiritual by regeneration (n. 10,156). All who are in the external without the internal, or with whom the spiritual internal is shut, are in hell (n. 9128, 10,483, 10,489).

The interiors of man are actually turned according to his loves (n. 10,702). In each and all things there must be an internal and an external that they may subsist (n. 9473).

"Above" and "high" in the Word, signifies the internal (n. 1725, 2148, 4210, 4599). Thence in the Word higher is interior, and lower is exterior (n. 3084).

48. *Of the natural and the spiritual.*

How perverse it is that the world at this day attributes so much to nature, and so little to the Divine (n. 3483). Why it is so (n. 5116). When nevertheless each and every particular in nature not only exists, but likewise continually subsists from the Divine, and through the spiritual world (n. 775, 8211). Divine, celestial, and spiritual things terminate in nature (n. 4240, 4939). Nature is the ultimate plane whereon they stand (n. 4240, 5651, 6275, 6284, 6299, 9216). Celestial, spiritual, and natural things follow and succeed each other in order; so do Divine things with them, because they are from the Divine (n. 880, 4938, 4939, 9992, 10,005, 10,017, 10,068). Celestial things are the head, spiritual things the body, and natural things the feet (n. 4938, 4939). They also inflow in an order similar to that wherein they follow and succeed each other (n. 4938, 4939). The good of the inmost or third heaven is called celestial, the good of the middle or second heaven is called spiritual, and the good of the ultimate or first heaven is called spiritual natural, whence it may be known what is the celestial, spiritual, and natural (n. 4279, 4286, 4938, 4939, 9992, 10,005, 10,017, 10,068); and in the work on *Heaven and Hell* (n. 20–28, 29–40).

All things of the natural world are from the Divine through the spiritual world (n. 5013). Consequently the spiritual is in every natural thing, just as the efficient cause is in the effect (n. 3562, 5711); or as effort is in motion (n. 5173), and as the internal is in the external (n. 3562, 5326, 5711). And since the cause is the very essential in the effect, as effort is in motion, and the internal in the external; hence it follows, that the spiritual, and consequently the Divine is the very essential in the natural (n. 2987–3002, 9701–9709). Spiritual things are presented to view in the natural, and the things manifested are representatives and correspondences (n. 1632, 2987–3002). Hence all nature is a theatre representative of the spiritual world, that is, of heaven (n. 2758, 2999, 3000, 4939, 8848, 9280). All things in nature are disposed in order and series according to ends (n. 4104). This is from the spiritual world, that is, from heaven, because ends, which are uses, reign there (n. 454, 696, 1103, 3645, 4054, 7038). Man is so created that Divine things descending according to order into nature, may be perceived in him (n. 3702).

With every man, who is in Divine order, there is an internal and an external, his internal is called the spiritual, or the spiritual man, and his external is called the natural, or the natural man (n. 978, 1015, 4459, 6309, 9701–9709). The spiritual man is in the light of heaven, and the natural man in the light of the world (n. 5965). The natural man can discern nothing from himself, but from the spiritual (n. 5286). The natural is like a face in which the interiors see themselves, and thus man thinks (n. 5165). The spiritual man thinks in the natural, consequently naturally, so far as it comes to the sensual perception of the natural (n. 3679, 5165, 6284, 6299). The natural is the plane, in which the spiritual terminates (n. 5651, 6275, 6284, 6299, 9216). The spiritual sees nothing, unless the natural be in correspondence (n. 3493, 3620, 3623). The spiritual or internal man can see what is being done in the natural or external, but not the contrary, because the spiritual flows into the natural, and not the natural into the spiritual (n. 3219, 4667, 5119, 5259, 5427, 5428 5477, 6322, 9109, 9110). The natural man from his own light, which is called the light [*lumen*] of nature, knows nothing concerning God, nor concerning heaven, nor concerning the life after death; neither does he believe, if he hears of such things, unless spiritual light, which is light from heaven, flows into that natural light [*lumen*] (n. 8944).

The natural man of himself, by birth, is opposite to the spiritual man (n. 3913, 3928). Therefore as long as they are opposite to each other, man feels it grievous to think of spiritual and celestial things, but delightful to think of natural and corporeal things (n. 4096). He nauseates the things of heaven, and even the bare mention of anything spiritual, from experience (n. 5006, 9109). Merely natural men regard spiritual good and truth as a servant (n. 5013, 5025). When nevertheless the natural man ought to be subordinate to the spiritual man, and serve him (n. 3019, 5168). The spiritual man is said to serve the natural, when the latter from the intellectual principle seeks confirmations of the objects of his concupiscence, particularly from the Word (n. 3019, 5013, 5025, 5168). How merely natural men appear in another life, and what is the quality of their state and lot there (n. 4630, 4633, 4940-4952, 5032, 5571).

The truths, which are in the natural man, are called scientifics and knowledges (n. 3293). The imagination of the natural man, when viewed in itself, is material, and his affections are like those of beasts (n. 3020). But there is a genuine thinking and imaginative principle from the internal or spiritual man, when the natural man sees, acts, and lives therefrom (n. 3493, 5422, 5423, 5427, 5428, 5477, 5510).

The things which are in the natural man, respectively to those which are in the spiritual man, are general (n. 3513, 5707); and consequently obscure (n. 6686).

There is an interior and an exterior natural with man (n. 3293, 3294, 3793, 5118, 5126, 5497, 5649). There is also a medium between them (n. 4570, 9216). The discharges of the spiritual man are made into the natural, and by it (n. 9572).

They who do good merely from a natural disposition, and not from religion, are not received in heaven (n. 8002, 8772).

49. *Of the light of heaven in which the spiritual man is.*
There is great light in the heavens (n. 1117, 1521, 1533, 1619–1632). The light in the heavens exceeds the meridian light on earth by many degrees (n. 1117, 1521, 4527, 5400, 8644). That light has been often seen by me (n. 1522, 4527, 7174). The light which the angels of the inmost or third heaven have is as the light from the sun, but the light which the angels of the second heaven have is as the light from the moon (n. 1529, 1530). The light in the inmost heaven is flamy, but in the second heaven it is bright white (n. 9570).

All light in the heavens is from the Lord as a sun there (n. 1053, 1521, 3195, 3341, 3636, 3643, 4415, 9548, 9684, 10,809). The Lord is the sun of the angelic heaven, and His Divine love is that sun (n. 1521, 1529, 1530, 1531, 1837, 4321, 4696, 7078, 7083, 7173). The Divine truth proceeding from the Lord in the heavens appears as light, and constitutes all the light of heaven; and consequently that light is spiritual light (n. 3195, 3322, 5400, 8644, 9399, 9548, 9684). Therefore the Lord in the Word is called light (n. 3195). Because that light is the Divine truth, there is in it Divine wisdom and intelligence (n. 3195, 3485, 3636, 3643, 3993, 4302, 4413, 4415, 9548, 9684). How light from the Lord flows into the heavens, illustrated by the circles of rays round the sun (n. 9407). The Lord is a sun to the heavens, and from Him is all the light there, may be seen in the work on *Heaven and Hell* (n. 116–125). And the light from that sun is the Divine truth, and the heat from it the Divine good of the Divine love (n. 126 to 140).

The light of heaven enlightens both the sight and the understanding of angels and spirits (n. 2776, 3138). They have light there according to their understanding and wisdom (n. 1524, 3339). Testified from the Word (n. 1529, 1530). There are as many differences of light in the heavens as there are angelic societies (n. 4414); since there are perpetual varieties in the heavens as to good and truth, thus as to wisdom and intelligence (n. 684, 690, 3241, 3744, 3745, 5598, 7236, 7833, 7836).

Heaven's being in light and heat signifies its being in wisdom and in love (n. 3643, 9399, 9400).

The light of heaven enlightens the understanding of man (n. 1524, 3138, 3167, 4408, 6608, 8707, 9128, 9399, 10,569). Man, when he is elevated from the sensual comes into a milder light [lumen], and at length into celestial light [lux] (n. 6313, 6315, 9407). There is elevation into the light of heaven when man comes into intelligence (n. 3190). What great light was perceived, when I have been withdrawn from worldly ideas (n. 1526, 6608). The sight of the internal man is in the light of heaven, and therefore man is able to think analytically and rationally (n. 1532). The light of heaven from the Lord is always present with man, but it flows in only so far as he is in truths from good (n. 4060, 4214). That light is according to truth from good (n. 3094). Truths shine in the spiritual world (n. 5219). Spiritual heat and spiritual light make the true life of man (n. 6032).

The light of the world is for the external man, and the light of heaven for the internal (n. 3223, 3324, 3337). The light of heaven flows into natural light [lumen] and the natural man is so far wise as he receives that light (n. 4302, 4408). There is a correspondence between those lights (n. 3225). The things which are in the light of heaven cannot be seen from the light of the world with man, which is called his natural light [lumen]; but the things in the light of the world may be seen from the light of heaven (n. 9577). Whence it follows, that they who are only in the light of the world, which is called natural light [lumen], do not perceive those things which are of the light of heaven (n. 3108). To those who are in falsities from evil, the light of heaven is thick darkness (n. 1783, 3337, 3413, 4060, 6907, 8197). The light of the world with the evil is glowing, and so far as it glows, so far the things which are of the light of heaven are dark to them (n. 6907). The light of the world does not appear to the angels (n. 1521, 1783, 1880).

In the heavens all light is from the Lord, and all shade from the ignorance and proprium of the angels and spirits; hence the modifications and variegations of light and shade, which are colors there (n. 3341). Concerning the variegations of light by the Urim and Thummim (n. 3862).

The light of those who are in faith separate from charity is snowy, and like the light of winter (n. 3412, 3413). That light is turned into mere darkness on the influx of light from heaven (n. 3412). Of the light of those who are in a persuasive faith, and in a life of evil (n. 4416). Of what quality the light appears with those who are in intelligence from the proprium, and what with those who are in intelligence from the Lord (n. 4419).

There is light [*lumen*] in the hells, but fatuous (n. 1528, 3340, 4214, 4418, 4531). This light is as light from a coal fire (n. 1528, 4418, 4531). They who are in the hells appear to themselves in their own light as men, but in the light of heaven as devils and monsters (n. 4532, 4533, 4674, 5057, 5058, 6605, 6626). All things in the light of heaven appear according to their true quality (n. 4674). The hells are said to be in thick darkness and darkness, because they are in falsities from evils (n. 3340, 4418, 4531). "Darkness" signifies falsities, and "thick darkness" the falsity of evil (n. 1839, 1860, 7688, 7711).

50. *Of the sensual man, who is the lowest degree natural (spoken of in the doctrine above, n. 45).*

The sensual is the ultimate of the life of man, adhering to and inhering in his corporeal (n. 5077, 5767, 9212, 9216, 9331, 9730). He who judges and concludes concerning everything from the bodily senses, and who believes nothing but what he can see with his eyes and touch with his hands, saying that these are something, and rejecting all things else, is a sensual man (n. 5094, 7693). Such a man thinks in outmosts, and not interiorly in himself (n. 5089, 5094, 6564, 7693). His interiors are shut, so that he sees nothing of truth therein (n. 6564, 6844, 6845). In a word, he is in gross natural light, and thus perceives nothing which is from the light of heaven (n. 6201, 6310, 6564, 6598, 6612, 6614, 6622, 6624, 6844, 6845). Consequently he is interiorly against the things which are of heaven and the church (n. 6201, 6316, 6844, 6845, 6948, 6949). The learned, who have confirmed themselves against the truths of the church, are sensual (n. 6316).

Sensual men reason sharply and shrewdly, because their thought is so near their speech as to be almost in it, and because they place all intelligence in discourse from the memory alone (n. 195, 196, 5700, 10,236). But they reason from the fallacies of the senses, with which the common people are captivated (n. 5084, 6948, 6949, 7693).

Sensual men are more crafty and malicious than others (n. 7693, 10,236). The avaricious, adulterers, the voluptuous, and the deceitful especially are sensual (n. 6310). Their interiors are foul and filthy (n. 6201). By means thereof they communicate with the hells (n. 6311). They who are in the hells are sensual in proportion to their depth (n. 4623, 6311). The sphere of infernal spirits conjoins itself with man's sensual from behind (n. 6312). They who reasoned from the sensual, and thereby against the truths of faith, were called by the ancients serpents of the tree of knowledge (n. 195–197, 6398, 6949, 10,313).

The sensual of man, and the sensual man himself, is further described (n. 10,236). And the extension of the sensual with man (n. 9731).

Sensual things ought to be in the last place, not in the first, and with a wise and intelligent man they are in the last place and subject to the interiors; but with an unwise man they are in the first place, and have dominion; these are they who are properly called sensual (n. 5077, 5125, 5128, 7645). If sensual things are in the last place, and are subject to the interiors, a way is opened through them to the understanding, and truths are refined by a kind of extraction (n. 5580).

The sensual things of man stand nearest to the world, and admit things that flow from the world, and as it were sift them (n. 9726). The external or natural man communicates with the world by means of those sensuals, and with heaven by means of rationals (n. 4009). Thus sensual things administer those things which are serviceable to the interiors of man (n. 5077, 5081). There are sensual things ministering to the intellectual part, and likewise to the will part (n. 5077).

Unless the thought is elevated from sensual things, man possesses but little wisdom (n. 5089). A wise man thinks above the sensual (n. 5089, 5094). Man, when his thought is elevated above sensual things, comes into a clearer light [*lumen*], and at length into heavenly light [*lux*] (n. 6183, 6313, 6315, 9407, 9730, 9922). Elevation above sensual things, and withdrawal from them, was known to the ancients (n. 6313).

Man with his spirit may see the things which are in the spiritual world, if he can be withdrawn from the sensual things of the body, and elevated by the Lord into the light of heaven (n. 4622). The reason is, because the body does not feel, but the spirit in the body; and so far as the spirit perceives in the body, so far is the perception gross and obscure, consequently in darkness; but so far as not in the body, so far is the perception clear and in the light (n. 4622, 6614, 6622).

The ultimate of the understanding is the sensual scientific, and the ultimate of the will the sensual delight, concerning which see (n. 9996). What is the difference between the sensual things that are common with beasts, and those that are not common with them (n. 10,236). There are sensual men who are not evil, inasmuch as their interiors are not so much closed; concerning whose state in another life (see n. 6311).

51. *Of sciences and knowledges, by which the internal spiritual man is opened.*

Those things are called scientifics, which are in the external or natural man, and its memory, but not those which are in the internal or spiritual man (n. 3019, 3020, 3293, 3309, 4967, 9918, 9922). Scientifics, as belonging to the external or natural man, are respectively instruments of service, inasmuch as the external or natural man is made to serve the internal or spiritual man, just as the world is made to serve heaven (n. 5077, 5125, 5128, 5786, 5947, 10,272, 10,471). The external man is respectively the world, because the laws of Divine order existing in the world are inscribed therein; and the internal man is respectively heaven, because the laws of Divine order existing in heaven are inscribed therein (n. 4523, 4524, 5368, 6013, 6057, 9278, 9279, 9283, 9709, 10,156, 10,472); and in the work on *Heaven and Hell* (n. 51–58).

There are scientifics which concern natural things, scientifics which relate to the civil state and life, scientifics which relate to the moral state and life, and scientifics which relate to the spiritual state and life (n. 5774, 5934). But for distinction's sake, those which relate to the spiritual state and life are called knowledges, consisting principally of doctrinals (n. 9945).

Man ought to be imbued with sciences and knowledges, since by these he learns to think, then to understand what is true and good (n. 129, 1450, 1451, 1453, 1548, 1802). Scientifics and knowledges are the first things, on which is built and founded the civil, moral, and spiritual life of man; but they are to be learned for the sake of the use of life as their end (n. 1489, 3310). Knowledges open the way to the internal man, and then conjoin it with the external according to uses (n. 1563, 1616). The rational is born by sciences and knowledges (n. 1895, 1900, 3086). Yet not by sciences and knowledges themselves, but by the affection of uses from them, and according to such affection (n. 1895). The internal man is opened and successively perfected by sciences and knowledges, provided man has some good use for an end, particularly a use that regards eternal life (n. 3086). Then the scientifics and knowledges which are in the natural man meet the spiritual things from the celestial and spiritual man and adopt those which agree (n. 1495). Uses of heavenly life are then extracted, refined, and elevated by the Lord, through the internal man, from the scientifics and knowledges which are in the natural man (n. 1895, 1896, 1900–1902, 5871, 5874, 5901). And the scientifics which are incongruous and adverse are rejected to the sides and exterminated (n. 5871, 5886, 5889). The sight of the internal man calls nothing forth from the scientifics and knowledges of the external man, but such as are of its love (n. 9394). Scientifics and knowledges are disposed in bundles, and conjoined according to the loves which introduced them (n. 5881). Then in the sight of the internal man, those which are of the love are in the middle and in clearness, but those which are not of the love are at the sides and in obscurity (n. 6068, 6084). Scientifics and knowledges with man are successively implanted in his loves, and dwell in them (n. 6325). Man would be born into every science, and thereby into intelligence, if he were born into love to the Lord and love towards the neighbor; but because he is born into the love of self and the world, he is born in total ignorance (n. 6323, 6325). Science, intelligence, and wisdom are the sons of love to the Lord and of love towards the neighbor (n. 1226, 2049, 2116).

Scientifics and knowledges, because they are of the external or natural man, are in the light of the world; but truths, which are become truths of love and faith, and have thus obtained life, are in the light of heaven (n. 5212). Nevertheless the truths, which have thus obtained life, are comprehended by man through natural ideas (n. 5510). Spiritual influx is through the internal man into the scientifics and knowledges which are in the external (n. 1940, 8005). Scientifics and knowledges are the receptacles and as it were the vessels of the truth and good of the internal man (n. 1469, 1496, 3068, 5489, 6004, 6023, 6052, 6071, 6077, 7770, 9922). Therefore by "vessels" in the Word, in the spiritual sense, are signified scientifics and knowledges (n. 3068, 3069, 3079, 9394, 9544, 9723, 9724). Scientifics are as it were mirrors, in which the truths and goods of the internal man appear, and are perceived as in an image (n. 5201). And there they are together as in their ultimate (n. 5373, 5874, 5886, 5901, 6004, 6023, 6052, 6071, 6077). Scientifics, because they are in the light of the world, are involved and obscure respectively to those things which are in the light of heaven; thus the things which are in the external man respectively to those in the internal (n. 2831). For which reason also by "involved" in the Word is signified what is scientific (n. 2831). So also by "the obscurity of a cloud" (n. 8443, 10,551).

Every principle is to be drawn from the truths of doctrine from the Word, which are first to be acknowledged, and then it is allowable to consult scientifics in order to confirm those truths, and thus they are corroborated (n. 6047). Thus it is allowable for those who are in the affirmative concerning the truths of faith, intellectually to confirm them by scientifics; but not for those who are in the negative, because a preceding affirmative draws all to favor its side, and a preceding negative draws all to its side (n. 2568, 2588, 3913, 4760, 6047). There is a doubting affirmative, and a doubting negative, the former with some who are good, and the latter with the evil (n. 2568). To enter from the truths of faith into scientifics is according to order; but on the other hand, to enter from scientifics into the truths of faith is contrary to order (n. 10,236). Inasmuch as influx is spiritual, and not physical or natural, thus from the truths of faith, because these are spiritual, into scientifics, because these are natural (n. 3219, 5119, 5259, 5427, 5428, 5478, 6322, 9109, 9110).

Whoever is in a doubting negative, which in itself is a negative, and says that he will not believe until he is persuaded by scientifics, will never believe (n. 2094, 2832). They who do so, become insane as to those things which are of the church and heaven (n. 128-130). They fall into the falsities of evil (n. 232, 233, 6047). And in the other life, when they think about spiritual things, they are as it were drunken (n. 1072). A further description of them (n. 196). Examples to illustrate that spiritual things cannot be comprehended, if the order of entering into them be inverted (n. 233, 2094, 2196, 2203, 2209). Many of the learned are more insane in spiritual things, than the simple, because they are in the negative, and have abundance of scientifics, by which they confirm the negative (n. 4760). An example of a learned man, who could understand nothing concerning spiritual life (n. 8629). They who reason from scientifics against the truths of faith, reason sharply, inasmuch as they do it from the fallacies of the senses, which captivate and persuade, for it is with difficulty these can be shaken off (n. 5700). They who understand nothing of truth, and they also who are in evil, can reason concerning the truths and goods of faith, and yet be in no enlightenment (n. 4214). Only to confirm a dogma, is not the part of an intelligent man, because falsity can be as easily confirmed as the truth (n. 1017, 2482, 2490, 4741, 5033, 6865, 7012, 7680, 7950, 8521, 8780). They who reason concerning the truths of the church, whether a thing be so or not, are evidently in obscurity respecting truths, and not yet in spiritual light (n. 215, 1385, 3033, 3428).

There are scientifics which admit Divine truths, and others which do not (n. 5213). Vain scientifics ought to be destroyed (n. 1489, 1492, 1499, 1500). Those are vain scientifics which regard for their end and confirm the loves of self and the world, and which withdraw from love to the Lord and love towards the neighbor because such scientifics shut up the internal man, so that he is not then capable of receiving anything from heaven (n. 1563, 1600). Scientifics are the means of becoming wise, and the means of becoming insane; and by them the internal man is either opened or shut; and thus the rational is either cultivated or destroyed (n. 4156, 8628, 9922).

Sciences after death are of no account, but only those things which man has imbibed in his understanding and life by means of sciences (n. 2480). Nevertheless all scientifics remain after death, but they are quiescent (n. 2476-2479, 2481-2486).

The same scientifics which with the evil are falsities because applied to evils, with the good are truths, because applied to goods (n. 6917). Scientific truths with the evil are not truths, however they may appear as truths when spoken, because within them there is evil, and consequently they are falsified; and the science of those men by no means deserves to be called science, inasmuch as it is destitute of life (10,331).

It is one thing to be wise, another to understand, another to know, and another to do; but still, with those who are in spiritual life, they follow in order, and correspond, and are together in doing or in deeds (n. 10,331). It is also one thing to know, another to acknowledge, and another to have faith (n. 896).

What is the quality of the desire of knowing, which spirits have, shown by an example (n. 1973). Angels have an immense desire of knowing and of becoming wise, inasmuch as science, intelligence and wisdom, are spiritual food (n. 3114, 4459, 4792, 4976, 5147, 5293, 5340, 5342, 5410, 5426, 5576, 5582, 5588, 5655, 6277, 8562, 9003).

The chief science with the ancients was the science of correspondences, but at this day it is lost (n. 3021, 3419, 4280, 4844, 4964, 4966, 6004, 7729, 10,252). The science of correspondences flourished with the orientals, and in Egypt (n. 5702, 6692, 7097, 7779, 9391, 10,407). Thence came their hieroglyphics (n. 6692, 7097). The ancients by the science of correspondences introduced themselves into the knowledges of spiritual things (n. 4749, 4844, 4966). The Word is written by mere correspondences, whence its internal or spiritual sense, the existence of which cannot be known without the science of correspondences, nor can the quality of the Word (n. 3131, 3472-3485, 8615, 10,687). How much the science of correspondences excels other sciences (n. 4280).

52. *Of the natural memory, which is of the external man, and of the spiritual memory, which is of the internal man.*

Man has two memories, an exterior and an interior memory, or a natural and a spiritual memory (n. 2469-2494). Man does not know that he has an interior memory (n. 2470, 2471). How much the interior memory excels the exterior memory (n. 2473). The things in the exterior memory are in natural light, but the things in the interior memory, in spiritual light (n. 5212). It is from the interior memory that man is able to think and speak intellectually and rationally (n. 9394). All and every particular which man has thought, spoken and done, and all that he has heard and seen, are inscribed on his interior memory (n. 2474, 7398). That memory is man's book of life (n. 2474, 9386, 9841, 10,505). In the interior memory are the truths which are become of faith, and the goods which are become of love (n. 5212, 8067). The things which are rendered habitual, and have become of the life, are in the interior memory (n. 9394, 9723, 9841). Scientifics and knowledges are of the exterior memory (n. 5212, 9922). They are very obscure and involved, respectively to those things which are of the interior memory (n. 2831). The languages which man speaks in the world are from the exterior memory (n. 2472, 2476). Spirits and angels speak from the interior memory, and consequently their language is universal, being such that all can converse together, of whatever land they may be (n. 2472, 2476, 2490, 2493); concerning which language, see the work on *Heaven and Hell* (n. 234–245); and concerning the wonders of the interior memory, which remains with man after death (see n. 463 of the same work).

53. *Of the fallacies of the senses, in which merely natural and sensual men are, mentioned above in this doctrine* (n. 45).

Merely natural and sensual men think and reason from the fallacies of the senses (n. 5084, 5700, 6948, 6949, 7693). Of what quality the fallacies of the senses are (n. 5084, 5094, 6400, 6948). To which the following particulars shall be added. There are fallacies of the senses in things natural, civil, moral, and spiritual, and many in each of them; but here I design to recite some of the fallacies in spiritual things. He who thinks from the fallacies of the senses, cannot understand: (1.) That man after death can appear as a man; nor that he can enjoy his senses as before; nor consequently that angels have such a capacity. (2.) They think that the soul is only a vital something, purely etherial, of which no idea can be formed. (3.)

That it is the body alone which feels, sees, and hears. (4.) That man is like a beast, with this difference only, that he can speak from thought. (5.) That nature is all, and the first source from which all things proceed. (6.) That man imbues and learns to think by an influx of interior nature and its order. (7.) That there is no spiritual, and if it is, that it is a purer natural. (8.) That man cannot enjoy any blessedness, if deprived of the delights of the love of glory, honor, or gain. (9.) That conscience is only a disease of the mind, proceeding from the infirmity of the body and from not having success. (10.) That the Divine love of the Lord is the love of glory. (11.) That there is no providence, but that all things come to pass from one's own prudence and intelligence. (12.) That honors and riches are real blessings which are given by God. Not to mention many other things of a similar nature. Such are the fallacies of the senses in spiritual things. Hence it may appear, that heavenly things cannot be comprehended by those who are merely natural and sensual. Those are merely natural and sensual whose internal spiritual man is shut, and whose natural only is open.

IV.

LOVE IN GENERAL.

54. The very life of man is his love, and such as the love is, such is the life, yea, such is the whole man. But it is the governing or ruling love which constitutes the man. That love has many loves subordinate to it, which are derivations. These appear under another form, but still they are all in the ruling love, and constitute, with it, one kingdom. The ruling love is as their king and head; it directs them, and, through them, as mediate ends, it regards and intends its own end, which is the primary and ultimate end of them all; and this it does both directly and indirectly. That which is of the ruling love is what is loved above all things.

55. That which man loves above all things is continually present in his thought, and also in his will, and constitutes his most essential life. As for example, he who loves riches above all things, whether money or possessions, continually revolves in his mind how he may obtain them. He inmostly rejoices when he acquires them, he grieves inmostly when he loses them; his heart is in them. He who loves himself above all things regards himself in each thing: he thinks of himself, he speaks of himself, he acts for the sake of himself, for his life is the life of self.

56. Man has for an end that which he loves above all things; he regards it in each and all things. It is in his will like the latent current of a river, which draws and bears him away, even when he is doing something else; for it is this which animates him. It is such that one man explores and also sees it in another, and either leads him according to it, or acts with him.

57. Man is altogether of such a quality as the ruling principle of his life is; by this he is distinguished from others; according to this is his heaven if he be good, and his hell if he be evil. It is his will itself, his proprium, and his nature, for it is the very *esse* of his life: this cannot be changed after death, because it is the man himself.

58. All the delight, pleasure, and happiness which any one has, are derived from his ruling love, and are according to it; for that which man loves, he calls delightful, because he feels it to be so: he may, indeed, also call that delightful which he thinks but does not love; but this is not the delight of his life. The delight of love is what he esteems good; and that which is undelightful is to him evil.

59. There are two loves, from which, as from their very fountains, all goods and truths exist; and there are two loves, from which all evils and falsities exist. The two loves, from which are all goods and truths, are love to the Lord and love towards the neighbor; and the two loves from which are all evils and falsities, are the love of self and the love of the world. The two latter loves are in direct opposition to the two former loves.

60. The two loves from which are all goods and truths, and which, as has just been stated, are love to the Lord and love towards the neighbor, constitute heaven with man, and therefore they reign in heaven; and since they constitute heaven with man, they also constitute the church with him. The two loves, whence are all evils and falsities, and which, as has just been said, are the love of self and the love of the world, constitute hell with man; wherefore also they reign in hell.

61. The two loves whence are all goods and truths, and which, as already observed, are the loves of heaven, open and form the internal spiritual man, because they reside there. But the two loves whence are all evils and falsities, when they rule, shut and destroy the internal spiritual man, and render man natural and sensual, in proportion to the extent and quality of their dominion.

FROM THE ARCANA CŒLESTIA.

62. Love is the *esse* of man's life (n. 5002). Man, spirit, and angel, are altogether as their love is (n. 6872, 10,177, 10,284). Man has for an end what he loves (n. 3796). What man loves and has for an end reigns universally with him, that is, in each and all things (n. 3796, 5130, 5949). Love is spiritul heat, and the very vital principle of man (n. 1589, 2146, 3338, 4906, 7081–7086, 9954, 10,740). All the interiors with man, which are of his understanding and will, are disposed in a form according to his ruling love (n. 2023, 3189, 6690). Love is spiritual conjunction (n. 1594, 2057, 3939, 4018, 5807, 6195, 6196, 7081–7086, 7501, 10,130). Hence all in the spiritual world are consociated according to their loves (*ibid.*). Affection is continuation of love (n. 3938). All delight, pleasure, happiness, and joy of heart, are of love; and their quality is according to the quality of the love (n. 994, 995, 2204). There are as many genera and species of delights and pleasures as there are of the affections which are of the love (n. 994, 995, 2204). The delight of the love is more vile in proportion as it is more external (n. 996). Man after death has such a life as is the quality of his love (n. 2363).

63. Further particulars respecting love and its essence and quality, may be known from what has been said and shown above, concerning good and truth; also from what has been said and quoted concerning the will and the understanding; and also from what has been said and quoted concerning the internal and the external man; because all things which are of the love refer themselves either to goods or to evils; and so also all things which are of the will: and since the two loves of heaven open and form the internal spiritual man; but the two loves of hell close and destroy it. Hence applications may be made and conclusions drawn respecting the quality of love in general and particular.

64. Love is also treated of in the work on *Heaven and Hell;* namely, that the Divine of the Lord in the heavens is love to Him and love towards the neighbor (n. 13–19). All who are in the hells are in evils, and thence in falsities from the loves of self and of the world (n. 551–565). The delights of every love in the other life are turned into corresponding things (n. 485–490). Spiritual heat in its essence is love (n. 133–140).

V.

THE LOVES OF SELF AND OF THE WORLD.

65. The love of self consists in willing well to ourselves alone, and not to others except for the sake of ourselves, not even to the church, to our country, to any human society, or to a fellow-citizen; and also in doing good to them only for the sake of our own fame, honor, and glory; for unless it sees these in the goods which it does to others, it says in its heart, What matters it? why should I do this? and what advantage will it be to me? and so omits them. Whence it is plain that he who is in the love of self does not love the church, nor his country, nor society, nor his fellow-citizens, nor anything good, but himself alone.

66. Man is in the love of self, when, in those things which he thinks and does, he has no regard for the neighbor, nor for the public, much less for the Lord, but only for himself and his own; consequently when everything which he does is for the sake of himself and his own, and when, if he does anything for the public and his neighbor it is only for the sake of appearance.

67. It is said for the sake of himself and his own, because he who loves himself also loves his own, who are, in particular, his children and relations, and in general, all who make one with him, and whom he calls his own. To love these is also to love himself, for he regards them as it were in himself, and himself in them. Among those whom he calls his own, are also all they who praise, honor, and pay their court to him.

68. That man is in the love of self, who despises the neighbor in comparison with himself, who esteems him his enemy if he does not favor him, and if he does not respect and pay his court to him: he is still more in the love of self who for such reasons hates the neighbor and persecutes him; and he is still more so who for such reasons burns with revenge against him, and desires his destruction: such persons at length delight in cruelty.

69. What the nature of the love of self is, may be evident from a comparison with heavenly love. Heavenly love is to love uses for the sake of uses, or goods for the sake of goods, which the man performs to the church, to his country, to human society, and to a fellow-citizen. But he who loves them for the sake of himself, does not love them otherwise than as his servants, because they are of service to him. It follows from this that he who is in the love of self wills that the church, his country, human societies, and his fellow-citizens serve him, and not he them. He puts himself above them, and them below him.

70. Moreover, as far as any one is in heavenly love, which is to love uses and goods, and to be affected with delight of heart when he performs them, so far he is led by the Lord, because that love is what He is in, and what is from Him. But as far as any one is in the love of self, so far he is led by himself; and as far as he is led by himself, he is so far led by his proprium; and man's proprium is nothing but evil; for evil is his heredity, which is to love himself above God, and the world above heaven.

71. The love of self is also such, that as far as the reins are relaxed, that is, as far as external bonds are removed, which are the fear of the law and its penalties, and the fear of the loss of reputation, honor, gain, office, and life, so far he rushes on, until he not only wishes to bear sway over the whole world, but even over heaven, and over the Divine itself. To him there is no bound or end. This lies hidden in every one who is in the love of self, though it is not manifest before the world, where such reins and bonds hold him back; and every such man where met by impossibility, waits there until it becomes possible. From these things, the man who is in such love does not know that such insane and unbounded desire lies hidden within him. That it is nevertheless so, every one can see in potentates and kings, for whom there are not such checks, bonds, and impossibilities, and who rush on and subjugate provinces and kingdoms as far as success attends them, and aspire to power and glory without limit; and still more in those who extend their dominion into heaven, and transfer all the Divine power of the Lord to themselves, and continually desire more.

72. There are two kinds of dominion, one that of love toward the neighbor, the other that of the love of self. These two kinds of dominion are in their essence altogether opposite to each other. He who rules from love toward the neighbor, wills good to all, and loves nothing more than to perform uses, thus to be of service to others. To serve others is to do good to them from good will, and to perform uses. This is his love, and this is the delight of his heart. He too, as far as he is elevated to dignities, is likewise glad; not, however, for the sake of the dignities, but for the sake of the uses which he is then able to perform in more abundance and in a greater degree. Such is the dominion in the heavens. But he who rules from the love of self wishes good to no one, but only to himself and his own. The uses which he performs are for the sake of his own honor and glory, which to him are the only uses. Serving others is to him for the end that he may be served, honored, and that he may rule. He seeks dignities, not for the sake of the goods he may perform, but to be in eminence and glory, and thence in the delight of his heart.

73. The love of dominion also remains with every one after his life in the world, but to those who have ruled from love toward the neighbor, rule is also entrusted in the heavens. But then they do not rule, but the uses and the goods which they love; and when uses and goods rule, the Lord rules. They, on the other hand, who in the world have ruled from the love of self, after their life in the world are in hell, and are in vile slavery there.

74. From these things it is now known who are in the love of self. But it matters not how they appear in outward form, whether elated or humble; for such things are in the interior man; and by most the interior man is concealed, and the exterior is instructed to feign the things which belong to love for the public and the neighbor, thus the opposite. And this is also done for the sake of self: for they know that the love of the public and the neighbor interiorly affect all, and that so far they will be loved and esteemed. The reason why that love affects all, is because heaven flows into it.

75. The evils which belong to those who are in the love of self, are, in general, contempt of others, envy, enmity against those who do not favor them, hostility on that account, hatreds of various kinds, revenge, cunning, deceit, unmercifulness, and cruelty; and where such evils exist, there is also contempt of the Divine, and of Divine things, which are the truths and goods of the church. If they honor these, it is only with the mouth, and not with the heart. And because such evils are thence, so there are similar falsities, for falsities are from evils.

76. But the love of the world consists in wishing to draw the wealth of others to ourselves by any artifice, in placing the heart in riches, and in suffering the world to draw us back, and lead us away from spiritual love, which is love towards the neighbor, consequently, from heaven. They are in the love of the world who desire to draw the goods of others to themselves by various artifices, especially they who do so by means of cunning and deceit, making no account of the good of the neighbor. They who are in that love covet the goods of others, and so far as they do not fear the laws and the loss of reputation for the sake of gain, they deprive others of their goods, yea commit depredations.

77. But the love of the world is not opposite to heavenly love in the same degree that the love of self is, inasmuch as such great evils are not concealed in it. This love is manifold: there is the love of riches as the means of obtaining honors; there is the love of honors and dignities as the means of obtaining riches; there is the love of riches for the sake of various uses with which they are delighted in the world; there is the love of riches for the sake of riches alone, which is avarice, and so on. The end for the sake of which riches are desired, is called their use, and it is the end or use from which the love derives its quality; for the quality of the love is the same as that of the end which it has in view, to which other things serve as means.

78. In a word, the love of self and the love of the world are altogether opposite to love to the Lord and love towards the neighbor; wherefore the love of self and the love of the world are infernal loves, for they also reign in hell, and also constitute hell with man; but love to the Lord and love towards the neighbor are heavenly loves. They also reign in heaven, and also constitute heaven with man.

79. From what has now been said, it may be seen that all evils are in and from those two loves; for the evils which were enumerated (n. 75) are common; the others, which were not enumerated, because they are specific, are derived and flow from them. Hence it may appear, that man, because he is born into these two loves, is born into evils of every kind.

80. In order that man may know evils, he ought to know their origins, and unless he knows evils, he cannot know goods, thus he cannot know of what quality he himself is: this is the reason that these two origins of evils are treated of here.

FROM THE ARCANA CŒLESTIA.

81. *The loves of self and of the world.*

As love to the Lord and love towards the neighbor, or charity, constitute heaven, so the love of self and the love of the world, where they reign constitute hell; and therefore these loves are opposites (n. 2041, 3610, 4225, 4776, 6210, 7366, 7369, 7489, 7490, 8232, 8678, 10,455, 10,741–10,743, 10,745). All evils proceed from the loves of self and of the world (n. 1307, 1308, 1321, 1594, 1691, 3413, 7255, 7376, 7488, 7489, 8318, 9335, 9348, 10,038, 10,742). From the loves of self and of the world proceed contempt of others, enmity, hatred, revenge, cruelty, and deceit, consequently all evil and all wickedness

(n. 6667, 7372–7374, 9348, 10,038, 10,742). These loves rush on in proportion as the reins are given them, and the love of self aspires to the throne of God (n. 7375, 8678). The love of self and the love of the world are destructive of human society and of heavenly order (n. 2045, 2057). The human race on account of those loves has formed governments, and has subjected itself to their rule for the sake of protection (n. 7364, 10,160, 10,814). Where those loves reign, the good of love and the good of faith are either rejected, suffocated or perverted (n. 2041, 7491, 7492, 7643, 8487, 10,455, 10,743). In these loves there is not life, but spiritual death (n. 7494, 10,731, 10,741). The quality of these loves described (n. 1505, 2219, 2363, 2364, 2444, 4221, 4227, 4948, 4949, 5721, 7366–7377, 8678). All cupidity and lust proceed from the loves of self and of the world (n. 1668, 8910).

The loves of self and of the world may serve as means, but not at all for an end (n. 7377, 7819, 7820). When man is reformed, those loves are inverted, and serve as means, and not as ends, thus that they are as the soles of the feet, and not as the head (n. 8995, 9210). With those who are in the loves of self and of the world, there is no internal, but an external without an internal; because the internal is shut towards heaven, but the external is open towards the world (n. 10,396, 10,400, 10,409, 10,411, 10,422, 10,429). They who are in the loves of self and of the world do not know what charity, conscience, and the life of heaven are (n. 7490). So far as a man is in the loves of self and of the world, so far he does not receive the good and truth of faith which continually flows in with man from the Lord (n. 7491).

They who are in the loves of self and the world are not bound by internal, but by external restraints; and on the removal thereof they rush into every wickedness (n. 10,744–10,746). All in the spiritual world turn themselves according to their loves; they who are in love to the Lord and in love towards the neighbor, to the Lord; but those who are in the love of self and in the love of the world, turn their backs on the Lord (n. 10,130, 10,189, 10,420, 10,742). The quality of the worship in which the love of self prevails (n. 1304, 1306–1308, 1321, 1322). The Lord rules the world by means of the evil, in leading them by their own loves, which have relation to the loves of self and the world (n. 6481, 6495). The evil as well as the good can discharge the duties of offices, and perform uses and goods, because they regard honors and gain as their rewards, for the sake of which they act in an external form like the good (n. 6481, 6495).

All who are in the hells are in evils and thence in falsities, and are in the loves of self and the world, see the work on *Heaven and Hell* (n. 551–565).

82. *Of the proprium of man, spoken of above* (n. 70), *that it is the love of self and of the world.*

The proprium of man is nothing but dense evil (n. 210, 215, 731, 874–876, 987, 1047, 2307, 2308, 3518, 3701, 3812, 8480, 8550, 10,283, 10,284, 10,286, 10,731). The proprium of man is his will (n. 4328). The proprium of man consists in loving himself more than God, and the world more than heaven, and in making his neighbor of no account respectively to himself, thus it is the love of self and of the world (n. 694, 731, 4317, 5660). Not only every evil, but also every falsity, springs from the proprium of man, and this falsity is the falsity of evil (n. 1047, 10,283, 10,284, 10,286). The proprium of man is hell with him (n. 694, 8480). Therefore he who is led by his proprium cannot be saved (n. 10,731). The good which man does from the proprium is not good, but in itself is evil, because done for the sake of self and the world (n. 8478).

The proprium of man must be separated, in order that the Lord may be present with him (n. 1023, 1044). And it is actually separated when man is reformed (n. 9334–9336, 9452–9454, 9938). This is done by the Lord alone (n. 9445). Man by regeneration receives a heavenly proprium (n. 1937, 1947, 2881, 2883, 2891). This appears to man as his own proprium, but it is not his, but the Lord's with him (n. 8497). They who are in this proprium are in liberty itself, because liberty consists in being led by the Lord, and by His proprium (n. 892, 905, 2872, 2886, 2890–2892, 4096, 9586, 9587, 9589–9591). All liberty is from the proprium, and its quality according thereto (n. 2880). What is the quality of the heavenly proprium (n. 164, 5660, 8480). How the heavenly proprium is implanted (n. 1712, 1937, 1947).

83. *Of the heredity of man, spoken of above* (n. 70–79), *it is the love of self and of the world.*

All men are born into evils of every kind, insomuch that their proprium is nothing but evil (n. 210, 215, 731, 874–876, 987, 1047, 2307, 2308, 3701, 3812, 8480, 8550, 10,283, 10,284, 10,286, 10,731). Therefore man is to be born again, that is, regenerated, in order that he may receive a new life from the Lord (n. 3701).

Hereditary evils are derived, increased and accumulated from parents and ancestors in a long backward series, and not as is believed, from the first man's eating of the tree of knowledge (n. 313, 494, 2910, 3469, 3701, 4317, 8550). Therefore hereditary evils are at this day more malignant than formerly (n. 2122). Infants who die such, and are educated in heaven, are from heredity nothing but evils (n. 2307, 2308, 4563). Hence they are of various dispositions and inclinations (n. 2300). Every man's interior evils are from the father, and the exterior from the mother (n. 1815, 3701).

Man superadds of himself new evils to such as are hereditary, which are called actual evils (n. 8551). No one suffers punishment in the other life for hereditary evils, but for actual evils, which return (n. 966, 2308). The more malignant hells are kept separate lest they should operate on the hereditary evils with men and spirits (n. 1667, 8806).

Hereditary evils are those of the loves of self and the world, which consist in man's loving himself more than God, and the world more than heaven, and in making his neighbor of no account (n. 694, 4317, 5660). And because these evils are contrary to the goods of heaven and to Divine order, man cannot but be born in mere ignorance (n. 1050, 1902, 1992, 3175). Natural good is connate with some, but nevertheless it is not good, because prone to all evils and falsities; and that good is not accepted in heaven unless it be made spiritual good (n. 2463, 2464, 2468, 3304, 3408, 3469, 3470, 3508, 3519, 7761).

VI.

LOVE TOWARDS THE NEIGHBOR, OR CHARITY.

84. It shall first be shown what the neighbor is, for it is the neighbor who is to be loved, and towards whom charity is to be exercised. For unless it be known what the neighbor is, charity may be exercised in a similar manner, without distinction, towards the evil as well as towards the good, whence charity ceases to be charity: for the evil, from benefactions, do evil to the neighbor, but the good do good.

85. It is a common opinion at this day, that every man is equally the neighbor, and that benefits are to be conferred on every one who needs assistance; but it is in the interest of Christian prudence to examine well the quality of a man's life, and to exercise charity to him accordingly. The man of the internal church exercises his charity with discrimination, consequently with intelligence; but the man of the external church, because he is not able thus to discern things, does it indiscriminately.

86. The distinctions of neighbor, which the man of the church ought altogether to know, are according to the good which is with every one; and because all good proceeds from the Lord, therefore the Lord is the neighbor in the highest sense and in a supereminent degree, and the origin is from Him. Hence it follows that so far as any one has the Lord with himself, so far he is the neighbor; and because no one receives the Lord, that is, good from Him, in the same manner as another, therefore no one is the neighbor in the same manner as another. For all who are in the heavens, and all the good who are on the earths, differ in good; no two ever received a good that is altogether one and the same; it must be various, that each may subsist by itself. But all these varieties, thus all the distinctions of the neighbor, which are according to the reception of the Lord, that is, according to the reception of good from Him, can never be known by any man, nor indeed by any angel, except in general, thus their genera and species: neither does the Lord require any more of the man of the church, than to live according to what he knows

87. Because good varies with every one, it therefore follows, that the quality of good determines in what degree and in what proportion any one is the neighbor. That this is the case is plain from the Lord's parable concerning him that fell among robbers, whom, when half dead, the priest passed by, and also the Levite; but the Samaritan, after he had bound up his wounds, and poured in oil and wine, took him up on his own beast, and led him to an inn, and ordered that care should be taken of him: because he exercised the good of charity, he is called the neighbor (*Luke* x. 29–37). Hence it may be known that they are the neighbor who are in good: "the oil and wine," which the Samaritan poured into the wounds, also signify good and its truth.

88. It is plain from what has now been said, that in the universal sense, good is the neighbor, because man is the neighbor according to the quality of the good that is with him from the Lord. And because good is the neighbor, so is love, for all good is of love; thus every man is the neighbor according to the quality of the love which he receives from the Lord.

89. That love is what causes any one to be the neighbor, and that every one is the neighbor according to the quality of his love, appears manifestly from those who are in the love of self. These acknowledge for their neighbor those who love them most, that is, so far as they belong to themselves; these they embrace, they kiss them, they confer benefits on them and call them brothers; yea, because they are evil, they say, that these are the neighbor more than others: they esteem others as the neighbor in proportion as they love them, thus according to the quality and quantity of their love. Such persons derive the origin of neighbor from self, by reason that love constitutes and determines it. But they who do not love themselves more than others, as is the case with all who belong to the kingdom of the Lord, will derive the origin of neighbor from Him whom they ought to love above all things, consequently, from the Lord; and they will esteem every one as the neighbor according to the quality of his love to Him and from Him. From these things it appears from whence the origin of neighbor is to be drawn by the man of the church; and that every one is the neighbor according to the good which he possesses from the Lord, thus good itself is the neighbor.

90. That this is the case, the Lord also teaches in *Matthew*:—

For He said to those who were in good that they had given Him to eat, that they had given Him to drink, that they had gathered Him, had clothed Him, had visited Him, and had come to Him in prison; and afterwards that, so far as they had done it to one of the least of their brethren, they had done it unto Him (xxv. 34–40).

In these six kinds of good, understood in the spiritual sense, are comprehended all the genera of the neighbor. Hence, likewise, it is evident, that when good is loved the Lord is loved, for it is the Lord from whom good is, who is in good, and who is good itself.

91. But the neighbor is not only man singly, but also man collectively, as a less or greater society, our country, the church, the Lord's kingdom, and, above all, the Lord Himself; these are the neighbor to whom good is to be done from love. These are also the ascending degrees of neighbor, for a society of many is neighbor in a higher degree than a single man is; in a still higher degree is our country; in a still higher degree is the church; and in a still higher degree is the Lord's kingdom; but in the highest degree is the Lord. These ascending degrees are like the steps of a ladder, at the top of which is the Lord.

92. A society is the neighbor more than a single man, because it consists of many. Charity is to be exercised towards it in a like manner as towards a man singly, namely, according to the quality of the good that is with it; thus in a manner totally different towards a society of the upright, than towards a society of those not upright. The society is loved when its good is regarded from the love of good.

93. Our country is the neighbor more than a society, because it is like a parent; for a man is born therein, and it nourishes and protects him from injuries. Good is to be done to our country from love according to its necessities, which principally regard its sustenance, and the civil and spiritual life of those therein. He who loves his country, and does good to it from good will, in the other life loves the Lord's kingdom, for there the Lord's kingdom is his country, and he who loves the Lord's kingdom loves the Lord, because the Lord is the all in all things of His kingdom.

94. The church is the neighbor more than our country, for he who has regard for the church, has regard for the souls and eternal life of the men who are in his country; wherefore he who provides for the church from love, loves the neighbor in a higher degree, for he wishes and wills heaven and happiness of life to eternity to others.

95. The Lord's kingdom is the neighbor in a still higher degree, for the Lord's kingdom consists of all who are in good, both those on the earths, and those in the heavens; thus the Lord's kingdom is good with all its quality in the complex: when this is loved, the individuals are loved who are in good.

96. These are the degrees of neighbor, and love ascends, with those who are in love towards their neighbor, according to these degrees. But these degrees are degrees in successive order, in which what is prior or superior is to be preferred to what is posterior or inferior; and because the Lord is in the highest degree, and He is to be regarded in each degree as the end to which it tends, consequently he is to be loved above all persons and things. From these things it may now appear, how love to the Lord conjoins itself with love towards the neighbor.

97. It is a common saying, that every one is his own neighbor; that is, that every one should first consider himself; but the doctrine of charity teaches how this is to be understood. Every one should provide for himself the necessaries of life, such as food, raiment, habitation, and many other things which the state of civil life, in which he is, necessarily requires, and this not only for himself, but also for his own, and not only for the present time, but also for the future; for unless a man procures for himself the necessaries of life, he cannot be in a state to exercise charity, for he is in want of all things.

98. But how every one ought to be his own neighbor may appear from this comparison. Every one ought to provide food and raiment for his body; this must be the first object, but it should be done to the end that he may have a sound mind in a sound body. And every one ought to provide food for his mind, namely, such things as are of intelligence and wisdom, to the end that it may thence be in a state to serve his fellow-citizens, human society, his country, and the church, thus the

Lord. He who does this provides for his own good to eternity. Hence it is evident that the first is where the end is on account of which we should act, for all other things look to this. The case is like that of a man who builds a house: he first lays the foundation; but the foundation is for the house, and the house is for habitation. He who believes that he is his own neighbor in the first place, is like him who regards the foundation as the end, not the house and habitation; when yet the habitation is the very first and ultimate end, and the house with the foundation is only a means to the end.

99. The end declares how every one should be his own neighbor, and provide for himself first. If the end be to grow richer than others only for the sake of riches, or for the sake of pleasure, or for the sake of eminence, and the like, it is an evil end, and that man does not love the neighbor, but himself; but if the end be to procure himself riches, that he may be in a state of providing for his fellow-citizens, human society, his country, and the church, in like manner if he procures for himself offices for the same end, he loves the neighbor. The end itself, for the sake of which he acts, constitues the man; for the end is his love, for every one has for a first and ultimate end, that which he loves above all things.

What has hitherto been said is concerning the neighbor. Love towards him, or Charity, shall now be treated of.

100. It is believed by many, that love towards the neighbor consists in giving to the poor, in assisting the indigent, and in doing good to every one; but charity consists in acting prudently, and to the end that good may result. He who assists a poor or indigent evil doer does evil to the neighbor through him, for through the assistance which he renders, he confirms him in evil, and supplies him with the means of doing evil to others. It is otherwise with him who gives support to the good.

101. But charity extends itself much more widely than to the poor and indigent; for charity consists in doing what is right in every work, and our duty in every office. If a judge does justice for the sake of justice, he exercises charity; if he punishes the guilty and absolves the innocent, he exercises charity, for thus he consults the welfare of his fellow-citizens, and of his country. The priest who teaches the truth, and leads to good, for the sake of truth and good, exercises charity. But he who does such things for the sake of self and the world, does not exercise charity, because he does not love the neighbor, but himself.

102. The case is the same in all other instances, whether a man be in any office or not; as with children towards parents, and with parents towards childen; with servants towards masters, and with masters towards servants; with subjects towards the king, and with a king towards subjects: whoever of these does his duty from a principle of duty, and what is just from a principle of justice, exercises charity.

103. The reason why such things belong to love towards the neighbor, or charity, is because, as was said above, every man is the neighbor, but in a different manner. A less and greater society is more the neighbor; our country is still more the neighbor; the Lord's kingdom still more; and the Lord above all; and in a universal sense, good, which proceeds from the Lord, is the neighbor; consequently also sincerity and justice. Wherefore he who does any good for the sake of good, and he who acts sincerely and justly for the sake of sincerity and justice, loves the neighbor and exercises charity; for he does so from the love of what is good, sincere, and just, and consequently from the love of those in whom good, sincerity, and justice are.

104. Charity therefore is an internal affection, from which man wills to do good, and this without remuneration; the delight of his life consists in doing it. With them who do good from internal affection, there is charity in each thing which they think and speak, and which they will and do; it may be said that a man and an angel, as to his interiors, is charity, when good is his neighbor. So widely does charity extend itself.

105. They who have the love of self and of the world for an end, cannot in any wise be in charity; they do not even know what charity is; and they cannot at all comprehend that to will and do good to the neighbor without reward as an end, is heaven in man, and that there is in that affection a happiness as great as that of the angels of heaven, which is ineffable;

for they believe, if they are deprived of the joy from the glory of honors and riches, that nothing of joy can be given them any longer; when yet it is then that heavenly joy first begins, which infinitely transcends the other.

FROM THE ARCANA CŒLESTIA.

106. Heaven is distinguished into two kingdoms, one of which is called the celestial kingdom, and the other the spiritual kingdom; the love in the celestial kingdom is love to the Lord, and is called celestial love; and the love in the spiritual kingdom is love towards the neighbor, or charity, and is called spiritual love (n. 3325, 3653, 7257, 9002, 9835, 9961). Heaven is distinguished into two kingdoms, see the work on *Heaven and Hell* (n. 20–28); and the Divine of the Lord in the heavens is love to Him, and charity towards the neighbor (n. 13–19, in the same).

It cannot be known what good is and what truth is, unless it be known what love to the Lord and love towards the neighbor are, because all good is of love, and all truth is of good (n. 7255, 7366). To know truths, to will truths, and to be affected with them for the sake of truths, that is, because they are truths, is charity (n. 3876, 3877). Charity consists in an internal affection of doing truth, and not in an external affection without an internal one (n. 2429, 2442, 3776, 4899, 4956, 8033). Thus charity consists in performing uses for the sake of uses (n. 7038, 8253). Charity is the spiritual life of man (n. 7081). The whole Word is the doctrine of love and charity (n. 6632, 7262). It is not known at this day what charity is (n. 2417, 3398, 4776, 6632). Nevertheless man may know from the light of his own reason, that love and charity make the man (n. 3957, 6273). Also that good and truth agree together, and that one is of the other, and so also love and faith (n. 7627).

The Lord is the neighbor in the highest sense, because He is to be loved above all things; and hence all is the neighbor which is from Him, and in which he is, thus good and truth (n. 2425, 3419, 6706, 6819, 6823, 8124). The distinction of neighbor is according to the quality of good, thus according to the presence of the Lord (n. 6707–6710). Every man and every society, also our country and the church, and, in the universal sense, the kingdom of the Lord, are the neighbor, and to do good to them according to the quality of their state from the love of good, is to love the neighbor; thus the neighbor is their good, which is to be consulted (n. 6818–6824, 8123). Civil good, which is justice, and moral good, which is the good of life in society, and is called sincerity, are also the neighbor (n. 2915, 4730, 8120–8122). To love the neighbor does not consist in loving his person, but in loving that with him from which he is, consequently good and truth (n. 5028, 10,336). They who love the person, and not that which is with him from which he is, love evil as well as good (n. 3820). And they do good to the evil as well as to the good, when nevertheless doing good to the evil is doing evil to the good, which is not loving the neighbor (n. 3820, 6703, 8120). The judge who punishes the evil that they may be amended, and that the good may not be contaminated by them, loves the neighbor (n. 3820, 8120, 8121).

To love the neighbor is to do what is good, just, and right, in every work and in every office (n. 8120–8122). Hence charity towards the neighbor extends itself to each and everything which man thinks, wills, and does (n. 8124). To do what is good and true is to love the neighbor (n. 10,310, 10,336). They who do this love the Lord, who in the highest sense is the neighbor (n. 9210). The life of charity is a life according to the commandments of the Lord; and to live according to Divine truths is to love the Lord (n. 10,143, 10,153, 10,310, 10,578, 10,645).

Genuine charity is not meritorious (n. 2027, 2343, 2400, 3887, 6388–6393). Because it is from internal affection, consequently from the delight of the life of doing good (n. 2373, 2400, 3887, 6388–6393). They who separate faith from charity, in another life hold faith and the good works which they have done in the external form as meritorious (n. 2373). They who are in evils from the love of self or the love of the world, do not know what it is to do good without remuneration, thus what that charity is which is not meritorious (n. 8037).

The doctrine of the Ancient Church was the doctrine of life, which is the doctrine of charity (n. 2385, 2417, 3419, 3420,

4844, 6628). Thence they had intelligence and wisdom (n. 2417, 6629, 7259–7262). Intelligence and wisdom increase immensely in the other life with those who have lived a life of charity in the world (n. 1941, 5859). The Lord flows in with Divine truth into charity, because into the essential life of man (n. 2063). The man with whom charity and faith are conjoined is like a garden; but like a desert with whom they are not conjoined (n. 7626). Man recedes from wisdom in proportion as he recedes from charity; and they who are not in charity, are in ignorance concerning Divine truths, however wise they think themselves (n. 2417, 2435). The angelic life consists in performing the goods of charity, which are uses (n. 454). The spiritual angels, who are they that are in the good of charity, are forms of charity (n. 553, 3804, 4735).

All spiritual truths regard charity as their beginning and end (n. 4353). The doctrinals of the church effect nothing unless they regard charity as their end (n. 2049, 2116).

The presence of the Lord with men and angels is according to their state of love and charity (n. 549, 904). Charity is the image of God (n. 1013). Love to the Lord, consequently the Lord, is within charity, although man does not know it (n. 2227, 5066, 5067). They who live a life of charity are accepted as citizens both in the world and in heaven (n. 1121). The good of charity is not to be violated (n. 2359).

They who are not in charity cannot acknowledge and worship the Lord except from hypocrisy (n. 2132, 4424, 9833). The forms of hatred and of charity cannot exist together (n. 1860).

107. To the above shall be added some particulars concerning the doctrine of love to the Lord, and the doctrine of charity, as it was held by the ancients with whom the church was, in order that the former quality of that doctrine, which at this day exists no longer, may be known. The particulars are extracted from the *Arcana Cœlestia* (n. 7257–7263).

The good which is of love to the Lord, is called celestial good; and the good which is of love towards the neighbor, or charity, is called spiritual good. The angels who are in the inmost or third heaven, are in the good of love to the Lord, being called celestial angels; but the angels of the middle or second heaven, are in the good of love towards the neighbor, being called spiritual angels.

The doctrine of celestial good, which is that of love to the Lord, is of most wide extent, and at the same time most full of arcana; being the doctrine of the angels of the inmost or third heaven, which is such, that if it were delivered from their mouths, scarcely a thousandth part of it would be understood: the things also which it contains are ineffable. This doctrine is contained in the inmost sense of the Word; but the doctrine of spiritual love, in the internal sense.

The doctrine of spiritual good, which is that of love towards the neighbor, is also of wide extent and full of arcana, but much less so than the doctrine of celestial good, which is that of love to the Lord. That the doctrine of love towards the neighbor, or charity, is of wide extent, may appear from the fact, that it reaches to all the things which man thinks and wills, consequently to all which he speaks and does, even to the most minute particulars; and also from the fact, that charity does not exist alike with two different persons, and that no two persons are alike the neighbor.

As the doctrine of charity was so extensive, therefore the ancients, with whom it was the very doctrine of the church, distinguished charity towards the neighbor into several classes, which they again subdivided, and gave names to each class, and taught how charity was to be exercised towards those who are in one class, and towards those who are in another; and thus they reduced the doctrine and the exercises of charity into order, that they might fall distinctly into the understanding.

The names which they gave to those towards whom they were to exercise charity were many; some they called "the blind," some "the lame," some "the maimed," some "the poor," some "the miserable," and "afflicted," some "the fatherless," some "widows," but in general they called them "the hungry," to whom they should give to eat; "the thirsty," to whom they should give to drink; "strangers," whom they should take in; "the naked," whom they should clothe; "the sick," whom they should visit, and "the bound in prison," to whom they should come.

Who they were whom they meant by these particulars, has been made known already in the *Arcana Cœlestia*, as whom they meant by "the blind" (n. 2383, 6990); by "the lame" (n. 4302); "the poor" (n. 2129, 4459, 4958, 9209, 9253, 10,227); "the miserable" (n. 2129); "the afflicted" (n. 6663, 6851, 9196); "the fatherless" (n. 4844, 9198–9200); and "widows" (n. 4844, 9198, 9200); "the hungry" (n. 4958, 10,227); "the thirsty" (n. 4958, 8568); "the strangers" (n. 4444, 7908, 8007, 8013, 9196, 9200); "the naked" (n. 1073, 5433, 9960); "the sick" (n. 4958, 6221, 8364, 9031); "the bound in prison" (n. 5037, 5038, 5086, 5096). It may be seen that the whole doctrine of charity is comprehended in the offices towards those who are called by the Lord "the hungry," "the thirsty," "strangers," "the naked," "the sick," and "the bound in prison" (*Matt.* xxv. 34–36, and the verses following) [n. 4954–4959].

These names were given from heaven to the ancients who were of the church, and by those who were so named they understood those who were spiritually such. Their doctrine of charity not only taught who these were, but also the quality of the charity to be exercised towards each. Hence it is, that the same names are in the Word, and signify those who are such in the spiritual sense. The Word in itself is nothing but the doctrine of love to the Lord, and of charity towards the neighbor, as the Lord also teaches:—

Thou shalt love the Lord thy God with all thy heart, and with all thy soul, and with all thy mind; this is the first and great commandment. The second is like unto it, Thou shalt love thy neighbor as thyself. On these two commandments hang all the law and the prophets (*Matt.* xxii. 37–40).

"The law and the prophets" are the whole Word (2606, 3382, 6752, 7643).

The reason why those same names are in the Word, is that the Word, which is in itself spiritual, might in its ultimate be natural; and because they who are in external worship are to exercise charity towards such as are so named, and they who are in internal worship towards such spiritually understood; thus that the simple might understand and do the Word in simplicity, and the wise, in wisdom; also, that the simple, by the externals of charity, might be initiated into its internals.

VII.

FAITH.

108. No one can know what faith is in its essence, unless he knows what charity is, because where there is no charity there is no faith, for charity makes one with faith as good does with truth. For what man loves or holds dear, this to him is good, and what man believes, this to him is truth; whence it is plain that there is a like union of charity and faith, as there is of good and truth; the quality of which union may appear from what has been said above concerning Good and Truth.

109. The union of charity and faith is also like that of the will and the understanding with man; for these are the two faculties which receive good and truth, the will receiving good and the understanding truth; thus, also, these two faculties receive charity and faith, since good is of charity and truth is of faith. Every one knows that charity and faith are with man, and in him, and because they are with man, and in him, they must be in his will and understanding, for all the life of man is therein, and from thence. Man has also memory, but this is only the outer court, where those things are collected together which are to enter into the understanding and the will. Thence it is evident that there is a like union of charity and faith, as there is of the will and the understanding; the quaiity of which union may appear from what has been said above concerning the Will and the Understanding.

110. Charity conjoins itself with faith with man, when man wills that which he knows and perceives; to will is of charity, and to know and perceive is of faith. Faith enters into man, and becomes his, when he wills and loves that which he knows and perceives; meanwhile it is without him.

111. Faith does not become faith with man, unless it becomes spiritual, and it does not become spiritual, unless it becomes of the love; and it then becomes of the love, when man loves to live truth and good, that is, to live according to those things which are commanded in the Word.

112. Faith is the affection of truth from willing truth because it is truth; and to will truth because it is truth is the spiritual itself of man; for it is abstracted from the natural, which is to will truth not for the sake of truth, but for the sake of one's own glory, reputation or gain. Truth withdrawn from such things is spiritual, because it is from the Divine. That which proceeds from the Divine is spiritual, and this is conjoined to man by love, for love is spiritual conjunction.

113. Man may know, think, and understand much, but when he is left to himself alone, and meditates, he rejects from himself those things which do not agree with his love; and therefore he also rejects them after the life of the body when he is in the spirit, for that only remains in the spirit of man which has entered into his love: other things after death are regarded as foreign, and because they are not of his love he casts them out. It is said in the spirit of man, because man lives a spirit after death.

114. An idea concerning the good which is of charity, and concerning the truth which is of faith, may be formed from the light and heat of the sun. When the light which proceeds from the sun is conjoined to heat, as is the case in the time of spring and summer, then all things of the earth germinate and flourish; but when there is no heat in the light, as in the time of winter, then all things of the earth become torpid and die; also spiritual light is the truth of faith, and spiritual heat is love. From these things an idea may be formed concerning the man of the church, what his quality is when faith with him is conjoined to charity, namely, that he is like a garden and paradise; and what his quality is when faith with him is not conjoined to charity, that he is like a desert and earth covered with snow.

115. The confidence or trust, which is said to be of faith, and is called saving faith itself, is not spiritual confidence or trust, but natural, when it is of faith alone. Spiritual confidence or trust has its essence and life from the good of love, but not from the truth of faith separate. The confidence of faith separate is dead; wherefore true confidence cannot be given with those who lead an evil life. The confidence also that salvation is on account of the Lord's merit with the Father, whatever a man's life may have been, is not from truth. All those who are in spiritual faith have confidence that they are saved by the Lord, for they believe that the Lord came into the world to give eternal life to those who believe and live according to the precepts which He taught, and that He regenerates them, and renders them fit for heaven, and that He alone does this from pure mercy without the aid of man.

116. To believe those things which the Word teaches, or which the doctrine of the church teaches, and not to live according to them, appears as if it were faith, and some also assert that they are saved by it; but by this alone no one is saved, for it is persuasive faith, the quality of which shall now be stated.

117. Faith is persuasive, when the Word and the doctrine of the church are believed and loved, not for the sake of truth and of a life according to it, but for the sake of gain, honor, and the fame of erudition, as ends; wherefore they who are in that faith, do not look to the Lord and to heaven, but to themselves and the world. They who in the world aspire after great things, and covet many things, are in a stronger persuasion that what the doctrine of the church teaches is true, than they who do not aspire after great things and covet many things: the reason is, because the doctrine of the church is to the former only a means to their own ends, and so far as the ends are coveted, so far the means are loved, and are also believed. But the case in itself is this: so far as they are in the fire of the loves of self and of the world, and from that fire speak, preach, and act, so far they are in that persuasion, and then they know no other than that it is so; but when they are not in the fire of those loves, then they believe little, and many not at all. Thence it is evident, that persuasive faith is a faith of the mouth and not of the heart, thus that in itself it is not faith.

118. They who are in persuasive faith do not know, from any internal enlightenment, whether the things which they teach be true or false; yea, neither do they care, provided they be believed by the common people; for they are in no affection of truth for the sake of truth. Wherefore they recede from faith, if they are deprived of honors and gains, provided their reputation be not endangered. For persuasive faith is not inwardly with man, but stands without, in the memory only, out of which it is taken when it is taught. Wherefore also that faith with its truths vanishes after death; for then there remains only that faith which is inwardly in man, that is, which is rooted in good, thus which has become of the life.

119. They who are in persuasive faith are meant by these in *Matthew* :—

> Many will say to me in that day, Lord, Lord, have we not prophesied by Thy name, and by Thy name cast out demons, and in Thy name done many virtues? But then I will confess to them, I have not known you, ye workers of iniquity (vii. 22, 23).

Also in *Luke* :—

> Then will ye begin to say, We have eaten before Thee, and have drunk, and Thou hast taught in our streets; but He will say, I say to you, I have not known you whence you are; depart from Me all ye workers of iniquity (xiii. 26, 27).

They are meant also by the five foolish virgins who had no oil in their lamps, in *Matthew* :—

> At length came those virgins, saying, Lord, Lord, open to us; but He answering will say, Verily I say unto you, I have not known you (xxv. 11, 12).

"The oil in the lamps" is the good of love in faith.

FROM THE ARCANA CŒLESTIA.

120. They who do not know that all things in the universe have relation to truth and good, and to the conjunction of both, that anything may be produced, do not know that all things of the church have relation to faith and love, and to the conjunction of both, that the church may be with man (n. 7752–7762, 9186, 9224). All things in the universe, which are according to Divine order have relation to good and truth, and to their conjunction (n. 2452, 3166, 4390, 4409, 5232, 7256, 10,122, 10,555). Truths are of faith and goods are of love (n. 4352, 4997, 7178, 10,367). This is the reason that good and truth have been treated of in this doctrine; wherefore from what has been adduced, it may be concluded respecting faith and love; and it may be known what their quality is when they are conjoined, and what it is when they are not conjoined, by putting love in the place of good, and faith in the place of truth, and making applications accordingly.

They who do not know that each and all things in man have relation to the understanding and will, and to the conjunction of both, in order that man may be man, do not know clearly that all things of the church have relation to faith and love, and to the conjunction of both, in order that the church may be with man (n. 2231, 7752–7754, 9224, 9995, 10,122). Man has two faculties, one of which is called the understanding and the other the will (n. 641, 803, 3623, 3539). The understanding is designed for receiving truths, thus the things of faith; and the will for receiving goods, thus the things of love (n. 9300, 9930, 10,064). This is the reason why the will and the understanding have been also treated of in this doctrine; for from what has been adduced, conclusions may be drawn respecting faith and love, and it may be known what their quality is when they are conjoined, and what it is when they are not conjoined, by thinking of love in the will, and faith in the understanding.

They who do not know that man has an internal and an external, or an internal and an external man, and that all things of heaven have relation to the internal man, and all things of the world to the external, and that their conjunction is like the conjunction of the spiritual world and the natural world, do not know what spiritual faith and spiritual love are (n. 4392, 5132, 8610). There is an internal and an external man, and the internal is the spiritual man, and the external the natural (n. 978, 1015, 4459, 6309, 9701–9709). Faith is so far spiritual, thus so far faith, as it is in the internal man; and love likewise (n. 1594, 3987, 8443). And so far as the truths which are of faith are loved, so far they become spiritual (n. 1594, 3987). This is the reason why the internal and the external man have been treated of, for from what has been adduced, conclusions may be drawn respecting faith and love, what their quality is when they are spiritual, and what when they are not spiritual; consequently how far they are of the church, and how far they are not of the church.

121. Faith separate from love or charity is like the light of winter, in which all things on earth are torpid, and no harvests, fruits, or flowers, are produced; but faith with love or charity is like the light of spring and summer, in which all things flourish and are produced (2231, 3146, 3412, 3413). The wintry light of faith separate from charity is changed into dense darkness when light from heaven flows in; and they who are in that faith then come into blindness and stupidity (n. 3412, 3413). They who separate faith from charity, in doctrine and life, are in darkness, thus in ignorance of truth, and in falsities, for these are darkness (n. 9186). They cast themselves into falsities, and into evils thence (n. 3325, 8094). The errors and falsities into which they cast themselves (n. 4721, 4730, 4776, 4783, 4925, 7779, 8313, 8765, 9224). The Word is shut to them (n. 3773, 4783, 8780). They do not see or attend to all those things which the Lord so often spake concerning love and charity, and concerning their fruits, or goods in act, concerning which (n. 1017, 3416). Neither do they know what good is, nor thus what celestial love is, nor what charity is (n. 2517, 3603, 4136, 9995).

Faith separate from charity is no faith (n. 654, 724, 1162, 1176, 2049, 2116, 2343, 2349, 2417, 3849, 3868, 6348, 7039, 7342, 9783). Such a faith perishes in the other life (n. 2228, 5820). When faith alone is assumed as a principle, truths are contaminated by the falsity of the principle (n. 2335). Such persons do not suffer themselves to be persuaded, because it is against their principle (n. 2385). Doctrinals concerning faith alone destroy charity (n. 6353, 8094). They who separate faith from charity were represented by Cain, by Ham, by Reuben, by the first-born of the Egyptians, and by the Philistines (n. 3325, 7097, 7317, 8093). They who make faith alone saving, excuse a life of evil, and they who are in a life of evil have no faith, because they have no charity (n. 3865, 7766, 7778, 7790, 7950, 8094). They are inwardly in the falsities of their own evil, although they do not know it (n. 7790, 7950). Therefore good cannot be conjoined with them (n. 8981, 8983). In the other life they are against good, and against those who are in good (n. 7097, 7127, 7317, 7502, 7545, 8096, 8313). Those who are simple in heart and yet wise, know what the good of life is, thus what charity is, but not what faith separate is (n. 4741, 4754).

All things of the church have relation to good and truth, consequently to charity and faith (n. 7752–7754). The church is not with man before truths are implanted in his life, and thus become the good of charity (n. 3310). Charity constitutes the church, and not faith separate from charity (n. 809, 916, 1798, 1799, 1834, 1844). The internal of the church is charity (n. 1799, 7755). Hence there is no church where there is no charity (n. 4766, 5826). The church would be one if all were regarded from charity, although men might differ as to the doctrinals of faith and the rituals of worship (n. 1285, 1316, 1798, 1799, 1834, 1844, 2385, 2982, 3267, 3451). How much of good would be in the church if charity were regarded in the first place, and faith in the second (n. 6269, 6272). Every church begins from charity, but in process of time turns aside to faith, and at length to faith alone (n. 1834, 1835, 2231, 4683, 8094). There is no faith at the last time of the church, because there is no charity (n. 1843). The worship of the Lord consists in a life of charity (n. 8254, 8256). The quality of the worship is according to the quality of the charity (n. 2190). The men of the external church have an internal if they are in charity (n. 1100, 1102, 1151, 1153). The doctrine of the ancient churches was the doctrine of life, which is the doctrine of charity, and not the doctrine of faith separate (n. 2385, 2417, 3419, 3420, 4844, 6628, 7259–7262).

The Lord inseminates and implants truth in the good of charity when He regenerates man (n. 2063, 2189, 3310). Otherwise the seed, which is the truth of faith, cannot take root (n. 880). Then goods and truths increase, according to the quality and quantity of the charity received (n. 1016). The light of a regenerate person is not from faith, but from charity by faith (n. 854). The truths of faith, when man is regenerated, enter with the delight of affection, because he loves to do them, and they are reproduced with the same affection, because they cohere (n. 2484, 2487, 3040, 3066, 3074, 3336, 4018, 5893).

They who live in love to the Lord, and in charity towards the neighbor, lose nothing to eternity, because they are conjoined to the Lord; but it is otherwise with those who are in separate faith (n. 7506, 7507). Man remains such as is his life of charity, not such as his faith separate (n. 8256). All the states of delight of those who have lived in charity, return in the other life, and are increased immensely (n. 823).

Heavenly blessedness flows from the Lord into charity, because into the very life of man; but not into faith without charity (n. 2363). In heaven all are regarded from charity, and none from faith separate (n. 1258, 1394). All are associated in the heavens according to their loves (n. 7085). No one is admitted into heaven by thinking, but by willing good (n. 2401, 3459). Unless doing good is conjoined with willing good and with thinking good, there is no salvation neither any conjunction of the internal man with the external (n. 3987). The Lord, and faith in Him, are received by no others in the other life, than those who are in charity (n. 2343).

Good is in the perpetual desire and consequent endeavor of conjoining itself with truths, and charity with faith (n. 9206, 9207, 9495). The good of charity acknowledges its own truth of faith, and the truth of faith its own good of charity (n. 2429, 3101, 3102, 3161, 3179, 3180, 4358, 5807, 5835, 9637). Hence there is a conjunction of the truth of faith and the good of charity, concerning which (n. 3834, 4096, 4097, 4301, 4345, 4353, 4364, 4368, 5365, 7623–7627, 7752–7762, 8530, 9258, 10,555). Their conjunction is like a marriage (n. 1904, 2173, 2508). The law of marriage is that two be one, according to the Word of the Lord (n. 10,130, 10,168, 10,169). So also faith and charity (n. 1094, 2173, 2503). Therefore faith which is faith, is, as to its essence, charity (n. 2228, 2839, 3180, 9783). As good is the *esse* of a thing, and truth the *existere* thence, so also is charity the *esse* of the church, and faith the *existere* thence (n. 3409, 3180, 4574, 5002, 9145). The truth of faith lives from the good of charity, thus a life according to the truths of faith is charity (n. 1589, 1947, 2571, 4070, 4096, 4097, 4736, 4757, 4884, 5147, 5928, 9154, 9667, 9841, 10,729). Faith cannot be given but in charity, and if not in charity, there is not good in faith (n. 2261, 4368). Faith does not live with man when he only knows and thinks the things of faith, but when he wills them, and from will does them (n. 9224).

There is no salvation by faith, but by a life according to the truths of faith, which life is charity (n. 379, 389, 2228, 4663, 4721). They are saved who think from the doctrine of the church that faith alone saves, if they do what is just for the sake of justice, and good for the sake of good, for thus they are still in charity (n. 2442, 3242, 3459, 3463, 7506, 7507). If a mere cogitative faith could save, all would be saved (n. 2361, 10,659). Charity constitutes heaven with man, and not faith without it (n. 3513, 3584, 3815, 9832, 10,714, 10,715, 10,721, 10,724). In heaven all are regarded from charity, and not from faith (n. 1258, 1394, 2361, 4802). The conjunction of the Lord with man is not by faith, but by a life according to the truths of faith (n. 9380, 10,143, 10,153, 10,310, 10,578, 10,645, 10,648). The Lord is the tree of life, the goods of charity the fruits, and faith the leaves (n. 3427, 9337). Faith is the "lesser luminary," and good the "larger luminary" (n. 30-38).

The angels of the Lord's celestial kingdom do not know what faith is, so that they do not even name it, but the angels of the Lord's spiritual kingdom speak of faith, because they reason concerning truths (n. 202, 203, 337, 2715, 3246, 4448, 9166, 10,786). The angels of the Lord's celestial kingdom say only yea, yea or nay, nay, but the angels of the Lord's spiritual kingdom reason whether it be so or not so, when there is discourse concerning spiritual truths, which are of faith (n. 2715, 3246, 4448, 9166, 10,786), where the Lord's words are explained:—

Let your discourse be yea, yea, nay, nay; what is beyond these is from evil (*Matt.* v. 37).

The reason why the celestial angels are such, is, because they admit the truths of faith immediately into their lives, and do not deposit them first in the memory, as the spiritual angels do; and hence the celestial angels are in the perception of all things of faith (n. 202, 585, 597, 607, 784, 1121, 1387, 1398, 1442, 1919, 5113, 5897, 6367, 7680, 7877, 8521, 8780, 9936, 9995, 10,124).

Trust or confidence, which in an eminent sense is called saving faith, is given with those only who are in good as to life, consequently with those who are in charity (n. 2982, 4352, 4683, 4689, 7762, 8240, 9239-9245). Few know what that confidence is (n. 3868, 4352).

What difference there is between believing those things which are from God, and believing in God (n. 9239, 9243). It is one thing to know, another to acknowledge, and another to have faith (n. 896, 4319, 5664). There are scientifics of faith, rationals of faith and spirituals of faith (n. 2504, 8078). The first thing is the acknowledgment of the Lord (n. 10,083). All that flows in with man from the Lord is good (n. 1614, 2016, 2751, 2882, 2883, 2891, 2892, 2904, 6193, 7643, 9128).

There is a persuasive faith, which nevertheless is not faith (n. 2343, 2682, 2689, 3427, 3865, 8148).

It appears from various reasonings as though faith were prior to charity, but this is a fallacy (n. 3324). It may be known from the light of reason, that good, consequently charity, is in the first place, and truth, consequently faith, in the second (n. 6273). Good, or charity, is actually in the first place, or is the first of the church, and truth, or faith, is in the second place, or is the second of the church, although it appears otherwise (n. 3324, 3325, 3330, 3336, 3494, 3539, 3548, 3556, 3570, 3576, 3603, 3701, 3995, 4337, 4601, 4925, 4926, 4928, 4930, 5351, 6256, 6269, 6272, 6273, 8042, 8080, 10,110). The ancients disputed concerning the first or primogeniture of the church, whether it be faith or whether it be charity (n. 367, 2435, 3324).

122. The twelve disciples of the Lord represented the church as to all things of faith and charity in the complex, as did also the twelve tribes of Israel (n. 2129, 3354, 3488, 3858, 6397). Peter, James, and John represented faith, charity, and the goods of charity in their order (n. 3750). Peter represented faith (n. 4738, 6000, 6073, 6344, 10,087, 10,580). And John represented the goods of charity, see the preface to the eighteenth and twenty-second chapters of Genesis. That there would be no faith in the Lord, because no charity, in the last time of the church, was represented by Peter's thrice denying the Lord before the cock crew the third[1] time; for Peter there, in a representative sense, is faith; (n. 6000, 6073). "Cock-crowing," as well as "twilight," signifies in the Word the last time of the church (n. 10,134). And "three" or "thrice," signifies what is complete to the end (n. 2788, 4495, 5159, 9198, 10,127). The like is signified by the Lord's saying to Peter, when Peter saw John follow the Lord:—

What is it to thee, Peter? follow thou Me, John; for Peter said of John, What is this? (*John* xxi. 21, 22); (n. 10,087).

John lay on the breast of the Lord, because he represented the good of charity (n. 3934, 10,081). The good of charity constitutes the church, is also signified by the words of the Lord from the cross to John:—

> Jesus saw His mother, and the disciple whom He loved, who stood by, and He said to His mother, Woman, behold thy son: and He said to that disciple, Behold thy mother; and from that hour that disciple took her to himself (*John* xix. 26, 27).

"John" signifies the good of charity, and "woman" and "mother," the church; and the whole passage signifies that the church will be where the good of charity is; that "woman" in the Word means the church (see n. 252, 253, 749, 770, 3160, 6014, 7337, 8994). And likewise "mother" (n. 289, 2691, 2717, 3703, 4257, 5580, 8897, 10,490). All the names of persons and places in the Word signify things abstractly from them (n. 768, 1888, 4310, 4442, 10,329).

VIII.

PIETY.

123. It is believed by many, that spiritual life, or the life which leads to heaven, consists in *piety*, in *external sanctity*, and in the *renunciation of the world;* but piety without charity, and external sanctity without internal sanctity, and a renunciation of the world without a life in the world, do not constitute spiritual life; but piety from charity, external sanctity from internal sanctity, and a renunciation of the world with a life in the world, constitute it.

124. Piety consists in thinking and speaking piously, in devoting much time to prayers, in behaving humbly at that time, in frequenting temples and harkening devoutly to the preaching there, in frequently every year receiving the Sacrament of the Supper, and in performing the other parts of worship according to the ordinances of the church. But the life of charity consists in willing well and doing well to the neighbor, in acting in every work from justice and equity, from good and truth, and in like manner in every office; in a word, the life of charity consists in performing uses. Divine worship primarily consists in this life, but secondarily in the former; wherefore he who separates one from the other, that is, who lives the life of piety, and not at the same time the life of charity, does not worship God. He thinks indeed of God, but not from God but from himself, for he thinks continually of himself, and nothing of the neighbor; and if he thinks of the neighbor, he holds him in low estimation, if he be not also such as himself. And likewise he thinks of heaven as a reward, thence in his mind there is merit, and also the love of self, as also contempt or neglect of uses, and thus of the neighbor, and at the same time he cherishes a belief that he is blameless. Hence it may appear that the life of piety, separate from the life of charity, is not the spiritual life which should be in Divine worship. (Compare *Matt.* vi. 7, 8.)

125. External sanctity is like such piety, and especially[1] consists in this, that man places all Divine worship in sanctity when he is in temples; but this is not holy with man unless his internal be holy; for such as man is as to his internal, such he also is as to his external, for this proceeds from the former as action does from its spirit; wherefore external sanctity without internal sanctity is natural and not spiritual. Hence it is that external sanctity is given with the evil as well as with the good; and they who place the whole of worship therein are for the most part empty; that is, without the knowledges of good and truth. And yet goods and truths are the real sanctities which are to be known, believed and loved, because they are from the Divine, and thus the Divine is in them. Internal sanctity, therefore, consists in loving good and truth for the sake of good and truth, and justice and sincerity for the sake of justice and sincerity. So far also as man thus loves them, so far he is spiritual, and also his worship, for so far also he is willing to know them and to do them; but so far as man does not thus love them, so far he is natural, and his worship also, and so far also he is not willing to know them and do them. External worship without internal may be compared with the life of the respiration without the life of the heart; but external worship from internal may be compared with the life of the respiration conjoined to the life of the heart.

126. But as to what relates to the renunciation of the world: it is believed by many, that to renounce the world, and to live in the spirit and not in the flesh, is to reject worldly things, which are chiefly riches and honors; to be continually engaged in pious meditation concerning God, concerning salvation, and concerning eternal life; to lead a life in prayers, in the reading of the Word and pious books; and also to afflict one's self: but this is not renouncing the world; but to renounce the world is to love God and to love the neighbor; and God is loved when man lives according to His commandments, and the neighbor is loved when man performs uses. Therefore in order that man may receive the light of heaven, it is altogether necessary that he should live in the world, and in offices and business there. A life abstracted from worldly things is a life of thought and faith separate from the life of love and charity, in which life the will of good and the doing of good to the neighbor perishes. And when this perishes, spiritual life is as a house without a foundation, which either sinks down successively, or becomes full of chinks and cracks, or totters till it falls.

127. That to do good is to worship the Lord, appears from the Lord's words :—

Every one who heareth My words and doeth them, I will liken to a prudent man who built a house upon a rock; but he who heareth My words and doeth them not, I will liken to a foolish man who built a house upon the sand, or upon the ground without a foundation (*Matt.* vii. 24–27; *Luke* vi. 47–49).

128. Hence now it is manifest, that a life of piety so far avails, and is accepted by the Lord, as a life of charity is conjoined to it; for this is the primary, and such as this is, such is that. Also, that external sanctity so far avails, and is accepted by the Lord, as it proceeds from internal sanctity; for such as this is, such is that. And also, that the renunciation of the world so far avails, and is accepted by the Lord, as it is practised in the world; for they renounce the world who remove the love of self and the world, and act justly and sincerely in every office, in every business, and in every work, from an interior, thus from a heavenly origin; which origin is in that life when man acts well, sincerely, and justly, because it is according to the Divine laws.

FROM THE ARCANA CŒLESTIA.

129. A life of piety without a life of charity, is of no avail, but when united therewith aids (n. 8252, *seq.*). External sanctity without internal sanctity is not holy (n. 2190, 10,177). Of the quality of those in another life, who have lived in external sanctity, and not from internal (n. 951, 952).

There is an internal and external of the church (n. 1098). There is internal worship and external worship, and the quality of each (n. 1083, 1098, 1100, 1151, 1153). Internals are what make worship (n. 1175). External worship without internal is no worship (n. 1094, 7724). There is an internal in worship, if man's life is a life of charity (n. 1100, 1151, 1153). Man is in true worship when he is in love and charity, that is, when he is in good as to life (n. 1618, 7724, 10,242). The quality of worship is according to good (n. 2190). Worship itself consists in a life according to the precepts of the church from the Word (n. 7884, 9921, 10,143, 10,153, 10,196, 10,645).

True worship is from the Lord with man, not from man himself (n. 10,203, 10,299). The Lord desires worship from man for the sake of man's salvation, and not for the sake of his own glory (n. 4593, 8263, 10,646). Man believes that the Lord desires worship for the sake of glory; but they who thus believe know not what Divine glory is, nor that it consists in the salvation of the human race, which man has when he attributes nothing to himself, and when he removes his proprium by humiliation; because the Divine is then first able to flow in (n. 4347, 4593, 5957, 7550, 8263, 10,646). Humiliation of heart with man exists from an acknowledgment of himself, which is, that he is nothing but evil, and that he can do nothing from himself; and from a consequent acknowledgment of the Lord, which is, that nothing but good is from the Lord, and that the Lord can do all things (n. 2327, 3994, 7478). The Divine cannot flow in except into a humble heart, since so far as man is in humiliation, so far he is absent from his proprium, and thus from the love of self (n. 3994, 4347, 5957). Hence the Lord does not desire humiliation for His own sake, but for man's sake, that man may be in a state for receiving the Divine (n. 4347, 5957). Worship is not worship without humiliation (n.

2327, 2423, 8873). The quality of external humiliation without internal (n. 5420, 9377). The quality of humiliation of heart, which is internal (n. 7478). There is no humiliation of heart with the evil (n. 7640).

They who have not charity and faith are in external worship without internal worship (n. 1200). If the love of self and of the world reigns interiorly with man, his worship is external without internal, however it may appear in the external form (n. 1182, 10,307–10,309). External worship in which the love of self reigns inwardly, as is the case with those who are of Babylon, is profane (n. 1304, 1306–1308, 1321, 1322, 1326). To imitate heavenly affections in worship, when man is in evils from the love of self, is infernal (n. 10,309).

What the quality of external worship is when it proceeds from internal, and when it does not, may be seen and concluded from what has been said and adduced above concerning the INTERNAL and the EXTERNAL MAN.

Concerning those who renounce the world and those who do not renounce it, their quality, and their lot in the other life, may be seen in the work on *Heaven and Hell*, under the following heads: Of the Rich and Poor in Heaven (n. 357–365); and of the Life that leads to Heaven (n. 528–535).

IX.

CONSCIENCE.

130. Conscience is formed with man from the religious principle in which he is, according to its reception inwardly in himself.

131. Conscience, with the man of the church, is formed by the truths of faith from the Word, or from doctrine out of the Word, according to their reception in the heart; for when man knows the truths of faith, and comprehends them in his own manner, and then wills them and does them, he then acquires conscience. Reception in the heart is reception in the will, for the will of man is what is called the heart. Hence it is that they who have conscience, speak from the heart the things which they speak, and do from the heart the things which they do. They have also an undivided mind, for they act according to that which they understand and believe to be true and good.

132. A more perfect conscience can be given with those who are enlightened in the truths of faith more than others, and who are in a clear perception above others, than with those who are less enlightened, and are in obscure perception.

133. In a true conscience is man's spiritual life itself, for there his faith is conjoined to charity. On which account to act from conscience is to them to act from their spiritual life; and to act against conscience is to them to act contrary to that life of theirs. Hence it is that they are in the tranquillity of peace, and in internal happiness, when they act according to conscience, and in intranquillity and pain, when they act against it. This pain is what is called remorse of conscience.

134. Man has a conscience of what is good, and a conscience of what is just. The conscience of what is good is the conscience of the internal man, and the conscience of what is just is the conscience of the external man. The conscience of what is good consists in acting according to the precepts of faith from internal affection; but the conscience of what is just consists in acting according to civil and moral laws from external affection. They who have the conscience of what is good, have also the conscience of what is just; but they who have only the conscience of what is just, are in a faculty of receiving the conscience of what is good; and they also do receive it when they are instructed.

135. Conscience, with those who are in charity towards the neighbor, is the conscience of truth, because it is formed by the faith of truth; but with those who are in love to the Lord, it is the conscience of good, because it is formed by the love of truth. The conscience of these is a superior conscience, and is called the perception of truth from good. They who have the conscience of truth, are of the Lord's spiritual kingdom; but they who have the superior conscience, which is called perception, are of the Lord's celestial kingdom.

136. But let examples illustrate what conscience is. He who has possession of another man's goods, whilst the other is ignorant of it, and thus can retain them without fear of the law, or of the loss of honor and reputation, and he still restores them to the other, because they are not his own, he has conscience, for he does what is good for the sake of what is good, and what is just for the sake of what is just. Again, if any one can obtain an office, but knows that another, who also desires it, would be more useful to his country, and gives way to the other for the sake of the good of his country, he has a good conscience. So in other cases.

137. From these instances it may be concluded, what quality they are of who have not conscience; they are known from the opposite. Thus, they who for the sake of any gain make what is unjust appear as just, and what is evil appear as good, and *vice versa*, have not conscience. Neither do they know what conscience is, and if they are instructed what it is, they do not believe; and some are not willing to know. Such are those who do all things for the sake of themselves and the world.

138. They who have not received conscience in the world, cannot receive it in the other life; thus they cannot be saved. The reason is, because they have no plane into which heaven, that is, the Lord through heaven, may flow in, and by which He may operate, and lead them to Himself. For conscience is the plane and receptacle of the influx of heaven.

FROM THE ARCANA CŒLESTIA.

139. *Of Conscience.*

They who have no conscience, do not know what conscience is (n. 7490, 9121). There are some who laugh at conscience, when they hear what it is (n. 721). Some believe that conscience is nothing; some that it is a sad, doleful, natural something, arising from bodily or worldly causes; and some that it is an effect of religion on the minds of the common people (n. 950). Some know not that they have conscience, when yet they have it (n. 2380).

The good have conscience, but not the evil (n. 831, 965, 7490). They who are in love to God and in love towards the neighbor have conscience (n. 2380). Conscience is especially with those who are regenerated by the Lord (n. 977). They who are in truths alone, and not in a life according to them, have no conscience (n. 1076, 1077, 1919). They who do good from natural good, and not from religion, have no conscience (n. 6208).

Man's conscience is from the doctrine of his church, or from some religious principle, and is according thereto (n. 9112). Conscience is formed with man from those things which are of his religion, and which he believes to be truths (n. 1077, 2053, 9113). Conscience is an internal bond, by which man is held to thinking, speaking, and doing good; and by which he is withheld from thinking, speaking, and doing evil; and this is not for the sake of self and the world, but for the sake of good, truth, justice, and uprightness (n. 1919, 9120). Conscience is an internal dictate, that one ought to do so or not so- (n. 1919, 1935). Conscience is in its essence a conscience of what is true and right (n. 986, 8081). The new will with the spiritual regenerate man is conscience (n. 927, 1023, 1043, 1044, 4299, 4328, 4493, 9115, 9596). The spiritual life of man is from conscience (n. 9117).

There is a true conscience, a spurious conscience, and a false conscience, concerning which (n. 1033). Conscience is more true, in proportion as it is formed from more genuine truths (n. 2053, 2063, 9114). In general, conscience is two-fold, interior and exterior, and interior conscience is of spiritual good, which in its essence is truth, and exterior conscience is of moral and civil good, which in its essence is sincerity and justice, in general, uprightness (n. 5140, 6207, 10,296).

Pain of conscience is anxiety of mind on account of injustice, insincerity, and any evil, which a man believes to be against God, and against the good of the neighbor (n. 7217). If anxiety is felt when a man thinks evil, it is from conscience (n. 5470). Pain of conscience is an anguish felt on account of the evil which man does, and also on account of the privation of good and truth (n. 7217). Since temptation is a combat of truth and falsity in the interiors of man, and since in temptations there is pain and anxiety, therefore no others are admitted into spiritual temptations, but those who have conscience (n. 847).

They who have conscience speak and act from the heart (n. 7935, 9114). They who have conscience do not swear in vain (n. 2842). They who have conscience are in interior blessedness when they do what is good and just according to conscience (n. 9118). They who have conscience in the world, have conscience in the other life, and are there amongst the happy (n. 965). The influx of heaven flows into conscience with man (n. 6207, 6213, 9122). The Lord rules the spiritual man by conscience, which is an internal bond (n. 1835, 1862). They who have conscience, have interior thought; but they who have no conscience, have only exterior thought (n. 1919, 1935). They who have conscience, think from the spiritual, but they who have no conscience, think only from the natural (n. 1820). They who have no conscience, are only external men (n. 4459). The Lord rules those who have no conscience by external bonds, which are all those things which are of the love of self and of the world, and which thence relate to the fear of the loss of reputation, honor, office, gain, wealth, and the fear of the law, and of the loss of life (n. 1077, 1080, 1835). They who have no conscience, and yet suffer themselves to be ruled by these external bonds, are capable of discharging the duties of high offices in the world, and of doing good, as well as those who have conscience; but the former do it in an external form, and from external bonds, whereas the latter do it in an internal form, and from internal bonds (n. 6207).

They who have no conscience would destroy conscience with those who have it (n. 1820). They who have no conscience in the world, have no conscience in the other life (n. 965, 9122). Hence those who are in hell have no torment of conscience for their evils in the world (n. 965, 9122).

Who and of what quality, and how troublesome, the scrupulously conscientious are, and what they correspond to in the spiritual world (n. 5386, 5724).

They who are in the Lord's spiritual kingdom, have conscience, and it is formed in their intellectual part (n. 863, 865, 875, 895, 927, 1043, 1044, 1555, 2256, 4328, 4493, 5113, 6367, 8521, 9596, 9915, 9995, 10,124). It is otherwise with those who are in the Lord's celestial kingdom (n. 927, 2256, 5113, 6367, 8521, 9915, 9995, 10,124).

140. *Of Perception.*

Perception consists in seeing what is true and good by influx from the Lord (n. 202, 895, 7680, 9128). Perception is given only with those who are in the good of love from the Lord to the Lord (n. 202, 371, 1442, 5228). Perception is given with those in heaven who, whilst they lived in the world, brought the doctrinals of the church which are from the Word immediately into the life, and who did not first commit them to memory; thus the interiors of their minds were formed to the reception of the Divine influx; and thence their understanding is in heaven in continual enlightenment (n. 104, 495, 503, 521, 536, 1616, 1791, 5145). They know innumerable things, and are wise beyond measure (n. 2718, 9543). They who are in perception, do not reason concerning the truths of faith, and if they reasoned their perception would perish (n. 586, 1398, 5897). They who believe that they know and are wise from themselves, cannot have perception (n. 1386). The learned do not comprehend what this perception is, from experience (n. 1387).

They who are in the Lord's celestial kingdom, have perception; but they who are in the spiritual kingdom, have no perception, but conscience in its place (n. 805, 2144, 2145, 8081). They who are in the Lord's celestial kingdom do not think from faith, like those in the Lord's spiritual kingdom, because they who are in the celestial kingdom are in perception from the Lord of all things of faith (n. 202, 597, 607, 784, 1121, 1387, 1398, 1442, 1919, 7680, 7877, 8780). Wherefore the celestial angels say concerning the truths of faith only, Yea, yea, or Nay, nay, because they perceive them and see them; but the spiritual angels reason concerning the truths of faith, whether a thing be so or not (n. 2715, 3246, 4448, 9166, 10,786); where the words of the Lord are explained:—

Let your discourse be Yea, yea, Nay, nay: what is beyond these is from evil (*Matt.* v. 37).

The celestial angels, because they know the truths of faith from perception, are not even willing to name faith (n. 202, 337). The distinction between the celestial angels and the spiritual angels (n. 2088, 2669, 2708–2715, 3235, 3240, 4788, 7068, 8521, 9277, 10,295). Of the perception of those who were of the Most Ancient Church, which was a celestial church (n. 125, 597, 607, 784, 895, 1121, 5121).

There is interior and exterior perception (n. 2145, 2171, 2831, 5920). There is in the world a perception of what is just and equitable, but rarely a perception of spiritual truth and good (n. 2831, 5937, 7977). The light of perception is altogether different from the light of confirmation; and it is not like it, although it may appear so to some persons (n. 8521, 8780).

X.

FREEDOM.

141. All freedom is of love, for what man loves, this he does freely; hence also all freedom is of the will, for what man loves, this he also wills; and because love and the will make the life of man, so also does freedom. From these things it may appear what freedom is, namely, it is that which is of the love and the will, and thence of the life of man. Hence it is, that what a man does from freedom, appears to him as if from his own proprium.

142. To do evil from freedom, appears as freedom, but it is slavery, because that freedom is from the love of self and from the love of the world, and these loves are from hell. Such freedom is actually turned into slavery after death, for the man who has been in such freedom then becomes a vile servant in hell. But to do good from freedom is freedom itself, because it is from love to the Lord and from love towards the neighbor, and these loves are from heaven. This freedom also remains after death, and then becomes freedom indeed, for the man who has been in such freedom, becomes in heaven like a son of the house. This the Lord thus teaches:—

Every one that doeth sin is the servant of sin; the servant abideth not in the house forever: the son abideth forever; if the Son shall have made you free, you shall be truly free (*John* viii. 34-36).

Now, because all good is from the Lord, and all evil from hell, it follows that freedom consists in being led by the Lord, and slavery is being led by hell.

143. That man has the freedom of thinking evil and falsity, and also of doing it, so far as the laws do not withhold him, is in order that he may be capable of being reformed; for goods and truths are to be implanted in his love and will, so that they may become of his life, and this cannot be done unless he have the freedom of thinking evil and falsity as well as good and truth. This freedom is given to every man by the Lord, and so far as he does not love evil and falsity, so far, when he thinks what is good and true, the Lord implants them in his love and will, consequently in his life, and thus reforms him. What is inseminated in freedom, this also remains, but what is inseminated in a state of compulsion, this does not remain, because what is from compulsion is not from the will of the man, but from the will of him who compels. Hence also it is, that worship from freedom is pleasing to the Lord, but not worship from compulsion; for worship from freedom is worship from love, but worship from compulsion is not so.

144. The freedom of doing good, and the freedom of doing evil, though they appear alike in the external form, are as different and distant from each other as heaven and hell are: the freedom of doing good also is from heaven, and is called heavenly freedom; but the freedom of doing evil is from hell, and is called infernal freedom; so far, also, as man is in the one, so far he is not in the other, for no one can serve two lords (*Matt.* vi. 24); which also appears from hence, that they who are in infernal freedom believe that it is slavery and compulsion not to be allowed to will evil and think falsity at their pleasure, but they who are in heavenly freedom abhor willing evil and thinking falsity, and would be tormented if they were compelled to do so.

145. Because acting from freedom appears to man as if from his own proprium, therefore heavenly freedom may also be called the heavenly proprium, and infernal freedom may be called the infernal proprium. The infernal proprium is that into which man is born, and this is evil; but the heavenly proprium is that into which man is reformed, and this is good.

146. From this it may appear what *Free-will* is; namely, that it consists in doing good from choice or will, and that they are in that freedom who are led by the Lord; and they are led by the Lord who love good and truth for the sake of good and truth.

147. Man may know what is the quality of the freedom in which he is, from the delight which he feels when he thinks, speaks, acts, hears, and sees; for all delight is of love.

FROM THE ARCANA CŒLESTIA.

148. All freedom is of love or affection, for what a man loves, he does freely (n. 2870, 3158, 8987, 8990, 9585, 9591). As freedom is of love, it is the life of every one (n. 2873). There is heavenly freedom and infernal freedom (n. 2870, 2873, 2874, 9589, 9590). Heavenly freedom is of the love of good and truth (n. 1947, 2870, 2872). And because the love of good and truth is from the Lord, that being led by the Lord is true freedom (n. 892, 905, 2872, 2886, 2890–2892, 9096, 9586, 9587–9591). Man by regeneration is introduced into heavenly freedom by the Lord (n. 2874, 2875, 2882, 2892). Man ought to be in freedom, that he may be regenerated (n. 1937, 1947, 2876, 2881, 3145, 3158, 4031, 8700). Otherwise the love of good and truth cannot be implanted in and appropriated to man, so as to appear his own (n. 2877, 2879, 2880, 2888). Nothing is conjoined to man which is done in compulsion (n. 2875, 8700). If man could be reformed by compulsion, all would be saved (n. 2881). Compulsion is hurtful in reformation (n. 4031).

Worship from freedom is worship, but not worship from compulsion (n. 1947, 2880, 7349, 10,097). Repentance should take place in a free state, and what is done in a forced state is of no avail (n. 8392). What forced states are (n. 8392).

Man is allowed to act from the freedom of reason, in order that good may be provided for him, and therefore man is in the freedom of thinking and willing, and even of doing evil, so far as the laws do not forbid (n. 10,777). Man is kept by the Lord between heaven and hell, and thus in equilibrium, that he may be in freedom for the sake of reformation (n. 5982, 6477, 8209, 8987). What is inseminated in freedom remains, but not what is inseminated in compulsion (n. 9588, 10,777). Therefore freedom is never taken away from any one (n. 2876, 2881). No one is compelled by the Lord (n. 1937, 1947). How the Lord leads man by means of freedom into good; by means of freedom he turns him from evil, and bends him to good, so gently and tactly that the man knows no other than that all proceeds from himself (n. 9587).

To compel himself is from liberty, but not to be compelled (n. 1937, 1947). Man ought to compel himself to resist evil (n. 1937, 1947, 7914). And also to do good as from himself, but still to acknowledge that it is from the Lord (n. 2883, 2891, 2892, 7914). Man has a stronger freedom in the combats of temptations in which he conquers, since he then interiorly compels himself to resist evils, although it appears otherwise (n. 1937, 1947, 2881). There is freedom in every temptation, but this freedom is interiorly with man from the Lord; and he therefore combats and wills to conquer, and not to be overcome, which he would not do without freedom (n. 1937, 1947, 2881). The Lord does this by means of an affection of truth and good impressed on the internal man, the man himself not knowing (n. 5044).

Infernal freedom consists in being led by the loves of self and of the world, and their lusts (n. 2870, 2873). They who are in hell do not know any other freedom (n. 2871). Heavenly freedom is as far from infernal freedom as heaven is from hell (n. 2873, 2874). Infernal freedom in itself regarded is slavery (n. 2884, 2890). Because it is slavery to be led by hell (n. 9586, 9589–9591).

All freedom is as the proprium, and according to it (n. 2880). Man receives a heavenly proprium from the Lord by regeneration (n. 1937, 1947, 2882, 2883, 2891). The nature of the heavenly proprium (n. 164, 5660, 8480). This proprium appears to man as his own, but it is not his, but the Lord's with him (n. 8497). They who are in this proprium are in true liberty, because true liberty consists in being led by the Lord and His proprium (n. 892, 905, 2872, 2886, 2890–2892, 4096, 9586, 9587, 9589–9591).

149. Freedom originates from the equilibrium between heaven and hell, and man, without freedom, cannot be reformed, is shown in the work on *Heaven and Hell*, in the articles concerning that equilibrium (n. 589–596), and concerning freedom (n. 597 to the end); but for the sake of instruction respecting what freedom is, and to show that man is reformed by means of it, I will here quote the following extracts from that work.

"It has been shown, that the eqilibrium between heaven and hell is an equilibrium between the good which is from heaven and the evil which is from hell; and thus it is a spiritual equilibrium, which in its essence is freedom. The reason that spiritual equilibrium is, in its essence, freedom, is, because it is an equilibrium between good and evil, and between truth and falsity, which are spiritual things; wherefore, the power of willing either good or evil, and of thinking either truth or falsity, and of choosing the one in preference to the other, is freedom. This freedom is given to every one by the Lord, nor is it ever taken away from him. In its origin, indeed, it does not belong to man, but to the Lord, because it is from the Lord; but, nevertheless, it is given to man, together with life, as his own: and it is given him to this end, that he may be reformed and saved; for without freedom there can be no reformation and salvation. Every one who takes any rational view of things may see, that man has freedom to think either ill or well, sincerely or insincerely, justly or unjustly; and also, that he is at liberty to speak and to act well, sincerely, and justly, but is withheld from speaking and acting ill, insincerely, and unjustly, by spiritual, moral, and civil laws, by which his external is kept in bonds. From these things it is evident, that the spirit of man, which is that which thinks and wills, is in freedom. Not so the external of man, which speaks and acts, except in conformity with the above-mentioned laws. The reason that man cannot be reformed, unless he is in freedom, is because he is born into evils of all kinds. These must be removed, in order that he may be saved; and they cannot be removed, unless he sees them in himself, and acknowledges them; and afterwards ceases to will them, and at length holds them in aversion. It is then that they are first removed. This could not be done, unless man possessed in him good as well as evil; for he is capable, from good, of seeing evils, but not, from evil, of seeing goods. The spiritual goods which man can think, he learns from infancy by reading the Word and hearing sermons; and he learns moral and civil goods from life in the world. This is the first reason why man ought to be in freedom. Another is, that nothing is appropriated to man, but what he does from an affection that is of his love; other things may indeed enter his mind, but no further than into his thought; and not into his will; and what does not enter into the will does not become his own, for the thought draws its ideas from the memory, but the will from the life itself. Nothing that man ever does or thinks is free, but what proceeds from this will, or, what is the same thing, from an affection belonging to his love. Whatever a man wills or loves, he does freely; in consequence of which, a man's freedom, and the affection which is that of his love or of his will, are one: on which account, therefore, man must have freedom, in order that he may be affected by truth and good, or love them, and that they may become as it were his own. In a word, whatever does not enter man in freedom, does not remain, because it is not of his love or will; and whatever is not of a man's love or will is not of his spirit: for the *esse* of the spirit of man is his love or will.

"That man may be in freedom, as necessary to his being reformed, he is conjoined, as to his spirit, with heaven and with hell; for spirits from hell, and angels from heaven, are with every man. By the spirits from hell, man is held in his evil; but by the angels from heaven, he is held in good by the Lord. Thus he is in spiritual equilibrium, that is, in freedom. That angels from heaven, and spirits from hell, are adjoined to every man, may be seen in the Section on the Conjunction of Heaven with the Human Race" (n. 291–302).

XI.

MERIT.

150. They who do good that they may merit, do not do good from the love of good, but from the love of reward, for he who wills to merit, wills to be rewarded; they who do so, regard and place their delight in the reward, and not in good; wherefore they are not spiritual, but natural.

151. To do good, which is good, must be from the love of good, thus for the sake of good. They who are in that love are not willing to hear of merit, for they love to do, and perceive satisfaction therein, and, on the other hand, they are sorrowful if it be believed that what they do is for the sake of anything of themselves. This is almost like those who do good to their friends for the sake of friendship; to a brother for the sake of brotherhood, to wife and children for the sake of wife and children, to the country for the sake of the country, thus from friendship and love. They who think well, also say and insist, that they do not do good for the sake of themselves, but for the sake of others.

152. They who do good for the sake of reward, do not do good from the Lord, but from themselves, for they regard themselves in the first place, because they regard their own good; and the good of the neighbor, which is the good of fellow-citizens, of human society, of the country, and of the church, they regard no otherwise than as a means to an end. Hence it is, that the good of the love of self and of the world lies concealed in the good of merit, and that good is from man and not from the Lord, and all good which is from man is not good; yea, so far as self and the world lies concealed in it, it is evil.

153. Genuine charity and genuine faith is without any [thought of] merit, for good itself is the delight of charity, and truth itself is the delight of faith; wherefore they who are in that charity and faith know what unmeritorious good is, but not they who are not in charity and faith.

154. That good is not to be done for the sake of reward, the Lord Himself teaches in *Luke:*—

> If ye love those who love you, what grace have you? for sinners do the same: rather love your enemies, and do good, and lend, hoping for nothing; then shall your reward be great, and ye shall be the sons of the Most High (vi. 32–35).

That man cannot do good that is good from himself, the Lord also teaches in *John:*—

> A man cannot take anything unless it be given Him from heaven (iii. 27).

And in another place:—

> Jesus said, I am the vine, ye are the branches: as the branch cannot bear fruit from itself, unless it shall abide in the vine, so neither can ye unless ye shall abide in Me: He who abideth in Me and I in him, he beareth much fruit, for except from Me ye cannot do anything (xv. 4–8).

155. Because all good and truth are from the Lord, and nothing of them from man, and because good from man is not good, it follows that merit belongs to no man, but to the Lord alone. The merit of the Lord consists in this, that from his own power He has saved the human race, and also, that He saves those who do good from Him. Hence it is that in the Word, he is called "just" to whom the merit and justice of the Lord are ascribed, and he is called "unjust" to whom are ascribed his own justice and the merit of self.

156. The delight itself, which is in the love of doing good without an end to reward, is a reward which remains to eternity, for heaven and eternal happiness are insinuated into that good by the Lord.

157. To think and believe that they who do good will come into heaven, and also that good is to be done in order that they may come into heaven, is not to regard reward as an end, thus neither is it to place merit in works; for even they who do good from the Lord think and believe so, but they who thus think, believe and do, and are not in the love of good for the sake of good, have regard to reward as an end, and place merit in works.

FROM THE ARCANA CŒLESTIA.

158. Merit and justice belong to the Lord alone (n. 9715, 9979). The merit and justice of the Lord consist in His having saved the human race by His own power (n. 1813, 2025, 2026, 2027, 9715, 9809, 10,019). The good of the Lord's justice and merit is the good which reigns in heaven, and is the good of His Divine love from which He saved the human race (n. 9486, 9979). No man can of himself become justice, nor claim it by any right (n. 1813). The quality of those in the other life who claim justice to themselves (n. 942, 2027). In the Word, the man to whom the justice and merit of the Lord are ascribed, is called "just;" and the man to whom his own justice and merit are ascribed, "unjust" (n. 5069, 9263). Whoever is once just from the Lord, will be continually just from Him; for justice never becomes man's own, but is continually the Lord's (n. 3686). They who believe in the justification taught in the church, know little of regeneration (n. 5398).

Man is so far wise as he ascribes all goods and truths to the Lord, and not to himself (n. 10,227). As all good and truth which are good and truth are from the Lord, and nothing is from man, and as good from man is not good, it follows that merit belongs to no man, but to the Lord alone (n. 9975, 9981, 9988). They who enter heaven put off all merit of their own (n. 4007). And they do not think of reward for the good they have done (n. 6478, 9174). They who think from merit so far do not acknowledge all things to be of mercy (6478, 9174). They who think from merit, think of reward and remuneration, and therefore to will to merit is to will to be remunerated (n. 5660, 6392, 9975). Such persons cannot receive heaven in themselves (n. 1835, 8478, 9977). Heavenly happiness consists in the affection of doing good, without an end of remuneration (n. 6388, 6478, 9174, 9984). In the other life so far as any one does good without an end of remuneration, so far happiness inflows with increase from the Lord; and it is immediately dissipated when remuneration is thought of (n. 6478, 9174).

Good is to be done without an end of remuneration (n. 6392, 6478); illustrated (n. 9981). Genuine charity is without any thing meritorious (n. 2343, 2371, 2400, 3887, 6388–6393). Because it is from love, thus from the delight of doing good (n. 3816, 3887, 6388, 6478, 9174, 9984). "Reward" in the Word, means the delight and happiness in doing good to others without an end of reward, and this delight and happiness is felt and perceived by those who are in genuine charity (n. 3816, 3956, 6388).

They who do good for the sake of reward, love themselves and not the neighbor (n. 8002, 9210). "Mercenaries," in the spiritual sense of the Word, mean those who do good for the sake of reward (n. 8002). They who do good for the sake of remuneration, in the other life desire to be served, and are never contented (n. 6393). They despise the neighbor, and are angry at the Lord Himself, because they do not receive a reward, saying that they have merited it (n. 9976). They who have separated faith from charity, in the other life make their faith, and also the good works which they have done in an external form, thus for the sake of themselves, meritorious (n. 2371). Further particulars respecting the quality of those in the other life who have placed merit in works (n. 942, 1774, 1877, 2027). They are there in the lower earth, and appear to themselves to cut wood (n. 1110, 4943, 8740). Because wood, especially shittim wood, signifies the good of merit in particular (n. 2784, 2812, 9472, 9486, 9715, 10,178).

They who have done good for the sake of remuneration, are servants in the Lord's kingdom (n. 6389, 6390). They who place merit in works, fall in temptations (n. 2273, 9978). They who are in the loves of self and of the world, do not know what it is to do good without a view to remuneration (n. 6392).

XII.

REPENTANCE AND THE REMISSION OF SINS.

159. He who would be saved must confess his sins, and do the work of repentance.

160. *To confess sins*, is to know evils, to see them in one's self, to acknowledge them, to make himself guilty, and to condemn himself on account of them. When this is done before God, it is the confession of sins.

161. *To do the work of repentance*, is to desist from sins after he has thus confessed them, and from a humble heart has made supplication for remission, and to live a new life according to the precepts of charity and faith.

162. He who only acknowledges universally that he is a sinner, and makes himself guilty of all evils, and yet does not explore himself, that is, see his own sins, makes confession, but not the confession of repentance; he, because he does not know his own evils, lives afterwards as he did before.

163. He who lives the life of charity and faith does the work of repentance daily; he reflects upon the evils which are with him, he acknowledges them, he guards against them, he supplicates the Lord for help. For man of himself continually lapses, but he is continually raised by the Lord, and led to good. Such is the state of those who are in good. But they who are in evil lapse continually, and are also continually elevated by the Lord, but are only withdrawn from falling into the most grievous evils, to which of themselves they tend with all their endeavor.

164. The man who explores himself that he may do the work of repentance, must explore his thoughts and the intentions of his will, and must there explore what he would do if it were permitted him, that is, if he were not afraid of the laws, and of the loss of reputation, honor, and gain. There the evils of man reside, and the evils which he does in the body are all from thence. They who do not explore the evils of their thought and will, cannot do the work of repentance, for they think and will afterwards as they did before, and yet to will evils is to do them. This is to explore one's self.

165. Repentance of the mouth and not of the life is not repentance. Sins are not remitted by repentance of the mouth, but by repentance of the life. Sins are continually remitted to man by the Lord, for He is mercy itself, but sins adhere to man, however he may suppose that they are remitted; nor are they removed from him but by a life according to the precepts of true faith. So far as he lives according to them, so far sins are removed; and so far as they are removed, so far they are remitted.

166. It is believed that sins are washed away, or are washed off, as filth is by water, when they are remitted; but sins are not washed away, but they are removed; that is, man is withheld from them when he is kept in good by the Lord; and when he is kept in good, it appears as if he were without them, thus as if they were washed away; and so far as man is reformed, so far he is capable of being kept in good. How man is reformed will be shown in the following doctrinal concerning regeneration. He who believes that sins are in any other manner remitted, is much deceived.

167. The signs that sins are remitted, that is, removed, are these which follow. They whose sins are remitted, perceive a delight in worshiping God for the sake of God, and in serving their neighbor for the sake of their neighbor, thus in doing good for the sake of good, and in speaking truth for the sake of truth; they are unwilling to claim merit by anything of charity and faith; they shun and are averse to evils, as enmities, hatreds, revenges, adulteries, and the very thoughts of such things with intention. But the signs that sins are not remitted, that is, removed, are these which follow. They whose sins are not remitted, worship God not for the sake of God, and serve the neighbor not for the sake of the neighbor, thus they do not do good and speak truth for the sake of good and truth, but for the sake of themselves and the world; they wish to claim merit by their deeds; they perceive nothing undelightful in evils, as in enmity, in hatred, in revenge, in adulteries; and they think of them and concerning them in all license.

168. The repentance which takes place in a free state is of avail, but that which takes place in a state of compulsion is of no avail. States of compulsion are states of sickness, states of dejection of mind from misfortune, states of imminent death, as also every state of fear which takes away the use of reason. He who is evil, and in a state of compulsion promises repentance, and also does good, when he comes into a free state returns to his former life of evil; it is otherwise with the good.

169. After a man has explored himself, and acknowledged his sins, and has done the work of repentance, he must remain constant in good even to the end of life. For if he afterwards relapses into his former life of evil and embraces it, he then profanes, for he then conjoins evil with good; whence his latter state becomes worse than his former, according to the words of the Lord:—

When the unclean spirit goes out from a man, he walks through dry places, seeking rest, but doth not find; then he saith, I will return into my house whence I went out; and when he cometh and findeth it empty, and swept, and adorned for him, then he goeth away, and adjoineth to himself seven other spirits worse than himself, and, entering in, they dwell there, and the latter things of the man become worse than the first (*Matt.* xii. 43–45).

FROM THE ARCANA CŒLESTIA.

170. *Of Sin or Evil.*

There are innumerable kinds of evil and falsity (n. 1188, 1212, 4818, 4822, 7574). There is evil from falsity, there is falsity from evil, and evil and falsity again from thence (n. 1679, 2243, 4818). The nature and quality of the evil of falsity (n. 2408, 4818, 7272, 8265, 8279). The nature and quality of the falsity of evil (n. 6359, 7272, 9304, 10,302). Of blamable evils, and of those which are not so blamable (n. 4171, 4172¹). Of evils from the understanding and of evils from the will (n. 9009). The difference between transgression, iniquity, and sin (n. 6563, 9156).

All evils adhere to man (n. 2116). Evils cannot be taken away from man, but man can only be withheld from them, and kept in good (n. 865, 868, 887, 894, 1581, 4564, 8206, 8393, 8988, 9014, 9333, 9446–9448, 9451, 10,057, 10,059). To be withheld from evil and kept in good, is effected by the Lord alone (n. 929, 2406, 8206, 10,060). Thus evils and sins are only removed, and this is effected successively (n. 9334–9336). This is done by the Lord by means of regeneration (n. 9445, 9452–9454, 9938). Evils shut out the Lord (n. 5696). Man ought to abstain from evils, that he may receive good from the Lord (n. 10,109). Good and truth inflow in proportion as man is withheld from evils (n. 2388, 2411, 10,675). To be withheld from evil and kept in good, constitutes remission of sins (n. 8391, 8393, 9014, 9444–9450). The signs whether sins are remitted or not (n. 9449, 9450). It is a consequence of the remission of sins to look at things from good and not from evil (n. 7697).

Evil and sin are a separation and turning away from the Lord; and this is signified by "evil" and "sin" in the Word (n. 4997, 5229, 5474, 5746, 5841, 9346); they are and signify separation and aversion from good and truth (n. 7589). They are and signify what is contrary to Divine order (n. 4839, 5076). Evil is damnation and hell (n. 3513, 6279, 7155). It is not known what hell is, unless it be known what evil is (n. 7181). Evils are as it were heavy, and fall of themselves into hell; and so also falsities that are from evil (n. 8279, 8298). It is not known what evil is unless it be known what the love of self and the love of the world are (n. 4997, 7178, 8318). All evils are from those loves (n. 1307, 1308, 1321, 1594, 1691, 3413, 7255, 7376, 7488, 7489, 8318, 9335, 9348, 10,038, 10,742).

All men whatever are born into evils of every kind, even so that their proprium is nothing but evil (n. 210, 215, 731, 874–876, 987, 1047, 2307, 2308, 3518, 3701, 3812, 8480, 8550, 10,283,

10,284, 10,731). Man must therefore be born again or regenerated, in order to receive a life of good (n. 3701).

Man casts himself into hell when he does evil from consent, afterwards from purpose, and at last from delight (n. 6203). They who are in evil of life, are in the falsities of their own evil, whether they know it or not (n. 7577, 8094). Evil would not be appropriated to man, if he believed, as is really the case, that all evil is from hell, and all good from the Lord (n. 4151, 6206, 6324, 6325). In the other life evils are removed from the good and goods from the evil (n. 2256). All in the other life are let into their interiors, thus the evil into their evils (n. 8870).

In the other life evil contains its own punishment, and good its own reward (n. 696, 967, 1857, 6559, 8214, 8223, 8226, 9048). Man is not punished in the other life for hereditary evils, as he is not to blame for these, but for his actual evils (n. 966, 2308). The interiors of evil are foul and filthy, however they may appear otherwise in an external form (n. 7046).

Evil is attributed in the Word to the Lord, and yet nothing but good proceeds from Him (n. 2447, 6071, 6991, 6997, 7533, 7632, 7677, 7926, 8227, 8228, 8632, 9306). So also anger (n. 5798, 6997, 8284, 8483, 9306, 10,431). Why it is so said in the Word (n. 6071, 6991, 6997, 7632, 7643, 7679, 7710, 7926, 8282, 9010, 9128). What is signified by "bearing iniquity," where it is predicated of the Lord (n. 9937, 9965). The Lord turns evil into good with the good who are infested and tempted (n. 8631). To leave man from his own liberty to do evil, is permission (n. 1778). Evils and falsities are governed by the laws of permission by the Lord; and they are permitted for the sake of order (n. 7877, 8700, 10,778). The permission of evil by the Lord is not as of one who wills, but as of one who does not will, but who cannot bring aid on account of the end (n. 7877).

171. *Of Falsity.*

There are innumerable kinds of falsity, namely, as many as there are evils, and evils and falsities are according to their origins, which are many (n. 1188, 1212, 4729, 4822, 7574). There is falsity from evil, or the falsity of evil; and there is evil from the falsity, or the evil of falsity; and falsity again from thence (n. 1679, 2243). From one falsity that is assumed as a principle, falsities flow in a long series (n. 1510, 1511, 4717, 4721). There is falsity from the lusts of the love of self and of the world; and there is falsity from the fallacies of the senses (n. 1295, 4729). There are falsities of religion; and there are falsities of ignorance (n. 4729, 8318, 9258). There is falsity which contains good, and falsity which does not contain good (n. 2863, 9304, 10,109, 10,302). There is what is falsified (n. 7318, 7319, 10,648).

The quality of the falsity of evil (n. 6359, 7272, 9304, 10,302). The quality of the evil of falsity (n. 2408, 4818, 7272, 8265, 8279). The falsities from evil appear like mists, and impure waters over the hells (n. 8138, 8146, 8210). Such waters signify falsities (n. 739, 790, 7307). They who are in hell speak falsities from evil (n. 1695, 7351, 7352, 7357, 7392, 7699). They who are in evil cannot do otherwise than think what is false when they think from themselves (n. 7437).

There are falsities of religion which agree with good, and falsities which disagree (n. 9258). Falsities of religion, if they do not disagree with good, do not produce evil but with those who are in evil of life (n. 8318). Falsities of religion are not imputed to those who are in good, but to those who are in evil (n. 8051, 8149). Every falsity may be confirmed, and then it appears like truth (n. 5033, 6865, 8521, 8780). Care should be taken lest falsities of religion be confirmed, since the persuasion of falsity principally arises from thence (n. 845, 8780). How hurtful the persuasion of falsity is (n. 794, 806, 5096, 7686). A persuasion of falsity is perpetually exciting such things as confirm falsities (n. 1510, 1511, 2477). They who are in the persuasion of falsity are interiorly bound (n. 5096). In the other life, they who are in a strong persuasion of falsity, when they approach others, close up their rational, and as it were suffocate it (n. 3895, 5128).

Truths which are not genuine, and also falsities, may be consociated with genuine truths; but falsities which contain good, and not falsities in which is evil (n. 3470, 3471, 4551, 4552, 7344, 8149, 9298). Falsities which contain good are received by the Lord as truths (n. 4736, 8149). The good which has its quality from falsity is accepted by the Lord, if there is ignorance, and therein is innocence and a good end (n. 7887).

Evil falsifies truth, because it draws aside and applies truth to evil (n. 8094, 8149). Truth is said to be falsified, when it is applied to evil by confirmations (n. 8602). Falsified truth is contrary to truth and good (n. 8602). For further particulars respecting the falsification of truth (see n. 7318, 7319, 10,648).

172. *Of the Profane and Profanation, spoken of above at* (n. 169).

Profanation is a commixture of good and evil, as also of truth and falsity in man (n. 6348). None can profane goods and truths, or the holy things of the church and the Word, except those who first acknowledge, believe, and still more live according to them, and afterwards recede from and do not believe, and who live to themselves and the world (n. 593, 1008, 1010, 1059, 3398, 3399, 3898, 4289, 4601, 8394, 10,287). He who believes truths in his childhood, and afterwards does not believe them, profanes lightly; but he who confirms truths in himself and after that denies them, profanes grievously (n. 6959, 6963, 6971). They who believe truths, and live evilly, commit profanation; as also they who do not believe truths and live holily (n. 8882). If man, after repentance of heart, relapses to his former evils, he profanes, and then his latter state is worse than his former (n. 8394). Those in the Christian world who defile the holy things of the Word by unclean thoughts and discourses, profane (n. 4050, 5390). There are various kinds of profanation (n. 10,287).

They who do not acknowledge holy things cannot profane them, still less they who do not know them (n. 1008, 1010, 1059, 9188, 10,287). They who are within the church, can profane holy things, but not they who are out of it (n. 2051). The Gentiles, because out of the church, and who do not have the Word, cannot profane (n. 1327, 1328, 2051, 9021). Neither can the Jews profane the holy interior things of the Word and the church, because they do not acknowledge them (n. 6963). Therefore interior truths were not revealed to the Jews, for if they had been revealed and acknowledged, they would have profaned them (n. 3398, 3479, 6963). Profanation is meant by the words of the Lord above quoted at n. 169:—

When the unclean spirit goes out of a man, he walks through dry places, seeking rest, but finding none; then he saith, I will return into my house from whence I went out; and when he comes and finds it empty, and swept, and garnished, then he goes away, and takes to himself seven other spirits worse than himself, and entering in they dwell there, and the latter things of the man become worse than the first (*Matt.* xii. 43–45).

"The unclean spirit going out of a man," signifies the repentance of him who is in evil; his "walking through dry places and not finding rest," signifies, that, to such a person, a life of good is of that quality; "the house" into which he returned, and which he found empty, swept, and garnished, signifies the man himself, and his will, as being without good. "The seven spirits" which he took to himself and with whom he returned, signify evil conjoined to good; "his state then being worse than his former," signifies profanation. This is the internal sense of these words, for the Lord spoke by correspondences. The same thing is meant by the words of the Lord to the man whom He healed in the Pool of Bethesda:—

Behold, thou art made whole; sin no more, lest a worse thing come unto thee (*John* v. 14).

Also by these words of the Lord:—

He hath blinded their eyes, and hardened their heart; that they should not see with their eyes, nor understand with their heart, and be converted, and I should heal them (*John* xii. 40).

"To be converted and healed," signifies to profane, which takes place when truth and good are acknowledged, and afterwards rejected, which would have been the case if the Jews had been converted and healed.

The lot of profaners in the other life is the worst of all, because the good and truth which they have acknowledged remain, and also the evil and falsity; and because they cohere, a tearing asunder of the life takes place (n. 571, 582, 6348). The greatest care is therefore taken by the Lord, to prevent profanation (n. 2426, 10,287). Therefore man is withheld from acknowledgment and faith, if he cannot remain therein to the end of life (n. 3398, 3402). On this account also man is rather kept in ignorance, and in external worship (n. 301–303, 1327, 1328). The Lord also stores up the goods and truths which man has received by acknowledgment, in his interiors (n. 6595).

Lest interior truths should be profaned, they are not revealed before the church is at its end (n. 3398, 3399). Wherefore the Lord came into the world, and opened interior truths, when the church was wholly vastated (n. 3398). See what is adduced on this subject in the work on *The Last Judgment and Babylon Destroyed* (n. 73, 74).

In the Word "Babel" signifies the profanation of good, and "Chaldea," the profanation of truth (n. 1182, 1283, 1295, 1304, 1306–1308, 1321, 1322, 1326). These profanations correspond to the prohibited degrees, or foul adulteries, spoken of in the Word (n. 6348). Profanation was represented in the Israelitish and Jewish church by eating blood, wherefore this was so severely prohibited (n. 1003).

XIII.

REGENERATION.

173. He who does not receive spiritual life, that is, who is not begotten anew by the Lord, cannot come into heaven; which the Lord teaches in *John:*—

Verily, verily, I say unto thee, except any one be begotten again, he cannot see the kingdom of God (iii. 3).

174. Man is not born of his parents into spiritual life, but into natural life. Spiritual life consists in loving God above all things, and in loving his neighbor as himself, and this according to the precepts of faith, which the Lord has taught in the Word. But natural life consists in loving ourselves and the world more than the neighbor, yea, more than God Himself.

175. Every man is born of his parents into the evils of the love of self and of the world. Every evil, which by habit has acquired as it were a nature, is derived into the offspring; thus it descends successively from parents, from grandfathers, and from great-grandfathers, in a long series backwards; whence the derivation of evil at length becomes so great, that the whole of man's own life is nothing else but evil. This continual derivation of evil is not broken and altered, except by the life of faith and charity from the Lord.

176. Man continually inclines to, and lapses into, what he derives from heredity: hence he confirms with himself that evil, and also superadds more from himself. These evils are altogether contrary to spiritual life; they destroy it; wherefore, unless man receives new life, which is spiritual life, from the Lord, thus unless he is conceived anew, is born anew, is educated anew, that is, is created anew, he is damned; for he wills nothing else, and thence thinks nothing else, but what is of self and the world, in like manner as they do in hell.

177. No man can be regenerated unless he knows such things as are of the new life, that is, of spiritual life. The things which are of the new life, or which are of the spiritual life, are truths which are to be believed and goods which are to done; the former are of faith, the latter of charity. These things no one can know from himself, for man apprehends only those things which are obvious to the senses, from which he procures to himself a light which is called natural light, from which he sees nothing else than what relates to the world and to self, but not the things which relate to heaven and to God. These he must learn from revelation. As that the Lord, who is God from eternity, came into the world to save the human race; that He has all power in heaven and in earth; that the all of faith and the all of charity, thus all truth and good, is from Him; that there is a heaven, and a hell; and that man is to live to eternity, in heaven if he has done well, in hell if he has done evil.

178. These and many other things belong to faith, which the man who is regenerating ought to know; for he who knows them, may think them, afterwards will them, and lastly do them, and so have new life. Whilst he who does not know that the Lord is the Saviour of the human race, cannot have faith in Him, love Him, and thus do good for the sake of Him. He who does not know that all good is from Him, cannot think that his own salvation is from Him, still less can he will it to be so, thus he cannot live from Him. He who does not know that there is a hell and a heaven, nor that there is eternal life, cannot even think about the life of heaven, nor apply himself to receive it, and so in other cases.

179. Every one has an internal man and an external man; the internal is what is called the spiritual man, and the external is what is called the natural man, and each is to be regenerated, that the man may be regenerated. With the man who is not regenerated, the external or natural man rules, and the internal serves; but with the man who is regenerated, the internal or spiritual man rules, and the external serves. Whence it is manifest that the order of life is inverted with man from his birth, namely, that serves which ought to rule, and that rules which ought to serve. In order that man may be saved, this order must be inverted; and this inversion can by no means exist, but by regeneration from the Lord.

180. What it is for the internal man to rule and the external to serve, and *vice versa*, may be illustrated by this:—If a man places all his good in pleasure, in gain, and in pride, and has delight in hatred and revenge, and inwardly in himself seeks for reasons which confirm them, then the external man rules and the internal serves. But when a man perceives good and delight in thinking and willing well, sincerely, and justly, and in outwardly speaking and doing in like manner, then the internal man rules and the external serves.

181. The internal man is first regenerated by the Lord, and afterwards the external, and the latter by means of the former. For the internal man is regenerated by thinking those things which are of faith and charity, but the external by a life according to them. This is meant by the words of the Lord:—

Unless any one be begotten of water and the spirit, he cannot enter into the kingdom of God (*John* iii. 5).

"Water," in the spiritual sense, is the truth of faith, and "the spirit" is a life according to it.

182. The man who is regenerated is, as to his internal man, in heaven, and is an angel there with the angels, among whom he also comes after death; he is then able to live the life of heaven, to love the Lord, to love the neighbor, to understand truth, to relish good, and to perceive the happiness thence derived.

FROM THE ARCANA CŒLESTIA.

183. *What Regeneration is, and why it is effected.*

At this day little is known concerning regeneration; the reason (n. 3761, 4136, 5398). Man is born into evils of every kind, and thence as to his proprium by birth, he is nothing but evil (n. 210, 215, 731, 874–876, 987, 1047, 2307, 2308, 3518, 3701, 3812, 8480, 8549, 8550, 8552, 10,283, 10,284, 10,286, 10,731). Man's hereditary nature is nothing but evil, see the extracts above in this doctrine (n. 83). Man's proprium is nothing but evil, see the same (n. 82). Man of himself, so far as he is under the influence of his hereditary nature and the proprium, is worse than the brute animals (n. 637, 3175). Therefore of himself he continually looks to hell (n. 694, 8480). Therefore, if man should be led by his own proprium, he could not possibly be saved (n. 10,731).

Man's natural life is contrary to spiritual life (n. 3913, 3928). The good which he does from himself or from proprium, is not good, because he does it for the sake of self, and the world (n. 8480). Man's proprium must be removed that the Lord and heaven may be able to be present (n. 1023, 1044). It is actually removed when he is regenerated by the Lord (n. 9334–9336, 9452, 9454, 9938). Therefore he must be created anew, that is, regenerated (n. 8548, 8549, 9452, 9937). "Creating" man, in the Word, signifies to regenerate him (n. 16, 88, 10,634).

Man is conjoined to the Lord by regeneration (n. 2004, 9338). And consociated with angels in heaven (n. 2474). He does not come into heaven, until he is in a state to be led by the Lord by means of good, which is the case when he is regenerated (n. 8516, 8539, 8722, 9139, 9832, 10,367).

The external or natural man rules, and the internal man serves, in the man who is not regenerated (n. 3167, 8743). Thus the state of man's life is inverted from his birth, and must be entirely inverted again in order that he may be saved (n. 6507, 8552, 8553, 9258). The end of regeneration is, that the internal or spiritual man may rule, and the external or natural man serve (n. 911, 913). This is actually effected after man is regenerated (n. 5128, 5651, 8743). For after regeneration the love of self and the world no longer reigns, but love to the Lord and towards the neighbor, thus the Lord and not man (n. 8856, 8857). Hence it is plain that man cannot be saved unless he is regenerated (n. 5280, 8548, 8772, 10,156).

Regeneration is a plane to perfect the life of man to eternity (n. 9334). The regenerate man is perfected to eternity (n. 6648, 10,048). The quality of the regenerate and the unregenerate man described (n. 977, 986, 10,156).

184. *Who is regenerated.*

Man cannot be regenerated unless he be instructed in the truths of faith and the goods of charity (n. 677, 679, 711, 8635, 8638–8640, 10,729). They who are only in truths and not in good, cannot be regenerated (6567, 8725). No one is regenerated unless he is in charity (n. 989). None can be regenerated but such as have conscience (n. 2689, 5470). Every one is regenerated according to his faculty of receiving the good of love to the Lord, and of charity towards the neighbor, by the truths of faith from the doctrine of the church, which is from the Word (n. 2967, 2975). Who can be regenerated, and who cannot (n. 2689). They who live the life of faith and charity, and who are not regenerated in the world, are regenerated in the other life (n. 989, 2490).

185. *Regeneration is from the Lord alone.*

The Lord alone regenerates man, and neither man nor angel contributes thereto (n. 10,067). Man's regeneration is an image of the Lord's glorification, that is, as the Lord made His Human Divine, so He makes spiritual the man whom He regenerates (n. 3043, 3138, 3212, 3296, 3490, 4402, 5688, 10,057, 10,076). The Lord wills to have the whole man whom He regenerates, and not part of him (n. 6138).

186. *Further particulars concerning regeneration.*

Man is regenerated by the truths of faith, and by a life according to them (n. 1904, 2046, 9088, 9959, 10,028). This is meant by the words of the Lord:—

Unless a man be born of water and of the spirit, he cannot enter the kingdom of God (*John* iii. 5).

"Water" signifies the truth of faith, and "spirit" a life according thereto (n. 10,240). "Water" in the Word signifies the truth of faith (n. 2702, 3058, 5668, 8568, 10,238). Spiritual purification, which is from evils and falsities, is effected by the truths of faith (n. 2799, 5954, 7044, 7918, 9088, 10,229, 10,237). When man is regenerated, truths are inseminated and implanted in good, that they may become of the life (n. 880, 2189, 2574, 2697). What the quality of truths must be that they may be implanted in good (n. 8725). In regeneration truth is initiated and conjoined to good, and good reciprocally to truth (n. 5365, 8516). How this reciprocal initiation and conjunction is effected (n. 3155, 10,067). Truth is implanted in good when it becomes of the will, since it then becomes of the love (n. 10,367).

There are two states of the man who is regenerated; first when he is led by truth to good; second, when he acts from good, and from good sees truth (n. 7992, 7993, 8505, 8506, 8510, 8512, 8516, 8643, 8648, 8658, 8685, 8690, 8701, 8772, 9227, 9230, 9274, 9736, 10,048, 10,057, 10,060, 10,076). The quality of man's state when truth is in the first place, and good in the second (n. 3610). Hence it appears that when man is regenerating, he looks to good from truth; but when regenerated, he regards truth from good (n. 6247). Thus a turning over as it were takes place, in that the state of man is inverted (n. 6507).

But it is to be known, that when man is regenerating, truth is not actually in the first place and good in the second, but only apparently; but when man is regenerated, good is in the first place and truth in the second, actually and perceptibly (n. 3324, 3325, 3330, 3336, 3494, 3539, 3548, 3556, 3563, 3570, 3576, 3603, 3701, 4243, 4245, 4247, 4337, 4925, 4926, 4928, 4930, 4977, 5351, 6256, 6269, 6273, 8516, 10,110). Thus good is the first and last of regeneration (n. 9337). Since truth appears to be in the first place and good in the second, when man is regenerating, or, which is the same thing, when man becomes a church, on account of this appearance it was a matter of controversy among the ancients, whether the truth of faith or the good of charity is the first-born of the church (n. 367, 2435). The good of charity is actually the first-born of the church, but the truth of faith only apparently (n. 3325, 3494, 4925, 4926, 4928, 4930, 8042, 8080). "First-born" in the Word signifies the first of the church, to which priority and superiority belongs (n. 3325). The Lord is called the first-born, because in Him and from Him is all the good of love, of charity, and of faith (n. 3325).

Man ought not to return from the latter state wherein truth is regarded from good, to the former state, wherein good is regarded from truth, and why (n. 2454, 3650-3655, 5895, 5897, 7857, 7923, 8505, 8506, 8510, 8512, 8516, 9274, 10,184). Where these words of the Lord are explained:—

Let not him who is in the field return back to take his garments (*Matt.* xxiv. 18);

also,

Whosoever shall then be in the field, let him not return to those things which are behind him. Remember Lot's wife (*Luke* xvii. 31, 32):

for this is signified by those words.

The process of the regeneration of man described, and how it is effected (n. 1555, 2343, 2490, 2657, 2979, 3057, 3286, 3310, 3316, 3332, 3470, 3701, 4353, 5113, 5126, 5270, 5280, 5342, 6717, 8772, 8773, 9043, 9103, 10,021, 10,057, 10,367). The arcana of regeneration are innumerable, since regeneration continues during the whole life of man (n. 2679, 3179, 3584, 3665, 3690, 3701, 4377, 4551, 4552, 5122, 5126, 5398, 5912, 6751, 9103, 9258, 9296, 9297, 9334). Scarcely any of these arcana come to the knowledge and perception of man (n. 3179, 9336). This is what is meant by the words of the Lord:—

The wind bloweth where it listeth, and thou hearest the sound thereof, but knowest not whence it cometh and whither it goeth; so is every one that is born of the Spirit (*John* iii. 8).

Concerning the process of the regeneration of the man of the spiritual church (n. 2675, 2678, 2679, 2682). And concerning the process of regeneration of the man of the celestial church, with the difference (n. 5113, 10,124).

The case of the regenerate man is similar to that of an infant, who first learns to speak, then to think, afterwards to live well, until all those things flow from him spontaneously, as from himself (n. 3203, 9296, 9297). Thus he who is regenerated is first led by the Lord as an infant, then as a boy, and afterwards as an adult (n. 3665, 3690, 4377-4379, 6751).

When man is regenerated by the Lord, he is first in a state of external innocence, which is his state of infancy, and is afterwards successively led into a state of internal innocence, which is his state of wisdom (n. 9334, 9335, 10,021, 10,210). The nature and quality of the innocence of infancy, and of the innocence of wisdom (n. 1616, 2305, 2306, 3494, 4563, 4797, 5608, 9301, 10,021). A comparison between the regeneration of man, and the conception and formation of an embryo in the womb (n. 3570, 4931, 9258). Therefore "generations and nativities" in the Word signify spiritual generations and nativities, which belong to regeneration (n. 613, 1145, 1255, 2020, 2584, 3860, 3868, 4070, 4668, 6239, 10,204). The regeneration of man illustrated by the germinations in the vegetable kingdom (n. 5115, 5116). The regeneration of man represented in the rainbow (n. 1042, 1043, 1053).

The internal or spiritual man, and the external or natural man, must each of them be regenerated, and the one by means of the other (n. 3868, 3870, 3872, 3876, 3877, 3882). The internal man must be regenerated before the external, since the internal man is in the light of heaven, and the external man in the light of the world (n. 3321, 3325, 3469, 3493, 4353, 8746, 9325). The external or natural man is regenerated by means of the internal or spiritual (n. 3286, 3288, 3321). Man is not regenerate before the external or natural man is regenerated (n. 8742–8747, 9043, 9046, 9061, 9325, 9334). The spiritual man is shut unless the natural man is regenerated (n. 6299). And it is as it were blind as to the truths and goods of faith and love (n. 3493, 3969, 4353, 4588). When the natural man is regenerated the whole man is regenerated (n. 7442, 7443). This is signified by "the washing of the disciples feet," and by these words of the Lord:—

He that is washed hath no need to be washed except as to his feet, and the whole is clean (*John* xiii. 9, 10; n. 10,243).

"Washing" in the Word signifies spiritual washing, which is purification from evils and falsities (n. 3147, 10,237, 10,241). And "feet" signify those things that are of the natural man (n. 2162, 3761, 3986, 4280, 4938–4952). Therefore "to wash the feet," is to purify the natural man (n. 3147, 10,241).

How the natural man is regenerated (n. 3502, 3508, 3509, 3518, 3573, 3576, 3579, 3616, 3762, 3786, 5373, 5647, 5650, 5651, 5660). The quality of the natural man when it is regenerated, and when it is not regenerated (n. 8744, 8745). So far as the natural man does not combat with the spiritual man, so far the man is regenerated (n. 3286). When a man is regenerated, the natural man perceives spiritual things by influx (n. 5651).

The sensual, which is the ultimate of the natural man, is not regenerated at this day, but man is elevated above it (n. 7442). All who are regenerated are actually elevated from the sensual into the light of heaven (n. 6183, 6454). The nature and quality of the sensual man may be seen in the extracts above (n. 50).

Man is regenerated by influx into the knowledges of good and truth which he has (n. 4096, 4097, 4364). When man is regenerated, he is introduced through mediate goods and truths into genuine goods and truths, and afterwards the mediate goods and truths are left, and the genuine succeed in their place (n. 3665, 3686, 3690, 3974, 4063, 4067, 4145, 6384, 9382). Then another order is induced amongst truths and goods (n. 4250, 4251, 9931, 10,303). They are disposed according to ends (n. 4104). Thus according to the uses of spiritual life (n. 9297). They who are regenerated undergo many states, and are continually brought more interiorly into heaven, thus nearer to the Lord (n. 6645). The regenerate man is in the order of heaven (n. 8512). His internal is open into heaven (n. 8512, 8513). Man by regeneration comes into angelic intelligence, which however lies concealed in his interiors so long as he remains in the world, but is opened in the other life, and his wisdom is then like that of the angels (n. 2494, 8747). The states as to enlightenment of those who are regenerated described (n. 2697, 2701, 2704). By regeneration man receives a new understanding (n. 2657). How the case is with respect to the fructification of good, and the multiplication of truth, with those who are regenerated (n. 984). With a regenerate person truths from good form as it were a constellation by successive derivations, and continually multiply themselves round about (5912). With a regenerate person, truths from good are disposed into such order, that the genuine truths of good, from which, as their parents, the rest proceed, are in the middle, whilst the rest succeed in order according to their relationship and affinities, even to the ultimates, where there is obscurity (n. 4129, 4551, 4552, 5134, 5270). With a regenerate person truths from good are arranged in the form of heaven (n. 3316, 3470, 3584, 4302, 5704, 5709, 6028, 6690, 9931, 10,303); and in the work on *Heaven and Hell,* under the article Concerning the Form of Heaven, according to which are the consociations and communications there (n. 200-212); and Concerning the Wisdom of the Angels of Heaven (n. 265-275).

With a regenerate person, there is a correspondence between spiritual things and natural things (n. 2850). His order of life is altogether inverted (n. 3332, 5159, 8995). He is altogether a new man as to his spirit (n. 3212). He appears like the unregenerate man as to externals, but not as to internals (n. 5159). Spiritual good, which is to will and to do good from the affection of the love of good, can only be given to man by means of regeneration (n. 4538). Truths, which enter with affection, are reproduced (n. 5893). Truths, so far as they are deprived of life from the proprium of man, are so far conjoined to good, and receive spiritual life (n. 3607, 3610). So far as evils from the love of self and the love of the world are removed, so far there is life in truths (n. 3610).

The first affection of truth with the man who is regenerated is not pure, but is purified successively (n. 3089, 8413). Evils and falsities, with the man who is regenerated, are removed slowly, and not quickly (n. 9334, 9335). The evils and falsities of the proprium of man still remain, and are only removed by regeneration (n. 865, 868, 887, 929, 1581, 2406, 4564, 8206, 8393, 8988, 9014, 9333-9336, 9445, 9447, 9448, 9451-9454, 9938, 10,057, 10,060). Man can never be so far regenerated as to be called perfect (n. 894, 5122, 6648). Evil spirits dare not assault the regenerate (n. 1695). They who believe the justification taught in the church, know little of regeneration (n. 5398).

Man must have freedom, to be capable of being regenerated (n. 1937, 1947, 2876, 2881, 3145, 3146, 3158, 4031, 8700).

Man is introduced into heavenly freedom by regeneration (n. 2874, 2875, 2882, 2892). There is no conjunction of good and truth by compulsion, and thus no regeneration (n. 2875, 2881, 4031, 8700). Other particulars respecting freedom as it regards regeneration, may be seen in the doctrine above, where it treats of Freedom.

He who is regenerated, must necessarily undergo temptations (n. 3696, 8403). Because temptations take place for the sake of the conjunction of good and truth, and also on account of the conjunction of the internal and the external man (n. 4248, 4272, 5773).

XIV.

TEMPTATION.

187. Those only who are being regenerated, undergo spiritual temptations; for spiritual temptations are pains of mind induced by evil spirits, with those who are in goods and truths. While those spirits excite the evils which are with them, there arises the anxiety of temptation. Man does not know whence this anxiety comes, because he does not know his origin.

188. For there are both evil and good spirits with every man; the evil spirits are in his evils, and the good spirits in his goods. When the evil spirits approach they draw forth his evils, while the good spirits, on the contrary, draw forth his goods; whence arise collision and combat, from which the man has interior anxiety, which is temptation. Hence it is plain that temptations are not induced by heaven, but by hell; which is also the faith of the church, which teaches that God tempts no one.

189. Interior anxieties are also experienced by those who are not in goods and truths; but they are natural, not spiritual anxieties; the two are distinguished by this, that natural anxieties have worldly things for their objects, but spiritual anxieties, heavenly things.

190. In temptations, the dominion of good over evil, or of evil over good, is contended for. Evil which wills to have dominion, is in the natural or external man, and good is in the spiritual or internal man. If evil conquers, the natural man has dominion; if good conquers, the spiritual has dominion.

191. These combats are carried on by the truths of faith which are from the Word. From these man must combat against evils and falsities; for if he combats from any other principles, he cannot conquer, because in these alone the Lord is present. Because this combat is carried on by the truths of faith, therefore man is not admitted into it until he is in the knowledges of good and truth, and has thence obtained some spiritual life; therefore such combats do not take place till man has arrived at years of maturity.

192. If man succumbs in temptation, his state after it becomes worse than before, because evil has acquired power over good, and falsity over truth.

193. Since at this day faith is rare because there is no charity, for the church is at its end, therefore few at this day are admitted into any spiritual temptations; hence it is scarcely known what they are, and to what they are conducive.

194. Temptations conduce to acquire for good dominion over evil, and for truth dominion over falsity; also to confirm truths, and conjoin them to goods, and at the same time to disperse evils and the falsities thence derived. They serve also to open the internal spiritual man, and to subject the natural man to it; as also to break the loves of self and the world, and to subdue the lusts which proceed from them. When these things are effected, man acquires enlightenment and perception as to what are truth and good, and what falsity and evil are; whence man obtains intelligence and wisdom, which afterwards increase continually.

195. The Lord alone combats for man in temptations. If man does not believe that the Lord alone combats and conquers for him, he undergoes only external temptation; which is not serviceable to him.

FROM THE ARCANA CŒLESTIA.

196. Before a summary is given of what is written in the *Arcana Cœlestia*, respecting temptations, something shall first be said concerning them, in order that it may be known still more clearly from whence they proceed. It is called spiritual temptation when the truths of faith which a man believes in his heart, and according to which he loves to live, are assaulted within him, especially when the good of love, in which he places his spiritual life, is assaulted. Those assaults take place in various ways; as by influx of scandals against truths and goods into the thoughts and the will; also by a continual drawing forth, and bringing to remembrance, of the evils which one has committed, and of the falsities which he has thought, thus by inundation of such things; and at the same time by an apparent shutting up of the interiors of the mind, and, consequently, of communication with heaven, by which the capacity of thinking from his own faith, and of willing from his own love, are intercepted. These things are effected by the evil spirits who are present with man; and when they take place, they appear under the form of interior anxieties and pains of conscience; for they affect and torment man's spiritual life, because he supposes that they proceed, not from evil spirits, but from his own interiors. Man does not know that such assaults are[1] from evil spirits, because he does not know that spirits are present with him, evil spirits in his evils, and good spirits in his goods; and that they are in his thoughts and affections. These temptations are most grievous when they are accompanied with bodily pains; and still more so, when those pains are of long continuance, and no deliverance is granted, even although the Divine mercy is implored; hence results despair, which is the end.

Some particulars shall first be adduced from the *Arcana Cœlestia*, concerning the spirits that are with man, because temptations proceed from them.

Spirits and angels are with every man (n. 697, 5846–5866). They are in his thoughts and affections (n. 2888, 5846, 5848). If spirits and angels were taken away, man could not live (n. 2887, 5849, 5854, 5993, 6321). Because by spirits and angels man has communication and conjunction with the spiritual world, without which he would have no life (n. 697, 2796, 2886, 2887, 4047, 4048, 5846–5866, 5976–5993). The spirits with man are changed according to the affections of his love (n. 5851). Spirits from hell are in the loves of man's proprium (n. 5852, 5979–5993). Spirits enter into all things of man's memory (n. 5853, 5857, 5859, 5860, 6192, 6193, 6198, 6199). Angels are in the ends from which and for the sake of which man thinks, wills, and acts thus and not otherwise (n. 1317, 1645, 5844). Man does not appear to spirits, nor spirits to man (n. 5885). Thence spirits cannot see what is in our solar world through man (n. 1880). Although spirits and angels are with man, in his thoughts and affections, yet still he is in freedom of thinking, willing, and acting (n. 5982, 6477, 8209, 8307, 10,777); and in the work on *Heaven and Hell*, where the Conjunction of Heaven with the Human Race is treated of (n. 291–302).

197. *Whence and of what quality temptations are.*

Temptations exist from the evil spirits who are with man, who inject scandals against the goods and truths which a man loves and believes, and likewise they also excite the evils which he has done and the falsities which he has thought (n. 741, 751, 761, 3927, 4307, 4572, 5036, 6657, 8960). Then evil spirits use all sorts of cunning and malice (n. 6666). The man who is in temptations is near to hell (n. 8131). There are two forces which act in temptations, a force from the interior from the Lord, and a force from the exterior from hell (n. 8168).

The ruling love of man is assaulted in temptations (n. 847, 4274). Evil spirits attack those things only which are of man's faith and love, thus those things which relate to his spiritual life; wherefore at such times it is about his eternal life (n. 1820). A state of temptations compared with the state of a man among robbers (n. 5246). In temptations angels from the Lord keep man in the truths and goods which are with him, but evil spirits keep him in the falsities and evils which are with him, whence arises a conflict and combat (n. 4249).

Temptation is a combat between the internal or spiritual man, and the external or natural man (n. 2183, 4256). Thus between the delights of the internal and external man, which are then opposite to each other (n. 3928, 8351). It takes place on account of the disagreement between those delights (n. 3928). Thus it is concerning the dominion of one over the other (n. 3928, 8961.)

No one can be tempted unless he is in the acknowledgment, and likewise in the affection of truth and good, because there is otherwise no combat, for there is nothing spiritual to act against what is natural, thus there is no contest for dominion (n. 3928, 4299). Whoever has acquired any spiritual life, undergoes temptations (n. 8963). Temptations exist with those who have conscience, that is, with those who are in spiritual love; but more grievous ones with those who have perception, that is, with those who are in celestial love (n. 1668, 8963). Dead men, that is they who are not in faith and love to God, and in love towards the neighbor, are not admitted into temptations, because they would fall (n. 270, 4274, 4299, 8964, 8968). Therefore very few at this day are admitted into spiritual temptations (n. 8965). But they have anxieties on account of various causes in the world, past, present, or future, which are generally attended with infirmity of mind and weakness of body, which anxieties are not the anxieties of temptations (n. 762, 8164). Spiritual temptations are sometimes attended with bodily pains, and sometimes not (n. 8164). A state of temptation is an unclean and filthy state, inasmuch as evils and falsities are injected, and also doubts concerning goods and truths (n. 5246). Also, because in temptations there are indignations, pains of the mind, and many affections that are not good (n. 1917, 6829). There is also obscurity and doubt concerning the end (n. 1820, 6829). And likewise concerning the Divine Providence and hearing, because prayers are not heard in temptations as they are out of them (n. 8179). And because man when he is in temptation, seems to himself to be in a state of damnation (n. 6097). Because man perceives clearly what is doing in his external man, consequently the things which evil spirits inject and call forth, according to which he thinks of his state; but he does not perceive what is doing in his internal man, consequently the things which flow in by means of angels from the Lord, and therefore he cannot judge of his state therefrom (n. 10,236, 10,240).

Temptations are generally carried to desperation, which is their ultimate (n. 1787, 2694, 5279, 5280, 6144, 7147, 7155, 7166, 8165, 8567). The reasons (n. 2694). In the temptation itself there are also despairings, but that they terminate in a general one (n. 8567). In a state of despair a man speaks bitter things, but the Lord does not attend to them (n. 8165). When the temptation is finished, there is at first a fluctuation between the truth and falsity (n. 848, 857). But afterwards truth shines, and becomes serene and joyful (n. 3696, 4572, 6829, 8367, 8370).

They who are regenerated undergo temptations not once only, but many times, because many evils and falsities are to be removed (n 8403). If they who have acquired some spiritual life do not undergo temptations in the world, they undergo them in the other life (n. 7122). How temptations take place in the other life, and where (n. 537–539, 699, 1106–1113, 1122, 2694, 4728, 4940–4951, 6119, 6928, 7090, 7122, 7127, 7186, 7317, 7474, 7502, 7541, 7542, 7545, 7768, 7990, 9331, 9763). Concerning the state of enlightenment of those who come out of temptation, and are raised into heaven, and their reception there (n. 2699, 2701, 2704).

The quality of the temptation from lack of truth, and the desire thereof at the same time (n. 2682, 8352). The temptation of infants in the other life, whereby they learn to resist evils, their quality (n. 2294). The difference between temptations, infestations, and vastations (n. 7474).

198. *How and when temptations take place.*

Spiritual combats chiefly take place by the truths of faith (n. 8962). Truth is the first of combat (n. 1685). The men of the spiritual church are tempted as to the truths of faith, wherefore with them the combat is by truths; but the men of the celestial church are tempted as to the goods of love, wherefore with them the combat is by goods (n. 1668, 8963). Those who are of the spiritual church, for the most part, do not combat from genuine truths, but from such as they believe to be true from the doctrinals of their church; which doctrinals however ought to be such, as to be capable of being conjoined with good (n. 6765).

Whoever is regenerated must undergo temptations, and he cannot be regenerated without them (n. 5036, 8403); and temptations therefore are necessary (n. 7090). The man who is regenerating comes into temptations, when evil endeavors to gain dominion over good, and the natural man over the spiritual man (n. 6657, 8961). And he comes into them when good ought to have the precedence (n. 4248, 4249, 4256, 8962, 8963). They who are regenerated, are first let into a state of tranquillity, then into temptations, and afterwards return into a state of tranquillity of peace, which is the end (n. 3696).

199. *What good is effected by temptations.*

The effect of temptations, a summary (n. 1692, 1717, 1740, 6144, 8958-8969). By temptations the spiritual or internal man acquires dominion over the natural or external man; consequently good over evil, and truth over falsity; because good resides in the spiritual man, which cannot exist without it, and evil resides in the natural man (n. 8961). Since temptation is a combat between them, it follows that dominion is the object of the contest, that is, whether the spiritual man shall have dominion over the natural man, thus whether good shall have dominion over evil, or *vice versa;* consequently, whether the Lord or hell shall have dominion over man (n. 1923, 3928). The external or natural man, by means of temptations, receives truths corresponding to the affection thereof in the internal or spiritual man (n. 3321, 3928). The internal spiritual man is opened and conjoined with the external by means of temptations, in order that man as to each may be elevated, and look to the Lord (n. 10,685). The internal spiritual man is opened and conjoined with the external by means of temptations, because the Lord acts from the interior, and flows in thence into the external, and removes and subjugates the evils therein, and at the same time subjects and renders it subordinate to the internal (n. 10,685).

Temptations take place for the sake of the conjunction of good and truth, and the dispersion of the falsities which adhere to truths and goods (n. 4572). Consequently that good is conjoined to truths by temptations (n. 2272). The vessels recipient of truth are softened by temptations, and put on a state receptive of good (n. 3318). Truths and goods, thus the things which belong to faith and charity, are confirmed and implanted by temptations (n. 8351, 8924, 8966, 8967). And evils and falsities are removed, and room made for the reception of goods and truths (n. 7122). By temptations the loves of self and the world, from whence proceed all evils and falsities, are broken (n. 5356). And thus man is humbled (n. 8966, 8967). Evils and falsities are subdued, separated, and removed, but not abolished, by temptations (n. 868). By temptations corporeal things with their lusts are subdued (n. 357, 868). Man by temptations learns what good and truth are, even from their relation to their opposites, which are evils and falsities (n. 5356). He also learns that of himself he is nothing but evil, and that all the good with him is from the Lord, and from His mercy (n. 2334).

By the temptations in which man conquers, evil spirits are deprived of the power of rising up against him any further (n. 1695, 1717). The hells dare not rise up against those who have suffered temptations and have conquered (n. 2183, 8273).

After temptations in which man has conquered, there is joy arising from the conjunction of good and truth, although the man does not know that the joy is thence (n. 4572, 6829). There is then the enlightenment of the truth which is of faith, and the perception of the good which is of love (n. 8367, 8370). Thence he has intelligence and wisdom (n. 8966, 8967) Truths after temptations increase immensely (n. 6663). And good has the precedence, or is in the first place, and truth in the second (n. 5773). And man, as to his internal spiritual man, is admitted into the angelic societies, thus into heaven (n. 6611).

Before a man undergoes temptations, the truths and goods which are with him are arranged in order by the Lord, that he may be able to resist the evils and falsities which are with him, and are excited from hell (n. 8131). In temptations the Lord provides good where the evil spirits intend evil (n. 6574). After temptations the Lord reduces truths with goods into a new order, and arranges them in a heavenly form (n. 10,685). The interiors of the spiritual man are arranged into a heavenly form, see the work on *Heaven and Hell*, in the chapter on the Form of Heaven, according to which are the consociations there (n. 200, 212).

They who fall in temptations, come into damnation, because evils and falsities conquer, and the natural man prevails over the spiritual man, and afterwards has the dominion; and then the latter state becomes worse than the former (n. 8165, 8169, 8961).

200. *The Lord combats for man in temptations.*

The Lord alone combats for man in temptations, and man does not combat at all from himself (n. 1692, 8172, 8175, 8176,

8273). Man cannot by any means combat against evils and falsities from himself, because that would be to fight against all the hells, which the Lord alone can subdue and conquer (n. 1692). The hells fight against man, and the Lord for him (n. 8159). Man combats from truths and goods, thus from the knowledges and affections thereof which are with him; but it is not man who combats, but the Lord by them (n. 1661). Man thinks that the Lord is absent in temptations, because his prayers are not heard as they are out of them, but nevertheless the Lord is then more present with him (n. 840). In temptations man ought to combat as from himself, and not to hang down his hands and expect immediate help; but nevertheless he ought to believe that it is from the Lord (n. 1712, 8179, 8969). Man cannot otherwise receive a heavenly proprium (n. 1937, 1947, 2882, 2883, 2891). The quality of that proprium, that it is not man's, but the Lord's with him (n. 1937, 1917, 2882, 2883, 2891, 8497).

Temptation is of no avail, and productive of no good, unless a man believes, at least after the temptations, that the Lord has fought and conquered for him (n. 8969). They who place merit in works, cannot combat against evils, because they combat from their own proprium, and do not permit the Lord to combat for them (n. 9978). They who believe they have merited heaven by their temptations, are with much difficulty saved (n. 2273).

The Lord does not tempt, but liberates, and leads to good (n. 2768). Temptations appear to be from the Divine, when yet they are not (n. 4299). In what sense the petition in the Lord's prayer, "Lead us not into temptations," is to be understood, from experience (n. 1875). The Lord does not concur in temptations by permitting them, according to the idea which man has of permission (n. 2768).

In every temptation there is freedom, although it does not appear so, but the freedom is interiorly with man from the Lord, and he therefore combats and is willing to conquer, and not to be conquered, which he would not do without freedom (n. 1937, 1947, 2881). The Lord effects this by means of the affection of truth and good impressed on the internal man, although the man does not know it (n. 5044). For all freedom is of affection or love, and according to its quality (n. 2870, 3158, 8987, 8990, 9585, 9591).

201. *Of the Lord's temptations.*

The Lord endured the most grievous and dreadful temptations, which are but little described in the sense of the letter of the Word, but much in the internal sense (n. 1663, 1668, 1787, 2776, 2786, 2795, 2814, 9528). The Lord fought from the Divine love towards the whole human race (n. 1690, 1691, 1812, 1813, 1820). The love of the Lord was the salvation of the human race (n. 1820). The Lord fought from His own power (n. 1692, 1813, 9937). The Lord alone was made justice and merit, by the temptations, and victories which He gained therein from His own power (n. 1813, 2025–2027, 9715, 9809, 10,019). By temptations the Lord united the Divine itself, which was in Him from conception, to His Human, and made this Divine, as He makes man spiritual by temptations (n. 1725, 1729, 1733, 1737, 3318, 3381, 3382, 4286). The temptations of the Lord were attended with despair at the end (n. 1787). The Lord, by the temptations admitted into Himself, subjugated the hells, and reduced to order all things in them, and in heaven, and at the same time glorified His Human (n. 1737, 4287, 9315, 9528, 9937). The Lord alone fought against all the hells (n. 8273). He admitted temptations into Himself from thence (n. 2816, 4295).

The Lord could not be tempted as to the Divine, because the hells cannot assault the Divine, wherefore He assumed a human from the mother, such as could be tempted (n. 1414, 1444, 1573, 5041, 5157, 7193, 9315). By temptations and victories He expelled all the hereditary from the mother, and put off the human from her, until at length He was no longer her son (n. 2159, 2574, 2649, 3036, 10,830). Jehovah, who was in Him from conception, appeared in His temptations as if absent (n. 1815). This was His state of humiliation (n. 1785, 1999, 2159, 6866). His last temptation and victory, by which He fully subjugated the hells, and made His Human Divine, was in Gethsemane and on the cross (n. 2776, 2803, 2813, 2814, 10,655, 10,659, 10,828).

"To eat no bread and drink no water for forty days," signifies an entire state of temptations (n. 10,686). "Forty years," "months," or "days," signify a plenary state of temptations from beginning to end; and such a state is meant by the duration of the flood, "forty days"; by Moses abiding "forty days" upon Mount Sinai; by the sojourning of the sons of Israel "forty years" in the desert; and by the Lord's temptation in the desert "forty days" (n. 730, 862, 2272, 2273, 8098).

XV.
BAPTISM.

202. Baptism was instituted to be a sign that a man is of the church, and as a memorial that he is to be regenerated; for the washing of baptism is nothing else than spiritual washing, which is regeneration.

203. All regeneration is effected by the Lord, through the truths of faith, and a life according to them. Baptism therefore testifies that the man is of the church, and that he can be regenerated: for in the church the Lord is acknowledged, who alone regenerates, and there also is the Word, which contains the truths of faith, by which regeneration is effected.

204. This the Lord teaches in *John*:—

Except a man be begotten of water and of the spirit, he cannot enter into the kingdom of God (chap. iii. 5).

"Water" in the spiritual sense is the truth of faith from the Word; "the spirit" is a life according to that truth; and "to be begotten" is to be regenerated thereby.

205. Since every one who is regenerated also undergoes temptations, which are spiritual combats against evils and falsities, therefore by the water of baptism these also are signified.

206. As baptism is for a sign and memorial of these things, therefore man may be baptized as an infant, and if not then, he may be baptized as an adult.

207. Let those therefore who are baptized know, that baptism itself does not give faith nor salvation, but it testifies that they may receive faith and be saved, if they are regenerated.

208. Hence may be seen what is meant by the Lord's words in *Mark:*—

He that believeth and is baptized, shall be saved; but he that believeth not shall be condemned (chap. xvi. 16).

"He who believeth" is he who acknowledges the Lord, and receives Divine truths from Him through the Word; "he who is baptized" is he who is regenerated by the Lord by means of those truths.

FROM THE ARCANA CŒLESTIA.

209. Baptism signifies regeneration by the Lord through the truths of faith from the Word (n. 4255, 5120, 9088, 10,239, 10,386–10,388, 10,392). Baptism is for a sign that man is of the church, where the Lord is acknowledged, from whom is regeneration, and which has the Word, from which are the truths of faith, by which regeneration is effected (n. 10,386–10,388). Baptism gives neither faith nor salvation, but testifies that faith and salvation will be received by those who are regenerated (n. 10,391).

The washings in the ancient churches, and in the Israelitish church, represented and thence signified purifications from evils and falsities (n. 3147, 9088, 10,237, 10,239). "The washings of garments" signified the purification of the understanding from falsities (n. 5954). "The washing of the feet" signified the purification of the natural man (n. 3147, 10,241). What is signified by "the washing of the disciples' feet" by the Lord, is explained (n. 10,243).

"Waters" signify the truths of faith (n. 28, 2702, 3058, 5668, 8568, 10,238). "A fountain" and "a well of living waters" signifies the truths of faith from the Lord, thus the Word (n. 3424). "Bread and water" signify all the goods of love and truths of faith (n. 4976, 9323). "Spirit" signifies the life of truth, or the life of faith (n. 5222, 9281, 9818). What "the spirit" and "the flesh" signify, that "the spirit" signifies life from the Lord, and "flesh," life from man (n. 10,283). Hence it is evident what is signified by these words of the Lord:—

Except a man be begotten of water and the spirit, he cannot enter into the kingdom of God (*John* iii. 5).

Namely, that unless man is regenerated by the truths of faith, and by a life according to them, he cannot be saved (n. 10,240). All regeneration is effected by the truths of faith, and by a life according to them (n. 1904, 2046, 9088, 9959, 10,028).

The total washing, which was effected by immersion in the waters of the Jordan, signified regeneration itself, in the same manner as baptism (n. 9088, 10,239). What "the waters of Jordan," and "Jordan" signified (n. 1585, 4255).

"A flood" and "inundation of waters" signify temptations (n. 660, 705, 639, 756, 790, 5725, 6853). "Baptism" signifies the same (n. 5120, 10,389). In what manner baptism was represented from heaven (n. 2299).

XVI.
THE HOLY SUPPER.

210. The Holy Supper was instituted by the Lord, that by it there may be conjunction of the church with heaven, thus with the Lord: therefore it is the most holy thing of worship.

211. But how conjunction is effected by it is not understood by those who do not know the internal or spiritual sense of the Word, since they do not think beyond the external sense, which is the sense of the letter. It is known from the internal or spiritual sense of the Word, what is signified by the "body" and "blood," and by the "bread" and "wine"; and also what is signified by "eating."

212. In the spiritual sense, the Lord's "body" or "flesh," and the "bread," signifies the good of love; and the Lord's "blood" and the "wine," the good of faith; and "eating" is appropriation and conjunction. The angels who are with the man who goes to the Sacrament of the Supper, understand those things in no other way, for they perceive all things spiritually. Hence it is, that the holiness of love and the holiness of faith then flow into man from the angels, thus through heaven from the Lord, and hence conjunction is effected.

213. From these things it is evident, that when man partakes of the bread, which is the body, he is conjoined to the

Lord by the good of love to Him from Him; and when he partakes of the wine, which is the blood, he is conjoined to the Lord by the good of faith in Him from Him. But it is to be known that conjunction with the Lord by the Sacrament of the Supper, is effected with those alone who are in the good of love and faith in the Lord from the Lord. With these there is conjunction by the Holy Supper; with others there is presence, but not conjunction.

214. Besides, the Holy Supper includes and comprehends the whole of the Divine worship instituted in the Israelitish Church; for the burnt-offerings and sacrifices, in which the worship of that church principally consisted, in one expression were called "bread"; hence also the Holy Supper is its completion.

FROM THE ARCANA CŒLESTIA.

Since what is involved in the Holy Supper cannot be known, unless it be known what its particulars signify, for they correspond to spiritual things, therefore some passages shall be quoted respecting what is signified by "body" and "flesh," by "bread" and "wine," and by "eating" and "drinking"; as also concerning the sacrifices, wherein the worship of the Israelitish church principally consisted, showing that they were called "bread."

215. *Of Supper.*

"Dinners" and "suppers" signified consociation by love (n. 3596, 3832, 4745, 5161, 7996). The "paschal supper" signified consociation in heaven (n. 7836, 7997, 8001). "The feast of unleavened bread," or of "the passover," signified deliverance from damnation, by the Lord (n. 7093, 7867, 9286–9292, 10,655); in the inmost sense, the remembrance of the glorification of the Lord's Human, because deliverance comes therefrom (n. 10,655).

216. *Of Body and Flesh.*

The Lord's "flesh" signifies the Divine good of His Divine love, that is, of His Divine Human (n. 3813, 7850, 9127, 10,283). His "body" has a like signification (n. 2343, 3735, 6135). "Flesh" in general signifies the will or proprium of man, which regarded in itself is evil; but which when vivified by the Lord, signifies good (n. 148, 149, 780, 999, 3813, 8409, 10,283). Hence "flesh" in the Word, is the whole man, and every man (n. 574, 1050, 10,283).

It is said here and in what follows, that these things signify, because they correspond; for whatever corresponds, signifies (see n. 2896, 2979, 2987, 2989, 3002, 3225). The Word is written by mere correspondences, and hence its internal or spiritual sense, the nature of which cannot be known, and scarcely its existence, without a knowledge of correspondences (n. 3131, 3472–3485, 8615, 10,687). Therefore there is a conjunction of heaven with the man of the church by the Word (n. 10,687). For further particulars on this head see in the work on *Heaven and Hell* (n. 303–310), where it treats of the Conjunction of Heaven with the Man of the Church by means of the Word.

217. *Of Blood.*

The Lord's "blood" signifies the Divine truth proceeding from the Divine good of His Divine love (n. 4735, 6978, 7317, 7326, 7846, 7850, 7877, 9127, 9393, 10,026, 10,033, 10,152, 10,210). The "blood" sprinkled upon the altar round about, and at its foundation, signified the unition of Divine truth and the Divine good in the Lord (n. 10,047). "The blood of grapes" signifies the truth of faith from the good of charity (n. 6378). "A grape" and "a cluster" signify spiritual good, which is the good of charity (n. 5117). "To shed blood" is to offer violence to the Divine truth (n. 374, 1005, 4735, 5476, 9127). What is signified by "blood and water" going out of the Lord's side (n. 9127). What by the Lord's redeeming men by "His blood" (n. 10,152).

218. *Of Bread.*

"Bread," when mentioned in relation to the Lord, signifies the Divine good of the Lord's Divine love, and the reciprocal of the man who eats it (n. 2165, 2177, 3478, 3735, 3813, 4211, 4217, 4735, 4976, 9323, 9545). "Bread" involves and signifies all food in general (n. 2165, 6118). "Food" signifies every thing that nourishes the spiritual life of man (n. 4976, 5147, 5915, 6277, 8418). Thus "bread" signifies all celestial and spiritual food (n. 276, 680, 2165, 2177, 3478, 6118, 8410). Consequently, "everything which proceeds out of the mouth of God," according to the Lord's words (*Matt.* iv. 4; n. 681).

"Bread" in general signifies the good of love (n. 2165, 2177, 10,686). The same is signified by "wheat," of which bread is made (n. 3941, 7605). "Bread and water" when mentioned in the Word, signify the good of love and the truth of faith (n. 9323). Breaking of bread was a representative of mutual love in the ancient churches (n. 5405). Spiritual food is science, intelligence, and wisdom, thus good and truth, because the former are derived from the latter (n. 3114, 4459, 4792, 5147, 5293, 5340, 5342, 5410, 5426, 5576, 5582, 5588, 5655, 8562, 9003). And because they nourish the mind (n. 4459, 5293, 5576, 6277, 8418). Sustenance by food signifies spiritual nourishment, and the influx of good and truth from the Lord (n. 4976, 5915, 6277).

The "bread" on the table in the tabernacle, signified the Divine good of the Lord's Divine love (n. 3478, 9545). The "meal-offerings" of cakes and wafers in the sacrifices, signified worship from the good of love (n. 4581, 10,079, 10,137). What the various meal-offerings signified in particular (n. 7978, 9992–9994, 10,079).

The ancients, when they mentioned bread, meant all food in general (see *Gen.* xliii. 16, 31; *Exod.* xviii. 12; *Judges* xiii. 15, 16; 1 *Sam.* xiv. 28, 29; xx. 24, 27; 2 *Sam.* ix. 7, 10; 1 *Kings* iv. 22, 23; 2 *Kings* xxv. 29).

219. *Of Wine.*

"Wine," when mentioned concerning the Lord, signifies the Divine truth proceeding from His Divine good, in the same manner as "blood" (n. 1071, 1798, 6377). "Wine" in general signifies the good of charity (n. 6377). "Must" signifies truth from good in the natural man (n. 3580). Wine is called "the blood of grapes" (n. 6378). "A vineyard" signifies the church as to truth (n. 3220, 9139). The "drink-offering" in the sacrifices, which was wine, signified spiritual good, which is holy truth (n. 1072). The Lord alone is holy, and hence all holiness is from Him (n. 9229, 9680, 10,359, 10,360). The Divine truth proceeding from the Lord is what is called "holy" in the Word (n. 6788, 8302, 9229, 9820, 10,361).

220. *Of Eating and Drinking.*

"To eat" signifies to be appropriated and conjoined by love and charity (n. 2187, 2343, 3168, 3513, 5643). Hence it signifies to be consociated (n. 8001). "To eat" is predicated of the appropriation and conjunction of good, and "to drink," of the appropriation and conjunction of truth (n. 3168, 3513, 3832, 9412). What "eating and drinking in the Lord's kingdom" signifies (n. 3832). Hence it is, that "to be famished" and "hungry," in the Word, signifies to desire good and truth from affection (n. 4958, 10,227).

The angels understand the things here spoken of according to their internal or spiritual sense alone, because the angels are in the spiritual world (n. 10,521). Hence holiness from heaven flows in with the men of the church, when they receive the Sacrament of the Supper with sanctity (n. 6789). And thence is conjunction with the Lord (n. 3464, 3735, 5915, 10,519, 10,521, 10,522).

221. *Of Sacrifices.*

"Burnt-offerings" and "sacrifices" signified all things of worship from the good of love, and from the truths of faith (n. 923, 6905, 8680, 8936, 10,042). "Burnt-offerings" and "sacrifices" also signified Divine celestial things, which are the internal things of the church, from which worship is derived (n. 2180, 2805, 2807, 2830, 3519). With a variation and difference according to the varieties of worship (n. 2805, 6905, 8936). Therefore there were many kinds of sacrifices, and various processes to be observed in them, and various beasts from which they were (n. 2830, 9391, 9990). The various things which they signified in general, may appear from unfolding the particulars by the internal sense (n. 10,042). What "the beasts" which were sacrificed signified in particular (n. 10,042). Arcana of heaven are contained in the rituals and processes of the sacrifices (n. 10,057). In general they contained the arcana of the glorification of the Lord's Human; and in a respective sense, the arcana of the regeneration and purification of man from evils and falsities; wherefore they were prescribed for various sins, crimes, and purifications (n. 9990, 10,022, 10,042, 10,053, 10,057). What is signified by "the imposition of hands" on the beasts which were sacrificed (n. 10,023). What by "the inferior parts of the slain beasts being put under their superior parts" in the burnt-offerings (n. 10,051). What by "the meal-offerings" that were offered at the same time (n. 10,079). What by "the drink-offering" (n. 4581, 10,137). What by "the salt" which was used (n. 10,300). What by "the altar" and all the particulars of it (n. 921, 2777, 2784, 2811, 2812, 4489, 4541, 8935, 8940, 9388, 9389, 9714, 9726, 9963, 9964, 10,028, 10,123, 10,151, 10,242, 10,245, 10,344). What by "the fire of the altar" (n. 934, 6314, 6832). What by "eating together of the things sacrificed" (n. 2187, 8682). Sacrifices were not commanded, but charity and faith, thus that they were only permitted, shown from the Word (n. 922, 2180). Why they were permitted (n. 2180, 2818).

The burnt-offerings and sacrifices, which consisted of lambs, she-goats, sheep, kids, he-goats, and bullocks, were in one word called "*Bread,*" is evident from the following passages:—

And the priest shall burn it upon the altar; it is the bread of the offering made by fire unto Jehovah (*Lev.* iii. 11, 16).

The sons of Aaron shall be holy unto their God, neither shall they profane the name of their God; for the offerings of Jehovah made by fire, the bread of their God, they do offer. Thou shalt sanctify him, for he offereth the bread of thy God. A man of the seed of Aaron, in whom there shall be a blemish, let him not approach to offer the bread of his God (*Lev.* xxi. 6, 8, 17, 21).

Command the sons of Israel, and say unto them, My offering, My bread, for My sacrifices made by fire for an odor of rest, ye shall observe, to offer unto Me in its stated time (*Num.* xxviii. 2).

He who shall have touched an unclean thing shall not eat of the holy things, but he shall wash his flesh in water; and shall afterwards eat of the holy things, because it is his bread (*Lev.* xxii. 6, 7).

They who offer polluted bread upon My altar (*Mal.* i. 7).

Hence now, as has been said above (n. 214), the Holy Supper includes and comprehends all of the Divine worship instituted in the Israelitish Church; for the burnt-offerings and sacrifices in which the worship of that church principally consisted were called by the one word "bread." Hence, also, the Holy Supper is its fulfilling.

From what has been observed, it may now be seen what is meant by bread in *John:*—

Jesus said to them, Verily, verily, I say unto you, Moses gave them not that bread from heaven, but My Father giveth you the true bread from heaven; for the bread of God is He who came down from heaven, and giveth life unto the world. They said unto Him, Lord, evermore give us this bread. Jesus said unto them, I am the bread of life; he that cometh to Me shall never hunger, and he that believeth on Me shall never thirst. He that believeth on Me hath eternal life. I am the bread of life. This is the bread which cometh down from heaven; that any one may eat thereof, and not die. I am the living bread which came down from heaven; if any one shall eat of this bread, he shall live for ever (vi. 31–35, 47–51).

From these passages, and from what has been said above, it appears that "bread" is all the good which proceeds from the Lord, for the Lord Himself is in His own good; and thus that "bread and wine" in the Holy Supper are all the worship of the Lord from the good of love and faith.

222. To the above shall be added some particulars from the *Arcana Cœlestia* (n. 9127): "He who knows nothing of the internal or spiritual sense of the Word, knows no other than that 'flesh and blood,' when they are mentioned in the Word, mean flesh and blood. But in the internal or spiritual sense, it does not treat of the life of the body, but of the life of man's soul, that is, of his spiritual life, which he is to live to eternity. This life is described in the literal sense of the Word, by things which belong the life of the body, that is, by 'flesh and blood;' and as the spiritual life of man subsists by the good of love and the truth of faith, therefore in the internal sense of the Word the good of love is meant by 'flesh,' and the truth of faith by 'blood.' These are understood by 'flesh and blood,' and by 'bread and wine,' in heaven; for 'bread' means altogether the same there as 'flesh,' and 'wine' as 'blood.' They who are not spiritual men, do not apprehend this; let such abide therefore in their own faith, only believing that in the Holy Supper, and in the Word, there is holiness, because they are from the Lord, although they may not know where that holiness resides. On the other hand, let those who are endowed with interior perception, consider whether 'flesh' means flesh, and 'blood,' blood, in the following passages. In the *Apocalypse:*—

I saw an angel standing in the sun, and he cried with a great voice, saying unto all the birds that fly in the midst of heaven, Come and gather yourselves together to the supper of the great God; that ye may eat the flesh of kings, and the flesh of commanders of thousands, and the flesh of the mighty, and the flesh of horses and of them that sit on them, and the flesh of all, free and bond, small and great (xix. 17, 18).

Who can understand these words, unless he knows what 'flesh,' 'kings,' 'commanders of thousands,' 'the mighty,' 'horses,' 'them that sit on them', and 'freemen' and 'bondmen,' signify in the internal sense? And in *Ezekiel*:—

> Thus saith the Lord Jehovih, Say to every bird of heaven, and to every beast of the field, Gather yourselves together and come; gather yourselves together from every side to My sacrifice that I sacrifice for you, a great sacrifice upon the mountains of Israel, that ye may eat flesh and drink blood; ye shall eat the flesh of the mighty, and drink the blood of the princes of the earth; and ye shall eat fat to satiety, and drink blood even to drunkenness, of My sacrifice which I have sacrificed for you: thus shall ye be satisfied at My table, with horse and chariot, with the mighty, and with every man of war; thus will I give My glory among the nations (xxxix. 17-21).

This passage treats of the calling together of all to the kingdom of the Lord, and in particular of the establishment of the church with the Gentiles; and 'eating flesh and drinking blood,' signify to appropriate to themselves Divine good and Divine truth, thus the holiness which proceeds from the Lord's Divine Human. Who cannot see, that 'flesh' does not here mean flesh, nor 'blood,' blood; as when it said, that 'they should eat the flesh of the mighty,' and 'drink the blood of the princes of the earth'; and that 'they should drink blood even to drunkenness'; also that 'they should be satisfied with horses, with chariots, with mighty men, and with all men of war'? What 'the birds of heaven' and 'the beasts of the field' signify in the spiritual sense, may be seen in the work on *Heaven and Hell* (n. 110 and the notes). Let us now consider what the Lord said concerning His flesh and His blood, in *John*:—

> The bread which I will give, is My flesh. Verily, verily, I say unto you, Except ye eat the flesh of the Son of man, and drink His blood, ye have no life in you. Whoso eateth My flesh and drinketh My blood, hath eternal life, and I will raise him up at the last day; for My flesh is meat indeed, and My blood is drink indeed. He that eateth My flesh and drinketh My blood, dwelleth in Me, and I in him. This is the bread which came down from heaven (vi. 50-58).

'The flesh' of the Lord is the Divine good, and His 'blood,' the Divine truth, each from Him, is evident, because these nourish the spiritual life of man; hence it is said, 'My flesh is meat indeed, and My blood is drink indeed,' and as man is conjoined to the Lord by the Divine good and truth, it is also said, 'Whoso eateth My flesh and drinketh My blood, hath eternal life'; and, 'He dwelleth in Me and I in him'; and in the former part of the chapter:—

> Labor not for the food which perisheth, but for that food which endureth to eternal life (verse 27).

'To abide in the Lord' is to be in love to Him, the Lord Himself teaches in *John* (chap. xv. 2–12)".

XVII.
THE RESURRECTION.

223. Man is so created that as to his internal he cannot die; for he can believe in and also love God, and thus be conjoined to God by faith and love; and to be conjoined to God is to live to eternity.

224. This internal is with every man who is born; his external is that by which he brings into effect the things which are of his faith and love. The internal is called the spirit, and the external is called the body. The external, which is called the body, is accommodated to the uses in the natural world, this is rejected when man dies; but the internal, which is called the spirit, is accommodated to the uses in the spiritual world, this does not die. This internal is then a good spirit and an angel, if the man had been good in the world; but an evil spirit if man had been evil in the world.

225. The spirit of man after the death of the body, appears in the spiritual world in a human form, in every respect as in the world. He enjoys the faculty of seeing, of hearing, of speaking, and of feeling, as in the world; and he is endowed with every faculty of thinking, of willing, and of acting, as in the world; in a word, he is a man as to each and everything, except that he is not encompassed with the gross body which he had in the world. This he leaves when he dies, nor does he ever resume it.

226. This continuation of life is meant by the resurrection. The reason why men believe that they will not rise again before the Last Judgment, when the whole visible world will perish, is because they have not understood the Word, and because sensual men place all their life in the body, and believe that unless this shall live again, it will be all over with the man.

227. The life of man after death is the life of his love and the life of his faith; hence such as his love and faith had been, when he lived in the world, such his life will remain to eternity. With those who loved themselves and the world above all things, it is the life of hell; and with those who had loved God above all things, and the neighbor as themselves, it is the life of heaven. The latter are they who have faith; but the former are they who have no faith. The life of heaven is called eternal life; and the life of hell is called spiritual death.

228. That man lives after death, the Word teaches; as that:—

God is not the God of the dead, but of the living (*Matt.* xxii. 31).

Lazarus after death was carried into heaven, but the rich man was cast into hell (*Luke* xvi. 22, 23, *seq.*).

Abraham, Isaac, and Jacob are there (*Matt.* viii. 11; xxii. 31, 32; *Luke* xx. 37, 38).

Jesus said to the robber, To-day shalt thou be with Me in paradise (*Luke* xxiii. 43).

FROM THE WORK ON HEAVEN AND HELL.

229. It is unnecessary here to adduce anything from the *Arcana Cœlestia*, since the things concerning the resurrection and the life of man after death have been fully treated in the work on *Heaven and Hell*, where they may be seen under the following articles:

I. Every Man is a Spirit as to His Interiors (n. 432–444).

II. Of Man's Resuscitation from the Dead, and His Entrance into Eternal Life (n. 445–452).

III. After Death Man is in a Perfect Human Form (n. 453–460).

IV. After Death Man has every Sense, and all the Memory, Thought, and Affection, which He had in the World; and that He Leaves Nothing but His Terrestrial Body (n. 461–469).

V. Man after Death is Such as his Life had Been in the World (n. 470–484).

VI. The Delights of Every one's Life are Turned into Corresponding Things (n. 485–490).

VII. Of Man's First State after Death (n. 491–498).

VIII. Of Man's Second State after Death (n. 499–511).

IX. Of Man's Third State after Death, which is a State of Instruction for Those that Come into Heaven (n. 512–520).

X. That Heaven and Hell are from the Human Race (311–317).

Concerning the Last Judgment, spoken of above at n. 226, see the work on *The Last Judgment, and Babylon Destroyed*, from the beginning to the end; where it is shown that the Last Judgment will not be attended with the destruction of the world.

XVIII.

HEAVEN AND HELL.

230. There are two things which constitute the life of man's spirit, namely, love and faith; love constituting the life of his will, and faith the life of his understanding. The love of good and the faith of truth thence derived, constitute the life of heaven; and the love of evil, and the faith of falsity thence derived, constitute the life of hell.

231. Love to the Lord and love towards the neighbor constitute heaven; and also faith, so far as it has life from those loves. And because both the love and the faith thence derived, are from the Lord, it is evident that the Lord Himself constitutes heaven.

232. Heaven is with every man according to his reception of love and faith from the Lord; and they who receive heaven from the Lord while they live in the world, come into heaven after death.

233. They who receive heaven from the Lord are they who have heaven in themselves, for heaven is in man, as the Lord also teaches:—

Neither shall they say, The kingdom of God, lo it is here, or lo there, for the kingdom of God is in you (*Luke* xvii. 21).

234. Heaven is with man in his internal, thus in his willing and thinking from love and faith, and thence in his external, which is in acting and speaking from love and faith. But heaven is not in man's external without the internal; for all hypocrites can act and speak well, but they cannot will and think well.

235. When man comes into the other life, which takes place immediately after death, it is evident whether heaven is in him or not; but not while he lives in the world. For in the world the external appears, and not the internal, but in the other life the internal is made manifest, because man then lives as to his spirit.

236. Eternal happiness, which is also called heavenly joy, is imparted to those who are in love and faith in the Lord, from the Lord; for this love and faith have that joy in them; into it the man comes after death who has heaven in him; in the meantime it lies hidden in his internal man. In the heavens there is a communion of all goods; there the peace, the intelligence, the wisdom, and the happiness of all are communicated to each; yet to every one according to his reception of love and faith from the Lord. Hence it may appear how great is the peace, intelligence, wisdom and happiness in heaven.

237. As love to the Lord and love towards the neighbor constitute the life of heaven with man, so the love of self and the love of the world, when they reign, constitute the life of hell with him; for these loves are opposite to those. Therefore they with whom the loves of self and of the world reign, can receive nothing from heaven, but what they receive is from hell; for whatever a man loves, and whatever he believes, is either from heaven or from hell.

238. Those with whom the love of self and the love of the world reign, do not know what heaven and heavenly happiness are; and it appears incredible to them that happiness is given in any other loves than in them. Nevertheless, the happiness of heaven enters so far as the loves of self and the world, regarded as ends, are removed; and the happiness which succeeds on their removal is so great as to exceed all human comprehension.

239. The life of man cannot be changed after death. It then remains such as it had been. For the quality of man's spirit is in every respect the same as that of his love, and infernal love can never be transcribed into heavenly love, because they are opposite. This is meant by the words of Abraham to the rich man in hell:—

> Between us and you there is a great gulf; so that they which would pass to you cannot; neither can they pass to us from thence (*Luke* xvi. 26).

Hence it is evident that all who come into hell remain there to eternity; and they who come into heaven remain there to eternity.

240. Since the subject of heaven and hell has been treated of in a separate work, wherein is also adduced what is contained in the *Arcana Cœlestia* concerning it, it is therefore unnecessary here to add anything further.

XIX.
THE CHURCH.

241. That which constitutes heaven with man, also constitutes the church; for as love and faith constitute heaven, so they also constitute the church; thus, from what has been already said concerning heaven, it is evident what the church is.

242. The church is said to be where the Lord is acknowledged and where the Word is, for the essentials of the church are love and faith in the Lord from the Lord; and the Word teaches how man must live that he may receive love and faith from the Lord.

243. That there may be a church, there must be doctrine from the Word, since without doctrine the Word is not understood. Doctrine alone, however, does not constitute the church with man, but a life according to it. Hence it follows that faith alone does not constitute the church with man, but the life of faith, which is charity. Genuine doctrine is the doctrine of charity and faith together, and not the doctrine of faith separate from charity; for the doctrine of charity and faith together is the doctrine of life; but not the doctrine of faith without the doctrine of charity.

244. They who are out of the church and acknowledge one God, and live according to their religious principle, and in some charity towards the neighbor, are in communion with those who are of the church; for no man who believes in God and lives well, is condemned. Hence it is evident, that the church of the Lord is in the whole world, although specifically, where the Lord is acknowledged, and where the Word is.

245. Every one with whom the church exists, is saved; but every one in whom it is not, is condemned.

FROM THE ARCANA CŒLESTIA.

246. The church exists specifically where the Word is, and and where the Lord is thereby known, and thus where Divine truths are revealed (n. 3857, 10,761). Still they who are born where the Word is, and where the Lord is thereby known, are not of the church, but they who are regenerated by the Lord by the truths of the Word, that is, they who live the life of charity (n. 6637, 10,143, 10,153, 10,578, 10,645, 10,829). They who are of the church, or in whom the church is, are in the affection of truth for the sake of truth, that is, they love truth because it is truth; and they examine from the Word whether the doctrinals of the church in which they were born are true (n. 5432, 6047). Otherwise the truth possessed by every one would be derived from another, and from his native soil (n. 6047).

The church of the Lord is with all in the whole world who live in good according to their religious principles (n. 3263, 6637, 10,765). All who live in good wherever they are, and acknowledge one God, are accepted by the Lord and come into heaven; since all who are in good acknowledge the Lord, because good is from the Lord, and the Lord is in good (n. 2589–2604, 2861, 2863, 3263, 4190, 4197, 6700, 9256). The universal church on earth before the Lord is as one man (n. 7396, 9276). As heaven is, because the church is heaven or the kingdom of the Lord on earth (n. 2853, 2996, 2998, 3624–3629, 3636–3643, 3741–3745, 4625). But the church, where the Lord is known and where the Word is, is like the heart and lungs in man in respect to the other parts of the body, which live from the heart and lungs as from the fountains of their life (n. 637,

931, 2054, 2853). Hence it is, that unless there were a church where the Word is, and where the Lord is thereby known, the human race could not be saved (n. 468, 637, 931, 4545, 10,452). The church is the foundation of heaven (n. 4060).

The church is internal and external (n. 1242, 6587, 9375, 9680, 10,762). The internal of the church is love to the Lord and charity towards the neighbor. Thence they who are in the affection of good and truth from love to the Lord and from charity towards the neighbor, constitute the internal church; and they who are in external worship from obedience and faith, constitute the external church (n. 1083, 1098, 4288, 6380, 6587, 7840, 8762). To know truth and good, and to act from thence, is the external of the church, but to will and love truth and good, and to act from thence, is the internal of the church (n. 4899, 6775). The internal of the church is in the worship of those who are of the external church, although in obscurity (n. 6775). The internal and external church make one church (n. 409, 10,762). Man has an internal and an external, an internal after the image of heaven, and an external after the image of the world; and therefore, in order that the man may be a church, his external must act in unity with his internal (n. 3628, 4523, 4524, 6057, 6314, 9706, 10,472). The church is in the internal of man and at the same time in the external, but not in the external without the internal (n. 1795, 6580, 10,691). The internal of the church is according to truths and their quality, and according to their implantation in good by life (n. 1238).

The church like heaven is in man, and thus the church in general consists of the men in whom the church is (n. 3884). In order that a church may exist, there must be the doctrine of life, that is, the doctrine of charity (n. 3445, 10,763, 10,764). Charity makes the church, and not faith separated from charity (n. 916). Consequently, not the doctrine of faith separated from charity, but the doctrine of faith conjoined therewith, and a life comformable to it (n. 809, 1798, 1799, 1834, 1844, 4468, 4672, 4689, 4766, 5826, 665.'). The church is not with man, unless the truths of doctrine are implanted in the good of charity with him, thus in the life (n. 3310, 3963, 5826). There is no church with man, if he is only in the truths, which are called the truths of faith (n. 5826). How much good would be in the church, if charity were in the first place and faith in the second (n. 6269). And how much evil, if faith is in the first place (n. 6272). In the ancient churches charity was the principal and essential of the church (n. 4680). The church would be like heaven, if all had charity (n. 2385, 2853). If good were the characteristic of the church, and not truth without good, thus if charity were its characteristic, and not faith separate, the church would be one, and differences with respect to the doctrinals of faith, and external worship, would be accounted as nothing (n. 1285, 1316, 2982, 3267, 3445, 3451).

Every church begins from charity, but declines therefrom in process of time (n. 494, 501, 1327, 3773, 4689). Thus to falsities from evil, and at length to evils (n. 1834, 1835, 2910, 4683, 4689). A comparison of the church at its beginning and decline with the infancy and old age of man (n. 10,134). And also with the rising and the setting of the sun (n. 1837). Concerning the successive states of the Christian Church even to its last state; wherein are explained the particulars which the Lord foretold concerning "the consummation of the age," and His "coming," in *Matt.* chap. xxiv. from the beginning to the end (n. 3353–3356, 3486–3489, 3650–3655, 3571–3757, 3897–3901, 4057–4060, 4229–4231, 4332–4335, 4422–4424, 4635–4638, 4807–4810, 4954–4959, 5063–5071). The Christian church is at this day in its last states, there being no faith therein because there is no charity (n. 3489, 4689). The Last Judgment is the last time of the church (n. 2118, 3353, 4057, 4333, 4535). Of the vastation of the church (n. 407–411). The consummation of the age and the coming of the Lord is the last time of the old church and the beginning of the new (n. 2243, 4535, 10,622). When the old church is vastated, interior truths are revealed for the service of the new church which is then established (n. 3398, 3786). Concerning the establishment of the church with the Gentiles (n. 1366, 2986, 4747, 9256).

247. *Of the Ancient Churches.*

The first and Most Ancient Church on this earth, which is described in the first chapters of *Genesis*, was a celestial church, and the chief of all the rest (n. 607, 895, 920, 1121–1124, 2896, 4493, 8891, 9942, 10,545). Of the quality of those in heaven who belonged to it (n. 1114–1125). They are in the highest degree of light (n. 1116, 1117). There were various churches after the flood, called in one word, the Ancient Church, concerning which (n. 1125–1127, 1327, 10,355). Through how many kingdoms of Asia the Ancient Church was extended (n. 1238, 2385). The quality of the men of the Ancient Church (n. 609, 895). The Ancient Church was a representative church, and its representatives were collected into one by certain men of the Most Ancient Church (n. 519, 521, 2896). The Ancient Church had a Word, but it was lost (n. 2897). The quality of the Ancient Church when it began to decline (n. 1128). The difference between the Most Ancient and the Ancient Churches (n. 597, 607, 640, 641, 765, 784, 895, 4493). The Most Ancient Church and the Ancient were also in the land of Canaan, and hence came the representatives of the places therein (n. 3686, 4447, 4454). Of the church that began from Eber, which was called the Hebrew Church (n. 1238, 1241, 1343, 4516, 4517). The difference between the Ancient and the Hebrew Churches (n. 1343, 4874). Eber instituted sacrifices which were wholly unknown in the Ancient Churches (n. 1343). The Ancient Churches agreed with the Christian Church as to internals, but not as to externals (n. 3478, 4489, 4772, 4904, 10,149). In the Most Ancient Church there was immediate revelation; in the Ancient Church, revelation by correspondences; in the Jewish Church, by a living voice; and in the Christian Church, by the Word (n. 10,355). The Lord was the God of the Most Ancient Church, and was called Jehovah (n. 1343, 6846). The Lord is heaven, and He is the church (n. 4766, 10,125, 10,151, 10,157). The Divine of the Lord makes heaven, see the work on *Heaven and Hell* (n. 7–12, and 78–86); and thus also the church, since what constitutes heaven with man, constitutes also the church, as was shown in the doctrine above.

248. *Of the Jewish Church and of the Jews.*

The statutes, judgments, and laws, which were commanded in the Jewish Church, were in part like those in the Ancient Church (n. 4449, 4835). In what respect the representative rites of the Jewish Church differed from those of the Ancient Church (n. 4288, 10,149). A representative church was instituted with that nation, but there was no church in that nation itself (n. 4899, 4912, 6304). Therefore as to that nation itself, it was the representative of a church, but not a church (n. 4281, 4288, 4311, 4500, 6304, 7048, 9320, 10,396, 10,526, 10,535, 10,698). The Israelitish and Jewish nation was not elected, but only received, in order that it might represent a church, on account of the obstinacy with which their fathers and Moses insisted (n. 4290, 4293, 7051, 7439, 10,430, 10,535, 10,632). Their worship was merely external, without any internal worship (n. 1200, 3147, 3479, 8871). They were entirely unacquainted with the internals of worship, and were not willing to know them (n. 301–303, 3479, 4429, 4433, 4680, 4844, 4847, 10,396, 10,401, 10,407, 10,694, 10,701, 10,707). In what manner they consider the internals of worship, of the church, and the Word (n. 4865). Their interiors were filthy, full of the loves of self and of the world, and of avarice (n. 3480, 9962, 10,454–10,457, 10,462–10,466, 10,575). On this account the internals of the church were not disclosed to them, because they would have profaned them (n. 2520, 3398, 3480, 4289). The Word is wholly shut to them (n. 3769). They see the Word from without and not from within (n. 10,549–10,551). Therefore their internal, when in worship, was shut (n. 8788, 8806, 9320, 9377, 9380, 9962, 10,396, 10,401, 10,407, 10,492, 10,498, 10,500, 10,575, 10,629, 10,694). That nation was of such a quality, that they could be in a holy external, when the internal was shut, more than others (n. 4293, 4311, 4903, 9373, 9377, 9380). Their state at that time (n. 4311). They are therefore preserved to this day (n. 3479). Their holy external was miraculously elevated by the Lord into heaven, and the interior things of worship, of the church, and the Word perceived there (n. 3480, 4307, 4311, 6304, 8588, 10,492, 10,500, 10,602). For this purpose they were forced by external means strictly to observe their rites in their external form (n. 3147, 4281, 10,149). Because they could be in a holy external without an internal, they could represent the holy things of the church and heaven (n. 3479, 3881, 4208, 6306, 8588, 9377, 10,430, 10,500, 10,570). Still those holy things did not affect them (n. 3479). The quality of the person who represents is of no importance, because the representation regards the thing represented, and not the person (n. 665, 1097, 1361, 3147, 3881, 4208, 4281, 4288, 4292, 4307, 4444, 4500, 6304, 7048, 7439, 8588, 8788, 8806).

That nation was worse than other nations, their quality also described from the Word of both Testaments (n. 4314, 4316, 4317, 4444, 4503, 4750, 4751, 4815, 4820, 4832, 5057, 5998, 7248, 8819, 9320, 10,454–10,547, 10,462–10,466). The tribe of Judah departed into worse things than the other tribes (n. 4815). How cruelly they treated the Gentiles, from delight (n. 5057, 7248, 9320). That nation was idolatrous in heart, and more than other nations worshiped other gods (n. 3732, 4208, 4444, 4825, 5998, 6877, 7401, 8301, 8871, 8882). Even their worship was idolatrous when considered as to that nation itself, because it was external without internal (n. 4281, 4825, 8871, 8882). They worshiped Jehovah only in name (n. 6877, 10,559–10,561, 10,566). And only on account of miracles (n. 4299). They who believe that the Jews will be converted at the end of the church, and brought again into the land of Canaan, think erroneously (n. 4847, 7051, 8301). Many passages adduced from the Word concerning this matter, but which are to be understood according to the internal sense, and differently from the sense of the letter (n. 7051). The Word was changed on account of that nation, as to its external sense, but not as to its internal sense (n. 10,453, 10,461, 10,603, 10,604). Jehovah appeared to them on Mount Sinai, according to their quality, in a consuming fire, a thick cloud, and smoke as of a furnace (n. 1861, 6832, 8814, 8819, 9434). The Lord appears to every one according to his quality, as a vivifying and re-creating fire to those who are in good, and as a consuming fire to those who are in evil (n. 934, 1861, 6832, 8814, 8819, 9434, 10,551). One origin of that nation was from a Canaanitess and the two others from whoredom with a daughter-in-law (n. 1167, 4818, 4820, 4874, 4899, 4913). These origins signify the nature of their conjunction with the church, as being like conjunction with the Canaanitess, and whoredom with a daughter-in-law (n, 4868, 4874, 4899, 4911, 4913). Of the state of the Jews in the other life (n. 939, 940, 5057).

Since this nation, although of such a quality, represented the church; and since the Word was written among them and concerning them; therefore Divine celestial things were signified by their names, as by "Reuben," "Simeon," "Levi," "Judah," "Ephraim," "Joseph," and the rest. That "Judah," in the internal sense, signifies the Lord as to celestial love, and His celestial kingdom (n. 3654, 3881, 5583, 5603, 5782, 6363). The prophecy of Israel concerning Judah, in which the Lord is treated of, explained, *Gen.* xlix. 8–12 (n. 6362–6381). "The tribe of Judah" and "Judea" signify the celestial church (n. 3654, 6364). The twelve tribes represented, and thence signified all things of love and faith in the complex (n. 3858, 3926, 4060, 6335); thus also heaven and the church (n. 6337, 6637, 7836, 7891). They signify according to the order in which they are named (n. 3862, 3926, 3939, 4603, *seq.*, 6337, 6640). The twelve tribes were divided into two kingdoms, in order that the Jews might represent the celestial kingdom, and the Israelites the spiritual kingdom (n. 8770, 9320). "The seed of Abraham," of "Isaac," and of "Jacob," signifies the goods and truths of the church (n. 3373, 10,445).

XX.

THE SACRED SCRIPTURE, OR THE WORD.

249. Without a revelation from the Divine, man cannot know anything concerning eternal life, nor even anything concerning God, and still less concerning love to, and faith in Him; for man is born into mere ignorance, and must therefore learn everything from worldly things, from which he must form his understanding. He is also born hereditarily into every evil which is from the love of self and of the world; the delights from thence reign continually, and suggest such things as are diametrically contrary to the Divine. Hence it is that man knows nothing concerning eternal life; wherefore there must necessarily be a revelation from which he may know.

250. That the evils of the love of self and of the world induce such ignorance concerning those things which are of eternal life, appears manifestly from those within the church; who, although they know from revelation that there is a God, that there is a heaven and a hell, that there is eternal life, and that eternal life is to be acquired by the good of love and faith, still lapse into denial concerning those things, both the learned and the unlearned. Hence it is further evident how great ignorance there would be, if there were no revelation.

251. Since therefore man lives after death, and then lives to eternity, and a life awaits him according to his love and faith, it follows that the Divine, out of love towards the human race, has revealed such things as may lead to that life, and conduce to man's salvation. What the Divine has revealed, is with us the Word.

252. The Word, because it is a revelation from the Divine, is Divine in each and all things; for what is from the Divine cannot be otherwise. What is from the Divine descends through the heavens even to man; wherefore in the heavens it is accommodated to the wisdom of the angels who are there, and on earth it is accommodated to the apprehension of the men who are there. Wherefore in the Word there is an internal sense, which is spiritual, for the angels, and an external sense, which is natural, for men. Hence it is that the conjunction of heaven with man is effected through the Word.

253. No others understand the genuine sense of the Word but they who are enlightened; and they only are enlightened who are in love to, and faith in, the Lord; for their interiors are elevated by the Lord into the light of heaven.

254. The Word in the letter cannot be understood, but by doctrine from the Word drawn by one who is enlightened. The sense of its letter is accommodated to the apprehension even of simple men, wherefore doctrine from the Word must serve them for a lamp.

FROM THE ARCANA CŒLESTIA.

255. *Of the Necessity and Excellence of the Word.*

From the light of nature, nothing is known concerning the Lord, concerning heaven and hell, concerning the life of man after death, and concerning the Divine truths by which man has spiritual and eternal life (n. 8944, 10,318–10,320). This may be manifest from this, that many, and among them the learned, do not believe them, although they were born where the Word is, and are thereby instructed concerning them (n. 10,319). It was therefore necessary that there should be some revelation from heaven, because man was born for heaven (n. 1775). Therefore in all time there has been a revelation (n. 2895). Concerning the various kinds of revelation which have been successively made on this earth (n. 10,355, 10,632). The most ancient people who lived before the flood, and whose age was called the golden age, had immediate revelation, and hence Divine truth was inscribed on their hearts (n. 2896). In the ancient churches which were after the flood, there was a Word, both historical and prophetical (n. 2686, 2897); concerning which churches see above (n. 247). Its historical parts were called the *Wars of Jehovah*, and its prophetical parts, *Enunciations* (n. 2897). That Word was like our Word as to inspiration (n. 2897). It is mentioned by Moses (n. 2686, 2897). But that Word is lost (n. 2897). There were also prophetic revelations with others, as appears from the prophecies of Balaam (n. 2898).

The Word is Divine in each and every particular (n. 639, 680, 10,321, 10,637). The Word is Divine and holy as to every jot and tittle, from experience (n. 9349). How it is explained at this day, that the Word is inspired as to every jot (n. 1886).

The church exists specifically where the Word is, and where the Lord is thereby known and Divine truths are revealed (n. 3857, 10,761). But it does not follow from hence, that they are of the church who are born where the Word is, and where the Lord is thereby known, but they who by means of truths from the Word are regenerated by the Lord, that is, who live according to the truths therein, thus who lead a life of love and of faith (n. 6637, 10,143, 10,153, 10,578, 10,645, 10,829).

256. *The Word is not understood except by those who are enlightened.*

The human rational cannot apprehend Divine things, nor even spiritual things, unless it is enlightened by the Lord (n. 2196, 2203, 2209, 2654). Thus only they who are enlightened apprehend the Word (n. 10,323). The Lord enables those who are enlightened to understand truth, and to see how to reconcile those things in the Word which may appear to contradict each other (n. 9382, 10,659). The Word in the sense of the letter is not consistent with itself, and sometimes it appears contradictory (n. 9025). And therefore it may be explained and strained by those who are not enlightened, to confirm any opinion or heresy whatever, and to patronize any worldly and corporeal love (n. 4783, 10,399, 10,400). They who read the Word from the love of truth and good, are enlightened from it, but not they who read it from the love of fame, gain, or honor, thus from the love of self (n. 9382, 10,548–10,550). They who are in the good of life, and thereby in the affection of truth, are enlightened (n. 8694). They whose internal is open, and who thus as to their internal man are capable of being elevated into the light of heaven, are enlightened (n. (10,400, 10,402, 10,691, 10,694). Enlightenment is an actual opening of the interiors of the mind, and elevation of them into the light of heaven (n. 10,330). Holiness from the internal, that is, through the internal from the Lord, inflows with those who esteem the Word to be holy, though they themselves do not know it (n. 6789). They who are led by the Lord are enlightened, and see truths in the Word, but not they who are led by self (10,638). They who love truth because it is truth, that is, who love to live according to Divine truths, are led by the Lord (n. 10,578, 10,645, 10,829). The Word is vivified with man, according to his life of love and faith (n. 1776). Those things which are from one's own intelligence have no life in them, since nothing good proceeds from man's proprium (n. 8491, 8944). They who have much confirmed themselves in false doctrine cannot be enlightened (n. 10,640).

It is the understanding that is enlightened (n. 6608, 9300). Because the understanding is recipient of truth (n. 6222, 6608, 10,659). There are ideas concerning every doctrinal of the church, according to which is the understanding of the subject (n. 3310, 3825). A man's ideas, so long as he lives in the world, are natural, because he then thinks in the natural, but nevertheless spiritual ideas lie concealed therein with those who are in the affection of truth for the sake of truth (n. 10,237, 10,240, 10,551). There is no perception of any subject without ideas (n. 3825). The ideas concerning the things of faith are opened in the other life, and their quality is then seen by the angels (n. 1869, 3310, 5510, 6200, 8885). Therefore the Word is not understood except by a rational man; for to believe anything without having an idea of the subject, and without a rational view of it, is only to retain words in the memory, destitute of all the life of perception and affection, which is not believing (n. 2553). The literal sense of the Word is what is enlightened (n. 34, 36, 9824, 9905, 10,548).

257. *The Word cannot be understood but by means of doctrine from the Word.*

The doctrine of the church must be from the Word (n. 3464, 5402, 6832, 10,763, 10,765). The Word without doctrine is not understood (n. 9025, 9409, 9424, 9430, 10,324, 10,431, 10,582). True doctrine is a lamp to those who read the Word (n. 10,400). Genuine doctrine must be formed by those who are in enlightenment from the Lord (n. 2510, 2516, 2519, 9424, 10,105). The Word is understood by means of doctrine formed by one who is enlightened (n. 10,324). They who are in enlightenment form doctrine for themselves from the Word (n. 9382, 10,659). The difference between those who teach and learn from the doctrine of the church, and those who teach and learn only from the sense of the letter, their quality (n. 9025). They who are in the sense of the letter without doctrine, come into no understanding of Divine truths (n. 9409, 9410, 10,582). They fall into many errors (n. 10,431). They who are in the affection of truth for the sake of truth, when they arrive at adult age, and can see from their own understanding, do not simply abide in the doctrinals of their own church, but examine from the Word whether they are truths (n. 5402, 5432, 6047). Otherwise every man's truth would be derived from others, and from his native soil, whether he was born a Jew or a Greek (n. 6047). Nevertheless such things as are become of faith from the literal sense of the Word, ought not to be extinguished till after a full view (n. 9039).

The true doctrine of the church is the doctrine of charity and faith (n. 2417, 4766, 10,763, 10,764). The doctrine of faith does not make the church, but the life of faith, which is charity (n. 809, 1798, 1799, 1834, 4468, 4672, 4766, 5826,

6637). Doctrinals are nothing unless one lives according to them (n. 1515, 2049, 2116). In the churches at this day the doctrine of faith is taught, and not the doctrine of charity, the latter being degraded into a science which is called moral theology (n. 2417). The church would be one, if men were acknowledged as members of the church from life, thus from charity (n. 1285, 1316, 2982, 3267, 3445, 3451, 3452). How much superior the doctrine of charity is to that of faith separate from charity (n. 4844). They who do not know anything concerning charity, are in ignorance concerning heavenly things (n. 2435). Into how many errors they fall who only hold the doctrine of faith, and not that of charity at the same time (n. 2338, 2417, 3146, 3325, 3412, 3413, 3416, 3773, 4672, 4730, 4783, 4925, 5351, 7623–7627, 7752–7762, 7790, 8094, 8313, 8530, 8765, 9186, 9224, 10,555). They who are only in the doctrine of faith, and not in the life of faith, which is charity, were formerly called uncircumcised, or Philistines (n. 3412, 3413, 8093). The ancients held the doctrine of love to the Lord, and of charity towards the neighbor, and made the doctrine of faith subservient thereto (n. 2417, 3419, 4844, 4955).

Doctrine made by one enlightened may be afterwards confirmed by means of rational things, and thus it is more fully understood, and is corroborated (n. 2553, 2719, 2720, 3052, 3310, 6047). See more on this subject (at n. 51 above). They who are in faith separate from charity would have the doctrinals of the church implicitly believed without any rational intuition (n. 3394).

It is not the part of a wise man to confirm a dogma, but to see whether it is true before he confirms it, as is the case with those who are in enlightenment (n. 1017, 4741, 7012, 7680, 7950). The light of confirmation is natural light, and not spiritual, and may exist even with the evil (n. 8780). All things, even falsities, can be confirmed so as to appear like truths (n. 2480, 2490, 5033, 6865, 8521).

258. *In the Word there is a spiritual sense, which is called the internal sense.*

No one can know what the internal sense of the Word is, unless he knows what correspondence is (n. 2895, 4322). The whole and every part, even to the most minute, of the natural world, corresponds to spiritual things, and thence is significative of them (n. 1886–1889, 2987–3003, 3213–3227). The spiritual things to which natural things correspond assume another appearance in the natural, so that they are not distinguished (n. 1887, 2395, 8920). Scarcely any one knows at this day, where, or in what part is the Divine of the Word, when nevertheless it is in its internal or spiritual sense, which at this day is not known (n. 2899, 4989). The mystic things of the Word are nothing else than what its internal or spiritual sense contains, which treats of the Lord, of His kingdom, and of the church, and not of the natural things which are in the world (n. 4923). The prophetic parts of the Word are in many places unintelligible, and therefore of no use without the internal sense; illustrated by examples (n. 2608, 8020, 8398). As what is signified by "the white horse," mentioned in the *Apocalypse* (n. 2760, *seq.*). By "the keys of the kingdom of the heavens" that were given to Peter, see the Preface to the 22nd chapter of *Genesis* (n. 9410). By "the flesh," "blood," "bread," and "wine," in the Holy Supper, and thus why it was instituted by the Lord (n. 8682). By the prophecies of Jacob concerning his sons in the 49th chapter of *Genesis* (n. 6306, 6333–6465). By many prophecies concerning Judah and Israel, which by no means tally with that people, nor in the literal sense have any coincidence with their history (n. 6333, 6361, 6415, 6438, 6444). Besides innumerable other instances (n. 2608).

Of the spiritual or internal sense of the Word in a summary (n. 1767–1777, 1869–1879). There is an internal sense in the whole and in every particular part of the Word (n. 1143, 1984, 2135, 2333, 2395, 2495, 2619). Such things do not appear in the sense of the letter, but nevertheless they are contained within it (n. 4442).

259. *The internal sense of the Word is principally for the use of angels, and it is also for the use of men.*

In order that it may be known what the internal sense is, of what quality it is, and whence it is, it may here be observed in general, that they speak and think in heaven differently from the way they do in the world; in heaven spiritually, but in the world naturally; therefore when man reads the Word, the angels who are with him perceive it spiritually, whilst he perceives it naturally; consequently, the angels are in the internal sense, whilst men are in the external sense; nevertheless these two senses make one by correspondence.

The Word is understood differently by the angels in the heavens and by men on earth, the angels perceiving the internal or spiritual sense, but men the external or natural sense (n. 1887, 2395). The angels perceive the Word in its internal sense, and not in its external sense, proved from the experience of those who spake with me from heaven, whilst I was reading the Word (n. 1769–1772). The ideas and speech of the angels are spiritual, but the ideas and speech of men are natural; therefore there is an internal sense, which is spiritual, for the use of the angels, illustrated by experience (n. 2333). Nevertheless the sense of the letter of the Word serves the spiritual ideas of the angels as a means of conveyance, just as the words of speech serve men to convey the sense of the subject (n. 2143). The things relating to the internal sense of the Word, fall into such things as belong to the light of heaven, thus into the perception of angels (n. 2618, 2619, 2629, 3086). The things which the angels perceive from the Word are on this account precious to them (n. 2540, 2541, 2545, 2551). The angels do not understand a single syllable of the sense of the letter of the Word (n. 64, 65, 1434, 1929). They do not know the names of persons and places mentioned in the Word (n. 1434, 1888, 4442, 4480). Names cannot enter heaven, nor be pronounced there (n. 1876, 1888). All names mentioned in the Word signify things, and in heaven are changed into the ideas of the thing (n. 768, 1888, 4310, 4442, 5225, 5287, 10,329). The angels think abstractly from persons (n. 6613, 8343, 8985, 9007). How elegant the internal sense of the Word is, even where nothing but mere names occur, shown by examples from the Word (n. 1224, 1888, 2395). Many names in a series express one thing in the internal sense (n. 5095). All numbers in the Word signify things (n. 482, 487, 647, 648, 755, 813, 1963, 1988, 2075, 2252, 3252, 4264, 6175, 9488, 9659, 10,217, 10,253). Spirits also perceive the Word in its internal sense, so far as their interiors are open into heaven (n. 1771). The sense of the letter of the Word, which is natural, is changed instantly with the angels into the spiritual sense, because there is a correspondence (n. 5648). And this is effected without their hearing or knowing what is contained in the literal or external sense (n. 10,215). Thus the literal or external sense is only with man, and proceeds no further (n. 2015).

There is an internal sense of the Word, and likewise an inmost or supreme sense, concerning which see (n. 9407, 10,604, 10,614, 10,627). The spiritual angels, that is, those who belong to the spiritual kingdom of the Lord, perceive the Word in its internal sense, and the celestial angels, that is, those who belong to the celestial kingdom of the Lord, perceive the Word in its inmost sense (n. 2157, 2275).

The Word is for men, and also for angels, being accommodated to each (n. 7381, 8862, 10,322). The Word is the means of uniting heaven and earth (n. 2310, 2495, 9212, 9216, 9357). The conjunction of heaven with man is effected by means of the Word (n. 9396, 9400, 9401, 10,452). Therefore the Word is called "a covenant" (n. 9396). Because "covenant" signifies conjunction (n. 665, 666, 1023, 1038, 1864, 1996, 2003, 2021, 6804, 8767, 8778, 9396, 10,632). There is an internal sense in the Word, because the Word has descended from the Lord through the three heavens to man (n. 2310, 6597). And thereby it is accommodated to the angels of the three heavens, and also to men (n. 7381, 8862). Hence it is that the Word is Divine (n. 2989, 4989); and is holy (n. 10,276); and is spiritual (n. 4480); and is divinely inspired (n. 9094). This is the meaning of inspiration (n. 9094).

The regenerate man also, is actually in the internal sense of the Word, although he knows it not, since his internal man, which is endowed with spiritual perception, is open (n. 10,400). But in this case the spiritual of the Word flows into natural ideas, and thus is presented naturally, because, while man lives in the world, he thinks in the natural (n. 5614). Hence the light of truth, with the enlightened, is from their internal, that is, through their internal from the Lord (n. 10,691, 10,694). By the same way holiness flows in with those who esteem the Word holy (n. 6789). As the regenerate man is actually in the internal sense of the Word, and in the sanctity of that sense, although he does not know it, therefore after death he comes into it, and is no longer in the sense of the letter (n. 3226, 3342, 3343).

260. *The internal or spiritual sense of the Word contains innumerable arcana.*

The Word in its internal sense contains innumerable things, which exceed human comprehension (n. 3085, 3086). It also contains inexplicable things (n. 1965). Which are represented only to angels, and understood by them (n. 167). The internal sense of the Word contains arcana of heaven, which relate to the Lord and His kingdom in the heavens and on earth (n. 1-4, 937). Those arcana do not appear in the sense of the letter (n. 937, 1502, 2161). Many things in the prophets appear to be disconnected, when yet in their internal sense they cohere in a regular and beautiful series (n. 7153, 9022). Not a single word, nor even a single iota can be omitted in the sense of the letter of the Word, without an interruption in the internal sense, and therefore, by the Divine Providence of the Lord, the Word has been preserved so entire as to every word and every point (n. 7933). Innumerable things are contained in every particular of the Word (n. 6617, 6620, 8920); and in every expression (n. 1689). There are innumerable things contained in the Lord's prayer, and in every part thereof (n. 6619). And in the precepts of the Decalogue; in the external sense of which, notwithstanding, some things are such as are known to every nation without revelation (n. 8867, 8900).

In the Word, and particularly in the prophetical parts of it, two expressions are used that seem to signify the same thing, but one expression has relation to good, and the other to truth; thus one relates to what is spiritual, the other to what is celestial (n. 683, 707, 2516, 8339). Goods and truths are conjoined in a wonderful manner in the Word, and that conjunction is apparent only to him who knows the internal sense (n. 10,554). And thus there is a Divine marriage and a heavenly marriage in the Word, and in every part thereof (n. 683, 793, 801, 2173, 2516, 2712, 5138, 7022). The Divine marriage is the marriage of Divine good and Divine truth, thus it is the Lord, in whom alone that marriage exists (n. 3004, 3005, 3009, 5138, 5194, 5502, 6343, 7945, 8339, 9263, 9314). "Jesus" signifies the

Divine good, and "Christ" the Divine truth; and both the Divine marriage in heaven, which is the marriage of the Divine good and the Divine truth (n. 3004, 3005, 3009). This marriage is in every part of the Word, in its internal sense; thus the Lord, as to the Divine good and the Divine truth, is in every part of the Word (n. 5502). The marriage of good and truth from the Lord in heaven and the church, is called the heavenly marriage (n. 2508, 2618, 2803, 3004, 3211, 3952, 6179). Therefore in this respect the Word is a kind of heaven (n. 2173, 10,126). Heaven is compared in the Word to a marriage, on account of the marriage of good and truth therein (n. 2758, 3132, 4434, 4835).

The internal sense is the very doctrine of the church (n. 9025, 9430, 10,400). They who understand the Word according to the internal sense, know the essential true doctrine of the church, inasmuch as the internal sense contains it (n. 9025, 9430, 10,400). The internal of the Word is also the internal of the church, and likewise the internal of worship (n. 10,460). The Word is the doctrine of love to the Lord, and of charity towards the neighbor (n. 3419, 3420).

The Word in the letter is as a cloud, and in the internal sense it is glory, see the Preface to the 18th chapter of *Genesis* (n. 5922, 6343), where the words, "The Lord shall come in the clouds of heaven with glory," are explained. "A cloud" in the Word signifies the Word in the sense of the letter, and "glory" signifies the Word in the internal sense, see the Preface to the 18th chapter of *Genesis* (n. 4060, 4391, 5922, 6343, 6752, 8106, 8781, 9430, 10,551, 10,574). Those things which are in the sense of the letter, respectively to those which are in the internal sense, are like rude projections round a polished optical cylinder, by which nevertheless is exhibited in the cylinder a beautiful image of a man (n. 1871). In the other life, they who only allow and acknowledge the sense of the letter of the Word, are represented by a deformed old woman; but they who allow and acknowledge the internal sense, together with the literal sense, are represented by a virgin beautifully clothed (n. 1774). The Word in its whole complex is an image of heaven, since the Word is the Divine truth, and the Divine truth makes heaven; and as heaven relates to one man, therefore the Word is in that respect as an image of man (n. 1871). Heaven in one complex relates to one man, may be seen in the work on *Heaven and Hell* (n. 59–67). And the Divine truth proceeding from the Lord makes heaven (n. 126–140, 200–212). The Word is beautifully and agreeably exhibited before the angels (n. 1767, 1768). The sense of the letter is as the body, and the internal sense, as the soul of that body (n. 8943). Thence the life of the Word is from its internal sense (n. 1405, 4857). The Word is pure in the internal sense, and does not appear so in the literal sense (n. 2362, 2395). The things which are in the sense of the letter of the Word are holy from the internal (n. 10,126, 10,728).

In the historical parts of the Word there is also an internal sense, but within them (n. 4989). Thus the historical as well as the prophetic parts of the Word contain arcana of heaven (n. 755, 1659, 1709, 2310, 2333). The angels do not perceive those historical things, but spiritually (n. 6884). The reason why the interior arcana which are in the historicals, are less evident to man than those that are in the propheticals (n. 2176, 6597).

The quality of the internal sense of the Word further shown (n. 1756, 1984, 2004, 2663, 3035, 7089, 10,604, 10,614). And illustrated by comparisons (n. 1873).

261. *The Word is written by correspondences, and thus by representatives.*

The Word, as to its literal sense, is written by mere correspondences, thus by such things as represent and signify spiritual things which relate to heaven and the church (n. 1404, 1408, 1409, 1540, 1619, 1659, 1709, 1783, 2179, 2763, 2899). This was done for the sake of the internal sense, which is contained in every part (n. 2899). For the sake of heaven, since those who are in heaven do not understand the Word according to the sense of the letter, which is natural, but according to its internal sense, which is spiritual (n. 2899). The Lord spake by correspondences, representatives, and significatives, because He spake from the Divine (n. 9048, 9063, 9086, 10,126, 10,728). Thus the Lord spake at the same time before the world and before heaven (n. 2533, 4807, 9048, 9063, 9086). The things which the Lord spake filled the entire heaven (n. 4637). The historicals of the Word are representative, and the words significative (n. 1540, 1659, 1709, 1783, 2686). The Word could not be written in any other style, that by it there might be a communication and conjunction with the heavens (n. 2899, 6943, 9481). They who despise the Word on account of the apparent simplicity and rudeness of its style, and who fancy that they would receive the Word, if it were written in a different style, are in a great error (n. 8783). The mode and style of writing, which prevailed amongst the most ancient people, was by representatives and significatives (n. 605, 1756, 9942). The ancient wise men were delighted with the Word, because of the representatives and significatives therein, from experience (n. 2592, 2593). If a man of the Most Ancient Church had read the Word, he would have seen the things which are in the internal sense clearly, and those which are in the external sense obscurely (n. 4493). The sons of Jacob were brought into the land of Canaan, because all the places in that land, from the most ancient times, were made representative (n. 1585, 3686, 4447, 5136, 6516). And thus that the Word might there be written, in which Word those places were to be mentioned for the sake of the internal sense (n. 3686, 4447, 5136, 6516). But nevertheless the Word was changed, for the sake of that nation, as to the external sense, but not as to the internal sense (n. 10,453, 10,461, 10,603, 10,604). In order that it may be known what the correspondences and representatives in the Word are, and what is their quality, something shall also be said concerning them.

All things which correspond are likewise representative, and thereby significative, thus that correspondences and representatives are one (n. 2896, 2897, 2973, 2987, 2989, 2990, 3002, 3225). What correspondences and representations are, from experience and examples (n. 2763, 2987–3002, 3213–3226, 3337–3352, 3472–3485, 4218–4228, 9280). The science of correspondences and representations was the chief science amongst the ancients (n. 3021, 3419, 4280, 4748, 4844, 4964, 4966, 6004, 7729, 10,252). Especially with the Orientals (n. 5702, 6692, 7097, 7779, 9391, 10,252, 10,407); and in Egypt more than in other countries (n. 5702, 6692, 7097, 7779, 9391, 10,407). Also among the Gentiles, as in Greece and other places (n. 2762,

7729). But at this day it is among the sciences which are lost, particularly in Europe (n. 2894, 2895, 2994, 3630, 3632, 3747–3749, 4581, 4966, 10,252). Nevertheless this science is more excellent than all other sciences, since without it the Word is not understood, nor the signification of the rites of the Jewish church, which are recorded in the Word; neither is it known what heaven is, nor what the spiritual is, nor in what manner spiritual influx takes place into what is natural, with many other things (n. 4280, and in the places above cited). All the things which appear before angels and spirits, are representatives, according to correspondences of such things as relate to love and faith (n. 1971, 3213–3226, 3449, 3475, 3485, 9481, 9574, 9576, 9577). The heavens are full of representatives (n. 1521, 1532, 1619). Representatives are more beautiful, and more perfect, in proportion as they are more interiorly in the heavens (n. 3475). Representatives there are real appearances, being derived from the light of heaven, which is Divine truth, and which is the very essential of the existence of all things (n. 3485).

The reason why each and all things in the spiritual world are represented in the natural world, is because what is internal assumes a suitable clothing in what is external, whereby it makes itself visible and apparent (n. 6275, 6284, 6299). Thus the end assumes a suitable clothing, that it may exist as the cause in a lower sphere, and afterwards that it may exist as the effect in a sphere lower still; and when the end, by means of the cause, becomes the effect, it then becomes visible, or appears before the eyes (n. 5711). This may be illustrated by the influx of the soul into the body, whereby the soul assumes a clothing of such things in the body, as enable all the things which it thinks and wills, to appear and become visible; wherefore the thought, when it flows down into the body, is represented by gestures and actions which correspond thereto (n. 2988). The affections, which are of the mind, are manifestly represented in the face, by the variations of the countenance, so that they may be seen therein (n. 4791–4805, 5695). Hence it is evident, that each and all things in nature have in them a latent cause and end from the spiritual world (n. 3562, 5711). Since the things in nature are ultimate effects, which contain prior things (n. 4240, 4939, 5051, 6275, 6284, 6299, 9216). Internal things are represented, and external things represent (n. 4292).

Since all things in nature are representative of spiritual and celestial things, therefore, in ancient times, there were churches, wherein all the externals, which are rituals, were representative; wherefore those churches were called representative churches (n. 519, 521, 2896). The church founded with the sons of Israel was a representative church (n. 1003, 2179, 10,149). All its rituals were external things, which represented the internal things of heaven and the church (n. 4288, 4874). Representatives of the church and of worship ceased when the Lord came into the world, because the Lord opened the internal things of the church, and because all the externals of the church in the highest sense regarded Him (n. 4832).

262. *Of the literal or external sense of the Word.*

The sense of the letter of the Word is according to appearances in the world (n. 589, 926, 1408, 2719, 2720, 1832, 1874, 2242, 2520, 2533). And is adapted to the capacity of the simple (n. 2533, 9048, 9063, 9086). The Word in its literal sense is natural (n. 8783). Because what is natural is the ultimate wherein spiritual and celestial things terminate, and upon which they rest like a house upon its foundation; and otherwise the internal sense of the Word without the external, would be like a house without a foundation (n. 9360, 9430, 9433, 9824, 10,044, 10,436). The Word is the containant of a spiritual and celestial sense, because it is of such a quality (n. 9407). And that it is holy and Divine in the sense of the letter as to each and all things therein, even to every iota, because it is of such a quality (n. 639, 680, 1869, 1870, 9198, 10,321, 10,637). The laws enacted for the sons of Israel, are yet the Holy Word, notwithstanding their abrogation, on account of the internal sense which they contain (n. 9211, 9259, 9349). Of the laws, judgments and statutes, for the Israelitish and Jewish church, which was a representative church, there are some which are still in force, both in their external and internal sense; some which ought to be strictly observed in their external sense; some which may be of use, if people are disposed to observe them; and some which are altogether abrogated (n. 9349). The Word is Divine, even as to those which are abrogated (n. 10,637).

The quality of the Word as to the sense of the letter, if not understood at the same time as to the internal sense, or what is the same thing, according to true doctrine from the Word (n. 10,402). Innumerable heresies arise from the sense of the letter without the internal sense, or without true doctrine from the Word (n. 10,400). They who are in an external without an internal cannot endure the interior things of the Word (n. 10,694). The Jews were of such a quality, and they are also such at this day (n. 301–303, 3479, 4429, 4433, 4680, 4844, 4847, 10,396, 10,401, 10,407, 10,694, 10,701, 10,707).

263. *The Lord is the Word.*

The Word in its inmost sense treats only of the Lord, and describes all the states of the glorification of His Human, that is, of its union with the Divine itself; and likewise all the states of the subjugation of the hells, and of the ordination of all things therein and in the heavens (n. 2249, 7014). Thus the Lord's whole life in the world is described in that sense, and thereby the Lord is continually present with the angels (n. 2523). Consequently the Lord alone is in the inmost of the Word, and the Divinity and sanctity of the Word is from thence (n. 1873, 9357). The Lord's saying that all the Scripture concerning Him was fulfilled, signifies that all things which are contained in the inmost sense were fulfilled (n. 7933).

The Word signifies the Divine truth (n. 4692, 5075, 9987). The Lord is the Word because He is the Divine truth (n. 2533). The Lord is the Word also because the Word is from Him, and treats of Him (n. 2859). And because it treats of the Lord alone in its inmost sense, thus because the Lord Himself is therein (n. 1873, 9357). And because in each and all things of the Word there is a marriage of Divine good and Divine truth (n. 3004, 5502). "Jesus" is the Divine good, and "Christ" the Divine truth (n. 3004, 3005, 3009). The Divine truth is alone real, and that in which Divine truth is, which is from the Divine, is alone substantial (n. 5272, 6880, 7004, 8200). And as the Divine truth proceeding from the Lord is light in heaven, and the Divine good is heat in heaven; and as all things in heaven derive their existence from the Divine good and the Divine truth; and as the natural world has its existence through heaven, or the spiritual world; it is plain that all things which were created, were created from the Divine truth, or from the Word, according to these words in *John:*—

In the beginning was the Word, and the Word was with God, and God was the Word, and by it were all things made which were made; and the Word was made flesh (i. 1, 3, 14; n. 2803, 2894, 5272, 6880).

Further particulars concerning the creation of all things by the Divine truth, consequently by the Lord, may be seen in the work on *Heaven and Hell* (n. 137). And more fully in the two articles therein (n. 116–125, and n. 126–140). The conjunction of the Lord with man is effected through the Word, by means of the internal sense (n. 10,375). Conjunction is effected by each and all things of the Word, and the Word is therefore more wonderful than all other writings (n. 10,632–10,634). Since the Word has been written, the Lord thereby speaks with men (n. 10,290).

264. *Of those who are against the Word.*

Of those who despise, mock at, blaspheme, and profane the Word (n. 1878). Their quality in the other life (n. 1761, 9322). They may be compared to the viscous parts of the blood (n. 5719). The danger of profaning the Word (n. 571–582). How hurtful it is if principles of falsity, particularly those which favor the loves of self and of the world, are confirmed by the Word (n. 589). They who are in no affection of truth for the sake of truth, utterly reject the internal sense of the Word, and nauseate it, from experience (n. 5702). Some in the other life who have rejected the interior things of the Word, are deprived of rationality (n. 1879).

265. *Further particulars concerning the Word.*

The term "Word" in the Hebrew tongue signifies various things, as speech, thought of the mind, everything that has a real existence, and also anything (n. 9987). "Word" signifies the Divine truth and the Lord (n. 4692, 5075, 9987). "Words" signify truths (n. 4692, 5075). They signify doctrinals (n. 1288). The "ten words" signify all Divine truths (n. 10,688). They signify things which really exist (n. 1785, 5075, 5272).

In the Word, particularly in the propheticals, there are two expressions to signify one thing, and the one has relation to good and the other to truth, which are thus conjoined (n. 683, 707, 2516, 8339). It cannot be known what expression has relation to good, and what to truth, but from the internal sense of the Word; for there are appropriate words by which the things relating to good are expressed, and appropriate words by which the things relating to truth are expressed (n. 793, 801). And this so that it may be known merely from the words predicated, whether the subject treated of is good, or whether it is truth (n. 2722). Frequently one expression implies a general, and the other expression implies a certain specific particular of that general (n. 2212). That there is a species of reciprocation in the Word, concerning which see (n. 2240). Most things in the Word have also an opposite sense (n. 4816). The internal sense proceeds regularly according to the subject predicated (n. 4502).

They who have been delighted with the Word, in the other life receive the heat of heaven, wherein is celestial love, according to the quality and quantity of their delight from love (n. 1773).

266. *What are the Books of the Word.*

The books of the Word are all those which have the internal sense; but those books which have not the internal sense, are not the Word. The books of the Word, in the Old Testament, are the five *Books of Moses*, the *Book of Joshua*, the *Book of Judges*, the two *Books of Samuel*, the two *Books of Kings*, the *Psalms of David*, the Prophets *Isaiah, Jeremiah, Lamentations, Ezekiel, Daniel, Hosea, Joel, Amos, Obadiah, Jonah, Micah, Nahum, Habakkuk, Zephaniah, Haggai, Zechariah, Malachi:* and in the New Testament, the four Evangelists, *Matthew, Mark, Luke, John;* and the *Apocalypse*. The rest have not the internal sense (10,325).

XXI.

PROVIDENCE.

267. The government of the Lord in the heavens and in the earths is called Providence; and because all the good of love and all the truth of faith, from which is salvation, are from Him, and nothing at all from man, it is evident therefrom that the Divine Providence of the Lord is in each and all the things which conduce to the salvation of the human race. This the Lord thus teaches in *John*:—

> I am the way, the truth, and the life (xiv. 6);

and in another place:—

> As the branch cannot bear fruit of itself, unless it shall abide in the vine, so neither can ye, unless ye shall abide in Me; without Me ye cannot do anything (xv. 4, 5).

268. The Divine Providence of the Lord extends to the most minute things of a man's life; for there is only one fountain of life, which is the Lord, from whom we are, we live, and we act.

269. They who think from worldly things concerning the Divine Providence, conclude from them that it is only universal, and that the particulars appertain to man. But they do not know the arcana of heaven, for they form their conclusions only from the loves of self and of the world, and their pleasures; wherefore, when they see the evil exalted to honors, and acquire wealth more than the good, and also succeed in evils according to their arts, they say in their heart, that it would not be so if the Divine Providence were in each and all things; but they do not consider that the Divine Providence does not regard that which soon passes away, and ends with the life of man in the world, but that it regards that which remains to eternity, thus which has no end. What has no end, that is; but what has an end, that respectively is not. Let him who can, think whether a hundred thousand years are anything compared to eternity, and he will perceive that they are not; what then are some years of life in the world?

270. Every one who rightly considers, may know that eminence and opulence in the world are not real divine blessings, notwithstanding man, from his pleasure in them, calls them so; for they pass away, and also seduce many, and turn them away from heaven; but that eternal life, and its happiness, are real blessings, which are from the Divine: this the Lord also teaches in *Luke:*—

Make to yourselves a treasure in the heavens that faileth not, where the thief approacheth not, neither the moth corrupteth; for where your treasure is, there will your heart be also (xii. 33, 34).

271. The reason why the evil succeed in evils according to their arts is, because it is according to Divine order that every one should act what he acts from reason, and also from freedom; wherefore, unless man were left to act from freedom according to his reason, and thus unless the arts which are thence derived were to succeed, man could by no means be disposed to receive eternal life, for this is insinuated when man is in freedom, and his reason is enlightened. For no one can be compelled to good, because nothing that is compelled inheres with him, for it is not his own: that becomes a man's own, which is done from freedom according to his reason, and that is done from freedom which is done from the will or love, and the will or love is the man himself. If a man were compelled to that which he does not will, his mind would continually incline to that which he wills; and besides, every one strives after what is forbidden, and this from a latent cause, because he strives for freedom. Whence it is evident that unless man were kept in freedom, good could not be provided for him.

272. To leave man from his own freedom also to think, to will, and, so far as the laws do not restrain him, to do evil, is called permitting.

273. To be led to felicities in the world by arts, appears to man as if it were from his own prudence, but still the Divine providence continually accompanies by permitting and continually leading away from evil. But to be led to felicities in heaven is known and perceived to be not from man's own prudence, because it is from the Lord, and is effected of His Divine providence by disposing and continually leading to good.

274. That this is so, man cannot comprehend from the light of nature, for from that light he does not know the laws of Divine order.

275. It is to be known that there is providence, and there is foresight; good is what is provided by the Lord, but evil is what is foreseen by the Lord. The one must accompany the other, for what comes from man is nothing but evil, but what comes from the Lord is nothing but good.

FROM THE ARCANA CŒLESTIA.

Since all the good which is provided for man by the Lord flows in, we will therefore adduce from the *Arcana Cœlestia* the particulars there concerning *Influx:* and since the Lord provides all things according to Divine order, we will also adduce from that work the particulars concerning *Order*.

276. *Of Providence.*

Providence is the government of the Lord in the heavens and on the earth (n. 10,773). The Lord, from providence, rules all things according to order, and thus providence is government according to order (n. 1755, 2447). And He rules all things either from will or from leave, or from permission; thus in various respects according to man's quality (n. 1755, 2447, 3704, 9940). Providence acts invisibly (n. 5508). Most things which are done from providence appear to man as contingencies (n. 5508). Providence acts invisibly, in order that man may not be compelled to believe from visible things, and thus that his free-will may not be injured; for unless man has freedom he cannot be reformed, thus he cannot be saved (n. 1937, 1947, 2876, 2881, 3854, 5508, 5982, 6477, 8209, 8987, 9588, 10,409, 10,777). The Divine providence does not regard temporary things which soon pass away, but eternal things (n. 5264, 8717, 10,776; illustrated n. 6491).

They who do not comprehend this, believe that opulence and eminence in the world are the only things to be provided, and call such things blessings from the Divine, when nevertheless they are not regarded as blessings by the Lord, but only as means conducive to the life of man in the world; but that those things are regarded by the Lord which conduce to man's eternal happiness (n. 10,409, 10,776). They who are in the

Divine providence of the Lord, are led in each and all things to eternal happiness (n. 8478, 8480). They who ascribe all things to nature and man's own prudence, and nothing to the Divine, do not think or comprehend this (n. 6481, 10,409, 10,775).

The Divine providence of the Lord is not, as believed in the world, universal only, and the particulars and single things dependent on man's prudence (n. 8717, 10,775). No universal exists but from and with single things, because single things taken together are called a universal, as particulars taken together are called a general (n. 1919, 6159, 6338, 6482–6484). Every universal is such as the single things of which it is formed, and with which it is (n. 917, 1040, 6483, 8857). The providence of the Lord is universal, because existing in the most single things (n. 1919, 2694, 4329, 5122, 5904, 6058, 6481–6486, 6490, 7004, 7007, 8717, 10,774); confirmed from heaven (n. 6486). Unless the Divine providence of the Lord were universal, from and in the most single things, nothing could subsist (n. 6338). All things are disposed by it into order, and kept in order both in general and in particular (n. 6338). How the case herein is comparatively with that of a king on earth (n. 6482, 10,800). Man's own proper prudence is like a small speck of dirt in the universe, whilst the Divine providence is respectively as the universe itself (n. 6485). This can hardly be comprehended by men in the world (n. 8717, 10,775, 10,780). Because many fallacies assail them, and induce blindness (n. 6481). Of a certain person in the other life, who believed from confirmation in the world, that all things were dependent on man's own prudence, and nothing on the Divine providence; the things belonging to him appeared infernal (n. 6484).

The quality of the Lord's providence with respect to evils (n. 6481, 6495, 6574, 10,777, 10,779). Evils are ruled by the Lord by the laws of permission, and they are permitted for the sake of order (n. 8700, 10,778). The permission of evil by the Lord is not that of one who wills, but of one who does not will, but who cannot bring aid on account of the urgency of the end, which is salvation (n. 7887). To leave man from his own freedom to think and will evil, and so far as the laws do not forbid, to do evil, is to permit (n. 10,778). Without freedom, thus without this permission, man could not be reformed, thus could not be saved, may be seen above in the doctrine of *Freedom* (n. 141–149).

The Lord has providence and foresight, and the one does not exist without the other (n. 5195, 6489). Good is provided by the Lord, and evil foreseen (n. 5155, 5195, 6489, 10,781).

There is no such thing as predestination or fate (n. 6487). All are predestined to heaven, and none to hell (n. 6488). Man is under no absolute necessity from providence, but has full liberty, illustrated by comparison (n. 6487). The "elect" in the Word are they who are in the life of good, and thence of truth (n. 3755, 3900, 5057, 5058). How it is to be understood that "God would deliver one man into another's hand" (*Exod.* xxi. 13) (n. 9010).

Fortune, which appears in the world wonderful in many circumstances, is an operation of the Divine providence in the ultimate of order, according to the quality of man's state; and this may afford proof, that the Divine providence is in the most single of all things (n. 5049, 5179, 6493, 6494). This operation and its variations are from the spiritual world, proved from experience (n. 5179, 6493, 6494).

277. *Of Influx.*

Of the influx of heaven into the world, and of the influx of the soul into all things of the body, from experience (n. 6053–6058, 6189–6215, 6307–6327, 6466–6495, 6598–6626). Nothing exists of or from itself, but from what is prior to itself, thus all things from the First (n. 4523, 4524, 6040, 6056). As all things existed, they also subsist, because subsistence is perpetual existence (n. 2886, 2888, 3627, 3628, 3648, 4523, 4524, 6040, 6056). Influx takes place according to that order (n. 7270). Hence it is plain that all things subsist perpetually from the first *esse*, because they exist from it (n. 4523, 4524, 6040, 6056). The all of life flows in from the First, because it is thence derived, thus from the Lord (n. 3001, 3318, 3337, 3338, 3344, 3484, 3628, 3629, 3741–3743, 4318–4320, 4417, 4524, 4882, 5847, 5986, 6325, 6468–6470, 6479, 9279, 10,196). Every *existere* is from an *esse*, and nothing can exist unless its *esse* be in it (n. 4523, 4524, 6040, 6056).

All things which a man thinks and wills flow into him, from experience (n. 904, 2886–2888, 4151, 4319, 4320, 5846 5848, 6189, 6191, 6194, 6197–6199, 6213, 7147, 10,219). Man's ability of examining things, and of thinking and forming analytic conclusions, is from influx (n. 2888, 4319, 4320). Man could not live a moment if the influx from the spiritual world were taken away from him; but still man is in freedom, from experience (n. 2887, 5849, 5854, 6321). The life which flows in from the Lord is varied according to man's state and according to reception (n. 2069, 5986, 6472, 7343). With the evil, the good which flows from the Lord is turned into evil, and the truth into falsity, from experience (n. 3643, 4632.) The good and truth, which continually flow from the Lord, are so far received, as evil and falsity do not oppose their reception (n. 2411, 3142, 3147, 5828).

All good flows in from the Lord, and all evil from hell (n. 904, 4151). At this day man believes all things to be in himself and from himself, when nevertheless they inflow, as he might know from the doctrinal of the church, that all good is from heaven, and all evil from hell (n. 4249, 6193, 6206). But if he would believe as the thing is, he would not appropriate evil to himself, but cast it back from himself into hell, neither would he make good his own, and thus would not claim any merit from it (n. 6206, 6324, 6325). How happy the state of man would then be, as he would view both good and evil from within, from the Lord (n. 6325). They who deny heaven, or know nothing about it, do not know there is any influx thence (n. 4322, 5649, 6193, 6479). What influx is, illustrated by comparisons (n. 6128, 6190, 9407).

Influx is spiritual, and not physical, thus it is from the spiritual world into the natural, and not from the natural world into the spiritual (n. 3219, 5119, 5259, 5427, 5428, 5477, 6322, 9109, 9110). Influx is through the internal man, into the external, and not contrariwise (n. 1702, 1707, 1940, 1954, 5119, 5259, 5779, 6322, 9380). Because the internal man is in the spiritual world, and the external in the natural world (n. 978, 1015, 3628, 4459, 4523, 4524, 6057, 6309, 9701–9709, 10,156, 10,472). It appears as if influx is from externals into internals; this is a fallacy (n. 3721). Influx is into man's rational and through this into things scientific, and not contrariwise (n. 1495, 1707, 1940). The order of influx (n. 775, 880, 1096, 1495, 7270).

There is immediate influx from the Lord, and also mediate influx through the spiritual world or heaven (n. 6063, 6307, 6472, 9682, 9683). The immediate influx from the Lord enters into the most single of all things (n. 6058, 6474-6478, 8717, 8728). Of the mediate influx of the Lord through heaven (n. 4067, 6982, 6985, 6996). It is effected through the spirits and angels who are adjoined to man (n. 697, 5846-5866). The Lord, by means of angels, flows into the ends from which, and for the sake of which, a man so thinks, wills, and acts (n. 1317, 1645, 5846, 5854). And thus into those things which are of conscience with man (n. 6207, 6213). But by means of spirits into the thoughts, and thence into the things of the memory (n. 4186, 5854, 5858, 6192, 6193, 6198, 6199, 6319). This can with difficulty be believed by man (n. 6214). The Lord inflows into firsts and at the same time into ultimates, or into inmosts and at the same time into outmosts, how (n. 5147, 5150, 6473, 7004, 7007, 7270). The influx of the Lord is into good with man, and through good into truth, and not contrariwise (n. 5482, 5649, 6027, 8685, 8701, 10,153). Good gives the faculty of receiving influx from the Lord, but not truth without good (n. 8321). It is not what enters the thought, but what enters the will, that is hurtful, because this is appropriated to the man (n. 6308). The Divine in the highest is tacit and pacific, but as it descends towards lower things in man, it becomes unpacific and tumultuous, on account of the things therein being in disorder (n. 8823). The quality of the Lord's influx with the prophets (n. 6212).

There is a general influx, its quality (n. 5850). It is a continual effort of acting according to order (n. 6211). This influx takes place into the lives of animals (n. 5850). And also into the subjects of the vegetable kingdom (n. 3648). That thought is formed into speech and will into gestures with man, according to this general influx (n. 5862, 5990, 6192, 6211).

278. *Of the influx of life with man in particular.*

There is one only fountain of life, from which all live both in heaven and in the world (n. 1954, 2021, 2536, 2658, 2886-

2889, 3001, 3484, 3742, 5847, 6467). This life is from the Lord alone, illustrated by various things (n. 2886–2889, 3344, 3484, 4319, 4320, 4524, 4882, 5986, 6325, 6468–6470, 9276, 10,-196). The Lord is life itself, may be seen (*John* i. 1, 4; chap. v. 26; chap. xiv. 6). Life from the Lord flows in with angels, spirits, and men, in a wonderful manner (n. 2886–2889, 3337, 3338, 3484, 3742). The Lord flows in from His Divine love, which is of such that it wills what is its own should be another's (n. 3742, 4320). All love is such; thus the Divine love infinitely more so (n. 1820, 1865, 2253, 6872). Hence life appears as if it were in man, and not as inflowing (n. 3742, 4320). Life appears as if it were in man, because the principal cause, which is life from the Lord, and the instrumental cause, which is the recipient form, act as one cause, which is felt in the instrumental (n. 6325). The chief of the wisdom and intelligence of the angels consists in perceiving and knowing that the all of life is from the Lord (n. 4318). Concerning the joy of angels perceived and shown by their discourse to me, from this that they do not live from themselves, but from the Lord (n. 6469). The evil are not willing to be convinced that life inflows (n. 3743). Doubts concerning the influx of life from the Lord cannot be removed, so long as fallacies, ignorance, and the negative reign (n. 6479). All in the church know that all good and truth is from heaven, that is, through heaven from the Lord, and that all evil and falsity is from hell; and yet the all of life has relation to good and truth, and to evil and falsity, there being nothing of life without them (n. 2893, 4151). The doctrinal of the church derived from the Word teaches the same thing (n. 4249). Nevertheless man does not believe that life inflows (n. 4249). If communication and connection with spirits and angels were taken away, man would instantly die (n. 2887). It is evident from hence, that the all of life flows in from the first *esse* of life, because nothing exists from itself, but from things prior to itself, thus each and all things exist from the First; and because everything must subsist from the same source from which it first existed, since subsistence is perpetual existence (n. 4523, 4524). Angels, spirits, and men, were created to receive life, thus they are only forms recipient of life (n. 2021, 3001, 3318, 3344, 3484, 3742, 4151, 5114, 5986).

Their forms are such as the quality of their reception (n. 2888, 3001, 3484, 5847, 5986, 6467, 6472). Men, spirits, and angels, are therefore such as are their forms recipient of life from the Lord (n. 2888, 5847, 5986, 6467, 6472). Man is so created, that in his inmost, and hence in those which follow in order, he can receive the Divine, and be elevated to the Divine, and be conjoined with the Divine by the good of love and the truths of faith, and on this account he lives to eternity, otherwise than beasts (n. 5114).

Life from the Lord flows in also with the evil, thus also with those who are in hell (n. 2706, 3743, 4417, 10,196). But they turn good into evil and truth into falsity, and thus life into spiritual death, for such as the man is, such is his reception of life (n. 4319, 4320, 4417). Goods and truths from the Lord also continually inflow with them, but they either reject, suffocate, or pervert them (n. 3743). They who are in evils, and thence in falsities, have no real life; the quality of their life (n. 726, 4623, 4747, 10,284, 10,286).

279. *Of Order.*

The Divine truth proceeding from the Lord is the source of order, and the Divine good is the essential of order (n. 1728, 2258, 8700, 8988). The Lord is order, since the Divine good and the Divine truth are from the Lord, yea, are the Lord, in the heavens and on earth (n. 1919, 2011, 5110, 5703, 10,336, 10,619). Divine truths are the laws of order (n. 2447, 7995). Where order is, the Lord is present, but where order is not, the Lord is not present (n. 5703). As the Divine truth is order, and the Divine good the essential of order, therefore each and all things in the universe have relation to good and truth, that they may be anything, because they have relation to order (n. 2452, 3166, 4390, 4409, 5232, 7256, 10,122, 10,555). Good, because it is the essential of order, disposes truths into order, and not *vice versa* (n. 3316, 3470, 4302, 5704, 5709, 6028, 6690). The entire heaven, as to all the angelic societies, is arranged by the Lord according to His Divine order, because the Divine of the Lord with the angels makes heaven (n. 3038, 7211, 9128, 9338, 10,125, 10,151, 10,157). Hence the form of heaven is a form according to Divine order (n. 4040–4043, 6607, 9877).

So far as man lives according to order, thus so far as he lives in good according to Divine truths, which are the laws of order, so far is he a man (n. 4839). Yea, as far as a man thus lives, so far he appears in the other life as a perfect and beautiful man, but so far as he does not thus live, so far he appears as a monster (n. 4839, 6605, 6626). Hence it appears that all things of Divine order are collected together in man, and that from creation he is Divine order in form (n. 4219, 4220, 4223, 4523, 4524, 5114, 5368, 6013, 6057, 6605, 6626, 9706, 10,156, 10,742). Every angel is in the human form because he is a recipient of Divine order from the Lord, perfect and beautiful according to reception (n. 322, 1880, 1881, 3633, 3804, 4622, 4735, 4797, 4985, 5199, 5530, 6054, 9879, 10,177, 10,594). The angelic heaven also in its whole complex is in the human form, because the whole heaven as to all its angelic societies, is disposed by the Lord according to Divine order (n. 2996, 2998, 3624–3629, 3636–3643, 3741–3745, 4625). Hence it is evident, that the Divine Human is the source from which all these things are derived (n. 2996–2998, 3624–3649, 3741–3745). Hence also it follows that the Lord is the only Man, and that they are men who receive the Divine from Him (n. 1894). So far as they receive it, so far they are images of the Lord (n. 8547).

Man is not born into good and truth, but into evil and falsity, thus not into Divine order, but into what is contrary to order, and on this account into mere ignorance, and he ought therefore necessarily be born anew, that is regenerated, which is done by Divine truths from the Lord, and by a life according to them, to the intent that he may be inaugurated into order, and thus become a man (n. 1047, 2307, 2308, 3518, 3812, 8480, 8550, 10,283, 10,284, 10,286, 10,731). When the Lord regenerates man, He disposes all things with him according to order, that is, according to the form of heaven (n. 5700, 6690, 9931, 10,303). The man who is led by the Lord, is led according to Divine order (n. 8512). The interiors which are of the mind are open into heaven, even to the Lord, with the man who is in Divine order, but shut with him who is not in Divine order (n. 8513). So far as man lives according to order, so far he has intelligence and wisdom (n. 2592).

The Lord rules the firsts and the ultimates of order, and the firsts from the ultimates and the ultimates from the firsts; and thus keeps all things in connection and order (n. 3702, 3739, 6040, 6056, 9828). Of successive order; and of the ultimate of order, in which things successive are together in their order (n. 634, 3691, 4145, 5114, 5897, 6239, 6326, 6465, 8603, 9215, 9216, 9828, 9836, 10,044, 10,099, 10,329, 10,335).

Evils and falsities are contrary to order, and still they are ruled by the Lord, not according to order, but from order (n. 4839, 7877, 10,778). Evils and falsities are ruled by the laws of permission, and this is for the sake of order (n. 7877, 8700, 10,778). What is contrary to Divine order is impossible, as that a man who lives in evil can be saved from mercy alone, as likewise that the evil can be consociated with the good in the other life, and many other things (n. 8700).

XXII.

THE LORD.

280. There is One God, who is the Creator and Conservator of the universe; thus who is the God of heaven and the God of the earth.

281. There are two things which make the life of heaven with man, the good of love and the truth of faith. Man has this life from God, and nothing at all of it is from man. Therefore the primary principle of the church is, to acknowledge God, to believe in God, and to love Him.

282. They who are born within the church ought to acknowledge the Lord, His Divine and His Human, and to believe in Him and love Him; for all salvation is from the Lord. This the Lord teaches in *John*:—

He that believeth on the Son hath eternal life; and he that believeth not the Son shall not see life; but the anger of God abideth on him (iii. 36).

Again:—

This is the will of Him that sent Me, that every one which seeth the Son, and believeth on Him, may have eternal life; and I will raise him up at the last day (vi. 40).

In the same:—

Jesus said, I am the resurrection and the life; he that believeth in Me, though he die, shall live; but whosoever liveth and believeth in Me shall not die to eternity (xi. 25, 26).

283. Therefore, they within the church who do not acknowledge the Lord and His Divine, cannot be conjoined to God, and thus cannot have any lot with the angels in heaven; for no one can be conjoined to God but from the Lord, and in the Lord. That no one can be conjoined to God but from the Lord, the Lord teaches in *John*:—

No one hath seen God at any time; the Only-begotten Son, who is in the bosom of the Father, He hath manifested Him (i. 20).

In the same:—

Ye have never heard the voice of the Father, nor seen His shape (v. 37).

In *Matthew*:—

No one knoweth the Father but the Son, and he to whom the Son will reveal Him (xi. 27).

And in *John*: —

I am the way, the truth, and the life; no one cometh to the Father but by Me (xiv. 6).

The reason why no one can be conjoined to God but in the Lord, is because the Father is in Him, and they are one, as He also teaches in *John*:—

If ye know Me, ye know My Father also; He who seeth Me seeth the Father; Philip, believest thou not that I am in the Father and the Father in Me? believe Me that I am in the Father and the Father in Me (xiv. 7–11).

And in the same:—

The Father and I are One; that ye may know and believe that I am in the Father and the Father in Me (x. 30, 38).

284. Because the Father is in the Lord, and the Father and the Lord are one; and because we must believe in Him, and he that believes in Him has eternal life, it is evident that the Lord is God. That the Lord is God, the Word teaches, as in *John:*—

In the beginning was the Word, and the Word was with God, and God was the Word; all things were made by Him, and without Him was not any thing made which was made; and the Word was made flesh, and dwelt among us, and we saw His glory, the glory as of the Only-begotten of the Father (i. 1, 3, 14).

In *Isaiah:*—

A Boy is born to us, a Son is given to us, on whose shoulder is the government, and His name shall be called God, Hero, the Father of Eternity, the Prince of Peace (ix. 6).

In the same:—

A virgin shall conceive and bring forth, and His name shall be called God with us (vii. 14; *Matt.* i. 23).

And in *Jeremiah:*—

Behold the days shall come when I will raise up to David a just Branch, who shall reign King, and shall prosper; and this is His name which they shall call Him, Jehovah our Justice (xxiii. 5, 6; xxxiii. 15, 16).

285. All they who are of the church, and in light from heaven, see the Divine in the Lord; but they who are not in light from heaven, see nothing but the Human in the Lord; when yet the Divine and the Human are in Him so united, that they are one; as the Lord also taught in another place in *John:*—

Father, all Mine are Thine, and all Thine Mine (xvii. 10).

286. That the Lord was conceived from Jehovah the Father, and thus was God from conception, is known in the church; and also that He rose again with the whole body, for He left nothing in the sepulchre; of which He also afterwards confirmed the disciples, saying:—

See My hands and My feet, that it is I Myself; feel Me and see; for a spirit hath not flesh and bones as ye see Me have (*Luke* xxiv. 39).

And although He was Man as to flesh and bones, still He entered through the closed doors, and, after He had manifested Himself, became invisible (*John* xx. 19, 26; *Luke* xxiv. 31). The case is otherwise with every man, for man only rises again, as to the spirit, and not as to the body, wherefore when He said, that He is not as a spirit, He said that He is not as another man. Hence it is evident that the Human in the Lord is also Divine.

287. Every man has his *esse* of life, which is called his soul, from the father; the *existere* of life thence derived is what is called the body; hence the body is the effigy of its soul, for the soul, by means of the body, exercises its life at will. Hence it is that men are born into the likeness of their parents, and that families are distinguished from each other. From this it is evident what was the quality of the body or Human of the Lord, namely, that it was as the Divine itself, which was the *esse* of His life, or the soul from the Father, wherefore He said:—

He that seeth Me, seeth the Father (*John* xiv. 9).

288. That the Divine and Human of the Lord is one Person, is from the faith received in the whole Christian world, which is to this effect:—

Although Christ is God and Man, still He is not two, but one Christ; yea, He is altogether one and a single Person; because as the body and the soul are one man, so also God and Man are one Christ.

This is from the Athanasian creed.

289. They who, concerning the Divinity, have the idea of three Persons, cannot have the idea of one God; if with the mouth they say one, still they think three; but they who, concerning the Divinity, have the idea of three in one Person, can have the idea of one God, and can say one God, and also think one God.

290. The idea of three in one Person is had, when it is thought that the Father is in the Lord, and that the Holy Spirit proceeds from Him; the Trinity is then in the Lord, the Divine itself which is called the Father, and the Divine Human which is called the Son, and the Divine proceeding which is called the Holy Spirit.

291. Because all the Divine is in the Lord, therefore He has all power in the heavens and in the earths; which he also says in *John:*—

The Father hath given all things into the hand of the Son (iii. 35).

In the same:—

The Father hath given to the Son power over all flesh (xvii. 2).

In *Matthew:*—

All things are delivered to Me by the Father (xi. 27).

In the same:—

All power is given to Me in heaven and in earth (xxviii. 18).

Such power is Divine.

292. They who make the Human of the Lord like the human of another man, do not think of His conception from the Divine itself, nor do they consider that the body of every one is an effigy of his soul. Neither do they think of His resurrection with the whole body; nor of His appearance when He was transformed, that His face shone as the sun. Neither do they think, respecting those things which the Lord said concerning faith in Him, concerning His unity with the Father, concerning His glorification, and concerning His power over heaven and earth, that these are Divine, and were said of His Human. Neither do they remember that the Lord is omnipresent also as to His Human (*Matt.* xxviii. 20); when yet the faith of His omnipresence in the Holy Supper is thence derived; omnipresence is Divine. Yea, perhaps they do not think that the Divine, which is called the Holy Spirit, proceeds from His Human; when yet it proceeds from His glorified Human, for it is said:—

The Holy Spirit was not yet, because Jesus was not yet glorified (*John* vii. 39).

293. The Lord came into the world that He might save the human race, which otherwise would have perished in eternal death; and He saved them by this, that He subjugated the hells, which infested every man coming into the world and going out of the world; and at the same time by this, that He glorified His Human: for thus He can keep the hells in subjugation to eternity. The subjugation of the hells, and the glorification of His Human at the same time, were effected by means of temptations admitted into the human which He had from the mother, and by continual victories therein. His passion on the cross was the last temptation and full victory.

294. That the Lord subjugated the hells, He Himself teaches in *John:* when the passion of the cross was at hand, then Jesus said:—

Now is the judgment of this world; now the prince of this world shall be cast out (xii. 27, 28, 31).

In the same:—

Have confidence, I have overcome the world (xvi. 33).

And in *Isaiah:*—

Who is this that cometh from Edom, going on in the multitude of His strength, great to save? My own arm brought salvation to Me; so He became to them for a Saviour (lxiii. 1-19; lix. 16-21).

That He glorified His Human, and that the passion of the cross was the last temptation and full victory, by which He glorified it, He teaches also in *John:*—

After Judas went out, Jesus said, Now is the Son of man glorified, and God will glorify Him in Himself, and will immediately glorify Him (xiii. 31, 32).

In the same:—

Father, the hour has come; glorify Thy Son, that Thy Son also may glorify Thee (xvii. 1, 5).

In the same:—

Now is my soul troubled; Father, glorify Thy name; and a voice came out from heaven, saying, I have both glorified it, and will glorify it again (xii. 27, 28).

And in *Luke:*—

Ought not Christ to suffer this, and to enter into His glory? (xxiv. 26.)

These words were said in relation to His passion: "to glorify" is to make Divine. Hence, now, it is manifest, that, unless the Lord had come into the world, and been made Man, and in this manner had liberated from hell all those who believe in Him and love Him, no mortal could be saved; this is understood by the saying, that without the Lord there is no salvation.

295. When the Lord fully glorified His Human, He then put off the human from the mother, and put on the Human from the Father, which is the Divine Human, wherefore He was then no longer the son of Mary.

296. The first and primary principle of the church is, to know and acknowledge its God; for without that knowledge and acknowledgment there is no conjunction; thus, in the church, without the acknowledgment of the Lord. This the Lord teaches in *John*:—

> He who believeth in the Son hath eternal life, but he who believeth not the Son shall not see life, but the anger of God abideth with him (iii. 36).

And in another place:—

> Except ye believe that I am, ye shall die in your sins (viii. 24).

297. That there is a Trine in the Lord, namely, the Divine itself, the Divine Human, and the Divine proceeding, is an arcanum from heaven, and is for those who will be in the holy Jerusalem.

FROM THE ARCANA CŒLESTIA.

298. *The Divine was in the Lord from His very conception.*

The Lord had the Divine from the Father (n. 4641, 4963, 5041, 5157, 6716, 10,125). The Lord alone had Divine seed (n. 1438). His soul was Jehovah (n. 1999, 2004, 2005, 2018, 2025). Thus the inmost of the Lord was the Divine itself, the covering[1] was from the mother (n. 5041). The Divine itself was the Lord's *esse* of life from which the human afterwards went forth, and became an *existere* from that *esse* (n. 3194, 3210, 10,270, 10,372).

299. *The Divine of the Lord is to be acknowledged.*

Within the church where the Word is, and where the Lord is thereby known, the Divine of the Lord ought not to be denied, nor the holy proceeding from Him (n. 2359). They within the church who do not acknowledge the Lord, have no conjunction with the Divine, which is not the case with those who are out of the church (n. 10,205). It is an essential of the church to acknowledge the Divine of the Lord, and His unition with the Father (n. 10,083, 10,112, 10,370, 10,730, 10,738, 10,816–10,818, 10,820).

300. *The Lord glorified His Human in the world.*

The glorification of the Lord is treated of in many places in the Word (n. 10,828); and everywhere in the internal sense (n.

2249, 2523, 3245). The Lord glorified His Human, but not His Divine, as this was glorified in itself (n. 10,057). The Lord came into the world to glorify His Human (n. 3637, 4287, 9315). The Lord glorified His Human by the Divine which was in Him from conception (n. 4727). The idea of the regeneration of man may give an idea of the glorification of the Lord's Human, since the Lord regenerates man in the same manner as He glorified His Human (n. 3043, 3138, 3212, 3296, 3490, 4402, 5688). Some of the arcana respecting the glorification of the Lord's Human (n. 10,057). The Lord saved the human race by glorifying His Human (n. 1676, 4180). Concerning the Lord's state of glorification and humiliation (n. 1785, 1999, 2159, 6866). Glorification, when predicated of the Lord, is the unition of His Human with the Divine, and to glorify is to make Divine (n. 1603, 10,053, 10,828).

301. *The Lord from His Human subjugated the hells when He was in the world.*

The Lord, when He was in the world, subjugated all the hells, and He then reduced all things to order both in the heavens and in the hells (n. 4075, 4287, 9937.) The Lord then delivered the spiritual world from the antediluvians (n. 1266). What quality they were of (n. 310, 311, 560, 562, 563, 570, 581, 607, 660, 805, 808, 1034, 1120, 1265–1272). By the subjugation of the hells, and the glorification of His Human at the same time, the Lord saved mankind (n. 4180, 10,019, 10,152, 10,655, 10,659, 10,828).

302. *The glorification of the Lord's Human, and the subjugation of the hells, were effected by temptations.*

The Lord more than all endured the most grievous temptations (n. 1663, 1668, 1787, 2776, 2786, 2795, 2816, 4295, 9528). The Lord fought from His Divine love toward the Human race (n. 1690, 1691, 1812, 1813, 1820). The Lord's love was the salvation of the human race (n. 1820). The hells fought against the Lord's love (n. 1820). The Lord alone, from His own proper power, fought against the hells, and overcame them (n. 1692, 1813, 2816, 4295, 8273, 9937). Thence the Lord alone became justice and merit (n. 1813, 2025–2027, 9715, 9809, 10,019). The last temptation of the Lord was in Gethsemane and on the cross, at which time He gained a full victory, by which

He subjugated the hells, and at the same time glorified His Human (n. 2776, 2803, 2813, 2814, 10,655, 10,659, 10,828). The Lord could not be tempted as to the Divine itself (n. 2795, 2803, 2813, 2814). Therefore He assumed an infirm human from the mother, into which He admitted temptations (n. 1414, 1444, 1573, 5041, 5157, 7193, 9315). By means of temptations and victories He expelled all that was hereditary from the mother, and put off the human which He had from her, till at length He was no longer her son (n. 2159, 2574, 2649, 3036, 10,830). Jehovah, who was in Him, appeared in temptations as if absent, and this so far as He was in the human from the mother (n. 1815). This state was the Lord's state of humiliation (n. 1785, 1999, 2159, 6866). The Lord by temptations and victories arranged all things in the heavens into order (n. 4287, 4295, 9528, 9937). By the same means He also united His Human with His Divine, that is, He glorified His Human (n. 1725, 1729, 1733, 1737, 3318, 3381, 3382, 4286, 4287, 4295, 9528, 9937).

303. *The Lord's Human, when He was in the world, was Divine truth.*

The Lord, when He was in the world, made His Human Divine truth from the Divine good which was in Him (n. 2803, 3194, 3195, 3210, 6716, 6864, 7014, 7499, 8127, 8724, 9199). The Lord then arranged all things in Himself into a heavenly form, which is according to the Divine truth (n. 1928, 3633). Consequently, that heaven was then in the Lord, and the Lord was as heaven (n. 911, 1900, 1928, 3624–3631, 3634, 3884, 4041, 4279, 4523–4525, 6013, 6057, 6690, 9279, 9632, 9931, 10,303). The Lord spake from the Divine truth itself (n. 8127). Therefore the Lord spake in the Word by correspondences (n. 3131, 3472–3485, 8615, 10,687). Hence the Lord is the Word, and is called the Word, which is the Divine truth (n. 2533, 2813, 2859, 2894, 3393, 3712). In the Word "the Son of man" signifies the Divine truth, and "the Father" the Divine good (n. 2803, 3704, 7499, 8724, 9194). Because the Lord was the Divine truth, He was the Divine wisdom (n. 2500, 2572). The Lord alone had perception and thought from Himself, above all angelic perception and thought (n. 1904, 1914, 1919). The Divine truth could be tempted, but not the Divine good (n. 2814).

304. *The Lord united the Divine truth to the Divine good, thus His Human to the Divine itself.*

The Lord was instructed as another man (n. 1457, 1461, 2523, 3030). The Lord successively advanced to union with the Father (n. 1864, 2033, 2632, 3141, 4585, 7014, 10,076). So far as the Lord was united with the Father, so far He spake as with Himself; but at other times as with another (n. 1745, 1999, 7058). The Lord united His Human with the Divine from His own power (n. 1616, 1749, 1752, 1813, 1921, 2025, 2026, 2523, 3141, 5005, 5045, 6716). The Lord united the Divine truth, which was Himself, with the Divine good which was in Himself (n. 10,047, 10,052, 10,076). The unition was reciprocal (n. 2004, 10,067). The Lord, when He went out of the world, made His Human the Divine good (n. 3194, 3210, 6864, 7499, 8724, 9199, 10,076). Thus He came forth from the Father, and returned to the Father (n. 3194, 3210). Thus He became one with the Father (n. 2751, 3704, 4766). The Lord, in His unition with the Divine itself which was in Him, regarded the conjunction of Himself with the human race (n. 2034). After the unition, the Divine truth proceeds from the Lord (n. 3704, 3712, 3969, 4577, 5704, 7499, 8127, 8241, 9199, 9398). How the Divine truth proceeds, illustrated (n. 7270, 9407).

Unless the Divine had been in the Lord's Human from conception, the Human could not have been united with the Divine itself, on account of the ardor of the infinite love in which the Divine itself is (n. 6849). Therefore no angel can ever be united with the Divine itself except at a distance, and by means of a veiling; for otherwise he would be consumed (n. 6849). The Divine love is of such a quality (n. 8644). Hence it may appear that the Human of the Lord was not like the human of another man (n. 10,125, 10,826). His union with the Father, from whom was His soul, was not like a union between two, but like that between soul and body (n. 3737, 10,824). Union is said of the Lord's Human and the Divine, but conjunction between man and the Divine (n. 2021).

305. *Thus the Lord made His Human Divine.*

The Human of the Lord is Divine, because it was from the *esse* of the Father, which was His soul, illustrated by the likeness of a father and children (n. 10,269, 10,372, 10,823). And

because it was from the Divine love which was in Him (n.
6872). Every man is such as his love is, and he is his
own love (n. 6872, 10,177, 10,284). The Lord was the Divine
love (n. 2077, 2253). The Lord made all His Human, both the
internal and the external Divine (n. 1603, 1815, 1902, 1926,
2093, 2803). Therefore He rose again as to the whole body,
differently from any man (n. 1729, 2083, 5078, 10,825). The
Lord's Human is Divine, is acknowledged from the omnipresence of His Human in the Holy Supper (n. 2343, 2359). And
it is evident from His transfiguration before the three disciples
(n. 3212). And likewise from the Word (n. 10,154). And
He was there called Jehovah (n. 1603, 1736, 1815, 1902, 2921,
3035, 5110, 6281, 6303, 8864, 9194, 9315). In the sense of the
letter there is a distinction made between the Father and the
Son, or Jehovah and the Lord, but not in the internal sense,
in which the angels are (n. 3035). The Christian world does
not acknowledge the Human of the Lord to be Divine, in consequence of a decree passed by a council in favor of the Pope,
that he might be acknowledged as the Lord's vicar; from conversation with them in another life (n. 4738).

The Divine Human from eternity was the Divine truth in
heaven, thus the Divine *existere*, which was afterwards made
in the Lord the Divine *esse*, from which is the Divine *existere*
in heaven (n. 3061, 6280, 6880, 10,579). The previous state of
heaven described (n. 6371–6373). The Divine was not per-
ceptible, and therefore not capable of being received, until it
passed through heaven (n. 6982, 6996, 7004). The Lord from
eternity was the Divine truth in heaven (n. 2803, 3195, 3704).
This is the Son of God born from eternity (n. 2628, 2798).

In heaven no other Divine is perceived but the Divine Human (n. 6475, 9303, 9356, 9571, 10,067). The most ancient
people could not adore the infinite *esse*, but the infinite *existere*, which is the Divine Human (n. 4687, 5321). The ancients
acknowledged the Divine, because it appeared in a human form,
and this was the Divine Human (n. 5110, 5663, 6846, 10,737).
The inhabitants of all the earths adore the Divine under a
human form, and they rejoice when they hear that God actually
became Man (n. 6700, 8541–8547, 9361, 10,736–10,738). See
also the little work *On the Earths in our Solar System, and in*

the Starry Heaven. God cannot be thought of, but in a Human form, and that which is incomprehensible can not fall into any idea (n. 9359, 9972). Man can worship what he has some idea of, but not what he has no idea of (n. 4733, 5110, 5663, 7211, 9356, 10,067). Therefore the Divine is worshiped under a Human form by most in the whole globe, and this is through an influx from heaven (n. 10,159). All who are in good as to life, when they think of the Lord, think of a Divine Human, but not of the Human separated from the Divine (n. 2326, 4724, 4731, 4766, 8878, 9193, 9198). They in the church at this day who are in evil as to life, and they who are in faith separate from charity, think of the Human of the Lord without the Divine, and do not comprehend what the Divine Human is, the causes thereof (n. 3212, 3241, 4689, 4692, 4724, 4731, 5321, 6371, 8878, 9193, 9198).

306. *The Trinity is in the Lord.*

Christians were examined in the other life concerning the idea they had of one God, and it was found that they had an idea of three Gods (n. 2329, 5256, 10,736–10,738, 10,821). The Divine Trinity may be conceived of in one Person, and thus as one God, but not in three Persons (n. 10,738, 10,821, 10,822). The Trinity in one Person, thus in the Lord, is the Divine itself, which is called the Father, the Divine Human, which is called the Son, and the Divine proceeding, which is called the Holy Spirit; thus the Trinity is one (n. 2149, 2156, 2288, 2321, 2329, 2447, 3704, 6993, 7182, 10,738, 10,822, 10,823). The Divine Trinity in the Lord is acknowledged in heaven (n. 14, 15, 1729, 2005, 5256, 9303). The Lord is one with the Father, thus He is the Divine itself, and the Divine Human (n. 1729, 2004, 2005, 2018, 2025, 2751, 3704, 3736, 4766). His Divine proceeding is also His Divine in heaven, which is called the Holy Spirit (n. 3969, 4673, 6788, 6993, 7499, 8127, 8302, 9199, 9228, 9229, 9278, 9407, 9818, 9820, 10,330). Thus the Lord is the alone and only God (n. 1607, 2149, 2156, 2329, 2447, 2751, 3194, 3704, 3712, 3938, 4577, 4687, 5321, 6280, 6371, 6849, 6993, 7014, 7091, 7182, 7209, 8241, 8724, 8760, 8864, 8865, 9194, 9303).

307. *Of the Lord in heaven.*

The Lord appears in heaven both as a sun and a moon; as a sun to those who are in the celestial kingdom, and as a moon

to those who are in the spiritual kingdom (n. 1053, 1521, 1529–
1531, 3636, 3641, 4321, 5097, 7078, 7083, 7173, 7270, 8812,
10,809). The light which proceeds from the Lord as a sun is
the Divine truth, from which the angels derive all their wisdom and intelligence (n. 1053, 1521–1533, 2776 3138, 3195,
3222, 3223, 3225, 3339, 3341, 3636, 3643, 3993, 4180, 4302,
4415, 5400, 9399, 9407, 9548, 9571, 9684). And the heat which
proceeds from the Lord as a sun, is the Divine good, from
which the angels derive their love (n. 3338, 3636, 3643, 5215).
The Lord's Divine itself is far above His Divine in heaven
(n. 7270, 8760). The Divine truth is not in the Lord, but proceeds from the Lord, as light is not in the sun, but proceeds
from the sun (n. 3969). *Esse* is in the Lord, and *existere* from
the Lord (n. 3938). The Lord is the common centre to which
all the angels in heaven turn (n. 3633, 9828, 10,130, 10,189).
Nevertheless the angels do not turn themselves to the Lord,
but the Lord turns them to Himself (n. 10,189); because the
angels are not present with the Lord, but the Lord is present
with the angels (n. 9415). The Lord's presence with the angels is according to their reception of the good of love and
charity from Him (n. 904, 4198, 4206, 4211, 4320, 6280, 6832,
7042, 8819, 9680, 9682, 9683, 10,106, 10,810). The Lord is
present with all in heaven, and also in hell (n. 2776, 3642,
3644). The Lord from His Divine love wishes to draw all men
to Himself into heaven (n. 6645). The Lord is in a continual
endeavor of conjunction with man, but the influx and conjunction are impeded by the loves of man's proprium (n. 2041,
2053, 2411, 5696).

The Divine Human of the Lord flows into heaven, and
makes heaven, and there is no conjunction with the Divine itself in heaven, but with the Divine Human (n. 3038, 4211,
4724, 5663). And the Divine Human flows in with men out
of heaven and through heaven (n. 1925). The Lord is the all
of heaven, and the life of heaven (n. 7211, 9128). The Lord
dwells with the angels in what is His own (n. 9338, 10,125,
10,151, 10,157). Hence they who are in heaven are in the
Lord (n. 3637, 3638). Heaven corresponds to the Divine Human of the Lord, and man as to each and all things, corresponds to heaven, whence heaven in general is as one man, and

is therefore called the Greatest Man (n. 2988, 2996, 3624–3629, 3636–3643, 3741–3745, 4625). The Lord is the only Man, and they only are men who receive the Divine from Him (n. 1894). So far as they receive, so far they become images of the Lord (n. 8547). The angels are forms of love and charity in a human form, and this is from the Lord (n. 3804, 3735, 4797, 4985, 5199, 5530, 9879, 10,177).

308. *All good and truth are from the Lord.*

The Lord is good itself and truth itself (n. 2011, 5110, 10,336, 10,619). All good and truth, consequently all peace, innocence, love, charity, and faith, are from the Lord (n. 1614, 2016, 2751, 2882, 2883, 2891, 2892, 2904). And all wisdom and intelligence are from Him (n. 109, 112, 121, 124). Nothing but good comes from the Lord, but the evil turn the good which is from the Lord into evil (n. 7643, 7679, 7710, 8632). The angels know that all good and truth are from the Lord, but the evil are not willing to know this (n. 6193, 9128). The angels at the presence of the Lord, are more in good, but the infernals, at the presence of the Lord, are more in evils (n. 7989). The evil cast themselves into hell at the mere presence of the Lord (n. 8137, 8265). The Lord judges all from good (n. 2335). The Lord regards all from mercy (n. 223). The Lord is never angry with any one, nor does evil to any one, and does not send any one to hell (n. 245, 1683, 2335, 8632). In what sense those parts of the Word are to be understood, where it is said, that Jehovah or the Lord is angry, that He kills, that He casts into hell, and other things of the like nature (n. 592, 696, 1093, 1874, 1875, 2395, 2447, 3605, 3607, 3614, 6071, 6997).

309. *The Lord has all power in the heavens and on earth.*

The entire heaven is the Lord's (n. 2751, 7086). And He has all power in the heavens and on earth (n. 1607, 10,089, 10,827). As the Lord rules the whole heaven, He also rules all things which depend thereon, thus all things in the world (n. 2026, 2027, 4523, 4524). He also rules the hells (n. 3642). The Lord rules all things from the Divine, by the Divine Human (n. 8864, 8865). The Lord rules all things according to Divine order, and the Divine order has relation to those things which are of His will, to those things which are done from leave, and to those things which are done from permission (n. 1755, 2447,

6574, 9940); concerning order, see above (n. 279). The Lord rules ultimates from firsts, and firsts from ultimates, and this is the reason why He is called "the First and the Last" (n. 3702, 6040, 6056). The Lord alone has the power of removing the hells, of withholding from evils, and of keeping in good, thus of saving (n. 10,019). Judgment belongs to the Lord (n. 2319–2321, 10,810, 10,811). What the Lord's priesthood is, and what His royalty is (n. 1728, 2015).

310. *In what manner some expressions in the Word, which relate to the Lord, are to be understood.*

What is meant by "the seed of the woman," in the prophecy concerning the Lord (n. 256). What "the Son of man" and "the Son of God" signify in the Word (n. 2159, 2813). What the two names "Jesus Christ" signify (n. 3004–3011). What is signified by the Lord's being said to be "sent by the Father" (n. 2397, 6831, 10,561). How it is to be understood, that the Lord bore the iniquities of all (n. 9937). How it is to be understood, that the Lord redeemed man by His blood (n. 10,152). How it is to be understood that the Lord fulfilled all things of the law (n. 10,239). How it is to be understood, that the Lord intercedes for man (n. 2250, 8573, 8705). How it is to be understood, that without the Lord there is no salvation (n. 10,828). Salvation is not effected by looking to the Father, or by praying Him to have mercy for the sake of His Son; for the Lord says, "I am the way, the truth, and life; no one cometh to the Father but by me" (*John* xiv. 6; n. 2854). The contradictions which are involved in the received faith, that the Lord reconciled the human race to the Father, by the passion of the cross (n. 10,659). The coming of the Lord is His presence in the Word (n. 3900, 4060). The Lord does not desire glory from man for the sake of Himself, but of man's salvation (n. 5957, 10,646). Wherever the name "Lord" occurs in the Word, it signifies the Divine good (n. 4973, 9167, 9194). Where the name "Christ" occurs, it signifies the Divine truth (n. 3004–3009).

The true acknowledgment and true worship of the Lord is to do His commandments, shown from the Word (n. 10,143, 10,153, 10,578, 10,645, 10,829).

XXIII.

ECCLESIASTICAL AND CIVIL GOVERNMENT.

311. There are two things which ought to be in order with men, namely, the things which are of heaven, and the things which are of the world. The things which are of heaven are called ecclesiastical, and those which are of the world are called civil.

312. Order cannot be maintained in the world without governors, who are to observe all things which are done according to order, and which are done contrary to order; and who are to reward those who live according to order, and punish those who live contrary to order. If this be not done, the human race will perish; for the will to command others, and to possess the goods of others, from heredity is connate with every one, whence proceed enmities, envyings, hatreds, revenges, deceits, cruelties, and many other evils. Wherefore, unless they were kept under restraint by the laws, and by rewards suited to their loves, which are honors and gains for those who do goods; and by punishments contrary to those loves, which are the loss of honors, of possessions, and of life, for those who do evils; the human race would perish.

313. There must therefore be governors to keep the assemblages of men in order, who should be skilled in the law, wise, and who fear God. There must also be order among the governors, lest any one, from caprice or ignorance, should permit evils which are contrary to order, and thereby destroy it. This is guarded against when there are superior and inferior governors, among whom there is subordination.

314. Governors over those things with men which relate to heaven, or over ecclesiastical affairs, are called priests, and their office is called the priesthood. But governors over those things with men which relate to the world, or over civil affairs, are called magistrates, and their chief, where such a form of government prevails, is called king.

315. With respect to the priests, they ought to teach men the way to heaven, and also to lead them; they ought to teach them according to the doctrine of their church from the Word, and to lead them to live according to it. Priests who teach truths, and thereby lead to the good of life, and so to the Lord, are good shepherds of the sheep; but they who teach and do not lead to the good of life, and so to the Lord, are evil shepherds.

316. Priests ought not to claim to themselves any power over the souls of men, because they do not know in what state the interiors of a man are; still less ought they to claim the power of opening and shutting heaven, since that power belongs to the Lord alone.

317. Dignity and honor ought to be paid to priests on account of the holy things which they administer; but they who are wise give the honor to the Lord, from whom the holy things are, and not to themselves, but they who are not wise attribute the honor to themselves; these take it away from the Lord. They who attribute honor to themselves, on account of the holy things which they administer, prefer honor and gain to the salvation of souls, which they ought to provide for; but they who give the honor to the Lord, and not to themselves, prefer the salvation of souls to honor and gain. The honor of any employment is not in the person, but is adjoined to him according to the dignity of the thing which he administers; and what is adjoined does not belong to the person himself, and is also separated from him with the employment. All personal honor is the honor of wisdom and the fear of the Lord.

318. Priests ought to teach the people, and to lead them by truths to the good of life, but still they ought to compel no one, since no one can be compelled to believe contrary to what he thinks from his heart to be true. He who believes otherwise than the priest, and makes no disturbance, ought to be left in peace; but he who makes disturbance, ought to be separated; for this also is of order, for the sake of which the priesthood is established.

319. As priests are appointed to administer those things which relate to the Divine law and worship, so kings and magistrates are appointed to administer those things which relate to civil law and judgment.

320. Because the king alone cannot administer all things, therefore there are governors under him, to each of whom a province is given to administer, which the king cannot and is not able to administer alone. These governors, taken together, constitute the royalty, but the king himself is the chief.

321. Royalty itself is not in the person, but is adjoined to the person. The king who believes that royalty is in his own person, and the governor who believes that the dignity of the government is in his own person, is not wise.

322. Royalty consists in administering according to the laws of the realm, and in judging according to them from justice. The king who regards the laws as above himself, is wise, but he who regards himself as above the laws, is not wise. The king who regards the laws as above himself places the royalty in the law, and the law has dominion over him, for he knows that the law is justice, and that all justice which is justice, is Divine. But he who regards himself as above the laws, places the royalty in himself, and either believes himself to be the law, or the law, which is justice, to be from himself; hence he arrogates to himself that which is Divine, under which nevertheless he ought to be.

323. The law which is justice ought to be enacted in the realm by persons skilled in the law, wise, and who fear God; then both the king and his subjects ought to live according to it. The king who lives according to the enacted law, and in this precedes his subjects by his example, is truly a king.

324. A king who has absolute power, who believes that his subjects are such slaves that he has a right to their possessions and lives, and if he exercises it, is not a king, but a tyrant.

325. There ought to be obedience to the king according to the laws of the realm, nor should he be injured by any means either by deeds or words; for on this the public security depends.

THE END.

A Brief Exposition

OF

The Doctrine of The New Church

A Brief Exposition

OF

The Doctrine of The New Church

WHICH IS MEANT BY

"THE NEW JERUSALEM" IN THE
APOCALYPSE

BY

EMANUEL SWEDENBORG

A SWEDE

Being a translation of his work, "SUMMARIA EXPOSITIO DOCTRINÆ NOVÆ HIEROSOLYMÆ, quæ per Novam Hierosolymam in Apocalypsi intelligitur: ab Emanuele Swedenborg, Sueco."
Amstelodami, 1769

Apocalypse XXI. 2, 5

"I, John, saw the holy city, New Jerusalem, coming down from God out of heaven, prepared as a Bride adorned for her Husband. And He that sat upon the throne said, Behold, I make all things new; and He said unto me, Write, for these words are true and faithful."

CONTENTS.

	Sections
INTRODUCTION	1
The Doctrinals of the Roman Catholics concerning justification, from the Council of Trent.	2–8
The Doctrinals of the Protestants concerning justification, from the Formula Concordiæ	9–15
A Sketch of the Doctrinals of the New Church	16

The Disagreement between the Doctrinals of the Old and the New Church, considered under XXV. Articles.

I. The churches, which, by the Reformation, separated themselves from the Roman Catholic Church, differ in various things; but they all agree in the articles concerning a Trinity of Persons in the Divinity, original sin from Adam, imputation of the merit of Christ, and justification by faith alone........................... 17–18

II. The Roman Catholics, before the Reformation, taught exactly the same things as the Reformed did after it, concerning the four articles above mentioned, namely, a Trinity of Persons in the Divinity, original sin, imputation of the merit of Christ, and justification by faith therein; only with this difference, that they conjoined that faith with charity or good works......... 19, 20

III. The leading Reformers, Luther, Melancthon, and Calvin, retained all the Dogmas concerning a Trinity of Persons in the Divinity, original sin, imputation of the merit of Christ, and justification by faith, just as they were and had been with the Roman Catholics; but they separated charity or good works from that faith, and declared that they were not at the same time saving, with a view to be totally severed from the Roman Catholics, as to the very essentials of the church, which are faith and charity... 21–23

IV. Nevertheless the leading Reformers adjoined good works, and also conjoined them, to their faith, but in man as a passive subject; whereas the Roman Catholics conjoin them in man as an active subject; and that notwithstanding this, there is actually a conformity between the one and the other as to faith, works, and merits... 24–29

V. The whole theology in the Christian world at this day is founded on an idea of three Gods, arising from the doctrine of a Trinity of Persons..................... 30–38

CONTENTS

Sections

VI. The dogmas of that theology appear to be erroneous, after the idea of a Trinity of Persons, and thence of three Gods, has been rejected, and the idea of One God, in Whom there is a Divine Trinity, is received in its stead.   39, 40

VII. Then truly saving faith, which is a faith in One God, united with good works, is acknowledged and received.   41, 42

VIII. And this is a faith in God the Saviour Jesus Christ, which in its simple form is as follows:—I. That there is One God, in Whom is the Divine Trinity, and He is the Lord Jesus Christ. II. Saving faith is to believe in Him. III. Evils ought to be shunned, because they are of the devil and from the devil. IV. Goods ought to be done, because they are of God and from God. V. And they ought to be done by man as of himself, but it is to be believed that they are from the Lord, with him and through him...   43, 44

IX. The faith of the present day has separated religion from the church, since religion consists in the acknowledgment of One God, and in the worship of Him, from the faith of charity...................................   45, 46

X. The faith of the church at this day cannot be conjoined with charity, and produce any fruits, which are good works...   47–50

XI. From the faith of the church at this day there results a worship of the mouth and not of the life, whereas the worship of the mouth is accepted by the Lord, according to the worship of the life.......................   51, 52

XII. The doctrine of the church at this day is interwoven with many paradoxes, which are to be embraced by faith; and therefore its dogmas gain admission into the memory only; and not into any part of the understanding above the memory, but merely into confirmation below it.   53–57

XIII. The dogmas of the church at this day cannot be learned and retained without great difficulty, nor can they be preached or taught without using great care and caution to conceal their nakedness, because true reason neither perceives nor receives them...................   58, 59

XIV. The doctrine of the faith of the church at this day ascribes to God human properties; as that He regarded man from anger, that He required to be reconciled, that He is reconciled through the love He bore towards the Son, and by His intercession; and that He required to be appeased by the sight of His Son's sufferings, and thus to be brought back to mercy; and that He imputes the justice of His Son to an unjust man who supplicates it from faith alone; and that thus from an enemy He makes him a friend, and from a child of wrath a child of grace..   60–63

CONTENTS

		Sections
XV.	The faith of the church at this day has produced monstrous births; such as instantaneous salvation from immediate mercy; predestination; that God pays no attention to the actions of men, but to faith alone; that there is no connection between charity and faith; that man in conversion is like a stock, with many more; likewise concerning the Sacraments of Baptism and the Holy Supper, as to the advantages reasonably to be expected from them, when considered according to the doctrine of justification by faith alone; as also with regard to the Person of Christ: and that the heresies from the first ages to the present day, have sprung up from no other source than from the doctrine founded on the idea of three Gods..	64–69
XVI.	The last state of the church at this day, when it is at its end, is meant by the consummation of the age, and then the coming of the Lord (*Matt.* xxiv. 3)...........	70–73
XVII.	The infestation from falsities, and thence the consummation of every truth, or the desolation which at this day prevails in the Christian churches, is meant by the great affliction, such as was not from the beginning of the world, nor ever shall be (*Matt.* xxiv. 21)........	74–76
XVIII.	There would be neither love, nor faith, nor the knowledges of good and truth, in the last time of the Christian Church, when it draws to an end, is understood by these words in the same chapter of *Matthew* (xxiv.), "After the affliction of those days, the sun shall be darkened, and the moon shall not give her light, and the stars shall fall from heaven, and the powers of the heavens shall be shaken" (verse 29)........	77–81
XIX.	They who are in the present justifying faith, are meant by the he-goats in *Daniel* and in *Matthew*	82–86
XX.	They who have confirmed themselves in the present justifying faith, are meant in the *Apocalypse* by the dragon and his two beasts, and by the locusts; and that this same faith, when confirmed, is there meant by the great city which is spiritually called Sodom and Egypt, where the two witnesses were slain, as also by the pit of the abyss from which the locusts went forth........	87–90
XXI.	Unless the New Church be established by the Lord, no one can be saved; and this is meant by these words, "Unless those days should be shortened, there should no flesh be saved" (*Matt.* xxiv. 22)..................	91–94
XXII.	The opening and rejection of the dogmas of the faith of the church at this day, and the revelation and reception of the dogmas of the faith of the New Church, is meant by these words in the *Apocalypse:* "He that sat upon the throne said, Behold I make all things new; and He said, Write, for these words are true and faithful"(chap. xxi. 5)	95–98

CONTENTS

                                                                                                                        Sections

XXIII. The New Church about to be established by the Lord, is the New Jerusalem, treated of in the *Apocalypse* (chap. xxi. and xxii.), which is there called the Bride and the Wife of the Lamb.............................. 99–101

XXIV. The faith of the New Church cannot by any means be together with the faith of the former church, and if they be together, such a collision and conflict will take place that everything of the church with man will perish... 102–104

XXV. The Roman Catholics of this day know nothing of the imputation of the merit of Christ, and of justification by faith therein, into which their church was first initiated, because it is entirely concealed under their externals of worship, which are many; for which reason, therefore, if they recede but in part from the externals of their worship, and immediately approach God the Saviour Jesus Christ, and receive the Holy Eucharist in both kinds, they may be brought into the New Jerusalem, that is, into the New Church of the Lord, more easily than the Reformed..................... 105–108

On Imputation... 109–113

Two Relations from *The Apocalypse Revealed*................ 114, 115

APPENDIX.

The faith of the New Heaven and the New Church in its universal form....................................... 116, 117

Three Relations from *The Apocalypse Revealed*.............. 118–120

A Brief Exposition

OF THE

Doctrine of The New Church

WHICH IS MEANT BY

THE NEW JERUSALEM IN THE APOCALYPSE

---

1. Several works and tracts having been published by me, during some years past, concerning the New Jerusalem, by which is meant the New Church about to be established by the Lord; and the *Apocalypse* having been revealed, I have come to a determination to bring to light the entire doctrine of that church in its fulness. But, as this is a work of some years, I have thought it advisable to draw up some sketch thereof, in order that a general idea may first be formed of that church and its doctrine; because when general principles precede, each and everything will afterwards appear extant in its breadth in light, for these enter into generals, as things homogeneous into their receptacles. This compendium, however, is not designed for critical examination, but is only offered to the world by way of information, as its contents will be fully demonstrated in the work itself. But the doctrinals at present maintained concerning justification shall be prefixed, that the following contrast between the doctrines of the present church, and those of the New Church, may be clearly understood.

THE DOCTRINALS OF THE ROMAN CATHOLICS CONCERNING JUSTIFICATION, FROM THE COUNCIL OF TRENT.

2. In the bull of Pope Pius IV., dated 13th November, 1564, are the following words: "I embrace and receive each and everything which the most holy Council of Trent hath determined and declared concerning *Original Sin and Justification*."

3. *From the Council of Trent, concerning Original Sin.*

(*a*) That Adam, by the offense of his transgression, experienced an entire change and depravation of nature, both in body and soul; and that the ill effects of Adam's transgression were not confined to himself, but also extended to his posterity; and that it not only transmitted death and corporal sufferings upon all mankind, but likewise sin, which is the death of the soul (Sess. v. 1, 2). (*b*) That this sin of Adam, which originally was a single transgression, and has been transmitted by propagation, and not by imitation, is so implanted in the proprium of every man, and cannot be taken away by any other means than by the merit of the only Saviour our Lord Jesus Christ, who has reconciled us to God by His blood, being made unto us justice, sanctification, and redemption (Sess. v. 3). (*c*) That by the transgression of Adam, all men lost their innocence, and became unclean, and by nature the sons of wrath (Sess. vi. chap. 1).

4. *Concerning Justification.*

(*a*) That our heavenly Father, the Father of mercies, sent Christ Jesus His Son to men, in the blessed fulness of time, as well to the Jews who were under the law, as to the Gentiles who followed not justice, that they might all lay hold of justice, and all receive the adoption of sons. Him God offered to be a propitiation through faith in His blood, not only for our sins, but likewise for the sins of the whole world (Sess. vi. chap. 2). (*b*) Nevertheless all do not receive the benefit of His death, but only they to whom the merit of His passion is communicated; so that unless they are born again in Christ, they can never be justified (Sess. vi. chap. 3). (*c*) That the beginning of justification is to be derived from the preventing grace of God through Christ Jesus, that is, from His call (Sess. vi. chap. 5). (*c*) That men are disposed to justice, when being stirred up by Divine grace, and conceiving faith from hearing, they are freely moved towards God, believing those things to be true which are Divinely revealed and promised; and especially this, that the ungodly are justified by God through His grace, through redemption, which is by Christ Jesus; and when, being convinced of sin from the fear of Divine justice, by which they are profitably disquieted, they are encouraged in hope, trusting that God, for Christ's sake, will be propitious to them (Sess. vi. chap. 6). (*d*) That the consequence of this disposition and preparation is actual justification, which is not only a remission of sins, but likewise a sanctification and renovation of the interior man by the reception of Divine grace and gifts, whereby man from being unjust, becomes just, and from being an enemy becomes a friend, so as to be an heir according to the hope of eternal life (Sess. vi. chap. 7). (*e*) The *final cause* of justification is the glory of God and of Christ, and life eternal. The *efficient cause* is God, who freely cleanses and sanctifies. The *meritorious cause* is the Dearly-Beloved and Only-Begotten of God, our Lord Jesus Christ, who when we were enemies, through the great charity wherewith He loved us, by His most holy passion upon the wood of the cross, merited for us justification, and made satisfaction for us to God the Father. The *instrumental cause* is the sacrament of baptism which is a sacrament of faith, without which no one can ever reach justification. The *formal cause* is the sole justice of God; not that whereby He is just Himself, but that whereby He makes us just, with which being gifted by Him, we are renewed in the spirit of our mind; and are not only reputed just, but are truly called and are just, each according to his own measure, which the Holy Spirit imparts to every one as it pleases Him (Sess. vi. chap. 7, § 2). (*f*) That justification is a translation from that state, wherein man is born a son of the first Adam, into a state of grace and adoption of the sons of God by the second Adam, our Saviour Jesus Christ (Sess. vi. chap. 4).

5. *Concerning Faith, Charity, Good Works and Merits.*

(*a*) When the apostle says, that man is justified by faith and freely, these words are to be understood in the sense wherein the Catholic church has uniformly held and expressed them; namely, that we are said to be justified by faith, because faith is the commencement of man's salvation, the foundation and root of all justification, without which it is impossible to please God, and attain to the fellowship of His sons. But we are said to be justified freely, because none of those things which precede justification, whether faith or works, merit the actual grace of justification; for if it be grace, it is not from works, otherwise grace would not be grace (Sess. vi. chap. 8). (*b*)

Although no one can be just, but they to whom the merits of the passion of our Lord Jesus Christ are communicated, nevertheless that is effected in justification, when by the merit of the same most holy passion, the charity of God is infused by the Holy Spirit into the hearts of those who are justified, and abides in them. Hence in the act of justification, man receives, together with the remission of his sins, all these things infused into him at once by Jesus Christ, in whom he is ingrafted by faith, hope, and charity. For faith, unless charity be added to it, neither unites perfectly with Christ, nor constitutes a living member of His body (Sess. vi. chap. 7, § 3). (c) That Christ is not only the Redeemer in whom they have faith, but also a Lawgiver, whom they obey (Sess. vi. chap. 16, Can. 21). (d) That faith without works is dead and vain, because in Christ Jesus neither circumcision availeth anything, nor uncircumcision, but faith which worketh through charity. For faith without hope and charity cannot avail unto eternal life; wherefore also they hearken to the word of Christ, "If thou wilt enter into life, keep the commandments." Thus they who are born again, receiving true Christian justice, are commanded to keep it white and unspotted, as their first robe, given them by Jesus Christ, instead of that which Adam lost both for himself and us by his disobedience, that they may present it before the tribunal of our Lord Jesus Christ, and obtain eternal life (Sess. vi. chap. 7, § 4). (e) That there is a continual influx of power from Jesus Christ Himself into those who are justified, as from a head into the members, and from a vine into the branches; which power always precedes, accompanies, and follows their good works, and without which they could not by any means be acceptable and meritorious in the sight of God; wherefore we are to believe, that nothing more is wanting to those who are justified, but they may be fully assured, that by those works which have been wrought in God, they have merited eternal life, which will be bestowed upon them in due time (Sess. vi. chap. 16). (f) We do not mean our own justice, as though it were our own from ourselves; for that which is termed our justice, is the justice of God, because it is infused into us by God through the merit of Christ. Far be it, therefore, from any Christian man either to trust or glory in himself, and not in the Lord, whose goodness towards us men is so great, that He vouchsafes to regard those things as our merits, which are His own gifts (Sess. vi. chap. 16). (*g*) For of ourselves, as of ourselves, we can do nothing; but by His co-operation, who strengthens us, we can do all things. Thus man has not whereof to glory, but all our glory is in Christ, in whom we live, in whom we merit, in whom we make satisfaction, bringing forth fruits worthy of repentance, which have their efficacy from Him, are offered unto the Father by Him, and are accepted by the Father through Him (Sess. xiv. chap. 8). (*h*) Whosoever shall say that man may be justified in the sight of God, by his own works, which are done either through the powers of human nature, or through the teaching of the law, without Divine grace through Christ Jesus, let him be accursed (Sess. vi. Can. 1). (*i*) Whosoever shall say that man may believe, hope, and love (that is, have faith, hope, and charity), as is necessary in order that the grace of justification may be conferred upon him, without the preventing inspiration of the Holy Spirit, and its assistance, let him be accursed (Sess. vi. Can. 2). (*k*) Whosoever shall say that man is justified without the justice of Christ, whereby He has merited for us, let him be accursed (Sess. vi. Can. 10). Not to mention many more passages, principally relating to the conjunction of faith with charity or good works, and the condemnation of their separation.

6. *Concerning Free-will.*

(*a*) That free-will is by no means destroyed by Adam's sin, although it is debilitated and warped thereby (Sess. vi. chap. 1). (*b*) Whosoever shall say that the free-will of man, when moved and stirred up by God, cannot at all co-operate by concurring with God, who stirs it up and calls it, whereby man may dispose and prepare himself to receive the grace of justification; or that he cannot dissent if he will, but that, like a thing inanimate, he can do nothing at all, and is merely passive, let him be accursed (Sess. vi. Can. 4).

7. *The Doctrinals of the Roman Catholics concerning Justification, collected from the Decrees of the Council of Trent may be summed up and arranged in a series thus.* That the sin of Adam was transfused into the whole human race, whereby his state, and likewise the state of all men, became perverted, and alienated from God, and thus they were made enemies and sons of wrath; that therefore God the Father graciously sent His Son to reconcile, expiate, atone, satisfy, and thus redeem, and this by His being made justice. That Christ accomplished and fulfilled all this, by offering up Himself a sacrifice to God the Father upon the wood of the cross, thus by His passion and blood. That Christ alone has merited, and that this His merit is graciously imputed, attributed, applied, and transferred to the man who is recipient thereof, by God the Father through the Holy Spirit; and that thus the sin of Adam is removed from man; lust, however, still remaining in him as an incentive to sin. That justification is the remission of sins, and that from thence a renovation of the interior man takes place, whereby man from an enemy becomes a friend, and from being a son of wrath, a son of grace; and that thus union with Christ is effected, and being re-born he becomes a living member in His body.

8. That faith comes by hearing, when a man believes those things to be true which are Divinely revealed, and believes in the promises of God. That faith is the beginning of man's salvation, the foundation and root of all justification, without which it is impossible to please God, and enter into the fellowship of His children. That justification is effected by faith, hope, and charity; and that unless faith be accompanied by hope and charity, it is not living but dead, which cannot unite with Christ. That man ought to co-operate; that he has the power to approach and recede, otherwise nothing could be given unto him, for he would be like an inanimate body. That inasmuch as the reception of justification renews man, and as this is effected by the application of the merit of Christ, during man's co-operation, it follows that works are meritorious; but inasmuch as they are done from grace, and by the Holy Spirit, and as Christ alone has merited, therefore God considers His own gifts in man as meritorious; whence it follows, that no one ought to attribute anything of merit to himself.

THE DOCTRINALS OF THE PROTESTANTS CONCERNING JUSTIFICATION, FROM THE FORMULA CONCORDIÆ.

9. The book from which the following extracts are collected, is called the *Formula Concordiæ*, and was composed by men attached to the Augsburg Confession; and as the pages will be cited where the quotations are to be met with, it is proper to observe, that I have made use of the edition printed at Leipsic in the year 1756.

10. *From the Formula Concordiæ, concerning original sin.*

(*a*) That since the fall of Adam, all men naturally descended from him are born with sin, which condemns, and brings eternal death upon those who are not born again, and that the merit of Christ is the only means whereby they are regenerated, consequently the only remedy whereby they are healed (pp. 9, 10, 52, 53, 55, 317, 641, 644, and Appendix, pp. 138, 139). (*b*) That original sin is such a total corruption of nature, that there is no spiritual soundness in the powers of man either as to his soul or body (p. 574). (*c*) That it is the source of all actual sins (pp. 317, 577, 639, 640, 942; Appendix, p. 139). (*d*) That it is a total absence or privation of the image of God (p. 640). (*e*) That we ought to distinguish between our nature, such as God created it, and original sin which dwells in our nature (p. 645). (*f*) Moreover, original sin is there called the work of the devil, spiritual poison, the root of all evils, an accident and a quality; whereas our nature is there called the work and creature of God, the personality of man, a substance, and an essence; and that the difference between them is the same as the difference between a man infected with a disease and the disease itself.

11. *Concerning justification by faith.*

The *general principles* are these. (*a*) That by the Word and the sacraments the Holy Spirit is given, who effects faith when and where He pleases, in those who hear the Gospel. (*b*) That contrition, justification by faith, renovation, and good works, follow in order; that they are to be properly distinguished; and that contrition and good works contribute nothing to salvation, but faith alone. (*c*) That justification by faith alone, is remission of sins, deliverance from damnation, reconciliation with the Father, adoption as sons, and is effected by the imputation of the merit or justice of Christ. (*d*) That hence faith is that justice itself, whereby we are accounted just before God, and that it is a trust and confidence in grace. (*e*) That renovation, which follows, is vivification, regeneration, and sanctification. (*f*) That good works, which are the fruits of faith, being in themselves works of the Spirit, follow that renovation. (*g*) That this faith may be lost by grievous evils. *The general principles concerning the Law and the Gospel* are these. (*h*) That we must carefully distinguish between the Law and the Gospel, and between the works of the Law and the works of the Spirit, which are the truths of faith. (*i*) That the Law is doctrine which shows that man is in sins, and therefore in condemnation and the wrath of God, thus exciting terror; but that the Gospel is doctrine which teaches atonement for sins, and the deliverance from damnation by Christ, and thus of consolation. (*k*) That there are three uses of the Law, namely, to keep the wicked within bounds, to bring men to acknowledgment of their sins, and to teach the regenerate a rule of life. (*l*) That the regenerate are in the Law, but not under the Law, for they are under grace. (*m*) That it is the duty of the regenerate to exercise themselves in the Law, because, during their life in the world, they are prompted to sin by the flesh; but that they become pure and perfect after death. (*n*) That the regenerate are also reproved by the Holy Spirit, and endure various afflictions, but that nevertheless they do the Law spontaneously, and thus being the sons of God, they live in the Law. (*o*) That with those who are not regenerated, the veil of Moses still remains before their eyes, and the old Adam bears rule; but that with the regenerate the veil of Moses is taken away, and the old Adam is put to death.

12. *Particulars from the Formula Concordiæ, concerning justification by faith without the works of the Law.*

(*a*) That faith is imputed for justice without works, on account of the merit of Christ which is laid hold of by faith (pp. 78, 79, 80, 584, 689). (*b*) That charity follows justifying faith, but that faith does not justify as being formed by charity, as the Papists say (pp. 81, 89, 94, 117, 688, 691; Appendix, p. 169). (*c*) That neither the contrition which precedes faith, nor the renovation and sanctification which follow after it, nor the good works then performed, have anything to do with justification by faith (pp. 688, 689). (*d*) That it is folly to dream that the works of the second table of the Decalogue justify before God, for with that table we act with men, and not properly with God; and in justification we act with God and appease His wrath (p. 102). (*e*) If any one, therefore, believes he can obtain the remission of his sins, because he has charity, he brings a reproach on Christ; because he has an impious and vain confidence in his own justice (pp. 87, 89). (*f*) That good works are utterly to be excluded, in treating of justification and eternal life (p. 589). (*g*) That good works are not necessary as a meritorious cause of salvation, and that they do not enter into the act of justification (pp. 589, 590, 702, 704; Appendix, p. 173). (*h*) That the position, that good works are necessary to salvation, is to be rejected, because it takes away the consolation of the gospel, gives occasion to doubt of the grace of God, instils an opinion of one's own justice, and because they are accepted by the Papists to support a bad cause (p. 704). (*i*) The expression that good works are necessary to salvation, is rejected and condemned (p. 591). (*k*) That expressions implying that works are necessary unto salvation, ought not to be taught and defended, but rather exploded and rejected by the churches as false (p. 705). (*l*) That works which do not proceed from a true faith, are regarded as sins before God, that is, they are defiled with sin, because an evil tree cannot bring forth good fruit (p. 700). (*m*) That faith and salvation are neither preserved nor retained by good works, because these are only evidences that the Holy Spirit is present, and dwells in us (pp. 590, 705; Appendix, p. 174). (*n*) That the decree of the Council of Trent is deservedly to be rejected, which affirms that good works preserve salvation, or that justification by faith, or even faith itself, is maintained and preserved, either in the whole, or in the least part, by our works (p. 707).

13. *Particulars from the Formula Concordiæ, Concerning the fruits of faith.*

(*a*) That a difference is to be observed between the works of the Law, and the works of the Spirit, and that the works which a regenerate person performs with a free and willing mind are not works of the Law, but works of the Spirit, which are the fruits of faith; because they who are born again are not under the Law, but under grace (pp. 589, 590, 721, 722). (*b*) That good works are the fruits of repentance (p. 12). (*c*) That the regenerate receive by faith a new life, new affections, and new works, and that these are from faith in repentance (p. 134). (*d*) That man after conversion and justification begins to be renewed in his mind, and at length in his understanding, and that then his will is not inactive in performing daily exercises of repentance (pp. 582, 673, 700). (*e*) That we ought to repent as well on account of original sin, as on account of actual sins (p. 321; Appendix, p. 159). (*f*) That repentance with Christians continues until death, because they have to wrestle with the remains of sin in the flesh throughout life (p. 327). (*g*) That we must enter upon, and advance more and more in the practice of the Law of the Decalogue (pp. 85, 86). (*h*) That the regenerate, although delivered from the curse of the Law, ought nevertheless still to exercise themselves in the Divine Law (p. 718). (*i*) That the regenerate are not without the Law, though not under the Law, for they live according to the Law of the Lord (p. 722). (*k*) That the Law ought to be considered by the regenerate as a rule of religion (pp. 596, 717; Appendix, p. 156). (*l*) That the regenerate do good works, not by compulsion, but spontaneously and freely, as though they had received no command, had heard of no threats, and expected no reward (pp. 596, 701). (*m*) That with them faith is always occupied in some good work, and he who does not thus perform good works, is destitute of true faith, for where there is faith, there are good works (p. 701). (*n*) That charity and good fruits follow faith and regeneration (pp. 121, 122, 171, 188, 692). (*o*) Faith and works agree well together, and are inseparably connected; but faith alone lays hold of the blessing without works, and yet it is not alone; hence it is that faith without works is dead (pp. 692, 693). (*p*) That after man is justified by faith, his faith being then true and alive is operative by charity, for good works always follow justifying faith, and are most certainly discovered with it; thus faith is never alone, but is always accompanied by hope and charity (p. 586). (*q*) We confess that where good works do not follow faith, in such case it is a false and not a true faith (p. 336). (*r*) That it is as impossible to separate good works from faith, as heat and light from fire (p. 701). (*s*) That as the old Adam is always inherent in our very nature, the regenerate have continual need of admonition, doctrine, threatenings, and even of chastisements of the Law, for they are reproved and corrected by the Holy Spirit through the Law (pp. 719, 720, 721). (*t*) That the regenerate must wrestle with the old Adam, and that the flesh must be kept under by exhortations, threatenings, and stripes, because renovation of life by faith is only begun in the present life (pp. 595, 596, 724). (*u*) That there remains a perpetual wrestling between the flesh and the spirit, in the elect and truly regenerate (pp. 675, 679). (*x*) That the reason why Christ promises remission of sins to good works, is, because they follow reconciliation, and also because good fruits must necessarily follow, and because they are the signs of the promise (pp. 116, 117). (*y*) That saving faith is not in those who have not charity, for charity is the fruit which certainly and necessarily follows true faith (p. 688). (*z*) That good works are necessary on many accounts, but not as a meritorious cause (pp. 11, 17, 64, 95, 133, 589, 590, 702; Appendix, p. 172). (*aa*) That a regenerate person ought to co-operate with the Holy Spirit, by the new powers and gifts which he has received, but in a certain way (pp. 582, 583, 674, 675; Appendix, p. 144). (*bb*) *In the Confession of the Churches in the Low Countries, which was received in the Synod of Dort, we read as follows:* "Holy faith cannot be inactive in man, for it is a faith working by charity; and works, which proceed from a good root of faith, are good and acceptable before God, like fruits of a good tree; for we are bound by God to good works, but not God to us, inasmuch as it is God that doeth them in us."

14. *Concerning merits, from the Formula Concordiæ.*

(*a*) That it is false that our works merit remission of sins; false, that men are accounted just by the justice of reason; and false, that reason of its own strength can love God above all things, and do the law of God (p. 64). (*b*) That faith does not justify because it is in itself so good a work, and so excellent a virtue, but because it lays hold of the merit of Christ in the promise of the gospel (pp. 76, 684). (*c*) That the promise of remission of sins, and justification for Christ's sake, does not involve any condition of merit, because it is freely offered (p. 67). (*d*) That a sinner is justified before God, or absolved from his sins, and from the most just sentence of damnation, and adopted into the number of the sons of God, without any merit of his own, and without any works of his own, whether past, present, or future, of mere grace, and only on account of the sole merit of Christ, which is imputed to him for justice (p. 684). (*e*) That good works follow faith, remission of sins, and regeneration; and whatever of pollution or imperfection is in them, is not accounted sinful or defective, and that for Christ's sake; and thus that the whole man, both as to his person and his works, is rendered and pronounced just and holy, out of mere grace and mercy in Christ, shed abroad, displayed, and magnified towards us; wherefore we cannot glory on account of merit (pp. 74, 92, 93, 336). (*f*) He who trusts in works, thinking he can merit anything thereby, despises the merit and grace of Christ, and seeks a way to heaven without Christ, by human strength (pp. 16, 17, 18, 19). (*g*) Whosoever desires to ascribe something to good works in the article of justification, and to merit the grace of God thereby, to such a man works are not only useless, but even pernicious (p. 708). (*h*) The works of the Decalogue are enumerated, and other necessary works, which God vouchsafes to reward (pp. 176, 198). (*i*) We teach that good works are meritorious, not indeed of remission of sins, grace, and justification, but of other temporal rewards, and even spiritual rewards in this life, and after this life, because Paul says, "Every one shall receive a reward according to his labor"; and Christ says, "Great will be your reward in the heavens"; and it is often said, that "it shall be rendered unto every one according to his works"; wherefore we acknowledge eternal life to be a reward, because it is our due according to promise, and because God crowns His own gifts, but not on account of our merits (pp. 96, 133, 134, 135, 136, 137, 138). (*k*) That the good works of believers, when they are performed on account of true causes, and directed to right ends, such as God requires from the regenerate, are signs of eternal salvation; and that God the Father accounts them acceptable and pleasing for Christ's sake, and promises to them excellent rewards of the present life, and of that which is to come (p. 708). (*l*) That although good works merit rewards, yet neither from their worthiness nor fitness do they merit the remission of sins, or the glory of eternal life (pp. 96, 135, 139, *seq.;* Appendix, p. 174). (*m*) That Christ at the Last Judgment will pass sentence on good and evil works, as the proper effects and evidences of men's faith (p. 134; Appendix, p. 187). (*n*) That God rewards good works, but that it is of grace that He crowns His own gifts, is asserted in the *Confession of the Churches in the Low Countries.*

15. *Concerning free-will, from the Formula Concordiæ.* (*a*) That man has plenary impotence in spiritual things (pp. 15, 18, 219, 318, 579, 656, *seq.*; Appendix, p. 141). (*b*) That man by the fall of his first parents is become so totally corrupt, that he is by nature blind with respect to spiritual things which relate to conversion and salvation, and judges the Word of God to be a foolish thing; and that he is and continues to be an enemy to God, until by the power of the Holy Spirit, through preaching and hearing of the Word, he is of mere grace, without any the least co-operation on his part, converted, gifted with faith, regenerated and renewed (pp. 656, 657). (*c*) That man is altogether corrupt and dead to what is good, so that in the nature of man, since the fall, and before regeneration, there is not so much as a spark of spiritual strength subsisting or remaining, whereby he can prepare himself for the grace of God, or apprehend it when offered, or of and by himself be capable of receiving it, or understand, believe, embrace, think, will, begin, perfect, act, operate, co-operate in spiritual things, or apply or accommodate himself to grace, or contribute anything towards his conversion, either in the whole, the half, or the least part (pp. 656, 658). (*d*) That man in spiritual and Divine things, which regard salvation, is like the statue of salt into which Lot's wife was turned, and like a stock or a stone without life, which have neither the use of eyes, mouth, nor any of the senses (pp. 661, 662). (*e*) That still man has a locomotive power, by virtue whereof he can govern his outward members, attend public assemblies, and hear the Word and the Gospel; but that in his private thoughts he despises it as a foolish thing; and in this respect is worse than a stock, unless the Holy Spirit is efficacious in him (pp. 662, 671, 672, 673). (*f*) That still it is not with man in his conversion, as in the forming of a stone into a statue, or the stamping an impression upon wax, which have neither knowledge, sense, nor will (pp. 662, 681). (*g*) That man in his conversion is a merely passive subject, and not an active one (pp. 662, 681). (*h*) That man in his conversion does not at all cooperate with the Holy Spirit (pp. 219, 579, 583, 672, 676; Appendix, pp. 143, 144). (*i*) That man since the fall retains and possesses the faculty of knowing natural things, as also free-will in some measure to choose natural and civil good (pp. 14, 218, 641, 664; Appendix, p. 142). (*j*) That the assertions of certain fathers, and modern doctors, that God draws man, but draws him in a manner consistent with his will, are not consonant with Holy Scripture (pp. 582–583). (*k*) That man, when he is born again by the power of the Holy Spirit, cooperates, though in much weakness, from the new powers and gifts, which the Holy Spirit has begun to operate in him at his conversion, not indeed forcibly, but spontaneously (pp. 582, *seq.*, 673–675); Appendix, p. 144). (*l*) That in the regenerate, not only the gifts of God, but likewise Christ Himself dwells by faith, as in His temples (pp. 695, 697, 698; Appendix, p. 130). (*m*) There is an immense difference between baptized and not baptized men; for it is the doctrine of Paul, that all who have been baptized, have put on Christ, and are truly regenerate, having thereby acquired a freedom of will, that is to say, being again made free, as Christ testifies, whence they not only hear the Word of God, but are likewise enabled, though in much weakness, to assent to it and embrace it by faith (p. 675).

It is proper to observe, that the foregoing extracts are taken from a book called *Formula Concordiæ*, which was composed by men attached to the Augsburg Confession; but that nevertheless the like doctrines concerning *justification by faith alone* are maintained and taught by the Reformed in England and Holland; wherefore the following treatise is intended for all; see below (n. 17, 18).

A SKETCH

OF THE

DOCTRINALS OF THE NEW CHURCH.

16. There now follows a brief Exposition of the Doctrine of the New Church, which is meant by the New Jerusalem in the *Apocalypse* (chaps. xxi. and xxii.). This doctrine, which is not only a doctrine of faith, but also of life, will be divided in the work itself into three parts.

THE FIRST PART will treat:—

    I. *Of the Lord God the Saviour, and of the Divine Trinity in Him.*
    II. *Of the Sacred Scripture, and its Two Senses, the Natural and the Spiritual, and of its Holiness thence derived.*
    III. *Of Love to God, and Love towards our Neighbor, and of their Agreement.*
    IV. *Of Faith, and its Conjunction with those Two Loves.*
    V. *The Doctrine of Life from the Commandments of the Decalogue.*
    VI. *Of Reformation and Regeneration.*
    VII. *Of Free-Will, and Man's Co-operation with the Lord thereby.*
    VIII. *Of Baptism.*
    IX. *Of the Holy Supper.*
    X. *Of Heaven and Hell.*
    XI. *Of Man's Conjunction therewith, and of the State of Man's Life after Death according to that Conjunction.*
    XII. *Of Eternal Life.*

THE SECOND PART will treat:—

    I. *Of the Consummation of the Age, or End of the present Church.*
    II. *Of the Coming of the Lord.*
    III. *Of the Last Judgment.*
    IV. *Of the New Church, which is the New Jerusalem.*

THE THIRD PART will point out the *Disagreements between the dogmas of the present church, and those of the New Church.* But we will dwell a little upon these now, because it is believed both by the clergy and laity, that the present church is in the light itself of the Gospel and in its truths, which cannot possibly be disproved, overturned, or controverted, not even by an angel if one should descend from heaven: neither does the present church see any otherwise, because it has withdrawn the understanding from faith, and yet has confirmed its dogmas by a kind of sight beneath the understanding, for falsities may there be confirmed even so as to appear like truths; and falsities there confirmed acquire a fallacious light, before which the light of truth appears as thick darkness. For this reason we shall here dwell a little upon this subject, mentioning the disagreements, and illustrating them by brief remarks, that such as have not their understanding closed by a blind faith, may see them as at first in twilight, and afterwards as in morning light, and at length, in the work itself, as in the light of day. The disagreements in general are as follows.

I.

17. *The churches which by the Reformation separated themselves from the Roman Catholic Church, differ in various things; but they all agree in the articles concerning a Trinity of Persons in the Divinity, original sin from Adam, imputation of the merit of Christ, and justification by faith alone.*

BRIEF ANALYSIS.

18. The churches which by the Reformation separated themselves from the Roman Catholic Church, are from those who call themselves Evangelical and Reformed, likewise Protestants, or from the names of their leaders, Lutherans and Calvinists, among which the church of England holds the middle place. We shall say nothing here of the Greek church, which long ago separated from the Roman Catholic church. That the Protestant churches differ in various things, particularly concerning the Holy Supper, Baptism, election, and the Person of Christ, is known to many; but that they all agree in the articles of a Trinity of Persons in the Divinity, original sin, imputation of the merit of Christ, and justification by faith alone, is not universally known. The reason of this is, because few study into the differences of dogmas among the churches, and consequently the agreements. It is only the clergy that study the dogmas of their church, while the laity rarely enter deeply into them, and consequently into their differences. That nevertheless they agree in the four articles above mentioned, both in their general principles, and in most of the particulars, will appear evident to any one if he will consult their books, or attend to their sermons. This, however, is premised and brought to the attention, on account of what follows.

II.

19. *The Roman Catholics, before the Reformation, taught exactly the same things as the Reformed did after it, concerning the four articles above mentioned, namely, a Trinity of Persons in the Divinity, original sin, the imputation of the merit of Christ, and justification by faith therein, only with this difference, that they conjoined that faith with charity or good works.*

BRIEF ANALYSIS.

20. That there is such a conformity between the Roman Catholics and the Protestants in these four articles, so that there is scarcely any important difference, except that the former conjoin faith and charity, while the latter divide between them, is scarcely known to any one, and indeed is so unknown, that the learned themselves will wonder at the assertion. The reason of this ignorance is, because the Roman Catholics rarely approach God our Saviour, but instead of Him, the Pope as His vicar, and likewise the saints; hence they have deeply buried in oblivion their dogmas concerning the imputation of the merit of Christ, and justification by faith. Nevertheless that these dogmas are received and acknowledged by them, evidently appears from the decrees of the Council of Trent, quoted above (n. 3–8) and confirmed by Pope Pius IV. (n. 2). If these be compared with the dogmas extracted from the Augsburg Confession, and from the Formula Concordiæ thence derived (n. 9–12), the difference between them will be found to be more verbal than real. The doctors of the church, by reading and comparing the above passages together, may indeed see some conformity between them, but still rather obscurely; that these, therefore, as well as those who are less learned, and also the laity, may see this, the subject shall be more clearly illustrated in what follows.

III.

21. *The leading reformers, Luther, Melancthon, and Calvin, retained all the dogmas concerning a Trinity of Persons in the Divinity, original sin, imputation of the merit of Christ, and justification by faith, just as they were and had been with the Roman Catholics; but they separated charity or good works from that faith, and declared that they were not at the same time saving, with a view to be totally severed from the Roman Catholics as to the very essentials of the church, which are faith and charity.*

BRIEF ANALYSIS.

22. That the four articles above mentioned, as at present taught in the churches of the Reformed were not new, and first broached by those three leaders, but were handed down from the time of the Council of Nice, and taught by the writers after that period, and thus preserved in the Roman Catholic church, is evident from the books of ecclesiastical history. The reason why the Roman Catholics and the Reformed agree in the article of a Trinity of Persons in the Divinity, is, because they both acknowledge the three creeds, the Apostles', the Nicene, and the Athanasian, in which a Trinity is taught. That they agree in the article of the imputation of the merit of Christ, is evident from the extracts from the Council of

Trent (n. 3–8) compared with those from *The Formula Concordiæ* (n. 10–15). Their agreement in the article of justification shall now be the subject of discussion.

23. The Council of Trent delivers this concerning justifying faith: "It has always been the consensus of the Catholic church, that faith is the beginning of man's salvation, the foundation and root of all justification, without which it is impossible to please God, and attain to the fellowship of His sons," see above (n. 5). (*a*) Also, "That faith comes by hearing the Word of God" (n. 4). (*c*) Moreover that Roman Catholic council joined faith and charity, or faith and good works, may clearly be seen from the quotations above (n. 4, 5, 7, 8). But that the Reformed churches, from their leaders, have separated them, declaring salvation to consist in faith, and not at the same time in charity or works, to the intent that they might be totally severed from the Roman Catholics, as to the very essentials of the church, which are faith and charity, I have frequently heard from the above mentioned leaders themselves. As also, that they established such separation by the following considerations, namely, "that no one can do good which confers salvation of himself, nor can he fulfil the law"; and moreover, lest thereby any merit in man should enter into faith. That from these principles, and with this view, they excluded the goods of charity from faith, and thereby also from salvation, is plain from the quotations from *The Formula Concordiæ* above (n. 12); among which are these: "That faith does not justify, as being formed by charity, as the Papists allege (n. 12). (*b*) That the position, that good works are necessary to salvation, ought to be rejected for many reasons, and among others, because they are accepted by the Papists to support an evil cause (n. 12). (*h*) That the decree of the Council of Trent that good works preserve and retain salvation and faith, is deservedly to be rejected" [n. 12 (*n*)]; besides many other things there. That still, however, the Reformed conjoin faith and charity into one at the same time saving, and only differ from the Roman Catholics respecting the quality of the works, will be shown in the following article.

IV.

24. *Nevertheless the leading reformers adjoined good works, and also conjoined them, to their faith, but in man as a passive subject: whereas the Roman Catholics conjoin them in man as an active subject; and that notwithstanding this, there is actually a conformity between the one and the other as to faith, works, and merits.*

BRIEF ANALYSIS.

25. That the leading reformers, although they separated faith and charity, still adjoined and even conjoined them, but would not admit of their being united into one, so as to be both together saving, is evident from their books, sermons, and declarations; for after they have separated them, they conjoin them, and even express this conjunction in clear terms, and not in such as admit of two senses; as for instance in the following. That faith after justification is never alone, but is accompanied by charity or good works, and if not, that faith is not living but dead, see above [n. 13 (*o*) (*p*) (*q*) (*r*) (*y*) (*bb*)]. Yea that good works necessarily follow faith [n. 13 (*x*) (*y*) (*z*)]. Then that the regenerate person, by new powers and gifts, co-operates with the Holy Spirit [n. 13 (*aa*)]. That the Roman Catholics teach exactly the same is plain from the passages collected from the Council of Trent (n. 4–8).

26. That the reformers profess nearly the same things with the Roman Catholics concerning the merits of works, is evident from the following quotations from *The Formula Concordiæ*. That good works are rewarded by virtue of the promise and by grace, and that from thence they merit rewards both temporal and spiritual [n. 14 (*i*) (*k*) (*l*) (*n*)]. And that God crowns His own gifts with a reward [n. 14 (*n*)]. The like is asserted in the Council of Trent, namely, That God of His grace makes His own gifts to be merits [n. 5 (*f*)]. And moreover, that salvation is not of works, but of promise and grace, because God operates them by the Holy Spirit [n. 5 (*e*) (*f*) (*g*) (*h*) (*i*) (*k*)].

27. From comparing the one and the other, it appears at the first view, as though there was an entire conformity between them; but lest this should be the case, the reformers distinguished between the works of the law proceeding from man's purpose and will, and works of the spirit proceeding from faith as from a free and spontaneous source, which latter they called the fruits of faith, as may be seen above [n. 11. (*h*) (*l*)], and [n. 13 (*a*) (*i*) (*l*)], and [n. 15 (*k*)]. Hence, on an accurate examination and comparison, there does not appear to be any difference in the works themselves, but only in the quality of them, namely, that the latter sort proceed from man as from a passive subject, but the former as from an active subject; consequently they are spontaneous when they proceed from man's understanding, and not at the same time from his will. This is said, because man, while he does good works, cannot but be conscious that he is doing them, and consciousness is from the understanding. Nevertheless, as the Reformed likewise preach the exercise of repentance, and wrestlings with the flesh [n. 13 (*d*) (*e*) (*f*) (*g*) (*h*) (*k*)], and these cannot be done by man but from his purpose and will, and thus by him as from himself, it follows, that there is still an actual conformity.

28. As regards free-will in conversion, or in the act of justification, it appears as if their dogmas were entirely opposite to each other; but that they still agree, may be seen if we duly consider and compare the passages transcribed from the Council of Trent [n. 6 (*a*) (*b*)], with those from *The Formula Concordiæ* [n. 15 (*m*)]; for in Christian countries all are baptized, and from thence are in a state of free-will, so as to be enabled not only to hear the Word of God, but likewise to assent to the same, and embrace it by faith; consequently no one in the Christian world is like a stock.

29. Hence then appears the truth of what is asserted (n. 19 and n. 21), namely, that the reformers derived their opinions concerning a Trinity of Persons in the Divinity, original sin, the imputation of the merit of Christ, and justification by faith, from the Roman Catholics. These things have been advanced, in order to point out the origin of their dogmas, especially the origin of the separation of faith from good works, or the doctrine of faith alone, and to show that it was with no other view than to be severed from the Roman Catholics, and that, after all, their disagreement is more in words than in reality. From the passages above adduced, it evidently appears upon what foundation the faith of the Reformed churches has been erected and from what inspiration it took its rise.

V.

30. *The whole system of Theology in the Christian world, at this day, is founded on an idea of Three Gods, arising from the doctrine of a Trinity of Persons.*

BRIEF ANALYSIS.

31. We will first say something concerning the origin or source from whence the idea of a Trinity of Persons in the Divinity, and thereby of three Gods, proceeded. There are three Creeds, which are called the Apostles', the Nicene, and the Athanasian, which specifically teach a Trinity: the Apostles' and the Nicene assert simply a Trinity, but the Athanasian a Trinity of Persons. These three Creeds are to be met with in many Psalters, the Apostles' Creed next the Psalm which is sung, the Nicene after the Decalogue, and the Athanasian apart by itself.* The Apostles' Creed was written after the times of the Apostles; the Nicene Creed at the Council of Nice, a city of Bithynia, to which all the bishops in Asia, Africa, and Europe, were summoned by the Emperor Constantine, in the year 325[1]; but the Athanasian Creed was composed since that council by one or more persons, with an intent utterly to overthrow the Arians and was afterwards received by the churches as œcumenical. In the two former creeds the confession of a Trinity was evident, but from the third or Athanasian Creed the profession of a Trinity of Persons was spread abroad: that hence arose the idea of three Gods, shall now be shown.

32. That there is a Divine Trinity, is manifest from the Lord's words in *Matthew:*—

Jesus said, go make disciples of all nations, baptizing them in the name of the Father, of the Son, and of the Holy Spirit (chap. xxviii. 19).

And from these words in the same:—

When Jesus was baptized, lo, the heavens were opened unto Him, and He saw the Holy Spirit descending like a dove, and coming upon Him, and lo, a voice from heaven, this is My beloved Son, in whom I am well pleased (chap. iii. 16, 17).

* This relates to the Protestant churches on the continent of Europe.

The reason why the Lord sent His disciples to baptize in the name of the Father, Son and Holy Spirit, was, because in Him then glorified there was the Divine Trinity; for in the preceding verse 18, He says:—

All power is given unto Me in heaven and in earth.

And in the 20th verse following:—

Lo; I am with you all the days, even unto the consummation of the age.

Thus He spoke of Himself alone, and not of three. And in *John:*—

The Holy Spirit was not yet, because Jesus was not yet glorified (chap. vii. 39).

The former words He uttered after His glorification, and His glorification was His complete unition with His Father, Who was the Divine itself in Him from conception; and the Holy Spirit was the Divine proceeding from Him glorified (*John* xx. 22).

33. The reason why the idea of three Gods has principally arisen from the Athanasian Creed, where a Trinity of Persons is taught, is, because the word Person begets such an idea, which is further implanted in the mind by the following words in the same Creed: "*There is one Person of the Father, another of the Son, and another of the Holy Spirit*"; and afterwards: "*The Father is God and Lord, the Son is God and Lord, and the Holy Spirit is God and Lord*"; but more especially by these: "*For like as we are compelled by the Christian verity to acknowledge every Person by Himself to be God and Lord, so are we forbidden by the Catholic religion to say there be three Gods or three Lords*"; the result of which words is this, that by the Christian verity we are bound to confess and acknowledge three Gods and three Lords, but by the Catholic religion we are not allowed to say, or to name three Gods and Lords; consequently we may have an idea of three Gods and Lords, but not an oral confession of them. Nevertheless, that the doctrine of the Trinity in the Athanasian Creed is agreeable to the truth, if only instead of a Trinity of Persons there be substituted a Trinity of Person, which Trinity is in God the Saviour Jesus

Christ, may be seen in *The Doctrine of the New Jerusalem concerning the Lord*, published at Amsterdam, in the year 1763 (n. 55–61.)

34. It is to be observed, that in the Apostles' Creed it is said, "*I believe in God the Father, in Jesus Christ, and in the Holy Spirit*"; in the Nicene Creed, "*I believe in one God, the Father, in one Lord Jesus Christ, and in the Holy Spirit,*" thus only in one God; but in the Athanasian Creed it is, "*In God the Father, God the Son, and God the Holy Spirit,*" thus in three Gods. But whereas the authors and favorers of this creed clearly saw that an idea of three Gods would unavoidably result from the expressions therein used, therefore, in order to remedy this, they asserted that one substance or essence belongs to the three; but still there arises from thence no other idea, than that there are three Gods unanimous and agreeing together: for when it is said of the three that their substance or essence is one and indivisible, it does not remove the idea of three, but confounds it, because the expression is a metaphysical one, and the science of metaphysics, with all its ingenuity, cannot of three Persons, each whereof is God, make one; it may indeed make of them one in the mouth, but never in the idea.

35. That the whole Christian theology at this day is founded on an idea of three Gods, is evident from the doctrine of justification, which is the head of the doctrines of the church with Christians, both among Roman Catholics and Protestants. That doctrine sets forth that God the Father sent His Son to redeem and save men, and give the Holy Spirit to operate the same; every man who hears, reads, or repeats this, cannot but in his thought, that is, in his idea, divide God into three, and perceive that one God sent another, and operates by a third. That the same thought of a Divine Trinity distinguished into three Persons, each whereof is God, is continued throughout the rest of the doctrinals of the present church, as from a head into its body, will be demonstrated in its proper place. In the meantime consult what has been premised concerning justification, consult theology in general and in particular, and at the same time, consult yourself, while listening to preachings in temples, or while praying at home, whether you have any other perception and thought thence resulting than of three

Gods; and especially while you are praying or singing first to one, and then to the other two separately, as is often done. Hence is established the truth of the proposition, that the whole theology in the Christian world at this day, is founded on an idea of three Gods.

36. That a trinity of Gods is contrary to the Sacred Scripture, is known, for we read:—

Am not I Jehovah, and there is no God else beside Me, a just God and a Saviour, there is none beside Me (*Isa.* xlv. 21, 22).

I Jehovah am thy God, and thou shalt acknowledge no God beside Me, and there is no Saviour beside Me (*Hos.* xiii. 4).

Thus said Jehovah the King of Israel and his Redeemer, Jehovah of Hosts, I am the First and the Last, and beside Me there is no God (*Isa.* xliv. 6).

Jehovah of Hosts is His name, and thy Redeemer the Holy One of Israel, the God of the whole earth shall He be called (*Isa.* liv. 5).

In that day Jehovah shall be King over the whole earth; in that day there shall be one Jehovah, and His name One (*Zech.* xiv. 9).

Beside many more passages elsewhere.

37. That a trinity of Gods is contrary to enlightened reason, may appear from many considerations. What man of sound reason can bear to hear that three Gods created the world; or that creation and preservation, redemption and salvation, together with reformation and regeneration, are the work of three Gods, and not of one God? And on the other hand, what man of sound reason is not willing to hear that the same God who created us, redeemed us, and regenerates and saves us? As the latter sentiment, and not the former, enters into the reason, there is therefore no nation upon the face of the whole earth, possessed of religion and sound reason, but what acknowledges one God. That the Mohammedans, and certain nations in Asia and Africa, abhor Christianity, because they believe that it worships three Gods, is known; and the only answer of the Christians is, that the three have one essence, and thus are one God. I can affirm, that from the reason which has been given me, I can clearly see, that neither the world, nor the angelic heaven, nor the church, nor anything therein, could have existed, nor can subsist, but from one God.

38. Here I will add something from the *Confession of the Dutch Churches* received at the *Synod of Dort,* which is this:

"I believe in one God, who is one essence, in which are three Persons, truly and really distinct, incommunicable properties from eternity, namely, the Father, the Son, and the Holy Spirit; the Father is of all things, both visible and invisible, the cause, origin, and beginning; the Son is the Word, wisdom, and image of the Father; the Holy Spirit is the eternal virtue and power proceeding from the Father and the Son. However, it must be confessed, that this doctrine far exceeds the comprehension of the human mind; we must therefore wait till we come to heaven for a perfect knowledge thereof."

VI.

39. *The dogmas of that theology appear to be erroneous, after the idea of a Trinity of Persons, and thence of three Gods has been rejected, and the idea of One God, in whom is the Divine Trinity, is received in its stead.*

BRIEF ANALYSIS.

40. The reason why the dogmas of the present church, which are founded upon the idea of three Gods, derived from the doctrine of a Trinity of Persons literally understood, appear erroneous, after the idea of one God, in whom is the Divine Trinity, has been received in its stead, is, because, till this truth is received, we cannot see what is erroneous. The case herein is like a person, who in the night time, by the light of some stars only, sees various objects, especially images, and believes them to be living men; or like one, who in the twilight before sunrise, as he lies in his bed, fancies he sees spectres in the air, and believes them to be angels; or like a person, who sees many things in the delusive light of fantasy, and believes them to be real; such things, it is known, do not appear according to their true qualities, until the person comes into the light of the day, that is, until he comes into the light of the understanding awake. The case is the same with the spiritual things of the church, which have been erroneously and falsely perceived, and also confirmed, when genuine truths also present themselves to be seen in their own light, which is the light of heaven. Who is there that cannot understand, that all dogmas founded on the idea of three Gods, must be interiorly erroneous and false? I say interiorly, because the idea of God enters into all things of the church, religion, and worship; and theological matters have their residence above all others in the human mind, and the idea of God is in the supreme place there; wherefore if this be false, all beneath it, in consequence of the principle from whence they flow, must likewise be false or falsified: for that which is supreme, being also the inmost, constitutes the very essence of all that is derived from it; and the essence, like a soul, forms them into a body, after its own image; and when in its descent it lights upon truths, it even infects them with its own blemish and error. The idea of three Gods in theology may be compared to a disease seated in the heart or lungs, in which the patient fancies himself to be in health, because his physician, not knowing his disease, persuades him that he is so; but if the physician knows it, and still persuades, he may justly be charged with deep malignity.

VII.

41. *Then truly saving faith, which is faith in one God, united with good works, is acknowledged and received.*

BRIEF ANALYSIS.

42. The reason why this faith, which is a faith in one God, is ackowledged and received as truly saving, when the former faith, which is a faith in three gods, is rejected, is because till this is the case it cannot be seen in its own form; for the faith of the present day is set forth as the only saving faith, because it is a faith in one God, and a faith in the Saviour; but still there are two faces of that faith, the one internal and the other external; its internal face is formed from the perception of three Gods, for who perceives or thinks otherwise? let every one consult himself; but its external face is formed from the confession of one God, for who confesses or speaks otherwise? let every one consult himself. These two faces are altogether discordant with each other; so that the external is not acknowledged by the internal, nor is the internal known by the external. From this disagreement, and the vanishing of the one out of sight of the other, a confused idea of things pertaining to salvation has been conceived and brought forth in the church. It is otherwise when the internal and external faces agree together, and mutually regard and acknowledge each other as one unanimous thing; that this is the case, when one God, in whom is the Divine Trinity, is not only perceived by the mind, but is likewise acknowledged by the mouth, is self-evident. That the dogma of the Father's being alienated from mankind, is then abolished, and thence also that of His reconciliation; and that an altogether different doctrine goes forth concerning imputation, remission of sins, regeneration, and salvation thence derived, will clearly be seen in the work itself, in the light of reason illustrated by Divine truths from the Sacred Scripture. This faith is called a faith united with good works, because faith in one God without union with good works is not given.

VIII.

43. *And this faith is in God the Saviour Jesus Christ, which in its simple form is as follows:*—I. *That there is One God in Whom is the Divine Trinity, and He is the Lord Jesus Christ.* II. *Saving Faith is to believe in Him.* III. *Evils ought to be shunned, because they are of the devil, and from the devil.* IV. *Goods ought to be done, because they are of God, and from God.* V. *And they ought to be done by man as of himself, but it is to be believed that they are from the Lord, with him and through him.*

BRIEF ANALYSIS.

44. This is the faith of the New Church in its simple form, which will appear more fully in the Appendix, and in its full form in the work itself, in its First Part; where we shall treat of the Lord God the Saviour, and of the Trinity in Him; of love to God, and love towards the neighbor; of faith and its conjunction with those two loves; and also in the other parts, which will follow in order there. But it is necessary that this preliminary concerning that faith should here be briefly illustrated. Its *first*, namely, That there is one God, in whom there is the Divine Trinity, and He is the Lord Jesus Christ, is summarily illustrated in the following manner. It is a certain and established truth, that God is one, and His essence is indivisible, and that there is a Trinity; since, therefore, God is One, and His essence is indivisible, it follows, that God is one Person, and when He is one Person, that the Trinity is in that Person. That this is the Lord Jesus Christ, appears from this, that He was conceived from God the Father (*Luke* i. 34, 35); and thus as to His soul and life itself He is God; and therefore, as He Himself said, that:—

The Father and He are One (*John* x. 30).
He is in the Father, and the Father in Him (*John* xiv. 10, 11).
He who seeth Him and knoweth Him, seeth and knoweth the Father (*John* xiv. 7, 9).
No one seeth and knoweth the Father, but He who is in the bosom of the Father (*John* i. 18).
All things of the Father are His (*John* iii. 35; xvi. 15).
He is the Way, the Truth, and the Life, and no one cometh unto the Father but by Him (*John* xiv. 6);

thus from Him, because He is in Him, and thus is He Himself; and according to Paul that:—

All the fulness of the Divinity dwells in Him bodily (*Col.* ii. 9).

And according to *Isaiah:*—

Unto us a Boy is born, unto us a Son is given, whose name is God, *Father of Eternity* (ix. 5).

And again, that:—

He hath power over all flesh (*John* xvii. 2).

And:—

He hath all power in heaven and on earth (*Matt.* xxviii. 18).

Thence it follows that He is the God of heaven and earth. *Second*, That saving faith is to believe in Him, is illustrated by these:—

Jesus said, he that believeth in Me, shall not die to eternity, but shall live (*John* xi. 25, 26).

This is the will of the Father, that every one who believeth in the Son may have eternal life (*John* vi. 40).

God so loved the world, that He gave His Only-begotten Son, that whosoever believeth in Him, should not perish, but have eternal life (*John* iii. 15, 16).

He that believeth in the Son, hath eternal life, but he that believeth not the Son, shall not see life, but the wrath of God abideth on him (*John* iii. 36).

The three remaining propositions, namely, That evils ought to be shunned, because they are of the devil and from the devil; and that goods ought to be done, because they are of God and from God; but that it is to be believed that they are from the Lord, with him and through him. There is no need to illustrate and demonstrate these; for the whole Sacred Scripture, from beginning to end, proves them, and, in short, teaches nothing else but to shun evils, and do goods, and to believe in the Lord God. Besides, without these three there is not any religion, for religion is of the life; and life is to shun evils and do goods, and man cannot do goods and shun evils except as of himself. Wherefore if these three are removed from the church, the Sacred Scripture, together with religion, is likewise removed at the same time: which being removed the church is not a church. For a further account of the faith of the New Church, in its universal and particular form, see below (n. 116, 117); all which will be demonstrated in the work itself.

IX.

45. *The faith of the present day has separated religion from the church, since religion consists in the acknowledgment of One God, and in the worship of Him from the faith of charity.*

BRIEF ANALYSIS.

46. What nation is there in the whole world, which has religion and sound reason, that does not know and believe, that there is one God, and that to do evils is contrary to Him, and that to do goods is with Him, and that man must do this from his soul, from his heart, and from his strength, although they inflow from God, and that herein religion consists? Who therefore does not see, that to confess three Persons in the Divinity, and to declare that in good works there is nothing of salvation, is to separate religion from the church? For it is declared that in good works there is not salvation, in these words: That faith justifies without good works [n. 12 (*a*) (*b*)]; that works are not necessary to salvation, nor to faith, because salvation and faith are neither preserved nor retained by good works [n. 12 (*g*) (*h*) (*m*) (*n*)]; consequently, that there is no bond of conjunction between faith and good works. It is indeed said afterwards, that good works nevertheless spontaneously follow faith, as fruit is produced from a tree [n. 13 (*l*) (*n*)]. But then who does them, yea, who thinks of them, or who is spontaneously led to perform them, while he knows and believes that they contribute nothing to salvation, and also, that no one can do any good thing towards salvation of himself, and so on? If it is said, that still they have conjoined faith with good works; we reply, this conjunction when closely inspected, is not conjunction, but it is mere adjunction, and this only like a superfluous appendage, that neither coheres nor adheres in any other manner than as a dark background to a picture, from which the picture appears more living. And because religion is of the life, and this consists in good works according to the truths of faith, it is evident that religion is the picture itself, and not the mere appendage; yea, with many it is like the tail of a horse, which because it avails nothing, may be cut off at pleasure. Who can rationally conclude otherwise, while he perceives such expressions as these according to their obvious meaning: That it is a folly to dream that the works of the second table of the Decalogue justify before God [n. 12 (*d*)]; and these: That if any one believes he shall therefore obtain salvation, because he hath charity, he brings reproach upon Christ [n. 12 (*e*)]; as also these: That good works are utterly to be excluded, in treating of justification and eternal life [n. 12 (*f*)]; with more to the same purpose? Who, therefore, when he reads afterwards, that good works necessarily follow faith, and that if they do not follow, the faith is a false and not a true faith [n. 13 (*p*) (*q*) (*y*)], with more to the same purpose, attends to it? or if he attends to it, understands whether such good works are attended with any perception? Yet good flowing forth from man without perception is inanimate as if from a statue. But if we inquire more deeply into the rise of this doctrine, it will appear as though the leading reformers first laid down faith alone as their rule, in order that they might be severed from the Roman Catholics, as mentioned above (n. 21, 22, 23); and that afterwards they adjoined thereto the works of charity, that it might not appear to contradict the Sacred Scripture, but have the semblance of religion, and thus be healed.

X.

47. *The faith of the present church cannot be conjoined with charity, and produce any fruits, which are good works.*

BRIEF ANALYSIS.

48. Before this is demonstrated, we shall first explain the origin and nature of charity, and the origin and nature of faith, and thus the origin and nature of good works, which are called fruits. Faith is truth, wherefore the doctrine of faith is the doctrine of truth; and the doctrine of truth is of the understanding, and thence of the thought, and from this of the speech; wherefore it teaches what we are to will and do, thus that evils and what evils are to be shunned, and that goods and what goods are to be done. When man does goods then goods thence conjoin themselves with truths, because the will is conjoined with the understanding, for good is of the will, and truth is of the understanding; from this conjunction the affection of good exists, which in its essence is charity, and the affection of truth, which in its essence is faith, and these two united together constitute a marriage. From this marriage good works are produced, as fruits from a tree; and hence they are the fruits of good, and the fruits of truth; the latter are signified in the Word by grapes, but the former by olives.

49. From this generation of good works, it is evident, that faith alone cannot possibly produce or beget any works, that are called fruits, any more than a woman alone without a man can produce any offspring; wherefore the fruits of faith is an empty expression and word. Besides, in the whole world nothing ever was or can be produced, but from a marriage, one of which has relation to good, and the other to truth, or in the opposite sense, one to evil, and the other to falsity; consequently no works can be conceived, much less be born, but from such marriage, good works from the marriage of good and truth, and evil works from the marriage of evil and falsity.

50. The reason why charity cannot be conjoined with the faith of the present church, and consequently why good works cannot be born from any marriage, is because imputation supplies everything, remits guilt, justifies, regenerates, sanctifies, imparts the life of heaven and thus salvation, and all this freely, without any works of man; what then is charity, which ought to be united with faith, but something superfluous and vain, and a mere addition and supplement to imputation and justification, to which nevertheless it is of no avail? Besides, a faith founded on the idea of three Gods is erroneous, as has been shown above (n. 39, 40); and with an erroneous faith, charity, that in itself is charity, cannot be conjoined. There are two reasons given for believing that there is no bond of union between that faith and charity; the one is, because they make their faith spiritual, but charity natural moral, thinking that there is not given any conjunction of the spiritual with the natural; the other reason is, lest anything of man, and so anything of merit, should inflow into their faith alone, as saving. Furthermore, between charity and that faith there is no bond, but there is with the new faith, which may be seen below (n. 116, 117).

XI.

51. *From the faith of the present church there results a worship of the mouth and not of the life, whereas the worship of the mouth is accepted by the Lord according to the worship of the life.*

BRIEF ANALYSIS.

52. This is testified by experience. How many are there at this day, who live according to the commandments of the Decalogue, and other precepts of the Lord, from religion? And how many are there at this day, who desire to look their own evils in the face, and to perform actual repentance, and thus enter upon the worship of the life? And who among those that cultivate piety, perform any other repentance than oral and oratorical, confessing themselves to be sinners, and praying, according to the doctrine of the church, that God the Father, for the sake of His Son, who suffered upon the cross for their sins, took away their damnation, and atoned for them with His blood, would mercifully forgive their transgressions, that so they might be presented without spot or blemish before the throne of His judgment? Who does not see, that this worship is of the lungs only, and not of the heart, consequently that it is external worship, and not internal? for he prays for the remission of sins, when yet he does not know one sin with himself; and if he did know of any, he would cover it over with favor and indulgence, or with a faith that is to purify and absolve him, without any works of his. But this is comparatively like a servant going to his master with his face and clothes defiled with soot and filth, and saying, Sir, wash me. Would not his master say to him, Thou foolish servant, what is it thou sayest? See! there is water, soap, and a towel, hast thou not hands, and ability to use them? wash thyself. Thus also the Lord God will say, The means of purification are from Me, and from Me also thou hast will and power, wherefore use these My gifts and talents, as thy own, and thou shalt be purified. Take another example by way of illustration. Suppose you should pray a thousand times at home and in temples, that God the Father, for the sake of His Son, would preserve you from the devil, and should not at the same time, from the freedom in which you are perpetually held by the Lord, keep yourself from evil, and so from the devil; you could not in this case be preserved even by legions of angels sent from the Lord; for the Lord cannot act contrary to His own Divine order, and His order is that man should examine himself, see his evils, resist them, and this as of himself, yet from the Lord. This does not indeed at this day appear to be the Gospel, nevertheless it is the Gospel, for the Gospel is salvation by the Lord. The reason why the worship of the mouth is accepted by the Lord according to the worship of the life, is because the speech of man before God, and before angels, has its sound from the affection of his love and faith, and these two are in man according to his life; wherefore, if the love of God and faith in Him are in your life, the sound of your voice will be like that of a dove; but if self-love and self-confidence are in your life, the sound of your voice will be like that of an owl, howsoever you may bend your voice to imitate the voice of a turtle-dove. The spiritual, which is within the sound, effects this.

XII.

53. *The doctrine of the present church is interwoven with many paradoxes, which are to be embraced by faith; and therefore its dogmas gain admission into the memory only, and not into any part of the understanding above the memory, but merely into confirmations below it.*

BRIEF ANALYSIS.

54. The rulers of the church insist, that the understanding is to be kept under obedience to faith, yea that faith, properly speaking, is a faith in what is unknown, which is blind, or a faith of the night. This is the first paradox; for faith is of truth, and truth is of faith; and truth, before it can become an object of faith, should be in its own light and be seen; otherwise what is false may be believed. The paradoxes flowing from such a faith are many; as that God the Father begat a Son from eternity, and that the Holy Spirit proceeds from both, and that each is a Person by Himself, and God; that the Lord both as to His soul and body, is from the mother; that those three Persons, consequently three Gods, created the universe; and that one of them descended, and assumed the Human, to reconcile the Father, and thus to save men; and that they who by grace obtain faith, and believe these paradoxes, are saved by the imputation, application, and translation of His justice to themselves; and that man, at his first reception of that faith, is like a statue, a stock or a stone, and that faith inflows by the mere hearing of the Word; and that faith alone without the works of the law, and not formed from charity, is saving; and that it produces the remission of sins without any previous repentance; and that, merely by virtue of such remission of sins, the impenitent are justified, regenerated, and sanctified; and that afterwards charity, good works, and repentance, spontaneously follow. Besides many similar things, which, like offspring from an illegitimate bed, have all issued from the doctrine founded on the idea of three Gods.

55. What wise man does not see, that such things enter only into the memory, and not into the understanding above the memory, although they may be confirmed by reasonings from appearances and fallacies below it? for to the human understanding there are two kinds of light, one from heaven, and the other from the world. The light from heaven, which is spiritual, flows into the human mind above the memory, but the light from the world, which is natural, below it. That man, from this latter light, can confirm whatever he pleases, and falsities equally as well as truths, and that after confirmation he sees falsities altogether as truths, has been shown in a Relation inserted in the work lately published concerning *Conjugial Love* (n. 233).

56. To these things shall be added this arcanum from heaven. All these paradoxes, according to their confirmations, abide in the minds of men, bound together as into one bundle, or wound up together as into one ball, and they enter at the same time into every individual proposition that is stated from the doctrine of the church; so that when either faith, charity, or repentance, and still more when imputation or justification is mentioned, they all enter and are included in each particular. Man himself does not perceive that congeries or aggregation of the paradoxes in every individual proposition; but the angels that are with man perceive it, and they call it *malua,* that is, confusion and darkness.

57. I foresee that very many at this day, tinctured with the paradoxes of this faith, will say, how can theological things be perceived by the understanding? are they not spiritual which transcend it? Explain, therefore, if you can, the mystery of redemption and justification, that reason may see it and acquiesce. This mystery then shall be opened in the following manner. Who does not know that God is one, and that besides Him there is no other, and that God is love itself, and wisdom itself, or that He is good itself, and truth itself; and that the very God Himself as to Divine truth, which is the Word, descended and assumed the Human to remove the hells, and consequently damnation from man, which he effected by combats with, and victories over the devil, that is, over all the hells, which at that time infested and spiritually slew every man coming into the world; and that afterwards He glorified His Human, by uniting in it the Divine truth with Divine good, and thus He returned to the Father from whom He came forth? When these things are perceived, then the following passage in *John* may be understood:—

> The Word was with God, and God was the Word, and the Word became flesh (chap. i. 1, 14).

And also the following in the same:—

> I went forth from the Father, and came into the world; again I leave the world and go to the Father (xvi. 28, 29).

Hence also it is evident, that without the coming of the Lord into the world, no mortal could have been saved, and they are saved who believe in Him, and live well. This face of faith presents itself as clear as the day to those who are enlightened by the Word, and it is the face of the faith of the New Church. See the FAITH OF THE NEW HEAVEN AND OF THE NEW CHURCH IN ITS UNIVERSAL AND IN ITS PARTICULAR FORM, below (n. 116, 117).

XIII.

58. *The dogmas of the present church cannot be learned and retained without great difficulty, nor can they be preached or taught without using great care and caution to conceal their nakedness, because true reason neither perceives nor receives them.*

BRIEF ANALYSIS.

59. That the understanding is to be kept under obedience to faith, is set as a motto before the dogmas of the present church, to denote that their interiors are mysteries, or arcana, which, because they transcend, cannot flow into the superior region of the understanding, and be there perceived, see above (n. 54). Those ministers of the church who are ambitious to be eminent for their reputation of wisdom, and wish to be looked upon as oracles in spiritual things, imbibe and swallow down in the schools, such things especially as surpass the comprehension of others, which they do with avidity, but nevertheless with difficulty. And because they are thence accounted wise, and they who have distinguished and enriched themselves from such hidden stores are honored with doctors' caps and episcopal robes, they revolve in their thoughts, and teach from their pulpits, scarce anything else but mysteries concerning justification by faith alone, and good works as her humble attendants. And from their erudition concerning both faith and good works, they in a wonderful manner sometimes separate them, and sometimes conjoin them; comparatively as if they held faith by itself in one hand, and the works of charity in the other, and at one time extend their arms and so separate them, and at another time bring their hands together and so conjoin them. But this shall be illustrated by examples. They teach, that good works are not necessary to salvation, because if done by man they are meritorious; at the same time they also teach, that good works necessarily follow faith, and that both together make one in the article of salvation. They teach that faith without good works, as being alive, justifies; and at the same time, that faith without good works, as being dead, does not justify. They teach, that faith is neither preserved nor retained by good works; and at the same time, that good works proceed from faith, as fruit from a tree, light from the sun, and heat from fire. They teach, that good works being adjoined to faith make it perfect; and at the same time, that being conjoined as in a marriage, or in one form, they deprive faith of its saving essence. They teach, that a Christian is not under the law; and at the same time, that he must be in the daily practice of the law. They teach, that if good works are intermixed in the business of salvation by faith, as in the remission of sins, justification, regeneration, vivification, and salvation, they are hurtful; but if not intermixed, that they are profitable. They teach, that God crowns His own gifts, which are good works, with rewards also spiritual, but not with salvation and eternal life, because faith without works, they say, is entitled to the crown of eternal life. They teach, that faith alone is like a queen, who walks in a stately manner with good works as her train of attendants behind her; but if these join themselves to her in front, and kiss her, she is cast from her throne and called an adulteress. But particularly, when they teach faith and good works at the same time, they view merit on the one hand, and no merit on the other, making choice of expressions which they use in two different senses; one for the laity, and the other for the clergy; for the laity, that its nakedness may not appear, and for the clergy, that it may. Consider now, whether any one hearing such things can draw from them any doctrine leading to salvation, or whether he will not rather, from the apparent contradictions therein, become blind, and afterwards grope for the objects of salvation, like one walking in the dark. Who in this case can tell from the evidence of works, whether he has any faith or not; and whether it is better to omit good works on account of the danger of merit, or to do them for fear of the loss of faith? But do you, my friend, tear yourself away from such contradictions, and shun evils as sins, and do goods, and believe in the Lord, and saving justification will be given you.

XIV.

60. *The doctrine of the faith of the present church ascribes to God human properties; as, that He regarded man from anger, that He wished to be reconciled, that He is reconciled through the love He bore toward the Son, and by His intercession; and that He wished to be appeased by the sight of His Son's sufferings, and thus to be brought back to mercy; and that He imputes* *the justice of His Son to an unjust man who supplicates it from faith alone; and that thus from an enemy He makes him a friend, and from a child of wrath, a child of grace.*

BRIEF ANALYSIS.

61. Who does not know that God is mercy and clemency itself, because He is love itself, and good itself, and that these are His *esse* or essence? And who does not thence see, that it is a contradiction to say, that mercy itself, or good itself, can look at man from anger, become his enemy, turn Himself away from him, and determine on his damnation, and still continue to be the same Divine *esse* or God? Such things can scarcely be attributed to an upright man, but only to a wicked man, nor to an angel of heaven, but only to an angel of hell; wherefore it is heinous to ascribe them to God. That they have been ascribed to Him, appears evident from the declarations of many fathers, councils, and churches, from the first ages to the present day; and also from the inferences which have necessarily followed from first principles into their derivatives, or from causes into their effects, as from a head into the members; such as, that He wishes to be reconciled; that He is reconciled through love to the Son, and through His intercession and mediation; that He wishes to be appeased by the view of the extreme sufferings of His Son, and so to be brought back and as it were compelled to mercy, and thus from an enemy to be made a friend, and to adopt those who were the sons of wrath as the sons of grace. That to impute the justice and merits of His Son to an unjust man, who supplicates it from faith alone, is also merely human, will be seen in the last analysis of this little work.

62. They who have seen that merely human properties are unworthy of God, and yet are attributed to Him, in order to defend the system of justification once conceived, and to veil that appearance, have said that anger, revenge, damnation, and the like, are predicated of His justice, and are therefore mentioned in many parts of the Word, and as it were appropriated to God. But by the anger of God in the Word, is signified evil in man, which, because it is against God, is called the anger of God; not that God is angry with man, but that man from his evil is angry with God; and because there is in evil its own punishment, as in good its own reward, therefore while evil punishes the evil-doer, it appears as if God did it. For this is like a criminal, who attributes his punishment to the law, or like one who blames the fire for burning him when he puts his hand into it, or a drawn sword for wounding him when he rushes upon the point of it, while in the hand of one defending himself. Such is the justice of God. But of this more may be seen in *The Apocalypse Revealed*, where it treats of justice and judgment in God and from God (n. 668). That anger is ascribed to Him, may be seen (n. 635); as likewise revenge (n. 658); but this is in the sense of the letter, because that sense is written by appearances and correspondences, yet not in the spiritual sense, wherein truth is in its own light. This I can affirm, that whenever the angels hear any one say, that God from anger determined on the damnation of the human race, and as an enemy was reconciled by His Son, as by another God begotten from Himself, they are affected in a manner similar to those, who from an uneasiness in their bowels and stomach are excited to vomiting; saying, What can be more insane than to affirm such things of God?

63. The reason why they have ascribed human properties to God, is, because all spiritual perception and illustration is from the Lord alone; for the Lord is the Word or the Divine truth, and:—

He is the true light which enlighteneth every man (*John* i. 9).

He also says:—

I am come a light into the world, that whosoever believeth in Me, may not abide in darkness (*John* xii. 46).

And this light, and the perception thence derived, inflows with those who acknowledge Him as the God of heaven and earth and approach Him alone, and not with those who cherish an idea of three Gods, which has been the case from the time the Christian church began to be established. This idea of three Gods, being a merely natural idea, receives no other light than natural, and cannot be opened to the afflux and reception of spiritual light; hence it is, that they have seen no other properties in God, than natural. Furthermore, had they seen how incongruous these human properties are to the Divine essence, and had they removed them from the article of justification, they must then have entirely departed from the religion, which from the beginning was founded on the worship of three Gods, before the time appointed for the New Church, when the fulness and restoration will take place.

XV.

64. *From the faith of the present church have been produced, and still may be produced, monstrous births; such as, instantaneous salvation from immediate mercy; predestination; the notion that God pays no attention to the actions of man, but to faith alone; that there is no connection between charity and faith; that man in conversion is like a stock, with many more heresies of the same kind; likewise concerning the Sacraments of Baptism and the Holy Supper, as to the advantages reasonably to be expected from them, when considered according to the doctrine of justification by faith alone; as also with regard to the Person of Christ. The heresies from the first ages to the present day, have sprung up from no other source than from the doctrine founded on the idea of three Gods.*

BRIEF ANALYSIS.

65. That no other salvation is believed at this day, than instantaneous salvation from immediate mercy, is evident from this, that an oral faith alone, at the same time a confidence of the lungs, and not with charity at the same time, whereby oral faith becomes real, and the confidence of the lungs becomes that of the heart, is believed to complete all the work of salvation; for if the co-operation is taken away, which is effected through the exercises of charity by man as of himself, the spontaneous co-operation which is said to follow faith of itself, becomes passive action, which is a frivolous expression. For what need would there then be of anything more than this instantaneous and immediate prayer, "Save me, O God, for the sake of the sufferings of Thy Son, who hath washed me from my sins in His own blood, and presents me pure, just, and holy, before Thy throne"? And this ejaculation of the mouth might avail even at the hour of death, if not sooner, as a seed of justification. That nevertheless instantaneous salvation, from immediate mercy, is at this day a fiery flying serpent in the church, and that by it religion is abolished, security induced, and damnation imputed to the Lord, may be seen in the work concerning *The Divine Providence*, published at Amsterdam in the year 1764 (n. 340).

66. Predestination is also an offspring of the faith of the present church, because it is born from a belief in instantaneous salvation from immediate mercy, and from a belief in absolute impotence and no free-will in spiritual things, concerning which, see below (n. 68, 69). That this follows from them, as one fiery flying serpent from another, or one spider from another, may be seen above. Predestination also follows from the supposition, that man is as it were inanimate in the act of conversion, that he is like a stock, and that afterwards he is unconscious whether he is a stock made alive by grace, or not; for it is said, that God, by the hearing of the Word, gives faith, when and where He wills [n. 11 (*a*)], consequently of His good pleasure; and likewise that election is of the mere grace of God, independently of any action on man's part, whether such activity proceed from the powers of nature or of grace: *Formula Concordiæ* (p. 821; Appendix, p. 182). The works which follow faith as evidences thereof, appear to the mind while it reflects on them like the works of the flesh, while the spirit which operates them does not make manifest from what origin they are, but makes them, like faith, to be the effects of grace, and thus of the good pleasure of God. Hence it is plain, that the dogma of predestination has sprung from the faith of the present church, as a sucker from its root; and I can say, that it has followed as the almost unavoidable consequence of that faith. This was first broached by the Predestinarians, and afterwards by Godoschalcus, then by Calvin and his followers, and lastly established and confirmed by the Synod of Dort, whence it was conveyed into the church, by the Supra and Infra Lapsarians, as the palladium of religion, or rather as the head of Gorgon or Medusa engraved on the shield of Pallas.

But what more hurtful, or more cruel notion could have been hatched out and believed concerning God, than that any part of the human race are predestined to damnation? For it would be a cruel belief, that the Lord, who is love itself and mercy itself, willed that a multitude of men should be born for hell, or that myriads of myriads should be born devoted to destruction, or in other words, born to be devils and satans; and that, out of His Divine wisdom, which is infinite, He would not and did not provide for those who live well, and acknowledge God, that they should not be cast into everlasting fire and torment; whereas the Lord is the Creator and Saviour of all, and He alone leads all, and wills not the death of any. What then can be believed and thought more monstrous, than that multitudes of nations and peoples, should under His auspices, and in His sight, from a predestined decree, be delivered up to the devil as his prey, to satiate his maw? Yet this is an offspring of the faith of the present church; but the faith of the New Church abhors it as a monster.

67. That God has no respect unto the actions of men, but unto faith alone, is a new heresy, the offspring of the two former, concerning which we have already spoken above (n. 64, 65); and what is wonderful, it is derived from faith alone deeply examined and attentively considered, which has been done by the most sagacious of this age, and is a third offspring, begotten by that faith, and brought forth by predestination, that she-wolf, as a mother; but whereas it is insane, impious, and machiavelian, it has hitherto been kept included as it were in the uterine coats, or secundines, that came from the mother, lest its hideous form should appear; but the insanity and impiety of it may be seen described and exploded in *The Apocalypse Revealed* (n. 463).

68. That there is not any connection between charity and faith, follows from these passages in their doctrine of justification, namely: That faith is imputed for justice without works [n. 12 (*a*)]. That faith does not justify as being formed from charity [n. 12 (*b*)]. That good works are to be altogether excluded in treating of justification and eternal life [n. 12 (*f*)]. That good works are not necessary to salvation, and the assertion of their necessity ought to be totally rejected by the church [n. 12 (*g*) (*h*) (*i*) (*k*)]. That salvation and faith are neither preserved nor retained by charity and the works thereof [n. 12 (*m*) (*n*)]. That good works when mixed with the business of justification, are pernicious [n. 14 (*g*)]. That the works of the spirit, or of grace, which follow faith as its fruits, contribute nothing to man's salvation [n. 14 (*d*)], and elsewhere; from all which it inevitably follows, that this faith has no connection with charity, and if it had, it would become injurious to salvation, because injurious to faith, which thus would no longer be the only means of salvation. That no connection between charity and that faith can actually exist, has been shown above (n. 47, 48, 49, 50); wherefore it may be said, that it was providentially ordered, that the reformers should be so zealous to reject charity and good works from their faith; for had they conjoined them, it would have been like conjoining a leopard with a sheep, a wolf with a lamb, or a hawk with a dove. That this faith is also described in the *Apocalypse* by a leopard, may be seen (chap. xiii. 2); and also in the explanation thereof, in *The Apocalypse Revealed* (n. 572). But what is a church without faith, and what is faith without charity, consequently what is a church without the marriage of faith and charity (n. 48)? This marriage is the church itself, and is the New Church which is now being established by the Lord.

69. That man in his conversion is like a stock, the faith of the present church acknowledges as its natural offspring in these express words. That man is altogether impotent in spiritual things [n. 15 (*a*) (*b*) (*c*)]. That in conversion he is like a stock, a stone, and a statue; and that he cannot so much as accommodate and apply himself to receive grace, but is like something that has not the use of any of the senses [n. 15 (*c*) (*d*)]. That man has only a locomotive power, whereby he is capable of going to assemblies to hear the Word and the Gospel [n. 15 (*e*)]. But that a person who is regenerate by virtue of the Holy Spirit, from the new powers and gifts which he has received, does in a certain manner co-operate [n. 15 (*k*)], besides many other passages. This description of man in his conversion, and during his repentance from evil works, is also an offspring produced from the same egg or womb, that is, from justification by faith alone, to the intent that man's works may be totally abolished, and not suffered to have the least conjunction with faith, not even to touch it. But because such ideas are repugnant to the common perception of all men concerning man's conversion and repentance, they have added the following words. *" There is an immense difference between men baptized, and unbaptized, for it is according to the doctrine of Paul, that all who are baptized have put on Christ, and are truly regenerated; they are then endowed with a freedom of will, whereby they not only can hear the Word of God, but can also assent to the same, and embrace it by faith* [n. 15 (*m*)], and in the *Formula Concordiæ* (p. 675). I appeal to the wise, to consider, whether this latter quotation be any way consistent with the preceding ones, and whether it be not a contradiction to say that a Christian in a state of conversion is like a stock or a stone, so that he is not able so much as to accommodate himself to the receiving of grace, when yet every Christian is baptized, and from baptism became possessed, not only of a power to hear the Word of God, but also to assent to it, and embrace it by faith; wherefore the comparing of a Christian man to a stock or a stone is a simile that ought to be banished from all churches in the Christian world, and to be done away with, like a meteor that vanishes from before the eyes of a man waking out of sleep; for what can be more repugnant to reason? But in order to elucidate the doctrine of the New Church concerning man's conversion, I will transcribe the following passage from a certain *Relation* in *The Apocalypse Revealed.*

"Who cannot see, that every man has freedom to think about God, or not to think about Him, consequently that every man has the same freedom in spiritual things, as he has in civil and moral things. The Lord gives this freedom continually to all; wherefore man becomes guilty or not guilty as he thinks. Man is man by virtue of this power, whereas a beast is a beast in consequence of its not possessing such a power; so that man is capable of reforming and regenerating himself as of himself, provided he only acknowledge in his heart that his ability is from the Lord. Every man who does the work of repentance, is reformed and regenerated. Both must be done by man as of himself, but this as of himself is also from the Lord, because the Lord gives both the power to will and perform, and never takes it away from any one. It is true that man cannot contribute anything thereunto, nevertheless he is not created a statue, but a man, to do the work of repentance from the Lord as from himself. In this alone consists the reciprocality of love and faith, and of conjunction thereby, which the Lord altogether wills to be done by man from Him. In a word, act of yourselves, and believe that it is from the Lord, for thus you will act as of yourselves. But the power so to act is not implanted in man by creation, because to act of himself is the Lord's alone, but it is given continually; and in this case in proportion as man does good and learns truth as of himself, he is an angel of heaven; but in proportion as he does evil, and thence confirms falsity, which also is done as of himself, in the same proportion he is a spirit of hell. That in this latter case also man acts as of himself, is evident from his prayers, as when he prays that he may be preserved from the devil, lest he should seduce him, and bring his own evils upon him. Every one, however, contracts guilt, who believes that he does of himself either good or evil; but not he who believes that he acts as of himself. For whatsoever a man believes that he does of himself, that he appropriates to himself; if he believes that he does good of himself, he appropriates to himself that good, and makes it his own, when nevertheless it is of God and from God; and if he believes that he does evil of himself, he also appropriates that evil to himself, and makes it his own, when yet it is of the devil and from the devil."

That many other false dogmas, even concerning the sacraments of Baptism and the Holy Supper, as to the benefits reasonably to be expected from them, when considered according to the doctrine of justification by faith alone; as likewise concerning the Person of Christ; together with all the heresies from the first ages down to the present day; have flowed from no other source, than from a doctrine founded on the idea of three Gods. This we have not room to demonstrate within the limits of this epitome; but it will be shown and proved at large in the work itself.

XVI.

70. *The last state of the present church, when it is at its end, is meant by the consummation of the age, and then the coming of the Lord* (*Matt.* xxiv. 3).

BRIEF ANALYSIS.

71. We read in *Matthew:*—

> The disciples came to Jesus, and showed Him the buildings of the temple; and Jesus said unto them, Verily, I say unto you, there shall not be left here one stone upon another, which shall not be thrown down. And the disciples said unto Him, tell us when these things shall be, especially what shall be the sign of *Thy coming, and of the consummation of the age* (chap. xxiv. 1–3).

At this day the learned clergy and laity understand by the destruction of the temple, its destruction by Vespasian; and by the coming of the Lord, and the consummation of the age, they understand the end and destruction of the world. But by the destruction of the temple is not only meant the destruction thereof by the Romans, but likewise the destruction of the present church; and by the consummation of the age, and the coming of the Lord at that time, is meant the end of the present church and the establishment of a New Church by the Lord. That these things are there meant, is evident from the whole of that chapter from beginning to end, which treats solely of the successive decline and corruption of the Christian church, even to its destruction, when it is at an end. That by "the temple," in a limited sense is meant the temple at Jerusalem; in a wide sense the church of the Lord; in a wider sense the angelic heaven; and, in the widest sense, the Lord as to His Human may be seen in *The Apocalypse Revealed* (n. 529). That by "the consummation of the age" is meant the end of the church, which comes to pass when there does not remain any truth of doctrine from the Word that is not falsified, and thus consummated (n. 658, 676, 750, of the same work). That by "the coming of the Lord" is meant His coming in the Word, and at the same time the establishment of a New Church instead of the former consummated one, evidently appears from His own words in the same chapter, from verse 30 to 34; as likewise from the last two chapters, xxi. and xxii., of the *Apocalypse*, where also are these words:—

I, Jesus, am the Root and the Offspring of David, the bright and morning Star. And the Spirit and the Bride say, Come; and let him that heareth say, Come; and him that thirsteth let him come. Yea, I come quickly: Amen, even so come, Lord Jesus (chap. xxii. 16, 17, 20).

72. That the church is then at an end, when there are no longer any truths of faith, and thence neither any goods of charity, is self-evident. That falsities of faith extinguish the truths of doctrine, and evils of life burn up the goods of charity, and that where there are falsities of faith, there likewise are evils of life, and that where there are evils of life, there likewise are falsities of faith, will be demonstrated in detail in its own chapter. The reason why it has been hitherto unknown that by "the consummation of the age" is meant the end of the church, is because when falsities are taught, and when the doctrine resulting from them is believed and honored as orthodox, then it cannot possibly be known that the church is to be brought to a consummation, for falsities are regarded as truths, and truths as falsities, and then the falsity explodes the truth and blackens it, like ink poured into clear water, or soot thrown upon white paper. For it is believed, and the most learned of the present age proclaim it, that they are in the clearest light of the Gospel, although as to the whole face they are in thick darkness; thus the white speck has covered over the pupils of their eyes.

73. That in *Matt.* xxiv., *Mark* xiii., and *Luke* xxi., where similar passages occur, the destruction of the temple and Jerusalem is not described, but the successive changes of the state of the Christian church are foretold, in regular order, even to its last state, when its end is, will be shown in the work itself, where those chapters will be explained; and in the meantime, it may appear from these words in those evangelists:—

Then shall appear the sign of the Son of man, and then shall all the tribes of the earth wail; and they shall see the Son of man coming in the clouds of heaven with power and glory. And He shall send His angels with a great sound of a trumpet, and they shall gather together His elect from one end of the heavens to the other end thereof (*Matt.* xxiv. 30, 31; *Mark* xiii. 26, 27; *Luke* xxi. 27).

It is known that these things were neither seen nor heard at the destruction of Jerusalem, and that it is believed at this day, that they will come to pass at the time of the Last Judgment. We likewise read of similar things in the *Apocalypse*, which from beginning to end treats solely of the last state of the church, where are these words:—

Behold, Jesus Christ cometh in the clouds, and all the tribes of the earth shall wail because of Him (i. 5, 7).

The particular explanation of these words may be seen in *The Apocalypse Revealed* (n. 24–28); also what is signified by "the tribes of the earth," and their "wailing" (n. 27, 348, 349).

XVII.

74. *The infestation from falsities, and thence the consummation of every truth, or the desolation, which at this day prevails in the Christian churches, is meant by "the great affliction, such as was not from the beginning of the world, nor ever shall be"* (*Matt.* xxiv. 21).

BRIEF ANALYSIS.

75. That the successive decline and corruption of the Christian church is foretold and described by the Lord in *Matt.* xxiv., may be seen above (n. 73). After having spoken of false prophets that should arise, and of the abomination of desolation wrought by them (verses 11, 15), He says:—

Then shall be great affliction, such as was not from the beginning of the world until now, nor ever shall be (verse 21).

Whence it is evident, that by "great affliction," in this as well as in other places throughout the Word, is meant the infestation of truth by falsities, until there remains no genuine truth derived from the Word which is not falsified, and thus consummated. This has come to pass, because the churches have not acknowledged the Unity of God in the Trinity, and His Trinity in Unity, in one Person, but in three, and hence have founded a church in the mind upon the idea of three Gods, and in the mouth upon the confession of one God; for by this means they have separated themselves from the Lord, and at length to such a degree, that they have no idea left of the Divinity in His Human nature (see *The Apocalypse Revealed* n. 294), when nevertheless the Lord as to His Human is the Divine truth itself, and the Divine light itself, as He fully teaches in the Word; hence is the great affliction at the present day. That this has been principally brought on by the doctrine of justification and imputation through the means of faith alone, will be shown in the following pages.

76. This affliction, or infestation of truth by falsities, is treated of in seven chapters of the *Apocalypse*, and is what is meant by:—

The black horse and the pale horse going forth from the book, the seals whereof the Lamb had opened (vi. 5–8).

Then:—

By the beast ascending out of the abyss, which made war against the two witnesses, and slew them (xi. 7, *seq.*).

As also by:—

The dragon which stood before the woman who was ready to be delivered, in order to devour her offspring, and pursued her into the desert, and there cast out of his mouth water as a flood, that he might swallow her up (xii.).

And likewise by:—

The beast out of the sea, the body of which was like that of a leopard, his feet like those of a bear, and his mouth like that of a lion (xiii. 2).

Also by:—

The three unclean spirits like frogs, which came out of the mouth of the dragon, out of the mouth of the beast, and out of the mouth of the false prophet (xvi. 13).

And moreover by these particulars, that:—

After the seven angels had poured out the vials of the wrath of God, wherein were the seven last plagues, upon the earth, upon the sea, upon the rivers and fountains, upon the sun, upon the throne of the beast, upon Euphrates, and at length upon the air, there was a great earthquake, such as had not been since men were created upon the earth (xvi.).

"The earthquake" here signifies an inversion of the church, which is effected by falsities and falsifications of truth. The like things are meant by these:—

> The angel sent in his sickle, and gathered the vineyard of the earth, and cast it into the great wine-press of the wrath of God; and the wine-press was trodden, and blood came out even unto the horses' bridles, for a thousand and six hundred stadia (xiv. 19, 20).

There "blood" signifies truth falsified: besides many other things in those seven chapters. But see, if you will, the explanations, and the Relations at the end of the chapters.

XVIII.

77. *There would be neither love, nor faith, nor the knowledges of good and truth, in the last time of the Christian Church, when it draws to an end, is meant by these words:* "*After the affliction of those days, the sun shall be darkened, and the moon shall not give her light, and the stars shall fall from heaven, and the powers of the heavens shall be shaken*" (*Matt.* xxiv. 29).

BRIEF ANALYSIS.

78. In the prophetic Word, the like things are said of the "sun," "moon," and "stars," as here (*Matt.* xxiv. 29). Thus in *Isaiah*:—

> Behold, the cruel day of Jehovah cometh; the stars of the heavens and the constellations thereof shall not shine with their light, the sun shall be darkened at his rising, and the moon shall not cause her light to shine (xiii. 9, 10).

In *Ezekiel*:—

> When I shall put thee out, I will cover the heavens, and make the stars thereof dark; I will cover the sun with a cloud, and the moon shall not cause her light to shine, and I will give darkness upon thy land (xxxii. 7, 8).

In *Joel*:—

> The day of Jehovah cometh, a day of darkness, the sun and moon shall not cause their light to shine, and the stars shall withdraw their shining (ii. 1, 2, 10).

In the same:—

> The sun shall be turned into darkness, and the moon into blood, before the great day of Jehovah cometh (iii. 4).
>
> The day of Jehovah is near in the valley of decision; the sun and moon are darkened (iv. 14, 15).

In the *Apocalypse:*—

> The fourth angel sounded, and the third part of the sun was smitten, and the third part of the stars, and the day shone not for a third part of it (vii. 12).

And in another place:—

> The sun became black as sackcloth of hair, and the moon became as blood (vi. 12).

In all these passages it treats of the last time of the Jewish Church, which was when the Lord came into the world; in like manner here in *Matthew* and in the *Apocalypse*, only in reference to the last time of the Christian Church, when the Lord is to come again, but in the Word, which is Himself, and in which He is; wherefore, immediately after those words (*Matt.* xxiv. 29), it follows:—

> And then shall appear the sign of the Son of man coming in the clouds of the heavens (verse 30).

By "the sun" in the above passages is meant love; by "the moon" faith; and by "the stars" the knowledges of good and truth; and by "the powers of the heavens" those three as the supports and firmaments of the heavens where the angels are, and of the churches where men are; by the above, therefore, collected into one sense, is meant, that there would be no love, nor faith, nor knowledges of good and truth, remaining in the Christian Church, in the last time thereof, when it draws to its end. That "the sun" signifies love, has been shown in *The Apocalypse Revealed* (n. 53, 54, 413, 796, 831, 961). That "the moon" signifies faith (n. 53, 332, 413, 423, 533). That "the stars" signify the knowledges of good and truth (n. 51, 74, 333, 408, 419, 954).

79. That, according to the above prediction, there is at this day such thick darkness throughout the Christian churches, that the sun gives no light by day, nor the moon and stars any light by night, is occasioned solely by the *doctrine of justifica-*

tion by faith alone; for it teaches faith as the only means of salvation; of the influx, progress, indwelling, operation, and efficacy of which no one has hitherto seen any sign; and into which neither the Law of the Decalogue, nor charity, nor good works, nor repentance, nor striving after a new life, have any entrance, or are in the smallest degree connected with it; for it is asserted, that they spontaneously follow, without being of any use either to contain faith or to procure salvation. The above doctrine likewise teaches, that faith alone imparts to the regenerate, or those who are possessed of it, full liberty, so as to be no longer under the law; moreover that Christ covers over their sins before God the Father, who forgives them as though they were not seen, and crowns them with renovation, sanctity, and eternal life. These and many other things of a like nature are the interiors of that doctrine; the exteriors, which do not gain admission, are valuable sayings concerning charity, good works, acts of repentance, and exercises of the law; yet these are accounted by them merely as slaves and drudges, which follow their mistress, faith, without contiguity. But because they know that the laity account these things as equally necessary to salvation with faith, they carefully subjoin them in their sermons and discourses, and pretend to conjoin them with and insert them into justification. This, however, they do merely to tickle the ears of the common people, and to defend their oracles, that they may not appear mere riddles, or like the vain responses of soothsayers.

80. In order to confirm the above assertions, I will adduce the following passages from the *Formula Concordiæ* (concerning which see n. 9), lest any one should think that these things have been unjustly laid to their charge. That the works of the second table of the Decalogue are civil duties, and belong to external worship, which man is able to do of himself; and that it is a folly to dream that they justify (pp. 84, 85, 102). That good works are to be utterly excluded from the business of justification by faith (pp. 589–591, 704–708). That good works do not in any wise enter into justification (pp. 589, 702; Appendix, 62, 173). That good works do not preserve salvation nor faith (pp. 590, 705; Appendix, p. 174). That neither does repentance enter into justification by faith (pp. 165, 320; Appendix, p. 158). That repentance is nothing more than invoking God, confessing the gospel, giving of thanks, being obedient to the magistracy, and following one's calling (pp. 12, 198; Appendix, 158, 159, 172, 266). That renovation of life has likewise nothing to do with justification (pp. 585, 685, 688, 689; Appendix, p. 170). That striving after new obedience neither enters into faith, nor justifies (pp. 90, 91, 690; Appendix, p. 167). That the regenerate are not under the law, but are delivered from the bondage thereof, and are only in the law, and under grace (p. 722, and elsewhere). That the sins of the regenerate are covered over by the merit of Christ (pp. 641, 686, 687, 719, 720); besides many other passages to the same purport. It is to be known, that all Protestants, both the Evangelical and the Reformed, teach in like manner justification by faith alone, see above (n. 17, 18).

81. It is wonderful, that the doctrine of justification by faith alone prevails at this day over every other doctrine throughout the whole Reformed Christian world, and is esteemed in the sacred order almost as the only important point of theology. This is what all young students among the clergy greedily learn and imbibe at the universities, and what they afterwards teach in temples, and publish in books, as if they were inspired with heavenly wisdom, and whereby they endeavor to acquire to themselves a name, and the reputation of superior learning, as well as diplomas, licenses, and other honorary rewards. And these things are done, notwithstanding it is owing to this doctrine alone, that the sun is at this day darkened, the moon deprived of her light, and the stars of the heavens have fallen, that is, have perished. It has been testified to me, that the doctrine of faith in imputed justice has blinded the minds of men at this day to such a degree, that they will not, and therefore as it were cannot, see any Divine truth by the light of the sun, nor by the light of the moon, but only by the light of a fire-place by night; on which account I will venture to assert, that supposing Divine truths concerning the conjunction of charity and faith, concerning heaven, the Lord, and eternal happiness, to be sent down from heaven engraven in silver characters, they would not be thought worthy to be read by the sticklers for justification; but the case would be quite otherwise supposing a paper concerning justification by faith alone to be brought up from hell. It is also said in the *Formula Concordiæ*, that the article of justification by faith alone, or the justice of faith, is the chief article in the whole Christian doctrine; and that the works of the law are utterly to be excluded from this article (pp. 17, 61, 62, 72, 89, 683; Appendix, p. 164).

XIX.

82. *They who are in the present justifying faith, are meant by "the he-goats" in Daniel and in Matthew.*

BRIEF ANALYSIS.

83. It is written in *Daniel*:—

I saw in a vision a ram, which had two horns that were high, but the higher came up last; and the horn pushed westward, and northward, and southward, and made itself great. Then I saw a he-goat coming from the west, over the face of the whole earth, which had a horn between its eyes; and he ran to the ram in the fury of his strength, and broke his two horns, and cast him down to the earth, and trampled him: but the great horn of the he-goat was broken, and instead of it there came up four horns; and out of one of them came forth a little horn which waxed exceeding great towards the south, towards the east, and towards honorableness, and even to the host of heaven; and it cast down of the host and of the stars to the earth, and trampled them: yea, he extolled himself to the prince of the host, and took from him the daily sacrifice, and cast away the place of his sanctuary, for he cast down truth to the earth. And I heard one saint saying, how long shall this vision be, the daily sacrifice, and the wasting transgression, that both the holy place and the host should be given to be trodden under foot? And he said, even to the evening the morning, then shall the holy place be justified (viii. 2–14).

That this vision is a prediction of the future states of the church is very evident, for it declares, that "the daily sacrifice was taken away from the prince of the host, the habitation of his sanctuary cast down, and the he-goat cast down truth to the earth"; moreover, that "a saint said, How long shall this vision be, that both the holy place and the host should be given to be trodden under foot?" and that this should be "even to the evening the morning, when the holy place shall be justified." By "the evening the morning" is meant the end of the old church, when a New Church commences.

84. We read these words in *Matthew*:—

> Then shall the Son of man say to the he-goats on His left hand, depart from Me, for I was hungry, and ye gave Me no meat; I was thirsty, and ye gave Me no drink; I was a stranger, and ye took Me not in; I was naked, and ye clothed Me not, I was sick and in prison, and ye visited Me not; and these shall go away into eternal punishment.

That the same are here meant by "he-goats" and "sheep" as by the "he-goat" and "ram" in *Daniel*, is very evident. That by "he-goats" are meant those who are in the present justifying faith, appears from this, that to the sheep are enumerated works of charity, and it is said that they did them; and that to the he-goats the same works of charity are enumerated, but it is said that they did them not, and that they are therefore condemned. For they who are in the present justifying faith, neglect works, because they deny them to have anything of salvation or of the church in them. When charity is thus removed, good works, which are of charity, slip away from the mind, and are obliterated; so that they are never remembered, nor is the least effort made to recall them to mind from the Law of the Decalogue. It is a general rule of religion, that as far as any one does not will goods, and hence does not do them, so far he wills evils, and hence does them; and on the contrary, that as far as any one does not will evils, and hence does not do them, so far he wills goods, and hence does them. These latter are the "sheep," but the former are the "he-goats." If all the evil had been there meant by the "he-goats," instead of the works of charity which they had not done, the evils which they had done would have been enumerated.

85. That no other than the above described are meant by the "he-goats," has been manifested to me by experience in the spiritual world. In that world there appear all things that are in the natural world, such as houses and palaces, paradises and gardens, with trees of every kind; likewise fields and fallow lands, as also plains and green pastures, and also herds and flocks; all resembling those upon our earth; nor is there any other difference, than that in the natural world they are from a natural origin, but in the spiritual world from a spiritual origin. There I have often seen sheep and he-goats, also combats between them, like that described in *Daniel* (chap. viii.). I have seen he-goats with horns bent forwards and backwards, and rushing with fury upon the sheep; I have seen some he-goats with two, and others with four horns, with which they vehemently struck at the sheep; and when I looked to discover what this meant, I saw some persons disputing together about faith conjoined with charity, and faith separated from charity; from whence it plainly appeared, that the present justifying faith, which considered in itself is a faith disjoined from charity, is "the he-goat," and that faith conjoined with charity is "the sheep."

86. The like are meant by "he-goats" in *Zechariah*:—

Mine anger was kindled against the shepherds, and I will visit the he-goats (x. 3).

And in *Ezekiel*:—

Behold I judge between cattle and cattle, between the rams and the he-goats; seemeth it a small thing unto you, to have eaten up the good pasture, but ye must trample down with your feet also the residue of the pastures? Ye thrust all the infirm sheep with your horns, until ye have dispersed them; therefore will I save My flock, that it will be no more a prey (xxxiv. 17, 18, 22, *seq.*).

XX.

87. *They who have confirmed themselves in the present justifying faith are meant in the Apocalypse by "the dragon, and his two beasts," and by "the locusts"; and this same faith, when confirmed, is there meant by "the great city which is spiritually called Sodom and Egypt, where the two witnesses were slain," as also by "the pit of the abyss, from which the locusts went forth."*

BRIEF ANALYSIS.

88. That in seven chapters of the *Apocalypse* it treats of the perverted state of the church with the Reformed, and in two chapters of the perverted state of the church with the Roman Catholics, and that the states of both churches, as existing at the present day, are condemned, has been shown in the explanation thereof, in the work entitled, *The Apocalypse Revealed*, and that not by vain conjectures, but by full proofs. That by "the dragon" treated of in chapter xii., are meant those in the church of the Reformed who make God three, and the Lord two, and who separate charity from faith, by making their faith spiritual and saving, and not charity, see there (n. 532–565), and the *Relation* adjoined (n. 566). That they are further described by "the two beasts," one rising out of the sea, and the other out of the earth (as related in chap. xiii.), see (n. 567–610), and the *Relation* (n. 611). That they are also described by "the locusts," which came forth out of the pit of the abyss (as mentioned in chap. ix.), see (n. 419–442). That this same faith, when confirmed, is meant, by "the great city, which is spiritually called Sodom and Egypt," where the two faithful witnesses were slain (as related in chap. xi.), see (n. 485–530), particularly (n. 500–503), and the *Relation* (n. 531). That they are also meant by "the pit of the abyss," out of which issued smoke as out of a great furnace, and the sun and the air were darkened, and then locusts came forth (chap. ix.), see (n. 421–424).

89. That I might be confirmed and fully convinced, that by "the pit of the abyss" nothing else is meant than that draconic faith, which is a faith conceived from the idea of three Gods, and from having no idea of the Divinity of the Human nature of Christ, and which is called faith alone justifying, regenerating, quickening, sanctifying, and saving; it was given me to look into that abyss, then to speak with those who are there, and likewise to see the locusts which came out thence; from which ocular demonstration, that pit together with the abyss is described by me in *The Apocalypse Revealed;* and because a description from ocular demonstration testifies what is certain, it shall be transcribed from that work, where it is described as follows.

"That pit, which is like the mouth of a furnace, appears in the southern quarter; and the abyss beneath it is of great extent towards the east; they have light even there, but if light from heaven be let in, there is immediate darkness; wherefore the pit is closed up at the top. There appear in the abyss huts constructed as of brick, which are divided into distinct cells, in each of which is a table, whereon lie papers, with some books. Every one there sits at his own table, who in this world had confirmed justification and salvation by faith alone, making charity a merely natural and moral act, and the works thereof only works of civil life, whereby men may reap rewards in the world; but if done for the sake of salvation, they condemn them, and some even rigorously, because human reason and will are in them. All who are in this abyss, have been scholars and learned men in the world; and among them are some metaphysicians and scholastics, who are there esteemed above the rest. But their lot is as follows: when first they come thither, they take their seats in the first cells, but as they confirm faith by excluding the works of charity, they leave the first seats, and enter into cells nearer the east, and thus successively till they come towards the end, where they are who confirm those dogmatic things from the Word; and because they then cannot but falsify the Word, their huts vanish, and they find themselves in a desert. There is also an abyss beneath that abyss, where those are who in like manner have confirmed justification and salvation by faith alone, but who in their spirits have denied God, and in their hearts have made a jest of the holy things of the church; there they do nothing but quarrel, tear their garments, get upon the tables, stamp with their feet, and assail each other with reproaches; and because it is not permitted them to do evil to any one, they threaten with the mouth and fists.

90. That I might also be confirmed and convinced, that they who have confirmed themselves in the present justifying faith, are meant by the dragon, it was given me to see many thousands of them assembled together, and they then appeared at a distance like a dragon with a long tail, which seemed full of spikes like thorns, which signified falsities. Once also there appeared a still greater dragon, which raising up his back, lifted his tail towards heaven, and endeavored to draw down the stars from thence; "stars" there signify truths.

XXI.

91. *Unless the New Church be established by the Lord, no one can be saved; and this is meant by these words, " Unless those days should be shortened, there should no flesh be saved"* (*Matt.* xxiv. 22).

BRIEF ANALYSIS.

92. By "shortening those days," is meant the putting an end to the present church, and establishing the New Church; for, as has been said above, in *Matt.* xxiv., it treats of the successive decline and the perversions of the Christian church, even to the consummation and end thereof, and then of the coming of the Lord. The reason why no flesh could be saved, unless those days should be shortened, is because the faith of the present church is founded on the idea of three Gods, and with this idea no one can enter heaven; consequently no one can enter heaven with the faith of the present church, because the idea of three Gods is in all and every part thereof; and besides, in that faith there is no life from the works of charity. That the faith of the present church cannot be conjoined with charity, and produce any fruits which are good works, was shown above (n. 47–50). There are two things which form heaven in man, namely, the truths of faith and the goods of charity; the truths of faith effect the presence of the Lord, and show the way to heaven, and the goods of charity effect conjunction with the Lord, and introduce into heaven. And every one is there introduced into light according to his affection of truth, and into heat according to his affection of good. That the affection of truth is faith in its essence, and the affection of good charity in its essence, and that the marriage of them both constitutes the church, may be seen above (n. 48). The church and heaven make one. That these three are not in the churches of the present day, which are built upon faith alone, has been fully shown in the preceding pages.

93. I have sometimes in the spiritual world spoken with the justifiers of men by faith alone, and I said that their doctrine is erroneous, and likewise absurd, that it brings on security, blindness, sleep, and night in spiritual things, thereby death to the soul, thus exhorting them to desist from it. But I have received for answer, Why should we desist? Does not the pre-eminence of the clergy above the laity, in point of erudition, depend upon this doctrine? To which I replied, that thus they do not regard the salvation of souls, but their own pre-eminence; and that because they had applied the truths of the Word to their own false principles, and thereby had adulterated them, they were angels of the abyss, called "Abaddons" and "Apollyons" (*Apoc.* ix. 11); by whom are signified the destroyers of the church by a total falsification of the Word. See the explanation thereof (n. 440), and the *Relation* (n. 566), in *The Apocalypse Revealed*. But they answered, What is this? Are we not, by our knowledge of the mysteries of that doctrine, oracles? And do we not from that doctrine give answers as from the sanctuary? wherefore we are not Apollyons, but Apollos. Being indignant at this I said, If ye are Apollos, ye are also Leviathans, the first class of you are crooked Leviathans, and the second class of you are oblong Leviathans, whom God will visit with His hard and great sword (*Isa.* xxvii. 1). But they laughed at these things. What is meant by "being visited and perishing by the sword," may be seen in *The Apocalypse Revealed* (n. 52).

94. The great arcanum, why, unless the New Church be established by the Lord, no flesh can be saved, is this: that as long as the dragon with his crew remains in the world of spirits, into which he was cast from heaven, so long no Divine truth, united with Divine good, can pass from the Lord to men on earth, but it is either annihilated or perverted, whence there is no salvation. This is what is meant by this in the *Apocalypse:*—

And the dragon was cast out into the earth, and his angels were cast out with him; woe to the inhabitants of the earth and the sea, for the devil is come down unto them, having great wrath; and he persecuted the woman, who brought forth a son (chap. xii. 9, 12, 13).

But after the dragon was cast into hell (xx. 10), then it was that John saw the new heaven and the new earth, and saw the new holy Jerusalem coming down from God out of heaven (*Apoc.* xxi. 1, 2, *seq.*). What is meant by "the dragon," and who the dragons are, may be seen above (n. 87).

XXII.

95. *The opening and rejection of the dogmas of faith of the present church, and the revelation and reception of the tenets of the faith of the New Church, is meant by these words in the Apocalypse:* "*He that sat upon the throne said, Behold I make all things new; and He said unto me, Write, for these words are true and faithful*" (chap. xxi. 5).

BRIEF ANALYSIS.

96. "He that sat upon the throne," that is, the Lord, said these things to John, when he saw "the New Jerusalem coming down from God out of heaven." That by "the New Jerusalem" is meant the New Church, will be shown in the following chapter. The reason why the falsities of the dogmas of the faith of the present church must first be opened and rejected, before the truths of the dogmas of the New Church can be revealed and received, is, because they do not agree together, no not in one single point or particular; for the dogmas of the present church are founded upon a faith, in which it is unknown whether there be any essential of the church, or not. The essentials of the church, which conjoin themselves with a faith in one God, are charity, good works, repentance, and a life according to the Divine laws; and because these together with faith affect and move the will and thought of man, they conjoin man with the Lord, and the Lord with man. Since, therefore, none of these essentials enter into the faith of the present church at its first approach, which is called the act of justification, it cannot possibly be known whether this faith be in man, or not, consequently whether it be anything, or whether it be only an idea; for it is said, that man in that act is like a stock or a stone, and that he can neither will, think, co-operate, no, nor even apply or accommodate himself to the reception thereof in the smallest degree, see above [n. 15 (*c*) (*d*)]. Since, therefore, the case is such, that no one can guess, much less know, whether that faith be in him, and thus whether it be in him like a painted flower, or like a flower of the field in him; or whether it be like a bird flying by him, or like a bird that has built her nest in him; I ask by what tokens or signs is this to be known? If it be answered, that it is to be known from charity, good works, repentance, and exercises of the law, which follow after this faith, and yet have no connection with it; I leave it to men of sagacity to determine, whether things that have no connection with faith, can possibly be signs testifying thereof. For this faith of theirs, they say, is neither preserved nor retained by the things above mentioned, see above [n. 12 (*m*) (*n*)]. From what has been said we may draw the following conclusion, that in the faith of the present day there is nothing of the church, and thus that it is not anything, but only an idea of something. Since then this faith is of such a nature, it is deservedly to be rejected, yea, it rejects itself, as that of which nothing of the church can be predicated.

97. But widely different is the case with the dogmas or doctrinals of the New Church; these are all essentials, in each of which there is heaven and the church; and they regard this as their end, that man may be in the Lord, and the Lord in man, according to His own words in *John* (xiv. 20; xv. 4–6). It is this conjunction alone which constitutes the Christian Church. From these few observations it may clearly appear what is meant by these words of the Lord:—

> He that sat upon the throne said, Behold, I make all things new; and He said, Write, for these words are true and faithful (xxi. 5).

98. The sole reason why the Christian world has fallen into a faith, which has put away from itself all the truths and goods of heaven and the church, even to the separation thereof, is because they have divided God into three, and have not believed the Lord God the Saviour to be one with God the Father, and thus have not approached Him immediately; when nevertheless He alone as to His Human is the Divine truth itself:—

> Which is the Word, that was God with God, and is the true Light which enlighteneth every man; and became flesh (*John* i. 1, 2, 9, 14).

That He is the truth itself, and thus the light itself, is also testified in other places; for He says:—

> I am the Light of the world (*John* viii. 22; ix. 5).

And in another place:—

While ye have the Light, believe in the Light, that ye may be sons of the Light. I am come a Light into the world, that whosoever believeth in Me, may not abide in darkness (John xii. 36, 46).

In the *Apocalypse:*—

I am the Alpha and the Omega, the Beginning and the End, the First and the Last, the bright and morning Star (chap. xxii. 13, 16).

And in *Matthew:*—

When Jesus was transformed, His face shone as the sun and His raiment became as the light (chap. xvii. 1, 2).

Hence it appears why and whence this imaginary faith came into the world, namely, because they have not approached the Lord. And I can, from all experience, and thence testimony from heaven, declare with certainty, that it is impossible to derive a single genuine theological truth from any other source than from the Lord alone; nay, that to derive it from any other source is as impossible, as it is to sail from England or Holland to the Pleiades, or to ride on horseback from Germany to Orion in the sky.

XXIII

99. *The New Church about to be established by the Lord is the New Jerusalem, treated of in the Apocalypse* (chap. xxi. and xxii.) *which is there called "the Bride and the Wife of the Lamb."*

BRIEF ANALYSIS.

100. The reason why the New Church is meant by "the New Jerusalem coming down from God out of heaven" (*Apoc.* xxi.), is because Jerusalem was the metropolis of the land of Canaan, and there was the temple, the altar, there the sacrifices were offered, thus Divine worship, to which every male throughout the land was commanded to come three times a year. Then, because the Lord was in Jerusalem, and taught in its temple, and afterwards glorified His Human there; hence it is, that by "Jerusalem" is signified the church. That by "Jerusalem" is meant the church, is very clear from the prophecies in the Old Testament concerning a New Church to be established by the Lord, wherein it is called "Jerusalem." The following passages only shall be quoted, from which any one of interior reason may clearly see, that by "Jerusalem" is meant the church:—

Behold I create a *new heaven and a new earth*, and the former shall not be remembered; behold *I will create Jerusalem*, an exultation, and her people a gladness, that I may exult over *Jerusalem*, and be glad over My people. Then the wolf and the lamb shall feed together: they shall not do evil in all the mountain of My holiness (*Isa.* lxv. 17, 18, 19, 25).

For Zion's sake I will not be silent, and for *Jerusalem's* sake I will not rest, until her justice go forth as splendor, and her salvation as a lamp that burneth. Then the Gentiles shall see thy justice, and all kings thy glory; and thou shalt be called by a new name; which the mouth of Jehovah shall utter; and thou shalt be a crown of beauty, and a tiara of a kingdom, in the hand of thy God. Jehovah shall be well pleased in thee, and thy land shall be married. Behold thy salvation shall come, behold His reward is with him: and they shall call them the people of holiness, the redeemed of Jehovah; and thou shalt be called a city sought out, not deserted (*Isa.* lxii. 1–4, 11, 12).

Awake, awake, put on thy strength, O Zion; put on the garments of thy beauty, *O Jerusalem*, the city of holiness; for henceforth there shall no more come into thee the uncircumcised and the unclean. Shake thyself from the dust, arise, sit down, *O Jerusalem*. The people shall know My name in that day; for I am He that doth speak, behold it is I. Jehovah hath comforted His people, He hath redeemed *Jerusalem* (*Isa.* lii. 1, 2, 6, 9).

Shout O daughter of Zion, be glad with all the heart, O daughter of *Jerusalem;* the king of Israel is in the midst of thee; fear not evil any more; he will be glad over thee with joy, he will rest in thy love, he will exult over thee with shouting; I will give you for a name and a praise among all the people of the earth (*Zeph.* iii. 14–17, 20).

Thus saith Jehovah, thy Redeemer, saying to *Jerusalem*, thou shalt be inhabited (*Isa.* xliv. 24, 26).

Thus saith Jehovah, I will return to Zion, and dwell in the midst of *Jerusalem*, whence *Jerusalem* shall be called the city of truth, and the mountain of Jehovah of Hosts the mountain of holiness (*Zech.* viii. 3, 20–23).

Then shall ye know that I am Jehovah your God, dwelling in Zion, the mountain of holiness, and *Jerusalem* shall be holiness. And it shall come to pass in that day, that the mountains shall drop must, and the hills shall flow with milk, and *Jerusalem* shall sit from generation to generation (*Joel* iv. 17–21).

In that day shall the branch of Jehovah be for ornament and glory; and it shall come to pass that he that is left in Zion, and he that remaineth in *Jerusalem*, shall be called holy, every one that is written for life in *Jerusalem* (*Isa.* iv. 2, 3).

In the last days the mountain of the house of Jehovah shall be established on the head of the mountains, for out of Zion shall go forth doctrine, and the Word of Jehovah from *Jerusalem* (*Micah* iv. 1, 2, 8).

At that time they shall call *Jerusalem* the throne of Jehovah, and all nations shall be gathered to *Jerusalem* for the name of Jehovah, neither shall they go any more after the confirmation of their own evil heart (*Jer.* iii. 17).

Look upon Zion, the city of our stated feasts, thine eyes shall see *Jerusalem*, a quiet habitation, a tabernacle that shall not be destroyed; the pins thereof shall not be removed forever, and the cords thereof shall not be torn out (*Isa.* xxxiii. 20); besides other passages, as (*Isa.* xxiv. 23; xxxvii. 32; lxvi. 10–14; *Zech.* xii. 3, 6–10; xiv. 8, 11, 12, 21; *Mal.* iii. 2, 4; *Ps.* cxxii. 1–7; *Ps.* cxxx. 4–6).

That by "Jerusalem" in the above passages is meant a church to be established by the Lord, and not the Jerusalem inhabited by the Jews, is plain from every particular of the description in the passages quoted; as that "Jehovah God was about to create a new heaven and a new earth," and also "Jerusalem" at the same time; and that "this would be a crown of beauty, and a tiara of a kingdom"; that it is to be called "holiness," and "the city of truth, the throne of Jehovah," "a quiet habitation," "a tabernacle that shall not be taken down"; that "the wolf and the lamb shall feed together therein," and that "the mountains shall drop down with new wine, and the hills flow with milk," and that "it should remain from generation to generation"; besides other circumstances, as respecting the people therein, that they should be "holy, all written for life," and should be called "the redeemed of Jehovah." Moreover, all those passages treat of the coming of the Lord, and particularly of His second coming, when Jerusalem shall be such as is there described; for heretofore she has not been married, that is, has not been "the Bride and the Wife of the Lamb," as "the New Jerusalem" is said to be in the *Apocalypse*. The former or present church is meant by "Jerusalem," and its beginning is there described in these words in *Daniel*:—

Know and perceive, that from the going forth of the Word, unto the restoring and building of *Jerusalem*, even unto Messiah the Prince, shall be seven weeks; afterwards in sixty and two weeks it shall be restored, and the street and the ditch shall be built, but in distress of times (ix. 25).

But its end is described by these words:—

At length upon the bird of abominations shall be desolation, and even to the consummation and decision it shall drop upon the devastation (ver. 27).

This last passage is meant by the following words of the Lord in *Matthew:*—

When ye shall see the abomination of desolation foretold by *Daniel* the prophet, standing in the holy place, let him that readeth note it well (chap. xxiv. 15).

That "Jerusalem" in the places above adduced, does not mean the Jerusalem inhabited by the Jews, may appear from those places in the Word, where it is said of that city that it was entirely destroyed, and that it was to be destroyed, as in (*Jer.* v. 1; vi. 6, 7; vii. 17, 18, *seq.;* viii. 6, 7, 8, *seq.;* ix. 10, 11, 13, *seq.;* xiii. 9, 10, 14; xiv. 16; *Lam.* i. 8, 9, 17; *Ezek.* iv. 1 to the end; v. 9 to the end; xii. 18, 19; xv. 6–8; xvi. 1–63; xxiii. 1–40; *Matt.* xxiii. 37, 38; *Luke* xix. 41–44; xxi. 20–22; xxiii. 28–30); besides many other passages; and also where it is called "Sodom" (*Isa.* iii. 9; *Jer.* xxiii. 14; *Ezek.* xvi. 46, 48); and in other places.

101. That the church is the Lord's, and that from the spiritual marriage, which is that of good and truth, the Lord is called "the Bridegroom" and "the Husband," and the church "the Bride" and "the Wife," is known to Christians from the Word, particularly from the following passages: John said of the Lord:—

He that hath *the Bride is the Bridegroom*, but the friend of the *Bridegroom* is he who standeth and heareth Him, and rejoiceth because of the *Bridegroom's* voice (*John* iii. 29).

Jesus said, while the *Bridegroom* is with them, the *sons of the marriage* cannot fast (*Matt.* ix. 15; *Mark* ii. 19, 20; *Luke* v. 34, 35).

I saw the holy city, New Jerusalem, coming down from God out of heaven, prepared as *a Bride adorned for her Husband* (*Apoc.* xxi. 2).

The angel said unto John, Come, and I will show thee *the Bride, the Lamb's Wife*; and from a mountain he showed him the holy city Jerusalem (*Apoc.* xxi. 9).

The time of *the marriage of the Lamb is come, and His Wife* hath made herself ready; happy are they who are called unto *the marriage supper of the Lamb* (*Apoc.* xix. 7, 9).

I am the Root and Offspring of David, the bright and morning Star. *The Spirit and the Bride* say, Come; and let him who heareth say, Come; and him that thirsteth let him come: and whosoever will, let him take the water of life freely (*Apoc.* xxii. 16, 17).

XXIV.

102. *The faith of the New Church cannot by any means be together with the faith of the former church, and if they are together, such a collision and conflict will take place that everything of the Church with man will perish.*

BRIEF ANALYSIS.

103. The reason why the faith of the New Church cannot by any means be together with the faith of the former or present church, is, because they do not agree together in one third, no, nor even in one tenth part. The faith of the former church is described in the *Apocalypse* (chap. xii.) by "the dragon," but the faith of the New Church by "the woman encompassed with the sun, having upon her head a crown of twelve stars, whom the dragon pursued, and at whom he cast water as a flood, that he might swallow her up," see above (n. 87–90). These two cannot be together in one city, much less in one house, consequently they cannot be together in one mind; and if they should be together, the unavoidable consequence must be, that the woman would be continually exposed to the anger and insanity of the dragon, and in fear lest he should devour her son; for it is said in the *Apocalypse*, that:—

The dragon stood before the woman who was ready to be delivered, in order to devour her offspring, and the woman, after she had brought forth, fled into the wilderness (xii. 1, 4, 6, 14–17).

The faith of the former church is a faith of the night, for human reason has no perception of it; wherefore it is also said, that the understanding must be kept in obedience thereto; yea, it is not known whether it be within man or without him, because nothing of man's will and reason enters into it, no, nor charity, good works, repentance, the Law of the Decalogue, with many other things which really exist in the mind of man. That this is the case, may be seen above (n. 79, 80, 96–98). But the faith of the New Church enters into a conjugial covenant with all these, and conjoins itself to them; and because it is thus in the heat of heaven, it is also in the light thereof, and is a faith of light. Now a faith of night and a faith of light cannot be together any more than an owl and a dove in one nest. For in such case the owl would lay her eggs, and the dove hers, and after sitting, the young of both would be hatched, and then the owl would tear in pieces the young of the dove, and would give them to her own young for food; for the owl is a bird of prey. There is a further reason why the faith of the former church and the faith of the New Church cannot possibly be together, and that is, because they are heterogeneous; for the faith of the former church springs from an idea of three gods, see (n. 30–38), but the faith of the New Church from the idea of one God; and as there hence arises a heterogeneity between them, there must inevitably, if they are together, be such a collision and conflict, that everything of the church would perish; that is, man would either fall into a delirium or into a swoon, as to spiritual things, until at length he would scarcely know what the church is, or whether there be any church. From what has been said, it follows, that they who have confirmed themselves in the faith of the old church, cannot, without endangering their spiritual life, embrace the faith of the New Church, until they first have disproved its particulars, and thus have extirpated the former faith, together with its offspring or eggs, that is, its dogmas; the nature of which has been already shown in the foregoing pages, particularly at (n. 64–69).

104. The like would happen if any one should embrace the faith of the New Church, and retain the faith of the old church concerning the imputation of the justice or merit of the Lord; for from this, as from their root, all its dogmas, like so many offshoots, have sprung forth. If this should be the case, it would comparatively be like any one extricating himself from three heads of the dragon, and becoming entangled in his four remaining ones; or like one who fled from a leopard, and met a lion; or like one escaping out of a pit where there is no water, and falling into a pit full of water, and being drowned. That this is the case, will be seen after the exposition of the following proposition, where something will be advanced concerning imputation.

XXV.

105. *The Roman Catholics at this day know nothing of the imputation of the merit of Christ, and of justification by faith therein, into which their church was formerly initiated, because it is entirely concealed under their externals of worship, which are many; for which reason, therefore, if they recede but in part from their externals of worship, and immediately approach God the Saviour Jesus Christ, and administer the Holy Eucharist in both kinds, they may be brought into the New Jerusalem, that is, into the New Church of the Lord, more easily than the Reformed.*

BRIEF ANALYSIS.

106. That the primates and leaders of the Romish church, at their inauguration into the ministry, swear to observe the decrees of the council of Trent, appears from the bull of the Roman pontiff Pius IV., where, in the form of the oath of their profession of faith, dated the 18th of November, 1564, we find these words: "*I firmly believe and profess all and every thing contained in the creed used by the holy church of Rome; and I receive, without any doubt, all such things as are maintained and declared in her holy canons, and general councils, and especially by the most holy council of Trent; so help me God.*" That they also bind themselves by an oath to believe and profess what the council of Trent has established, concerning the imputation of the merit of Christ, and justification by faith therein, is evident from these words in the same bull: "*I embrace and receive each and all things, which have been determined and declared in the most holy council of Trent, concerning original sin and justification.*" What these are, may be seen from the extracts taken from that council, see above (n. 3–8). From these principles established in that council, the following consequences have been drawn, namely, "That the Roman Catholics, before the Reformation, held precisely the same doctrines as the Reformed have done after it, with respect to the imputation of the merit of Christ, and justification by faith therein, only with this difference, that they conjoined the same faith with charity and good works," see above (n. 19,

20). Also, "That the leading reformers, Luther, Melancthon, and Calvin, retained all the dogmas concerning the imputation of the merit of Christ, and justification by faith, just as they then were and had been with the Roman Catholics; but that they separated charity and good works from that faith, and declared them to have no saving efficacy, to the intent that they might be severed from the Roman Catholics, as to the very essentials of the church, which are faith and charity," see above (n. 21–23). Moreover, "That nevertheless the aforesaid reformers adjoined good works, and even conjoined them, to their faith, but in man as a passive subject; but the Roman Catholics conjoin them in him as an active subject; and that nevertheless there actually is a conformity of sentiment between both the one and the other, as to faith, works, and merits," see above (n. 24–29). From what has been shown, then, it is evident, that this faith is a faith which the Roman Catholics swear to observe, equally as well as the Reformed.

107. Nevertheless this faith is so far obliterated with the Roman Catholics at this day, that they scarcely know a jot about it; not that it has been reprobated by any papal decree, but because it has been concealed by the externals of worship, which are in general the adoration of Christ's vicar, the invocation of saints, the veneration of images; and moreover by such things as, from being accounted holy, affect the senses, as masses in an unknown tongue, garments, lights, incense, the pomp of processions; also mysteries respecting the Eucharist. By these things, and others of a like nature, faith justifying by the imputation of the merit of Christ, although a primitive tenet of the Roman church, has been so removed out of sight, and withdrawn from the memory, that it is like something buried in the earth, and covered over with a stone, which the monks have set a watch over, to prevent its being dug up and recalled; for were it recalled, the belief of their possessing a supernatural power of forgiving sins, and thus of justifying, sanctifying, and saving, would cease, and therewith all their sanctity, pre-eminence, and prodigious gains.

108. *The first reason* why the Roman Catholics may be brought into the New Jerusalem, or the New Church, more easily than the Reformed, is because the faith of justification by the imputation of the merit of Christ, which is an erroneous faith, and cannot be together with the faith of the New Church (n. 102–104), is with them obliterated, yea, is to be altogether obliterated; but it is as it were engraven upon the Reformed, inasmuch as it is the principal tenet of their church. *The second reason* is, because the Roman Catholics entertain an idea of Divine majesty in the Human of the Lord, more than there is with the Reformed, as is evident from their most devout veneration of the host. *The third reason* is, because they hold charity, good works, repentance, and attention to amendment of life, to be essentials of salvation, and these are also the essentials of the New Church; but the case is otherwise with the Reformed, who are confirmed in faith alone; with these the above are neither regarded as essentials nor formalities belonging to faith, and consequently they contribute nothing to salvation. These are three reasons, why the Roman Catholics, if they approach God the Saviour Himself, not mediately but immediately, and likewise administer the Holy Eucharist in both kinds, may more easily than the Reformed receive a living faith in the place of a dead faith, and be conducted by angels from the Lord to the gates of the New Jerusalem or the New Church, and be introduced therein with joy and shouting.

109. The imputation of the justice or merits of Christ, enters at this day like a soul into the whole system of theology throughout the Reformed Christian world. It is from imputation that faith, which is therein accounted the only means of salvation, is affirmed to be justice before God, see above [n. 11 (*d*)]; and it is from imputation that man, by means of that faith, is said to be clothed with the gifts of justice, as a king when elected is invested with the insignia of royalty. But nevertheless imputation, from the mere assertion that a man is just, effects nothing, for it passes only into the ears, and does not operate in man, unless the imputation of justice be also the application of justice by its being communicated and so induced. This follows from its effects, which are said to be the remission of sins, regeneration, renovation, sanctification, and thus salvation. It is asserted further, that by means of that faith Christ dwells in man, and the Holy Spirit operates in him, and that hence the regenerate are not only called just, but they also are just. That not only the gifts of God, but likewise Christ Himself, yea, all the Holy Trinity, dwells by faith in the regenerate, as in their temples, see above [n. 15 (*l*)]; and that man both as to person and works, is just, and is called so, see above [n. 14 (*e*)]. From which it clearly follows, that by the imputation of the justice of Christ is meant its application, and thereby its being induced, from which man is made partaker thereof. Now, because imputation is the root, the beginning, and the foundation of faith, and all its operations towards salvation, and hence is as it were the sanctuary or sacred recess in the Christian temples at this day, it is necessary to subjoin here something concerning *Imputation* by way of corollary; but this shall be distinctly arranged in articles in the following order:—

I. That to every one after death is imputed the evil in which he is, and in like manner the good.

II. That the induction of the good of one into another, is impossible.

III. That a faith of the imputation or application of the justice or merits of Christ, because it is impossible, is an imaginary faith.

110. I. *That to every one, after death, is imputed the evil in which he is, and in like manner the good.* In order to illustrate this with some degree of evidence, it shall be considered under the following distinctions. 1. That every one has his own life. 2. That his own life remains with every one after death. 3. That to the evil is then imputed the evil of his life, and that to the good is imputed his good.

1. *That every one has his own life*, thus a life distinct from that of another, is known. For there is a perpetual variety, and no two things are alike; hence it is that every one has his own. This manifestly appears from the faces of men, there is not given one face exactly like that of another, nor ever can be to eternity, because there do not exist two minds alike, and the face is from the mind, for it is, as is said, the type of the mind, and the mind derives it origin and form from the life. Unless

a man had his own life as he has a mind and face of his own, he would not have any life after death distinct from that of another; nay, heaven could not exist, for this consists of perpetual varieties; the form of this is solely from the varieties of souls and minds disposed into such an order, as to make one; and they constitute one from that One whose life is in the whole and every particular there, as the soul is in man. Unless this were the case, heaven would be dispersed, because its form would be dissolved. The One from whom the life of all and every one proceeds, and from whom that form coheres together, is the Lord.

2. *That the life of every one remains with him after death*, is known in the church from the Word, and particularly from the following passages:—

The Son of man shall come, and then He shall render unto every one according to his deeds (*Matt.* xvi. 27).

I saw the books opened, and all were judged according to their works (*Apoc.* xx. 12, 13).

In the day of judgment God will render unto every one according to his works (*Rom.* ii. 6; 2 *Cor.* v. 10).

The works, according to which it shall be rendered unto every one, are the life, for the life effects them, and they are according to the life. Forasmuch as it has been granted me for many years to be with angels, and to speak with new comers from the world, I can testify as a matter of certainty, that every one is there explored as to the quality of his past life, and that the life which he had contracted in the world, abides with him to eternity. I have spoken with those who lived many ages ago, whose life was known to me from history, and I found them similar to the description. I have also heard from the angels, that no one's life can be changed after death, because it is organized according to his love and faith, and hence according to his works; and that if the life were changed, the organization would be destroyed, which never can be done. They further added, that a change of organization can only take place in the material body, and by no means in the spiritual body, after the former is rejected.

3. *That to the evil is then imputed the evil of his life, and that to the good is imputed his good.* The imputation of evil

after death, does not consist in accusation, blame, censure, or in passing judgment, as in the world; but the evil itself effects this. For the evil of their own accord separate themselves from the good, because they cannot be together; the delights of the love of evil are averse to the delights of the love of good, and delights exhale from every one, as odors from every vegetable on earth; for they are no longer absorbed and concealed by the material body as before, but freely flow forth into the spiritual atmosphere from their loves; and inasmuch as evil is there perceived as it were in its odor, it is this which accuses, blames, inculpates, and judges; not before any judge, but before every one who is in good; and this is what is meant by imputation. The imputation of good is effected in the same manner; this takes place with those who in the world had acknowledged that every good in them was and is from the Lord, and nothing thereof from themselves. These, after they have been prepared, are let into the interior delights of their own good, and then a way is opened for them towards a society in heaven, whose delights are homogeneous. This is done by the Lord.

111. II. *That the induction of the good of one person into another, is impossible.* The proof hereof may also appear from the following observations in their order: 1. That every man is born in evil. 2. That man is led into good through regeneration by the Lord. 3. That this is effected by faith in the Lord, and by a life according to His commandments. 4. Wherefore the good of one cannot by application be transferred to another, and so imputed.

1. *That every man is born in evil,* is known in the church. This evil is said to be hereditary from Adam; but it is from parents, from whom every one derives his disposition or inclination. That it is so experience and reason proves; for the likenesses of parents may be traced in the faces, characters, and manners of their children, and their posterity. Hence families are distinguished by many, and their propensities are also judged of: wherefore, the evils which parents have contracted, are transmitted by propagation to their posterity, under a species of inclination towards them; hence are derived the evils into which men are born.

2. *That man is led into good through regeneration by the Lord.* That there is regeneration, and that unless one is regenerated, he cannot enter into heaven, is very evident from the Lord's words in (*John* iii. 3, 5). That regeneration is purification from evils, and thus renovation of life, cannot lie hidden in the Christian world, for reason also sees this, whilst it acknowledges that every one is born in evil, and that evil cannot be washed and wiped away, like filth by soap and water, but by repentance.

3. *That this is effected by faith in the Lord, and by a life according to His commandments.* The precepts of regeneration are five, as may be seen above (n. 43, 44); among which are these. That evils ought to be shunned, because they are of the devil and from the devil; that goods ought to be done, because they are of God and from God; and that the Lord is to be approached, that He may lead us so to do. Let every one consider and weigh with himself, whether good can be derived to man from any other source; and if he has not good he cannot be saved.

4. *Wherefore the good of one cannot by application be transferred to another, and so imputed.* From what has been said above, it follows, that man by regeneration is renewed as to his spirit, and that this is effected by faith in the Lord, and at the same time by a life according to His commandments. Who does not see, that this renewal can only be effected from time to time, nearly in like manner as a tree takes root, and grows successively from a seed, and is perfected? They who have a different notion of regeneration and renovation, know nothing of the state of man, nor anything about evil and good, as that they are diametrically opposite to each other, and that good cannot be implanted but in proportion as evil is removed; neither do they know, that so long as any one is in evil, he is averse to good which in itself is really good; wherefore if the good of one were to be applied and so induced into another who is in evil, it would be like casting a lamb to a wolf, or fastening a pearl to a hog's snout. From what has been said it is evident, that the induction of the good of one into another is impossible.

112. III. *That the faith of imputation, or application of the justice or merit of Christ, inasmuch as such imputation or appli-*

cation is impossible, is an imaginary faith. That to every one is imputed the evil in which he is, and in like manner the good, was demonstrated above (n. 110). Hence it is evident, that if by imputation is meant the application and thence the induction of the good of one into another, it is an imaginary thought. In the world, merits may be as it were transcribed by men, that is, benefits may be conferred on children for the sake of their parents, or on the friends of any adherent from favoritism; yet the good of merit cannot be inscribed on their souls, but only externally adjoined. The like cannot take place with men in respect to their spiritual life. This, as was shown above, must be implanted, and if not implanted by a life according to the above-mentioned precepts of the Lord, man remains in the evil in which he was born. Until this is done, no good can approach him, or if it does, it is instantly repelled, and rebounds like an elastic ball falling on a rock, or is absorbed like a diamond thrown into a swamp. An unreformed man is, as to his spirit, like a panther or an owl, and may be compared to a thorn or a nettle; but a regenerate man is like a sheep or a dove, and may be compared to an olive-tree or a vine. Consider then, I pray, if thou art disposed, how can a man a panther be converted into a man a sheep, or an owl into a dove, or a thorn into an olive-tree, or a nettle into a vine, by any imputation, if thereby is meant transcription? In order that conversion may take place, must not the ferocious nature of the panther and the owl, and the noxious properties of the thorn and the nettle, be first removed, and thus the truly human and inoffensive properties be implanted? How this is effected, the Lord also teaches in *John* (xv. 1–7).

113. To the above shall be added the following observations. It is said in the church, that no one can fulfil the law, especially since whosoever offends against one commandment of the Decalogue, offends against all. This form of speaking, however, is not such as it sounds; for this is to be understood in this manner, that whosoever from purpose or from confirmation acts against one commandment, acts against all the rest, since to act thus from purpose or from confirmation is to deny altogether that it is a sin, and he who denies it to be sin, makes light of acting against all the rest of the commandments. Who does not know, that he who is a fornicator is not therefore a murderer, a thief, or a false witness, nor even willing to be such? But he who is an adulterer from purpose and confirmation, makes light of all things relating to religion, and consequently pays no regard to murders, thefts, and false witness, not abstaining from them because they are sins, but for fear of the law or loss of reputation. The case is similar, if any one from purpose or confirmation acts against any other commandment of the Decalogue; he then also offends against the rest, because he does not account anything a sin. It is very similar with those who are in good from the Lord. These, if from the will and understanding, or from purpose and confirmation, they abstain from one evil because it is a sin, abstain from all, and still more if they abstain from many; for whenever any one abstains, from purpose and confirmation, from any evil, because it is a sin, he is kept by the Lord in the purpose of abstaining from the rest; wherefore if through ignorance, or any predominant lust of the body, he does an evil, it nevertheless is not imputed to him, because he did not purpose it to himself, nor confirm it with himself. A man comes into this kind of purpose, if he examines himself once or twice a year, and repents of the evil he discovers in himself. It is otherwise with him who never examines himself. It is permitted to confirm this by the following. I have met with many in the spiritual world, who have lived like other people in the natural world, feasting sumptuously, being splendidly clothed, making interest by trade like others, frequenting play-houses, joking on amatory affairs as if from lust, with other things of a similar nature, and yet the angels charged such things as evils of sin in some, and did not impute them as evils in others, declaring the latter innocent, and the former guilty. On being asked the reason of of such distinction, when both had indulged in like practices, they replied, that they consider all according to their purpose, intention, and end, and distinguish them accordingly; and therefore that they excuse and condemn those whom the end excuses or condemns, inasmuch as good is the end that influences all who are in heaven, and evil is the end that influences all who are in hell. From what has been said it now plainly appears, to whom sin is imputed, and to whom it is not imputed.

114. To the above shall be added two *Relations* taken from *The Apocalypse Revealed*. The *First* is this: I was seized suddenly with a disease almost deadly. My whole head was oppressed with pain; a pestilential smoke was let in from the great city which is spiritually called Sodom and Egypt (*Apoc.* xi. 8). I was half dead with severe anguish, I expected the end. Thus I lay in bed through three days and a half; my spirit became such, and from it my body. Then I heard about me voices saying, "Lo! he lieth dead in the street of our city, who preached repentance for the remission of sins, and Christ the man as the only God." And they asked some of the clergy, whether he was worthy of burial, as was said concerning the two witnesses slain in that city (*Apoc.* xi. 8–10). And they answered, "No, let him lie, let him be looked at"; and they passed to and fro, and mocked. All this befell me of a truth, when that chapter of the *Apocalypse* was being explained. Then there were heard severe speeches from them, such as the following: "How can repentance be performed without faith? And how can Christ, the man, be adored as God? Whilst we are saved freely without any merit of our own, what need is there of anything besides faith alone, that God the Father sent the Son to take away the damnation of the law, to impute His merit to us, and so to justify us in His sight, and absolve us from our sins, and then to give the Holy Spirit to operate all good in us? Are not these things agreeable to Scripture, and to reason also?" The crowd standing by applauded these things. I heard all this without any power to reply, being almost dead. But after three days and a half my spirit recovered, and as to the spirit I went forth from the street into the city, and again said, "Repent, and believe in Christ, and your sins will be remitted, and you will be saved, but otherwise you will perish. Did not the Lord Himself preach repentance for the remission of sins, and that men should believe in Him? Did He not command His disciples to preach the same? Does not a full security of life follow the dogma of your faith?" But they said, "What idle talk! Has not the Son made satisfaction? And does not the Father impute it to us, and justify us who have believed this? Thus we are led by the spirit of grace, then what sin is in us, what death is with us? Dost thou comprehend this gospel, thou preacher of sin and repentance?" But then a voice went forth from heaven, saying, "What is the faith of an impenitent man, but a dead faith? The end is come, the end is come upon you that are secure, unblamable in your own eyes, justified in your own faith, devils." And suddenly a deep gulf was then opened in the midst of that city, which spread itself far and wide, and the houses fell one upon another, and were swallowed up; and presently water began to bubble up from a large whirlpool, and overflowed the waste.

When they were thus submerged, and seemed inundated, I desired to know their lot in the deep; and it was said to me from heaven, "Thou shalt see and hear." And immediately the waters wherein they seemed to be inundated disappeared, for waters in the spiritual world are correspondences, and consequently appear around those who are in falsities; and then they appeared to me in a sandy bottom, where were large heaps of stones, among which they ran, and lamented that they were cast out of their great city: and they shouted and cried, "Why has all this befallen us? Are we not, through our faith, clean, pure, just, and holy?" Others exclaimed, "Are we not, through our faith, cleansed, purified, justified, and sanctified?" And others cried, "Are we not, through our faith, rendered worthy to be reputed and esteemed clean, pure, just, and holy, before God the Father, and before the whole Trinity, and to be declared such before the angels? Are not we reconciled, atoned for, expiated, and thereby absolved, washed and cleansed from sins? And is not the curse of the law taken away by Christ? Why then are we cast down hither like the condemned? We have heard from an audacious preacher of sin in our great city, *Believe in Christ, and do the work of repentance.* Have we not believed in Christ, whilst we believed in His merit? And have we not done the work of repentance, whilst we confessed ourselves sinners? Why then has all this befallen us?" But then a voice from one side said to them, "Do you know any one sin in which you are? Have you ever examined yourselves? Have you in consequence thereof shunned any evil as sin against God? And whosoever does not shun it, remains in it. Is not sin the devil? Wherefore you are they of whom the Lord says:—

Then shall ye begin to say, we have eaten and drunk in Thy presence, and Thou hast taught in our streets; but He shall answer, I say unto you, I know you not, whence ye are; depart from Me all ye workers of iniquity (*Luke* xiii. 26, 27; *Matt.* vii. 22, 23).

Depart therefore every one to his place; you see the openings into those caverns, enter therein, and work shall be given each of you to do, and afterwards food in proportion to your work; but if not, still presently you will be compelled by hunger to enter.

Afterwards there came a voice from heaven to some on that land, who were without the great city, and who are also described in the *Apocalypse* (xi. 13), crying aloud, "Take heed to yourselves, take heed how you associate yourselves with such persons. Cannot you understand, that evils, which are called sins and iniquities, render man unclean and impure? How can man be cleansed and purified from them, but by actual repentance, and faith in the Lord God the Saviour? Actual repentance consists in a man's examining himself, in knowing and acknowledging his sins, in making himself guilty, in confessing them before the Lord, in imploring help and power to resist them, and thus in desisting from them, and leading a new life, and doing all these things as of himself. Do this once or twice in a year, when you come to the Holy Communion; and afterwards when the sins, whereof you made yourselves guilty, recur, then say to yourselves, we will not consent to them, because they are sins against God; this is actual repentance. Who cannot understand, that he who does not examine himself and see his sins, remains in them? For all evil is delightful to a man from his birth; it is a delight to revenge, to commit whoredom, to defraud and to blaspheme; does not the delight cause them not to be seen? And, if perchance it is said that they are sins, do you not on account of that delight excuse them? Yea, do you not by falsities confirm them, and persuade yourselves that they are not sins, and so remain in them, and afterwards do them more than before; even till you do not know what sin is, or whether there be any sin? But the case is otherwise with every one who performs actual repentance; the evils which he has known and acknowledged he calls sins, and therefore he begins to shun and be averse to them, and to feel their delight as undelightful; and in proportion as this is the case, so far he sees and loves goods, and at length feels the delights of these, which are the delights of heaven. In a word, so far as any one rejects the devil to the back, so far he is adopted by the Lord, and by Him is taught, led, withheld from evils, and held in goods. This is the way, and there is no other from hell to heaven." This is wonderful, that there is in the Reformed a certain deep-rooted opposition and aversion to actual repentance, which is so great, that they cannot force themselves to self-examination, and to see their sins, and to confess them before God; they are seized as it were with horror when they intend it. I have inquired of many in the spiritual world concerning this, and they all said, that it is above their power. When they heard that the papists practise such duties, namely, that they examine themselves, and confess their sins openly before a monk, they greatly wondered, and likewise that the Reformed cannot do the same in private before God, although it is alike enjoined them previous to their approaching the Holy Supper. Some have examined into the cause of this, and found, that faith alone induces such an impenitent state and such a heart; and then it was given them to see, that such of the papists as approach and adore Christ, and do not adore, but only honor, the primates and leaders of their church are saved.

After the above admonition, was heard as it were thunder, and a voice speaking from heaven, saying, "We are amazed; say unto the assembly of the Reformed, believe in Christ, and do the work of repentance, and you shall be saved." And I told them; and added further, "Is not *baptism a sacrament of repentance*, and thereby an introduction into the church? What else do the sponsors promise for the person to be baptized, but that he will renounce the devil and his works? Is not the *Sacred Supper a sacrament of repentance*, and thereby an introduction into heaven? Is it not declared to the communicants, that they must altogether do the work of repentance before they approach? Is not the *Decalogue, which teaches repentance, the doctrine of the whole Christian Church?* Is it not there said, in the six commandments of the second table, thou shalt not do this and that evil, and not said, thou shalt do this and that good? Hence you may know, that in proportion as any one shuns evil, in the same proportion he loves good, and that before this, he does not know either what good is, nor what evil is."

115. *The Second Relation* is this. An angel once said to me, "You wish to see clearly what faith and charity are, and thereby what faith is when separate from charity, and what it is when conjoined with charity; I will also demonstrate it to the eye." I replied, "Show it me." And he said, "Instead of faith and charity, think of light and heat, and you will see clearly. For faith in its essence is the truth of wisdom, and charity in its essence is the affection of love, and the truth of wisdom in heaven is light, and the affection of love in heaven is heat; the light and heat which the angels have, are nothing else. Hence you can see clearly what faith is when separate from charity, and what it is when conjoined with charity. Faith separate from charity is like the light in winter, and faith conjoined with charity is like the light in spring; the light in winter, which is light separate from heat, and in consequence thereof conjoined with cold, strips the trees of all their leaves, kills the grass, hardens the earth and freezes the water; but the light in spring, which is light conjoined with heat, causes the trees to vegetate, first into leaves, then into blossoms, and lastly into fruits; it opens and softens the earth whereby it yields grass, herbs, flowers, and fruits; and it also dissolves the ice, so that the waters flow from their fountains. Exactly similar is the case with faith and charity; faith separate from charity deadens all things, and faith conjoined with charity vivifies all things. The nature of such deadening and vivifying may be seen to the life in our spiritual world, because here faith is light, and charity, heat; for where faith is conjoined with charity, there are paradisal gardens, flower beds, and lawns, in their pleasantness according to conjunction. But where faith is separate from charity, there does not grow even grass, nor any green thing, except it be on thorns and briers." There were then not far from us some of the clergy, whom the angel called justifiers and sanctifiers of men by faith alone, and also arcanists; we said to them the same things and likewise demonstrated them even so that they saw it to be so. But when we asked them whether it was so, they turned themselves away, and said, "We did not hear"; whereupon we cried aloud to them saying, "Hear us now, then"; but immediately they stopped their ears with both hands, and exclaimed, "We do not wish to hear."

CONCLUSION.

From *Jeremiah* (vii. 2–4, 9–11).

Stand in the gate of the house of Jehovah, and proclaim there this word: Thus saith Jehovah of Hosts, the God of Israel: Render good your ways and your works; trust ye not upon the words of a lie, saying, the temple of Jehovah, the temple of Jehovah, the temple of Jehovah is here (that is the church). Will ye steal, kill, commit adultery, and swear falsely, and after that come and stand before Me in this house, whereon My name is called, and say, we are delivered, whilst ye do all these abominations? Is not this house become a den of robbers? Even I, behold, I have seen, saith Jehovah.

APPENDIX.

116. THE FAITH OF THE NEW HEAVEN AND THE NEW CHURCH IN ITS UNIVERSAL FORM, is this: That the Lord from eternity who is Jehovah, came into the world that He might subdue the hells, and glorify His Human; and that without this no mortal could have been saved; and that they are saved who believe in Him.

It is said in the universal form, because this is the universal of faith, and the universal of faith is what must enter into each and all things. It is a universal of faith, that God is one in essence and Person, in whom is the Trinity, and that the

Lord God the Saviour Jesus Christ is He. It is a universal of faith, that no mortal could have been saved, unless the Lord had come into the world. It is a universal of faith, that He came into the world to remove hell from man, and He removed it by combats against it, and by victories over it; thus He subdued it, and reduced it to order, and under obedience to Himself. It is a universal of faith, that He came into the world to glorify the Human which He assumed in the world, that is, to unite it with the Divine from which it was; thus, having subdued hell, He keeps it in order and under obedience to Himself to eternity. Inasmuch as both these could only be effected by means of temptations admitted into His Human, even to the last, which was the passion of the cross, therefore He endured that. These are the universals of faith concerning the Lord.

The universal of Christian faith on man's part is, that he should believe in the Lord, for by believing in Him conjunction with Him is effected, and by conjunction salvation. To believe in Him, is to have confidence that He will save; and because none can have such confidence but he who lives well, therefore this is also meant by believing in Him.

117. THE FAITH OF THE NEW HEAVEN AND THE NEW CHURCH, IN ITS PARTICULAR FORM, is this: That Jehovah God is love itself and wisdom itself, or that He is good itself and truth itself; and that as to the Divine truth itself, which is the Word, and which was God with God, He came down and assumed the Human, for the purpose of restoring to order all things which were in heaven, and all things which were in hell, and all things which were in the church; inasmuch as at that time, the power of the devil, that is, of hell, prevailed over the power of heaven, and on earth the power of evil over the power of good; and thence a total damnation stood before the door and threatened. This impending damnation Jehovah God removed by His Human, which was the Divine truth, and thus He redeemed both angels and men; and afterwards He united in His Human the Divine truth to the Divine good, and thus He returned into His Divine, in which He was from eternity, together with His glorified Human. This is signified by these words in *John:*—

The Word was with God, and God was the Word; and the Word became flesh (i. 1, 14).

And by this in the same:—

I went forth from the Father, and am come into the world; again I leave the world, and go to the Father (xvi. 28).

Hence it appears, that without the coming of the Lord into the world, no one could have been saved. The case is similar at this day; wherefore, unless the Lord come again into the world in Divine truth, which is the Word, no one can be saved.

The particulars of faith on the part of man are these:—I. That God is one, in whom is the Divine Trinity, and that He is the Lord God the Saviour Jesus Christ. II. That saving faith is to believe in Him. III. That evils ought to be shunned, because they are of the devil and from the devil. IV. That goods ought to be done, because they are of God and from God. V. And that they should be done by man as of himself, but that he must believe that they are from the Lord with him and through him. The first two have relation to faith; the next two to charity; and the fifth respects the conjunction of charity and faith, and thereby of the Lord and man: see also what has been said above on these subjects (n. 44).

THE THREE FOLLOWING RELATIONS ARE TAKEN FROM THE APOCALYPSE REVEALED.

118. *The First Relation.* When I was engaged in the explanation of chap. xx. of the *Apocalypse*, and was meditating about the dragon, the beast, and the false prophet, an angelic spirit appeared to me, and asked, "What do you meditate about?" I answered, "About the false prophet." Then he said, "I will lead you to the place where they are who are meant by the false prophet; and who are the same that are meant in chap. xiii. by the beast out of the earth, which had two horns like a lamb, and spake like a dragon." I followed him, and lo, I saw a multitude, in the midst of which there were leaders of the church, who taught that nothing saves man but faith in the merit of Christ, and that works are good, but not for salvation, and that still they are to be taught from the Word, in order that the laity, especially the simple, may be kept more strictly within the bond of obedience to the magistracy, and forced, as if from religion, therefore interiorly, to exercise moral charity. Then one of them observing me, said, "Do you wish to see our shrine, wherein is an image representative of our faith?" I approached and saw it, and lo, it was magnificent. In the midst of it there was the image of a woman clothed in a scarlet robe, and holding in her right hand a gold coin and in her left a string of pearls. But both the image and the shrine were induced by fantasy; for infernal spirits can by fantasies represent magnificent objects, by closing the interiors of the mind, and opening only its exteriors. When I perceived, however, that they were such sorceries, I prayed to the Lord, and suddenly the interiors of my mind were opened, and then, instead of a magnificent shrine, I saw a house full of clefts from the roof to the bottom, in which nothing cohered together; and instead of the woman I saw hanging up in that house an image, the head of which was like a dragon's, the body like a leopard's, and the feet like a bear's, and a mouth like a lion's; thus altogether like the beast out of the sea which is described (*Apoc.* xiii. 2); and instead of a floor there was a swamp containing a multitude of frogs; and I was informed, that beneath the swamp was a large hewn stone, under which the Word lay deeply hidden. On seeing this, I said to the juggler, "Is this your shrine?" and he said, "It is"; but then suddenly his interior sight was opened also, and he saw the same things that I did; whereupon he cried with a great cry, and said, "What and whence is this?" And I said, "This is from light from heaven, which discloses the quality of every form, and thus the quality of your faith separate from spiritual charity." Then immediately an east wind blew, and carried away that shrine with the image, and also dried up the swamp, and thereby exposed the stone under which lay the Word; and afterwards there breathed as it were a vernal warmth from heaven, and lo, then in the same place, there appeared a tabernacle, as to its outward form simple. And the angels who were with me said, "Behold, the tabernacle of Abraham, such as it was when the three angels came to him and announced the future birth of Isaac. It appears indeed simple to the eye, but nevertheless according to the influx of light from heaven it becomes more and more magnificent." And they were permitted to open the heaven, in which were the spiritual angels who excel in wisdom, and then from the influx of light from heaven thence, the tabernacle appeared as a temple resembling that of Jerusalem; and on looking into it, I saw that the stone in the floor, under which the Word was deposited, was set with precious stones, from which there issued forth bright rays as of lightning that shone upon the walls, and caused beautiful variegations of color on certain cherubic forms that were sculptured on them. As I was admiring these things, the angels said, "Thou shalt yet see something still more wonderful." And it was permitted them to open the third heaven, in which were the celestial angels who are in love, and then from the light thence inflowing that whole temple disappeared, and in its stead was seen the Lord alone, standing on the foundation stone, which was the Word, in the same form that He appeared to John (*Apoc.* i.). But because holiness then filled the interiors of the minds of the angels, occasioning in them an inclination to fall on their faces, suddenly the way of light from the third heaven was closed by the Lord, and the way from the second heaven opened; in consequence of which the former appearance of the temple returned, and also of the tabernacle, but this was in the temple. Hereby was illustrated the meaning of these words in chap. xxi. of the *Apocalypse:*—

Behold, the tabernacle of God is with men, and He will dwell with them (ver. 3).

And by these:—

And I saw no temple in the New Jerusalem, for the Lord God Omnipotent and the Lamb are the temple of it (ver. 22).

119. The *Second Relation* from *The Apocalypse Revealed.* Once on waking from sleep, I fell into a profound meditation concerning God; and when I looked up, I saw above me in heaven a very bright light in an oval form; and when I fixed my attention on that light, it receded to the sides, and entered into the circumference. And then behold, heaven was opened to me, and I saw some magnificent things, and angels standing in the form of a circle on the southern side of the opening, speaking with one another. And because I was enkindled with the desire of hearing what they were saying, it was therefore given me first to hear the sound, which was full of heavenly love, and afterwards their speech, which was full of wisdom from that love. They were talking with one another of the *One God*, of *Conjunction with Him*, and of *Salvation* thence. They spoke ineffable things, the most of which cannot be expressed by any natural language. But as I had many times been in consociation with angels in heaven itself, and then in similar speech with them, because in a similar state, I could therefore now understand them, and gather some things from their discourse, which can be expressed rationally in the words of natural language.

They said that the *Divine Esse is One, the Same, the Itself, and Indivisible;* thus also the Divine Essence, because the Divine *Esse* is the Divine Essence; and thus also God, because the Divine Essence, which is also the Divine *Esse*, is God. They illustrated this by spiritual ideas, saying that the Divine *Esse* cannot fall into many, every one of which has the Divine *Esse*, and yet be One, the Same, Itself, and Indivisible; for each would think from his *Esse* from himself and by himself; if he should at the same time also think from the others and by the others unanimously, there would be many unanimous gods, and not one God. For unanimity, as it is the consent of many, and at the same time of each one from himself, and by himself, does not agree with the unity of God, but with a plurality; they did not say *of Gods*, because they could not; for the light of heaven, from which was their thought, and in which their discourse proceeded, resisted.

They also said, that when they wished to pronounce the word Gods, and each as a Person by himself, the effort of utterance immediately fell of itself into One, yea, into the Only God. To this they added that the Divine *Esse* is the Divine *Esse* in Itself, not from Itself; because *from Itself* supposes an *Esse* in Itself from another, and thus supposes a God from

God, which is not given. That which is from God is not called God, but is called the Divine; for what is a God from God; and thus what is a God from God born from eternity; and what is a God from God proceeding through a God born from eternity, but words in which there is not the least light from heaven?

They said further, that the Divine *Esse*, which in itself is God, is the *Same:* not the Same simply, but Infinite; that is, the Same from eternity to eternity: it is the Same everywhere, and the Same with every one and in every one; but that all the variety and variableness is in the recipient; the state of the recipient does this. That the Divine *Esse*, which is God in Himself, is the *Itself*, they illustrated thus. God is the Itself, because He is Love Itself, Wisdom Itself, or what is the same, He is Good Itself, and Truth Itself, and thence Life Itself; which unless they were the Itself in God, would not be anything in heaven and in the world; because there would not be anything of them having relation to the Itself. Every quality derives its quality from this, that there is an Itself from which it is, and to which it has relation, that it may be such. This Itself, which is the Divine *Esse*, is not in place, but is with those and in those who are in place, according to reception; since of love and wisdom, and of good and truth, and thence of life, which are the Itself in God, yea, are God Himself, place cannot be predicated, or progression from place to place, but without place, whence is omnipresence. Wherefore the Lord says, that "He is in the midst of them"; also "He in them, and they in Him." But because He cannot be received by any one as He is in Himself, He appears as He is in Himself as the sun above the angelic heavens, the proceeding from which as light is Himself as to wisdom, and as heat is Himself as to love. He Himself is not the sun; but the Divine love and Divine wisdom, going forth from Himself proximately, round about Himself, appear before the angels as the sun. He Himself in the sun is a Man, He is our Lord Jesus Christ both as to the Divine from which, and as to the Divine Human: since the Itself, which is Love Itself and Wisdom Itself, was His soul from the Father, and thus the Divine Life, which is Life in itself. It is otherwise in every man: in him the soul is not life, but a recipient of life. The Lord also teaches this, saying:—

I am the Way, the Truth, and the Life;

and again:—

As the Father hath life in Himself, so hath He given to the Son to have life in Himself.

Life in Himself is God. They added to this, that he who is in any spiritual light, can perceive that the Divine *Esse*, which is also the Divine Essence, because it is One, the Same, the Itself, and thence Indivisible, cannot be given in many; and that if it were said to be given, manifest contradictions would follow.

After hearing these things, the angels perceived in my thought the common ideas of the Christian Church concerning a Trinity of Persons in Unity and their Unity in Trinity, respecting God, as also concerning the birth of a Son of God from eternity: and they then said, "What are you thinking of? Are you not thinking those things from natural light, with which our spiritual light does not agree? Wherefore, unless you remove the ideas of that thought, we close heaven to you, and go away." But I then said to them, "Enter, I pray, more deeply into my thought and perhaps you will see agreement." And they did so, and saw that by three Persons I understand three proceeding Divine Attributes, which are Creation, Salvation, and Reformation; and that these Attributes are of the one God: and that by the birth of a Son of God from eternity I understand His birth foreseen from eternity and provided in time. And I then related that my natural thought concerning a Trinity and Unity of Persons, and concerning the birth of a Son of God from eternity, I received from the doctrine of faith of the church, which has its name from Athanasias; and that that doctrine is just and right, provided that instead of a Trinity of Persons there be there understood a Trinity of Person, which is given only in the Lord Jesus Christ; and instead of the birth of a Son of God there be understood His birth foreseen from eternity and provided in time; because as to the Human, which He took to Himself in time, He is called openly the *Son of God*.

The angels then said, "Well, well," and they requested that I would say from their mouth, that if any one does not go to the God of heaven and earth Himself, he cannot come into heaven; because heaven is heaven from that Only God; and that this God is Jesus Christ, who is Jehovah the Lord, Creator from eternity, Redeemer in time, and to eternity Regenerator; thus who is at the same time the Father, the Son, and the Holy Spirit; and that this is the Gospel which is to be preached. After this the heavenly light before seen above the opening returned and gradually descended, and filled the interiors of my mind, and enlightened my natural ideas of the Unity and Trinity of God: and then the ideas received about them in the beginning, which were merely natural, I saw separated, as the chaff is separated from the wheat by the motion of a fan, and carried away as by a wind into the north of heaven, and dispersed.

120. The *Third Relation* from *The Apocalypse Revealed*. Since it has been given me by the Lord to see the wonderful things which are in the heavens and below the heavens, I must, from command, relate what has been seen. There appeared a magnificent palace, and in its inmost a temple. In the midst of the latter was a table of gold, upon which was the Word, beside which two angels were standing. Around it were seats in three rows: the seats of the first row were covered with silken cloth of a purple color; the seats of the second row, with silken cloth, of a blue color; and the seats of the third row, with white cloth. Under the roof, high above the table, there appeared a wide-spread canopy, shining with precious stones, from the splendor of which there shone forth as it were a rainbow, as when heaven clears up after a shower. There then suddenly appeared a number of the clergy, occupying all the seats, clothed in the garments of their priestly office. At one side was a wardrobe, where an angel keeper stood; and within there lay splendid garments in beautiful order. It was a *Council convoked by the Lord;* and I heard a voice from heaven, saying, "*Deliberate.*" But they said, "Upon what?" It was said, "*Concerning the Lord the Saviour and concerning the Holy Spirit.*" But when they thought upon these subjects, they were not in enlightenment; wherefore they supplicated, and then light descended from heaven, which first illumined the back part of their heads, and afterwards their temples, and at length their faces: and then they began; and, as it was commanded, first, concerning the *Lord the Saviour.* The first question proposed and discussed was, "*Who assumed the Human in the Virgin Mary?*" And an angel standing at the table upon which was the Word, read before them these words in *Luke:*—

The angel said to Mary, Behold, thou shalt conceive in thy womb, and shalt bring forth a Son, and shalt call His name Jesus; He shall be great, and shall be called the Son of the Most High. And Mary said to the angel, How shall this be, since I know not a man? And the angel answering said, The Holy Spirit shall come upon thee; and the power of the Most High shall overshadow thee; whence the Holy One that is born of thee shall be called the Son of God (i, 31, 32, 34, 35).

As also what is in *Matt.* (i. vers. 20–25); and what is in verse 25 there he read emphatically. Besides these, he read many things from the Evangelists, as *Matt.* iii. 17; and *Matt.* xvii. 5, *John* xx. 31; and elsewhere, where the Lord as to His Human is called "the Son of God," and where He from His Human calls Jehovah His "Father," as also from the Prophets, where it is foretold that Jehovah Himself would come into the world; among which also are these two in *Isaiah:*—

It shall be said in that day, Lo, this is our God, whom we have waited for, that He may free us; this is Jehovah, whom we have waited for; let us exult and rejoice in His salvation (xxv. 9).

The voice of him that crieth in the wilderness, prepare ye the way for Jehovah, make straight in the desert a highway for our God: for the glory of Jehovah shall be revealed, and all flesh shall see it together: Behold, the Lord Jehovih cometh in strength; He shall feed His flock as a shepherd (*Isa.* xl. 3, 5, 10, 11).

And the angel said, "Since Jehovah Himself came into the world, and assumed the Human, and thereby saved and redeemed men, He is therefore called 'the Saviour' and 'the Redeemer' in the prophets." And then he read before them these passages following:—

Surely God is in thee, and there is no God besides; verily Thou art a hidden God, O God of Israel the Saviour (*Isa.* xlv. 14, 15).

Am not I Jehovah? and there is no God else besides Me, a just God and a Saviour, there is none besides Me (*Isa.* xlv. 21, 22).

I am Jehovah, and besides Me there is no Saviour (*Isa.* xliii. 11).

I Jehovah am thy God, and thou shalt acknowledge no God besides Me, and there is no Saviour besides Me (*Hos.* xiii. 4).

That all flesh may know that I Jehovah am thy Saviour, and thy Redeemer (*Isa.* xlix. 26; lx. 16).

As for our Redeemer, Jehovah of Hosts in His name (*Isa.* xlvii. 4).

Their Redeemer is strong, Jehovah of Hosts is His name (*Jer.* l. 34).

O Jehovah my Rock and my Redeemer (*Ps.* xix. 14).

Thus said Jehovah thy Redeemer, the Holy One of Israel, I Jehovah am thy God (*Isa.* xlviii. 17; xliii. 14; xlix. 7; liv. 8).

Thou O Jehovah art our Father, our Redeemer, Thy name is from an age (*Isa.* lxiii. 16).

Thus said Jehovah thy Redeemer, I am Jehovah that maketh all things, and alone by Myself (*Isa.* xliv. 24).

Thus said Jehovah King of Israel, and His Redeemer Jehovah of Hosts, I am the First and the Last, and besides Me there is no God (*Isa.* xliv. 6).

Jehovah of Hosts is His name, and thy Redeemer, the Holy One of Israel, the God of the whole earth shall He be called (*Isa.* liv. 5).

Behold, the days come, that I will raise up unto David a just Branch who shall reign King, and this is His name, Jehovah our Justice (*Jer.* xxiii. 5, 6; xxxiii. 15, 16).

In that day shall Jehovah be King over all the earth; in that day shall Jehovah be one; and His name One (*Zech.* xiv. 9).

Being confirmed from all these passages, those that sat upon the seats said unanimously that Jehovah Himself assumed the Human to redeem and save men. But there was then heard a voice from the Roman Catholics, who had hid themselves behind the altar, saying, "How can Jehovah the Father become Man? is He not the Creator of the universe?" And one of them that sat upon the seats of the second row turned himself, and said, "Who then?" And he behind the altar answered, "The Son from eternity." But he received for answer, "Is not the Son from eternity, according to your confession, the Creator of the universe also? And what is a Son or a God born from eternity? And how can the Divine essence, which is one and indivisible, be separated, and some of it descend and take on the Human, and not at the same time the whole?"

The second discussion concerning the Lord was, whether God the Father and He thus are one, as the soul and the body are one? They said that this is a consequence, because the soul is from the Father. And then one of those who sat upon the seats in the third row, read from the Creed which is called *Athanasian* these words: "Although our Lord Jesus Christ, the Son of God, is God and Man, still they are not two, but one Christ; yea, He is altogether one, He is one Person; since as the soul and the body make one man, so God and Man are one Christ." The reader said that this faith is received in the whole Christian world, even by the Roman Catholics. And they then said, "What need is there of more? God the Father and He are one, as the soul and the body are one." And they said, "As it is so, we see that the Lord's Human is Divine, because it is the Human of Jehovah; then that the Lord as to the Divine Human is to be approached; and that thus and not otherwise can the Divine which is called the Father be approached." This conclusion of theirs the angel confirmed by many more passages from the Word, among which were these in *Isaiah* :—

Unto us a Boy is born, unto us a Son is given, whose name is Wonderful, Counsellor, God, Hero, the Father of eternity, the Prince of peace (ix. 6).

In the same:—

Abraham hath not known us, and Israel doth not acknowledge us; Thou, O Jehovah, art our Father, our Redeemer, from everlasting is Thy name (lxiii. 16).

And in *John* :—

Jesus said, He that believeth in Me, believeth in Him that sent Me, and He that seeth Me seeth Him who sent Me (xii. 44, 45).

Philip said unto Jesus, Show us the Father; Jesus saith unto him, He that seeth Me seeth the Father; how sayest thou then, show us the Father? Believest thou not that I am in the Father, and the Father in Me? Believe Me that I am in the Father and the Father in Me (*John* xiv. 8–11).

Jesus said, I and the Father are one (*John* x. 30).

Then:—

All things which the Father hath are Mine, and all Mine are the Father's (*John* xvi. 15; xvii. 10).

And lastly this:—

Jesus said, I am the Way, the Truth, and the Life; no one cometh to the Father but by Me (*John* xiv. 6).

On hearing these, they all said with one voice and heart, that the Lord's Human is Divine, and that this is to be approached that the Father may be approached; since Jehovah God, who is the Lord from eternity, through it sent Himself into the world, and made Himself visible to the eyes of men, and thus accessible. Likewise He made Himself visible to the eyes of men, and thus accessible in the human form to the ancients, but then through an angel.

After this followed the deliberation concerning the Holy Spirit. And first was disclosed the idea of many respecting God the Father, the Son, and the Holy Spirit, which was as if God the Father was sitting on high, and the Son at His right hand, and they were sending forth the Holy Spirit from them, to enlighten and teach men. But a voice was then heard from heaven, saying, "We cannot endure that idea of thought. Who does not know that Jehovah God is omnipresent? He who knows and acknowledges this, will also acknowledge that He Himself enlightens and teaches; and that there is not an intermediate God, distinct from Him, and still less from two, as one person from another. Therefore let the former idea, which is vain, be removed; and let this which is just be received; and you will see this clearly." But a voice was then heard again from the Roman Catholics, who had hid themselves behind the altar of the temple, saying, "What then is the Holy Spirit, who is named in the Word in the Evangelists and in Paul, by whom so many of the learned men from the clergy, especially from ours, say that they are led? Who in the Christian world at this day denies the Holy Spirit and its operation?" At this one of those who were sitting upon the second row of seats, turned himself and said, "You say that the Holy Spirit is a Person by Himself and a God by Himself. But what is a person going forth and proceeding from a person, but operation going forth and proceeding? One person cannot go forth and proceed from another through a third, but operation can. Or what is a God going forth and proceeding from a God, but the Divine going forth and proceeding? One God cannot go forth and proceed from another through a third, but the Divine can. Is not the Divine Essence one and indivisible? And as the Divine Essence or the Divine *Esse* is God, is not God one and indivisible?" On hearing these things, they who sat upon the seats concluded unanimously that the Holy Spirit is not a Person by itself, nor a God by itself; but that it is the Holy

Divine going forth and proceeding from the Only Omnipresent God, who is the Lord. At this the angels that stood by the golden table upon which was the Word, said, "It is well. We do not anywhere read in the Old Testament, that the prophets spoke the Word from the Holy Spirit, but from Jehovah the Lord; and where 'the Holy Spirit' is mentioned in the New Testament, the proceeding Divine is meant, which is the Divine enlightening, teaching, vivifying, reforming, and regenerating."

After this there followed another discussion concerning the Holy Spirit, which was, From whom does the Divine which is called the Holy Spirit proceed? is it from the Divine which is called the Father, or from the Divine Human which is called the Son? And when they were discussing this, the light shone on them from heaven, from which they saw that the Holy Divine, which is meant by the Holy Spirit, proceeds from the Divine in the Lord through His glorified Human, which is the Divine Human, comparatively as all activity proceeds from the soul through the body with man. This the angel standing at the table confirmed from the Word by these passages:—

He whom the Father hath sent, speaketh the words of God; He hath not given the Spirit by measure unto Him; the Father loveth the Son, and hath given all things into His hand (*John* iii. 34, 35).

There shall come forth a Rod out of the stem of Jesse, the Spirit of Jehovah shall rest upon Him, the Spirit of wisdom and intelligence, the Spirit of counsel and might (*Isa.* xi. 1, 2).

That the Spirit of Jehovah was given upon Him, and that it was in Him (*Isa.* xlii. 1; lix. 19, 20; lxi. 1; *Luke* iv. 18).

When the Holy Spirit shall come, which I will send unto you from the Father (*John* xv. 26).

He shall glorify Me, for He shall receive of mine, and announce it unto you: all things that the Father hath are mine; therefore I said that He shall receive of mine, and announce it unto you (*John* xvi. 14, 15).

If I go away, I will send the Comforter unto you (*John* xvi. 7).

The Comforter is the Holy Spirit (*John* xiv. 26).

The Holy Spirit was not yet, because Jesus was not yet glorified (*John* vii. 39).

After the glorification, Jesus breathed on them, and said to the disciples, Receive ye the Holy Spirit (*John* xx. 22).

And in the *Apocalypse*:—

Who shall not glorify Thy name, O Lord? for Thou alone art holy (xv. 4).

Since the Lord's Divine operation from His Divine omnipresence is meant by the Holy Spirit, therefore when He spoke to the disciples concerning the Holy Spirit which He would send from God the Father, He also said:—

> I will not leave you orphans; I go away, and come unto you: and in that day ye shall know that I am in My Father, and ye in Me, and I in you (*John* xiv. 18, 20, 28).

And just before His departure out of the world, He said:—

> Lo, I am with you all the days until the consummation of the age (*Matt.* xxviii. 20).

Having read these words before them, the angel said, "From these and many other passages in the Word, it is manifest that the Divine which is called the Holy Spirit proceeds from the Divine in the Lord through His Divine Human." To this they that sat upon the seats said, "This is the Divine truth."

At length this decision was made, "That from the deliberations in this Council we have clearly seen, and thence acknowledge as the holy truth, that in the Lord God the Saviour Jesus Christ there is a Divine Trinity, which is the Divine from which, that is called the Father; the Divine Human, which is the Son; and the proceeding Divine, which is the Holy Spirit, crying out, That in Jesus Christ dwelleth all the fulness of the Divinity bodily (*Col.* ii. 9). Thus there is one God in the church."

After these things were concluded in that magnificent Council, they rose up: and the angel keeper of the wardrobe came and brought to each of those who sat upon the seats, splendid garments interwoven here and there with threads of gold, and said, "Receive these wedding garments." And they were conducted in glory into the New Christian Heaven, with which the Lord's church on earth, which is the New Jerusalem, will be conjoined.

> There shall be one day which is known to Jehovah, not day nor night, but about the time of evening it shall be light. It shall come to pass in that day that living waters shall go forth from Jerusalem. And Jehovah shall be King over all the earth; in that day Jehovah shall be one, and His name one (*Zech.* xiv. 7-9).

THE END.

The Intercourse
between
The Soul and The Body

The Intercourse

BETWEEN

The Soul and The Body

WHICH IS BELIEVED TO BE EITHER BY

PHYSICAL INFLUX, OR BY SPIRITUAL INFLUX,
OR BY PRE-ESTABLISHED HARMONY

BY

EMANUEL SWEDENBORG

Originally published at London, 1769

CONTENTS

                                                                         Nos.

I. There are two worlds, the spiritual world, where spirits and angels are; and the natural world, where men are......... 3

II. The spiritual world existed and subsists from its own sun, and the natural world from its own sun...................... 4

III. The sun of the spiritual world is pure love from Jehovah God, Who is in the midst of it................................ 5

IV. From that sun proceed heat and light, and the heat proceeding from it is in its essence love, and the light thence is in its essence wisdom....................................... 6

V. Both that heat and that light flow into man, the heat into his will, where it produces the good of love, and the light into his understanding, where it produces the truth of wisdom... 7

VI. Those two, namely, heat and light, or love and wisdom, flow conjointly from God into the soul of man, and through this into his mind, its affections and thoughts, and from these into the senses, speech, and actions of the body........... 8

VII. The sun of the natural world is pure fire, and by means of this sun the world of nature existed and subsists.............. 9

VIII. Therefore every thing which proceeds from this sun, regarded in itself, is dead....................................... 10

IX. The spiritual clothes itself with the natural, as a man clothes himself with a garment................................. 11

X. Spiritual things, thus clothed in a man, enable him to live a rational and moral man, thus a spiritually natural man.... 12

XI. The reception of that influx is according to the state of love and wisdom with man................................... 13

	Nos.
XII. The understanding in man can be elevated into the light, that is, into the wisdom in which the angels of heaven are, according to the cultivation of his reason; and in like manner his will can be elevated into the heat of heaven, that is, into love, according to the deeds of his life; but the love of the will is not elevated except so far as man wills and does those things which the wisdom of the understanding teaches.....	14
XIII. It is altogether otherwise with beasts.......................	15
XIV. There are three degrees in the spiritual world, and three degrees in the natural world, hitherto unknown, according to which all influx takes place..............................	16
XV. Ends are in the first degree, causes in the second, and effects in the third...	17
XVI. From these things it is evident what is the quality of spiritual influx from its origin to its effects.......................	18
A Relation concerning the disciples of Aristotle, Descartes, and Leibnitz..	19
A Relation concerning the spiritual meaning of a fisherman..	20

The Intercourse

between

The Soul and The Body

which is believed to be either by

PHYSICAL INFLUX, OR BY SPIRITUAL INFLUX, OR BY PRE-ESTABLISHED HARMONY.

---

1. Concerning the intercourse between the soul and the body, or the operation of one into the other, and of one with the other, there are three opinions and traditions, which are hypotheses. The first is called Physical Influx, the second Spiritual Influx, and the third Pre-established Harmony. The *first*, which is called Physical Influx, is from the appearances of the senses and the fallacies therefrom, since it appears as if the objects of sight, which affect the eyes, flow into thought and produce it; in like manner that speech, which moves the ears, flows into the mind and produces ideas there; and similarly with the senses of smell, taste, and touch. Since the organs of these senses first receive the impressions from contact with the world, and according as they are affected the mind appears to think and also to will; for this reason the ancient philosophers and schoolmen believed that influx was derived from these organs into the soul, and thus they adopted the hypothesis of physical or natural influx. The *second* hypothesis, which is called Spiritual Influx, by some occasional influx, is from order and its laws; since the soul is a spiritual substance, and therefore purer, prior, and interior, but the body is material, and therefore grosser, posterior, and exterior; and it is according to order that purer should flow into grosser, prior into posterior, and interior into exterior, thus spiritual into material, and not the reverse. Consequently it is of order that the thinking mind should flow into the sight according to the state induced on the eyes from objects, which state the mind also disposes at will; and likewise the perceptive mind into the hearing according to the state induced on the ears from speech. The *third* hypothesis, which is called Pre-established Harmony, is from the appearances and fallacies of reason, since the mind in its operation acts together and at the same time with the body. But yet every operation is first successive and afterward simultaneous. Successive operation is influx, and simultaneous operation is harmony; as when the mind thinks and afterward speaks, or when it wills and afterward acts. It is therefore a fallacy of reason to establish simultaneous operation and to exclude successive. Besides these three opinions concerning the intercourse of the soul and the body, no fourth is possible, for either the soul must operate on the body, or the body on the soul, or both continually together.

2. Since spiritual influx is from order and its laws, as was said, therefore this influx has been acknowledged and received by the wise in the learned world in preference to the other two hypotheses. All that which is from order is truth, and truth manifests itself by the light implanted in it, even in the shade of reason, in which hypotheses are. But there are three things that involve this hypothesis in shade, ignorance of what the soul is, ignorance of what the spiritual is, and ignorance of what influx is; therefore these three must first be unfolded before reason sees the truth itself. For hypothetical truth is not truth itself, but only a conjecture of truth. It is as a picture on the wall seen at night by the light of the stars, on which the mind induces various forms according to its fancy. It is otherwise when the light of the sun after the dawn shines upon it, and disposes and brings to view not only its generals, but also its particulars. So out of the shade of truth in which this hypothesis is, truth is opened when it is known what the spiritual is and what is its quality in comparison with the natural, also what the human soul is and its quality, as well as the nature of the influx that flows into the soul and through it into the perceptive and thinking mind, and from this into the body. But these things cannot be explained except by one to whom it has been granted by the Lord to associate with angels in the spiritual world and at the same time with men in the natural world. And because this has been granted to me, I have been able to describe both the spiritual and the natural, and their nature; which has been done in the work on *Conjugial Love*, the spiritual is described there in the Relation (n. 326-329); the human soul (n. 315); influx (n. 380); and more fully (n. 415-422). Who does not know, or may not know, that the good of love and the truth of faith flow from God into man, and that they flow into his soul, and are felt in his mind, and flow out from his thought into his speech, and from his will into his actions? That spiritual influx, and its origin and derivation, are from this, will be manifested in the following order:—

I. There are two worlds, the spiritual world, where spirits and angels are, and the natural world, where men are.

II. The spiritual world existed and subsists from its own sun, and the natural world from its sun.

III. The sun of the spiritual world is pure love from Jehovah God, Who is in the midst of it.

IV. From that sun proceed heat and light, and the heat proceeding from it is in its essence love, and the light thence is in its essence wisdom.

V. Both that heat and that light flow into man, the heat into his will, where it produces the good of love, and the light into his understanding, where it produces the truth of wisdom.

VI. These two, heat and light, or love and wisdom, flow conjointly from God into the soul of man, and through this into his mind, its affections and thoughts, and from these into the senses, speech, and actions of the body,

VII. The sun of the natural world is pure fire, and by means of this sun the world of nature existed and subsists.

VIII. Therefore everything which proceeds from this sun, regarded in itself, is dead.

IX. The spiritual clothes itself with the natural, as a man clothes himself with a garment.

X. Spiritual things thus clothed in a man enable him to live a rational and moral man, thus a spiritually natural man.

XI. The reception of that influx is according to the state of love and wisdom with man.

XII. The understanding in man can be elevated into the light, that is, into the wisdom in which the angels of heaven are, according to the cultivation of his reason; and his will can be elevated in like manner into heat, that is, into love, according to the deeds of his life; but the love of the will is not elevated, except so far as man wills and does those things which the wisdom of the understanding teaches.

XIII. It is altogether otherwise with beasts.

XIV. There are three degrees in the spiritual world, and three degrees in the natural world, according to which all influx takes place.

XV. Ends are in the first degree, causes in the second, and effects in the third.

XVI. From these things it is evident what is the quality of spiritual influx from its origin to its effects.

Each of these propositions shall now be briefly illustrated.

I.

There are two worlds, the spiritual world, where spirits and angels are, and the natural world, where men are.

3. That there is a spiritual world, in which spirits and angels are, distinct from the natural world in which men are, has hitherto been deeply hidden even in the Christian world. The reason is, because no angel has descended and taught it by word of mouth, and no man has ascended and seen it. Lest therefore from ignorance of that world, and the uncertain faith concerning heaven and hell resulting from it, man should be infatuated to such a degree as to become an atheistic naturalist, it has pleased the Lord to open the sight of my spirit, and to elevate it into heaven, and also to let it down into hell, and to present to view the quality of both. Thence it has thus been manifested to me that there are two worlds, which are distinct from each other; one in which all things are spiritual, which is therefore called the spiritual world, and the other in which all things are natural, and thence is called the natural world; and that spirits and angels live in their own world, and men in theirs; and also that every man passes by death from his own world into the other, and in this he lives to eternity. A knowledge of both of these worlds must be given first, in order that influx, which is here treated of, may be disclosed from its beginning; for the spiritual world flows into the natural world, and actuates it in all its parts, both with men and with beasts, and also constitutes the vegetative activity in trees and herbs.

II.

The spiritual world existed and subsists from its own sun, and the natural world from its own sun.

4. That there is one sun of the spiritual world and another of the natural world, is because those worlds are altogether distinct; and a world derives its origin from its sun; for a world in which all things are spiritual cannot arise from a sun all things from which are natural, for thus there would be physical influx, which however is contrary to order. That the world existed from the sun, and not the reverse, is manifest from the effect of the cause, namely, that the world, in each and every part subsists by means of the sun; and subsistence demonstrates existence, wherefore it is said that subsistence is perpetual existence; from which it is evident, that if the sun were removed, its world would fall into chaos, and this chaos into nothing. That in the spiritual world there is a sun other than that in the natural world, I can testify, for I have seen it. It appears fiery like our sun, of a nearly similar magnitude, it is distant from the angels as our sun is from men; but it does not rise nor set, but stands immovable at a middle altitude between the zenith and the horizon, whence the angels have perpetual light and perpetual spring. The man of reason, who knows nothing concerning the sun of the spiritual world, easily goes astray in his idea of the creation of the universe, which, when he deeply considers it, he perceives no otherwise than as being from nature; and as the origin of nature is the sun, no otherwise than as being from its sun as a creator. Moreover no one can apprehend spiritual influx, unless he also knows its origin; for all influx is from a sun, spiritual influx from its sun, and natural influx from its sun. The internal sight of man, which is that of his mind, receives influx from the spiritual sun, but his external sight, which is that of his body, receives influx from the natural sun; and both conjoin themselves together in operation, in like manner as the soul conjoins itself with the body. From these things it is evident into what blindness, thick darkness, and foolishness they may fall who know nothing about the spiritual world and its sun: into *blindness*, because the mind that depends on the sight of the eye alone becomes in its reasonings like a bat, which flies by night here and there to a suspended cloth; into *thick darkness*, because the sight of the mind, when the sight of the eye flows into it from within, is deprived of all spiritual light, and becomes like an owl; into *foolishness*, because the man still thinks, but from natural things concerning spiritual things, and not the reverse; thus insanely, stupidly, and foolishly.

III.

The sun of the spiritual world is pure love, from Jehovah God, who is in the midst of it.

5. Spiritual things cannot proceed from any other source than from love, and love cannot proceed from any other source than from Jehovah God, Who is love itself. Wherefore the sun of the spiritual world, from which all spiritual things flow forth as from their fountain, is pure love from Jehovah God, Who is in the midst of it. That sun itself is not God, but is from God, and is the nearest sphere around Him from Him. By means of this sun the universe was created by Jehovah God; by which universe are meant all worlds in the aggregate, which are as many as the stars in the expanse of our heaven. That creation was effected by means of that sun, which is pure love, thus by Jehovah God, is because love is the very *esse* of life, and wisdom is the *existere* of life therefrom, and all things were created from love by wisdom. This is meant by these words in *John:*—

The Word was with God, and God was the Word, all things were made by Him, and without Him nothing was made which was made; and the world was made by Him (i. 1, 3, 10).

"The Word" there is the Divine truth; thus also the Divine wisdom; wherefore also the Word is there called the light which enlightens every man (ver. 9), in like manner as does the Divine wisdom by Divine truth. Those who derive the origin of worlds from any other source than from the Divine love through the Divine wisdom, are deluded like persons of disordered brain, who see spectres as men, phantoms as lights, and imaginary beings as real figures. For the created universe is a connected work, from love by wisdom. You will see this if you are able to investigate the connections of things in their order from firsts to lasts. As God is one, so also the spiritual sun is one; for the extension of space cannot be predicated of spiritual things, which are the derivations of that sun; and essence and existence without space is everywhere in spaces without space; thus the Divine love is from the beginning of the universe to all its boundaries. That the Divine fills all things, and by filling preserves all things in the state in which they were created, reason sees remotely, and closely so far as it knows the quality of love as it is in itself, with its conjunction with wisdom for the perception of ends, its influx into wisdom for the exhibition of causes; and its operation through wisdom for the production of effects.

IV.

From that sun proceed heat and light, and the heat proceeding from it is in its essence love, and the light thence is in its essence wisdom.

6. It is known that in the Word, and thence in the common language of preachers, the Divine love is expressed by fire, as that heavenly fire fills the heart and kindles holy desires to worship God. The reason is because fire corresponds to love, and therefore signifies it. From this it is that Jehovah God was seen as fire in the bush before Moses, and in like manner on mount Sinai before the sons of Israel; and that it was commanded that fire should be perpetually kept upon the altar, and that the lights of the lampstand in the tabernacle should be lighted every evening. This was because fire signified love. That there is heat from that fire is clearly evident from the effects of love; for a man is kindled, grows warm, and is inflamed, as his love is exalted into zeal, or into the wrath of anger. The heat of the blood, or the vital heat of men, and of animals in general, is from no other source than from the love, which constitutes their life. Nor is infernal fire anything else than love opposite to heavenly love. This then is the reason that the Divine love appears to the angels as the sun in their world, fiery like our sun, as was said above, and that the angels are in heat according to their reception of love from Jehovah God through that sun. It follows from this that the light there is in its essence wisdom; for love and wisdom are indivisible, like *esse* and *existere*, for love exists through wisdom and according to it. This is very much as it is in our world, in that, in the time of spring, heat unites itself with light, and produces germinations and at length fructifications. Furthermore, every one knows that spiritual heat is love, and spiritual light is wisdom, for a man grows warm according as he loves, and his understanding is in light according as he is wise. I have often seen that spiritual light. It immensely exceeds natural light in brightness and also in splendor, for it is as brightness and splendor themselves, and appears like bright and dazzling snow, as the garments of the Lord appeared when He was transfigured (*Mark* ix. 3; *Luke* ix. 29). Since light is wisdom, therefore the Lord calls Himself:—

The Light which enlightens every man (*John* i. 9).

And says in other places that:—

He is the Light itself (*John* iii. 19; viii. 12; xii. 35, 36, 46).

That is, that He is the Divine truth itself, which is the Word, thus wisdom itself. It is believed that natural light which is also rational light, is from the light of our world; but it is from the light of the sun of the spiritual world; for the sight of the mind flows into the sight of the eye, thus also the lights, and not the reverse. If the reverse took place, there would be physical influx and not spiritual influx.

V.

Both that heat and that light flow into man, the heat into his will, where it produces the good of love, and the light into his understanding, where it produces the truth of wisdom.

7. It is known that all things universally have relation to good and truth, and that there is not given a single entity in which there is not what has relation to those two. From this it is that in man there are two receptacles of life, one which is the receptacle of good, which is called the will, and another which is the receptacle of truth, which is called the understanding; and as good is of love, and truth is of wisdom, the will is the receptacle of love, and the understanding is the receptacle of wisdom. That good is of love, is because what a man loves, this he wills, and when he does it he calls it good; and that truth is of wisdom, is because all wisdom is from truths; yea, the good which a wise man thinks, is truth, and this becomes good when he wills it and does it. He who does not rightly distinguish between these two receptacles of life, which are the will and the understanding, and does not form a clear notion concerning them, vainly endeavors to know spiritual influx; for there is influx into the will, and there is influx into the understanding; there is an influx of the good of love into man's will, and there is an influx of the truth of wisdom into his understanding, both of them from Jehovah God immediately through the sun in the midst of which He is, and mediately through the angelic heaven. These two receptacles, the will and the understanding, are as distinct as heat and light; for the will receives the heat of heaven, which in its essence is love, and the understanding receives the light of heaven, which in its essence is wisdom, as was said above. There is an influx from the human mind into the speech, and there is an influx into the actions; the influx into the speech is from the will through the understanding, but the influx into the actions is from the understanding through the will. They who know only of the influx into the understanding, and not at the same time into the will, and who reason and conclude from this, are like one-eyed persons, who see the objects on one side only, and not at the same time on the other; and like maimed persons, who do their work awkwardly with one hand only; and like the lame who hobble on one foot with a crutch. From these few things it is made plain, that spiritual heat flows into man's will, and produces the good of love, and that spiritual light flows into his understanding, and produces the truth of wisdom.

VI.

Those two, namely heat and light, or love and wisdom, flow conjointly from God into the soul of man, and through this into his mind, its affections and thoughts, and from these into the senses, speech, and actions of the body.

8. The spiritual influx hitherto treated of by men of learning, is the influx from the soul into the body, and not any influx into the soul, and through that into the body; although it is known that all the good of love, and all the truth of faith, flow from God into man, and that nothing of them is from man; and those things which flow in from God, flow directly into his soul and through the soul into the rational mind, and through this into those things which constitute the body. If any one investigates spiritual influx in any other manner, he is like one who stops up the source of a fountain, and still seeks there for unfailing waters; or like one who deduces the origin of a tree from the root and not from the seed; or like one who examines derivatives without the beginning. For the soul is not life in itself, but is a recipient of life from God, Who is life in itself; and all influx is of life, thus from God. This is meant by this passage:—

Jehovah God breathed into the nostrils of the man the soul of lives, and the man became a living soul (*Gen.* ii. 7).

"To breathe into the nostrils the soul of lives," signifies to implant the perception of good and truth. And the Lord also says of Himself:—

As the Father hath life in Himself, so hath He given also to the Son to have life in Himself (*John* v. 26).

"Life in Himself" is God; and the life of the soul is life that flows in from God. Now because all influx is of life, and life operates through its receptacles, and the inmost or first of the receptacles in man is his soul, therefore, that influx may be rightly perceived, it is necessary to begin from God, and not from an intermediate station. If the beginning were from an intermediate station, the doctrine of influx would be like a chariot without wheels, or like a ship without sails. Since it is so, therefore in the preceding articles the sun of the spiritual world has been treated of, in the midst of which is Jehovah God (n. 5); and the influx thence of love and wisdom, thus of life (n. 6, 7). The reason that life from God flows into man through the soul, and through this into his mind, that is, into its affections and thoughts, and from these into the senses, speech, and actions of the body, is because these are of life in successive order; for the mind is subordinate to the soul, and the body is subordinate to the mind. And the mind has two lives, one of the will and another of the understanding. The life of the will is the good of love, the derivations of which are called affections, and the life of the understanding is the truth of wisdom, the derivations of which are called thoughts. By these together the mind lives. But the senses, speech, and actions are the life of the body; that these are from the soul through the mind, follows from the order in which they are; and from this they manifest themselves before a wise man without investigation. The human soul, because it is a superior spiritual substance, receives influx immediately from God; but the human mind, because it is an inferior spiritual substance, receives influx from God mediately through the spiritual world; and the body, because it is from the substances of nature, which are called material, receives influx from God mediately through the natural world. That the good of love and the truth of wisdom flow from God into the soul of man conjointly, that is, united into one, but that they are divided by man in their progression, and are conjoined only with those who suffer themselves to be led by God, will be seen in the following articles.

VII.

The sun of the natural world is pure fire, and by means of this sun the world of nature existed and subsists.

9. That nature and its world, by which are meant the atmospheres, and the earths which are called planets, among which is the terraqueous globe on which we dwell, and also each and all of the things which yearly adorn its surface, subsist solely from the sun, which constitutes their centre, and which by the rays of its light and the temperings of its heat is everywhere present, every one knows with certainty from experience, from the testimony of the senses, and from the writings which treat of the way in which the world has become inhabited. And as the perpetual subsistence of these things is from the sun, reason may with certainty conclude that their existence also is thence; for perpetually to subsist is perpetually to exist as they first existed. From this it follows that the natural world was created by Jehovah God secondarily through this sun. That there are spiritual things and that there are natural things, which are entirely distinct from each other, and that the origin and maintenance of spiritual things is from a sun which is pure love, in the midst of which is the Creator and founder of the universe, Jehovah God, has been heretofore shown; but that the origin and maintenance of natural things is from a sun which is pure fire, and that the latter is from the former, and both from God, follows of itself, as the posterior follows from the prior, and the prior from the first. That the sun of nature and its worlds is pure fire, all its effects clearly show; as the concentration of its rays into a focus by optical instruments, from which proceeds fire burning with vehemence, and also flame; the nature of its heat, which is similar to heat from elementary fire; the graduation of that heat according to its angle of incidence, whence are the varieties of climate, and also the four seasons of the year; besides many things, from which reason, by the senses of its body, may confirm the truth that the sun of the natural world is mere fire, and also that it is fire in its purity itself. Those who know nothing concerning the origin of spiritual things from their own sun, but only concerning the origin of natural things from theirs, can scarcely avoid confounding spiritual things and natural things, and concluding, through the fallacies of the senses and thence of the reason, that spiritual things are nothing but pure natural things, and that from the activity of the latter, excited by light and heat, wisdom and love arise. Those, because they see nothing else with their eyes, and smell nothing else with their nostrils, and breathe nothing else with their breast than nature, therefore ascribe all rational things to it also, and thus absorb naturalism, as a sponge does waters. But these may be compared to charioteers who yoke the horses behind the chariot and not before it. It is otherwise with those who distinguish between spiritual things and natural things, and deduce the latter from the former; these also perceive that the influx of the soul into the body is spiritual, and that natural things, which are of the body, serve the soul for vehicles and means, that it may produce its effects in the natural world. If you conclude otherwise, you may be likened to a crab, which in walking assists its progress with its tail, and draws its eyes backward at every step; and your rational sight may be compared to the sight of the eyes of Argus in the back of his head, when those in his forehead were asleep. These persons also believe themselves to be Arguses when they reason; for they say, Who does not see that the origin of the universe is from nature? and what then is God but the inmost extension of nature? and the like irrational things; of which they boast more than the wise do of rational things.

VIII.

Therefore every thing which proceeds from this sun, regarded in itself, is dead.

10. Who does not see from the reason of his understanding, if this is a little elevated above the sensual things of the body, that love regarded in itself is alive, and that the appearance of its fire is life, and, on the contrary, that elementary fire regarded in itself is respectively dead; consequently, that the sun of the spiritual world, because it is pure love, is alive, and that the sun of the natural world, because it is pure fire, is dead; and similarly all things which proceed and exist from them? There are two things which produce all the effects in the universe, Life and Nature, and they produce them according to order when life from within actuates nature. It is otherwise when nature from within brings life to act, which takes place with those who place nature, which in itself is dead, above and within life, and thence who strive solely after the pleasures of the senses and the lusts of the flesh, and care nothing for the spiritual things of the soul and the truly rational things of the mind. Such persons, on account of that inversion, are they who are called "the dead"; such are all atheistic naturalists in the world, and all satans in hell. They are also called "the dead" in the Word, as in *David:*—

> They joined themselves to Baal-peor, and ate the sacrifices of the dead (*Ps.* cvi. 28).
>
> The enemy persecuteth my soul, he maketh me to sit in darkness like the dead of the world (*Ps.* cxliii. 3).
>
> To hear the groaning of the bound, and to open to the sons of death (*Ps.* cii. 21).

And in the *Apocalypse:*—

> I know thy works, that thou hast a name that thou livest, but thou art dead; be watchful and establish the things which remain that are ready to die (iii. 1, 2).

They are called "the dead," because spiritual death is damnation, and damnation is the lot of those who believe that life is from nature, and thus that the light of nature is the light of life, and thereby hide, suffocate, and extinguish every idea of God, of heaven, and of eternal life. Such persons are like owls, which see light in darkness and darkness in light, that is, falsities as truths and evils as goods; and because the delights of evil are the delights of their hearts, they are not unlike those birds and beasts which devour the bodies of the dead as dainties, and perceive the fetid odors from sepulchres as balsams. Such persons also do not see any other influx than physical or natural; if notwithstanding they affirm influx to be spiritual, this is not done from any idea of it, but from the mouth of a teacher.

IX.

The spiritual clothes itself with the natural, as a man clothes himself with a garment.

11. It is known that in every operation there is an active and a passive; and that from the active alone nothing exists, and nothing from the passive alone. It is the same with the spiritual and the natural; the spiritual, because it is a living force, is active, and the natural, because it is a dead force, is passive. Hence it follows that whatever has existed in this solar world from the beginning, and afterwards exists every moment, is from the spiritual through the natural, and this not only in the subjects of the animal kingdom, but also in the subjects of the vegetable kingdom. Another similar thing is also known, namely, that in every thing which is effected there is a principal and an instrumental, and that these two, when anything is done, appear as one, although they are distinctly two; wherefore this also is one of the canons of wisdom, that the principal cause and the instrumental cause make together one cause; so also do the spiritual and the natural. That these two in producing effects appear as one, is because the spiritual is within the natural as the fibre is within the muscle, and as the blood is within the arteries; or as the thought is within the speech, and the affection in sounds; and it makes itself felt by means of the natural. From these things, but still as if through a lattice, it is evident that the spiritual clothes itself with the natural, as a man clothes himself with a garment. The organic body with which the soul clothes itself is here likened to a garment, because it clothes the soul, and the soul also puts off the body, and casts it away as exuviae when by death it emigrates from the natural world into its own spiritual world. For the body grows old like a garment; but not the soul, because this is a spiritual substance, which has nothing in common with the changes of nature, which progress from their beginnings to their ends, and are periodically terminated. They who do not consider the body as the vesture or covering of the soul, and as being in itself dead, and only adapted to receive the living forces flowing in through the soul from God, cannot help concluding, from fallacies, that the soul lives by itself, and the body by itself, and that there is a pre-established harmony between the lives of the two; or even that the life of the soul flows into the life of the body, or the life of the body into the life of the soul, and thus they conceive influx as either spiritual or natural; when yet it is a truth which is proved by every thing that is created, that what is posterior does not act from itself, but from what is prior, from which it proceeded; thus that neither does this act from itself, but from something still prior; and thus that nothing acts except from the First which acts from itself, thus from God. Besides, there is only one life, and this is not capable of being created, but is eminently capable of flowing into forms organically adapted to its reception. Such forms are each and all of the things in the created universe. It is believed by many that the soul is life, and thus, that a man, because he lives from the soul, lives from his own life, thus from himself, and therefore not by an influx of life from God; but these cannot help tying a sort of Gordian knot of fallacies, and entangling in it all the judgments of their mind, whence are mere insanities in spiritual things; or constructing a labyrinth, from which the mind can never, by any thread of reason, retrace its way and extricate itself; they also actually let themselves down as it were in caverns under the earth, where they dwell in eternal darkness. For from such a belief proceed innumerable fallacies, each of which is horrible; as that God transfused and transcribed Himself into men, and that thus every man is a sort of Deity, which lives from itself, and thus that he does good and is wise from himself; likewise that he possesses faith and charity in himself, and thus derives them from himself, and not from God; besides many monstrous beliefs such as prevail with those in hell, who, when they were in the world, believed that nature lived, or produced life by its own activity. When these look towards heaven they see its light as mere thick darkness. I once heard the voice of one saying from heaven, that if a spark of life in man were his own, and not of God in him, there would be no heaven, nor anything therein, and hence that there would not be any church on earth, and consequently no life eternal. More upon this subject may be consulted in the Relation inserted in the work on *Conjugial Love* (n. 132–136).

X.

Spiritual things, thus clothed in a man, enable him to live a rational and moral man, thus a spiritually natural man.

12. From the principle established above, that the soul clothes itself with a body as a man clothes himself with a garment, this follows as a conclusion. For the soul flows into the human mind, and through this into the body, and carries life with it, which it continually receives from the Lord, and thus transfers it mediately into the body, where by the closest union it makes the body as it were to live. Thence from a thousand testimonies of experience, it is evident that the spiritual united to the material, as a living force with a dead force, causes man to speak rationally and to act morally. It appears as if the tongue and lips speak from a certain life in themselves, and that the arms and hands act in a like manner; but it is the thought, which in itself is spiritual, that speaks, and the will, which likewise is spiritual, that acts, and each through its own organs, which in themselves are material, because taken from the natural world. That it is so appears in the day, provided this is attended to: remove thought from speech, is not the mouth dumb in a moment? also remove will from action, do not the hands rest in a moment? The union of spiritual things with natural, and the appearance of life therefrom in material things, may be compared to generous wine in a clean sponge, and to the sweet must in a grape, and to the savory liquor in an apple, and also to the aromatic odor in cinnamon. The fibres containing all these things are matters which neither taste nor are fragrant from themselves, but from the fluids in and between them; wherefore if you squeeze out those juices, they are dead filaments. So are the organs proper to the body, if life is taken away. That man is rational from the union of spiritual things with natural, is evident from the analytical processes of his thought; and that he is moral from the honorableness of his conduct and the graces of his bearing. These he has from the faculty of receiving influx from the Lord through the angelic heaven, where is the very abode of wisdom and love, thus of rationality and morality. From these things it is perceived, that what is spiritual and what is natural, being united in man, cause him to live a spiritually natural man. The reason that he lives in a similar and yet dissimilar manner after death, is because his soul is then clothed with a substantial body, as in the natural world it was clothed with a material body. It is believed by many that the perceptions and thoughts of the mind, because they are spiritual, flow in naked, and not through organized forms. But those dream thus who have not seen the interiors of the head, where perceptions and thoughts are in their beginnings; and that the brains are there, interwoven and composed of the cineritious and medullary substances, and that there are glands, cavities, septa, and the meninges and matres, which surround them all; and that a man thinks and wills sanely or insanely according to the sound or perverted state of all those things; thence that he is rational and moral according to the organic formation of his mind. For nothing could be predicated of the rational sight of man, which is the understanding, without forms organized for the reception of spiritual light, just as nothing could be predicated of the natural sight without the eyes; and so in other instances.

XI.

The reception of that influx is according to the state of love and wisdom with a man.

13. That a man is not life, but an organ recipient of life from God, and that love together with wisdom is life, also that God is love itself and wisdom itself, and thus life itself, has been demonstrated above. Thence it follows that so far as a man loves wisdom, or so far as wisdom in the bosom of love is with him, so far he is an image of God, that is, a receptacle of life from God; and, on the contrary, so far as he is in opposite love, and thence in insanity, so far he does not receive life from God, but from hell, which life is called death. Love itself and wisdom itself are not life, but are the *esse* of life, but the delights of love and the pleasantnesses of wisdom, which are affections, constitute life, for the *esse* of life exists by these.

The influx of life from God carries with it those delights and pleasantnesses just as does the influx of light and heat in springtime, into human minds, and also into birds and beasts of every kind, yea into plants, which then germinate and become prolific; for the delights of love and the pleasantnesses of wisdom expand minds and adapt them to reception, as joys and gladnesses expand the face and adapt it to the influx of the cheerfulness of the soul. The man who is affected with the love of wisdom, is like the garden in Eden, in which are two trees, the one of life and the other of the knowledge of good and evil. The tree of life is the reception of love and wisdom from God, and the tree of the knowledge of good and evil is the reception of them from himself. But the latter is insane, and still believes that it is wise like God, while the former is truly wise, and believes that no one is wise but God alone, and that man is wise so far as he believes this, and more wise so far as he feels that he wills it. But more on this subject may be seen in the Relation inserted in the work on *Conjugial Love* (n. 132–136). I will here add an arcanum confirming these things from heaven. All the angels of heaven turn their forehead to the Lord as a sun, and all the angels of hell turn the back of the head to Him; and the latter receive influx into the affections of their will, which in themselves are lusts, and make the understanding favor them; but the former receive influx into the affections of their understanding, and make the will favor them. Hence these are in wisdom, but the others are in insanity; for the human understanding dwells in the cerebrum, which is under the forehead, and the will in the cerebellum, which is in the back of the head. Who does not know that a man who is insane from falsities, favors the cupidities of his own evil, and confirms them by reasons from the understanding; and that a wise man sees from truths the quality of the cupidities of his will, and curbs them? A wise man does this because he turns his face to God, that is, he believes in God, and not in himself; but an insane man does the other thing because he turns his face from God, that is, he believes in himself, and not in God. To believe in himself is to believe that he loves and is wise from himself, and not from God, and this is signified by eating of the tree of the knowledge of good and evil; but to believe in God is to believe that he loves and is wise from God, and not from himself, and this is to eat of the tree of life (*Rev.* ii. 7). From these things, but still only as in the light of the moon by night, it may be perceived that the reception of the influx of life from God is according to the state of love and wisdom with a man. This influx may further be illustrated by the influx of light and heat into plants, which blossom and bear fruit according to the structure of the fibres which form them, thus according to reception. It may also be illustrated by the influx of the rays of light into precious stones, which modify them into colors according to the situation of the parts composing them, thus also according to reception; and likewise by optical glasses and by drops of rain, which exhibit rainbows according to the incidences, refractions, and thus the receptions of light. The case is similar with human minds as to spiritual light, which proceeds from the Lord as a sun, and perpetually flows in, but is variously received.

XII.

The understanding in a man can be elevated into the light, that is, into the wisdom in which the angels of heaven are, according to the cultivation of his reason; and in like manner his will can be elevated into the heat of heaven, that is, into love according to the deeds of his life; but the love of the will is not elevated except so far as the man wills and does those things which the wisdom of the understanding teaches.

14. By the human mind are meant its two faculties, which are called the understanding and the will. The understanding is the receptacle of the light of heaven, which in its essence is wisdom, and the will is the receptacle of the heat of heaven, which in its essence is love, as was shown above. These two, wisdom and love, proceed from the Lord, as a sun, and flow into heaven universally and particularly, whence the angels have wisdom and love; and they also flow into this world universally and particularly, whence men have wisdom and love. But these two united proceed from the Lord, and likewise united flow into the souls of angels and men, but they are not received united in their minds. Light which makes the understanding is first received there, and love which constitutes the will is received gradually. This also is of providence, because every man is to be created anew, that is, reformed, and this is effected through the understanding; for from infancy he must acquire the knowledges of truth and good, which will teach him to live well, that is, to will and act rightly. Thus the will is formed through the understanding. For the sake of this end, there is given to man the faculty of elevating his understanding almost into the light in which the angels of heaven are, that he may see what he ought to will and thence to do, in order that he may be prosperous in the world for a time, and be happy after death to eternity. He becomes prosperous and happy if he procures for himself wisdom, and keeps his will under obedience to it; but unprosperous and unhappy if he subjects his understanding under obedience to his will. The reason is, because the will from birth inclines to evils, even to enormous ones; wherefore unless it were curbed by the understanding, a man would rush into heinous things, yea, from his inborn savage nature, he would depopulate and slaughter for the sake of himself all those who do not favor and indulge him. Furthermore, unless the understanding could be separately perfected, and the will by means of it, a man would not be a man, but a beast. For without that separation, and without the ascent of the understanding above the will, he would not be able to think, and from thought to speak, but only to express his affection by sounds; neither would he be able to act from reason, but only from instinct; still less would he be able to know the things which are of God, and God by means of them, and thus to be conjoined to Him, and to live to eternity. For a man thinks and wills as from himself, and this as from himself is the reciprocal of conjunction; for there cannot be conjunction without a reciprocal, just as there cannot be conjunction of the active with the passive without reaction. God alone acts, and man suffers himself to be acted on, and he reacts in all appearance as from himself, though interiorly it is from God. From these things rightly perceived it may be seen what is the quality of the love of a man's will if it is elevated by means of the understanding, and what is its quality if it is not elevated; consequently, what is the quality of the man. But this quality of a man if the love of his will is not elevated by means of the understanding shall be illustrated by comparisons. He is like an eagle which flies on high, and as soon as it sees the food below which is the object of its desire, as chickens, young swans, yea, young lambs, swoops down in a moment and devours them. He is also like an adulterer, who conceals a harlot in a cellar below, and by turns goes up to the highest part of the house, and talks wisely with those who dwell there about chastity, and by turns hastens away from his companions, and indulges his lasciviousness below with his harlot. He is also like a thief on a tower, who there pretends to keep watch, but who, as soon as he sees an object of plunder below, hastens down and seizes it. He may also be compared to marsh-flies, which fly in a column over the head of a running horse, but which fall down when the horse stops, and immerse themselves in their marsh. Such is the man whose will or love is not elevated by means of the understanding, for he then stands still below at the foot, immersed in the unclean things of nature and the lusts of the senses. It is altogether otherwise with those who subdue the allurements of the cupidities of the will by means of the wisdom of the understanding. With these the understanding afterwards enters into a conjugial covenant with the will, thence wisdom with love, and they dwell together above with delights.

XIII.

It is altogether otherwise with beasts.

15. Those who judge from the mere appearance to the senses of the body, conclude that beasts have will and understanding as well as men, and hence that the only distinction is that man can speak, and thus describe what he thinks and desires, while beasts can only express this by sounds. Yet beasts have not will and understanding, but only an image of each, which the learned call an analogue. That a man is a man, is because his understanding can be elevated above the desires of his will, and thus can know and see them from above, and also moderate them; but a beast is a beast because its desires impel it to do whatever it does. Wherefore a man is a man in that his will is under obedience to his understanding; but a beast is a beast in that its understanding is under obedience to its will. From these things this conclusion follows, that the understanding of man, because it receives the light that flows in from heaven, and apprehends and perceives this as its own, and from it thinks analytically with all variety, altogether as from itself; is alive, and thence a true understanding; and that the will of man, because it receives the inflowing love of heaven, and from it acts as from itself, is alive, and is thence truly will; but the contrary is the case with beasts. Wherefore those who think from the lusts of the will are likened to beasts, and also in the spiritual world they appear at a distance as beasts; they also act like beasts, with this difference only, that they can act otherwise if they will. But those who restrain the lusts of their will by means of the understanding, and therefore act rationally and wisely, appear in the spiritual world as men, and are angels of heaven. In a word, the will and the understanding in beasts always cohere; and because the will in itself is blind, for it is of heat and not of light, it makes the understanding blind also. Hence a beast does not know and understand its own actions; and yet it acts, for it acts from an influx from the spiritual world; and such action is instinct. It is believed that a beast thinks from the understanding what it does, but this is not so; it is impelled to act only from natural love, which is in it from creation, with the assistance of the senses of its body. That a man thinks and speaks is solely because his understanding can be separated from his will, and can be elevated even into the light of heaven; for the understanding thinks, and thought speaks. That beasts act according to the laws of order inscribed on their nature, and some beasts as it were morally and rationally, differently from many men, is because their understanding is blind obedience to the desires of their will, and therefore they are not able to pervert these by depraved reasonings, as men do. It is to be observed, that by the will and the understanding of beasts in the foregoing statements, is meant an image and analogue of them. Analogues are so named from appearance. The life of a beast may be compared with a somnambulist who walks and acts from the will while the understanding is in a deep sleep; and also with a blind man, who walks through the streets with a dog leading him; and also with a foolish person, who from custom and the habit thence acquired does his work according to rules; likewise with a person void of memory, and therefore deprived of understanding, who still knows or learns how to clothe himself, to eat dainties, to love the sex, to walk the streets from house to house, and to do such things as soothe the senses and gratify the flesh, by the allurements and pleasures of which he is carried along, though he does not think, and therefore cannot speak. From these things it is plain how much they are deceived who believe that beasts enjoy rationality, and are only distinguished from men by the external figure, and by their not being able to give utterance to the rational things which they hide within. From which fallacies many even conclude that if man lives after death beasts also will live after death, and, on the contrary, that if beasts do not live after death neither will man; besides many dreams arising from ignorance about the will and the understanding, and also about degrees, by means of which, as by a ladder, the mind of man mounts up to heaven.

XIV.

There are three degrees in the spiritual world, and three degrees in the natural world, hitherto unknown, according to which all influx takes place.

16. It is discovered, by the investigation of causes from effects, that there are degrees of two kinds, one in which are things prior and posterior, and another in which are things greater and less. The degrees which distinguish things prior and posterior are to be called *degrees of altitude*, and also *dis-*

crete degrees; but the degrees by which things greater and less are distinguished from each other are to be called, *degrees of latitude,* and also *continuous degrees.* Degrees of altitude, or discrete degrees, are like the generations and compositions of one thing from another; as, for example, of any nerve from its fibres, and of any fibre from its fibrils; or of any piece of wood, stone, or metal from its parts, and of any part from its particles. But degrees of latitude or continuous degrees are like the increments and decrements of the same degree of altitude as to breadth, length, height, and depth; as of greater and smaller volumes of water, or air, or ether; and as of large and small masses of wood, stone, or metal. All and each of the things in both worlds, the spiritual and the natural, are, from creation, in degrees of both these kinds. The whole animal kingdom in this world is in those degrees both in general and in particular; and the whole vegetable kingdom and the whole mineral kingdom likewise; as also is the expanse of atmospheres from the sun even to the earth. There are therefore three atmospheres discretely distinct according to the degrees of altitude, both in the spiritual world and in the natural world, because each world has its sun; but the atmospheres of the spiritual world, by virtue of their origin, are substantial, and the atmospheres of the natural world, by virtue of their origin, are material. And because the atmospheres descend from their origins according to those degrees, and are the containants, and, as it were, the carriers of light and heat, it follows that there are three degrees of light and heat. And because light in the spiritual world in its essence is wisdom, and heat there in its essence is love, as was shown above in its own article, it follows also that there are three degrees of wisdom and three degrees of love, hence three degrees of life; for they are graded by those things through which they pass. Hence it is that there are three angelic heavens: a highest, which is also called the third heaven, where are the angels of the highest degree; a middle, which is also called the second heaven, where are the angels of the middle degree; and a lowest, which is also called the first heaven, where are the angels of the lowest degree. Those heavens are also distinguished according to the degrees of wisdom and love. Those who are in the lowest heaven are in the love of knowing truths and goods; those who are in the middle heaven are in the love of understanding them; and those who are in the highest heaven are in the love of being wise, that is, of living according to those things which they know and understand. Since the angelic heavens are distinguished into three degrees, therefore the human mind is also distinguished into three degrees, because the human mind is an image of heaven, that is, it is a heaven in the least form. Hence it is that man can become an angel of one of those three heavens, and this is effected according to his reception of wisdom and love from the Lord: an angel of the lowest heaven if he receives only the love of knowing truths and goods; an angel of the middle heaven if he receives the love of understanding them; and an angel of the highest heaven if he receives the love of being wise, that is, of living according to them. That the human mind is distinguished into three regions, according to the three heavens, may be seen in the Relation inserted in the work on *Conjugial Love* (n. 270). From these things it is evident that all spiritual influx to man and into man descends from the Lord through these three degrees, and that it is received by man according to the degree of wisdom and love in which he is. The knowledge of these degrees is of the greatest use at the present day; since many, because they do not know them, subsist and inhere in the lowest degree, in which are the senses of their body, and from ignorance, which is intellectual thick darkness, cannot be elevated into spiritual light, which is above them. Hence naturalism invades them, as it were spontaneously, as soon as they enter on any investigation and inquiry concerning the human soul and mind, and its rationality, and still more if they inquire concerning heaven and the life after death. Thus they become comparatively like those who stand in the market places with telescopes in their hands, looking at the sky, and utter vain predictions; and also like those who chatter and also reason concerning every object they see, and everything they hear, without there being in it anything rational from the understanding. But such persons are like butchers, who believe themselves to be skilled in anatomy, because they have examined the viscera of oxen and sheep outwardly but not inwardly. But it is a truth, that to think from the influx of natural light, not enlightened by the influx of spiritual light, is nothing else than dreaming, and to speak from such thought is to talk nonsense. But more concerning these degrees may be seen in the work on *The Divine Love and The Divine Wisdom* (n. 173-281).

XV.

Ends are in the first degree, causes in the second, and effects in the third.

17. Who does not see that the end is not the cause, but that it produces the cause, and that the cause is not the effect, but that it produces the effect; consequently that they are three distinct things which follow in order? The end with man is the love of his will, for what a man loves, this he proposes to himself and intends; the cause with him is the reason of his understanding, for by means of it the end seeks for mediate or efficient causes; and the effect is the operation of the body from them and according to them. Thus there are three things in man, which follow each other in order, in like manner as the degrees of altitude follow each other. When these three things appear in act, then the end is inwardly in the cause, and the end through the cause is in the effect, wherefore the three co-exist in the effect. On this account it is said in the Word, that every one shall be judged according to his works; for the end, or the love of his will, and the cause, or the reason of his understanding, are together in the effects, which are the works of his body; thus the quality of the whole man is in them. They who do not know these things, and do not thus distinguish the objects of reason, cannot avoid terminating the ideas of their thought in the atoms of Epicurus, the monads of Leibnitz, or in the simple substances of Wolff, and thus they close up their understandings as with a bolt, so that they cannot even think from reason concerning spiritual influx, because they cannot think concerning any progression; for the author says concerning his simple substance, that if it is divided it falls into nothing.

Thus the understanding stands still in its first light, which is merely from the senses of the body, and does not advance a step further. Hence it is not known but that the spiritual is a subtile natural, and that beasts have a rational as well as men, and that the soul is a breath of wind such as is breathed forth from the breast when a person dies; besides many things which are not of light but of thick darkness. Since all things in the spiritual world and all things in the natural world proceed according to these degrees, as was shown in the preceding article, it is evident that intelligence properly consists in knowing and distinguishing them, and seeing them in their order. By means of these degrees, also, every man is known as to his quality, when his love is known; for, as was said above, the end which is of the will, and the causes which are of the understanding, and the effects which are of the body, follow from his love, as a tree from its seed, and as fruit from the tree. There are three kinds of loves, the love of heaven, the love of the world, and the love of self; the love of heaven is spiritual, the love of the world is material, and the love of self is corporeal. When the love is spiritual, all the things which follow from it, as forms from their essence, derive their spiritual nature; similarly if the principal love is the love of the world or of wealth, and thus is material, all the things which follow from it, as derivatives from their principle derive their material nature; likewise if the principal love is the love of self, or of eminence above all others, and thus is corporeal, all the things which follow from it derive their corporeal nature. The reason is, because the man who is in this love regards himself alone, and thus immerses the thoughts of his mind in his body. Wherefore, as was just now said, he who knows the ruling love of any one, and at the same time the progression of ends to causes and of causes to effects, which three things follow in order according to the degrees of altitude, knows the whole man. Thus the angels of heaven know every one with whom they speak; they perceive his love from the tone of his speech; and they see his image from his face, and his character from the gestures of his body.

XVI.

From these things it is evident what is the quality of spiritual influx from its origin to its effects.

18. Spiritual influx has hitherto been deduced from the soul into the body, but not from God into the soul and thus into the body. This has been done, because no one knew anything concerning the spiritual world, and concerning the sun there, from which all spiritual things flow as from their fountain, and thus nothing concerning the influx of spiritual things into natural things. Now because it has been granted me to be in the spiritual world and in the natural world at the same time, and thus to see each world and each sun, I am obliged by my conscience to manifest these things; for what is the use of knowing, unless what is known to one be also known to others? Without this, what is knowing but collecting and storing up riches in a casket, and only looking at them occasionally and counting them over, without any thought of use from them? Spiritual avarice is nothing else. But that it may be fully known what and of what quality spiritual influx is, it is necessary to know what *the spiritual* is in its essence, and what *the natural* is, and also what *the human soul* is. Lest therefore this short treatise should be defective through ignorance of these things, it is important to consult some Relations inserted in the work on *Conjugial Love;* concerning *the spiritual,* in the Relation there (n. 326–329); concerning *the human soul* (n. 315); and concerning *the influx of spiritual things into natural things* (n. 380); and more fully (n. 415–422).

19. To these things I will add this Relation. After these things were written, I prayed to the Lord that I might be permitted to converse with disciples of *Aristotle,* and at the same time with disciples of *Descartes,* and with disciples of *Leibnitz,* in order that I might draw forth the opinions of their minds concerning the intercourse between the soul and the body. After my prayer, there were present nine men, three Aristotelians, three Cartesians, and three Leibnitzians; and they stood around me, the admirers of Aristotle on the left side, the followers of Descartes on the right, and the supporters of Leibnitz behind. Quite a distance away, and at intervals from each other, were seen three persons as it were crowned with laurel, and I knew from an inflowing perception that they were those three great leaders or teachers themselves. Behind Leibnitz stood one holding in his hand the skirt of his garment, and I was told that it was Wolff. Those nine men, when they beheld one another, at first saluted and spoke to one another in a courteous tone. But presently there arose from below a spirit with a torch in his right hand, which he shook before their faces, whereupon they became enemies, three against three, and looked at one another with a fierce countenance; for they were seized with the lust of disputing and discussing. Then the Aristotelians, who were also schoolmen, began to speak, saying, Who does not see that objects flow in through the senses into the soul, as one enters through the doors into a chamber, and that the soul thinks according to such influx? When a lover sees a beautiful virgin or his bride, does not his eye sparkle and carry the love of her into the soul? When a miser sees bags of money, does he not burn for them with every sense, and thence convey this order into the soul, and excite the cupidity of possessing them? When a proud man hears his praises from another, does he not prick up his ears, and do not these transmit those praises to the soul? Are not the senses of the body like outer courts, through which alone there is entrance to the soul? From these things and innumerable others like them, who can conclude otherwise than that influx is from nature, or is physical? To these statements the followers of Descartes, who had held their fingers on their foreheads, and now withdrew them, replied, saying, Alas, you speak from appearances. Do you not know that the eye does not love a virgin or a bride from itself, but from the soul? Likewise that the senses of the body do not covet the bags of money from themselves, but from the soul? and similarly that the ears do not seize on the praises of flatterers in any other manner? Is it not perception that causes sensation? and perception is of the soul, and not of the organs. Tell, if you can, what else makes the tongue and lips to speak but the thought? and what else makes the hands to work but the will? and thought and will are of the soul, and not of the body. Thus what makes the eye to see, and the ears to hear, and the other organs to feel, but the soul? From these things, and innumerable others like them, every one whose wisdom is above the sensual things of the body, concludes, that there is no influx of the body into the soul, but of the soul into the body, which we call occasional, and also spiritual influx. When these had been heard, the three men who stood behind the former triads, who were the supporters of Leibnitz, lifted up their voices, saying, We have heard the arguments on both sides, and have compared them, and we have perceived that in many particulars the latter are stronger than the former, and that in many others the former are stronger than the latter; wherefore if it is permitted, we will settle the dispute. And on being asked how, they said, There is not any influx of the soul into the body, nor of the body into the soul, but there is a unanimous and instantaneous operation of both together, which a celebrated author has distinguished by a beautiful name, calling it pre-established harmony. Hereupon there appeared again the spirit with the torch in his hand, but now in his left, and he shook it at the back of their heads, whence their ideas of everything became confused, and they cried out together, Neither our soul nor body knows what part to take, wherefore let us decide this dispute by lot, and we will favor the lot which comes out first. And they took three pieces of paper, and wrote on one of them, *physical influx*, on another *spiritual influx*, and on the third, *pre-established harmony;* and they put these three pieces into a hat. Then they chose one of their number to draw, and he, putting in his hand, took hold of that on which was written *spiritual influx;* and when this was seen and read, they all said, yet some with a clear and flowing, some with a faint and smothered voice, Let us favor this because it came out first. But then an angel suddenly stood by, and said, Do not believe that the paper in favor of spiritual influx came out by chance, but from providence; for you do not see its truth because you are in confused ideas, but the truth itself presented itself to the hand of him that drew the lots, that you might favor it.

20. I was once asked how from a philosopher I became a theologian; and I answered, In the same manner that fishermen were made disciples and apostles by the Lord; and that I also from early youth had been a spiritual fisherman. On hearing this the inquirer asked, What is a spiritual fisherman? I replied that a fisherman in the spiritual sense of the Word, signifies a man who investigates and teaches natural truths, and afterwards spiritual truths rationally. To the question, How is this demonstrated? I said, From these passages in the Word:—

Then the waters shall fail from the sea, and the river shall be dried up and become dry, therefore the fishers shall mourn, and all that cast a hook into the sea shall be sad (*Isa.* xix. 5, 8).

In another place:—

Upon the river whose waters were healed, the fishers stood from Engedi; they were there in the spreading forth of nets; according to its kind was their fish, as the fish of the great sea, exceeding many (*Ezek.* xlvii. 9, 10).

And in another place:—

The saying of Jehovah, Behold, I will send to many fishers, who shall fish the sons of Israel (*Jer.* xvi. 16).

Thence it is evident, why the Lord chose fishermen for disciples, and said:—

Come ye after Me, and I will make you fishers of men (*Matt.* iv. 18, 19; *Mark* i. 16, 17).

And to Peter after he had caught a multitude of fishes:—

From henceforth thou shalt catch men (*Luke* v. 9, 10).

Afterwards I demonstrated the origin of this signification of fishermen from *The Apocalypse Revealed*; namely, because "water" signifies natural truths (n. 50, 932); likewise "a river" (n. 409, 932); "fish," those who are in natural truths (n. 405); and thence "fishermen" signify those who investigate and teach truths. On hearing this my interrogator raised his voice and said, Now I can understand why the Lord called and chose fishermen to be His disciples, and therefore I do not wonder that He has also called and chosen you, since, as you have said, you were from early youth a fisherman in a spiritual sense, that is, an investigator of natural truths; that you are now an investigator of spiritual truths, is because these are founded on the former. To this he added, because he was a man of reason, that the Lord alone knows who is adapted to perceive and to teach those things which are of His New Church, whether some one among the primates, or some one among their servants. Moreover, what theologian among Christians does not first study philosophy at college, before he is inaugurated as a theologian; and from what other source has he intelligence? At last he said, Since you are become a theologian, explain what is your theology. I replied, These are the two principles of it, *That God is one, and that there is a conjunction of charity and faith.* To which he replied, Who denies these? I answered, The theology of the present day, when interiorly examined.

THE END.

THE WHITE HORSE

THE WHITE HORSE

MENTIONED IN

THE APOCALYPSE CHAP. XIX.

WITH PARTICULARS RESPECTING

THE WORD AND ITS SPIRITUAL OR INTERNAL SENSE

EXTRACTED FROM THE ARCANA CŒLESTIA

FROM THE LATIN OF

EMANUEL SWEDENBORG

SERVANT OF THE LORD JESUS CHRIST

BEING A TRANSLATION OF HIS WORK ENTITLED

"DE EQUO ALBO de quo in Apocalypsi, Cap. xix., et dein de Verbo et ejus Sensu Spirituali seu Interno, ex Arcanis Cœlestibus."
Londini, MDCCLVIII.

CONTENTS

	Numbers
The Word and its spiritual or internal sense	1–5
The necessity and excellence of the Word	6
The Word cannot be understood except by those who are enlightened	7
The Word cannot be understood but by means of doctrine from the Word	8
In the Word there is a spiritual sense, which is called the internal sense	9
The internal sense of the Word is principally intended for the use of angels, and it is also for men	10
In the internal or spiritual sense of the Word there are innumerable arcana	11
The Word is written by correspondences, and thus by representatives	12
The literal or external sense of the Word	13
The Lord is the Word	14
Those who are against the Word	15
The books of the Word	16
Further particulars respecting the Word	17

THE WHITE HORSE

MENTIONED IN

THE APOCALYPSE CHAP. XIX.

1. In the *Apocalypse* of John the Word is thus described as to its spiritual or internal sense:—

I saw heaven opened, and behold a *white horse*, and He that sat upon him was called faithful and true, and in justice He doth judge and make war. His eyes were as a flame of fire; and upon His head were many diadems; and He hath a name written that no one knew but He Himself. And He was clothed with a vesture dipped in blood; and His name is called *The Word of God*. And the armies which were in the heavens followed Him upon white horses, clothed in fine linen white and clean. And He hath upon His vesture and upon His thigh a name written, *King of kings and Lord of lords* (xix. 11–14, 16).

No one can know what each of these expressions involves, except from the internal sense. It is manifest that every expression is in some respect representative and significative: as when it is said, that "heaven was opened"; that there was "a white horse"; that "there was One sitting upon him"; that "in justice He doth judge and make war"; that "His eyes were as a flame of fire"; that "on His head were many diadems"; that "He had a name that no man knew but He Himself"; that "He was clothed with a vesture dipped in blood"; that "the armies which were in heaven followed Him upon white horses"; that "they were clothed in fine linen white and clean"; and that "on His vesture and on His thigh He had a name written." It is expressly said, that it is "the Word" which is here described, and the Lord who is the Word; for it is said, "His name is called the *Word of God*"; and afterwards, "He hath on His vesture and on His thigh a name written, *King of kings and Lord of lords.*" From the interpretation of each expression it evidently appears, that the Word is here described as to its spiritual or internal sense. By "heaven being opened" is represented and signified, that the internal sense of the Word is seen in heaven, and thence by those in the world to whom heaven is opened. "The horse," which was white, represents and signifies the understanding of the Word as to its interiors; that this is the signification of "a white horse," will be shown presently. That "He that sat upon him" is the Lord as to the Word, thus the Word, is manifest, for it is said, "His name is called the Word of God"; who, from good, is called "faithful and judging in justice"; and from truth, is called "true, and who maketh war in justice"; for the Lord Himself is justice. "His eyes, as a flame of fire," signify the Divine truth, from the Divine good of His Divine love. "The many diadems upon His head," signify all the goods and truths of faith. "Having a name written that no one knew but He Himself," signifies that the quality of the Word in the internal sense is seen by no one but Himself, and those to whom He reveals it. "Clothed in a vesture dipped in blood," signifies the Word in the letter, to which violence has been offered. "The armies in the heavens which followed Him upon white horses," signify those who are in the understanding of the Word as to its interiors. "Clothed in fine linen, white and clean," signify the same persons in truth from good. "Upon His vesture and upon his thigh a name written" signifies truth and good, and their quality. From these particulars, and from those which precede and follow in that chapter, it is evident, that therein is predicted, that about the last time of the church the spiritual or internal sense of the Word would be opened; but what would come to pass at that time, is also described there (vers. 17–21). That this is the signification of the words mentioned, it is unnecessary to prove in this place, as they are particularly explained in *The Arcana Cœlestia;* where it is shown, That the Lord is the Word, because He is the Divine truth (n. 2533, 2803, 2884, 5272, 7835). That the Word is the Divine truth (n. 4692, 5075, 9987). That because the Lord is justice, therefore it is said, that "He who sat upon the horse in justice doth judge and make war"; and that the Lord is called "justice" for this reason, because of His own power He has saved the human race (n. 1813, 2025–2027, 9715, 9809, 10,019, 10,152). And that "justice" is the merit which belongs to the Lord alone (n. 9715, 9979). That

"His eyes, as a flame of fire," signify the Divine truth from the Divine good of the Divine love, is, because "the eyes" signify the understanding and the truth of faith (n. 2701, 4403–4421, 4523–4534, 6923, 9051, 10,569); and "a flame of fire" signifies the good of love (n. 934, 4906, 5215, 6314, 6832). That "the diadems which were upon His head" signify all the goods and truths of faith (n. 114, 3858, 6335, 6640, 9863, 9865, 9868, 9873, 9905). That "He hath a name written which no one knew but He Himself," signifies that the quality of the Word in the internal sense is seen by no one but Himself, and those to whom He reveals it, is because "a name" signifies the quality of a thing (n. 144, 145, 1754, 1896, 2009, 2724, 3006, 3237, 3421, 6674, 9310). That "clothed in a vesture dipped in blood," signifies the Word in the letter, to which violence has been offered, is because "a vesture" signifies truth because it clothes good (n. 1073, 2576, 5248, 5319, 5954, 9212, 9216, 9952, 10,536); especially truth in the ultimates, thus the Word in the letter (n. 5248, 6918, 9158, 9212); and because "blood" signifies violence offered to truth by falsity (n. 374, 1005, 4735, 5476, 9127). That "the armies in heaven followed Him upon white horses," signify those who are in the understanding of the Word as to its interiors, is because "armies" signify those who are in the truths and goods of heaven and the church (n. 3448, 7236, 7988, 8019). And "a horse" signifies the understanding (n. 3217, 5321, 6125, 6400, 6531, 6534, 7024, 8146, 8318). And "white" signifies truth which is in the light of heaven, consequently interior truth (n. 3301, 3993, 4007, 5319). That "clothed in fine linen white and clean," signifies the same persons in truth from good, is because "fine linen," or "linen,"signifies truth from a celestial origin, which is truth from good (n. 5319, 9469). That "a name written upon the vesture and upon the thigh," signifies truth and good, and their quality, is because "a vesture" signifies truth, and "a name" quality, as observed above, and "the thigh" signifies the good of love (n. 3021, 4277, 4280, 9961, 10.485). "King of kings, and Lord of lords," is the Lord as to the Divine truth and as to the Divine good; the Lord is called "King" from the Divine truth (n. 3009, 5068, 6148). And He is called "Lord" from the Divine good (n. 4973, 9167, 9194). Hence it appears what is the quality of the Word in its spiritual or internal sense, and that there is no expression therein which does not signify something spiritual, that is, something of heaven and the church.

2. In the prophetical parts of the Word mention is very often made of the horse, but heretofore no one has known that "a horse" signifies the understanding, and his "rider" one who is intelligent; and this possibly, because it seems strange and wonderful, that by "a horse" such a thing should be meant in the spiritual sense, and thence in the Word. But nevertheless that it is so, may evidently appear from many passages therein; some of which only I will here adduce. In the prophecy of Israel, it is said of Dan:—

> Dan is a serpent upon the way, an arrow-snake upon the highway, that biteth the horse's heels, so that his rider shall fall backward (*Gen.* xlix. 17, 18).

No one can understand what this prophecy concerning one of the tribes of Israel signifies unless he knows what is signified by "a serpent," and what by "a horse" and his "rider": every one, however, knows that there is something spiritual involved therein; what therefore each expression signifies, may be seen in *The Arcana Cœlestia* (n. 6398, 6399, 6400, 6401), where this prophecy is explained. In *Habakkuk:*—

> O God, Thou didst ride upon Thy horses. Thy chariots are salvation. Thou didst tread in the sea with Thy horses (iii. 8, 15).

That "horses" here signify what is spiritual, is evident, for they are said concerning God; in any other sense, what could be meant by saying, that "God rides upon His horses, and that He treads upon the sea with His horses?" In like manner in *Zechariah:*—

> In that day, there shall be upon the bells of the horses, holiness unto Jehovah (xiv. 20).

In the same:—

> In that day, saith Jehovah, I will smite every horse with astonishment, and his rider with madness; and I will open Mine eyes upon the house of Judah, and will smite every horse of the people with blindness (xii. 4).

It treats there of the vastation of the church, which takes place when there no longer remains the understanding of any truth;

and which is described thus by "the horse and his rider"; what else could be the meaning of "smiting every horse with astonishment," and of "smiting the horse of the people with blindness"? What has this to do with the church? In *Job:*—

> God hath caused her to forget wisdom, neither hath He imparted to her intelligence: what time she lifteth up herself on high, she scorneth the horse and his rider (xxxix. 17, 18, 19, *seq.*).

That "the horse" here signifies the understanding, is manifestly evident. In like manner in *David*, where it is said:—

> He rideth upon the word of truth (*Ps.* xlv. 4).

And in many other passages. Moreover, who can know the reason why Elijah and Elisha were called "the chariot of Israel and the horsemen thereof"; and why "the boy of Elisha saw the mountain full of horses and chariots of fire"; except it be known what is signified by "chariots," and what was represented by "Elijah and Elisha"? For Elisha said to Elijah:—

> My father, my father, the chariot of Israel and the horsemen thereof (2 *Kings* ii. 11, 12).

And Joash the king said to Elisha:—

> My father, my father, the chariot of Israel and the horsemen thereof (2 *Kings* xiii. 14).

And, speaking of the boy of Elisha, it is said:—

> Jehovah opened the eyes of the boy of Elisha, and he saw and behold the mountain was full of horses and chariots of fire round about Elisha (2 *Kings* vi. 17).

The reason why Elijah and Elisha were called "the chariot of Israel and the horsemen thereof," is because they both represented the Lord as to the Word, and "a chariot" signifies doctrine from the Word, and "horsemen" intelligence. That "Elijah" and "Elisha" represented the Lord as to the Word, may be seen in *The Arcana Cœlestia* (n. 5247, 7643, 8029, 9327). And that "chariots" signify doctrine drawn from the Word (n. 5321, 8215).

3. That a horse signifies the understanding, is from no other source than from the representatives in the spiritual world. In that world horses are frequently seen, and persons sitting upon horses, and also chariots; and there every one knows that they signify intellectual and doctrinal things. I have often observed, when any were thinking from their understanding, that at such times they appeared as if riding on horses; their meditation was thus represented before others, they themselves not knowing it. There is also a place there, where many assemble who think and speak from the understanding concerning the truths of doctrine; and when others approach, they see the whole plain full of chariots and horses; and novitiate spirits, who wonder whence this is, are instructed that it is an appearance resulting from their intellectual thought. That place is called the assembly of the intelligent and the wise. I have likewise seen bright horses and chariots of fire, when some were taken up into heaven, which was a sign that they were then instructed in the truths of heavenly doctrine, and became intelligent, and thus were taken up; on seeing which, it occurred to my mind, what is signified by "the chariot of fire and the horses of fire by which Elijah was taken up into heaven"; and what is signified by "the horses and chariots of fire" that were seen by the young man of Elisha, when his eyes were opened.

4. That such is the signification of "chariots" and "horses" was well known in the ancient churches; for those churches were representative churches, and with those who were in them, the science of correspondences and representations was the chief of all sciences. The signification of the horse, as being understanding, was derived by the wise round about, even to Greece, from those churches. Hence it was, when they would describe the sun, in which they placed their God of wisdom and intelligence, that they attributed to it a chariot and four horses of fire. And when they would describe the God of the sea, since by the sea were signified sciences derived from the understanding, that they also attributed horses to him. And when they would describe the origin of the sciences from the understanding, they represented it by a winged horse, which with its hoof broke open a fountain, at which sat nine virgins called the sciences. For from the ancient churches they received the knowledge that "the horse" signifies the understanding; "wings," spiritual truth; "the hoof," what is scientific from the understanding; and "a fountain," doctrine from which sciences are derived. Nor is anything else signified by "the

Trojan horse," than an artificial contrivance devised by their understanding for the purpose of destroying the walls. Even at this day, when the understanding is described after the manner received from those ancients, it is usual to figure it by a flying horse or Pegasus; so, likewise, doctrine is described by a fountain, and the sciences by virgins; but scarcely any one knows, that "the horse," in the mystic sense, signifies the understanding; still less that those significatives were derived by the Gentiles from the ancient representative churches.

5. Since "the White Horse" signifies the understanding of the Word as to its spiritual or internal sense, those particulars concerning the Word and that sense, which are shown in *The Arcana Cœlestia*, are here subjoined: for in that work the whole contents of *Genesis* and *Exodus* are explained according to the spiritual or internal sense of the Word.

THE WORD, AND ITS SPIRITUAL OR INTERNAL SENSE, FROM THE ARCANA CŒLESTIA.

6. *The necessity and excellence of the Word.* From the light of nature nothing is known concerning the Lord, concerning heaven and hell, concerning the life of man after death, nor concerning the Divine truths by which man acquires spiritual and eternal life (n. 8944, 10,318, 10,319, 10,320). This may appear manifest from the consideration, that many, and among them men of learning, do not believe those things, although they are born where the Word is, and are thereby instructed concerning them (n. 10,319). Therefore it was necessary that there should be some revelation from heaven because man was born for heaven (n. 1775). Therefore in every age of the world there has been a revelation (n. 2895). Of the various kinds of revelation which have successively been made on this earth (n. 10,355, 10,632). To the most ancient men, who lived before the flood, whose time was called the golden age, there was an immediate revelation, and thence Divine truth was inscribed on their hearts (n. 2896). The ancient churches, which existed after the flood, had a historical and prophetical Word (n. 2686, 2897): concerning which churches see *The New Jerusalem and its Heavenly Doctrine* (n. 247). Its historical parts were called *The Wars of Jehovah*, and its prophetical parts, *Enunciations* (n. 2897). That Word, as to inspiration was like our Word, but accommodated to those churches (n. 2897). It is mentioned by Moses (n. 2686, 2897). But that Word is lost (n. 2897). Prophetical revelations were also made to others, as appears from the prophecies of Balaam (n. 2898).

The Word is Divine in all and every particular part (n. 639, 680, 10,321, 10,637). The Word is Divine and holy as to every point and iota, from experience (n. 1349). How it is explained at this day, that the Word is inspired as to every iota (n. 1886).

The church is especially where the Word is, and where the Lord is thereby known, and Divine truths are revealed (n. 3857, 10,761). But it does not follow from thence, that they are of the church, who are born where the Word is, and where the Lord is thereby known; but they who, by means of truths from the Word, are regenerated by the Lord, who are they who live according to the truths therein, consequently, who lead a life of love and faith (n. 6637, 10,143, 10,153, 10,578, 10,645, 10,829).

7. *The Word is not understood, except by those who are enlightened.* The human rational faculty cannot comprehend Divine, nor even spiritual things, unless it be enlightened by the Lord (n. 2196, 2203, 2209, 2654). Thus they only who are enlightened comprehend the Word (n. 10,323). The Lord enables those who are enlightened to understand truths, and to discern those things which appear to contradict each other (n. 9382, 10,659). The Word in its literal sense appears inconsistent, and in some places seems to contradict itself (n. 9025). And therefore by those who are not enlightened, it may be so explained and applied, as to confirm any opinion or heresy, and to defend any worldly and corporeal love (n. 4738, 10,339, 10,401). They are enlightened from the Word, who read it from the love of truth and good, but not they who read it from the love of fame, of gain, or of honor, thus from the love of self (n. 9382, 10,548, 10,549, 10,550). They are enlightened who are in the good of life, and thereby in the affection of truth (n. 8694). They are enlightened whose internal is open, thus who as to their internal man are capable of elevation into the light of heaven (n. 10,401, 10,402, 10,691, 10,694). Enlightenment is an actual opening of the interiors of the mind, and also an elevation into the light of heaven (n. 10,330). There is an influx of holiness from the internal, that is, from the Lord through the internal, with those who regard the Word as holy, though they themselves are ignorant of it (n. 6789). They are enlightened, and see truths in the Word, who are led by the Lord, but not they who are led by themselves (n. 10,638). They are led by the Lord, who love truth because it is truth, who also are they that love to live according to Divine truths (n. 10,578, 10,645, 10,829). The Word is vivified with man according to the life of his love and faith (n. 1776). The things derived from one's own intelligence have no life in themselves, because from man's proprium there is nothing good (n. 8941, 8944). They cannot be enlightened who have much confirmed themselves in false doctrine (n. 10,640).

It is the understanding which is enlightened (n. 6608, 9300). The understanding is the recipient of truth (n. 6242, 6608, 10,659). In regard to every doctrine of the church, there are ideas of the understanding and of the thought thence, according to which the doctrine is perceived (n. 3310, 3825). The ideas of man during his life in the world are natural, because man then thinks in the natural; but still spiritual ideas are concealed therein, with those who are in the affection of truth for the sake of truth, and man comes into these ideas after death (n. 3310, 5510, 6201, 10,236, 10,240, 10,550). Without ideas of the understanding, and of the thought thence, on any subject, there can be no perception (n. 3825). Ideas concerning the things of faith are laid open in the other life, and their quality is seen by the angels, and man is then conjoined with others according to those ideas, so far as they proceed from the affection which is of love (n. 1869, 3320, 5510, 6201, 8885). Therefore the Word is not understood except by a rational man; for to believe anything without an idea thereof, and without a rational view of the subject, is only to retain in the memory words destitute of all the life of perception and affection, which is not believing (n. 2533). It is the literal sense of the Word which admits of enlightenment (n. 3619, 9824, 9905, 10,548).

8. *The Word cannot be understood but by means of doctrine from the Word.* The doctrine of the church must be from the Word (n. 3464, 5402, 6832, 10,763, 10,765). The Word without doctrine is not understood (n. 9025, 9409, 9424, 9430, 10,324, 10,431, 10,582). True doctrine is a lamp to those who read the Word (n. 10,401). Genuine doctrine must be from those who are in enlightenment from the Lord (n. 2510, 2516, 2519, 2524, 10,105). The Word is understood by means of doctrine formed by one enlightened (n. 10,324). They who are in enlightenment form for themselves doctrine from the Word (n. 9382, 10,659). What is the difference between those who teach and learn from the doctrine of the church, and those who teach and learn from the sense of the letter of the Word alone (n. 9025). They who are in the sense of the letter of the Word without doctrine, do not come into any understanding concerning Divine truths (n. 9409, 9410, 10,582). They may fall into many errors (n. 10,431). They who are in the affection of truth for the sake of truth, when they become adults, and can see from their own understanding, do not simply abide in the doctrinals of their churches, but examine from the Word whether they be true or not (n. 5402, 5432, 6047). Otherwise every one would have truth from another, and from his native soil, whether he were born a Jew or a Greek (n. 6047). Nevertheless such things as are become matters of faith from the literal sense of the Word, are not to be extinguished till after a full view (n. 9039).

The true doctrine of the church is the doctrine of charity and faith (n. 2417, 4766, 10,763, 10,765). The doctrine of faith does not constitute the church, but the life of faith, which is charity (n. 809, 1798, 1799, 1834, 4468, 4677, 4766, 5826, 6637). Doctrinals are of no account, unless one live according to them; and every one may see they are for the sake of life, and not merely for the memory and thought thence derived (n. 1515, 2049, 2116). In the churches at this day the doctrine of faith is taught, and not the doctrine of charity, the latter being rejected to a science, which is called moral philosophy (n. 2417). The church would be one, if they should be acknowledged as men of the church from the life, thus from charity (n. 1285, 1316, 2982, 3267, 3445, 3451, 3452). How much superior the doctrine of charity is to that of faith separate from charity (n. 4844). They who know nothing concerning charity, are in ignorance with respect to heavenly things (n. 2435). They who only hold the doctrine of faith, and not that of charity, fall into errors; which errors are also described (n. 2383, 2417, 3146, 3325, 3412, 3413, 3416, 3773, 4672, 4730, 4783, 4925, 5351, 7623–7677, 7752–7762, 7790, 8094, 8313, 8530, 8765, 9186, 9224, 10,555). They who are only in the doctrine of faith, and not in the life of faith, which is charity, were formerly called the uncircumcised, or Philistines (n. 3412, 3413, 3463, 8093, 8313, 9340). The ancients held the doctrine of love to the Lord and of charity towards the neighbor, and made the doctrine of faith subservient thereto (n. 2417, 3419, 4844, 4955).

Doctrine formed by one enlightened may afterwards be confirmed by things rational and scientific; and that thus it is more fully understood, and is corroborated (n. 2553, 2719, 2720, 3052, 3310, 6047). See more on this subject in *The New Jerusalem and its Heavenly Doctrine* (n. 51). They who are in faith separate from charity, would have the doctrinal of the church simply believed, without any rational intuition (n. 3394).

It is not the mark of a wise man to confirm a dogma, but to see whether it be true before it is confirmed; and that this is the case with those who are in enlightenment (n. 1017, 4741, 7012, 7680, 7950). The light of confirmation is a natural light, and not spiritual, and may exist even with the evil (n. 8780). All things, even falsities, may be so far confirmed, as to appear like truths (n. 2482, 2490, 5033, 6865, 8521).

9. *In the Word there is a spiritual sense, which is called the internal sense.* No one can know what the spiritual or internal sense of the Word is, unless he knows what correspondence is (n. 2895, 4322). Each and all things, even the most minute, which are in the natural world, correspond to spiritual things, and thence signify them (n 2890–2893, 2897–3003, 3213–3227). The spiritual things to which natural things correspond, assume another appearance in the natural, so that they are not recognized (n. 1887, 2396, 8920). Scarcely any one knows wherein resides the Divine of the Word, when nevertheless it is in its internal and spiritual sense, which at this day is not known even to exist (n. 2980, 4989). The mystical contents of the Word are no other than those of its internal or spiritual sense, which treats of the Lord, of the glorification of His Human, of His kingdom, and of the church, and not of the natural things which are in the world (n. 4923). The prophetic writings are in many places unintelligible, and therefore of no use, without the internal sense, illustrated by examples (n. 2608, 8020, 8398). As for instance, with respect to what is signified by "the white horse" in the *Apocalypse* (n. 2760, *seq.*). What by "the keys of the kingdom of the heavens," that were given to Peter, see the preface to *Genesis* xxii., and (n. 9410). What by "flesh," "blood," "bread," and "wine," in the Holy Supper (n. 8682). What by the prophecies of Jacob concerning his sons (*Gen.* xlix.; n. 6306, 6333–6465). What by many prophecies concerning Judah and Israel, which by no means tally with that nation, nor in the sense of the letter have any coincidence with their history (n. 6331, 6361, 6415, 6438, 6444). Besides many other instances (n. 2608). More may be seen of the nature of correspondence in the work on *Heaven and Hell* (n. 87–102, 103–115, and 303–310).

Of the internal or spiritual sense of the Word in a summary (n. 1767–1777, 1869–1879). In each and all things of the Word there is an internal sense (n. 1143, 1984, 2135, 2333 2395, 2495, 2619). Such things do not appear in the sense of the letter, but nevertheless they are within it (n. 4442).

10. *The internal sense of the Word is especially for the angels, and it is also for men.* In order that it may be known what the internal sense is, the quality thereof, and whence it is, it may here be observed in general, that thought and speech in heaven are different from thought and speech in the world; for in heaven they are spiritual, but in the world natural; when, therefore, man reads the Word, the angels who are with him perceive it spiritually, whilst men perceive it naturally; hence it follows, that angels are in the internal sense, whilst men are in the external sense; but that nevertheless these two senses make a one by correspondence. That angels not only think spiritually, but also speak spiritually; that they are likewise present with man; and that they have conjunction with man by means of the Word, may be seen in the work on *Heaven and Hell*, where it treats of The Wisdom of the Angels of Heaven (n. 265–275). Of their Speech (n. 234–245). Of their Conjunction with Man (n. 291–302). And of their Conjunction by the Word (n. 303–310).

The Word is understood differently by angels in the heavens, and by men on earth; the former perceiving the internal or spiritual sense, whilst the latter see only the external or natural sense (n. 1887, 2396). The angels perceive the Word in its internal sense, and not in its external sense, proved from the experience of those who have conversed with me from heaven, when I was reading the Word (n. 1769–1772). The ideas of the thought and also the speech of angels are spiritual, but the ideas and speech of men natural; that therefore there is an internal sense, which is spiritual, for the use of angels, illustrated from experience (n. 2333). Nevertheless the sense of the letter of the Word serves the spiritual ideas of angels as a means of conveyance, comparatively as the words of speech do with men to convey the sense of a subject (n. 2143). The things relating to the internal sense of the Word fall into such things as are of the light of heaven, thus into angelic perception (n. 2618, 2619, 2629, 3086). Therefore those things which the angels perceive from the Word, are precious to them (n. 2540, 2541, 2545, 2551). Angels do not understand a single expression of the Word in its literal sense (n. 64, 65, 1434, 1929). They do not know the names of persons and places recorded in the Word (n. 1434, 1888, 4442, 4480). Names cannot enter into heaven, nor be pronounced there (n. 1876, 1888). All the names in the Word signify things, and in heaven they are changed into ideas of the things (n. 768, 1888, 4310, 4442, 5225, 5287, 10,329). Angels also think abstractly from persons (n. 6613, 8343, 8985, 9007). How elegant the internal sense of the Word is, even where nothing but mere names occur, shown by examples from the Word (n. 1224, 1888, 2395). Many names also in series express one thing in the internal sense (n. 5905). Likewise all numbers in the Word signify things (n. 482, 487, 647, 648, 755, 813, 1963, 1988, 2075, 2252, 3152, 4264, 6175, 9488, 9659, 10,217, 10,253). Spirits also perceive the Word in its internal sense in proportion as their interiors are open into heaven (n. 1771). The sense of the letter of the Word, which is the natural sense, is instantly changed into the spiritual sense with the angels, because there is a correspondence (n. 5648). And this without their hearing or knowing what is in the literal or external sense (n. 10,215). Thus the sense of the letter or the external sense is only with man, and proceeds no further (n. 2015).

There is an internal sense in the Word, and likewise an inmost or supreme sense, concerning which (n. 9407, 10,604, 10,614, 10,627). The spiritual angels, or those who are in the spiritual kingdom of the Lord, perceive the Word in its internal sense; and the celestial angels, or those who are in the celestial kingdom of the Lord, perceive the Word in its inmost sense (n. 2157, 2275).

The Word is for men, and also for angels, being accommodated to each (n. 7381, 8862, 10,322). The Word is the means of uniting heaven and earth (n. 2310, 2493, 9212, 9216, 9357). The conjunction of heaven with man is through the Word (n. 9396, 9400, 9401, 10,452). Therefore the Word is called a covenant (n. 9396). Because a covenant signifies conjunction (n. 665, 666, 1023, 1038, 1864, 1996, 2003, 2021, 6804, 8767, 8778, 9396, 10,632). There is an internal sense in the Word, because the Word is from the Lord, it descended through the three heavens even to man (n. 2310, 6397). And thereby it is accommodated to the angels of the three heavens and also to men (n. 7381, 8862). Hence it is that the Word is Divine (n. 2980, 4989). And it is holy (n. 10,276). And it is spiritual (n. 4480). And it is Divinely inspired (n. 9094). This is inspiration (n. 9094).

The regenerate man is actually in the internal sense of the Word, although he does not know it, since his internal man, which has spiritual perception, is open (n. 10,401). But with him the spiritual of the Word flows into natural ideas, and thus is represented naturally, because while he lives in the world this spiritual thinks in the natural man, so far as it comes to the perception (n. 5614). Hence the light of truth, with those who are enlightened, is from their internal, thus through the internal, from the Lord (n. 10,691, 10,694). Also by the same way there is an influx of holiness with those who esteem the Word holy (n. 6789). Since the regenerate man is actually in the internal sense of the Word, and in the sanctity thereof, although he does not know it, therefore after death he comes into it of himself, and is no longer in the sense of the letter (n. 3226, 3342, 3343). The ideas of the internal man are spiritual; but man during his life in the world does not attend thereto, inasmuch as they are within his natural thought, and give it its rational faculty (n. 10,236, 10,240, 10,550). But man after death comes into those his spiritual ideas, because they are proper to his spirit, and then he not only thinks, but also speaks therefrom (n. 2470, 2478, 2479, 10,568, 10,604). Hence, as was said, the regenerate man knows not that he is in the spiritual sense of the Word, and that he receives enlightenment thence.

11. *In the internal or spiritual sense of the Word there are innumerable arcana.* The Word in the internal sense contains innumerable things which exceed human comprehension (n. 3085, 3086). It also contains things ineffable and inexplicable (n. 1965). Which are manifest only to angels, and are understood by them (n. 167). The internal sense of the Word contains arcana of heaven, which relate to the Lord and His kingdom in the heavens and on earth (n. 1–4, 937). Those arcana do not appear in the sense of the letter (n. 937, 1502, 2161). Many things in the writings of the prophets appear to be unconnected, which yet in the internal sense cohere in a beautiful series (n. 7153, 9022). Not a single expression, nor even a single iota, in its original language, can be taken from the sense of the letter of the Word, without an interruption in the internal sense; and therefore, by the Divine Providence of the Lord, the Word is preserved so entire as to every point (n. 7933). There are innumerable things in the particulars of the Word (n. 6637, 8920). And in every expression (n. 1689). There are innumerable things contained in the Lord's prayer and in every particular part thereof (n. 6619). And in the precepts of the Decalogue; in the external sense whereof, notwithstanding, some things are such as are known to every nation without revelation (n. 8867, 8900). In every tittle of the letter of the Word, in the original language, there is holiness, shown from heaven; see the work on *Heaven and Hell* (n. 260), where these words of the Lord are explained:—

Not one jot or one tittle shall pass from the law (*Matt.* v. 18).

In the Word, particularly in the prophetical parts, there are two expressions which seem to signify the same thing: but one has relation to good, and the other to truth (n. 683, 707, 2516, 8339). In the Word goods and truths are conjoined in a wonderful manner, and such conjunction appears to him only who knows the internal sense (n. 10,554). And thus in the Word, and in every part thereof, there is a Divine marriage and a heavenly marriage (n. 683, 793, 801, 2173, 2516, 2712, 5138, 7022). The Divine marriage is the marriage of Divine good and Divine truth, thus it is the Lord in heaven, in whom alone there is that marriage (n. 3004, 3005, 3009, 4158, 5194, 5502, 6343, 7945, 8339, 9263, 9314). Jesus also signifies the Divine good, and Christ the Divine truth, and thus both signify the Divine marriage in heaven (n. 3004, 3005, 3009). This marriage is in every particular part of the Word in its internal sense, and thus the Lord is therein as to the Divine good and the Divine truth (n. 5502). The marriage of good and truth from the Lord in heaven and in the church is called the heavenly marriage (n. 2508, 2618, 2803, 3004, 3211, 3952, 6179). Therefore in this respect the Word is as it were heaven (n. 2173, 10,126). Heaven is compared in the Word to a marriage, on account of the marriage of good and truth therein (n. 2758, 3132, 4434, 4834).

The internal sense is itself the genuine doctrine of the church (n. 9025, 9430, 10,401.) They who understand the Word according to the internal sense, know the true doctrine itself of the church, because the internal sense contains it (n. 9025, 9430, 10,401). The internal of the Word is also the internal of the church, as it is likewise the internal of worship (n. 10,460). The Word is the doctrine of love to the Lord, and of charity towards the neighbor (n. 3419, 3420).

The Word in the literal sense is as a cloud, and in the internal sense it is glory (see the preface to *Gen.* xviii. and n. 5922, 6343), where these words are explained: "The Lord shall come in the clouds of heaven with glory." "Clouds" also in the Word signify the Word in the sense of the letter, and glory the Word in its internal sense (see the preface of *Gen.* xviii. and n. 4060, 4391, 5922, 6343, 6752, 8106, 8781, 9430, 10,551, 10,574). Things contained in the literal sense, respectively to those which are in the internal sense, are like rude projections round a polished optical cylinder, from which nevertheless is exhibited in the cylinder a beautiful image of a man (n. 1871). In the spiritual world they who desire and acknowledge only the sense of the letter of the Word, are represented by a deformed old woman; but they who desire and acknowledge the internal sense at the same time, are represented by a virgin beautifully clothed (n. 1774). The Word in its whole complex is an image of heaven; for the Word is the Divine truth, and the Divine truth makes heaven, and heaven relates to one man, and therefore in this respect the Word is as it were an image of man (n. 187). Heaven in one complex resembles one man, may be seen in the work on *Heaven and Hell* (n. 59–67). And the Divine truth from the Lord makes heaven (n. 126–140, 200–212). The Word is represented before the angels under the most beautiful and agreeable forms (n. 1767, 1768). The sense of the letter is as the body, and the internal sense as the soul of that body (n. 8943). Hence the life of the Word is from the internal sense (n. 1405, 4857). The Word is pure in the internal sense, but it does not appear so in the sense of the letter (n. 2362, 2396). The things which are in the sense of the letter are holy from the internal contents (n. 10,126, 10,728).

The historical parts of the Word also have an internal sense, but within in them (n. 4989). Thus the historical as well as the prophetical parts of the Word contain arcana of heaven (n. 755, 1659, 1709, 2310, 2333). The angels do not perceive those parts historically, but dogmatically because spiritually (n. 6884). The interior arcana contained in the historical parts are less evident to man than those contained in the prophetical parts, by reason that the mind is engaged in viewing and considering the historical transactions (n. 2176, 6597).

The nature of the internal sense of the Word is further shown (n. 1756, 1984, 2004, 2663, 3033, 7089, 10,604, 10,614). And illustrated by comparisons (n. 1873).

12. *The Word is written by correspondences, and thus by representatives.* The Word as to the sense of the letter is written by mere correspondences, that is, by such things as represent and signify the spiritual things of heaven and the church (n. 1404,

1408, 1409, 1540, 1619, 1659, 1709, 1783, 2179, 2763, 2899). This was done for the sake of the internal sense, which is there in every part (n. 2899). Consequently for the sake of heaven, since those who are in heaven do not understand the Word according to the sense of its letter, which is natural, but according to the internal sense, which is spiritual (n. 2899). The Lord spake by correspondences, representatives, and significatives, because He spake from the Divine (n. 9049, 9063, 9086, 10,126, 10,728). The Lord thus spoke before the world, and at the same time before heaven (n. 2533, 4807, 9049, 9063, 9086). The things spoken by the Lord went through the whole heaven (n. 4637). The historicals of the Word are representatives, and the words significative (n. 1540, 1659, 1709, 1783, 2687). The Word could not be written in any other style, so that through it there might be communication and conjunction with the heavens (n. 2899, 6943, 9481). They greatly err, who despise the Word on account of the apparent simplicity and rudeness of its style, and who think that they would receive the Word if it had been written in a different style (n. 8783). The method and style of writing which prevailed amongst the most ancient people, was by correspondences and representatives (n. 605, 1756, 9942). The ancient wise men were delighted with the Word, because of the representatives and significatives therein, from experience (n. 2592, 2593). If a man of the Most Ancient Church had read the Word, he would have seen clearly the things contained in the internal sense, and obscurely the things contained in the external sense (n. 449). The sons of Jacob were brought into the land of Canaan, because all the places in that land, from the most ancient times, were made representative (n. 1585, 3686, 4441, 5136, 6516). And thus the Word might be there written, wherein those places should be mentioned for the sake of the internal sense (n. 3686, 4447, 5136, 6416). But nevertheless the Word, as to the external sense was changed for the sake of that nation, but not as to the internal sense (n. 10,453, 10,461, 10,603, 10,604). Many passages adduced from the Word concerning that nation, which must be understood according to the internal sense, and not according to the letter (n. 7051). Inasmuch as that nation represented the church, and the Word was written with them and concerning them, therefore Divine celestial things were signified by their names, as by Reuben, Simeon, Levi, Judah, Ephraim, Joseph, and the rest: and by "Judah" in the internal sense is signified the Lord as to celestial love, and His celestial kingdom (n. 3654, 3881, 3882, 5583, 5782, 6362–6381).

That it may be known what correspondences are and their nature, and what is the nature of representatives in the Word, something shall be here said concerning them. All things which correspond likewise represent, and thereby signify, so that correspondences and representations are one (n. 2890, 2897, 2971, 2987, 2989, 2990, 3002, 3225). The nature of correspondences and representations shown from experience and examples (n. 2703, 2987–3002, 3213–3226, 3337–3352, 3472–3485, 4218–4228, 9280). The science of correspondences and representations was the chief science with the ancients (n. 3021, 3419, 4280, 4749, 4844, 4964, 4965, 6004, 7729, 10,252). Especially with the Orientals (n. 5702, 6692, 7097, 7779, 9391, 10,252, 10,407). And in Egypt more than in other countries (n. 5702, 6692, 7097, 7779, 9391, 10,407) Also with the Gentiles, as in Greece, and in other places (n. 2762, 7729). But that at this day the science of correspondences and representations is lost, particularly in Europe (n. 2894, 2895, 2994, 3630, 3632, 3747, 3748, 3749, 4581, 4966, 10,252). Nevertheless this science is more excellent than all other sciences, inasmuch as without it the Word cannot be understood, nor the signification of the rites of the Jewish Church which are recorded in the Word, nor can it be known what the nature of heaven is, nor what the spiritual is, nor in what manner a spiritual influx takes place into what is natural, nor how the case is with respect to the influx of the soul into the body, with many other matters (n. 4180), and in the places above cited. All things which appear before spirits and angels, are representative according to correspondences (n. 1971, 3213–3226, 3457, 3475, 3485, 9481, 9574, 9576, 9577). The heavens are full of representatives (n. 1521, 1532, 1619). Representatives are more beautiful, and more perfect, in proportion as they are more interior in the heavens (n. 3475). Representatives there are real appearances, because they are from the light of heaven which is Divine truth, and which is the very essential of the existence of all things (n. 3485).

The reason why each and all things in the spiritual world are represented in the natural world, is, because what is internal assumes to itself a suitable clothing in what is external, whereby it makes itself visible and apparent (n. 6275, 6284, 6299). Thus the end assumes a suitable clothing that it may exist as the cause in a lower sphere, and afterwards that it may exist as the effect in a sphere still lower; and when the end, by means of the cause, becomes the effect, it then becomes visible, or appears before the eyes (n. 5711). This may be illustrated by the influx of the soul into the body, whereby the soul assumes a clothing of such things in the body as enable it to express all its thoughts and affections in a visible form; wherefore thought, when it flows down into the body, is there represented by such gestures and actions as correspond to it (n. 2988). The affections of the mind are manifestly represented in the face, by the variations of the countenance, so as to be there seen (n. 4791–4805, 5695). Hence is is evident, that in each and all things in nature there lies hidden a cause and an end from the spiritual world (n. 3562, 5711). Since those things which are in nature are the ultimate effects, within which are the prior things (n. 4240, 4939, 5051, 6275, 6284, 6299, 9216). That internal things are the objects represented, and external things the objects representing (n. 4292). What is further meant by correspondences and representations may be seen in the work on *Heaven and Hell*, where it treats of the Correspondence between all things of Heaven, and all things of Man (n. 87–102). Of the Correspondence of Heaven with all things on Earth (n. 103–115). And of Representatives and Appearances in Heaven (n. 170–176).

Since all things in nature are representative of spiritual and celestial things, therefore in the churches which existed in ancient times, all the externals, which were rituals, were representative, and therefore those churches were called representative churches (n. 519, 521, 2896). The church instituted with the sons of Israel was a representative church (n. 1003, 2179, 10,149). All the rituals therein were externals, which represented internals, which are of heaven and the church (n. 4288, 4874). The representatives of the church and of worship ceased when the Lord came into the world and manifested Himself, because the Lord opened the internals of the church, and because all things of that church in the highest sense regarded Him (n. 4832).

13. *Of the sense of the letter, or the external sense of the Word.* The sense of the letter of the Word is according to appearances in the world (n. 584, 926, 1719, 1720, 1832, 1874, 2242, 2520, 2533). And adapted to the conceptions of the simple (n. 2533, 9049, 9063, 9086). The Word, in the sense of the letter is natural (n. 8783). Because what is natural is the ultimate, wherein spiritual and celestial things find their limits, and upon which they rest like a house upon its foundation; and that otherwise the internal sense of the Word, without the external, would be like a house without a foundation (n. 9360, 9430, 9433, 9824, 10,044, 10,436). The Word because it is such contains both a spiritual and celestial sense (n. 9407). And of consequence, that it is holy and Divine in the sense of the letter as to all and every part thereof, even to every iota (n. 639, 680, 1319, 1870, 9198, 10,321, 10,637). The laws enacted for the sons of Israel, although abrogated, are yet the holy Word, on account of the internal sense in them (n. 9210, 9259, 9349). Among the laws, judgments and statutes, ordained in the Israelitish or Jewish Church, which was a representative church, there are some which are still in force both in their external and internal sense; which ought strictly to be observed in their external sense; some which may be of use, if one is so disposed; and some which are altogether abrogated (n. 9349). The Word is Divine even in those statutes which are abrogated, on account of the heavenly things which lie concealed in their internal sense (n. 10,637).

What the quality of the Word is in the sense of the letter, if not understood at the same time as to the internal sense, or, what is the same thing, according to true doctrine from the Word (n. 10,402). An immense number of heresies spring up from the sense of the letter of the Word without the internal sense, or without genuine doctrine drawn from the Word (n. 10,401). They who are in externals without internals, cannot bear the interior things of the Word (n. 10,694). The Jews were of this description and they are such also at the present day (n. 301–303, 3479, 4429, 4433, 4680, 4844, 4847, 10,396, 10,401, 10,407, 10,695, 10,701, 10,707).

14. *The Lord is the Word.* The Word in its inmost sense treats solely of the Lord, describing all the states of the glorification of His Human, that is, of its union with the Divine itself, and likewise all the states of the subjugation of the hells, and the reducing to order of all things therein, and in the heavens (n. 2249, 7014). Thus the inmost sense describes the Lord's whole life in the world, and thereby the Lord is continually present with the angels (n. 2523). Therefore the Lord alone is in the inmost part of the Word, and the Divinity and the holiness of the Word is from thence (n. 1873, 9357). The Lord's saying, that the Scripture was fulfilled concerning Him, signifies, that all things were fulfilled which are contained in the inmost sense (n. 7933).

The Word signifies the Divine truth (n. 4692, 5075, 9987). The Lord is the Word because He is the Divine truth (n. 2533). The Lord is the Word also because the Word is from Him, and treats of Him (n. 2859). And because it treats of the Lord alone in its inmost sense; thus the Lord Himself is therein (n. 1873, 9357). And because in each and all things of the Word there is a marriage of the Divine good and the Divine truth, which marriage is in the Lord alone (n. 3004, 3005, 3009, 4158, 5194, 5502, 6343, 7945, 8339, 9263, 9314). Divine truth is the only reality; and that in which it is, and which is from the Divine, is the only thing substantial (n. 5272, 6880, 7004, 8200). And because the Divine truth proceeding from the Lord as the sun in heaven is light there, and the Divine good is heat there; and inasmuch as all things in heaven derive their existence therefrom, as all things in the world derive their existence from light and heat, which are also in their own substances, and act by means thereof; and inasmuch as the natural world exists by means of heaven or the spiritual world; it is plain that all things were created from the Divine truth, thus from the Word, according to these words in *John:*—

In the beginning was the Word, and the Word was with God, and God was the Word, and by it all things were made that were made; and *the Word was made flesh* (i. 1–3. 14; n. 2803, 2884, 5272, 7830).

Further particulars concerning the creation of all things from the Divine truth, consequently by the Lord, may be seen in the work on *Heaven and Hell* (n. 137); and more fully in the article concerning the Sun in Heaven, where it is shown that the Lord is that Sun, and that it is His Divine love (n. 116–125). And that the Divine truth is Light, and the Divine good is Heat, proceeding from that sun in heaven (n. 126–140).

The conjunction of the Lord with man is effected by the Word, by means of the internal sense (n. 10,375). This conjunction is effected by each and all things of the Word, and herein the Word is more wonderful than all other writings (n. 10,632–10,634). Since the time of writing the Word, the Lord thereby speaks with men (n. 10,290). For further particulars respecting the Conjunction of Heaven with man by means of the Word, see the work on *Heaven and Hell* (n. 303–310).

15. *Of those who are against the Word.* Of those who despise, blaspheme, and profane the Word (n. 1878). Their quality in the other life (n. 1761, 9222). They relate to the viscous parts of the blood (n. 5719). How great the danger is from profaning the Word (n. 571–582). How hurtful it is, if principles of falsity, particularly those which favor self-love and the love of the world, are confirmed by the Word (n. 589). They who are in no affection of truth for its own sake, utterly reject the things appertaining to the internal sense of the Word, and nauseate them, from experience of such in the world of spirits (n. 5702). Of some in the other life, who endeavored altogether to reject the interior things of the Word; such are deprived of rationality (n. 1879).

16. *Which are the books of the Word.* The books of the Word are all those which have the internal sense; but those which have not the internal sense are not the Word. The books of the Word in the Old Testament are, THE FIVE BOOKS OF MOSES; THE BOOK OF JOSHUA; THE BOOK OF JUDGES; THE TWO BOOKS OF SAMUEL; THE TWO BOOKS OF KINGS; THE PSALMS OF DAVID; THE PROPHETS ISAIAH, JEREMIAH, LAMENTATIONS, EZEKIEL, DANIEL, HOSEA, JOEL, AMOS, OBADIAH, JONAH, MICAH, NAHUM, HABAKKUK, ZEPHANIAH, HAGGAI, ZECHARIAH, MALACHI. In the New Testament, the four Evangelists, MATTHEW, MARK, LUKE, JOHN; and the APOCALYPSE. The rest have not the internal sense (n. 10,325).

The book of Job is an ancient book, which indeed contains an internal sense, but not in series (n. 3570, 9942).

17. *Further particulars Concerning the Word.* The term WORD, in the Hebrew language, signifies various things; as speech, thought of the mind, every thing that really exists, and also something (n. 9987). The Word signifies the Divine truth and the Lord (n. 2533, 4692, 5075, 9987). Words signify truths (n. 4692, 5075). They signify doctrinals (n. 1288). The ten words signify all Divine truths (n. 10,688).

In the Word, particularly in the prophetic parts, there are two expressions that signify one thing, and the one has relation to good and the other to truth, which are thus conjoined (n. 683, 707, 5516, 8339). It can be known only from the internal sense of the Word, what expression refers to good and what to truth; for there are proper words by which things appertaining to good are expressed, and proper words by which things appertaining to truth are expressed (n. 793, 801). And this so determinately, that it may be known merely from the words made use of, whether the subject treated of is good, or whether it is truth (n. 2722). Sometimes also one expression involves a general, and the other expression implies a certain specific particular from that general (n. 2212). There is a species of reciprocation in the Word, concerning which see (n. 2240). Most expressions in the Word have also an opposite sense (n. 4816). That the internal sense proceeds regularly according to the subject predicated (n. 4502).

They who have been delighted with the Word, in the other life receive the heat of heaven, wherein is celestial love, according to the quality and degree of their delight from love (n. 1773).

END OF THE WHITE HORSE.

APPENDIX

TO THE

TREATISE ON THE WHITE HORSE

APPENDIX

TO

THE TREATISE

ON

THE WHITE HORSE

FROM THE LATIN OF
EMANUEL SWEDENBORG
SERVANT OF THE LORD JESUS CHRIST

APPENDIX

TO THE

TREATISE ON THE WHITE HORSE

1. That "a horse" should signify the understanding of truth, and, in the opposite sense reasonings, which appear as if they were the result of understanding, in confirmation of falsity, must needs appear strange at this day; I will therefore bring together still more passages from the Word, where the horse is mentioned. Thus in the following:—

Is Thy wrath against the sea, O Jehovah, that Thou ridest on Thine horses? Thy chariots are salvation. Thou hast trodden the sea with Thine horses, the mire of the waters (*Hab.* iii. 8, 15).

The hoofs of the horses of Jehovah are counted as rocks (*Isa.* v. 28).

At Thy rebuke both the chariot and the horse have fallen into a deep sleep (*Ps.* lxxvi. 7).

I will overthrow the throne of kingdoms, and I will overthrow the chariot, and those that ride in it, and the horses and their riders shall come down (*Hag.* ii. 22).

I will cut off the horse from Jerusalem; but to the Gentiles He will speak peace (*Zech.* ix. 10).

2. In these passages "horse" signifies the understanding of the truth of the church; and "chariot" doctrine thence derived; and "they who ride in the chariots, and on the horses," signify those who are in understanding, and in doctrine from the Word. But this may appear yet more evident from the following passages:—

Gather yourselves on every side, to My sacrifice; ye shall be filled at My table with horse and with chariot; thus will I set My glory among the Gentiles (*Ezek.* xxxix. 17, 20, 21).

Gather yourselves together unto the supper of the great God, that ye may eat the flesh of horses, and of them that sit on them (*Apoc.* xix. 17, 18).

It treats there of the New Church about to be established by the Lord, and that the understanding of the Word will then be opened, and they will be instructed in the doctrine of truth therefrom; otherwise would it not be ludicrous, that "they would be filled at the Lord's table with horse and chariot, and would eat the flesh of horses and of them that sit on them"? In addition to these, the signification of horse and chariot is evident from the following:—

> Gird Thy sword, O Mighty One, mount, ride upon the Word of truth (*Ps.* xlv. 4, 5).
> Sing ye, extol Him that rideth on the clouds (*Ps.* lxviii. 5).
> Jehovah is riding upon a cloud (*Isa.* xix. 1).
> Sing ye praises unto the Lord, who rideth on the heaven of heavens, which was of old (*Ps.* lxviii. 33, 34).
> God rode upon a cherub (*Ps.* xviii. 11).
> Then shalt thou delight thyself in Jehovah, and I will cause thee to ride upon the high places of the land (*Isa.* lviii. 14; *Deut.* xxxii. 12, 13).
> I will make Ephraim to ride (*Hos.* x. 11).

In these places "to ride" signifies to instruct and be instructed in the truths of doctrine, and so to be wise. "The high places of the land" signify the sublimer truths of the church, and "Ephraim" also signifies the understanding of the Word. The like are signified by the "horses" and "chariots" in *Zechariah*:—

> Four chariots went out from between mountains of brass, four horses were attached to them, that were red, black, white and grizzled; these are called "spirits," and they are said to have gone forth from standing before the Lord of the whole land (*Zech.* vi. 1-8, 15).

And also by these in the *Apocalypse*:—

> When the Lamb opened the seals of the book, there went forth in order horses, the first a white horse, the second a red horse, the third a black horse, and the fourth a pale horse (vi. 1-8).

By the "book" the seals of which the Lamb opened, is meant the Word, and from this Word it is evident that nothing but the understanding of it could go forth; for what else could be meant by "horses going forth from an open book"?

3. From the same expressions in an opposite sense it is evident that "horse" signifies the understanding of truth, and "chariot" doctrine; and in that opposite sense, however, "a horse" signifies the understanding of truth when falsified by reasonings; and "a chariot," the doctrine or heresy thence derived; as in the following:—

Woe to them that go down to Egypt for help, and stay on horses, and look not unto the Holy One of Israel; for Egypt is man and not God, and his horses flesh and not spirit (*Isa.* xxxi. 1, 3).

Then shalt thou set him as king over Israel whom Jehovah shall choose. But he shall not multiply horses to himself, nor bring back the people unto Egypt, to multiply horses (*Deut.* xvii. 14–16).

These things are said, because "Egypt" represents the natural man, who by reasonings drawn from the bodily senses, perverts the truths of the Word. For what else could be meant by "the horses of Egypt are flesh and not spirit," and by "the king shall not multiply horses," but falsities of religion:—

Ashur shall not save us, we will not ride upon a horse (*Hos.* xiv. 4).

Some trust in a chariot, and some in horses, but we will glory in the name of our God (*Ps.* xx. 8).

A horse is a lying thing for safety (*Ps.* xxxiii. 17).

Thus saith the Holy One of Israel, in confidence shall be your strength; but ye said, No; we will flee upon a horse, we will ride upon the swift (*Isa.* xxx. 15, 16).

Jehovah shall make the house of Judah as a horse of glory; and the riders on horses shall be ashamed (*Zech.* x. 3–5).

I will bring against Tyre the king of Babel, with horse, and with chariot, and with horsemen; by reason of the abundance of horses, their dust shall cover thee, thy walls shall shake at the voice of the horsemen and of the chariot; with the hoofs of his horses shall he tread down all thy streets (*Ezek.* xxvi. 7–11).

In the Word, "Tyre" signifies the church as to the knowledges of good and truth; and "the king of Babel" their falsification and profanation; and on this account it is said that "he would come with horse, and with chariot, and with horsemen, and that by reason of the abundance of horses their dust should cover it":—

Woe to the city of bloods, the whole is full of a lie, and the neighing horse and the bounding chariot (*Nah.* iii. 1–4).

"A city of blood" signifies doctrine from the falsified truths of the Word. Besides in other passages, as (*Isa.* v. 26, 28; *Jer.* vi. 23; viii. 16; xlvi. 4, 9; l. 37, 38, 43; *Ezek.* xvii. 15; xxiii. 5, 20; *Hab.* i. 6, 8–10; *Ps.* lxvi. 11, 12; cxlvii. 10). The understanding of the truth of the Word, falsified and destroyed, is also signified by "the red, the black, and the pale horses" in the *Apocalypse* (vi. 4, 5, 8). Since, then, the understanding of truth is signified by "a horse," and in the opposite sense the understanding of falsity, it may appear from this what the quality of the Word is in its spiritual sense.

4. It is known, that in Egypt there were hieroglyphics, and that they were inscribed on the columns and walls of the temples and other buildings; and that no one at this day is able to determine their signification. Those hieroglyphics were no other than the correspondences of natural and spiritual things, to which science the Egyptians more than any people in Asia applied themselves, and according to which the oldest peoples of Greece formed their fables; for this, and this only, was the most ancient style of composition; to which I will add this new information, that all things seen by spirits and angels in the spiritual world are solely correspondences; and the whole Sacred Scripture is on this account written by correspondences, that by it, because it is such, it might be the means of conjunction between the men of the church and the angels of heaven. But as the Egyptians, and with them the people of the kingdoms of Asia, began to convert these correspondences into idolatries, to which the sons of Israel were prone, these latter were forbidden to make any use of them. This is evident from the first commandment of the Decalogue, which says:—

Thou shalt not make unto thee any graven image, nor any likeness of what is in the heavens above, or that is in the earth beneath, or that is in the waters under the earth. Thou shalt not bow down thyself to them, nor serve them, for I Jehovah am thy God (*Deut.* v. 8, 9).

Besides many passages elsewhere. From that time, the science of correspondences became obliterated, and successively to such an extent, that at this day it is scarcely known that it ever existed, and that it is anything. But because the Lord is now about to establish the New Church, which will be founded on the Word, and which is meant by the New Jerusalem in the *Apocalypse;* it has pleased the Lord to reveal this science, and thus to open the Word what it is interiorly in its bosom or spiritual sense. This I have done in the works entitled *Arcana Cœlestia*, published at London, and *The Apocalypse Revealed*, published at Amsterdam. As the science of correspondences was esteemed by the ancients, the science of sciences, and constituted their wisdom, it is of importance for some of your Acad-

emy to devote his attention to that science; and this may be done especially from the correspondences disclosed in *The Apocalypse Revealed* and demonstrated from the Word. Should it be desired, I am willing to unfold the meaning of the EGYPTIAN HIEROGLYPHICS, *which are nothing else but correspondences, and give them to the public, which cannot be done by any one else.*
E. S.

END OF THE APPENDIX.

NOTE.

The following paragraph is from the Advertisement prefixed to the translation of the "Appendix," published at London, 1824, by T. Goyder.

" The history of this little work may be given in a few words: It was originally written in Latin, and sent by the author under the title of 'An Appendix to the Treatise on the White Horse,' to the Rev. Thomas Hartley. By this gentleman a copy was sent to Dr. Messiter, a name well known to the readers of the New Doctrines. After his decease, it came into the possession of his eldest daughter, along with his other papers; and I am indebted to her kindness for the copy, from which this translation has been made."

To this it may be added, that the original edition contains the particulars of the receipt of the "Appendix" by the Rev. T. Hartley, which have likewise been printed in the New Jerusalem Magazine, August, 1840: Boston, U. S. The Latin has been printed only in " Swedenborg's Drömmar," published by G. E. Klemming, Stockholm, 1859, pp. 73–77. The paragraphs are numbered in the present edition for convenience of reference, but there are no numbers in the original.

The Latin original is preserved in the Royal Library in Stockholm, to which it has been transferred from the Library of Count Engeström. See " Documents Concerning Swedenborg," Vol. II. p. 751.

THE
EARTHS IN THE UNIVERSE

THE EARTHS
IN OUR SOLAR SYSTEM

WHICH ARE CALLED

PLANETS

AND

The Earths in The Starry Heaven, and Their Inhabitants; Also The Spirits and Angels There

FROM THINGS HEARD AND SEEN

FROM THE LATIN OF

EMANUEL SWEDENBORG

SERVANT OF THE LORD JESUS CHRIST

BEING A TRANSLATION OF HIS WORK ENTITLED

"De Telluribus in Mundo Nostro Solari, quæ Vocantur Planetæ: et de Telluribus de Cœlo Astrifero: Deque Illarum Incolis; tum de Spiritibus et Angelis Ibi: ex Auditis et Visis." Londini: MDCCLVIII

CONTENTS.

	Nos.
The Earths in the Universe	1–8
The Earth or Planet Mercury	9–45
The Earth or Planet Jupiter	46–84
The Earth or Planet Mars	85–96
The Earth or Planet Saturn	97–104
The Earth or Planet Venus	105–110
The Spirits and Inhabitants of the Moon	111, 112
The Reasons why the Lord was willing to be born on our Earth, and not on another	113–122
The Earths in the Starry Heaven	123–126
The First Earth in the Starry Heaven	127–137
A Second Earth in the Starry Heaven	138–147
A Third Earth in the Starry Heaven	148–156
A Fourth Earth in the Starry Heaven	157–167
A Fifth Earth in the Starry Heaven	168–178

THE
EARTHS IN THE UNIVERSE

1. Since, from the Divine mercy of the Lord, the interiors, which are of my spirit, have been opened to me, and thereby it has been granted me to speak with spirits and angels, not only with those who are near our earth, but also with those who are near other earths; because I had a desire to know whether there are other earths, and what their nature is, and the quality of their inhabitants, therefore it has been granted me by the Lord to speak and converse with spirits and angels who are from other earths, with some for a day, with some for a week, and with some for months; and to be instructed by them concerning the earths, from which and near which they were; and concerning the lives, customs, and worship of the inhabitants thereof, and of various other things worthy to be related: and because in this manner it has been granted me to know these things, it is permitted to describe them from what has been heard and seen. It is to be known that all spirits and angels are from the human race;[1] and that they are near their own earths;[2] and that they know what is there; and that by them man may be instructed, if his interiors are so far opened that he can speak and converse with them; for man in his essence is a spirit,[3] and he is together with spirits as to his interiors;[4] wherefore he whose interiors are opened by the

---

FROM THE ARCANA CŒLESTIA;
WHERE THESE AND THE FOLLOWING NOTES ARE EXPLAINED AND SHOWN.

[1] There are no spirits and angels who are not from the human race (n. 1880).

[2] The spirits of every earth are near to their own earth, because they are from the inhabitants of that earth, and of a similar genius; and they are serviceable to those inhabitants (n. 9968).

[3] The soul, which lives after death, is the spirit of man, which is the real man in him, and also appears in the other life in a perfect human form (n. 322, 1880, 1881, 3633, 4622, 4735, 6054, 6605, 6626, 7021, 10,594).

[4] Man, even when he is in the world, as to his interiors, thus as to his spirit or soul, is in the midst of spirits and angels, of a quality such as he is himself (n. 2379, 3645, 4067, 4073, 4077).

Lord, may speak with them as man with man;[5] which has been granted me now for twelve years daily.

2. That there are many earths, and men upon them, and spirits and angels thence, is well known in the other life, for it is there granted to every one who desires it from a love of truth, and thence of use, to speak with the spirits of other earths, and thereby to be confirmed concerning a plurality of worlds, and to be informed that the human race is not from one earth only, but from innumerable earths; and moreover to be informed what is their genius, manner of life, and their Divine worship.

3. I have occasionally spoken on this subject with the spirits of our earth, and it was said that any man of keen understanding may conclude from many things that he knows that there are many earths, and that there are men there; for it may be concluded from reason that such great masses as the planets are, some of which exceed this earth in magnitude, are not empty masses, and created only to be conveyed in their revolutions round the sun, and to shine with their scanty light for one earth, but that their use must needs be more excellent than that. He who believes, as every one ought to believe, that the Divine created the universe for no other end than that the human race may exist, and thence heaven, for the human race is the seminary of heaven, must needs believe also, that wherever there is an earth, there are men. That the planets which are visible to our eyes, as being within the boundaries of this solar system, are earths, may be manifestly known from this, that they are bodies of earthy matter, because they reflect the light of the sun, and when seen through optical glasses, they appear, not as stars glittering by reason of their flame, but as earths variegated from darker portions. The same may further appear from this, that they, in like manner as our earth, are conveyed by a progressive motion round the sun, in the way of the zodiac, whence they have their years, and seasons of the year, as spring, summer, autumn, and winter; and in like manner, as our earth, revolve about their own axis, whence they have their days, and times of the day, as morn-

---

[5] Man can speak with spirits and angels, and the ancients on our earth frequently spoke with them (n. 67-69, 784, 1634, 1636, 7802). But at this day it is dangerous to speak with them, unless man is in true faith, and led by the Lord (n. 784, 9438, 10,751).

ing, noon, evening and night. Moreover some of them have moons, which are called satellites, and which revolve round their globes at stated times, as the moon does round our earth. Also the planet Saturn has besides a large luminous belt, because it is very far distant from the sun, which belt supplies that earth with much light, although reflected. Who that knows these things and from reason thinks about them can say that these are empty bodies?

4. Moreover, when I have spoken with spirits, I have said that men may believe that in the universe there are more earths than one, from this, that the starry heaven is so immense, and the stars therein are so innumerable, each of which in its place, or in its world, is a sun, and like our sun, in various magnitude. Whoever duly considers, concludes that so immense a whole must needs be a means to an end, which is the ultimate of creation, which end is the kingdom of heaven, wherein the Divine may dwell with angels and men; for the visible universe, or the heaven resplendent with stars so innumerable, which are so many suns, is only a means for the existence of earths, and of men upon them, of whom may be formed a heavenly kingdom. From these things a rational man must needs be led to conceive, that so immense a means, adapted to so great an end, was not constituted for a race of men and for a heaven thence derived from one earth only; for what would this be to the Divine, which is infinite, and to which thousands, yea, ten thousands of earths, all full of inhabitants, would be small and scarce anything.

5. Moreover, the angelic heaven is so immense, that it corresponds with all the particulars with man, myriads corresponding to every member, organ, and viscus, and to every affection of each; and it has been given to know, that this heaven, as to all its correspondences, can by no means exist, except from the inhabitants of very many earths.[6]

---

[6] Heaven corresponds to the Lord, and man as to each and all things corresponds to heaven, and hence heaven, before the Lord, is a man in a large effigy, and may be called the Greatest Man (n. 2996, 2998, 3624–3649, 3636–3643, 3741–3745, 4625). Concerning the correspondence of man, and of all things pertaining to him, with the Greatest Man, which is heaven, in general, from experience (n. 3021, 3624–3649, 3741–3751, 3883–3896, 4039–4051, 4218–4228, 4318–4331, 4403–4421, 4527–4533, 4622–4633, 4652–4660, 4791–4805, 4931–4953, 5050–5061, 5171–5189, 5377–5396, 5552–5573, 5711–5727, 10,030).

6. There are spirits whose sole study is to acquire to themselves knowledges, because they are delighted only with knowledges. Therefore these spirits are permitted to wander about, and even to pass out of this solar system into others, and to procure for themselves knowledges. They have declared that there are earths inhabited by men, not only in this solar system, but also out of it in the starry heaven, to an immense number. These spirits are from the planet Mercury.

7. As to what in general concerns the Divine worship of the inhabitants of other earths, those of them who are not idolaters, all acknowledge the Lord as the only God; for they adore the Divine not as invisible, but as visible, also for this reason, because when the Divine appears to them, He appears in the human form, as He also formerly appeared to Abraham and others on this earth;[7] and they who adore the Divine under a human form, are all accepted by the Lord.[8] They say also, that no one can rightly worship God, much less be joined to Him, unless He comprehends Him by some idea, and that God cannot be comprehended except in the human form; and if He be not so comprehended, the interior sight, which is of the thought, concerning God, is dissipated, as the sight of the eye when looking upon the boundless universe; and that in this case the thought cannot but sink into nature, and worship nature as God.

8. When they were told that the Lord on our earth assumed the Human, they mused awhile, and presently said, that it was done for the salvation of the human race.

---

[7] The inhabitants of all the earths adore the Divine under a human form, consequently the Lord (n. 8541–8547, 10,159, 10,736–10,738). And they rejoice when they hear that God actually became Man (n. 9361). It is impossible to think of God except in a human form (n. 8705, 9359, 9972). Man can worship and love what he has some idea of, but not what he has no idea of (n. 4733, 5110, 5633, 7211, 9267, 10,067).

[8] The Lord receives all who are in good, and who adore the Divine under a human form (n. 9359, 7173).

THE EARTH OR PLANET MERCURY, ITS SPIRITS AND INHABITANTS.

9. That the whole heaven resembles one man, which is therefore called the *Greatest Man,* and that each and all things with man, both his exteriors and interiors, correspond to that man or heaven, is an arcanum not yet known in the world; but that it is so, has been abundantly shown.[6] To constitute that Greatest Man, there is need of spirits from many earths, those who come from our earth into heaven not being sufficient for this purpose, being respectively few; and it is provided by the Lord, that whenever there is a deficiency in any place as to the quality or quantity of correspondence, immediately those are summoned from another earth who can fill up the deficiency, that the proportion may be preserved, and thus heaven be kept in due consistence.

10. It was also disclosed to me from heaven, in what relation to the Greatest Man the spirits from the planet Mercury stand, namely, that they have relation to the memory, but to the memory of things abstracted from terrestrial and merely material objects. Since however it has been granted to speak with them, and this during many weeks, and to learn their nature and quality, and to explore how the inhabitants of that earth are particularly circumstanced, I will adduce the experiences themselves.

11. Some spirits came to me, and it was declared from heaven, that they were from the earth which is nearest to the sun, and which in our earth is called by the name of the planet Mercury. Immediately on their coming, they sought from my memory what I knew. Spirits can do this most dexterously, for when they come to man, they see in his memory all things contained therein.[9] During their search for various things, and amongst others, for the cities and places where I had been, I observed they they did not wish to know anything of temples, palaces, houses, or streets, but only of those things which I

---
[6] See foot-note, page 403.
[9] Spirits enter into all the things of man's memory but not from their own memory into man's (n. 2488, 5863, 6192, 6193, 6198, 6199, 6214). Angels enter into the affections and ends, from which and for the sake of which man thinks, wills, and acts in such and such a manner and not otherwise (n. 1317, 1645, 5844).

knew were transacted in those places, also of whatever related to the government therein, and to the genius and manners of the inhabitants, and similar things: for such things cohere with places in man's memory; wherefore when the places are recalled, those things also are brought up. I wondered that they were of such a nature; wherefore I asked them, why they disregarded the magnificence of the places, and only attended to the things and deeds done there. They said they had no delight in looking at things material, corporeal, and terrestrial, but only at things real. Hence it was confirmed, that the spirits of that earth, in the Greatest Man, have relation to the memory of things abstracted from what is material and terrestrial.

12. It was told me, that such is the life of the inhabitants of that earth, namely, that they have no concern about things terrestrial and corporeal, but only about the statutes, laws, and forms of government, of the nations therein; also about the things of heaven, which are innumerable. And I was further informed, that many of the men of that earth speak with spirits, and that thence they have the knowledges of spiritual things, and of the states of life after death; and thence also their contempt of things corporeal and terrestrial. For they who know of a certainty, and believe in the life after death, are concerned about heavenly things, as being eternal and happy, but not about worldly things, only so far as the necessities of life require. Because the inhabitants of Mercury are such, therefore also the spirits who are from thence are of a like nature.[9]

13. With what eagerness they inquire into and imbibe the knowledges of things, such as appertain to the memory elevated above the sensual things of the body, was made manifest to me from this, that when they looked into those things which I knew respecting heavenly things, they passed hastily through them all, and continually saying that this and that were so and so. For when spirits come to man, they enter into all his memory, and excite thence whatever suits themselves: yea, what I have often observed, they read the things contained therein, as out of a book.[10] These spirits did this with greater dexterity

---

[9] See foot-note, page 405.
[10] That the spirits who are with man, are in possession of all things appertaining to his memory (n. 5853, 5857, 5859, 5860).

and expedition, because they did not stop at such things as are heavy and sluggish, and which confine and consequently retard the internal sight, as all terrestrial and corporeal things do, when regarded as ends, that is, when alone loved: but they looked into things themselves; for such things, which are not clogged with things terrestrial, carry the mind upwards, thus into a broad field; whereas mere material things carry the mind downwards, and at the same time limit and shut it up. Their eagerness to acquire knowledges, and to enrich the memory, was manifest also from the following experience. Once while I was writing something concerning things to come, and they were at a distance, so that they could not look into those things from my memory, because I was not willing to read them in their presence, they were very indignant, and contrary to their usual behavior, they were desirous to inveigh against me, saying that I was one of the worst of men, and the like; and that they might give proof of their resentment, they caused a kind of contraction attended with pain on the right side of my head even to the ear. But these things did not hurt me. Nevertheless, in consequence of having done evil, they removed themselves to a yet greater distance, but presently they stood still again, desirous to know what I had written; such is their eager thirst after knowledges.

14. The spirits of Mercury, above all other spirits, possess the knowledges of things, as well respecting this solar system, as respecting the earths which are in the starry heavens; and what they have once acquired to themselves, that they retain, and also recollect as often as anything similar occurs. Hence also it may appear manifest, that spirits have memory, and that it is much more perfect than the memory of men; and further, that what they hear, see, and apperceive, they retain, and especially such things as delight them, as these spirits are delighted with the knowledges of things. For whatever things cause delight, and affect the love, these flow in as it were spontaneously, and remain; other things do not enter, but only touch the surface and pass by.

15. When the spirits of Mercury come to other societies, they explore and collect from them what they know, and then they depart; for such communication is granted amongst spirits and especially amongst angels, that when they are in a society, if they are accepted and loved, all things which they know are communicated.[11]

16. In consequence of their knowledges, the spirits of Mercury are more proud than others; wherefore they were told, that although they knew innumerable things, yet there are infinite things which they do not know; and that if their knowledges should increase to eternity, the notice even of all general things would still be unattainable. They were told likewise of their pride and elation of mind, and that this is unseemly; but they replied, that it is not pride, but only a glorying by reason of the faculty of their memory; thus they were able to excuse their faults.

17. They are averse to vocal speech, because it is material; wherefore when I conversed with them without intermediate spirits, I could only do it by a species of active thought. Their memory, as consisting of things not of images purely material, supplies objects that are nearer to the thought; for the thought, which is above the imagination, requires for its objects things abstracted from material. But notwithstanding this, the spirits of Mercury are little distinguished for their judgment, having no delight in the exercise of that faculty, and the deducing of conclusions from knowledges; for bare knowledges alone are delightful to them.

18. They were asked whether they wished to make any use of their knowledges; for it is not enough to be delighted with knowledges, because knowledges have respect to uses, and uses ought to be the ends of knowledges; from knowledges alone no use results to them, but to others with whom they are disposed to communicate their knowledges; and that it is very inexpedient for any one who wishes to be wise, to rest satisfied with mere knowledges, these being only administering causes, intended to be subservient to the investigation of things appertaining to life: but they replied, that they were delighted with knowledges, and that knowledges to them are uses.

---

[11] That in the heavens there is given a communication of all goods, inasmuch as it is the property of heavenly love to communicate all its possessions with others; and that hence the angels derive wisdom and happiness (n. 549, 550, 1390, 1391, 1399, 10,130, 10,723).

19. Some of them are also unwilling to appear as men, like the spirits of other earths, and would rather appear as crystalline globes. The reason why they are desirous to appear so, although they do not so appear, is because the knowledges of things immaterial are represented in the other life by crystals.

20. The spirits of Mercury differ altogether from the spirits of our earth, for the spirits of our earth do not care so much about realities, but about worldly, corporeal, and terrestrial things, which are material; wherefore the spirits of Mercury cannot be together with the spirits of our earth, therefore wheresoever they happen to meet them, they flee away; for the spiritual spheres, which are exhaled from each, are almost contrary. The spirits of Mercury have a common saying, that they do not wish to look at a sheath, but at things stripped of their sheath, that is, at interior things.

21. There appeared a whitish flame, burning briskly, and this for nearly an hour. That flame signified the approach of spirits of Mercury, who for penetration, thought, and speech, were more prompt than the former spirits. When they were come, they instantly ran through the things contained in my memory, but I could not perceive what they observed by reason of their promptitude. I heard them afterwards saying that such is the case; in respect to what I had seen in the heavens and in the world of spirits, they said that they knew those things before. I perceived that a multitude of spirits consociated with them was behind, a little to the left in the plane of the occiput.

22. At another time I saw a multitude of such spirits, but at some distance from me, in front a little to the right, and thence they discoursed with me, but through intermediate spirits; for their speech was as quick as thought, which does not fall into human speech, but by means of other spirits. And what surprised me, they spake in a volume, and yet readily and rapidly. Their speech was perceived as undulatory, because of many together, and what is remarkable, it was conveyed towards my left eye, although they were to the right. The reason was, because the left eye corresponds to the knowledges of things abstracted from what is material, consequently to such things as appertain to intelligence: whereas the right eye corresponds to such things as appertain to wisdom.[12] They likewise perceived and judged of what they heard with the same promptitude with which they discoursed, saying of such a thing that it was so, and of such a thing that it was not so; their judgment was as it were instantaneous.

23. There was a spirit from another earth, who could speak dexterously with them, because he spoke promptly and quickly, but who affected elegance in his discourse. They instantly decided on whatever he spake, saying of this, that it was too elegant; of that, that it was too polished: so that the sole thing they attended to was, whether they could hear anything from him which they had never known before, rejecting thus the things which caused obscurity, which are especially affectations of elegance of discourse and erudition; for these hide real things, and instead thereof present expressions, which are only material forms of things; for the speaker keeps the attention fixed herein, and is desirous that his expressions should be regarded more than the meaning of them, whereby the ears are more affected than the mind.

24. The spirits of the earth Mercury do not abide long in one place, or within companies of the spirits of one world, but wander through the universe. The reason is, because they have relation to the memory of things, which memory must be continually enriched. Hence it is granted them to wander about, and to acquire to themselves knowledges in every place. During their sojourning in this manner, if they meet with spirits who love material things, that is, things corporeal and terrestrial, they avoid them, and betake themselves where they do not hear such things. Hence it may appear, that their mind is elevated above things of sense, and thus that they are in interior light. This was also given me actually to perceive, whilst they were near me, and discoursed with me: I observed at such times, that I was withdrawn from things of sense, insomuch that the light of my eyes began to grow dull and obscure.

---

[12] The eye corresponds to the understanding, because the understanding is the internal sight, and the sight of things immaterial (n. 2701, 4410, 4526, 9051, 10,569). The sight of the left eye corresponds to truths, consequently to intelligence; and the sight of the right eye corresponds to the goods of truth, consequently to wisdom (n. 4410).

25. The spirits of that earth go in companies and phalanxes, and when assembled together, they form as it were a globe. Thus they are joined together by the Lord, that they may act in unity, and that the knowledges of each may be communicated with all, and the knowledges of all with each, as is the case in heaven.[11] That they wander through the universe to acquire the knowledges of things, appeared to me also from this, that once, when they appeared very far from me, they discoursed with me thence, and said, that they were then gathered together, and journeying out of the sphere of this world into the starry heaven, where they knew such spirits existed as had no concern about terrestrial and corporeal things, but only about things elevated above them, with whom they wished to be. It was said, that they themselves do not know whither they are going, but that they are led from the Divine auspices to those places where they may be instructed concerning such things as they they do not yet know, and which agree with the knowledges that they have already. It was also said, that they do not know how to find the companions with whom they are joined together, and that this also is done from the Divine auspices.

26. Because of their thus journeying through the universe, and thereby being enabled to know more than others respecting the worlds and earths out of the sphere of our solar system, I have also spoken with them on this subject. They said that in the universe there are very many earths inhabited by men; and that they wonder how any should suppose, whom they called men of little judgment, that the heaven of the omnipotent God consisted only of spirits and angels who come from one earth, when these comparatively are so few that in respect to the omnipotence of God they are scarce anything, even if there should be myriads of worlds, and myriads of earths. They said, moreover, that they knew there were earths existing in the universe to the number of some hundred thousands and upwards; and yet what is this to the Divine, which is infinite?

27. The spirits of Mercury, who were with me whilst I was writing and explaining the Word as to its internal sense, and who perceived what I wrote, said that the things which I wrote were in a manner gross, and that almost all the expressions

---

[11] See foot-note, page 408.

appeared as material; but it was given to reply, that to the men of our earth what was written seemed subtle and elevated, and many things incomprehensible. I added, that many on this earth do not know that it is the internal man which acts into the external, and causes the external to live; and that they persuade themselves from the fallacies of the senses that the body has life, and that in consequence thereof, such as are evil and unbelieving entertain doubt respecting the life after death; also, that the part of man which is to live after death is not by them called spirit, but soul; and that they dispute what soul is, and where is its abode, and believe that the material body, although dispersed to all the winds, is to be joined again to it, in order that man may live as man; with many other things of a like nature. The spirits of Mercury, on hearing these things, asked, whether such men could become angels; and it was given to answer, that those become angels who have lived in the good of faith and charity, and that then they are no longer in external and material things, but in internal and spiritual; and when they come into that state, that they are in a light superior to that in which the spirits from Mercury are. That they might know that it was so, an angel was allowed to discourse with them, who had come into heaven from our earth, who had been such when he lived in the world, concerning whom more will be said presently.

28. Afterwards there was sent me by the spirits of Mercury a long piece of paper, of an irregular shape, consisting of several pieces pasted together, which appeared as if printed with types, as on this earth. I asked whether they had the art of printing amongst them; but they said they had not, nevertheless they knew that on our earth we had such printed papers. They did not wish to say more; but I perceived that they thought that knowledges in our earth were upon paper, and not so much in man, thus insinuating that the papers knew what man did not. But they were instructed how this really is. After some time they returned, and sent me another paper, which appeared also printed like the former, but not so pasted together and irregular, but neat and handsome. They said, that they were further informed, that in our earth there are such papers, and books made of them.

29. From what has now been said, it appears manifest, that spirits retain in the memory what they see and hear in the other life, and that they are capable of being instructed alike as when they were men in the world, consequently of being instructed in the things of faith, and thereby of being perfected. The more interior spirits and angels are, in the same proportion they receive instruction more readily, and in a greater fulness, and retain it more perfectly: and inasmuch as this faculty abides forever, it is evident that they are continually increasing in wisdom. With the spirits of Mercury there is a constant growth in the science of things, but not in wisdom thence derived, because they love knowledges, which are means, but not uses which are ends.

30. The genius of the spirits who are from the planet Mercury, may still further appear from the following account. It is to be known, that all spirits and angels whatsoever, were once men; for the human race is the seminary of heaven; also that the spirits are altogether such, as to affections and inclinations, as they were during their life in the world whilst men; for every one's life follows him.[13] This being the case, the genius of the men of every earth may be known from the genius of the spirits who are thence.

31. Inasmuch as the spirits of Mercury in the Greatest Man have relation to the memory of things abstracted from what is material, therefore when any one discourses with them concerning things terrestrial, corporeal, and merely worldly, they are altogether unwilling to hear him; and if they are forced to hear, they transmute the things spoken of into other things, and for the most part into things contrary, that they may avoid them.

32. That I might know for certain, that such is their genius, it was allowed to represent to them meadows, fallow lands, gardens, woods, and rivers; to represent such things is imaginatively to exhibit them before another, in which case, in another world, they appear to the life; but they instantly transmuted them, obscuring the meadows and fallow fields, and by repre-

---

[13] Every one's life remains with him and follows him after death (n. 4227, 7440). The externals of life are kept closed after death, and the internals opened (n. 4314, 5128, 6495). Then all and each of the things of thought are made manifest (n. 4633, 5128).

sentations filling them with snakes. The rivers they made black, so that the water no longer appeared limpid. When I asked them why they did so, they said that they did not wish to think of such things, but of things real, which are the knowledges of things abstracted from what is terrestrial, especially of such things as exist in the heavens.

33. Afterwards I represented to them birds of different sizes, both large and small, such as exist on our earth; for in the other life such things may be represented to the life. When they saw the birds represented, they at first wished to change them, but afterwards they were delighted with them and were satisfied. The reason was, because birds signify the knowledges of things, and the perception of this then flowed in also.[14] Thus they desisted from transmuting them, and thereby from averting the ideas of their memory. Afterwards it was allowed to represent before them a most pleasant garden full of lamps and lights; then they paused, and their attention was fixed, for the reason that lamps with lights signify truths which shine from good.[15] Hence it was made manifest that their attention might be fixed in viewing things material, if only the signification of those things in the spiritual sense was insinuated at the same time; for the things of the spiritual sense are not so abstracted from things material, since these are representatives of them.

34. Moreover I spoke with them concerning sheep and lambs, but they were not willing to hear of such things, because they were perceived by them as things terrestrial. The reason was, because they did not understand what innocence is, which lambs signify, as was perceivable from this, that when I told them that lambs, represented in heaven, signify innocence,[16] they immediately said that they did not know what innocence was, but only knew it as to the name; and this was because they are affected only with knowledges, and not with uses, which are the ends of knowledges, consequently they cannot know from internal perception what innocence is.

---

[14] Birds signify things rational, intellectual, thoughts, ideas, and knowledges (n. 40, 745, 776, 778, 866, 988, 993, 5149, 7441). And this with variety according to the genera and species of birds (n. 3219).

[15] Lamps with lights signify truths shining from good (n. 4638, 9548, 9783).

[16] Lambs in heaven, and in the Word, signify innocence (n. 3994, 7840, 10,132).

35. Some of the spirits of the earth Mercury came to me, being sent by others, to hear what I was employed about. One of the spirits of our earth said to them, that they might tell those who sent them not to speak anything but what was true, and not, according to their usual practice, suggest things opposite to those who questioned them; for if any of the spirits of our earth were to do so, he would be punished. But immediately the company which was at a distance, from which those spirits were sent, made answer, that if they were to be punished on that account, they must all be punished, since by reason of acquired habit they could not do otherwise. They said that when they speak with the men of their own earth, they also do so, but this not with any intention of deceiving, but to inspire the desire of knowing; for when they suggest things opposite, and conceal things in a certain manner, then the desire of knowing is excited, and thereby from the endeavor to search out those things, the memory is perfected. I also spoke with them at another time on the same subject, and because I knew that they spoke with the men of their earth, I asked them in what manner they instruct their inhabitants. They said that they do not instruct them how the matter is, but still they insinuate some perception thereof, that thus a desire of examining and knowing may be cherished and grow; which desire would perish, in case they answered everything. They added, that they suggest things opposite also, for this reason, that the truth afterwards may better appear; for all truth is made manifest by relation to its opposites.

36. It is their custom not to declare to another what they know, but still they desire to learn from all others what is known to them. But with their own society they communicate all things, insomuch that what one knows all know, and what all know each one there knows.[11]

37. Because the spirits of Mercury abound in knowledges, they are in a certain kind of pride; hence they imagine that they know so much, that it is almost impossible to know more. But it was told them by the spirits of our earth, that they do not know many, but few things, and that the things which they do not know are respectively infinite, and that those things

---

[11] See foot-note, page 408.

which they do not know, compared to the things they know, are like the waters of the largest ocean compared with the waters of a very small fountain; and further, that the first step to wisdom is to know, acknowledge, and perceive that what is known is little and scarce anything in comparison with what is unknown. To convince them that this is the case, it was granted, that a certain angelic spirit should speak with them, and should tell them in general what they knew, and what they did not know, and that there were infinite things which they did not know, also that to eternity they could not even know the general things. He spoke by angelic ideas much more readily than they did, and because he discovered to them what they knew, and what they did not know, they were struck with amazement. Afterwards I saw another angel speaking with them, who appeared in some altitude to the right. He was from our earth, and enumerated very many things which they did not know. Afterwards he spoke with them by changes of state, which they said they did not understand. Then he told them that every change of state contains infinite things, as did also every smallest part of such change. When they heard these things, inasmuch as they had been in pride on account of their knowledges, they began to humble themselves. Their humiliation was represented by the sinking downwards of their volume; for that company then appeared as a volume, in front at a distance towards the left, in the plane of the region below the navel, but the volume appeared as it were hollowed in the middle, and elevated on the sides; a reciprocal moving was also observed therein. They were likewise told what that signified, that is, what they thought in their humiliation, and that they who appeared elevated on the sides were not as yet in any humiliation. And I saw that the volume was separated, and that they who were not in humiliation were remanded back towards their orb, the rest remaining where they were.

38. Spirits of Mercury came to a certain spirit from our earth, who during his abode in the world had been most distinguished for his learning (it was Christian Wolf), desiring to receive information from him on various subjects. But when they perceived that what he said was not elevated above the sensual things of the natural man, because in speaking his thoughts were intent on honor, and he was desirous, as in the world (for in the other life every one is like his former self), to connect various things into series, and from those series again and continually to form other conclusions, and thus from such conclusions to link together still more, which they did not see or acknowledge to be true, and which therefore they declared to be chains which neither cohered in themselves, nor with the conclusions, calling them the obscurity of authority; they then desisted from asking him further questions, inquiring only, *how this is called, and how that;* and because he answered these inquiries also by material ideas, and by no spiritual ones, they retired from him. For every one, in the other life, speaks spiritually, or by spiritual ideas, so far as he had believed in God, and materially, so far as he had not believed. An occasion here offering itself, it is permitted to mention how it is in the other life with the learned who acquire intelligence from their own meditation, kindled with the love of knowing truths, for the sake of truths, thus for the sake of uses abstracted from worldly considerations, and how with those who acquire intelligence from others, without any meditation of their own, as they are wont to do who desire to know truths solely for the sake of a reputation for learning, and thereby for honor or gain in the world; thus who desire to know truth, not for the sake of uses abstracted from worldly considerations: concerning such, it is allowed to relate the following experience. A certain sound was perceived penetrating from beneath, near the left side even to the left ear. I observed that they were spirits, who there attempted to force a way; but of what sort they were I could not know. However, when they had forced a way, they spake with me, saying that they were logicians and metaphysicians, and that they had immersed their thoughts in such things, with no other end than to to be accounted learned, and thus to be advanced to honor and wealth, lamenting that they now led a miserable life in consequence of having acquired those sciences with no other end, and thus not having cultivated thereby their rational; their speech was slow, and of a low tone. In the meantime there were two discoursing with each other above my head, and on inquiring who they were, it was said that one of them was most renowned in the learned world, and it was given me to believe that it was Aristotle. Who the other was, was not stated. The former was then let into the state in which he was during his life in the world; for every one may easily be let into the state of his life which he had in the world, because he has with him every state of his former life. But, what surprised me, he applied himself to the right ear, and there spake, but in a hoarse tone of voice, yet sanely. From the purport of his speech I perceived, that he was altogether of a different genius from those schoolmen who first ascended, in that he evolved from his own thought the things he had written, and thence he produced his philosophy; so that the terms which he invented, and which he imposed on subjects of thought, were forms of expression by which he described interior things; also that he was excited to such things by a delight of the affection, and by a desire of knowing the things of the thought and understanding, and that he followed obediently whatever his spirit had dictated. Therefore he applied himself to the right ear, contrary to the custom of his followers, who are called schoolmen, and who do not go from thought to terms, but from terms to thoughts, thus in a contrary way; and many of them do not even proceed to thoughts, but stick solely in terms, which if they apply, it is to confirm whatever they desire, and to impose on falsities an appearance of truth according to their cupidity of persuading. Hence philosophical things are rather means of becoming insane than means of becoming wise; and hence they have darkness instead of light. Afterwards I spoke with him concerning the science of analysis, observing that a child, in half an hour, speaks more philosophically, analytically, and logically, than he could describe by a volume, inasmuch as all things of the thought, and thence of human speech are analytical, the laws whereof are from the spiritual world; and he who desires to think artificially from terms, is not unlike a dancer, who would learn to dance by the science of the moving fibres and muscles, in which science, if he should fix his mind whilst he is dancing, it would be almost impossible for him to move a foot; and yet without that science, he moves all the moving fibres throughout the whole body, and in subordination thereto he moves the lungs, the diaphragm, the sides, the arms, the neck, and other organs of the body, to describe all which volumes would not suffice; and it is similar with those who are desirous to think from terms. He approved of these things, saying, that to learn to think in that way, is proceeding in an inverted order, adding if any one will be so foolish, let him so proceed; but let him think continually concerning use, and from what is interior. He next showed me, what idea he had conceived of the Supreme Deity, namely, that he had represented Him to himself as having a human face, and encompassed about the head with a radiant circle; and that now he knew that the Lord is Himself that Man, and that the radiant circle is the Divine from Him, which not only flows into heaven, but also into the universe, disposing and ruling all things therein. He added, Whosoever disposes and rules heaven, also disposes and rules the universe, because the one cannot be separated from the other. He also said that he believed in one God only, whose attributes and qualities were distinguished by a variety of names, and that these names were by others worshiped as gods. There appeared to me a woman, who stretched out her hand, desiring to stroke my cheek, and when I wondered at this, he said that when he was in the world such a woman had often appeared to him, as it were stroking his cheek, and that her hand was beautiful. The angelic spirits said that such women sometimes appeared to the ancients, and were by them called Pallases, and that she appeared to him from the spirits, who, during their abode on earth, in ancient times, were delighted with ideas, and indulged in thoughts, but without philosophy: and because such spirits were with him, and were delighted with him, because he thought from the interior, therefore they representatively exhibited such a woman. Lastly, he informed me what idea he had conceived of the soul or spirit of man, which he called *pneuma*, namely, that it was an invisible vital principle, like somewhat of ether; and he said that he knew that his spirit would live after death, inasmuch as it was his interior essence, which cannot die, because it is capable of thinking; and that moreover he was not able to think clearly concerning it, but only obscurely, because he had not formed any thought about it from any other source than from himself, and a little also from the ancients. Moreover Aristotle is among sound spirits in the other life, and many of his followers are among the foolish.

39. I once saw that spirits of our earth were with spirits of the earth Mercury, and I heard them discoursing together, and the spirits of our earth, amongst other things, asked them in whom they believed. They replied that the believed in God; but when they inquired further concerning the God in whom they believed, they were unwilling to say, it being customary with them not to answer questions directly. Then the spirits from the earth Mercury, in their turn, asked the spirits from our earth in whom they believed. They said that they believed in the Lord God. The spirits of Mercury then said that they perceived that they believed in no God, and that they had contracted a habit of professing with the mouth that they believe, when yet they do not believe. The spirits of Mercury have exquisite perception, in consequence of their continually exploring, by means of perception, what others know. The spirits of our earth were of the number of those who in the world had made profession of faith agreeable to the doctrine of the church, but still had not lived the life of faith; and they who do not live the life of faith, in the other life have not faith, because it is not in the man.[17] On hearing this they were silent, inasmuch as, by apperception then given them, they acknowledged that it was so.

40. There were certain spirits who knew from heaven, that on a time a promise was made to the spirits of the earth Mercury, that they should see the Lord; wherefore they were asked by the spirits about me whether they recollected that promise. They said that they did recollect it; but that they did not know whether it had been promised in such a way as to be beyond doubt. Whilst they were thus discoursing together, the sun of heaven then appeared to them. The sun of heaven, which is the Lord, is seen only by those who are in the inmost or third

---

[17] They who make profession of faith from doctrine and do not live the life of faith, have no faith (n. 3865, 7766, 7778, 7790, 7950, 8094). And their interiors are contrary to the truths of faith, although in the world they do not know this (n. 7790, 7950).

heaven; others see the light thence derived. On seeing the sun, they said that this was not the Lord God, because they did not see a face. Meanwhile the spirits discoursed with each other, but I did not hear what they said. But suddenly, the sun again appeared, and in the midst of it the Lord, encompassed with a solar circle: on seeing this the spirits of Mercury humbled themselves profoundly and subsided. Then also the Lord, from that sun, appeared to the spirits of this earth, who, when they were men, saw Him in the world; and they all, one after another, and thus many in order, confessed that it was the Lord Himself. This confession they made before all the company. Then also the Lord, out of the sun, appeared to the spirits of the planet Jupiter, who declared aloud that it was He Himself whom they had seen on their earth when the God of the universe appeared to them.[18]

41. Certain of them, after the Lord appeared, were led away towards the front to the right, and as they advanced, they said that they saw a light much clearer and purer than they had ever seen before, and that it was impossible any light could exceed it; and it was then evening here. There were many who said this.[19]

42. It is to be known that the sun of the world does not appear to any spirit, nor anything of light thence. The light of that sun is as dense as thick darkness to spirits and angels. That sun remains only in the perception with spirits from having seen it during their abode in the world, and is presented to them in idea as somewhat darkish, and this behind at a considerable distance, in an altitude a little above the plane of the

---

[18] The Lord is the sun of heaven, from whom is all light there (n. 1053, 3636, 4060). And the Lord thus appears to those who are in His celestial kingdom, where love to Him reigns (n. 1521, 1529–1531, 1837, 4696). He appears at a middle distance above the plane of the right eye (n. 4321, 7078). Therefore by "sun" in the Word is signified the Lord as to Divine love (n. 2495, 4060, 7083). The sun of this world does not appear to spirits and angels, but in the place thereof there appears somewhat as it were darkish, not in front, but behind and opposite to the sun of heaven, or to the Lord (n. 9755).

[19] There is in the heavens great light, which exceeds, by many degrees, the noon-day light of this world (n. 1117, 1521, 1533, 1619–1632, 4527, 5400, 8644). All light in the heavens is from the Lord as a sun there (n. 1053, 1521, 3195, 3341, 3636, 3643, 4415, 9548, 9684, 10,809). The Divine truth proceeding from the Divine good of the Divine love of the Lord appears in the heavens as light, and furnishes all the light that is there (n. 3195, 3222, 5400, 8644, 9399, 9548, 9684). The light of heaven illumines both the sight and the understanding of the angels (n. 2776, 3138). When heaven is said to be in light and heat, it signifies being in wisdom and in love (n. 3643, 9399, 9401).

head. The planets which are within the system of that sun appear according to a determinate situation in respect to the sun; Mercury behind, a little towards the right; the planet Venus to the left, a little backwards; the planet Mars to the left in front; the planet Jupiter in like manner to the left in front, but at a greater distance; the planet Saturn directly in front, at a considerable distance; the Moon to the left, at a considerable height: the satellites also to the left in respect to their planet. Such is the situation of those planets in the ideas of spirits and angels; spirits also appear near their planets, but out of them. As to what particularly concerns the spirits of Mercury, they do not appear in any certain quarter, or at any certain distance, but sometimes in front, sometimes to the left, sometimes a little to the back; the reason is, because they are allowed to wander through the universe to procure for themselves knowledges.

43. Once the spirits of Mercury appeared to the left in a globe, and afterwards in a volume extending itself lengthways. I wondered whither they were desirous of going, whether to this earth or elsewhere; and presently I observed that they inclined to the right, and as they rolled along, approached to the earth or planet Venus towards the quarter in front. But when they came thither they said they were unwilling to be there, because the inhabitants were evil; wherefore they turned about to the back part of that earth, and then said that they would willingly stay there, because the inhabitants were good. When this took place, I felt a remarkable change in the brain, and a powerful operation thence proceeding. Hence I was led to conclude that the spirits of Venus, who were on that part of the planet, were in concord with the spirits of Mercury, and that they had relation to the memory of things material[a] which was in concord with the memory of things immaterial, to which latter memory the spirits of Mercury have relation: hence a more powerful operation was felt from them when they were there.

44. I was desirous to know what kind of face and body the men in the earth Mercury had, whether they were like the men on our earth. There was then presented before my eyes a woman exactly resembling the women in that earth. She had a beautiful face, but it was smaller than that of a woman of our earth; her body also was more slender, but her height was equal; she wore on her head a linen cap, which was put on without art, but yet in a manner becoming. A man also was presented to view, who was more slender in body than the men of our earth are. He was clad in a garment of dark blue color, closely fitted to his body, without any foldings or protuberances. It was said that such was the form of body and such the dress of the men of that earth. Afterwards there was presented to view a species of their oxen and cows, which indeed did not differ much from those on our earth, but were smaller, and in some degree approached to species of hinds and deer.

45. They were also asked about the sun of the world, how it appears from their earth. They said that it appears large, and larger there than when seen from other earths, and they said they knew this from the ideas of other spirits concerning the sun. They said further that they enjoy a middle temperature, neither too hot nor too cold. It was then granted me to tell them, that it was so provided of the Lord in regard to them that they should not be exposed to too much heat by reason of their greater nearness to the sun, inasmuch as heat does not arise from the sun's nearness, but from the altitude and density of the atmosphere, as appears from the cold on high mountains even in hot climates; also that heat is varied according to the direct or oblique incidence of the sun's rays, as is plain from the seasons of winter and summer in every region. These are the things which it was given me to know concerning the spirits and inhabitants of the earth Mercury.

THE EARTH OR PLANET JUPITER, ITS SPIRITS AND INHABITANTS.

46. It was granted me to enjoy longer intercourse with the spirits and angels of the planet Jupiter, than with the spirits and angels from the rest of the planets; wherefore I am at liberty to relate more concerning the state of their life, and of the inhabitants of that planet. That those spirits were from that planet was evident from many things, and it was also declared from heaven.

47. The earth itself or planet Jupiter does not indeed appear to spirits and angels: for to the inhabitants of the spiritual world no earth is visible, but only the spirits and angels who come thence. They who are from the planet Jupiter appear in front to the left, at a considerable distance, and this constantly, see above (n. 42); there also is the planet. The spirits of every earth are near their earth, because they are from its inhabitants, for every man after death becomes a spirit, and because they are thus of a similar genius, and can be with the inhabitants, and serve them.

48. They related that in the region of the earth where they had lived while in the world, the multitude of men therein was as great as the earth could support; that the earth was fertile, and it abounded in all things; and that there they did not desire more than the necessaries of life; that they accounted nothing useful but so far as it was necessary; and that hence the multitude of men was so great. They said that the education of their children was their greatest concern, and that they loved them most tenderly.

49. They further related that they are there distinguished into nations, families, and houses, and that they all live apart with their own kindred; and that hence their intercourse is confined to relatives; likewise, that no one ever covets the goods of another; and that it never enters into their minds to desire the possessions of another, still less to obtain them fraudulently, and least of all to break in and plunder. This they consider as a crime against human nature, and regard it as horrible. When I would have told them that on this earth there are wars, depredations, and murders, they then turned away, and were unwilling to hear. It was declared to me by the angels that the most ancient people on this earth lived in like manner, namely, that they were distinguished into nations, families, and houses; that all at that time were content with their own possessions; that it was a thing altogether unknown for one person to enrich himself from the goods of another, and to have dominion from self-love; and that on this account the ancient times, and especially the most ancient, were more acceptable to the Lord than succeeding times: and such being the state of the world, innocence also then reigned, and with it wisdom; every one then did what was good from good, and what was just from justice. To do what is good and just with a view to their own honor, or gain, was unknown. At the same time they spake nothing but what was true, and this not so much from truth as from good, that is, not from the understanding separate from the will, but from the will conjoined with the understanding. Such were the ancient times; wherefore angels could then converse with men, and convey their minds, almost separate from things corporeal, into heaven, yea, lead them about, and show them the magnificent and blessed things there, and likewise communicate to them their happinesses and delights. These times were known also to the ancient writers, and were by them called the golden and also Saturnian ages. The reason that those times were such, was owing to this, that men were then distinguished into nations, nations into families, and families into houses, and every house lived apart by itself; and it then never entered into any one's mind to invade another's inheritance, and thence acquire to himself opulence and dominion. Self-love and the love of the world were then far removed; every one rejoiced in his own, and not less in his neighbor's good. But in succeeding times this scene was changed, and totally reversed, when the lust of dominion and of large possessions invaded the mind. Then mankind, for the sake of self-defence, collected themselves into kingdoms and empires; and because the laws of charity and of conscience, which were inscribed on the hearts, ceased, it became necessary to enact laws in order to restrain violence, in which honors and gains were rewards, and privation of them punishments. When the state of the world was thus changed, heaven removed itself from man, and this more and more even to this age, when it is no longer known whether there is a heaven and a hell, yea, by some it is denied. These things are said, that it may be illustrated by the parallel, what is the state of the inhabitants of the earth Jupiter, and whence they have their probity, and also their wisdom, concerning which more will be said hereafter.

50. By long conversation with the spirits of the earth Jupiter, it was made manifest to me that they were more upright than the spirits of most other earths. The manner of their approach to me, their abode with me, and their influx at that time, was inexpressibly gentle and sweet. In the other life the quality of every spirit manifests itself by an influx, which is the communication of his affection; uprightness by gentleness and sweetness; by gentleness, in that he fears to do hurt, and by sweetness, because he loves to do good. I could clearly distinguish a difference between the gentleness and the sweetness of the influx proceeding from the spirits of Jupiter and of that which proceeds from the good spirits of our earth. When any slight disagreement exists among them, they said that there appears a sort of slender bright irradiation, like that of lightning, or like the little swath encompassing glittering and wandering stars; but all disagreements among them are soon adjusted. Glittering stars, which are at the same time wandering, signify what is false; but glittering and fixed stars signify what is true; thus the former signify disagreement.[20]

51. I could distinguish the presence of the spirits of Jupiter, not only by the gentleness and sweetness of their approach and influx, but also from this, that for the most part their influx was into the face, and made it smiling and cheerful, and this continually during their presence. They said that they comcommunicate a like cheerfulness of countenance to the inhabitants of their earth, when they come to them, being desirous thus to inspire them with tranquillity and delight of heart. That tranquillity and delight with which they inspired me filled my breast and heart very sensibly; at the same time cupidities and anxieties concerning things to come were removed, which cause unrest and undelightfulness, and excite various commotions in the mind. Hence it was evident to me what was the nature and quality of the life of the inhabitants of the earth Jupiter; for the disposition of the inhabitants of any earth may be known by the spirits who come thence, inasmuch as every one retains his own life after death, and continues to live it when he becomes a spirit. It was observed that they had a state of blessedness or happiness still more interior, which was manifest from this circumstance, that their interiors were perceived not to

---

[20] Stars in the Word signify the knowledges of good and truth, consequently truths (n. 2495, 2849, 4697). And in the other life truths are represented by fixed stars, but falsities by wandering stars (n. 1128).

be closed, but open to heaven; for in proportion as the interiors are more open to heaven, in the same proportion they are the more susceptible of receiving Divine good, and with it blessedness and interior happiness. The case is altogether otherwise with those who do not live in the order of heaven: the interiors with such are closed, and the exteriors open to the world.

52. It was further shown me what sort of faces the inhabitants of the earth Jupiter had; not that the inhabitants themselves appeared to me, but that the spirits appeared with faces similar to what they had when on their earth. But before it was shown, one of their angels appeared behind a bright cloud, who gave leave; and then two faces were shown. They were like the faces of the men of our earth, fair and beautiful; sincerity and modesty beamed forth from them. During the presence of the spirits of Jupiter, the faces of the men of our earth appeared less than usual, which was owing to this, that there was an influx from those spirits of the idea which they had concerning their own faces as being larger; for they believe, during their abode in their earth, that after their decease their faces will be larger and of a round shape; and because this idea is impressed on them, it consequently remains with them, and when they become spirits they appear to themselves as having larger faces. The reason why they believe that their faces will be larger is, because they say that the face is not body, because through it they see, hear, speak, and manifest their thoughts; and whereas the mind is thus transparent through the face, they hence form an idea of the face as of the mind in form; and because they know that they will be wiser after their life in the world, therefore they believe that the form of the mind or the face will become larger. They believe also that after their decease they will perceive a fire which will communicate warmth to their faces. This belief takes its rise from hence, that the wiser amongst them know that fire in the spiritual sense signifies the love, and that love is the fire of life, and from this fire the angels have life.[21] Those of them

---

[21] Fire in the Word is love in both senses (n. 934, 4906, 5215). The sacred and heavenly fire is the Divine love, and every affection which is of that love (n. 934, 6314, 6832). Infernal fire is the love of self and the world, and every concupiscence which is of these loves (n. 965, 1861, 5071, 6314, 6832, 7575, 10,747). Love is the fire of life, and life itself is actually thence (n. 4906, 5071, 6032).

also who have lived in heavenly love, obtain their wish, and perceive their face to grow warm; and then the interiors of their mind are kindled with love. For this reason the inhabitants of that earth also wash and cleanse their faces much, and protect them carefully from the heat of the sun. They have a covering made of the inner rind or bark of a tree, of a bluish color, which they wrap about the head and thus cover the face. Concerning the faces of the men of our earth, which they saw through my eyes,[22] they said that they were not beautiful, and that their beauty consisted in the external skin, but not in the fibres from the internal. They wondered that the faces of some were full of warts and pustules, or were otherwise deformed, saying that with them such faces were never seen. Some faces were always smiling, namely, those that were cheerful and merry, and those that were a little prominent about the lips.

53. The reason of the faces smiling that were prominent about the lips was, that the most of their speech is effected by the face, and especially by the region around the lips; and also because they never dissemble, that is, speak otherwise than they think. For this reason they do not constrain their face, but let it out freely. It is otherwise with those who from childhood have learned to dissemble. Their face is thus contracted interiorly, lest something of their thought should shine forth. Neither is it let forth outwardly, but is held ready to let itself out or contract itself, according as cunning suggests. The truth of this may be evident from an examination of the fibres of the lips and the parts around them. For there are manifold series of fibres there, folded together and intertwined, which were created not only for masticating and for speech by words, but also for expressing the ideas of the mind.

54. It was also shown how the thoughts are presented by the face. The affections of the love are manifested through the countenance and its changes, and the thoughts by variations as to the forms of the interiors therein; but they cannot be further described. The inhabitants of the earth Jupiter have also a vocal speech, but not as sonorous as ours. The

---

[22] Spirits and angels do not see what is in this solar world, but they saw through my eyes (n. 1881).

one speech assists the other, and their vocal speech is inspired with life by the speech of the face. I was informed by angels that the first speech of all men on every earth was speech by the face, and this from two sources, the lips and the eyes. The reason why such speech was the first, is, that the face was formed for portraying what man thinks and wills, and thence also the face was called the image and index of the mind; also because in the most ancient or earliest times there was sincerity, and man neither thought nor wished to think anything else than what he was willing should shine forth from his face. Thus also the affections of the mind, and the the thoughts therefrom, could be presented to the life, and fully. Thus also they were made apparent to the eye, very many, as it were, in a form together. This speech, therefore, as much surpassed vocal speech as sight excels hearing, or as seeing a landscape excels hearing of it, or apprehending it by verbal description. They added that such speech agrees with the speech of angels, with whom also men in those times were in communication; and further that when the face speaks, or the mind through the face, it is the angelic speech with man in ultimate natural form, but not when the mouth speaks by words. Every one, too, can comprehend that the most ancient people could not have the speech of words; since the words of language were not immediately infused into men, but had to be invented, and applied to things; which could be done only in process of time.[23] As long as sincerity and rectitude remained with man, so long also such speech remained. But as soon as the mind began to think one thing and speak another, which took place when man began to love himself and not his neighbor, then vocal speech began to develop, the face being silent or dissembling. Thus the internal form of the face was changed, contracted itself, hardened, and began to be almost void of life; but the external form, inflamed by the fire of self-love, began to appear to the eyes of men as if it were alive. For that absence of life which lies underneath, does not ap-

---

[23] The most ancient people on this earth had speech through the face and lips, by means of internal breathing (n. 607, 1118, 7361). The people on certain other earths have a similar speech (n. 4799, 7359, 8248, 10,587). Concerning the perfection and excellence of that speech (n. 7360, 10,587, 10,708).

pear to the eyes of men, but to the eyes of angels, since these see the interiors. Such are the faces of those who think one thing and speak another; for dissimulation, hypocrisy, cunning, and deceit, which are prudence at this day, induce such effects. But it is different in the other life, where it is not permitted to speak one thing and think another. Disagreement between the speech and the thought is also there clearly perceived in every word; and when it is perceived in a spirit, he is cast out of the community, and fined. Afterward he is reduced by various methods to speak as he thinks, and to think as he wills; even till he has one undivided mind; so that if he is good, he may will good and think and speak truth from good, and if he is evil, he may will evil and think and speak falsity from evil. Not before this is effected is the good spirit elevated into heaven, nor the evil spirit cast into hell; and this to the end, that there may be in hell nothing but evil and the falsity of evil, and in heaven nothing but good and the truth of good.

55. I was further informed by the spirits from that earth, concerning various particulars relating to its inhabitants, as concerning their manner of walking, their food, and their habitations. With respect to their manner of walking, they do not walk erect like the inhabitants of this and of many other earths, nor do they creep like animals; but as they go along, they assist themselves with their hands, and alternately half elevate themselves on their feet, and also at every third step turn the face sideways and behind them, and likewise at the same time bend the body a little, which is done suddenly; for with them it is thought unbecoming to be seen by others except in the face. In walking thus they always keep the face elevated as with us, that so they may look at the heavens as well as the earth. Holding the face downwards so as to look at the earth alone, they call accursed. The most vile amongst them do so, but if they continue and do not elevate the face, they are banished from the society. When they sit, they appear like men of our earth, erect as to the upper part of the body, but they usually sit cross-legged. They take special care, not only when they walk, but also when they sit, to be seen in the face, and not at the back. They are also very willing to have their faces seen, because thence their mind appears;

for with them the face is never at variance with the mind, nor indeed can they make it so. Those present also know clearly from this what dispositions they entertain towards them, especially whether their apparent friendship is sincere or forced, for this they never conceal. These particulars were shown to me by their spirits, and confirmed by their angels. Hence also their spirits are seen to walk, not erect like others, but almost like persons swimming, appearing to help themselves forward with their hands, and by turns to look around them.

56. They who live in their warm climates go naked, except with a covering about the loins; nor are they ashamed of their nakedness, for their minds are chaste, and they love their consorts only, and abhor adultery. They wondered exceedingly that the spirits of our earth, who on hearing of their method of walking, and also that they were naked, ridiculed it, and had lascivious thoughts, without attending at all to their heavenly life, but only to such things. They said that this was a sign that things corporeal and terrestrial were of more concern to them than heavenly things, and that things of an indecent nature had place in their minds. Those spirits of our earth were told that nakedness gives no occasion either of shame or of scandal to such as live in chastity and a state of innocence, but only to such as live in lasciviousness and immodesty.

57. When the inhabitants of that earth lie in bed, they turn their faces forward, or towards the chamber, but not backward, or towards the wall. This was told me by their spirits, who said the reason is, that they believe that in turning the face forward they turn it to the Lord, but if they turn it backward they avert it from the Lord. I have sometimes observed, in regard to myself, whilst I was in bed, such a direction of the face; but never knew before whence it was.

58. They take delight in making long meals; but not so much from enjoyment of the food, as from enjoyment of the conversation at that time. When they sit at table they do not sit on chairs or benches, or raised couches of turf, nor on the grass, but on the leaves of a certain tree. They were not willing to tell of what tree the leaves were; but when I named several by conjecture, they assented at last on my naming the leaves of the fig-tree. They said moreover, that they do not prepare food with reference to the taste, but especially with reference to the use; and they added that to them useful food was savory. On this subject a conversation arose among the spirits, and it was said that this is the right way for man; for thus it is in his heart to have a sound mind in a sound body, but it is otherwise with those whose taste governs, and whose body therefore sickens, or at least inwardly languishes, and consequently their mind also; for the action of this depends upon the interior state of the recipient parts of the body, as the sight and hearing upon the state of the eye and ear. Thus is seen the insanity of placing all the delight of life in luxury and pleasure. From this too, comes dulness in such things as are of thought and judgment, and shrewdness in such things as are of the body and the world. From this arises the likeness between a man and a brute animal, with which also such persons not inaptly compare themselves.

59. Their habitations were also shown me. They are low and of wood, but within they are lined with the bark or rind of a tree of a palish blue color, the walls and ceiling being spotted as with small stars, to represent the heavens; for they are fond of thus picturing the visible heavens and stars in the insides of their houses, because they believe the stars to be the abodes of angels. They have also tents, which are round above, and stretched out to a considerable length, spotted likewise within with little stars in a blue plane; in these they betake themselves in the middle of the day, lest their faces be injured from the heat of the sun. They take great care in the construction and in the cleanliness of these their tents. They have also their meals in them.

60. When the spirits of Jupiter saw the horses of this earth, the horses appeared to me smaller than usual, although they were tolerably robust and large. This was in consequence of the idea of those spirits concerning the horses there. They said that they also had horses with them, and much larger, but that they were wild, or in the woods, and that when they are seen, the inhabitants are terrified, although they do no harm. They added, that the fear of horses is innate or natural to them. This led me to a consideration of the cause of that fear; for "a horse" in the spiritual sense signifies the intellectual faculty formed of scientifics,[24] and because the inhabitants of Jupiter are afraid of cultivating the intellectual faculty by worldly sciences, hence comes an influx of fear. That they do not care for scientifics, which are of human erudition, will be seen in what follows.

61. The spirits of that earth are not willing to associate with the spirits of our earth, because they differ both in minds and manners. They say that the spirits of our earth are cunning, and that they are prompt and ingenious in the contrivance of evil; and that they know and think little about what is good. Moreover, the spirits of the earth Jupiter are much wiser than the spirits of our earth. They say also of our spirits, that they talk much and think little, and thus that they are not capable of an interior perception of many things, not even of what is good; hence they conclude, that the men of our earth are external men. Once also it was permitted evil spirits of our earth, by their evil arts, to act upon and infest the spirits of Jupiter who were with me. The spirits of Jupiter endured them for a long time, but at length confessed that they could endure no longer, and that they believed it impossible for worse spirits to exist, for they perverted their imagination and also their thoughts in such a manner that they seemed to themselves as it were bound, and that they could not be extricated and set at liberty without Divine aid. Whilst I was reading in the Word some passages concerning our Saviour's passion, then European spirits infused dreadful scandals, with intent to seduce the spirits of Jupiter. Inquiry was made who they were, and what had been their profession in the world, and it was discovered that some of them had been preachers; and that the greater part were of those who call themselves of the Lord's society, or Jesuits. I said that when they lived in the world, by their preaching concerning the Lord's passion, they were able to move the common people to tears. I added also the reason, that in the world they thought one way and spoke another, thus entertained one thing in the heart and professed

---

[24] A "horse" signifies the intellectual faculty (n. 2760–2762, 3217, 5321, 6125, 6400, 6534, 7024, 8146, 8148). And that "the white horse" in the *Apocalypse* signifies the understanding of the Word (n. 2760).

another with the mouth; but now it was not permitted them to speak thus deceitfully, because when they become spirits, they are compelled to speak just as they think. The spirits of Jupiter were greatly astonished that there could be given such a disagreement between a man's interiors and his exteriors, so that he could speak altogether differently from what he thought; which to them was impossible. They wondered when they heard that many who are from our earth also become angels, and are of an altogether different heart, supposing at the time that all on our earth were like those present. But it was said that there are many of a different nature, and that there are also those who think from good, and not as these from evil; and that they who think from good become angels. That they might know that it was so, there came out of heaven choirs of angels from our earth, one after another, which with one voice and in harmony together glorified the Lord.[25] Those choirs so greatly delighted the spirits of Jupiter who were with me, that they seemed to themselves, as if they were caught up into heaven. The glorification by the choirs lasted about an hour, and the delight they received was communicated to me and given me to feel. They said that they would tell their people about it who were elsewhere.

62. The inhabitants of the earth Jupiter place wisdom in thinking well and justly of all things that happen in life. This wisdom they derive from their parents from infancy, and it is successively transmitted to posterity, and increases from the love they have for it because of its belonging to their parents. Of sciences, such as are in our earth, they know nothing whatever, nor do they wish to know. They call them shades and compare them to clouds which hide the sun. This idea concerning the sciences they have conceived from some spirits from our earth who boasted that they were wise from sciences. The spirits from our earth who thus boasted were such as made wisdom to consist in things appertaining merely to the memory, as in languages, especially the Hebrew, Greek, and Latin, in a

---

[25] When many spirits speak together and unanimously they form what is called a choir, and concerning them (n. 2595, 2596, 3350). In their speech there is harmony (n. 1648, 1649). By choirs in the other life introduction into unanimity is effected (n. 5182).

knowledge of the things related in the literary world, in criticism, in mere experiments, and in terms, particularly such as are philosophical, with other things of a like nature, not using such things as means leading to wisdom, but making wisdom to consist in those things themselves. Such persons, because they have not cultivated their rational faculty by the sciences, as by means leading to wisdom, have little perception in the other life; for they see only in terms, and from terms, in which case those things are as clods and clouds obstructing the intellectual sight (see above, n. 38); and they who have been proud of their erudition therefrom, have still less perception; but they who have used the sciences as means of invalidating and annihilating the things appertaining to the church and to faith, have totally destroyed their intellectual faculty, and like owls they see in the thick darkness falsity for truth, and evil for good. The spirits of Jupiter, from the conversation they had with such, concluded that sciences induce shade and blindness. But they were informed that on our earth the sciences are means of opening the intellectual sight, which sight is in the light of heaven; but because such things as appertain to the mere natural and sensual life reign, therefore the sciences to the men of our earth are means of becoming insane, namely, of confirming them in favor of nature against the Divine, and in favor of the world against heaven. They were further informed that the sciences in themselves are spiritual riches, and that they who possess them are like those who possess worldly riches, which in like manner are means of performing uses to himself, his neighbor, and his country, and also means of doing evil. Moreover, that they are like garments, which serve for use and ornament, and also for pride, as with those who would be honored for these alone. The spirits of the earth Jupiter understood these things well; but they wondered that, being men, they should rest in means, and prefer things leading to wisdom before wisdom itself; and that they should not see, that to immerse the mind in such things, and not to elevate it above them, was to becloud and blind it.

63. A certain spirit ascending from the lower earth, came to me, and said that he had heard what I had been discoursing upon with other spirits, but that he did not understand at all what was said concerning spiritual life and the light thereof. He was asked whether he was willing to be instructed concerning it. He said that he had not come with that purpose. From which I concluded that he would not comprehend such things. He was very stupid; yet it was declared by the angels, that when he lived as a man in the world, he was much celebrated for his learning. He was cold, as was manifestly felt from his breathing, which was a sign of light merely natural, and of none spiritual, thus that by the sciences he had not opened, but had closed for himself the way to the light of heaven.

64. Because the inhabitants of the earth Jupiter procure intelligence for themselves by a way different from that of the inhabitants of our earth, and are moreover of a different genius from their life, therefore they cannot abide long together, but either shun them or remove them. There are spheres, which may be called spiritual spheres, which continually flow forth, yea, overflow from every spirit; they flow from the activity of the affections and consequent thoughts, thus from the life itself.[26] All consociations in the other life are regulated according to these spheres; those which agree being joined together according to their agreement, and those which disagree being separated according to their disagreement. The spirits and angels who are from the earth Jupiter, in the *Greatest Man* have relation to the *imaginative of thought*, and consequently to an active state of the interior parts; but the spirits of our earth have relation to the various functions of the exterior parts of the body, and when these are desirous to have dominion, the activity or imaginative of thought from the interior cannot flow in: hence come the oppositions between the spheres of the life of each.

65. As to what concerns their Divine worship, it is a principal characteristic thereof, that they acknowledge our Lord as the Supreme, who rules heaven and earth, calling Him the only Lord; and because they acknowledge and worship Him

---

[26] A spiritual sphere, which is the sphere of the life, flows forth and overflows from every man spirit, and angel, and encompasses them about (n. 4464, 5179, 7454). It flows forth from the life of their affections and consequent thoughts (n. 2489, 4464, 6206). In the other life consociations and also dissociations are according to spheres (n. 6206, 9606, 9607, 10,312).

during their life in the body, they hence seek Him after death and find Him; He is the same with our Lord. They were asked, whether they know that the only Lord is a Man. They replied that they all know that He is a Man, because in their world He has been seen by many as a Man; and that He instructs them concerning the truth, preserves them, and also gives eternal life to those who worship Him from good. They said further, that it is revealed to them from Him how they should live, and how they should believe; and that what is revealed is handed down from parents to children, and hence there flows forth doctrine to all the families, and thereby to the whole nation which is descended from one father. They added, that it seems to them as if they had the doctrine written on their minds, and they conclude so from this, because they perceive instantly, and acknowledge as of themselves, whether it be true or not what is said by others concerning the life of heaven with man. They do not know that their only Lord was born a man on our earth; they said that they care to know only that He is Man, and rules the universe. When I informed them that on our earth He is named Christ Jesus, and that Christ signifies Anointed or King, and Jesus, Saviour, they said that they do not worship Him as a King, because royalty savors of what is worldly, but that they worship Him as the Saviour. On this occasion a doubt was injected from the spirits of our earth, whether their only Lord was the same with our Lord; but they removed it by the recollection that they had seen Him in the sun, and had acknowledged that it was He Himself whom they saw on their earth (see above, n. 40). Once also with the spirits of Jupiter who were with me, there flowed in for a moment a doubt whether their only Lord was the same with our Lord; but this doubt, which flowed in for a moment, was also in a moment dispersed. It inflowed from some spirits of our earth; and then, what surprised me, they were so ashamed for having doubted this, though but for a moment, that they requested me not to publish it, lest they should be charged with incredulity, when yet they now know it more than others. These spirits were very much affected and rejoiced when they heard it declared that the only Lord is alone Man, and that all have from Him what entitles them to be called men; but that they are only so far men as they are images of Him, that is, as far as they love Him, and love their neighbor, thus, so far as they are in good; for the good of love and faith is the image of the Lord.

66. There were with me some spirits of the earth Jupiter, while I was reading the seventeenth chapter in *John* concerning the Lord's love, and concerning His glorification; and when they heard the things that are there, holiness filled them, and they confessed that all things therein were Divine. But then some spirits of our earth, who were unbelievers, continually suggested various scandals, saying that He was born an infant, lived as a man, appeared as another man, was crucified, with other circumstances of a like nature. But the spirits of the earth Jupiter paid no attention to these suggestions. They said that their devils are such, whom they abhor; adding, that nothing celestial has any place in their minds, but only earthly things, which they called dross. That it was so, they said they had also discovered from this, that when they heard that on their earth they go naked, obscene ideas immediately occupied their thoughts, and they paid no attention to their celestial life, about which they had heard at the same time.

67. The clear perception which the spirits of Jupiter have concerning spiritual things, was made manifest to me from their manner of representing how the Lord converts depraved affections into good affections. They represented the intellectual mind as a beautiful form, and impressed upon it an activity suitable to the form answering to the life of affection. This they executed in a manner which no words can describe, and with such dexterity that they were commended by the angels. There were then present some of the learned from our earth, who had immersed the intellectual faculty in scientific terms, and had written and thought much about form, about substance, about materiality and immateriality, and the like, without applying such things to any use; these could not even comprehend that representation.

68. They are exceedingly cautious on their earth, lest any one should fall into wrong opinions concerning the only Lord; and if they observe that any begin to think wrongly concerning Him, they first admonish him, then use threats, and lastly deter by punishment. They said that they had observed, if any such wrong opinions insinuate themselves into any family, that family is taken from amongst them, not by the punishment of death inflicted by their fellows, but by being deprived of respiration, and consequently of life, by spirits, when they have first threatened them with death. For in that earth spirits speak with the inhabitants, and chastise them if they have done evil, and even if they have intended to do evil, of which we shall say more presently. Hence if they think evil concerning the only Lord, and do not repent, they are threatened with death. In this manner the worship of the Lord is preserved, who is to them there the Supreme Divine.

69. They said that they have no festival days, but that every morning at sunrise, and every evening at sunset, they perform holy worship to their only Lord in their tents; and that they also sing psalms after their manner.

70. I was further instructed, that in that earth there are also some who call themselves saints, and who command their servants, of whom they wish to have great numbers, to give them the title of lords, under threat of punishment. They likewise forbid them to adore the Lord of the universe, saying that themselves are mediating lords and that they will present their supplications to the Lord of the universe. They call the Lord of the universe, who is our Lord, not only the Lord, as the rest do, but the Supreme Lord, by reason that they call themselves also lords. The sun of the world they call the face of the supreme Lord, and believe that His abode is there, wherefore they also adore the sun. The rest of the inhabitants hold them in aversion and are unwilling to converse with them, as well because they adore the sun as because they call themselves lords, and are worshiped by their servants as mediatory gods. There was shown me by spirits the covering of their head, which was a tower-shaped cap of darkish color. In the other life such appear to the left in a certain altitude, and there sit as idols, and in the beginning are also worshiped by the servants who have attended upon them, but are afterwards held in derision by them also. What surprised me was, that their faces shine there as from a fire, which is in consequence of their having believed that they were saints; but notwithstanding this fiery appearance of their faces, they are nevertheless cold, and have an intense desire to be made warm. Hence it is evident that the fire, from which they shine, is the fire of self-love, and is fatuous. In order to make themselves warm, they seem to themselves to cut wood, and whilst they are cutting, there appears underneath the wood something of a man, whom at the same time they attempt to strike. This appearance is in consequence of their attributing to themselves merit and sanctity; for all who do so in the world, seem to themselves in the other life to cut wood, as was the case likewise with some spirits from our earth, who have been spoken of elsewhere. For the further illustration of this subject, I will here adduce this experience concerning them. "In the lower earth beneath the soles of the feet, are those who have placed merit in their good deeds and works. Many of them appear to themselves to cut wood. The place where they are is very cold, and they seem to themselves to acquire warmth by their labor. I have also spoken with them, and it was granted me to ask them whether they wished to come out of that place. They said that they had not yet merited it by their labor. But when that state has been gone through, they are taken out. They are natural, because to wish to merit salvation is not spiritual; for it comes from the proprium, not from the Lord. Moreover they also prefer themselves to others, and some of them despise others. If they do not receive greater joy than others in the other life, they are indignant against the Lord; for which reason, when they are cutting wood, there appears as it were something of the Lord under the wood. This comes from their indignation."[27]

71. It is common on that earth for spirits to speak with the inhabitants and to instruct them, and also to chastise them if they have done evil, in regard to which since many things have been related to me by their angels, I wish to repeat them in order. The reason why spirits speak with the men there, is

---

[27] The Lord alone has merit and justice (n. 9715, 9975, 9979, 9981, 9982). They who place merit in works, or wish to merit heaven by their good deeds, wish to be served in the other life, and are never content (n. 6393). They despise the neighbor, and are angry with the Lord Himself if they do not receive reward (n. 9976). What their lot is in the other life (n. 942, 1774, 1877, 2027). They are of those who appear to cut wood in the lower earth (n. 1110, 4943).

that they think much about heaven and about the life after death, and have comparatively little solicitude about life in the world; for they know that they are to live after death, and in a state happy according to the state of their internal man, formed in the world. To speak with spirits and angels was also common on this earth in ancient times, and for the same reason, namely, because they then thought much of heaven and little of the world. But that living communication with heaven in process of time was closed, as man from internal became external, or what is the same, as he began to think much about the world and little about heaven; and still more when he no longer believed that there is a heaven or a hell, nor that man in himself is a spirit which lives after death; for at this day it is believed that the body lives from itself, and not from its spirit; wherefore unless man now believed that he will rise again with the body, he would have no belief in the resurrection.

72. As to what particularly regards the presence of spirits with the inhabitants of the earth Jupiter, there are some spirits who chastise, some who instruct, and some who rule over them. The spirits who chastise apply themselves to the left side, and incline themselves towards the back, and when they are there, they draw forth from the man's memory all that he has done and thought; for this is easy to spirits, for when they come near to a man, they come into all his memory. If they find that he has done evil, or thought evil, they reprove him, and also chastise him with pain of the joints, and of the feet or hands, or with a pain about the epigastric region. This also spirits can do dexterously when permitted. When such come to a man they inspire horror with fear, and thus the man knows of their approach. Evil spirits can inspire fear when they approach any one, especially those who while they lived in the world were robbers. That I might know how these spirits act when they come to a man of their earth, it was permitted that such a spirit should also come to me. When he was near, horror with fear manifestly took possession of me; yet the horror was not interior but exterior, because I knew that it was such a spirit. He was also seen, and appeared like a dark cloud, with moving stars in the cloud. Moving stars signify falsities, but fixed stars truths. He applied himself to my left side

toward the back, and also began to reprove me for the deeds and thoughts which he drew forth out of my memory, and also interpreted perversely; but he was prevented by angels. When he perceived that he was with one who was not a man of his earth, he began to speak with me, saying that when he came to a man, he knew each and all things that the man had done and thought; and that he reproved him severely, and also chastised him with various pains. Again at another time such a chastising spirit came to me, and applied himself to my left side below the middle of the body, like the former one, who also wished to punish me; but he too was prevented by angels. He, however, showed me the kinds of punishments which they are permitted to inflict upon the men of their earth, if they do and intend to do evil. They were, besides pain of the joints, a painful constriction also around the middle of the belly, which is felt as a compression by a sharp girdle. And then there was a taking away of the breath at intervals even to distress; and also the prohibition from eating anything but bread for a time; last of all the threat of death, if they should not leave off doing such things; and also privation from enjoyment of the consort, children, and companions. Pain therefrom is also then insinuated.

73. But the spirits who instruct, also, apply themselves to the left side, but more toward the front. They also rebuke, but mildly, and presently teach them how they ought to live. They appear dark also, yet not as the former like clouds, but as if clothed in sackcloth. These are called instructors, but the former chastisers. When these spirits are present, angelic spirits are also present, sitting at the head and filling it in a peculiar manner. Their presence is also perceived there as a gentle breathing; for they fear lest from their drawing near and their influx the man should perceive the least pain or anxiety. They rule the chastising and instructing spirits; preventing the former from doing worse to the man than is permitted by the Lord, and requiring the latter to tell the truth. When the chastising spirit was with me, the angelic spirits also were then present, and kept my face continually cheerful and smiling, and the region around the lips prominent, and my mouth a little open. This the angels do easily by influx, when permitted by the Lord. They said that they induce such a countenance upon the inhabitants of their earth, when they are present.

74. If a man after chastisement and instruction again does evil, or thinks to do evil, and does not restrain himself by the precepts of truth, then, when the chastising spirit returns, he is punished more severely. But the angelic spirits moderate the punishment according to the intention in the deeds, and according to the will in the thoughts. From this it may be evident that their angels who sit at the head, have a kind of judicial authority over the man; since they permit, moderate, restrain, and flow in. But it was said that they do not judge, for the Lord alone is the Judge; and all the things which they command to the chastising and instructing spirits flow in with them from Him, though it appears as if from them.

75. Spirits there speak with man, but not man in turn with the spirits, except these words when he is instructed *that he will do so no more.* Nor is it permitted him to tell any one that a spirit has spoken with him: if one does this, he is afterward punished. Those spirits of Jupiter, when they were with me, thought at first that they were with a man of their earth; but when I spoke in turn with them, and they saw that I thought of publishing these things, and thus of telling others, and it was not then permitted them to chastise or instruct me, they perceived that they were with another.

76. There are two signs that appear to those spirits when they are with a man. They see an old man with a pale face, which is a sign that they should say nothing but what is true, and do nothing but what is just. They also see a face in a window, which is a sign that they should depart thence. That old man was also seen by me, and likewise the face in the window was seen; on seeing which the spirits immediately departed from me.

77. Besides the spirits who have now been mentioned, there are also spirits who persuade the contrary. They are those who while they lived in the world, were banished from the society of others, because they were evil. When they approach, there appears as it were a flying fire, that glides down near the face. They place themselves low down behind the man, and speak thence toward the upper parts. They speak things contrary to what the instructing spirit has said from the angels, namely, that one should not live according to the instruction, but of his own will and license, and similar things. They come for the most part after the former spirits have gone away, but the men there know who and what these spirits are, and therefore care nothing for them; yet they learn in this way what evil is, and so what good is; for by evil it is learned what good is, since the quality of good is known from its opposite. All perception of a thing is according to reflection in regard to its distinctions from things contrary, in various ways and various degrees.

78. The chastising and instructing spirits do not go to those who call themselves saints and mediating lords of whom above (n. 70), as they do to others on that earth, because these do not suffer themselves to be instructed, nor are they amended by discipline. They are inflexible, because they do this from the love of self. The spirits said that they recognize them from their coldness, and when they perceive the cold, they depart from them.

79. There are also spirits among those of Jupiter, whom they call chimney-sweepers, because they appear in such garments, and also with a sooty face. Who and what they are, I am also permitted to describe. One such spirit came to me, and earnestly begged me to intercede for him that he might come into heaven. He said that he did not know that he had done evil, only that he had reproved the inhabitants of that earth; adding that after he had reproved, he instructed them. He applied himself to my left side under the elbow, and spoke as with a cracked voice; he could also move to pity. But I could only reply that I could bring him no help, and that this is of the Lord alone; and that I could not intercede, because I did not know whether it would be useful or not, but if he was worthy he might have hope. He was then sent back among the upright spirits from his earth; but they said that he could not be in their company, because he was not such as they. But because from his intense desire he still importuned to be let into heaven, he was sent into a society of upright spirits of this earth; but they also said that he could not be with them. He was of a black color in the light of heaven, but he said that he was not of a black, but of a brown color. It was told me that they are such at first, who are afterward received among those that constitute the province of the seminal vesicles in the Greatest Man, or heaven; for in those vesicles the semen is collected and enclosed around with a suitable material, fitted for preserving the prolific principle of the semen from being dissipated, but such as may be thrown off in the neck of the uterus, that thus what is reserved within may serve for conception, or for the impregnation of the ovulum. Hence also that seminal matter has an effort, and as it were a burning desire, to throw itself off and leave the semen to perform its use, similar to what was seen with that spirit. He still came to me, in vile garments, and said again that he burned to come into heaven, and that he now perceived that he was such that he could. I was then permitted to tell him, that perhaps this was an indication that he would shortly be received. He was then told by angels to cast off his garment, which from his desire he rejected so quickly, that scarce anything could be quicker. By this was represented what are the desires of those who are in the province to which the seminal vesicles correspond. It was said that these spirits when prepared for heaven, put off their garments and are clothed with shining new ones, and become angels. They were likened to caterpillars, which having passed through their vile state, are changed into chrysalises, and thus into butterflies; to which another dress is then given, and also wings of a blue, yellow, silver, or golden color; and then the liberty of flying in the air as in their heaven, of celebrating their marriages and laying their eggs, and thus of providing for the propagation of their kind; and at the same time there is allotted them sweet and pleasant food from the juices and odors of the various flowers.

80. Thus far nothing has been said of the quality of the angels who are from that earth; for those who come to the men of their earth and sit at their head, as mentioned above (n. 73), are not angels in their interior heaven, but are angelic spirits, or angels, in their exterior heaven. And as the nature of the angels of the interior heaven has also been disclosed to me, it is permitted to relate what has been given me to know. A certain one of the spirits of Jupiter who inspire fear, applied himself to my left side under the elbow and spoke thence. But his speech was harsh, nor were his words sufficiently distinct and separate; so that I had to wait some time before I could gather his meaning. And when he spoke he also injected something of fear, thus also admonishing me to receive the angels well when they they came. But it was given to answer, that this did not depend on me; since all were received with me as they are. Presently angels of that earth came to me, and I was able to perceive from their speech with me, that they were altogether different from the angels of our earth; for their speech was not by words, but by ideas, which diffused themselves everywhere through my interiors, and thus they had also an influx into my face, so that the face concurred in every particular, beginning from the lips and proceeding in every direction toward the circumference. The ideas which were in the place of spoken words were discrete, though in small degree. They afterwards spoke with me by ideas still less discrete, so that scarce any interstice was perceivable. To my perception it was like the meaning of words with those who only attend to the meaning abstractly from the words. This speech was more intelligible to me than the former, and was also more full. Like the former it flowed into the face, but the influx in accordance with the quality of the speech, was more continuous. It did not however begin like the former from the lips, but from the eyes. Afterward they spoke still more continuously and fully, so that my face was not then able to concur by fitting motion; but there was felt an influx into the brain, and that this was then acted upon in like manner. At last they so spoke that the discourse fell only into the interior understanding. Its volubility was like that of a thin aura. I felt the influx itself, but not distinctly the particulars. These kinds of speech were like fluids, the first kind like flowing water, the second like thinner water, the third comparatively like the atmosphere, and the fourth like a thin aura. The spirit mentioned above, who was on the left side, sometimes interrupted, especially warning me to act modestly with his angels; for there were spirits from our earth, who introduced such things as were displeasing. He said that he did not at first understand what the angels said, but that he did afterward when he was brought nearer to my left ear. Then also his speech was not harsh, as before, but like that of other spirits.

81. I afterward spoke with these angels about some notable things on our earth, especially about the art of printing, about the Word, and about the various doctrines of the church from the Word; and I said that the Word and the doctrines are published, and so are learned. They wondered exceedingly that such things could be published by writing and by types.

82. I was permitted to see how the spirits of that earth after they have been prepared, are taken up into heaven and become angels. There then appear chariots and horses bright as with fire, by which they are carried away like Elijah. Chariots and horses bright as with fire appear, because it is thus represented that they have been instructed and prepared to enter heaven; since "chariots" signify the doctrinals of the church, and "bright horses" the understanding enlightened.[28]

83. The heaven into which they are taken, appears on the right of their earth, thus apart from the heaven of the angels of our earth. The angels who are in that heaven appear clothed in shining blue, dotted with small golden stars, and this because they loved that color in the world. They also believed that it was the veriest celestial color, chiefly because they are in such good of love as that color corresponds to.[29]

84. There appeared to me a bald head, but only the top of it, which was bony; and it was said that those who are to die within a year see such a one, and that they then prepare themselves. They do not fear death there, except on account of leaving the consort, children or parents; for they know that they will live after death, and that they are not going out of life, because they are going into heaven. Therefore they do

---

[28] "Chariots" signify the doctrinals of the church (n. 2761, 5321, 8215). "Horses" signify the intellectual faculty (n. 2760, 2761, 2762, 3217, 5321, 6125, 6400, 6534, 7024, 8146, 8148, 8381). "The white horse" in the *Apocalypse* signifies the understanding of the Word (n. 2760). By "Elijah" in the representative sense is meant the Word (n. 2762, 5247). And because all the doctrine of the church and the understanding of it are from the Word, Elijah was called "the chariot of Israel and the horsemen thereof" (n. 2762). He was therefore taken up by a fiery chariot and horses of fire (n. 2762, 8029).

[29] Blue from red or flame corresponds to the good of celestial love, and blue from white or light corresponds to the good of spiritual love (n. 9868).

not call it dying, but being heaven-made. Those who have lived in love truly conjugial on that earth, and have taken care of their children as becomes parents, do not die of diseases, but tranquilly as in sleep; and thus they migrate from the world into heaven. The age of men there is usually thirty years, according to the years of our earth. The cause of their dying in so short a time is of the Lord's providence, lest the multitude of men should increase beyond what can be sustained by that earth; and because after they have fulfilled those years, they do not suffer themselves to be led by spirits and angels as those do who have not yet fulfilled them; for which reason spirits and angels rarely go to the more mature. They come to maturity also more quickly than on our earth. Even in the first flower of youth they form marriages, and then their delights are to love the consort, and to take care of their children. Other delights they indeed call delights, but respectively external.

THE EARTH OR PLANET MARS, ITS SPIRITS AND INHABITANTS.

85. The spirits of Mars are the best of all among the spirits who are from the earths of our solar system, for they are as to the most part celestial men, not unlike those who were of the Most Ancient Church on this earth.[30] When they are represented as to their quality, they are represented with the face in heaven and the body in the world of spirits; and those of them who are angels, with the face toward the Lord and the body in heaven.

86. The planet Mars in the idea of spirits and angels, like the other planets, appears constantly in its place, which is to the left in front, at some distance, in the plane of the breast, and so out of the sphere where the spirits of our earth are. The spirits of one earth are separate from the spirits of another

---

[30] The First and Most Ancient Church on this earth was a celestial church, which is the primary of all, see (n. 607, 895, 920, 1121–1124, 2896, 4493, 8891, 9942, 10,545). The church is called celestial in which the principal thing is love to the Lord, but spiritual in which the principal thing is charity toward the neighbor and faith (n. 3691, 6435, 9468, 9680, 9683, 9780).

earth, because the spirits of each earth refer to some particular province in the Greatest Man, and hence are in another and different state; and diversity of state makes them appear separate from each other, either to the right or to the left, at a greater or less distance.[31]

87. Spirits from Mars came to me and applied themselves to my left temple, where they breathed upon me with their speech; but I did not understand it. It was soft in its flow, softer I had never before perceived; it was like the softest aura. It first breathed upon my left temple, and upon my left ear from above; and the breathing proceeded thence to my left eye, and little by little to the right, and then flowed down, chiefly from the left eye to the lips; and when it reached the lips, it entered through the mouth, and through the passage within the mouth, and indeed through the Eustachian tube, into the brain. When the breathing arrived there, I then understood their speech; and it was granted to speak with them. I observed when they were speaking with me, that my lips were moved, and the tongue also a little; which was by reason of the correspondence of interior speech with exterior speech. Exterior speech is that of articulate sound finding its way to the external membrane of the ear, whence it is conveyed, by means of little organs, membranes, and fibres which are within the ear, into the brain. From this, it was granted, to know that the speech of the inhabitants of Mars was different from that of the inhabitants of our earth, namely, it was not sonorous, but almost tacit, insinuating itself into the interior hearing and sight by a shorter way; and being such it was more perfect, and more full of the ideas of thought, thus approaching nearer to the speech of spirits and angels. The very affection of the speech is also represented with them in the face, and its thought in the eyes; for the thought and the speech, also the affection and the face, with them act as one. They regard it as nefarious to think one thing and speak another, and to will one thing and show another in the face. They do not know what hypocrisy is, nor what fraudulent pretence and deceit are. That such was also the speech

---

[31] Distances in the other life are real appearances, which are presented by the Lord to be seen, according to the state of the interiors of angels and spirits (n. 5604, 9104, 9440, 10,146).

of the most ancient people on our earth, it has been given me to know by conversation with some of them in the other life; and that this matter may be made clearer, it is permitted to relate what I have heard, as follows: "It was shown me by an influx which I cannot describe, what kind of speech they had who were of the Most Ancient Church, namely, that it was not articulate, like the vocal speech of our time, but tacit, which was effected not by external respiration but by internal; thus it was the speech of thought. It was also granted to perceive what their internal respiration was, that it proceeded from the navel toward the heart, and so through the lips without being sonorous when they spoke; and that it did not enter into the ear of another by the external way, and beat upon what is called the drum of the ear, but by a certain internal way, and in fact by a certain passage now called the Eustachian tube. It was shown that by such speech they could much more fully express the feelings of the mind and the ideas of the thought, than can ever be done by articulate sounds or sonorous words; which speech is in like manner directed by respiration, but external: for there is no word, nor indeed anything in a word, which is not directed by applications of the respiration. But with them this was much more perfect, because it was effected by internal respiration, which is the more perfect, because more internal, and more applicable and better conformed to the very ideas of thought; and it is further effected also by the little motions of the lips and corresponding changes of the face. For, since they were celestial men, whatever they thought shone forth from their face and eyes, which were varied in conformity, the face as to form according to the life of the affection, and the eyes as to light. They could by no means present any other countenance than such as accorded with what they thought; and because they had speech by internal respiration, which is that of man's spirit itself, they were therefore able to associate and speak with angels. The respiration of the spirits of Mars was also communicated to me;[32] and it was perceived that it proceeded from the region of the thorax toward the navel, and thence flowed upward through the chest with an imperceptible

---

[32] That spirits and angels have respiration (n. 3884, 3885, 3891, 3893).

breathing toward the mouth. From this, as also from other proofs of experience, it was made plain to me that they were of a celestial genius; thus that they were not unlike those who were from the Most Ancient Church on this earth.

88. I have been instructed that the spirits of Mars have reference in the Greatest Man to what is mediate between the intellectual and the voluntary faculties, thus to *thought from affection;* and the best of them to *the affection of thought.* It is for this reason that their face acts as one with their thought, and that they cannot dissemble before any one. And as they have reference to this in the Greatest Man, the middle province, which is between the cerebrum and the cerebellum, corresponds to them. For with those with whom the cerebrum and the cerebellum are conjoined as to spiritual operations, the face acts as one with the thought; so that the very affection of the thought shines forth from the face, and from the affection, with the aid of some signs going forth from the eyes, the general of thought shines forth. For this reason when the spirits of Mars were with me, I perceived sensibly a drawing back of the front part of the head toward the occiput, thus of the cerebrum toward the cerebellum.[33]

89. Once when the spirits of Mars were with me, and occupied the sphere of my mind, some spirits from our earth came and wished to infuse themselves also into that sphere. But then these spirits from our earth became as it were insane, for the reason that they did not at all agree. For the spirits of our earth in the Greatest Man have reference to the external sense, and thus they were in an idea turned to the world and to self, while the spirits of Mars were in an idea turned from self to heaven and to the neighbor; hence there was contrariety. But angelic spirits of Mars then came, and at their approach communication was taken away, and so the spirits of our earth withdrew.

90. The angelic spirits spoke with me about the life of the inhabitants on their earth, that they are not under empires, but

---

[33] Human faces on our earth in ancient times received influx from the cerebellum, and the faces then acted as one with the interior affections of man; but that afterward they received influx from the cerebrum, when man began to dissemble and counterfeit in the face affections not his own, and concerning the changes brought upon faces therefrom in process of time (n. 4325-4328).

are arranged in societies larger and smaller, and that they consociate with themselves in their societies such as agree with them in mind, which they know at once from the face and speech, and are rarely deceived. Then they are friends at once. They said also that their consociations are delightful, and that they speak with one another of those things that are done in the societies, especially those done in heaven; for many of them have manifest communication with the angels of heaven. Those in their societies who begin to think perversely, and from this to will evil, are dissociated, and left to themselves alone, and thus they pass their time very miserably out of the society, among rocks or elsewhere; for the society no longer has a care over them. Certain societies try in various ways to compel such to repentance; but when they cannot effect this, they separate themselves from them. Thus they take care lest the lust of dominion and the lust of gain creep in; that is, lest any from the lust of dominion subject any society to themselves, and then many more; and lest any from the lust of gain seize the goods of others. Every one there lives content with his own goods, and every one with his own honor, in being esteemed just and one that loves his neighbor. This delight and tranquillity of mind would perish, if those that think and will what is evil were not cast out, and if the love of self and the love of the world were not met prudently and severely in the very beginnings. For these are the loves for the sake of which empires and kingdoms have been established, within which there are few who do not wish to have dominion, and to possess the goods of others. For there are few who do what is just and equitable from the love of what is just and equitable; still less who do what is good from charity itself, rather than from fear of the law, of life, of the loss of gain, of honor, and of reputation on account of those things.

91. Concerning the Divine worship of those that dwell on their earth, they said that they acknowledge and adore our Lord, saying that He is the Only God, and that He rules both heaven and the universe; and that all good is from Him, and and that He leads them; also that He often appears with them on their earth. It was then granted to say to them, that Christians also on our earth know that the Lord rules heaven and earth, from the words of the Lord Himself in *Matthew:*—

All power is given unto Me in heaven and in earth (xxviii. 18);

but that they do not believe this as those who are from the earth Mars do. They said also that there they believe that there is nothing in them but what is filthy and infernal, and that all good is the Lord's, yea, saying further, that of themselves they are devils, and that the Lord draws them out of hell, and continually withholds them. Once when the Lord was named, I saw that those spirits humbled themselves so interiorly and profoundly as cannot be described; for in their humiliation they had the thought that they were of themselves in hell; and that so they were altogether unworthy to look to the Lord, Who is holiness Itself. They were so profoundly in that thought, from belief, that they were as if out of themselves; and they remained in it upon their knees until the Lord lifted them up, and then as it were drew them out of hell. When they thus come forth out of their humiliation, they are full of good and of love, and thence of joy of heart. When they so humble themselves, they do not turn their face to the Lord, for this they do not then dare to do, but turn it away. The spirits who were around me said that they had never seen such humiliation.

92. Certain spirits who were from that earth wondered that there were about me so many spirits from hell, and that they also spoke with me. But it was given to answer, that this was permitted them in order that I might know their quality, and why they are in hell, and that this is according to their life. It was also given to say that there were many among them whom I had known when they lived in the world, and that some were then established in great dignity, who yet had nothing but the world in their heart; but that no evil spirit, even the most infernal, could do me any harm, because I was continually protected by the Lord.

93. There was presented before me an inhabitant of that earth. He was not indeed an inhabitant, but like one. His face was like that of the inhabitants of our earth, but the lower region of the face was black, not from a beard, for he had none, but from blackness in place of it. This blackness extended on both sides as far as the ears. The upper part of the face was yellowish, like the faces of the inhabitants of our earth who are not altogether white. These spirits said further that on their earth they feed on the fruits of trees, especially a certain round fruit which grows up out of the ground, and also leguminous plants. That they are there clothed with garments made out of fibres of the bark of certain trees. These have such consistence that they can be woven, and also glued together by a kind of gum which they have with them. They further related that they know there how to make fluid fires from which they have light during the evening and night.

94. I saw a most beautiful flame of varying color, purple, and also bright red, and the colors with a beautiful ruddy glow from the flame. I also saw a certain hand, to which this flame adhered, at first on the back, afterward in the palm, and thence it played round the hand on all sides. This lasted for some little time. Then the hand with its flamy light was removed to a distance, and where it rested there was a bright light. In that brightness the hand receded, and then the flame was changed into a bird, which at first was of the same colors as the flame, and the colors glittering in like manner; but gradually the colors were changed, and with the colors the vigor of life in the bird. It flew round about and at first around my head, then forward into a certain narrow chamber, which appeared like a shrine; and as it flew farther forward, so its life receded, till at length it became as of stone, at first of a pearl color, afterward dark; but though without life, it was still flying. When the bird was flying around my head and was still in the vigor of life, a spirit was seen rising from below through the region of the loins to the region of the breast, who wished to take the bird away. But because it was so beautiful, the spirits around me prevented him; for their eyes were all fastened on it. The spirit however who rose up from below, endeavored strongly to persuade them that the Lord was with him, and thus that he did this from the Lord. And then, though most of them did not believe this, they no longer prevented him from taking away the bird. But as heaven flowed in at that moment, he could not hold it, and presently let it go free out of his hand. When this was done, the spirits around me who had intently watched the bird and its successive changes, spoke with one another about it, and this for a considerable time. They perceived that such a sight could not but signify something celestial. They knew that the flame signified celestial love and its affections; that the hand to which the flame adhered, signified life and its power; the changes of colors, varieties of life as to wisdom and intelligence; and the bird also the same, but with the difference that the flame signified celestial love and the things of that love, and the bird signified spiritual love and the things of that love (celestial love is love to the Lord, and spiritual love charity toward the neighbor); and that the changes of the colors and at the same time of the life in the bird, until it became as of stone, signified successive changes of spiritual life as to intelligence. They knew also that spirits who ascend from below through the region of the loins to the region of the breast, are in a strong persuasion that they are in the Lord, and hence believe that all things they do, even though evil, they do by the Lord's will. But yet they could not know from this who were meant by this appearance. At length they were instructed from heaven that the inhabitants of Mars were meant, that their celestial love, in which very many still are, was signified by the flame which adhered to the hand, and that the bird in the beginning, when in the beauty of its colors and the vigor of its life, signified their spiritual love; but that the bird's becoming as of stone without life, and at length of a dark color, signified such of the inhabitants as have removed themselves from the good of love and are in evil, and yet still believe that they are in the Lord. The same was signified by the spirit who rose up and wished to take away the bird.

95. By the bird of stone were also represented the inhabitants of that earth who in a strange manner transmute the life of their thoughts and affections into almost no life, concerning which I have heard as follows. There was a certain spirit above my head who spoke with me, and from the sound of his voice it was perceived that he was as it were in a state of sleep. In this state he spoke many things, and with such prudence that if he were awake he could not speak more prudently. It

was given to perceive that he was a subject through which
angels spoke; and that in that state he perceived and brought
forth what they said,[34] for he spoke nothing but what was true.
If anything flowed in from any other source, he admitted it
indeed, but did not bring it forth. I questioned him about his
state, and he said that this state was to him peaceful, and without any anxiety about the future; and that at the same time he
performed uses, whereby he had communication with heaven.
It was told me that such spirits in the Greatest Man have reference to the longitudinal sinus in the brain, which lies between
its two hemispheres, and there he is in a quiet state, however
the brain may be disturbed on both sides. When I was in conversation with this spirit, some spirits introduced themselves
toward the fore part of the head, where he was, and pressed
upon him; wherefore he withdrew to one side, and gave them
place. The newly arrived spirits conversed with one another;
but neither the spirits around me, nor I myself, understood
what they were saying. I was instructed by angels that they
were spirits from the earth Mars, who were skilled in talking
with one another in such manner that the spirits present neither
understood nor perceived anything. I wondered that such
speech was possible, because all spirits have one kind of speech,
which flows from the thought, and consists of ideas, that are
heard as words in the spiritual world. It was said that those
spirits form in a certain manner ideas expressed by the lips
and the face, not intelligible to others, and at the same moment
artfully withdraw their thoughts, taking special care that nothing of the affection should manifest itself, because if anything
of the affection were perceived, the thought would then be
manifest; for the thought flows from the affection, and is as it
were in it. I was instructed further that the inhabitants of the
earth Mars who place heavenly life in knowledges alone, and
not in a life of love, contrived such speech, though not all of
them; and that when they become spirits, they retain it. It
is these who were signified in particular by the bird of stone;
for to present speech by modifications of the countenance and

---

[34] That communications are made through spirits sent forth by societies of spirits
and angels to other societies, and that these emissary spirits are called subjects (n.
4403, 5856, 5983, 5985–5989).

foldings of the lips, with the removal of the affections and withdrawal of the thoughts from others, is to take the soul out of speech, and to render it like a mere image, and by degrees they also become similar. But although they think that they are not understood by others in what they say among themselves, still angelic spirits perceive each and everything that they speak, for the reason that from them no thought can be concealed. This was also shown them by living experience. I was thinking of this, that the evil spirits of our earth are not affected with shame when they infest others, and this thought flowed in with me from angelic spirits who perceived their speech. These spirits of Mars then acknowledged that this was what they were speaking of among themselves, and they marvelled. Moreover, there were many things disclosed by an angelic spirit, both of what they spoke and of what they were thinking, notwithstanding they endeavored to withdraw their thoughts from him. Afterward those spirits flowed in from above into my face, and their influx was felt like a fine striated rain, which was a sign that they were not in any affection of truth and good, since that is represented by what is striated. They then spoke with me plainly, saying that the inhabitants of their earth speak with one another in like manner. It was then said to them, that this is evil, because in this way they obstruct internals, and recede from them to externals, which they also deprive of their life; and especially because it is not sincere to speak thus. For they who are sincere have no wish to speak nor even to think anything but what others may know, yea all, even the whole heaven. But they who do not wish others to know what they speak, judge concerning others, think evil of them, and well of themselves, and are at length carried by habit so far as to think and speak ill of the church, of heaven, and even of the Lord Himself. It was said that they who love knowledges, and not so much a life according to them, have reference to the interior membrane of the skull in the Greatest Man; but they who accustom themselves to speak without affection, and to draw the thought to themselves and withdraw it from others, have reference to that membrane when it is become bony, because from having some spiritual life they come to have no life.

96. As those who are in knowledges alone, and in no life of love, were also represented by the bird of stone, and as they have thence no spiritual life, I may therefore show here, by way of appendix, that those alone have spiritual life who are in heavenly love, and in knowledges therefrom; and that a love contains in itself all the power of knowing which is of that love. For example, the animals of the earth, and also the animals of the air, or the birds, have the knowledge of all things that are of their loves. These loves are, to nourish themselves, to dwell in safety, to propagate offspring, to bring up their young, and with some, to provide for themselves against winter. Consequently they have all the requisite knowledge, for this is in those loves, and it flows into them as into its very receptacles; which knowledge with some animals is such, that man cannot but be astonished. The knowledge is innate with them, and is called instinct; but it is of the natural love in which they are. If man were in his love, which is love to God and toward the neighbor (for this love is man's proper love, by which he is distinguished from the beasts, and is heavenly love), man would then be not only in all requisite knowledge, but also in all intelligence and wisdom; for these would flow into those loves from heaven, that is, through heaven from the Divine. But because man is not born into those loves, but into the opposite ones, namely, into the loves of self and the world, for that reason he cannot but be born into all ignorance and lack of knowledge. But by Divine means he is led on to something of intelligence and wisdom, yet not actually into anything of it, unless the loves of self and the world are removed, and the way is thus opened for love to God and the neighbor. That love to God and love toward the neighbor have in them all intelligence and wisdom, may be evident from those who in the world have been in these loves. When after death they come into heaven, they there come into such knowledge and wisdom as they had never known before; yea, they think and speak there, as do the rest of the angels, such things as the ear has never heard, nor the mind has ever known, and which are ineffable. The reason is, that those loves have in them the faculty of receiving such things.

THE EARTH OR PLANET SATURN, ITS SPIRITS AND INHABITANTS.

97. The spirits from the earth Saturn appear in front at a considerable distance, beneath in the plane of the knees, where the earth itself is; and when the eye is opened to see thither, a multitude of spirits come into view who are all from that earth. They are seen on this part of that earth, and to the right of it. It has also been granted to speak with them, and thereby to know their quality in comparison with others. They are upright and modest, and inasmuch as they esteem themselves little, therefore they also appear small in the other life.

98. In worship they are exceedingly humble, for in it they account themselves as nothing. They worship our Lord, and acknowledge Him as the only God. The Lord also appears to them at times under an angelic form, and thereby as a Man, and the Divine then shines forth from the face and affects the mind. The inhabitants also, when they arrive at a certain age, speak with spirits, by whom they are instructed concerning the Lord, how He ought to be worshiped, and likewise how they ought to live. When any wish to seduce the spirits who come from the earth Saturn, and to withdraw them from faith in the Lord, or from humiliation towards Him, and from uprightness of life, they say they wish to die. There then appear in their hands small knives, with which they seem desirous of striking their breasts. On being questioned why they do so, they say that they would rather die than be drawn away from the Lord. The spirits of our earth sometimes deride them on this account, and infest them with reproaches for so doing. But they reply, that they know well that they do not kill themselves, and that this is only an appearance flowing from the will of their mind, inclining them rather to die than to be withdrawn from the worship of the Lord.

99. They said that sometimes spirits from our earth come to them, and ask them what God they worship; to whom they reply, that they are insane, and that there cannot be a greater proof of insanity than to ask what God any one worships, when there is but one only God for all in the universe; and that they are still more insane in this, that they do not acknowledge the Lord to be that one only God, and that He rules the entire heaven, and thereby the whole world; for whosoever rules heaven also rules the world, inasmuch as the world is ruled through heaven.

100. They said that on their earth there are also some who call the nocturnal light, which is great, the Lord; but that they are separated from the rest, and are not tolerated by them. That nocturnal light comes from the great belt, which at a distance encompasses that earth, and from the moons which are called Saturn's satellites.

101. They related further that another kind of spirits, who go in companies, frequently come to them, desiring to know how things are with them; and that by various methods they draw out from them whatever they know. They said concerning these spirits, that they were not insane, only in this, that they desire to know so much for no other use than to know. They were afterwards instructed that these spirits were from the planet Mercury, or the earth nearest the sun, and that they are delighted with knowledges alone, and not so much with their uses.

102. The inhabitants and spirits of the planet Saturn have relation in the Greatest Man, to the *middle sense between the spiritual and the natural man*, but to that which recedes from the natural and accedes to the spiritual. Hence it is that those spirits appear to be carried or snatched away into heaven, and presently to be let back again; for whatever appertains to the spiritual sense is in heaven; but whatever appertains to the natural sense is beneath heaven. Inasmuch as the spirits of our earth, in the Greatest Man have relation to natural and corporeal sense, it was given me to know by manifest experience how the spiritual man and the natural fight and strive with each other, when the latter is not in faith and charity. The spirits of the earth Saturn came from afar into view, and there was then opened a living communication between them and such spirits of our earth. The latter, on thus perceiving the former, became as if insane, and began to infest them, by infusing unworthy suggestions concerning faith, and also concerning the Lord; and whilst abusing them with these invectives and insults, they also cast themselves into the midst of them, and from the insanity in which they were, they endeavored to do evil to them. But the spirits of Saturn feared nothing, because they were secure and in tranquillity; whereas the spirits of our earth, when they were in the midst of them, began to be tortured, and to respire with difficulty, and so they cast themselves out, one in this way and another that, till they all disappeared. The spirits who were present perceived from this, what is the quality of the natural man when separate from the spiritual, and when he comes into a spiritual sphere, namely, that he is insane; for the natural man separate from the spiritual is wise only from the world, and not from heaven; and he who is wise only from the world, believes nothing but what he can apprehend with his senses, and the things which he believes he believes from the fallacies of the senses, which, unless they are removed by an influx from the spiritual world, produce falsities. Hence it is that spiritual things to him are not anything, insomuch that he can scarcely bear to hear mention made of anything spiritual; wherefore such become insane when they are kept in a spiritual sphere. It is otherwise during their abode in the world, where they either think naturally concerning spiritual things, or avert their ears that they may not hear them; that is, they hear and do not attend. It was also manifest from this experience, that the natural man cannot introduce himself into the spiritual, that is, ascend; but when man is in faith, and thereby in spiritual life, in this case the spiritual man flows into the natural, and thinks therein. For there is given a spiritual influx, that is, an influx from the spiritual world into the natural, but not the reverse.[35]

103. I was further informed by the spirits of that earth respecting the inhabitants, what their consociations are, with several other particulars. They said that they live distinguished into families, every family apart by itself; each family consisting of a man and his wife with their children; and the children,

---

[35] Influx is spiritual, and not physical or natural, consequently influx is from the spiritual world into the natural, and not from the natural into the spiritual (n. 3219, 5119, 5259, 5427, 5428, 5477, 6322). It appears as if influx is from externals into man's internals, but this is a fallacy (n. 3721).

when they enter the married state, are separated from the parental house, and have no further care about it. Wherefore the spirits from that earth appear two and two. They are little solicitous about food and raiment, they feed on the fruits and legumes their earth produces; and they are clothed slightly, being encompassed with a coarse skin or coat, which repels the cold. Moreover, all on that earth know that they will live after death; and that on this account also they make light of their bodies, only so far as regards that life, which they say is to remain and serve the Lord. It is for this reason likewise that they do not bury the bodies of the dead, but cast them forth, and cover them with branches of forest trees.

104. They were asked concerning that great belt, which appears from our earth to rise above the horizon of that planet, and to vary its situations. They said, that it does not appear to them as a belt, but only as a snowy light in the heaven in various directions.

THE EARTH OR PLANET VENUS, ITS SPIRITS AND INHABITANTS.

105. The planet Venus, in the idea of spirits and angels, appears to the left a little backwards, at some distance from our earth. It is said, in the idea of spirits, because neither the sun of this world, nor any planet, appears to any spirit; but spirits have only an idea that they exist. It is in consequence of such idea that the sun of this world is presented behind as something quite dark, and the planets not movable as in the world, but remaining constantly in their several places; see above (n. 42).

106. In the planet Venus there are two kinds of men, of dispositions opposite to each other; the first mild and humane, the second savage and almost like wild beasts. They who are mild and humane appear on the further side of the earth, they who are savage and like wild beasts, appear on the side looking this way. But it is to be known that they appear thus according to the states of their life, for in the spiritual world the state of life determines every appearance of space and of distance.

107. Some of those who appear on the further side of the planet, and who are mild and humane, came to me and were presented visibly above the head, and I spake with them on various subjects. Amongst other things, they said that during their abode in the world, and more so since they were become spirits, they acknowledged our Lord as their only God. They added that on their earth they had seen Him, and they represented also how they had seen Him. These spirits in the Greatest Man have relation to *the memory of things material, agreeing with the memory of things immaterial,* to which the spirits of Mercury have relation: wherefore the spirits of Mercury have the fullest agreement with these spirits of Venus, and on this account, when they were together, a remarkable change, and a powerful operation in my brain, was perceivable from their influx; see above (n. 43).

108. But I did not speak with those spirits who are on the side that looks this way, and who are savage and almost like wild beasts; but I was informed by the angels concerning their quality, and whence they have so fierce a nature. The cause is this, that they are exceedingly delighted with rapine, and more especially with eating their plunder; the delight thence arising, when they think about eating their plunder, was communicated to me, and was perceived to be most extraordinary. That on our earth there have been inhabitants of a like fierce nature, appears from the histories of various nations; also from the inhabitants of the land of Canaan (1 *Sam.* xxx. 16); and likewise from the Jewish and Israelitish nation, even in the time of David, in that they made yearly excursions, and plundered the Gentiles, and rejoiced in feasting on the spoils. I was informed further, that those inhabitants are for the most part giants, and that the men of our earth reach only to their navels; also that they are stupid, making no inquiries concerning heaven or eternal life, but immersed solely in earthly cares and the care of their cattle.

109. Because they are such, when they come into the other life they are exceedingly infested there by evils and falsities. The hells, which appertain to them, appear near their earth, and have no communication with the hells of the wicked of our earth, because they differ altogether in genius and disposition: hence also their evils and falsities are altogether of a different sort.

110. Such, however, amongst them, as can be saved, are in places of vastation, and are there reduced to the last state of desperation; for there is no other method whereby evils and false persuasions of that kind can be subdued and removed. When they are in a state of desperation, they cry out that they are beasts, that they are abominations, that they are hatreds, and that thus they are damned. Some of them, when they are in this state, exclaim even against heaven; but as this proceeds from desperation, it is forgiven them. The Lord moderates that in their vituperations, they may not pour them forth except to certain limits. These, when they have passed through extreme suffering, are finally saved, inasmuch as corporeal things with them are as if dead. It was further declared concerning these spirits, that during their life on their earth they believed in a certain Supreme Creator without a Mediator; but when they are saved, they are also instructed that the Lord alone is God, the Saviour and Mediator. I have seen some of them, after they have passed through extreme suffering, taken up into heaven; and when they were received there, I have perceived such a tenderness of joy from them as drew tears from my eyes.

THE SPIRITS AND INHABITANTS OF THE MOON.

111. Certain spirits appeared above the head, and thence were heard voices like thunder; for they thundered with their voices like the thunder from the clouds after lightning. I asserted that it was a great multitude of spirits, who had the art of uttering voices attended with so loud a noise. The more simple spirits who were with me laughed at them, at which I greatly wondered. The cause of their laughter was presently discovered to be this, that the spirits who thundered were not many, but few, and were also as small as boys; and that before they had terrified them by such noises, and yet were unable to do them any harm. In order that I might know their quality, some of them let themselves down from on high where they were thundering; and what surprised me, one carried another on his back, and thus two of them approached me. Their faces appeared not unhandsome, but longer than the faces of other spirits. Their stature was like the stature of boys seven years old, but more robust; thus they were dwarfs. It was told me by the angels, that they were from the Moon. He who was carried on the other's back, on coming to me, applied himself to my left side under the elbow, and thence spake with me, saying that whenever they utter their voices they thus thunder; and that thereby they terrify the spirits who wish to do them evil; and put some to flight, and that thus they go with security whithersoever they will. That I might know certainly that they made this sound, he retired from me to some others, but not entirely out of sight, and thundered in like manner. They showed, moreover, that the voice being uttered from the abdomen, like an eructation, made this thundering sound. It was perceived that this was owing to the fact, that the inhabitants of the Moon do not speak from the lungs like the inhabitants of other earths, but from the abdomen, and thus from some air there collected, by reason that the Moon is not encompassed with an atmosphere like that of other earths. I was instructed that the spirits of the Moon, in the Greatest Man, have relation to the ensiform or zyphoid cartilage, to which the ribs in front are joined, and from which descends the *facia alba*, which is the fulcrum of the abdominal muscles.

112. That there are also inhabitants on the Moon, spirits and angels know, and in like manner that there are inhabitants on the moons or satellites which revolve about the earths Jupiter and Saturn. They who have not seen and spoken with spirits therefrom, still do not doubt but that there are also men upon them, because they are equally earths; and where there is an earth, there are men; for man is the end for which every earth was created, and nothing was made by the Great Creator without an end. That the human race is the end of creation, that from it there may be a heaven, may appear to every one who thinks from a somewhat enlightened reason.

THE REASONS WHY THE LORD WAS WILLING TO BE BORN ON OUR EARTH, AND NOT ON ANOTHER.

113. There are many reasons, concerning which I had information from heaven, why it pleased the Lord to be born and to assume the human on our earth, and not on another. The PRINCIPAL REASON *was because of the Word, in that it might be written on our earth; and when written be afterwards published throughout the whole earth; and when once published be preserved to all posterity; and that thus it might be made manifest, even to all in the other life, that God became Man.*

114. *That the principal reason was because of the Word*, is because the Word is the Divine truth itself, which teaches man that there is a God, that there is a heaven and a hell, and that there is a life after death; and teaches moreover how man ought to live and believe, in order to come into heaven, and thus into eternal happiness. All these things would have been altogether unknown without a revelation, thus on this earth without the Word; and yet man is so created that, as to his interiors, he cannot die.[36]

115. *That the Word might be written on our earth*, is because the art of writing has existed here from the most ancient time, first on the bark of trees, next on parchment, afterwards on paper, and lastly published by types. This was provided by the Lord for the sake of the Word.

116. *That the Word might afterwards be published throughout the whole earth*, is because there is commerce here between all nations, both by land and water, to all parts of the globe; hence that the Word once written might be conveyed from one nation to another, and be taught everywhere.

---

[36] From natural light alone nothing is known concerning the Lord, concerning heaven and hell, concerning the life of man after death, and concerning Divine truths, by which man has spiritual and eternal life (n. 8944, 10,318–10,320). This may appear from this, that many, and among them the learned, do not believe those things, although they are born where the Word is, and where there is instruction by the Word concerning those things (n. 10,319). Therefore it was necessary there should be a revelation from heaven, because man was born for heaven (n. 1775).

117. *That the Word once written might be preserved to all posterity,* consequently for thousands and thousands of years, and that it has been so preserved is well known.

118. *That thus it might be made manifest that God became Man;* for this is the first and most essential, for the sake of which the Word was revealed. For no one can believe in God, and love God, whom he cannot comprehend under some appearance; wherefore they who acknowledge what is invisible and thus incomprehensible, in thought sink into nature, and thus believe in no God. Hence it pleased the Lord to be born on this earth, and to make this manifest by the Word, that it might not only be known on this globe, but also *might be made manifest thereby to spirits and angels even from other earths, and likewise to the Gentiles from our own earth.*[37]

119. It is to be known that the Word on our earth, given through heaven from the Lord, is the union of heaven and the world; for which end there is a correspondence of all things contained in the letter of the Word with the Divine things in heaven; and the Word in its supreme and inmost sense treats of the Lord, of His kingdom in the heavens and the earths, and of love and faith from Him and in Him, consequently of life from Him and in Him. Such things are presented to the angels in heaven, when the Word of our earth is read and preached.[38]

120. In every other earth Divine truth is manifested by word of mouth through spirits and angels, as was said above in speaking of the inhabitants of the earths of this solar system. But this manifestation is confined within families; for the human race in most earths live distinct according to families; wherefore the Divine truth thus revealed through spirits and angels is not conveyed far beyond the limits of families, and unless a new revelation constantly succeeds, truth

---

[37] The Gentiles in the other life are instructed by angels, and they who have lived well according to their religious principles, receive the truths of faith, and acknowledge the Lord (n. 2049, 2595, 2598, 2600, 2601, 2603, 2661, 2863, 3263).

[38] The Word is understood by the angels in the heavens differently from what it is understood by men on the earths, and that the internal or spiritual sense is for the angels but the external or natural sense for men (n. 1769–1772, 1887, 2143, 2333, 2396, 2540, 2541, 2545, 2551). The Word is conjunctive of heaven and earth (n. 2310, 2495, 9212, 9216, 9357, 10,357). The Word therefore is written by mere correspondences (n. 1404, 1408, 1409, 1540, 1619, 1659, 1709, 1783, 8615, 10,687). In the inmost sense of the Word the Lord alone and His Kingdom are treated of (n. 1873, 2249, 2523, 7014, 9357).

is either perverted or perishes. It is otherwise on our earth, where the Divine truth, which is the Word, remains for ever in its integrity.

121. It is to be known that the Lord acknowledges and receives all, of whatsoever earth they be, who acknowledge and worship God under the human form, inasmuch as God under the human form is the Lord. And because the Lord appears to the inhabitants in the earths in an angelic form, which is the human form, therefore when the spirits and angels from those earths are informed by the spirits and angels of our earth that God is actually Man, they receive that Word, acknowledge it, and rejoice that it is so.

122. To the reasons above adduced, may be added, that the inhabitants and spirits of our earth, in the Greatest Man, have relation to the natural and external sense, which sense is the ultimate wherein the interiors of life close, and rest as on their common basis. The case is similar in regard to the Divine truth in the letter, which is called the Word, and which for this reason also was given on this earth, and not on any other:[39] and because the Lord is the Word, and is the First and the Last thereof, therefore, that all things might exist according to order, He was willing to be born on this earth, and be made the Word, according to what is written in *John:*—

In the beginning was the Word, and the Word was with God, and God was the Word. This was in the beginning with God. All things were made by Him, and without Him was not anything made which was made. *And the Word became flesh, and dwelt among us, and we beheld His glory, the glory as of the Only-begotten of the Father.* No one has seen God at any time; the Only-begotten Son, who is in the bosom of the Father, He hath brought Him forth to view (i. 1–14, 18).

The Word is the Lord as to the Divine truth, thus the Divine truth from the Lord.[40] But this is an arcanum which falls within the understanding of only a few.

---

[39] The Word in the sense of the letter is natural (n. 8783). By reason that what is natural is the ultimate, wherein spiritual and celestial things close, and on which they subsist as on their foundation, and that otherwise the internal or spiritual sense of the Word without the external or natural sense, would be as a house without a foundation (n. 9430, 9433, 9824, 10,044, 10,436).

[40] The Word is the Lord as to the Divine truth, thus the Divine truth from the Lord (n. 2859, 4692, 5075, 9987). By the Divine truth all things were created and made (n. 2803, 2884, 5272, 7835).

THE EARTHS IN THE STARRY HEAVEN.

123. They who are in heaven can speak and converse with angels and spirits who are not only from the earths in this solar system, but also with those who are from other earths in the universe out of this system; and not only with the spirits and angels there, but also with the inhabitants themselves, but only with those whose interiors are open, so that they can hear such as speak from heaven. The same is the case with man during his abode in the world, to whom it has been granted by the Lord to speak with spirits and angels. For man is a spirit as to his interiors, the body which he carries about in the world only serving him for performing functions in this natural or terrestrial sphere, which is the ultimate. But it is granted to no one to speak as a spirit with angels and spirits, unless he be such that he can consociate with angels as to faith and love; nor can he so consociate, unless he have faith and love to the Lord; for man is joined to the Lord by faith and love to Him, that is, by truths of doctrine and goods of life from Him; and when he is conjoined to the Lord, he is secure from the assaults of evil spirits from hell. With others the interiors cannot be so far opened, since they are not in the Lord. This is the reason why there are few at this day to whom it is granted to speak and converse with angels; a manifest proof whereof is, that the existence of spirits and angels is scarcely believed at this day, much less that they are with every man, and that by them man has connection with heaven, and through heaven with the Lord. Still less is it believed that man, when he dies as to the body, lives a spirit, even in a human form as before.

124. Because at this day with many in the church there is no belief in the life after death, and scarce any belief in heaven, nor in the Lord as the God of heaven and earth; therefore the interiors which are of my spirit have been opened by the Lord, so that while still in the body, I can at the same time be with angels in heaven, and not only speak with them, but also see the stupendous things there, and describe them; so that it may not chance to be said hereafter, "Who has come to us from heaven and told us that there is such a place, and what there is there?" But I know that they who in heart have before denied heaven and hell and the life after death, will still confirm themselves against them, and deny them; for it is easier to make a crow white, than to make those believe who have once rejected faith in the heart. The reason is, that they always think of such things from the negative, and not from the affirmative. Nevertheless, let what has been said hitherto, and what is still further to be said concerning angels and spirits, be for the few who are in faith. And that the rest also may be led along to something of acknowledgment, it has been conceded to relate such things as delight and attract the man who is desirous of knowing; and now about the earths in the starry heaven.

125. He who does not know the arcana of heaven, cannot believe that a man can see earths so distant, and relate anything about them from the experiences of the senses. But let him know that the spaces and distances, and thence the progressions in the natural world, are, in their origin and first cause, changes of the state of the interiors, and with angels and spirits appear according to these changes;[41] and that thus they can by these changes be apparently transferred from one place to another, and from one earth to another, even to the earths which are at the end of the universe. So also may a man be transferred as to his spirit, his body still remaining in its place. Thus it has been done with me, since by the Divine mercy of the Lord it has been given me to have intercourse with spirits as a spirit, and at the same time with men as a man. That a man can be so transferred as to his spirit, the sensual man cannot understand, since he is in space and time, and measures his movements according to them.

126. That there are many worlds, may be evident to every one, from there being so many constellations visible in the universe; and it is known in the learned world that every fixed star is like a sun in its place; for it remains fixed like the sun of our earth in its place; and that the distance makes it appear

---

[41] Movements, progressions, and changes of place in the other life are changes of state of the interiors of the life, and still they appear to spirits and angels as real changes of place (n. 1273-1277, 1377, 3356, 5605, 10,734).

small in form like a star. Consequently that like the sun of our world, it has round it planets, which are earths; and the reason that these do not appear to our eyes, is their being at such an immense distance, and having only the light of their star, which cannot be reflected again as far as here. For what other purpose is there so great a heaven with so many stars? For the end of the creation of the universe is man, that from man there may be an angelic heaven. What would the human race, and thence an angelic heaven, from one earth, be for the Infinite Creator, for Whom a thousand earths, nay, tens of thousands, would not be enough? By calculation it appears that if there were a million earths in the universe, and men on every earth to the number of three hundred millions, and two hundred generations in six thousand years, and if to each man or spirit were given the space of three cubic ells, the whole number of so many men or spirits, collected into one body, would still not fill the space of the thousandth part of this earth, thus perhaps not more than the space of a single satellite around the planet Jupiter or Saturn; which would be a space scarce discernible in the universe, for a satellite is hardly visible to the naked eye. What is this to the Creator of the universe? to Whom there would not be enough if the whole universe should be filled, for He is Infinite. On these matters I have spoken with angels, who said that they have a similar idea of the fewness of the human race in comparison with the infinity of the Creator, although they do not think from spaces, but from states; and that according to their idea, earths to the number of as many myriads as could be conceived by thought, would still be as nothing at all to the Lord. But in what now follows, the earths in the starry heavens shall be described from experience itself; from which it will also be evident how I was transferred thither as to my spirit, my body remaining in its place.

THE FIRST EARTH IN THE STARRY HEAVEN, ITS SPIRITS AND INHABITANTS; FROM THINGS HEARD AND SEEN.

127. I was led by the Lord by means of angels to a certain earth in the starry heaven, where it was given me to look into the earth itself, yet not to speak with the inhabitants there, but with the spirits who were from it. All the inhabitants or men of every earth, after the life in the world is finished, become spirits, and remain near their own earth. From these spirits, however, information is given about their earth, and about the state of the inhabitants there; for men who leave the body bring with them all their former life, and all their memory.[42] To be led to earths in the universe is not to be led and transferred thither as to the body, but as to the spirit; and the spirit is led by variations of the state of the interior life, which appear to it as progressions through space.[41] Approaches also are made according to agreements or similarities of states of life; for agreement or similarity of life conjoins, and disagreement and dissimilarity disjoin. From this may be evident how transference is made as to the spirit, and approach to what is distant, the man still remaining in his place. But to lead the spirit beyond its own world by variations of the state of its interiors, and to make the variations advance successively even to a state agreeing with or similar to that of those to whom it is led, is in the power of the Lord alone. For there must be continual direction and foresight from first to last, in going and returning; especially with a man who is still in the world of nature as to the body, and thereby in space. That this has been done, those who are in the bodily senses and think from them, cannot be induced to believe, for the reason that what is of bodily sense cannot comprehend progressions without space. But still they who think from the sense of their spirit, somewhat removed or withdrawn from the sense of the body, thus interiorly in themselves, may be led to believe and to comprehend; since in the idea of the in-

---

[42] Man after death retains the memory of all his affairs in the world (n. 2476–2486).
[41] See foot-note, page 470.

terior thought there is not space nor time, but instead thereof those things from which spaces and times exist. It is for such persons that what follows concerning the earths in the starry heaven is related, and not for others, unless they will suffer themselves to be instructed.

128. In a state of wakefulness I was led as to the spirit by the Lord, by means of angels, to a certain earth in the universe, accompanied by some spirits from this world. Our progress was made toward the right, and lasted two hours. Near the limit of our solar system, there appeared at first a shining bright cloud, but dense, and beyond it a fiery smoke ascending out of a great chasm. It was a vast gulf separating our solar world on that side from some worlds of the starry heavens. That fiery smoke appeared at a considerable distance. I was borne across the middle of it; and then there appeared beneath in that chasm or gulf very many men, who were spirits; for spirits all appear in the human form, and actually are men. I also heard them speaking with one another; but whence they were and their quality was not given me to know. Yet one of them said to me that they were guards, lest spirits should pass from this world into another in the universe without leave having been given. That it was so, was also confirmed; for some spirits who were in our company, but had not received the ability to pass over, when they came to that great interspace, began to cry out vehemently that they were perishing; for they were like those who are struggling in agony with death, and therefore they stopped on that side of the gulf, nor could they be taken any further, as the fiery smoke that exhaled from the gulf enveloped them and thus tortured them.

129. Afterwards I was carried along through that great chasm, and at length I arrived at a place where I stopped; and there then appeared to me spirits overhead with whom it was given me to speak. From their speech, and from their genius of apprehending and explaining things, I clearly perceived that they were from another earth; for they were quite different from the spirits of our solar system. They also perceived from my speech that I was from afar.

130. After we had spoken for some time on various matters, I asked what God they worshiped. They said they worshiped an angel, who appears to them as a Divine Man, shining with light; and that He instructs them and gives them to perceive what they ought to do. They said further that they know that the Most High God is in the sun of the angelic heaven; and that He appears to their angel, and not to themselves; and that He is too great for them to dare to adore Him. The angel whom they worshiped was an angelic society, to which it was given by the Lord to preside over them, and to teach the way of what is just and right. They therefore have light from a certain flame, which appears like a small torch, quite fiery and yellow. The reason is because they do not adore the Lord, and thus they do not have light from the sun of the angelic heaven, but from an angelic society. For an angelic society, when it is given by the Lord, can present such light to the spirits who are in a lower region. That angelic society was also seen by me, high above them; and there was also seen there the flamy appearance from which their light came.

131. As to the rest, they were modest, and somewhat simple, but yet they thought very well. From the light with them it might be concluded what their intellectual faculty is; for the understanding is according to the reception of the light which is in the heavens; since the Divine truth proceeding from the Lord as a sun is what shines there, and enables the angels not only to see, but also to understand.[43]

132. I was instructed that the inhabitants and spirits of that earth have reference in the Greatest Man to something in the spleen, of which I was confirmed by an influx into the spleen when they were speaking with me.

133. They were asked about the sun of their system, which illumines their earth. They said that the sun there appears flamy; and when I represented the size of the sun of our earth, they said that theirs is smaller; for their sun to our eyes is a star, and I was told by angels that it is among the smaller

---

[43] The light in the heavens is great (n. 1117, 1521, 1522, 1533, 1619–1632, 4527, 5400, 8644). All the light in the heavens is from the Lord as a sun there (n. 1053, 1521, 3195, 3341, 3636, 4415, 9548, 9684, 10,809). Divine truth proceeding from the Lord appears in the heavens as light (n. 3195, 3222, 5400, 8644, 9399, 9548, 9684). That light illumines both the sight and the understanding of angels and spirits (n. 2776, 3138). The light of heaven also illumines the understanding of man (n. 1524, 3138, 3167, 4408, 6608, 8707, 9128, 9399, 10,569).

stars. They also said that the starry heaven is likewise seen from their earth, and that a star larger than the rest appears to them toward the west. I was told from heaven that this is our sun.

134. Presently my sight was opened, so that I could look somewhat into that earth itself; and there appeared many meadows and woods with leafy trees, and also woolly sheep. I afterward saw some of the inhabitants, who were of the lower class, clothed in a dress much like that of peasants in Europe. There was also seen a man with his woman. She appeared of handsome figure and graceful carriage, and the man likewise. But, what I wondered at, he had a pompous gait, with a rather haughty step; while the woman, on the contrary, walked with a humble step. It was said by the angels that such is the custom on that earth, and that the men who are such are loved, because nevertheless they are good. I was further told that it is not permitted them to have many wives, because it is contrary to their laws. The woman whom I saw had before her breast a broad garment, with which she could screen herself, while it was so made that she could insert her arms and wrap it about herself, and so walk away. The lower part of it could be drawn up, and when drawn up and applied to the body, it appeared like an upper garment covering the chest, such as is worn by the women of our earth. But the same garment served also for the man, who was seen to take it from the woman and apply it to his back, loosening the lower part, which then flowed down to his feet, like a toga, and thus clothed he walked about. What I saw on that earth, was not seen with the eyes of my body, but with the eyes of my spirit; and the spirit can see the things that are on an earth, when it is granted by the Lord.

135. Since I know that it will be doubted whether it is in any way possible for a man to see with the eyes of his spirit anything on an earth so distant, it is allowed me to say how this thing is. Distances in the other life are not like distances on earth. In the other life distances are altogether according to the states of the interiors of any one. Those who are in a like state, are together in one society and in one place. Everything is present there according to similarity of state and everything is distant according to dissimilarity of state. Hence it was that I was near that earth when I was led by the Lord into a state similar to that of its spirits and inhabitants, and that being then present I spoke with them. From this it is plain that the earths in the spiritual world are not distant in the same way as in the natural world; but only apparently, according to the states of life of the inhabitants and spirits there. The state of life is the state of affections as to love and faith. In regard to a spirit being able to see the things which are on an earth, or what is the same, a man as to his spirit, it is allowed me to explain how this also is. Neither spirits nor angels can, by their own sight, see anything that is in the world; for to them the light of the world, or of the sun, is as dense thick darkness, just as man by his bodily sight cannot see anything that is in the other life; for to him the light of heaven is as dense thick darkness. But still, spirits and angels, when it is the Lord's good pleasure, can see the things that are in the world through the eyes of man. But this the Lord does not grant to any others than those whom He gives to speak with spirits and angels, and to be together with them. Through my eyes it has been given them to see the things which are in the world, and as plainly as I did; and also to hear men speaking with me. It has sometimes happened, that some through me have seen their friends whom they had in the life of the body, just at present as before, and they were astounded. They have also seen their husbands, or wives, and their children, and wished to tell them that they were present and saw them, and also wanted me to tell them about their state in the other life. But I was prohibited from telling them and revealing to them that they were thus seen, even for the reason that they would have called me insane, or would have thought that it was delirium of mind. For it was known to me, that although they acknowledged with the lips, still they did not believe in the heart, that there were spirits, and that the dead had risen and were among spirits, and that these could see and hear through a man. When my interior sight was first opened, and those who were in the other life saw through my eyes the world and the things that were in it, they were so astonished that they called this the miracle of miracles, and were affected with a new joy, that thus there was granted a communication of earth with heaven, and of heaven with earth. This joy lasted for months; but afterwards it became familiar. Now they have ceased to wonder. I have been instructed that the spirits and angels with other men, see nothing at all of what is in the world, but only perceive the thoughts and affections of those with whom they are. From this it may be evident that man was so created, that while living in the world among men, he might at the same time also live in heaven among angels, and the converse; thus that heaven and the world with a man might be together, and act as one; and that men might know what is in heaven, and angels what is in the world; and when men die, they might thus pass out of the Lord's kingdom on earth into the Lord's kingdom in heaven, not as into a different kingdom, but as into the same in which they also were when they lived in the body. But because man has become so corporeal, he has closed heaven to himself.

136. Lastly I spoke with the spirits who were from that earth about various things on our earth, especially about there being sciences here which are not elsewhere, as astronomy, geometry, mechanics, physics, chemistry, medicine, optics, philosophy; and also arts, which are not known elsewhere, as those of ship-building, of casting metals, of writing upon paper, and of printing what is written by types, and so of communicating it to others on the earth, and also of preserving it for posterity for thousands of years; as I told them had been done with the Word which is from the Lord; and therefore there is a permanent Revelation on our earth.

137. Lastly was shown me the hell of those who are from that earth. Those who were seen from it terrified one most exceedingly, and I dare not describe their monstrous faces. There were also seen there enchantresses, who practise direful arts. These appeared clothed in green, and they struck me with horror.

A SECOND EARTH IN THE STARRY HEAVEN, ITS SPIRITS AND INHABITANTS.

138. I was afterwards led by the Lord to an earth in the universe which was further distant from our earth than the foregoing of which we have been just speaking. That it was further distant was plain from this, that I was two days in being led thither as to my spirit. This earth was to the left, whereas the former was to the right. Inasmuch as remoteness in the spiritual world does not arise from distance of place, but from difference of state, as was said above, therefore from the slowness of my progression thither, which lasted two days, I might conclude that the state of the interiors with them, which is the state of the affections and thence of the thoughts, differed proportionately from the state of the interiors with spirits from our earth. Being conveyed thither as to the spirit by changes of the state of the interiors, I was enabled to observe the successive changes themselves before I arrived thither. This was done whilst I was awake.

139. When I arrived thither, the earth was not seen, but only the spirits who were from that earth; for, as also was said above, the spirits of every earth appear about their own earth, by reason that they are of a genius similar to that of the inhabitants, for they are from them, and in order that they may serve them. Those spirits were seen at a considerable height above my head whence they observed me as I approached. It is to be known that they who stand on high in the other life can look at those who are beneath them, and the higher they are the greater is the extent of their vision; and they can not only look at them, but likewise can speak with them. From their state of elevation they observed that I was not from their earth, but from another afar off; wherefore they addressed me inquiring concerning various things, to which it was given me to reply; and among other things I related to them from what earth I was, and what kind of earth it was. Afterwards I spake to them concerning the other earths in our solar system; and at the same time also concerning the spirits of the earth or planet Mercury, that they wander about to many earths for the purpose of procuring for themselves knowledges of various matters. On hearing this, they said that they had likewise seen those spirits with them.

140. It was told me by the angels from our earth, that the inhabitants and spirits of that earth have reference in the Greatest Man to *keenness of vision,* and for this reason they appear on high, and that they are also exceedingly clear-sighted. Because they had reference to that, and because they saw very clearly what was beneath them, in talking with them I also compared them to eagles, which fly on high, and have a clear and wide vision around them. But at this they were indignant, supposing that I believed them to be like eagles as to rapine, and thus that they were evil. But I replied that I did not liken them to eagles as to rapine, but as to keenness of sight.

141. They were asked about the God whom they worshiped; and they answered that they worshiped God visible and invisible, God visible under the Human form, and God invisible not under any form; and it was found from their speech, and also from the ideas of their thought as communicated to me, that the visible God was our Lord Himself, and they also called Him Lord. To this it was given to reply, that on our earth also God is worshiped as invisible and as visible; and that God invisible is called the Father, and visible the Lord, but that the two are one, as He Himself taught, saying that no man had ever seen the form of the Father, but that the Father and He are one; and that He who sees Him sees the Father; and that the Father is in Him, and He in the Father; consequently that the two are the Divine in one Person. That these are the words of the Lord Himself, may be seen in *John* (v. 37; x. 30; xiv. 7, 9–11).

142. After a while I saw other spirits from the same earth, who appeared in a place below the former, with whom also I spoke. But they were idolaters, for they worshiped an idol of stone, resembling a man, but not beautiful. It is to be known that all who come into the other life have at first a worship like their worship in the world, but that they are gradually withdrawn from it. The reason is, that all worship remains implanted in man's interior life, from which it cannot be removed and eradicated but by degrees. On seeing this, it was

given me to tell them that they ought not to worship what is
dead, but what is living; to which they answered that they know
that God lives, and that a stone does not; but that they think
of the living God when they look upon a stone in the form of
a man; and that otherwise the ideas of their thought cannot
be fixed and determined to the invisible God. Then it was
given me to tell them that the ideas of thought can be fixed
and determined to the invisible God when they are fixed and
determined to the Lord, Who is God visible in thought under
the Human form; and thus that man can be conjoined to the
invisible God in thought and affection, consequently in faith
and love, when he is conjoined to the Lord, but in no other
way.

143. The spirits who were seen on high were asked whether
on their earth they live under the rule of princes and kings;
to which they answered that they do not know what such rule
is; and that they live under themselves, distinguished into
nations, families, and houses. They were asked whether they
are secure in this way. They said that they are, since one
family does not envy another, nor wish to take anything away
from it. They were indignant at being asked such questions,
which seemed to imply that there was hostility among them,
or need of protection against robbers. What more is needed,
they said, than to have food and clothing, and so to dwell contented and quiet under themselves.

144. Being questioned further about their earth, they said
that they have meadows, flower gardens, woods full of fruit
trees, and also lakes in which are fish; and that they have
birds of a blue color with golden wings, and animals of various
sizes. Among the smaller they mentioned one kind which had
the back humped, like the camels on our earth. They do not,
however, eat the flesh of these animals, but only the flesh of
fishes, and also the fruits of trees and leguminous plants of the
earth. They said further that they do not dwell in built houses,
but in groves, in which they make a shelter for themselves
among the foliage against rain and the heat of the sun.

145. They were asked about their sun, which is seen as a
star from our earth, and they said that it appears fiery; not
larger to the sight than a man's head. I was told by angels

that the star which is their sun is among the smaller stars, not far distant from the celestial equator.

146. Spirits were seen, in a similar appearance to what they had when they were men on their earth. They had a face not unlike that of the men of our earth, except that the eyes and nose were smaller. As this seemed to me somewhat of a deformity, they said that to them small eyes and a small nose are marks of beauty. A woman was seen, dressed in a gown on which were roses of various colors. I inquired of what materials they make their garments on that earth. They answered that from plants they gather such things as they can spin into threads, and that they then lay the threads side by side in double and triple layers, and moisten them with a glutinous liquid, and so give it consistency, coloring it afterward with juices from herbs. I was likewise shown how they prepare the threads: they sit leaning back on a seat, and twist the thread with the toes; and when it is twisted, they draw it to them, and finish it with the hands.

147. They also said that on that earth a husband has only one wife, and not more, and that they have from ten to fifteen children. They added that harlots are also found there; but that after the life of the body, when they become spirits, they are sorceresses, and are cast into hell.

A THIRD EARTH IN THE STARRY HEAVEN, ITS SPIRITS AND INHABITANTS.

148. Some spirits appeared at a distance who were not willing to come near. The reason was that they could not be with the spirits of our earth who were then around me. From this I perceived that they were from another earth, and afterward I was told that they were from a certain earth in the universe; but where that earth is, I was not informed. These spirits were altogether unwilling to think of their body, and indeed of anything corporeal and material, differently from the spirits from our earth. This was why they were not willing to come near. But still after the removal of some of the spirits of our earth, they came nearer and spoke with me. But then anxiety was felt, arising from the collision of spheres; for spiritual spheres encompass all spirits and societies of spirits; and because they flow forth from the life of the affections and of the thoughts therefrom, therefore where there are opposing affections there arises collision, and thence anxiety. The spirits of our earth said that they did not dare to approach them, since when they were approaching, they not only were seized with anxiety, but also appeared to themselves as if bound hand and foot with serpents, from which they could not be loosed until they withdrew. This appearance had its origin from correspondence; for the spirits of our earth have reference in the Greatest Man to the external sense, thus to the corporeal sensual, and this sensual is represented in the other life by serpents.[44]

149. Because the nature of the spirits of that earth is such, they appear before the eyes of other spirits, not like others, in a manifest human form, but like clouds, and for the most part like a dark cloud, in which is mingled something of a bright human appearance. But they said that they are white within, and that when they become angels, the dark color is turned into a beautiful blue, as was also shown to me. I asked whether they had such an idea of their body, when they lived as men in the world. They said that the men of their earth make no account of their bodies, but only of the spirit in the body, because they know that this is to live to eternity, but the body to perish. They also said that many on their earth believe that the spirit of the body has been from eternity, and was infused into the body at conception. But they added that they now know it is not so, and that they repent having been in such a false opinion.

150. When I asked whether they wished to see anything on our earth, and said that this could be done through my eyes (see above n. 135), they answered at first that they could not, and then that they did not wish it; since they would see only

---

[44] Man's external sensual is represented in the spiritual world by serpents, because it is in the lowest things, and in comparison with the interiors with man, lies on the ground and as it were creeps; and that they were thence called serpents, who reasoned from that sensual (n. 195-197, 6398, 6949).

earthly and material things, from which they remove their thoughts as far as possible. But still there were represented before them magnificent palaces, like those of kings and princes on our earth, for such things can be represented before spirits, and when represented, they appear altogether as if they were there. But the spirits from that earth set no value upon them, calling them marble images; and then they told me that they had more magnificent ones, which are their sanctuaries, not of stone, but of wood. When it was said to them that these were still earthly, they answered that they were not, but heavenly; because when they look upon them, they have not an earthly, but a heavenly idea, believing that they will also see similar ones in heaven after death.

151. They then represented their sanctuaries before the spirits of our earth, who said that they had seen nothing more magnificent; and as I also saw them, I can therefore describe them. They are constructed of trees, not cut down, but growing in their native soil. They said that on their earth there were trees of wonderful growth and height. These from their beginnings they arrange in order, so that they serve for porticos and walks, and by cutting and pruning the branches when they are tender, they fit and prepare them so that while they are growing they may intertwine and unite to make the base and floor of the sanctuary, and rise on the sides for the walls, and bend above into arches for the roof. By these means they construct the sanctuary with admirable art, elevated high above the earth, and they also prepare an ascent into it by successive branches of the trees extending out and firmly connected. Moreover they adorn the sanctuary without and within in various ways, by bending the leafy bows into various forms. Thus they build entire groves. But what these sanctuaries are within, I was not permitted to see. It was only told me that the light of their sun is let into them through apertures between the branches, and is here and there transmitted through crystals, by which the light falling on the walls is variegated into colors like the rainbow, especially the colors blue and orange, which they love more than the rest. Such is their architecture, which they prefer to the most magnificent palaces of our earth.

152. They said, further, that the inhabitants do not live in high places, but on the earth in low cottages, for the reason that high places are for the Lord, who is in heaven, and low places for men, who are on earth. Their cottages were also shown to me. They were oblong, having within along the walls a continuous couch, on which they lie one after another. On the side opposite the door is a semicircular recess, before which is a table, and behind this a fireplace, by which the whole room is lighted. In the fireplace there is not a burning fire, but luminous wood which gives out as much light as the flame of a wood fire. They said that those pieces of wood appear in the evening like a fire of burning coals.

153. They said that they do not live in societies, but each house is by itself; and that they are societies when they meet for worship, and that then those who teach walk below[a] the sanctuary, and the rest in the porticos at the sides; and that in those meetings they have interior joys, from the sight of the sanctuary, and from the worship therein.

154. Respecting Divine worship they said that they acknowledge God under the Human form, thus our Lord; for whoever acknowledge the God of the universe under the Human form, are accepted by our Lord and led by Him. The rest cannot be led, because they think without a form. They added that the inhabitants of their earth are instructed in the things of heaven by a kind of immediate intercourse with angels and spirits, into which they can be led by the Lord more easily than others, because they reject what is corporeal from their thought and affection. I asked what becomes of those among them who are evil. They said that on their earth it is not permitted to be wicked; but that if any one thinks and does evil, he is reproved by a certain spirit, who threatens death to him if he persists in so doing; and that when he persists, he dies in a swoon; and that in this way the men of that earth are preserved from the contamination of the evil. One such spirit was also sent to me, and spoke with me as he did with his own people. Moreover he brought something of pain to the region of my abdomen, saying that thus he does to those who think and do evil, and threatens death to them, if they persist. They said that those who profane holy things are severely punished; and that before the punishing spirit comes there appear to them in vision the jaws of a lion, wide open, of a livid color, which seems as if it would swallow their head, and tear it from the body, whereby they are seized with horror. They call the punishing spirit the devil.

155. As they desired to know how it is with regard to revelation on our earth, I said that it is effected by writing and by preaching from the Word, and not by immediate intercourse with spirits and angels; and that what is written can be printed and published, and be read and comprehended by entire communities, and thus the life may be amended. They wondered greatly that such an art, entirely unknown elsewhere, should exist here. But they comprehended that on this earth, where corporeal and earthly things are so much loved, Divine things from heaven cannot flow in and be received in any other way; and that it would be dangerous for them to speak with angels.

156. The spirits of that earth appear above in the plane of the head, toward the right. All spirits are distinguished by their situation with respect to the human body; and this for the reason that the whole heaven corresponds to all things of man.[6] These spirits keep themselves in that plane and at that distance because their correspondence is not with the externals in man, but with the interiors. Their action is into the left knee, above and a little below, with a certain very sensible vibration; which is a sign that they correspond to *the conjunction of natural and heavenly things.*

A FOURTH EARTH IN THE STARRY HEAVEN, ITS SPIRITS AND INHABITANTS.

157. I was conducted to still another earth in the universe beyond our solar system, which was effected by changes of the state of my mind, and thus as to the spirit. For, as has been sometimes said before, the spirit is conducted from place to place in no other way than by changes of the state of its interiors, which changes appear to it altogether like movements

---

[6] See foot-note, page 403.

from place to place, or like journeyings. These changes lasted continuously for about ten hours, before from the state of my life I arrived at the state of their life; thus before I was brought thither as to my spirit. I was borne toward the east to the left, and I seemed to be sensibly elevated above the plane of the horizon. It was also given me to observe very clearly the progression and advance from the place where I had been before, until at length those from whom I departed were no longer in sight. Meanwhile I spoke on various subjects with the spirits who went with me. A certain spirit was also with us, who when he lived in the world had been a primate and a preacher, and likewise a very pathetic writer. From my idea of him the accompanying spirits supposed that in heart he must be eminently a Christian. For in the world an idea is received and a judgment formed from one's preaching and writings, and not from his life, unless this is conspicuous; and if there appears anything inconsistent in his life, still it is excused; for the idea, or the thought and perception concerning any one, draws everything to its own side.

158. After I had observed that as to my spirit I was in the starry heaven far beyond the world of our sun, for this might be observed from the changes of state and from the apparent continual progression thence, which lasted nearly ten hours, I at length heard spirits speaking near some earth, which was afterward also seen by me. When I came near to them, after some conversation, they said that visitors sometimes come to them from elsewhere, who speak with them about God and confuse the ideas of their thought. They also showed the way by which they come, from which it was perceived that they were of the spirits from our earth. Being then asked wherein their thoughts were confused, they answered that it was by those spirits saying that one must believe in the Divine as distinguished into three Persons, which they still call one God. And when they examine the idea of their thoughts, it is presented as a trine not continuous, but discrete; and with some, as three persons speaking together one to another; and with some, as two seated together, and a third hearkening to them, and then going from them; and though they call each Person God, and have a different idea concerning each, they still call them one

God. They complained exceedingly that they confuse them by thinking three and saying one, when yet one ought to think as he speaks, and speak as he thinks. The spirit who in the world had been a primate and a preacher, and was with me, was then examined as to what idea he had concerning one God and three Persons. He represented three Gods, but these as one by continuity, but he presented this trinal one as invisible because Divine; and when he presented this, it was perceived that he then thought only of the Father, and not of the Lord; and that his idea of the invisible God was no other than as of nature in its firsts; from which it resulted that to him the inmost of nature was his Divine, and thus that from this he could be easily led to acknowledge nature as God. It is to be known that in the other life the idea of any one upon any subject is presented to the life; and that by this means every one is explored as to what thought and perception he has concerning matters of faith; and that the idea of the thought concerning God is the chief of them all; for by that, if it is genuine, conjunction is effected with the Divine, and thence with heaven. Being then asked what idea they had of God, these spirits answered that they did not conceive of God as invisible, but as visible under the Human form; and that they know this not only from interior perception, but also from His appearing to them as a Man; adding that if according to the idea of some visitors they should conceive of God as invisible, thus without form and quality, they could not think at all of God, since what is thus invisible does not fall into any idea of thought. On hearing this, it was given me to say to them that they do well to think of God under the Human form; and that many from our earth think in like manner, especially when they think of the Lord; and that the ancients thought in no other way. I then told them about Abraham, Lot, Gideon, and Manoah and his wife, and what is related of them in our Word, namely, that they saw God under the Human form and acknowledged Him thus seen as the Creator of the universe, and called Him Jehovah, and this also from interior perception; but that at this day that interior perception has perished in the Christian world, and only remains with the simple who are in faith.

159. Before this was said, they believed that our company also was of those who wished to confuse them by the idea of three concerning God. When therefore they heard these things, they were affected with joy, and said that some were also sent to them by God, whom they then called the Lord, who teach them concerning Him; and that they were not willing to admit visitors who disturb them, especially by the idea of three Persons in the Divinity, since they know that God is one, consequently that the Divine is one, and not a unanimity of three, unless they would think of God as of an angel, in whom the inmost of life is something invisible, from which he thinks and is wise, and the external of life what is visible under the human form, from which he sees and acts, and the proceeding of life that which is the sphere of love and faith from him, for from every spirit and angel proceeds a sphere of life by which he is known at a distance; and as to the Lord, that the proceeding of life from Him is the Divine Itself which fills and constitutes the heavens, because it proceeds from the *esse* itself of the life of love and faith. They said that in this and in no other way could they perceive a Trine and a One at the same time. On hearing this, it was given me to say that such an idea of a Trine and a One together agrees with the angelic idea of the Lord; and that it is from the Lord's own teaching concerning Himself; for He teaches that the Father and He are one; that the Father is in Him, and He in the Father; that whoso sees Him, sees the Father; and that He who believes in Him, believes in the Father and knows Him; also that the Comforter, by whom is meant the proceeding Divine, and whom He calls the Spirit of truth, as also the Holy Spirit, proceeds from Him, and speaks not from Himself, but from Him. Moreover, that the idea of a Trine and of One at the same time agrees with the *esse* and *existere* of the Lord's life, when He was in the world. The *esse* of His life was the Divine Itself, for He was conceived of Jehovah, and the *esse* of any one's life is that from which he is conceived; the *existere* of life from that *esse* is the Human in form. The *esse* of every man's life which he has from his father, is called the soul; and the *existere* of life therefrom is called the body. The soul and the body constitute one man. The likeness between both is like that between that which is in effort and that which is in the act thence, for the act is the effort acting, and so the two are one. Effort in man is called the will, and effort acting is called action. The body is the instrument, by which the will, which is the principal, acts; and the instrument and the principal in acting are one; thus the soul and the body are one. The angels in heaven have such an idea concerning the soul and the body; and thus they know that the Lord made His Human Divine from the Divine in Himself, which He had as His soul from the Father. The faith also received everywhere in the Christian world does not dissent from this, for it teaches: "Although Christ is God and Man, yet He is not two, but one Christ; yea, He is altogether a one and only Person; for as the body and the soul are one man, so also God and Man is one Christ."[45] Because there was such a union, or such a One in the Lord, He therefore, otherwise than any man, rose not only as to the soul, but also as to the body, which He glorified in the world; concerning which He also instructed His disciples, saying:—

Handle Me, and see; for a spirit hath not flesh and bones, as ye see Me have.[46]

These things those spirits well understood, for such things fall into the understanding of angelic spirits. They then added that the Lord alone has power in the heavens, and that the heavens are His. To which it was given me to respond that the church on our earth also knows this, from the mouth of the Lord Himself, before He ascended into heaven; for He then said:—

All power is given unto Me in heaven and in earth.

160. I afterward spoke with those spirits concerning their earth; for all spirits know about their earth when their natural or external memory is opened by the Lord; since they have this with them from the world, but it is not opened except by the good pleasure of the Lord. The spirits then said

---

[45] From the Athanasian Creed.
[46] Man rises again as to his spirit immediately after death, and he is in the human form, and that as to each and every particular he is a man (n. 4527, 5006, 5078, 8939, 8991, 10,594, 10,597, 10,758). Man rises again only as to his spirit, and not as to his body (n. 10,593, 10,594). The Lord alone rose again as to the body also (n. 1729, 2083, 5078, 10,825).

respecting their earth from which they were, that when leave is given them, they appear to the inhabitants of their earth, and speak with them as men; and that this is done by their being let into their natural or external memory, and thus into such thought as they were in when they lived in the world; and that the inhabitants then have their interior sight, or the sight of their spirit, opened, from which they see them. They added that the inhabitants do not know that they are not men of their earth, and first perceive that they are not, when they are suddenly taken away from their sight. I told them that such was the case on our earth in ancient times, as with Abraham, Sarah, Lot, the inhabitants of Sodom, Manoah and his wife, Joshua, Mary, Elizabeth, and the prophets in general; and that the Lord appeared in like manner, and those who saw Him did not know otherwise than that He was a man of the earth, before He revealed Himself. But that this is rarely done at this day, lest by such things men should be compelled to believe; for a compelled faith, such as is that which enters through miracles, does not remain fixed, and would also be hurtful to those with whom faith might be implanted through the Word in a state not compelled.

161. The spirit who in the world had been a primate and a preacher, did not at all believe that there were any other earths than ours, because he had thought in the world that the Lord was born on this earth only, and that no one has salvation without the Lord. He was therefore reduced to such a state as the spirits are reduced when they appear on their earth as men (see just above), and thus was sent to that earth, so as not only to see it, but also to speak with its inhabitants. When this was done, communication was also thereby granted me, so that I in like manner saw the inhabitants, and some things also upon that earth (see above, n. 135). There then appeared four kinds of men, but one kind after another in succession. First were seen men clothed; next men naked of the color of human flesh; afterward men naked, but with bodies inflamed; and lastly black men.

162. When the spirit who had been a primate and a preacher was with those who were clothed, there appeared a woman of a very beautiful face, dressed in a simple garment, with a tunic that hung gracefully behind her and was brought up over the arms. She had a beautiful headdress, in the form of a chaplet of flowers. That spirit was greatly delighted at the sight of this virgin, and spoke with her, and also took her hand. But as she perceived that he was a spirit, and not of that earth, she hurried away from him. There afterward appeared to him on the right many other women, who were tending sheep and lambs, which they were then leading to a watering trough that was supplied with water by a small ditch from a lake. They were similarly clothed, and held shepherds' crooks in their hands, by which they guided the sheep and lambs to drink. They said that the sheep went in the way to which they pointed with their crooks. The sheep seen were large, with woolly tails, both broad and long. The faces of the women when seen nearer were full and beautiful. The men were also seen, and their faces were of the color of human flesh, as on our earth; but with the difference, that the lower part of the face, in place of a beard, was black, and the nose more the color of snow than of flesh. Afterward the spirit above mentioned, who had been a preacher in the world, was led on further, but unwillingly, because his thought was still on that woman with whom he was delighted, as was made manifest by somewhat of a shadow from him still appearing in the former place. He then came to those who were naked, and who were seen walking together two and two, being husband and wife, girded with a covering about the loins and a certain covering upon the head. That spirit when with them was led into that state in which he was in the world when he wished to preach, and said that he would preach to them the Lord crucified. But they said that they were not willing to hear any such thing, because they did not know what this meant, but they knew that the Lord lives. He then declared that he wished to preach the Lord living. But this also they refused to hear, saying that they perceived in his speech something not heavenly, because it had much regard to himself, his fame and honor, for they can tell from the very tone of one's voice whether it is from the heart, or not, and because he was such, he could not teach them. On this he was silent, for in the world he had had much pathetic power, so that he could strongly move his hearers to holiness; but this power had been acquired by art, and thus it was from himself and the world, and not from heaven.

163. They said further, that they have a perception whether the conjugial exists with those of their nation who are naked; and it was shown that they perceive this from a spiritual idea of marriage, which was communicated to me, to the effect that a similarity of interiors is formed by the conjunction of good and truth, thus of love and faith, and from that conjunction flowing down into the body conjugial love exists. For all things of the mind are presented in a certain natural appearance in the body, thus in the appearance of conjugial love, when the interiors of two mutually love each other, and from that love desire also to will and to think the one like the other, and so to be together and to be conjoined as to the interiors which are of the mind. Thus spiritual affection, which is of the minds, becomes natural affection in the body, and clothes itself with the sense of conjugial love. The spiritual affection which is of their minds is the affection of good and truth, and their conjunction; for all things of the mind, or of the thought and will, have relation to truth and good. They said also that what is given between one man and several wives is not at all conjugial, since the marriage of good and truth, which is of the minds, can be given only between two.

164. The spirit mentioned above then came to those who were naked, but with bodies inflamed, and at last to those that were black, of whom some were naked, and some clothed; but these different people dwelt in different places on the same earth, for a spirit can be led in a moment to remote parts of an earth, since he does not proceed and is not borne, as a man is, through spaces, but through changes of state (see above, n. 125, 127).[41]

165. At length I spoke with the spirits of that earth about the belief of the inhabitants of our earth concerning the resurrection, that they cannot conceive of men's coming into the other life immediately after death, and then appearing like men as to face, body, arms, feet, and all the senses, both external and internal; and still less of their being then clothed with garments and having mansions and dwellings. And the reason is

---

[41] See foot-note, page 470.

that most of them there think from the sensual things which are of the body, and therefore believe in the existence of nothing which they do not see and touch. And few of them can be drawn away from external sensual things to what is interior, and so be elevated into the light of heaven in which such interior things are perceived. Hence it is, that in regard to their soul or spirit they cannot have any idea of it as a man, but as of wind, air, or breath, without form, in which there is yet something vital. This is why they do not believe they are to rise until the end of the world, which they call the Last Judgment; when they believe the body, though fallen into dust and dissipated to all the winds, will be brought back and joined to its soul and spirit. I added that they are permitted to believe this, for the reason that those who think from what is external and sensual, as has been said, can form no other idea than that one's soul or spirit can live as a man in the human form, only by regaining the body which it bore about in the world. And therefore, unless it were said that this would rise again, they would reject in heart the doctrine of a resurrection and eternal life, as incomprehensible. But still that thought about the resurrection has this use in it, that they believe in a life after death, from which belief it follows that when they lie sick in bed and do not think as before from what is worldly and corporeal, thus not from things sensual, they then believe that they shall live immediately after death. They also speak then about heaven, and about the hope of living there immediately after death, laying aside their doctrine about the Last Judgment. I told these spirits further, that I sometimes wondered that when those who are in faith speak of the life after death, and of their friends who are dying or who have died, and do not at the same time think of the Last Judgment, they believe that they will live as men immediately after death. But this idea, as soon as the thought of the Last Judgment flows in, is changed into a material idea about their earthly body, that it is to be again joined to its soul. For they do not know that every man is a spirit as to his interiors, and that it is the spirit which lives in the body and in all its parts, and not the body of itself; and that it is from the spirit of every one that the body has its human form, and thus it is the spirit which is chiefly the man, and in a similar form, but invisible to the eyes of the body, yet visible to the eyes of spirits. Hence also when the sight of a man's spirit is opened, which takes place by the removal of the sight of the body, angels appear as men. Thus did the angels appear to the ancients, as related in the Word. I have also spoken sometimes with spirits whom I knew when they lived as men in the world, and have asked them whether they wished to be clothed again with their earthly body, as they had once thought. On hearing which, at the mere idea of conjunction with the body they fled away, being struck with amazement that in the world they should have thus thought from blind faith without any understanding.

166. Moreover, their dwellings on that earth were seen by me, and were long low houses, with windows on the sides according to the number of rooms or chambers into which they were divided. The roof was arched, and there was a door on each side at the end. They said that they were built of earth and roofed with sods, and the windows of threads of grass, so woven together that the light shone through. Children were also seen. And they said that their neighbors visited them, especially for the sake of their children, that they might be in company with other children, under the sight and auspices of their parents. There also appeared fields then whitening with the nearly ripened harvest. The seeds or grains of this harvest were shown, and they were like the grains of Chinese wheat. We were shown also loaves made of the grain, which were small in size and square in form. Moreover there also appeared grassy plains, with flowers therein, and trees with fruits similar to pomegranates; also shrubs, which were not vines, yet bearing berries from which wine is prepared.

167. Their sun which to us is a star, appears flaming there, and about one-fourth as large as our own sun. In their year are about two hundred days, and the days of fifteen hours length, as compared with the days on our earth. The earth itself is among the smallest in the starry heavens, being scarcely five hundred German miles* in circumference. This I learned from angels by comparison with such things as they saw in me,

---

*Or two thousand English geographical miles.

or in my memory, in relation to our earth. They formed these conclusions by angelic ideas, by which the measures of spaces and times are immediately known in their just relation to the spaces and times elsewhere. In such comparisons angelic ideas, which are spiritual, immensely exceed human ideas, which are natural.

A FIFTH EARTH IN THE STARRY HEAVEN, ITS SPIRITS AND INHABITANTS.

168. I was led again to another earth which is in the universe out of our solar system, and this also by changes of state, continued for nearly twelve hours. There were in company with me several spirits and angels from our earth, with whom I discoursed in the way or in that progression. I was carried at times obliquely upwards and obliquely downwards, continually towards the right, which in the other life is towards the south. In only two places I saw spirits, and in one I spoke with them. In the way or progression I was enabled to observe how immense is the Lord's heaven, which is for angels and spirits; for from the parts uninhabited I was led to conclude that it was so immense, that if there were many myriads of earths, and on each earth a multitude of men as great as in ours, there would still be a place of abode for them to eternity, and it would never be filled. This I was enabled to conclude from a comparison made with the extent of the heaven which is about our earth and designed for it, which extent was respectively so small, that it did not equal a hundred millionth part of the extent uninhabited.

169. When the angelic spirits who were from that earth came into view, they accosted us, asking who we were, and what we wanted. We said that we came for the sake of journeying, that we were directed thither, and that they had nothing to fear from us; for they were afraid we were of those who disturb them in regard to God, to faith, and things of a like nature, on account of whom they had betaken themselves to that quarter of their earth, shunning them as much as possible. We asked them by what they were disturbed. They replied, by an idea of three, and by an idea of the Divine without the Human, in God, when yet they know and perceive that God is one, and that He is Man. It was then perceived that they who disturbed them, and whom they shunned, were from our earth. This was manifest also from this, that there are from our earth those who thus wander about in the other life in consequence of their fondness for and delight in travelling, which they have contracted in the world; for on other earths there is no such custom of travelling as on ours. It was then discovered that they were monks, who had travelled on our globe from the zeal of converting the Gentiles; wherefore we told them they did well to shun them, because their intention was not to teach, but to secure gain and dominion; and that they study by various arts first to captivate men's minds, but afterwards to subject them to themselves as slaves. Moreover, that they did well in not suffering their ideas concerning God to be disturbed by such. They said further, that the above spirits confuse them by asserting that they ought to have faith and to believe the things they say; but they replied to them, that they know not what faith is nor what is meant by believing, since they perceive in themselves whether a thing be true or not. They were of the Lord's celestial kingdom, where all know from an interior perception the truths which with us are called the truths of faith, for they are in enlightenment from the Lord; but it is otherwise with those who are in the spiritual kingdom. That the angelic spirits of that earth were of the Lord's celestial kingdom, it was granted me to see from the flaming light whence their ideas flowed; for the light in the celestial kingdom is flaming, and in the spiritual kingdom it is white. They who are of the celestial kingdom, when the discourse is about truths, say no more than yea, yea, or nay, nay, and never reason about truths whether they be so or not so. These are they of whom the Lord speaks:—

Let your discourse be yea, yea, and nay, nay, for whatsoever is more than this is from evil.

Hence it was that those spirits said that they did not know what is meant by having faith or believing. They consider this, like a person's saying to his companion who sees houses or trees with his own eyes, that he ought to have faith or to believe that they are houses and trees, when he sees clearly that they are so. Such are they who are of the Lord's celestial kingdom, and such were these angelic spirits.[47] We told them that there are few on our earth who have interior perception, because in their youth they learn truths and do not do them. For man has two faculties, which are called the understanding and the will; they who admit truths no further than into the memory, and thence in some small degree into the understanding, and not into the life, that is, into the will, these, inasmuch as they are not capable of any enlightenment or interior sight from the Lord, say that those truths are to be believed, or that they are objects of faith, and also reason concerning them whether they be truths or not; yea, they are not willing that they should be perceived by any interior sight, or by any enlightenment in the understanding. They say this, because truths with them are without light from heaven, and to those who see without light from heaven, falsities may appear like truths, and truths like falsities; hence so great blindness has seized many there, that although they do not do truths or live according to them, still they say that they can be saved by faith alone, as if it were the knowledge of the things of faith which constitutes man, and not the life according to that knowledge. We afterwards discoursed with them concerning the Lord, concerning love to Him, concerning love toward the neighbor, and concerning regeneration; saying that to love the Lord is to love the commandments which are from Him, which is to live according to them from love.[48] That love toward the neighbor is to will good and thence do good to a fellow-citizen, to one's country, to the church, and to the Lord's kingdom, not for the sake of self, to be seen, or to merit, but from the affection of

---

[47] Heaven is distinguished into two kingdoms, one of which is called the celestial kingdom, the other the spiritual kingdom (n. 3887, 4138). The angels in the celestial kingdom know innumerable things and are immensely more wise than the angels in the spiritual kingdom (n. 2718). The celestial angels do not think and speak from faith, like the spiritual angels, but from an internal perception that a thing is so (n. 202, 597, 607, 784, 1121, 1387, 1398, 1442, 1919, 7680, 7877, 8780). The celestial angels say only concerning the truths of faith, yea, yea, or nay, nay, but the spiritual angels reason whether it be so or not so (n. 202, 337, 2715, 3246, 4448, 9196).

[48] To love the Lord is to live according to His commandments (n. 10,143, 10,153, 10,310, 10,578, 10,648).

good.[49] Concerning regeneration, we observed that they who are regenerated by the Lord, and commit truths immediately to life, come into an interior perception concerning them; but that they who receive truths first in the memory, and afterwards will them and do them, are they who are in faith; for they act from faith, which is then called conscience. They said that they perceived these things to be so, and thus perceived also what faith is. I discoursed with them by spiritual ideas, whereby such things may be exhibited and comprehended in light.

170. The spirits with whom I now discoursed were from the northern part of their earth. I was afterwards led to others who were on the western part. These also, wishing to discover who and what I was, immediately said that there was nothing in me but evil, thinking thus to deter me from approaching nearer. It was perceived that this was their manner of accosting all who came to them; but it was granted me to reply that I well knew it to be so, and that with them also there was nothing but evil, by reason that every one is born in evil, and therefore whatever comes from man, spirit, and angel, as from what is his own, or his proprium, is nothing but evil, inasmuch as all good with every one is from the Lord. Hence they perceived that I was in the truth, and I was admitted to speak with them. They then showed me their idea concerning evil with man, and concerning good from the Lord, how they are separated from each other. They placed one near the other, almost contiguous, but still distinct, yet as it were bound together in a manner inexpressible, so that the good led the evil, and restrained it, insomuch that it was not allowed it to act at pleasure; and thus the good bent the evil in whatever direction desired, without the evil knowing it. In this manner they exhibited the dominion of good over evil, and at the same time a state of freedom. They then asked how the Lord appeared with the angels from our earth. I said that He appears in the sun as Man, encompassed therein with solar fire, whence the angels in the heavens have all light; and that the heat which proceeds thence is the Divine good, and that the light which proceeds

---

[49] To love the neighbor is to do what is good, just, and right, in every work and in every function, from the affection of what is good, just, and right (n. 8120–8122, 10,310, 10,336). A life of love towards the neighbor is a life according to the Lord's commandments (n. 3249).

thence is the Divine truth, each from the Divine love, which is the fire appearing around the Lord in that sun. That sun, however, appears only to the angels in heaven, and not to the spirits who are beneath, since they are more removed from the reception of the good of love and of the truth of faith, than the angels who are in the heavens (see above, n. 40). It was granted them thus to inquire concerning the Lord, and concerning His appearance before the angels from our earth, because it then pleased the Lord to present Himself before them, and to reduce into order the things which had been disturbed by the evil spirits of whom they complained. This also was the reason why I was led thither, that I might see these things.

171. There was then seen a dark cloud toward the east, descending from on high, which in descending gradually appeared bright and in the human form; and this form at length appeared in a flaming radiance, around which were little stars of the same color. In this manner the Lord presented Himself before the spirits with whom I was speaking. To this Presence were then gathered together from every side all the spirits who were there; and when they came, the good were separated from the evil, the good to the right and the evil to the left, and this at once, as of their own accord. And those on the right were arranged according to the quality of their good, and those on the left according to the quality of their evil. The good were then left to form a heavenly society among themselves; but the evil were cast into the hells. I saw afterward that this flaming radiance descended quite deep into the lower parts of the earth there; and then it appeared, now flamy verging to brightness, now bright verging to obscurity, and now in obscurity. And I was told by angels that the appearance is according to the reception of truth from good, and of falsity from evil, with those who inhabit the lower parts of that earth; and that the flamy radiance itself did not at all undergo such variations. They said also that the lower parts of that earth were inhabited as well by the good as by the evil; but well separated, in order that the evil might be ruled through the good by the Lord. They added that the good were by turns taken up thence into heaven by the Lord, and others succeed in their place, and so on continually. In that descent the good were in like manner separated from the evil, and all things were reduced into order. For the evil, by various arts and crafty devices, had introduced themselves into the dwellings of the good there, and infested them; and this was the cause of that visitation. That cloud, which in descending gradually appeared bright and in the human form, and then as a flamy radiance, was an angelic society, in the midst of which was the Lord. From this it was given to know what is meant by the Lord's words in the Evangelists, where He speaks of the Last Judgment:—

That He will come with the angels in the clouds of heaven with glory and power.

172. Afterward some monkish spirits were seen, namely, those who had been travelling monks or missionaries in the world, and who have been spoken of above; and a crowd of spirits was also seen, who were from that earth, most of them evil, whom they had drawn over and seduced to their side. These were seen at the eastern quarter of that earth, from which they drove away the good, who betook themselves to the northern side of that earth, and have been spoken of above. That crowd, together with their seducers was collected into one body, to the number of some thousands, and was separated when the evil were cast into the hells. I was granted to speak with one spirit who was a monk, and to ask what he did there. He replied that he taught them concerning the Lord. I asked, what besides. He said, concerning heaven and hell. I asked, what further. He said, concerning a belief in all that he should say. I asked, what further. He said, concerning the power of remitting sins, and of opening and shutting heaven. He was then examined as to what he knew concerning the Lord, concerning the truths of faith, concerning the remission of sins, concerning man's salvation, and concerning heaven and hell; and it was discovered that he knew scarcely anything, and that he was in obscurity and falsity concerning all and each of them, and that he was possessed solely by the lust of gain and dominion which he had contracted in the world and brought with him thence. Wherefore he was told that, because he had travelled so far led by that lust, and was such as to doctrine, he must needs deprive the spirits of that earth of celestial light, and bring in the darkness of hell, and thus bring them under the dominion of hell, and not of the Lord. Moreover he was cunning in seducing, but stupid as to those things which are of heaven. Because he was such he was then cast thence into hell. Thus the spirits of that earth were liberated from them.

173. The spirits of that earth mentioned also, among other things, that those strangers, who, as has been said, were monkish spirits, used all their endeavors to persuade them to live together in society, and not separate and solitary; for spirits and angels dwell and associate in like manner as in the world; they who have dwelt in communities in the world, dwell also in a similar state in the other life; and they who have dwelt in a separate state, divided into houses and families, dwell also in a separate state in another life. These spirits on their earth, while they lived there as men, had dwelt in a separate state, house and house, families and families, and thus nation and nation apart, and hence they knew not what it was to dwell together in society. Wherefore when it was told them that those strangers wished to persuade them to dwell in society, to the intent that they might rule and have dominion over them, and that they could not otherwise subject them to themselves and make them slaves, they replied that they were totally ignorant what was meant by ruling and domineering. That they flee away at the very idea of rule and dominion, was made manifest to me from this, that one of them, who accompanied us back again, when I showed him the city in which I dwelt, at the first sight of it fled away, and was no more seen.

174. I then spoke with the angels who were with me concerning dominion, saying that there are two kinds of dominion, one of love towards the neighbor, and the other of self-love; and that the dominion of love towards the neighbor is among those who dwell separated into houses, families, and nations; whereas the dominion of self-love is among those who dwell together in society. Among those who live separated into houses, families, and nations, he has dominion who is the father of the nation, and under him the father of families, and under these the father of each house. He is called the father of the nation from whom the families originate, from which families the houses are derived; but all these exercise dominion from love, like that of a father towards his children, who teaches them how they ought to live, does good to them, and as far as he can, gives them of his own. It never enters into his mind to subject them to himself, as subjects or as servants, but he loves that they should obey him as sons obey their father. And because this love increases in descending, as is known, therefore the father of the nation acts from a more interior love than the father himself from whom the sons are next descended. Such also is the dominion in the heavens, inasmuch as such is the Lord's dominion; for His dominion is from the Divine love towards the whole human race. But the dominion of self-love, which is opposite to the dominion of love towards the neighbor, began when man alienated himself from the Lord; for in proportion as man does not love and worship the Lord, in the same proportion he loves and worships himself, and so far also he loves the world. Then from necessity that they might be safe, the nations with their families and houses, formed themselves into one body, and established governments under various forms. For in proportion as self-love increased, in the same proportion all kinds of evil, as enmity, envy, hatred, revenge, cruelty and deceit, increased with it, being exercised against all who opposed them. For from the proprium in which they are who are in self-love, nothing but evil springs, inasmuch as man's proprium is nothing but evil, and because the proprium is evil, it does not receive good from heaven. Hence self-love, while it has dominion, is the father of all such evils.[50] And that love is also of such a nature that as far as the reins are relaxed it rushes on, until at length every one possessed by it wishes to domineer over all others in the whole world, and to possess all the goods of others. Yea, even this is not enough, but he wishes to have dominion over the whole heaven, as may be evident from the Babylon of this day. This then is the

---

[50] Man's proprium, which he derives from his parents, is nothing but dense evil (n. 210, 215, 731, 874, 876, 987, 1047, 2307, 2318, 3518, 3701, 3812, 8480, 8550, 10,-283, 10,284, 10,286, 10,731). Man's proprium consists in loving himself more than God, and the world more than heaven, and in making light of his neighbor in respect to himself, except it be for the sake of himself, and thus from motives of self-love and the love of the world (n. 694, 731, 4317, 5660). All evils flow from self-love and the love of the world, when they have dominion (n. 1307, 1308, 1321, 1594, 1691, 3413, 7255, 7376, 7480, 7488, 8318, 9335, 9348, 10,038, 10,742). These evils are contempt of others, enmity, hatred, revenge, cruelty, and deceit (n. 6667, 7372-7374, 9348, 10,038, 10,742). And that from these evils every falsity flows (n. 1047, 10,283, 10,284, 10,286).

rule of self-love, from which the rule of the love of the neighbor differs as much as heaven does from hell. But however great such dominion of self-love is in societies or in kingdoms and empires, still even in these is found also the dominion of love towards the neighbor among those who are wise from faith in and love to God; for these love the neighbor. That these also dwell in the heavens distinguished into nations, families, and houses, although in societies together, but according to spiritual affinities, which are those of the good of love and the truth of faith, will by the Divine mercy of the Lord be told elsewhere.

175. I afterward questioned those spirits about various things on the earth from which they were, and first about their Divine worship and revelation. In regard to worship they said that the nations with their families assemble at one place every thirtieth day, and hear preaching; and that the preacher then, from a pulpit raised a little above the earth, teaches them Divine truths, which lead to the good of life. Concerning revelation they said that it came in the early morning, in a state midway between sleep and wakefulness, when they are in interior light not yet interrupted by the bodily senses and by worldly things. And that they then hear angels of heaven speaking of Divine truths, and of a life according to them; that when they awaken, an angel in a white garment appears to them by the bed, who then suddenly disappears from their sight; and that from this they know that what they have heard is from heaven. In this way Divine vision is distinguished from vision not Divine; for in vision not Divine no angel appears. They added that revelations are made in this manner to their preachers, also sometimes to others.

176. To an inquiry concerning their houses, they said that they are low, of wood, with a flat roof, around which project eaves sloping downward; and that in the front part dwell the husband and wife, in the next adjoining part the children, and after them the maid-servants and men-servants. Of their food they said that they drink milk with water, and that they have the milk from cows, which are woolly like sheep. Of their life they said that they walk naked, and that to them nakedness is not a cause of shame; also that their social intercourse is with those who are within their families.

177. In regard to the sun of that earth they related that to the inhabitants it has a flamy appearance; that the length of their years is two hundred days, and that a day equals nine hours of our time, which they could conclude from the length of the days of our earth perceived in me. And further, that they have perpetual spring and summer, and consequently that the fields are ever green, and the trees ever bearing fruit. The reason of this is, because their year is so short, being equal only to seventy-five days of our year; and when the years are so short, the cold does not continue long in winter nor the heat in summer, whence the ground is continually verdant.

178. Concerning betrothals and marriages in that earth, they related that a daughter, when she arrives at a marriageable age, is kept at home, nor is she allowed to leave the house till the day she is to be married; that then she is conducted to a certain connubial house, where there are also many other young women of marriageable age brought together, and there they are placed behind a screen, which reaches to the middle of the body, so that they appear naked as to the breast and face: and that then the young men come thither to choose for themselves a wife. And when a young man sees one that seems suited to him, and to whom his mind draws him, he takes her by the hand; and if she then follows him, he leads her to a house prepared, and she becomes his wife. For they see from the face whether they agree in mind, inasmuch as there every one's face is an index of the mind, and in nothing does it dissemble and deceive. That all things may be done decently and without lasciviousness, an old man is seated behind the virgins, and an old woman at the side of them, to make their observations. There are many such places to which the young women are conducted: and also stated times for the young men to make their choice. For if they do not find a maid to suit them in one place, they go to another; and if not at one time, they return again at a future time. They said further, that a husband has only one wife, and never more than one, because this is contrary to Divine order.

THE END.

THE LAST JUDGMENT

The Last Judgment

AND

Babylon Destroyed

ALL THE PREDICTIONS IN THE APOCALYPSE ARE AT
THIS DAY FULFILLED

FROM THINGS HEARD AND SEEN

FROM THE LATIN OF
EMANUEL SWEDENBORG
SERVANT OF THE LORD JESUS CHRIST

BEING A TRANSLATION OF HIS WORK ENTITLED

"De Ultimo Judicio et de Babylonia Destructa : ita quod omnia quæ in
Apocalypsi prædicta sunt, hodie impleta sint. Ex auditis
et visis." Londini, 1758

CONTENTS

		Nos.
I.	The Destruction of the World is not meant by the Day of the Last Judgment..................................	1–5
II.	The Procreations of the Human Race on the Earths will never cease.......................................	6–13
III.	Heaven and Hell are from the Human Race............	14–22
IV.	All who have ever been born Men from the Beginning of Creation, and are Deceased, are either in Heaven or in Hell	23–27
V.	The Last Judgment must be where all are together, thus in the Spiritual World, and not on Earth..............	28–32
VI.	The Last Judgment exists when the End of the Church is; and the End of the Church is when there is no Faith because there is no Charity.........................	33–39
VII.	All Things which are Predicted in the *Apocalypse* are at this day Fulfilled.................................	40–44
VIII.	The Last Judgment has been Accomplished.............	45–52
IX.	Babylon and its Destruction...........................	53–64
X.	The Former Heaven and its Abolishment...............	65–72
XI.	The State of the World and of the Church Hereafter...	73–74

THE LAST JUDGMENT

AND

BABYLON DESTROYED

I.

THE DESTRUCTION OF THE WORLD IS NOT MEANT BY THE DAY OF THE LAST JUDGMENT.

1. Those who have not known the spiritual sense of the Word, have understood that everything in the visible world will be destroyed in the day of the Last Judgment; for it is said, that heaven and earth are then to perish, and that God will create a New Heaven and a New Earth. In this opinion they have also confirmed themselves because it is said, that all are then to rise from their graves, and that the good are then to be separated from the evil, with more to the same purport. But it is thus said in the sense of the letter of the Word, because the sense of the letter of the Word is natural, and in the ultimate of Divine order, where each and every part contains a spiritual sense within it. For which reason, he who comprehends the Word only according to the sense of the letter, may be led into various opinions, as indeed has been the case in the Christian world, where so many heresies have thus arisen, and every one of them is confirmed from the Word. But since no one has hitherto known, that in the whole and in every part of the Word there is a spiritual sense, nor even what the spiritual sense is, therefore they who have embraced this opinion concerning the Last Judgment are excusable. But still they may now know, that neither the visible heaven nor the habitable earth will perish, but that both will endure; and that by "the New Heaven and the New Earth" is meant a New Church, both in the heavens and on the earth. It is said a New Church in the heavens, for there is a church in the heavens, as well as on the earth; for there also is the Word, and likewise preachings, and Divine worship as on the earth; but with a difference, that there all things are in a more perfect state, because there they are not in the natural world, but in the spiritual; hence all there are spiritual men, and not natural as they were in the world. That it is so, may be seen in the work on *Heaven*, in a special article there, on the Conjunction of Heaven with man by the Word (n. 303–310); and on Divine Worship in Heaven (n. 221–227).

2. The passages in the Word, in which mention is made of the destruction of heaven and earth, are the following:—

Lift up your eyes to heaven, and look upon the earth beneath; the heavens are about to perish like smoke, and the earth shall wax old like a garment (*Isa.* li. 6).

Behold, I am about to create new heavens, and a new earth; neither shall the former things be remembered (*Isa.* lxv. 17).

I will make new heavens and a new earth (*Isa.* lxvi. 22).

The stars of heaven have fallen to the earth, and heaven has departed like a book rolled together (*Apoc.* vi. 13, 14).

I saw a great throne, and One sitting thereon, from whose face the earth and the heaven fled away, and their place was not found (*Apoc.* xx. 11).

I saw a New Heaven and a New Earth, for the first heaven and the first earth had passed away (*Apoc.* xxi. 1).

In these passages, by "a New Heaven" is not meant the visible heaven, but heaven itself where the human race is collected; for a heaven was formed from all the human race, who had lived since the commencement of the Christian church; but they who were there were not angels, but spirits of various religions; this heaven is meant by "the first heaven" which was to perish: but how this was, shall be specially declared in what follows; here is related only so much as serves to show what is meant by "the first heaven" which was to perish. Every one even who thinks from a somewhat enlightened reason, may perceive, that it is not the starry heaven, the so immense firmament of creation, which is here meant, but that it is heaven in the spiritual sense, where angels and spirits are.

3. That by "the new earth" is meant a New Church on earth, has hitherto been unknown, for every one by "earth" in the Word has understood the earth, when yet by it is meant the church; in the natural sense, earth is the earth, but in the spiritual sense it is the church, because they who are in the spiritual sense, that is, who are spiritual, as the angels are, when "the earth" is named in the Word, do not understand the earth itself, but the nation which is there, and its Divine worship; hence it is that by "earth" is signified the church; that it is so, may be seen in the *Arcana Cœlestia*, as quoted below.[1]

I will here adduce one or two passages from the Word, by which in some measure it may be comprehended, that "earth" (land) signifies the church:—

The cataracts from on high were opened, and the foundations of the earth were shaken; in breaking, the earth is broken; in agitating, the earth is agitated; in reeling, the earth reels like a drunkard; it moves to and fro like a cottage; and heavy upon it is the transgression thereof (*Isa.* xxiv. 18–20).

I will cause a man to be more rare than pure gold; therefore I will remove the heaven, and the earth shall be removed out of her place, in the day of the fierce anger of Jehovah (*Isa.* xiii. 12, 13).

The earth was agitated before Him, the heavens have trembled, the sun and the moon are become black, and the stars have withdrawn their splendor (*Joel* ii. 10).

The land was shaken and agitated, and the foundations of the mountains trembled and were shaken (*Ps.* xviii. 7, 8, and in many other places).

FROM THE ARCANA CŒLESTIA.

[1] By "earth" (land) in the Word is signified the kingdom of the Lord and the church (n. 662, 1066, 1067, 1262, 1413, 1607, 2928, 3355, 4447, 4535, 5577, 8011, 9325, 9643). Chiefly for this reason, because by "earth" is meant the land of Canaan, and the church was there from the most ancient times; hence also it is, that heaven is called the heavenly Canaan (n. 567, 3686, 4447, 4454, 4516, 4517, 5136, 6516, 9325, 9327). And because in the spiritual sense by "earth" is understood the nation which is there, and its worship (n. 1262). Hence the "earth" signifies various things pertaining to the church (n. 620, 636, 1066, 2571, 3368, 3379, 3404, 8732). The people of the "earth" are they who are of the spiritual church (n. 2928). "An earthquake" is a change of the state of the church (n. 3355). "A New Heaven and a New Earth" signify the church (n. 1733, 1850, 2117, 2118, 3355, 4535, 10,373).

The Most Ancient Church, which was before the flood, and the Ancient Church, which was after the flood, were in the land of Canaan (n. 567, 3686, 4447, 4454, 4516, 4517, 5136, 6516, 9327). Thence all the places there became representative of such things as are in the Lord's kingdom and in the church (n. 1585, 3686, 4447, 5136). Therefore Abraham was commanded to go thither, since with his posterity from Jacob, a representative church was to be instituted, and the Word written, the ultimate sense of which should consist of the representatives and significatives which were there (n. 3686, 4447, 5136, 6516). Hence it is that by "earth" and by "the land of Canaan" is signified the church (n. 3038, 3481, 3705, 4447, 4517, 5757, 10,559).

4. "To create" in the spiritual sense of the Word also signifies to form, to establish, and to regenerate; so by "creating a new heaven and a new earth" signifies to establish a New Church in heaven and on earth, as may appear from the following passages:—

The people who shall be created shall praise Jah (*Ps.* cii. 18).

Thou sendest forth the spirit, they are created; and Thou renewest the faces of the earth (*Ps.* civ. 30).

Thus said Jehovah, thy Creator, O Jacob, thy Former, O Israel, for I have redeemed thee, and I have called thee by thy name, thou art Mine; every one called by My name, and for My glory I have created, I have formed him, yea, I have made him (*Isa.* xliii. 1, 7, and in other places).

Hence it is, that "the new creation" of man is his reformation, since he is made anew, that is, from natural he is made spiritual; and hence it is that "a new creature" is a reformed man.[2]

5. Concerning the spiritual sense of the Word, see in the small work on the *White Horse*, mentioned in the *Apocalypse*.

II.

THE PROCREATIONS OF THE HUMAN RACE ON THE EARTHS WILL NEVER CEASE.

6. They who have adopted as their belief concerning the Last Judgment, that all things in the heavens and on the earth are then to perish, and that a new heaven and a new earth will exist in their place, believe, because it follows of consequence, that the generations and procreations of the human race are therefore to cease. For they think that all things will be then accomplished, and that men will be in a different state from before. But since the day of the Last Judgment does not mean the destruction of the world, as was shown in the preceding article, it also follows that the human race will endure, and that procreations will not cease.

---

[2] "To create" is to create anew, or to reform and regenerate (n. 16, 88, 10,373, 10,634). "To create a New Heaven and a New Earth," is to institute a new church (n. 10,373). By "the creation of heaven and earth" in the first chapter of Genesis, in the internal sense, is described the institution of the celestial church, which was the Most Ancient Church (n. 8891, 9942, 10,545).

7. That the procreations of the human race will endure to eternity, is plain from many considerations, of which some are shown in the work on *Heaven*, especially from the following:—

I. *The human race is the basis on which heaven is founded.*
II. *The human race is the seminary of heaven.*
III. *The extension of heaven, which is for angels, is so immense that it cannot be filled to eternity.*
IV. *They are but few respectively, of whom heaven at present is formed.*
V. *The perfection of heaven increases according to its numbers.*
VI. *And every Divine work has respect to infinity and eternity.*

9. I. *The human race is the basis on which heaven is founded*, is because man was last created, and that which is last created is the basis of all that precedes. Creation commenced from the supreme or inmost, because from the Divine; and proceeded to ultimates or extremes, and then first subsisted. The ultimate of creation is the natural world, including the terraqueous globe, with all things on it. When these were finished, then man was created, and into him were collated all things of Divine order from firsts to lasts; into his inmost were collated those things of that order which are primary; and into his ultimates those which are ultimate; so that man was made Divine order in form. Hence it is that all things in man and with man, are both from heaven and from the world, those of his mind from heaven, and those of his body from the world; for the things of heaven flow into his thoughts and affections, and dispose them according to reception by his spirit, and the things of the world flow into his sensations and pleasures, and dispose them according to reception in his body, but still in accommodation to their agreement with the thoughts and affections of his spirit. That it is so, may be seen in several articles in the work on *Heaven and Hell*, especially in the following: That the Whole Heaven, in one complex, has reference to one man (n. 59–67); each society in the Heavens likewise (n. 68–72); that hence every Angel is in a perfect human form (n. 73–77); and that this is from the Divine Human of the Lord (n. 78–86). And moreover under the article on the Correspondence of all things of Heaven with all things of Man (n. 87–102). On the Correspondence of Heaven with all things on earth (n. 103–115). And on the Form of Heaven (n. 200–212). From this order of creation it may appear, that such is the binding chain of connection from firsts to lasts that all things together make one, in which the prior cannot be separated from the posterior (just as a cause cannot be separated from its effect); and that thus the spiritual world cannot be separated from the natural, nor the natural world from the spiritual; thence neither the angelic heaven from the human race, nor the human race from the angelic heaven. Wherefore it is so provided by the Lord, that each shall afford a mutual assistance to the other, that is, the angelic heaven to the human race, and the human race to the angelic heaven. Hence it is, that the angelic mansions are indeed in heaven, and to appearance separate from the mansions where men are; and yet they are with man in his affections of good and truth. Their presentation to sight, as separate, is from appearances; as may be seen in an article in the work on *Heaven and Hell*, where Space in Heaven is treated of (n. 191–199). That the mansions of angels are with men in their affections of good and truth, is meant by these words of the Lord:—

He who loveth Me, keepeth my words, and my Father will love him, and we will come unto him, and make our mansion with him (*John* xiv. 23).

By "the Father" and "the Lord" in the above passage is also meant heaven, for where the Lord is, there is heaven, since the Divine proceeding from the Lord makes heaven, as may be seen in the work on *Heaven and Hell* (n. 7–12; and n. 116–125). And likewise by these words of the Lord:—

The Comforter the Spirit of Truth abideth with you, and is in you (*John* xiv. 17).

"The Comforter" is the Divine truth proceeding from the Lord, for which reason He is also called "the Spirit of truth," and the Divine truth makes heaven, and also the angels, because they are recipients; that the Divine proceeding from the Lord is the Divine truth, and that the angelic heaven is from it, may be seen in the work on *Heaven and Hell* (n. 126–140). The like is also understood by these words of the Lord:—

The kingdom of God is within you (*Luke* xvii. 21).

"The kingdom of God" is the Divine good and truth, in which the angels are. That angels and spirits are with man, and in his affections, has been granted me to see a thousand times, from their presence and abode with me; but angels and spirits do not know with what men they are, neither do men know the angels and spirits they cohabit with, for the Lord alone knows and disposes this. In a word, there is an extension into heaven of all the affections of good and truth, and a communication and conjunction with those who are in the like affections there; and there is an extension into hell of all the affections of evil and falsity, and a communication and conjunction with those who are in the like affections there. The extension of the affections into the spiritual world, is almost like that of sight into the natural world; communications in both are nearly similar; yet with this difference, that in the natural world there are objects, but in the spiritual world angelic societies. Hence it appears, that the connection of the angelic heaven with the human race is such that the one subsists from the other, and that the angelic heaven without the human race would be like a house without a foundation, for heaven closes into it and rests upon it. The case herein is the same as with each particular man; his spiritual things, which pertain to his thought and will, inflow into his natural things, which pertain to his sensations and actions, and in these they terminate and subsist. If man were not in possession of them, that is, if he were without these boundings and ultimates, his spiritual things, which pertain to the thoughts and affections of his spirit, would flow away, like things unbounded, or like those which have no foundation. In like manner, when a man passes from the natural into the spiritual world, which takes place when he dies, then because he is a spirit, he no longer subsists on his own basis, but upon the common basis, which is the human race. He who knows not the arcana of heaven, may believe that angels subsist without men, and men without angels; but I can affirm from all my experience of heaven, and from all my discourse with the angels, that no angel or spirit subsists without man, and no man without spirits and angels, but that there is a mutual and reciprocal conjunction. From this, it may now be seen that the human race and the angelic heaven make one, and mutually and reciprocally subsist from each other, and thus that the one cannot be taken away from the other.

10. II. *The human race is the seminary of heaven*, will appear from a subsequent article, in which it will be shown, that heaven and hell are from the human race, and that therefore the human race is the seminary of heaven. It must, however, first be mentioned, that as heaven has been formed of the human race, from the first creation until now, so it will be formed and filled up from the same source hereafter. It is indeed possible that the human race on one earth may perish, which comes to pass when they separate themselves entirely from the Divine, for then man no longer has spiritual life, but only natural, like that of beasts; and when man is such no society can be formed, and held bound by laws, since without the influx of heaven, and thus without the Divine government, man would become insane, and rush unchecked into every wickedness, one against another. But although the human race, by separation from the Divine, might perish on one earth, which, however, is provided against by the Lord, yet still they would continue on other earths; for that there are earths in the universe to some hundreds of thousands, may be seen in the little work, *The Earths in our Solar System called Planets, and the Earths in the Starry Heaven*. It was said to me from heaven, that the human race on this earth would have perished, so that not one man would have existed on it at this day, if the Lord had not come into the world, and on this earth assumed the Human, and made it Divine; and also, unless the Lord had given here such a Word as might serve for a basis to the angelic heaven, and for its conjunction. That the conjunction of heaven with man is by the Word, may be seen in the work on *Heaven and Hell* (n. 303-310). But that such is the case can be comprehended only by those who think spiritually, that is, by those who through the acknowledgment of the Divine in the Lord are conjoined with heaven, for they alone are able to think spiritually.

11. III. *The extension of heaven, which is for angels, is so immense, that it cannot be filled to eternity*, appears from what has been said in the work on *Heaven and Hell*. On the Immensity of Heaven (n. 415-420); and *That they are but few* *respectively of whom heaven is at present formed*, in the little work on the *Earths in the Universe* (n. 126).

12. IV. *The perfection of heaven increases according to its numbers*, is evident from its form, according to which its associations are disposed in order, and its communications flow, for it is the most perfect of all; and in proportion to the increase of numbers in that most perfect form, there is given a direction and consent of more and more to unity, and therefore a closer and a more unanimous conjunction; the consent and the conjunction derived from it increase from numbers, for everything is there inserted as a mediate relation between two or more, and what is inserted confirms and conjoins. The form of heaven is like the form of the human mind, the perfection of which increases according to the increase of truth and good, from whence are its intelligence and wisdom. The form of the human mind, which is in heavenly wisdom and intelligence, is like the form of heaven, because the mind is the least image of that form; hence it is, that on all sides there is a communication of the thoughts and affections of good and truth in such men, and in angels, with surrounding societies of heaven; and an extension according to the increase of wisdom, and thus according to the plurality of the knowledges of truth implanted in the intellect and according to the abundance of the affections of good implanted in the will; and therefore in the mind, for the mind consists of the intellect and the will. The human and angelic mind is such that it may be infilled to eternity, and as it is infilled, so it is perfected; and this is especially the case, when man is led by the Lord, for he is then introduced into genuine truths, which are implanted in his intellect, and into genuine goods, which are implanted in his will, for the Lord then disposes all things of such a mind into the form of heaven, until at length it is a heaven in the least form. From this comparison, which is a true parallel, it is evident, that the increasing number of the angels perfects heaven. Moreover, every form consists of various parts; a form which does not consist of various parts, is not a form, for it has no quality, and no changes of state; the quality of every form results from the arrangement of various things within it, from their mutual relation, and from their consent to unity, from which every form is considered as one; such a form, in proportion to the multitude of the various things arranged within it, is the more perfect, for every one of them, as was said above, confirms, corroborates, conjoins, and so perfects. But this is still more evident from what has been shown in the work on *Heaven and Hell*, especially where it treats of this: That every Society of Heaven is a Heaven in a lesser form, and every Angel a heaven in the least form (n. 51–58); and also in the article, On the Form of Heaven, according to which Consociations and Communications have place there (n. 200–212); and On the Wisdom of the Angels of Heaven (n. 265–275).

13. V. *Every Divine work has respect to infinity and eternity*, is evident from many things which exist both in heaven and in the world: in neither of them is there ever given one thing exactly similar to, or the same as, another: no two faces are either alike or identical, nor will be to eternity: in like manner the mind of one is never altogether like that of another; wherefore there are as many faces and as many minds as there are men and angels. There never exists in any one man (in whom yet there are innumerable parts which constitute his body, and innumerable affections which constitute his mind) any one thing quite alike, or identical with any one thing in another man; hence it is that every one leads a life distinct from the life of another. The same order exists in the whole and in every part of nature. That such infinite variety is in each and in all, is because they all originate from the Divine, which is infinite; hence there is a certain image of infinity everywhere, to the end that the Divine may regard all things as His own work, and at the same time, that all things, as His work, may have respect to the Divine. A familiar instance may serve to illustrate the manner in which every thing in nature has respect to infinity and eternity. Any seed, be it the produce of a tree, or of grain, or of a flower, is so created, that it may be multiplied to infinity, and endure to eternity. For from one seed are produced many, five, ten, twenty, a hundred, and from each of these again as many more; such fructification from one seed continuing but for a century, would cover the surface not only of one, but of myriads of earths; the same seeds are so created, that their durations may be eternal. Hence it is evident, how the idea of infinity and eternity is in them; and the like is true in all other cases. The angelic heaven is the end for which all things in the universe were created, for it is the end on account of which the human race exists, and the human race is the end regarded in the creation of the visible heaven, and the earths included in it. Wherefore that Divine work, namely, the angelic heaven, primarily has respect to infinity and eternity, and therefore to its multiplication without end, for the Divine Himself dwells therein. Hence also it is clear, that the human race will never cease, for were it to cease, the Divine work would be limited to a certain number, and thus its looking to infinity would perish.

III.

HEAVEN AND HELL ARE FROM THE HUMAN RACE.

14. It is altogether unknown in the Christian world that heaven and hell are from the human race; for it is believed that angels were created at the beginning, and that heaven was formed of them; and that the Devil or Satan was an angel of light, who, becoming rebellious, was cast down with his crew, and that this was the origin of hell. The angels are greatly astonished at such a faith in the Christian world, and still more, that nothing at all is there known of heaven, when yet it is a primary doctrine in the church; and since such ignorance prevails, they are rejoiced in heart that it has now pleased the Lord to reveal to men many things concerning heaven, and also concerning hell; and by this means, as far as possible, to dissipate the darkness which daily increases, because the church has come to its end. Wherefore they wish me to declare from them, that there is in the universal heaven not one who was created an angel from the first, nor any devil in hell who was created an angel of light, and cast down, but that all both in heaven and in hell are from the human race; in heaven those who had lived in the world in heavenly love and faith, and in hell those who had lived in infernal love and faith; and that hell in the whole complex is called the Devil and Satan; that the hell behind, where those are who are called evil genii, is the Devil, and the hell in front, which is the abode of evil spirits, is Satan.[3] What the nature of one hell is, and what the other, may be seen in the work on *Heaven and Hell*, towards the end. The angels said, that the Christian world have conceived such a belief about those in heaven and hell, from certain passages in the Word no otherwise understood than according to the sense of the letter, and not illustrated and explained by genuine doctrine from the Word; when yet the sense of the letter, if the genuine doctrine of the church does not shine before it, draws the mind away into various opinions; whence come ignorance, heresies, and errors.[4]

15. Another cause of such a belief in the man of the church is, that he believes that no one can go to heaven or hell before the time of the Last Judgment; of which he has conceived this opinion that the visible world is then to perish, and a new one will come into existence, and that then the soul will return into its body, and from their conjunction man will again live a man. This belief involves another about the angels, that they were created from the beginning; for it is impossible to believe that heaven and hell are from the human race, when it is believed that no man goes there till the end of the world. But in order that man may be convinced that it is not so, it has been granted me to have fellowship with angels, and also to speak with those who are in hell, and this now for many years, sometimes continuously from morning even to evening, and thus to be informed concerning heaven and hell; to the end that the man of the church may no longer remain in his erroneous belief, about a resurrection at the day of judgment, about a state of the soul in the interval, as well as about angels, and about the Devil; which belief, since it is a belief in falsity,

---

[3] The hells, or the infernals, taken together, are called the Devil and Satan (n. 694). They who have been devils in the world, become devils after death (n. 968).

[4] The doctrine of the church must be from the Word (n. 3464, 5402, 6832, 10,-763, 10,765). The Word is not understood without doctrine (n. 9021, 9409, 9424, 9430, 10,324, 10,431, 10,582). True doctrine is a lamp to those who read the Word (n. 10,401). Genuine doctrine must be from those who are in illustration from the Lord (n. 2510, 2516, 2519, 9424, 10,105). They who are in the sense of the letter of the Word without doctrine, can come into no understanding of Divine truths (n. 9409, 9410, 10,582). And they are led into many errors (n. 10,431). The difference between those who teach and learn from the doctrine of the church from the Word, and those who teach and learn only from the sense of the letter of the Word (n 9025).

induces darkness; and with those who think of such things from their own intelligence, brings on doubt, and at length denial; for they say in heart, how can so vast a heaven, and so many stars, with sun and moon, be destroyed and dissipated? and how can the stars fall from heaven upon the earth, which yet are larger than the earth? and how can bodies, eaten up by worms, consumed by putrefaction, and scattered to all the winds, be collected again for its own soul? in the meantime, where is the soul, and what is it without the senses which it had in the body? with such like sayings on matters, which being incomprehensible, fall not within belief, and destroy in many the faith in man's eternal life, in heaven and hell, and with them, in all the remaining things of the faith of the church. That faith has thus been destroyed is evident from those who say, Who ever came from heaven and told us that it exists? What is hell? Is it anything at all? What is the meaning of man's being tormented with fire to eternity? What is the day of judgment? Has it not been expected for ages in vain? and many more questions which involve a denial of all things. Lest therefore, they who think thus (as do many who, from their knowledge in worldly matters are reputed skilful and learned), should any longer disturb and seduce the simple in faith and heart, and induce infernal darkness concerning God, heaven, eternal life, and other subjects dependent upon these, the interiors of my spirit have been opened by the Lord, and thus it has been granted me to speak with all those of the deceased whom I ever knew in the life of the body, with some for days, with some for months, and with some for a year, and also with so many others, that I should come short if I reckoned them at an hundred thousand, of whom many were in the heavens, and many in the hells. I have also spoken with some two days after their decease, and told them that solemn preparations were then making for their funerals; to which they said, that it was well to reject that which had served them for a body and its functions in the world: and they desired me to say that they are not dead, but alive and equally men as before, and that they had only passed out of one world into another; and they did not know that they had lost anything, since they are in a body and its senses as before, and in intellect and will as before, and have like thoughts and affections, like sensations, pleasures, and desires, as in the world. Most of those newly deceased, when they saw that they were living men as before, and in a similar state (for after death the state of every one's life is at first similar to what it was in the world, but is successively changed with him either into heaven or into hell), were affected with new joy at being alive, and said that they had not believed this. But they greatly wondered that they had been in such ignorance and blindness concerning the state of their own lives after death; and more especially, that the man of the church is in such a state, when yet he of all in the world can be in light concerning them.[5] Then for the first time they saw the cause of this blindness and ignorance, which is, that external things, which are worldly and corporeal, had occupied and filled their minds to such an extent, that they could not be elevated into the light of heaven and behold the things of the church, which are beyond its doctrinals. For mere darkness inflows from corporeal and worldly things, when they are so much loved as they are at the present day, when man wishes to think of the things of heaven, beyond the dictate of the doctrine of faith of his church.

16. Very many of the learned from the Christian world are amazed when they see themselves after death in a body, in garments, and in houses as they were in the world; and when they recall to memory what they had thought of the life after death, of the soul, of spirits, of heaven and of hell, they are affected with shame, declare that they have thought foolishly, and that the simple in faith are much wiser than they. The learned were explored, who had confirmed themselves in such things, and who had attributed all things to nature, and it was found,

---

[5] At this day few in Christendom believe that man rises again immediately after death, Pref. to chap. xvi. of *Gen.* and (n. 4622, 10,758). But at the time of the Last Judgment, when the visible world is to perish (n. 10,591). The cause of such belief (n. 10,594, 10,758). Nevertheless man does rise again immediately after death, and that then he is a man as to each and all things (n. 4527, 5006, 5078, 8939, 8991, 10,594, 10,758). The soul, which lives after death, is man's spirit, which is the real man in the man, and which also in the other life is in a perfect human form (n. 322, 1880, 1881, 3633, 4622, 4735, 5883, 6054, 6605, 6626, 7021, 10,594). The same from experience (n. 4527, 5006, 8939). And from the Word (n. 10,597). What is meant by the dead being seen in the holy city (*Matt.* xxvii. 53) is explained (n. 9229). How man is raised from the dead; by experience (n. 168–189). Of his state after resuscitation (n. 317–319, 2119, 5070, 10,596). False opinions about the soul and the resurrection (n. 444, 445, 4527, 4622, 4658).

that the interiors of their minds were closed, and the exteriors opened, so that they had not looked to heaven, but to the world, and hence also to hell; for so far as the interiors of the mind are opened, so far man looks to heaven; but so far as the interiors are closed, and the exteriors opened, so far he looks to hell; for the interiors of man are formed for the reception of all things of heaven, and his exteriors for the reception of all things of the world, and they who receive the world, and not at the same time heaven, receive hell.[6]

17. That the spirit of man, after its release from the body, is a man, and in a similar form, has been attested to me by the daily experience of many years; for I have seen, heard, and spoken with spirits a thousand times; and even on this very subject; that men in the world do not believe them to be such, and that they who do believe it, are accounted as simple by the learned. The spirits were grieved in heart, that such ignorance should still prevail in the world, and most of all in the church; but this, they said, proceeded principally from the learned, who thought of the soul from the sensual corporeal; wherefore they have conceived no other idea of it, than as of mere thought; which, when it is regarded without any subject in which and from which it is viewed, is like some volatile form of pure ether, which is necessarily dispersed when the body dies. But since the church from the Word believes in the immortality of the soul, they were obliged to ascribe it to some vital quality, such as belongs to thought, though not the sensation which man has, till it is again conjoined to its body. On this opinion is founded the doctrine of the resurrection at the time of the Last Judgment, and a belief in the conjunction of the soul and the body then; for from this hypothesis about the soul, coupled with the belief of the church in man's eternal life, no other conclusion can be reached: hence it is, that when any one thinks of the soul, from the doctrine and the hypothesis together, he does not at all comprehend that it is a spirit, and that this is in the human form. Add to this, that scarcely any one at this day knows what the spiritual is, and still less that they

---

[6] In man the spiritual and the natural worlds are conjoined (n. 6057). Man's internal is formed in the image of heaven, but his external in the image of the world (n. 3628, 4523, 4524, 6057, 6314, 9706, 10,156, 10,472).

who are spiritual, as all spirits and angels are, have any human form. Hence it is, that almost all who come from the world are greatly amazed that they are alive, and are equally men as before, with no difference whatever. But when they cease to be amazed at themselves, they then wonder that the church knows nothing of this state of men after death, when yet all who have ever lived in the world, are in the other life, and live as men. And because they have also wondered why this was not manifested to man by visions, it was told them from heaven, that this could be done, for nothing is easier, when the Lord pleases, but that still they who had confirmed themselves in falsities against it, would not believe, even though they themselves were to see it; and moreover that it is perilous to manifest anything from heaven to those who are in worldly and corporeal things, for in this case they would first believe and afterwards deny, and thus profane the very truth itself; for to believe and afterwards to deny, is to profane; and they who profane, are thrust down into the lowest and most grievous of all the hells. It is this danger which is meant by these words of the Lord:—

He hath blinded their eyes, and hardened their hearts, lest they should see with the eyes and understand with the heart, and convert themselves, and I should heal them (*John* xii. 40).

Also that they who are in worldly and corporeal loves, still would not believe, is meant by these words:—

Abraham said to the rich man in hell, They have Moses and the prophets, let them hear them; but he said, Nay, father Abraham, but if one from the dead come to them, they will be converted; but Abraham said to him, if they hear not Moses and the prophets, neither will they believe even if one rose from the dead (*Luke* xvi. 29-31).

18. That heaven is from the human race, is evident from this, that angelic and human minds are similar; both enjoying the faculty of understanding, of perceiving, and of willing; both being formed for receiving heaven. For the human mind possesses wisdom as well as the angelic; but it is not so wise in the world, because it is in a terrestrial body, in which its spiritual mind thinks naturally, for its spiritual thought, which it has in common with an angel, then flows down into the natural ideas corresponding with the spiritual, and is thus perceived in them. But it is otherwise when the mind of man is freed from its connection with the body; then it no longer thinks naturally but spiritually; and when spiritually it then thinks what is incomprehensible and ineffable to the natural man, as an angel does. Hence it is evident, that man's internal, which is called his spirit, in its essence is an angel.[7] That an angel is in a perfect human form, may be seen in the work on *Heaven and Hell* (n. 73–77): but when man's internal is not opened above, but only below, then still, after its removal from the body, it is in a human form, but a direful and diabolical one, for it cannot look upwards to heaven, but only downwards to hell.

19. That heaven and hell are from the human race, the church moreover might have known from the Word, and made it a part of its doctrine, if it had admitted enlightenment from heaven, and had attended to the Lord's words to the robber, that:—

To-day he should be with Him in paradise (*Luke* xxiii. 43);

and to those which the Lord spake concerning the rich man and Lazarus, that:—

The one went to hell, and spoke thence with Abraham, and that the other went to heaven (*Luke* xvi. 19–31).

Also to what the Lord told the Sadducees respecting the resurrection, that:—

God is not the God of the dead, but of the living (*Matt.* xxii. 32).

And furthermore they might have known it from the common faith of all who live well, especially from their faith in the hour of death, when they are no longer in worldly and corporeal things, in that they believe they will go to heaven, as soon as the life of their body departs. This faith prevails with all, so long as they do not think, from the doctrine of the church, of a resurrection at the time of the Last Judgment. Inquire into the subject and you will be confirmed that it is so.

---

[7] There are as many degrees of life in man, as there are heavens, and they are opened after death according to his life (n. 3747, 9594). Heaven is in man (n. 3884). The men who are living a life of love and charity, have angelic wisdom in them, but that it is then latent, and that they come into it after death (n. 2494). In the Word, the man who receives the good of love and of faith from the Lord, is called an angel (n. 10,528).

20. He who has been instructed concerning Divine order, may moreover understand, that man was created to become an angel, because in him is the ultimate of order (see above n. 9), in which *ultimate*, whatever belongs to celestial and angelic wisdom may be formed, renewed, and multiplied. Divine order never subsists in the mediate, so as to form anything there without an ultimate, for it is not in its own fulness and perfection, but it proceeds to the ultimate. But when it is in its ultimate, it then forms, and also by mediates there collated, renews and produces itself farther, which is effected by procreations; wherefore the seminary of heaven is there. This also is meant by the things related of man, and of his creation in the first chapter of *Genesis:*—

God said, Let us make man in our image, according to our likeness; and God created man in His image, in the image of God created He him; male and female created He them; and God blessed them, and God said unto them, be fruitful and multiply (vers. 26–28).

"To create in the image of God, and in the likeness of God," is to confer upon man all things of Divine order from firsts to ultimates, and thus to make him an angel as to the interiors of his mind.

21. That the Lord rose again not only as to the Spirit, but also as to the Body, is because the Lord, when He was in the world, glorified His whole Human, that is, made it Divine. For the soul, which He had from the Father, was the Divine Itself from Himself, and the body was made a similitude of the soul, that is of the Father, and therefore also Divine. Hence it is that He Himself, unlike any man, rose again as to both;[8] which He also manifested to His disciples, who believed they saw a spirit when they saw Him; for he said:—

Behold My hands and My feet, that it is I Myself: feel Me and see, for a spirit has not flesh and bones, as ye see Me have (*Luke* xxiv. 36–39).

By which He pointed out that He was not only Man as to the Spirit, but also as to the body.

---

[8] Man rises again as to the spirit only (n. 10,593, 10,594). The Lord alone rose as to the body also (n. 1729, 2083, 5078, 10,825).

22. Moreover that heaven and hell are from the human race, has been shown in many articles in the work on *Heaven and Hell* as in the following: Of the Nations and People in Heaven who are out of the Church (n. 318–328). Of Infants in Heaven (n. 329–345). Of the Wise and the Simple in Heaven (n. 346–356). Of the Rich and the Poor in Heaven (n. 357–365). Every Man is a Spirit, as regards his own interiors (n. 432–444). Man after Death is in a perfect human Form (n. 453–460). Man after Death is in all the sense, memory, thought, and affection, which he had in the world, and leaves nothing but his terrestrial body (n. 461–469). Of the First state of man after Death (n. 491–498). Of the Second State of man after Death (n. 499–511). Of his Third state (n. 512–517). See moreover what is said of the Hells (n. 536–588). From all these articles it may be seen, that heaven does not consist of any angels created in the beginning, nor hell of any devil and his crew, but solely of those who have been born men.

IV.

ALL WHO HAVE EVER BEEN BORN MEN FROM THE BEGINNING OF CREATION, AND ARE DECEASED, ARE EITHER IN HEAVEN OR IN HELL.

23. I. *This follows from what has been said and shown in the preceding article, namely, that heaven and hell are from the human race.*

II. *And from this, that every man after the life in the world, lives to eternity.*

III. *Thus all who have ever been born men from the creation of the world, and are deceased, are either in heaven or in hell.*

IV. *Since all who will be born hereafter, will also come into the spiritual world, that world is so vast, and is such that the natural world, in which are men on earth, cannot be compared with it.*

But in order that all these things may be the more distinctly perceived, and more plainly evident, I will expound and describe them one by one.

24. I. That all who have ever been born men from the beginning of creation, and are deceased, are either in heaven or in hell, *follows from those things which have been said and shown in the preceding article, namely, that heaven and hell are from the human race.* This is clear without explanation. It has been the common belief hitherto, that men will not come into heaven or into hell before the day of the Last Judgment, when souls will return into their own bodies, and thus to enjoy such things as are believed to belong only to the body. The simple have been led into this belief by men professing wisdom, who have investigated the interior state of man. Because these have thought nothing concerning the spiritual world, but only of the natural world, nor therefore of the spiritual man, they have not known that the spiritual man which is in every natural man, is in the human form, as well as the natural man. Hence it never entered their minds that the natural man draws his own human form from his spiritual man; although they might have seen that the spiritual man acts at will upon the whole, and upon every part of the natural man, and that the natural man of himself does nothing at all. It is the spiritual man who thinks and wills, for this the natural man of himself cannot do; and thought and will are the all in all of the natural man; for the natural man acts as the spiritual man wills, and also speaks as the spiritual thinks, and that so entirely, that action is nothing but will, and speech is nothing but thought, for on the removal of thought and will, speech and action cease in a moment. From this it is evident that the spiritual man is truly a man, and that he is in the whole, and in every part of the natural man, and that therefore their effigies are alike, for the part or particle of the natural man, in which the spiritual does not act, does not live. But the spiritual man cannot appear to the natural man, for the natural cannot see the spiritual, but the spiritual can see the natural; for this is according to order, but the converse is contrary to order; since there is given an influx, and therefore also a sight, of the spiritual into the natural, for sight too is influx, but not the reverse. It is the spiritual man who is called the spirit of man, and who appears in the spiritual world in a perfect human form, and lives after death. Because they who are intelligent have not known anything of the spiritual world, and therefore nothing of the spirit of man, as was said above, they have conceived therefore an idea that man cannot live a man, before his soul returns into the body, and again puts on the senses. Hence have arisen such vain ideas about man's resurrection, namely, that bodies, though eaten up by worms and fish, or entirely fallen to dust, are to be collected again by the Divine omnipotence, and re-united to souls; and that this is not to happen till the end of the world, when the visible universe is to perish; with many more like ideas, which are every one of them inconceivable, and at the first glance of the mind, strike it as impossible, and contrary to Divine order, tending thus to weaken the faith of many; for those who think wisely, cannot believe what they do not in some measure comprehend; and belief in impossibilities is not given, that is, a belief in such things as man thinks to be impossible. Hence also those who disbelieve the life after death, derive an argument in support of their denial. But that man rises again immediately after his decease, and that then he is in a perfect human form, may be seen in the work on *Heaven and Hell*, in many of its articles. These things have been said, that it may be still more confirmed that heaven and hell are from the human race, from which it follows, that all who were ever born men from the beginning of creation, and are deceased, are either in heaven or in hell.

25. II. *That every man after the life in the world lives to eternity*, is evident from this, that man is then spiritual, and no longer natural, and that the spiritual man, separated from the natural, remains such as he is to eternity, for man's state cannot be changed after death. Moreover, the spiritual of every man is in conjunction with the Divine, since it can think of the Divine, and also love the Divine, and be affected with all things which are from the Divine, such as those which the church teaches, and therefore it can be conjoined to the Divine by thought and will, which are the two faculties of the spiritual man, and constitute his life; and that which can thus be conjoined to the Divine, can never die, for the Divine is with it, and conjoins it to Himself. Man is also created to the form of heaven as to his mind, and the form of heaven is from the Divine itself, as may be seen in the work on *Heaven and Hell*, where it has been shown, That the Divine of the Lord makes and forms Heaven (n. 7–12, and n. 78–86). That Man is created to be a Heaven in the least form (n. 57). That Heaven in the whole complex, has reference to one Man (n. 59–66). That hence an Angel is in a perfect human Form (n. 73–77); an angel is a man as to his spiritual. On this subject moreover, I have often spoken with the angels, who wondered exceedingly, that of those who are called intelligent in the Christian world, and who also are believed by others to be intelligent, there are very many who utterly reject the belief in their own immortality, believing that the soul of man is dissipated at death, just as the soul of a beast is; not perceiving the distinction between the life of a man and the life of a beast; that man has the power of thinking above himself, of God, of heaven, of love, of faith, of good, spiritual and moral, of truths, and the like, and that thus he may be elevated to the Divine itself, and be conjoined by all those things to Him; but that beasts cannot be elevated above their own natural, to think of such things, and consequently that their spiritual cannot be separated from their natural after death,[9] so as to live by itself, as man's spiritual can: whence also it is, that the life of a beast ceases on the dissipation of its natural life. The reason why many of the so-called intelligent in the Christian world, have no belief in the immortality of their own lives, the angels declared to be this, that in heart they deny the Divine, and acknowledge nature instead of the Divine; and they who think from such principles, are not able to think of any eternity by conjunction with the Divine, nor consequently, of the state of man as dissimilar to that of beasts, for in rejecting the Divine from thought, they also reject eternity. They declared more-

---

[9] There is also an influx from the spiritual world into the lives of beasts, but that it is general, and not special as with man (n. 1633, 3646). The distinction between men and beasts is, that men can be elevated above themselves to the Lord, can think of the Divine, love it, and may thus be conjoined to the Lord, whence they have eternal life; but it is otherwise with beasts, which cannot be elevated to such things (n. 4525, 6323, 9231).

over, that with every man there is an inmost or supreme degree of life, or an inmost or supreme something into which the Divine of the Lord proximately inflows, and from which He disposes all the remaining interiors belonging to the spiritual and natural man, which are successive in both according to the degrees of order. This inmost or supreme they called the Lord's entrance into man, and His veriest dwelling place with him; and they said, that by this inmost or supreme, man is man, and is distinguished from brute animals which do not have it; and that hence it is, that men, as regards the interiors which are of the mind and disposition, unlike animals, can be elevated by the Lord to Himself, can have faith in Him, be affected by love to Him, and can receive intelligence and wisdom, and speak from reason. When I asked them concerning those who deny the Divine, and the Divine truths, by which the conjunction of the life of man with the Divine itself is effected, and who yet live to eternity, they replied, that these also have the faculty of thinking and of willing, and therefore of believing and loving the things which are from the Divine, as well as those who acknowledge the Divine, and that by this faculty, they too live to eternity; they added, that this faculty is from that inmost or supreme which is in every man, of which mention was made above; that even those who are in hell have that faculty, and that they derive from it the power of reasoning and speaking against Divine truths, has been shown in many places. Hence it is, that every man lives to eternity, whatever be his quality. Because every man after death lives to eternity, no angel or spirit ever thinks of death; indeed they do not at all know what it is to die; wherefore, when "death" is mentioned in the Word, the angels understand by it either damnation, which is death in the spiritual sense, or the continuation of life and the resurrection.[10] These things have been said in confirmation that all the men who have ever been born, and have died, from the beginning of creation, are alive, some in heaven, and some in hell.

---

[10] When "death" is mentioned in the Word, and spoken of the wicked, in heaven are understood damnation, which is spiritual death, and also hell (n. 5407, 6119, 9008). They who are in goods and truths are called "living," but they who are in evils and falsities "dead" (n. 81, 290, 7494). By "death," when spoken of the good who die, resurrection and continuation of life are understood in heaven, for at death man rises again, continues his own life, and advances in it to eternity (n. 3498, 3505, 4618, 4621, 6036, 6222).

26. III. *In order that I might know that all who have ever been born men from the beginning of creation, and are deceased, are either in heaven or in hell,* it has been granted me to speak with some who lived before the flood; and also with some who lived after the flood; and with certain of the Jewish nation, who are made known to us from the Word of the Old Testament; with some who lived in the Lord's time; with many who lived in the ages succeeding, even down to the present day; and moreover with all those of the dead, whom I had known during their lives in the body; and likewise with infants; and with many of the Gentiles. From this experience I have been fully convinced, that there is not even one, who was ever born a man, from the first creation of this earth, who is not in heaven or in hell.

27. IV. *Because all, who are to be born hereafter, must also come into the spiritual world, that world is so vast and such, that the natural world, in which men are on earth, cannot be compared with it;* this is evident from the immense multitude of men who have passed into the spiritual world since the first creation, and who are together there; as well as from the continual increase hereafter from the human race, which will be added to them, and this without end, according to what has been shown above, in an article for the purpose (n. 6–13), namely, that the procreations of the human race on the earths will never cease. When my eyes have been opened, it has sometimes been granted me to see how immense, even now, is the multitude of men who are there; it is so great that it can scarcely be numbered, such myriads are there, and this only in one place, towards one quarter; what then must the numbers be in the other quarters? For all are there collected into societies, and the societies exist in vast numbers, and each society, in its own place, forms three heavens, and three hells under them; wherefore there are some who are on high, some who are in the middle, and some who are below them; and underneath, there are those who are in the lowest places, or in the hells; and those who are above dwell among themselves as men dwell in cities, in which hundreds of thousands are together. Whence it is evident, that the natural world, the abode of men on earth, cannot be compared with that world, as regards the multitude of the human race; so that when man passes from the natural world into the spiritual, it is like going from a village into a great city. That the natural world cannot be compared with the spiritual world as to quality, may appear from this, that not only have all the things which are in the natural world an existence there, but innumerable others besides, which never were seen in this world, nor can be presented to the sight, for spiritual things there are effigied each to its own type by appearances, as if natural, each with an infinite variety; for the spiritual so far exceeds the natural in excellence, that the things are few which can be produced to the natural sense; the natural sense not receiving one of the thousands which the spiritual mind receives; and all things which belong to the spiritual mind, are presented, even in forms to their sight. This is the reason why it is impossible to describe what the spiritual world is, as regards its magnificent and stupendous things. These moreover increase in proportion to the multiplication of the human race in the heavens, for all things are there presented in forms which correspond to the state of each as to love and faith, and thence as to intelligence and wisdom; thus with a variety which increases continually, as the multitude increases. Whence it has been said by those who have been elevated into heaven, that they saw and heard things there, which no eye has ever seen, and no ear has ever heard. From these things, it may appear that the spiritual world is such, that the natural world cannot be compared with it. Moreover, what it is, may be seen in the work on *Heaven and Hell*, where it treats of the two Kingdoms of Heaven (n. 20–28). Of the Societies of Heaven (n. 41–50). Of Representatives and Appearances in Heaven (n. 170–176). Of the Wisdom of the Angels of Heaven (n. 265–275). The things there described, however, are very few.

V.

THE LAST JUDGMENT MUST BE WHERE ALL ARE TOGETHER, THUS IN THE SPIRITUAL WORLD, AND NOT ON EARTH.

28. Concerning the Last Judgment, it is believed that the Lord will then appear in the clouds of heaven with the angels in glory, and awaken from the sepulchres all who have ever lived since the beginning of creation, clothing their souls with their bodies; and thus summoned together He will judge them, those who have done well, to eternal life or heaven, those who have done ill, to eternal death or hell. The churches derive this belief from the sense of the letter of the Word, nor could it be removed, so long as men did not know that there is a spiritual sense within each thing which is said in the Word, and that this sense is the Word itself, to which the sense of the letter serves for a foundation or basis, and that without such a letter, the Word could not have been Divine, or have served in heaven, as in the world, for the doctrine of life and faith, and for conjunction. He therefore who knows the spiritual things corresponding to the natural things in the Word, can know that by "the Lord's coming in the clouds of heaven," is not meant such an appearance of Him, but His appearance in the Word; for "the Lord" is the Word, because He is the Divine truth; "the clouds of heaven" in which He is to come, are the sense of the letter of the Word, and "the glory" is its spiritual sense; "the angels" are the heaven from which He will appear, and they also are the Lord as to Divine truths.[11] Hence the meaning of these words is now evident, namely, that when

---

[11] The Lord is the Word, because He is the Divine truth in heaven (n. 2533, 2813, 2859, 2894, 3393, 3712). The Lord is the Word, also because it is from Him, and treats of Him (n. 2859); and because it treats of the Lord alone, and primarily of the glorification of His Human in its inmost sense, so that the Lord Himself is therein (n. 1873, 9357). The coming of the Lord is His presence in the Word, and revelation (n. 3900, 4060). "Clouds" in the Word signify the Word in the letter, or the sense of its letter (n. 4060, 4391, 5922, 6343, 6752, 8106, 8781, 9430, 10,551, 10,574). "Glory" in the Word signifies Divine truth, such as it is in heaven, and such as it is in the spiritual sense (n. 4809, 5922, 8267, 8427, 9429, 10,574). "Angels" in the Word signify Divine truths from the Lord, since angels are receptions of them, and do not speak them from themselves, but from the Lord (n. 1925, 2821, 3039, 4085, 4295, 4402, 6280, 8192, 8301). "Trumpets" or "cornets," which the angels then have, signify Divine truths in heaven and revealed from heaven (n. 8815, 8823, 8915).

the end of the church is, the Lord will open the spiritual sense of the Word, and thus the Divine truth, such as it is in itself; therefore that this is the sign that the Last Judgment is at hand. That there is a spiritual sense within each thing and expression in the Word, and what it is may be seen in the *Arcana Cœlestia*, in which each and all things of *Genesis* and *Exodus* are explained according to that sense; and a collection of passages extracted from it, concerning the Word and its spiritual sense, may be seen in the little work on *The White Horse, Mentioned in the Apocalypse*.

29. That the Last Judgment must be in the spiritual world, and not in the natural world, or on the earth, is evident from the two preceding articles, and also from those that follow. In the two preceding articles it has been shown, that heaven and hell are from the human race; and that all who were ever born men since the beginning of creation, and are deceased, are either in heaven or in hell, thus that all are there together; but in the articles which follow it shall be shown that the Last Judgment has already been accomplished.

30. Moreover, no one is judged from the natural man, thus not so long as he lives in the natural world, for man is then in a natural body; but every one is judged in the spiritual man, and therefore when he comes into the spiritual world, for man is then in a spiritual body. It is the spiritual in man which is judged, but not the natural, for this cannot be held guilty of any fault or crime, since it does not live of itself, but is only the servant, and instrument by which the spiritual man acts (see n. 24). Hence also it is, that judgment is effected upon men when they have put off their natural, and put on their spiritual bodies. In the spiritual body moreover, man appears such as he is with respect to love and faith, for every one in the spiritual world is the effigy of his own love, not only as to the face and the body, but also as to the speech and the actions (see the work on *Heaven and Hell*, n. 481). Hence it is, that the qualities of all are known, and they are immediately separated, whenever the Lord pleases. From what has been said it is plain, that judgment is effected in the spiritual world, but not in the natural world, or on the earth.

31. That the natural life in man effects nothing, but his spiritual life in the natural, since what is natural of itself is void of life; and that the life which appears in it, is from the life of the spiritual man, thus that this is what is judged; and moreover that being "judged according to deeds," means that man's spiritual is judged, may be seen in the work on *Heaven and Hell*, in the article headed, That Man after Death is such as his Life in the World was (n. 470–484).

32. To these things I will add a certain heavenly arcanum, which is indeed mentioned in the work on *Heaven and Hell*, but has not yet been described. Every one after death is bound to some society, even when first he comes into the spiritual world (see that work, n. 427–497). But a spirit in his first state is ignorant of it, for he is then in his externals and not yet in his internals. When he is in this state, he goes hither and thither, wherever the desires of his mind impel him; but still actually, he is where his love is, that is, in a society where those are who are in a love like his own. When a spirit is in such a state he then appears in many other places, in all of them also present as it were with the body, but this is only an appearance. Wherefore as soon as he is led by the Lord into his own ruling love, he vanishes instantly from the eyes of others, and is among his own, in the society to which he was bound. This peculiarity exists in the spiritual world, and is wonderful to those who are ignorant of its cause. Hence now it is, that as soon as spirits are gathered together, and separated, they are also judged, and every one is presently in his own place, the good in heaven, and in a society there among their own, and the evil in hell, and in a society there among their own. From these things it is moreover evident, that the Last Judgment can exist nowhere but in the spiritual world, both because every one there is in the likeness of his own life, and because he is with those who are in similar life, and thus everyone is with his own. But it is otherwise in the natural world; the good and the evil can dwell together there, the one ignorant of what the other is, nor are they separated from each other according to the love of their life. Indeed it is impossible for any one in the natural body, to be either in heaven or in hell;

wherefore in order that man may come into one or the other, it it necessary that he put off his natural body, and be judged in the spiritual body. Hence it is, as was said above, that the spiritual man is judged, and not the natural.

VI.

THE LAST JUDGMENT EXISTS, WHEN THE END OF THE CHURCH IS; AND THE END OF THE CHURCH IS, WHEN THERE IS NO FAITH, BECAUSE THERE IS NO CHARITY.

33. There are many reasons why the Last Judgment exists when the end of the church is. The principal reason is, that then the equilibrium between heaven and hell begins to perish, and with the equilibrium man's freedom itself; and when man's freedom perishes, he can no longer be saved, for he cannot then be led to heaven in freedom, but from freedom is borne to hell; for no man can be reformed without freedom, and all man's freedom is from the equilibrium between heaven and hell. That it is so, may appear from two articles in the work on *Heaven and Hell*, where it treats, Of the Equilibrium between Heaven and Hell (n. 589-596): and, That Man is in that Freedom by means of that Equilibrium between Heaven and Hell (n. 597-603); and further, that no man can be reformed except in freedom.

34. That the equilibrium between heaven and hell begins to perish at the end of the church, may appear from this, that heaven and hell are from the human race, as shown above in its own article, and that when few men come into heaven, and many into hell, evil on the one part increases over good on the other; for evil increases in proportion as hell increases, and all man's evil is from hell, and all his good is from heaven. Now since evil increases over good at the end of the church, all are then judged by the Lord, the evil are separated from the good, all things are reduced into order, and a new heaven is established, and also a new church upon earth, and thus the equilibrium is restored. It is this then which is called the Last Judgment, of which more will be said in the following articles.

35. It is known from the Word, that the end of the church is, when faith no longer exists within it, but it is not yet known, that there is no faith, if there is no charity; therefore something shall now be said upon this subject. It is predicted by the Lord that there is no faith at the end of the church:—

When the Son of Man comes shall He find faith on the earth (*Luke* xviii. 8);

and also that there is no charity then:—

In the consummation of the age iniquity will be multiplied, the charity of many will grow cold, and this gospel will be preached in all the world, and then shall the end come (*Matt.* xxiv. 12, 14).

"The consummation of the age" is the last time of the church. The state of the church successively decreasing as to love and faith, is described by the Lord in this chapter, but it is described there by mere correspondences, and therefore the things therein predicted by the Lord cannot be understood, unless the spiritual sense corresponding to each expression there is known; on which account it has been granted me by the Lord to explain in the *Arcana Cœlestia* the whole of that chapter and a part of the next, concerning the consummation of the age, His advent, the successive vastation of the church, and the Last Judgment; see in the *Arcana Cœlestia* (n. 3353–3356, 3486–3489, 3650–3655, 3751–3757, 3897–3901, 4056–4060, 4229–4231, 4332–4335, 4422–4424, 4635–4638, 4661–4664, 4807–4810, 4954–4959, 5063–5071).

36. Something shall now be said concerning this, that there is no faith, if there is no charity. It is supposed that faith exists, so long as the doctrinals of the church are believed; or that they who believe, have faith; and yet mere believing is not faith, but willing and doing what is believed, is faith. When the doctrinals of the church are merely believed, they are not in man's life, but only in his memory, and thence in the thought of his external man; nor do they enter into his life, before they enter into his will, and thence into his actions: then for the first time does faith exist in man's spirit; for man's spirit, the life of which is his life itself, is formed from his will, and from so much of his thought as proceeds from his will; the memory of man, and the thought derived from it, being only the outer court by which introduction is effected. Whether you say the will, or the love, it is the same, since every one wills what he loves, and loves what he wills; and the will is the receptacle of love, and the intellect, the function of which is to think, is the receptacle of faith. A man may know, think, and understand many things, but those which do not accord with his will or love, he rejects from him when he is left to himself, to meditate from his own will or love, and therefore he also rejects them after the life of the body, when he lives in the spirit; for that alone remains in man's spirit which has entered into his will or love, as was said above. Other things after death are viewed as foreign, which he casts out of doors, and regards with aversion, because they are not of his love. But it is another thing when man not only believes the doctrinals of the church which are from the Word, but wills them, and does them; then he has faith; for faith is the affection of truth from willing truth because it is truth; for to will truth itself because it is truth is the spiritual man, for it is withdrawn from the natural, which consists in willing truth, not for truth's sake, but for the sake of self-glory, fame and gain. Truth regarded apart from such things is spiritual, because in its essence it is Divine; wherefore, to will truth because it is truth, is also to acknowledge, and to love the Divine. These two are altogether conjoined, and are also regarded as one in heaven, for the Divine which proceeds from the Lord in heaven is Divine truth, as may be seen in the work on *Heaven and Hell* (n.128–132), and they are angels in the heavens, who receive it, and make it of their life. These things are said, in order that it may be known, that faith is not only to believe, but to will and do, therefore there is no faith if there is no charity. Charity or love is to will and to do.

37. That within the church at this day, faith is so rare, that it can scarcely be said to exist at all, was made evident, from many both learned and simple, whose spirits were explored after death, as to what their faith had been in the world; and it was found, that every one of them supposed faith to be merely to believe, and to persuade himself that it is so; and that the more learned of them placed it entirely in believing, with trust or confidence that they are saved by the Lord's passion and His intercession, and that scarcely one among them knew that there is no faith, if there is no charity, or love; yea, they did not know what charity to the neighbor is, nor the difference between thinking and willing. For the most part they turned their backs upon charity, saying that charity effects nothing, but faith only. When it was said to them, that charity and faith are one, like the will and the understanding, and that charity has its seat in the will, and faith in the understanding, and that to separate the one from the other, is like separating the will from the understanding, this they did not understand. Whence it was made evident to me that scarcely any faith exists at the present day. This also was shown them to the life. They who were in the persuasion that they had faith, were led to an angelic society, where genuine faith existed, and when they were made to communicate with it, they clearly perceived that they had no faith, which afterwards moreover, they confessed in the presence of many. The same thing was also shown by other means to those who had made a profession of faith, and had thought they believed, without having lived the life of faith, which is charity; and every one of them confessed that they had no faith, because they had nothing of it in the life of their spirits, but only in some thought extrinsic to it, whilst they lived in the natural world.

38. Such is the state of the church at this day, namely, that in it there is no faith because there is no charity; and where there is no charity, there is no spiritual good, for that good exists from charity alone. It was said from heaven that there is still good with some, but that it cannot be called spiritual, but natural good, because Divine truths themselves are in obscurity, and Divine truths introduce to charity, for they teach it, and regard it as their end and aim; whence no other charity can exist than such as the truths are which form it. The Divine truths from which the doctrines of the churches are derived, respect faith alone, on which account they are called the doctrines of faith, and do not look to life; and truths which only regard faith and not life, cannot make man spiritual; for so long as they are out of the life they are only natural, being merely known and thought of like other things. Hence it is that spiritual good is not given at the present day, but only natural good with some. Moreover every church in the beginning is spiritual, for it begins from charity; but in the course of time it turns aside from charity to faith, and then from being an internal church it becomes an external one, and when it becomes external its end is, since it then places everything in knowledge, and little or nothing in life. Thus also as far as man from being internal becomes external, spiritual light is darkened within him, until he no longer sees Divine truth from truth itself, that is from the light of heaven, for Divine truth is the light of heaven, but only from natural light; which is of such a nature, that when it is alone, and not illumined by spiritual light, it sees Divine truth as it were in night, and recognizes it as truth for no other reason than that it is so called by the leader, and is received as such by the common assembly. Hence it is, that their intellectual faculty cannot be illustrated by the Lord, for as far as natural light shines in the intellectual faculty, in so far spiritual light is obscured. Natural light shines in the intellectual faculty, when worldly, corporeal, and earthly things are loved in preference to spiritual, celestial, and Divine things; so far also man is external.

39. But since it is not known in the Christian world that there is no faith if there is no charity, nor what charity towards the neighbor is, nor even that the will constitutes the man himself, and the thought only in as far as it is derived from the will, therefore, in order that these subjects may come into the light of the understanding, I will adjoin a collection of passages concerning them from the *Arcana Cœlestia*, which may serve for illustration.

FROM THE ARCANA CŒLESTIA.

FAITH.

They who do not know that all things in the universe refer themselves to truth and good, and to the conjunction of both, in order to the production of anything, do not know that all things of the church refer themselves to faith and love, and to the conjunction of both (n. 7752–7762, 9186, 9224). All things in the universe refer themselves to truth and good, and to their conjunction (n. 2452, 3166, 4390, 4409, 5232, 7256, 10,122, 10,555). Truths belong to faith, and goods to love (n. 4352, 4997, 7178, 10,367).

They who do not know that each and all things in man have relation to the understanding and the will, and to the conjunction of both, in order that man may be man, also do not know that all things of the church have relation to faith and love, and to their conjunction, in order that the church may be in man (n. 2231, 7752–7754, 9224, 9995, 10,122). Man has two faculties, one of which is called the understanding, and the other the will (n. 641, 803, 3623, 3539). The understanding is dedicated to the reception of truths, or of those things which belong to faith; and the will to the reception of goods, or of those things which belong to love (n. 9300, 9930, 10,064). Hence it follows, that love or charity makes the church, and not faith alone, or faith separated from them (n. 809, 916, 1798, 1799, 1834, 1844, 4766, 5826).

Faith separated from charity is no faith (n. 654, 724, 1162, 1176, 2049, 2116, 2343, 2349, 2417, 3849, 3868, 6348, 7039, 7342, 9783). Such faith perishes in the other life (n. 2228, 5820). Doctrinals concerning faith alone, destroy charity (n. 6353, 8094). They who separate faith from charity are represented in the Word by Cain, by Ham, by Reuben, by the first-born of the Egyptians, and by the Philistines (n. 3325, 7097, 7317, 8093). As far as charity departs, in so far prevails a religion respecting faith alone (n. 2231). The church in process of time turns aside from charity to faith, and at length to faith alone (n. 4683, 8094). In the last time of the church there is no faith, because there is no charity (n. 1843, 3488, 4689). They who make faith alone saving, excuse a life of evil; and they who are in a life of evil, have no faith, because they have no charity (n. 3865, 7766, 7778, 7790, 7950, 8094). They are inwardly in the falsities of their own evil, although they do not know it (n. 7790, 7950). Therefore good cannot be conjoined to them (n. 8981, 8983). Also in the other life they are opposed to good, and to those who are in good (n. 7097, 7127, 7317, 7502, 7545, 8096, 8313). The simple in heart know better than the learned what the good of life is, and thus what charity is, but not what separated faith is (n. 4741, 4754).

Good is the *esse*, and truth the *existere* derived from it, and thus the truth of faith has its own *esse* of life from the good of charity (n. 3049, 3180, 4574, 5002, 9154). Hence the truth of faith lives from the good of charity, or charity is the life of faith (n. 1589, 1947, 1997, 2571, 4070, 4096, 4097, 4736, 4757, 4884, 5147, 5928, 9154, 9667, 9841, 10,729). Faith is not alive in man, when he only knows and thinks of the things of faith, but when he wills them, and from willing, does them (n. 9224). The conjunction of the Lord with man is not by faith, but by the life of faith, which is charity (n. 9380, 10,143, 10,153, 10,578, 10,645, 10648). Worship from the good of charity is true worship, but worship from the truth of faith, without the good of charity, is merely an external act (n. 7724).

Faith alone, or faith separated from charity, is as the light of winter, in which all things of the earth are torpid, and nothing is produced; but faith with charity is as the light of spring and of summer, in which they all bloom and are made productive (n. 2231, 3146, 3412, 3413). The wintry light, which is that of separated faith, in the other life is turned into dense darkness, when the light of heaven inflows; and they who are in that faith, then come into blindness and stupidity (n. 3412, 3413). They who separate faith from charity, are in darkness, and thus in ignorance of truth, and thence in falsities, for falsities are darkness (n. 9186). They cast themselves into falsities, and thence into evils (n. 3325, 8094). The errors and falsities into which they cast themselves (n. 4721, 4730, 4776, 4783, 4925, 7779, 8313, 8765, 9224). The Word is closed against them (n. 3773, 4783, 8780). They do not see and attend to all the things which the Lord so often spake concerning love and charity, which see (n. 1017, 3416). They neither know what good is, what heavenly love is, nor what charity is (n. 2517, 3603. 4136, 9995).

Charity makes the church, and not faith separated from charity (n. 809, 916, 1798, 1799, 1834, 1844). How much of good would exist in the church, if charity were regarded as primary (n. 6269, 6272). The church would be one, and not divided into many, if charity were its essential; and then it would be unimportant if men did differ on the doctrines of faith and of external worship (n. 1285, 1316, 2385, 2853, 2982,

3267, 3445, 3451, 3452). All in heaven are regarded from charity, and none from faith without it (n. 1258, 1394, 2364, 4802).

The twelve disciples of the Lord represented the church, as to the all of faith and charity, in one complex, as in like manner did the twelve tribes of Israel (n. 2129, 3354, 3488, 3858, 6397). Peter, James and John, represented faith, charity, and the goods of charity, in their order (n. 3750). Peter represented faith (n. 4738, 6000, 6073, 6073, 6344, 10,087, 10,580). And John the goods of charity (Pref. to chap. xviii. and xxii. of *Genesis*). In the last times, there would be no faith in the Lord, because no charity, was represented by Peter's denying the Lord three times, before the cock crew twice;[1] for Peter there in a representative sense is faith (n. 6000, 6073). "Cock-crowing," as well as "twilight," signifies in the Word the last time of the church (n. 10,134). And "three" or "thrice," signify what is complete to the end (n. 2788, 4495, 5159, 9198, 10,127). The like is signified by what the Lord said to Peter, when Peter saw John following the Lord:—

What is it to thee, Peter? Follow thou Me, John;

for Peter said of John:—

What is he (*John* xxi. 21, 22; n. 10,087)?

John rested on the breast of the Lord, because he represented the goods of charity (n. 3934, 10,081). All the names of persons and places in the Word signify things abstracted from them (n. 768, 1888, 4310, 4442, 10,329).

CHARITY.

That heaven is distinguished into two kingdoms, one of which is called the celestial kingdom, and the other the spiritual; love in the celestial kingdom is love to the Lord, and is called celestial love; and love in the spiritual kingdom is charity towards the neighbor, and is called spiritual love (n. 3325, 3653, 7257, 9002, 9835, 9961). Heaven is distinguished into those two kingdoms, may be seen in the work on *Heaven and Hell* (n. 20–28). And the Divine of the Lord in the heavens is love to Him, and charity towards the neighbor (n. 13–19), in the same work.

It is not known what good and truth are, unless it be known what love to the Lord and charity towards the neighbor are, because all good is of love and charity, and all truth is of good (n. 7255, 7366). To know truths, to will truths, and to be affected by truths for truth's sake, that is, because they are truths, is charity (n. 3876, 3877). Charity consists in an internal affection of doing truth, and not in an external affection without it (n. 2429, 2442, 3776, 4899, 4956, 8033). Therefore charity consists in performing uses for the sake of uses, and its kind is according to the uses (n. 7038, 8253). Charity is man's spiritual life (n. 7081). The whole Word is the doctrine of love and charity (n. 6632, 7262). Men at this day do not know what charity is (n. 2417, 3398, 4776, 6632). Still it may be known from the light of reason, that love and charity constitute man (n. 3957, 6273). Also that good and truth agree together, and one belongs to the other; therefore charity and faith do the like (n. 7627).

In the supreme sense the Lord is the neighbor, because He is to be loved above all things; hence all that is the neighbor which is from Him, and in which He is; therefore good and truth are the neighbor (n. 2425, 3419, 6706, 6819, 6823, 8124). The distinction of neighbor is according to the quality of good; thus according to the presence of the Lord (n. 6707–6710). Every man, and every society, also our country, and the church, and in the universal sense the kingdom of the Lord, are the neighbor; and to do well by them, from the good of love, according to their several states, is to love the neighbor; thus the neighbor is their good, which we ought to consult (n. 6818–6824, 8123). Civil good, which is justice, and moral good, which is the good of life in society, are also the neighbor (n. 2915, 4730, 8120–8122). To love the neighbor is not to love the person, but that in him which makes him the neighbor, that is, good and truth (n. 5028, 10,336). They who love the person, and not that which makes the neighbor in him, love the evil as well as the good (n. 3820). And they do service to the evil as well as to the good, when yet to serve the evil is to injure the good, and this is not to love the neighbor (n. 3820, 6703, 8120). The judge who punishes the evil to amend them, and lest they should corrupt the good, loves the neighbor (n. 3820, 8120, 8121).

To love the neighbor is to do what is good, just, and upright in every work, and in every function (n. 8120–8122). Hence charity towards the neighbor extends itself, both in general and in particular, to all that a man thinks, wills, and does (n. 8124). To do good and truth for the sake of good and truth, is to love the neighbor (n. 10,310, 10,336). They who do this, love the Lord, who in the supreme sense, is the neighbor (n. 9210). A life of charity is a life according to the Lord's precepts; so that to live according to Divine truths, is to love the Lord (n. 10,143, 10,153, 10,310, 10,578, 10,645).

Genuine charity is not meritorious (n. 2027, 2343, 2400, 3887, 6388–6393). Because it is from an internal affection, thus from the delight of doing good (n. 2373, 2400, 3887, 6388–6393). They who separate faith from charity, in the other life make a merit of faith, and of the good works they did, as matters of external form (n. 2373).

The doctrine of the ancient church was the doctrine of life, which is the doctrine of charity (n. 2385, 2417, 3419, 3420, 4844, 6628). The ancients, who were of the church, arranged the goods of charity in order, and distinguished them into classes, giving names to each, and this was the source of their wisdom (n. 2417, 6629, 7259–7262). Wisdom and intelligence increase immensely in the other life, with those who have lived a life of charity in the world (n. 1941, 5859). The Lord inflows with Divine truths into charity, because into the very life of man (n. 2363). Man is as a garden, when charity and faith are conjoined in him, but as a desert when they are not conjoined (n. 7626). Man recedes from wisdom in proportion as he recedes from charity (n. 6630). They who are not in charity, are in ignorance of Divine truths, howsoever wise they may think themselves (n. 2417, 2435). The angelic life consists in performing the goods of charity, which are uses (n. 454). The spiritual angels are forms of charity (n. 553, 3804, 4735).

THE WILL AND THE UNDERSTANDING.

Man has two faculties, one of which is called the understanding, and the other the will (n. 35, 641, 3539, 10,122). Those two faculties make the man himself (n. 10,076, 10,109, 10,110, 10,264, 10,284). The man is such, as those two faculties are in him (n. 7342, 8885, 9282, 10,264, 10,284). By them also man is distinguished from the beasts, because the understanding of man may be elevated by the Lord, and see Divine truths, and his will may be elevated equally, and perceive Divine goods; and thus man may be conjoined to the Lord by those two faculties, which make him man; but that it is not so with beasts (n. 4525, 5114, 5302, 6323, 9232). And since man, in that faculty, is above the beasts, he cannot die as to his interiors, which belong to his spirit, but he lives to eternity (n. 5302).

All things in the universe refer themselves to good and truth; thus in man to the will and the understanding (n. 803, 10,122). For the understanding is the recipient of truth, and the will of good (n. 3332, 3623, 5835, 6065, 6125, 7503; 9300, 9930). It amounts to the same whether you say truth, or faith, for faith is of truth, and truth is of faith; and also whether you say good, or love, for love is of good, and good is of love; for what a man believes, he calls truth; and what he loves, he calls good (n. 4353, 4997, 7178, 10,122, 10,367). Hence it follows, that the understanding is the recipient of faith, and the will is the recipient of love (n. 7179, 10,122, 10,367). And since man's understanding may be receptive of faith towards God, and his will of love towards God, that he may be conjoined to God by faith and love, and whoso can be conjoined to God by faith and love, can never die (n. 4525, 6323, 9231).

The will of man is the very *esse* of his life, since it is the receptacle of love or good, and the understanding is the *existere* of his life derived from it, since it is the receptacle of faith or truth (n. 3619, 5002, 9282). Thus the life of the will is the principal life of man, and the life of the understanding proceeds from it (n. 585, 590, 3619, 7342, 8885, 9282, 10,076, 10,109, 10,110). Just as light proceeds from fire or flame (n. 6032, 6314). The things which enter the understanding and the will at the same time, are appropriated to man, but not those which enter the understanding alone (n, 9009, 9069, 9071, 9133, 9182, 9386, 9393, 10,076, 10,109, 10,110). Those things become properties of man's life, which are received by the will (n. 3161, 9386, 9393). Hence it follows, that man is man from the will, and from the understanding thence (n. 8911, 9069, 9071, 10,076, 10,109, 10,110). Every man moreover is loved and esteemed by others, according to the good of his will and the understanding thence; for he who wills well, and understands well, is loved and esteemed, but he who understands well, and does not will well, is rejected and despised (n. 8911, 10,076). Man also after death remains as his will, and the understanding thence (n. 9069, 9071, 9386, 10,153). And those things which belong to the understanding, and not at the same time to the will, then vanish away, because they are not in man (n. 9282). Or, what amounts to the same, man remains after death as his love, and its derivative faith are, or as his good and its derivative truth are; and the things which belong to faith, and not at the same time to love, or the things which belong to truth, and not at the same time to good, then vanish away, because they are not in man, and thus not of man (n. 553, 2363, 10,153). Man may receive in the understanding what he does not do from the will, or he may understand what he cannot will, because it is against his love (n. 3539). The reason why man scarcely knows the distinction between thinking and willing (n. 9995).

How perverted is the state of those whose understanding and will do not act in unity (n. 9075). Such is the state of hypocrites, of deceivers, of flatterers, and of dissemblers (n. 2426, 3573, 4799, 8250).

All the will of good, and all the derivative understanding of truth are from the Lord; not so the understanding of truth, separated from the will of good (n. 1831, 3514, 5482, 5649, 6027, 8685, 8701, 10,153). It is the understanding which is enlightened by the Lord (n. 6222, 6608, 10,659). The understanding is enlightened as far as man receives truth in the will, that is, as far as he wills to do according to it (n. 3619). The understanding has light from heaven, as the sight has light from the world (n. 1524, 5114, 6608, 9128). The understanding is such, as are the truths from good of which it is formed (n. 10,064). The understanding is that which is from truths from good, but not that which is from falsities from evil (n. 10,675). The understanding is the seeing, from matters of experience and science, truths, the causes of things, connections, and consequences, in series (n. 6125). The understanding is the seeing and perceiving whether a thing be truth, before it is confirmed, but not the being able to confirm every thing (n. 4741, 7012,

7680, 7950, 8521, 8780). The seeing and perceiving whether a thing be truth before it is confirmed, is given to those only who are affected with truth for the sake of truth, and are thus in spiritual light (n. 8521). The light of confirmation is natural light, communicable even to the evil (n. 8780). That all dogmas, even false ones, may be confirmed, until they appear like truths (n. 2243, 2385, 4647, 4741, 5033, 6865, 7950).

VII.

ALL THE THINGS WHICH ARE PREDICTED IN THE APOCALYPSE, ARE AT THIS DAY FULFILLED.

40. No one can know what all the things which are contained in the *Apocalypse* signify and involve, unless he knows the internal or spiritual sense of the Word; for everything there is written in a style similar to that of the prophecies of the Old Testament, in which each Word signifies some spiritual thing, which does not appear in the sense of the letter. Besides, the contents of the *Apocalypse* cannot be explained as to their spiritual sense, except by one who also knows how it went with the church, even to its end, which can only be known in heaven, and is the thing contained in the *Apocalypse*. For the spiritual sense of the Word treats everywhere of the spiritual world, that is, of the state of the church in the heavens, as well as in the earth; hence the Word is spiritual and Divine. It is this state which is there expounded in its own order. Hence it may appear, that the things contained in the *Apocalypse* can never be explained by any one but him to whom a revelation has been made concerning the successive states of the church in the heavens; for there is a church in the heavens as well as on the earth, of which something shall be said in the following articles.

41. The quality of the Lord's church on earth, cannot be seen by any man, so long as he lives in the world, still less how the church in process of time has turned aside from good to evil. The reason is, that man whilst he is living in the world, is in externals, and only sees those things which appear before his natural man; but the quality of the church as to spiritual things, which are its internals, does not appear in the world. Yet it does appear in heaven as in clear day, for the angels are in spiritual thought, and also in spiritual sight, and hence see nothing but spiritual things. Furthermore, all the men who have been born in this world from the beginning of creation are together in the spiritual world, as shown above, and are all there distinguished into societies according to the goods of love and faith, as may be seen in the work on *Heaven and Hell* (n. 41–50); whence it is that the state of the church, and its progressions, are manifest in heaven before the angels. Now since the state of the church as to love and faith is described in the spiritual sense of the *Apocalypse*, therefore no one can know what all the things in its series involve, but he to whom it has been revealed from heaven, and to whom at the same time it has been granted to know the internal or spiritual sense of the Word. This I can assert, that each thing there, nay, that every word, contains within it a spiritual sense, and all things of the church, as to its spiritual state, from the beginning to the end, are fully described in that sense; and because every word there signifies some spiritual thing, therefore not a word can be wanting without the series of things in the internal sense thereby suffering a change; on which account, at the end of that book, it is said:—

If any one shall take away from the words of the book of this prophecy, God will take away his part out of the book of life, and from that holy city, and from those things which are written in that book (*Apoc.* xxii. 19).

It is the same with the books of the Old Testament; in them also every thing, and every word, contains an internal or spiritual sense, wherefore not one word can be taken away from them either. Hence it is that, of the Lord's Divine providence, those books have been preserved entire to an iota since the time in which they were written, and by the care of many who have enumerated their minutest particulars; this was provided by the Lord on account of the sanctity which is within each iota, letter, word, and thing they contain.

42. Since in like manner there is an internal or spiritual sense in every word in the *Apocalypse*, and since that sense contains the arcana of the state of the church in the heavens, and on the earth; and since those arcana can be revealed to no one, but to him who knows that sense, and to whom at the same time it has been granted to have consort with the angels, and to speak spiritually with them, therefore, lest the things which are therein written should be hidden to men, and should hereafter be disregarded, because they are not understood, its contents have been disclosed to me; but because they are many they cannot be described in this little work. On which account I will explain the whole book from beginning to end, and disclose the arcana which are within it. This explanation shall be published in less than two years, together with certain things in *Daniel*, which have hitherto lain hidden, because their spiritual sense was unknown.

43. He who does not know the internal or spiritual sense, never can divine what is meant in the *Apocalypse* by "the dragon," and by "the battle" of Michael and his angels with it; what by "the tail" with which the dragon drew down the third part of the stars from heaven; what by "the woman" who brought forth the son a male, which was caught up to God, and whom the dragon persecuted; what by "the beast ascending from the sea," and "the beast ascending from the earth," which had so many horns; what by "the harlot," with whom the kings of the earth committed whoredom; what by the first and second "resurrection," and by "the thousand years"; what by "the lake of sulphur and of fire," into which the dragon, the beast, and the false prophet were cast; what by "the white horse"; also what by "the former heaven, and the former earth" which passed away; and what by "the new heaven and the new earth," in the place of the former; and by "the sea," which was no more; also what by "the city New Jerusalem descending from heaven," and by its "measures," "wall," "gates," and "foundation of precious stones"; what by the various "numbers"; besides other things, which are the deepest mysteries to those who know nothing of the spiritual sense of the Word. But the meaning of all these things shall be unfolded in the promised explanation of that book.

44. It has been remarked before, that all the things which are contained in that book, in the heavenly sense, are now fulfilled. In this little work I will deliver some general account of the Last Judgment, the Babylon destroyed, the first heaven and the first earth which passed away, the new heaven, the new earth, and the New Jerusalem; in order that it may be known, that all things are now accomplished. But the details can only be delivered, where all these things are explained according to the description of them in the *Book of Revelation*.

VIII.

THE LAST JUDGMENT HAS BEEN ACCOMPLISHED.

45. It was shown above, in an article for the purpose, that the Last Judgment does not exist on the earth, but in the spiritual world, where all from the beginning of creation are together; and since it is so, it is impossible for any man to know when the Last Judgment is accomplished, for every one expects it to exist on earth, accompanied by a change of all things in the visible heaven, and on the earth and in the human race there. Lest therefore the man of the church from ignorance should live in such a belief, and lest they who think of the Last Judgment should expect it forever, whence at length the belief in those things which are said of it in the literal sense of the Word must perish, and lest perchance therefore many should recede from a belief in the Word, it has been granted me to see with my own eyes that the Last Judgment is now accomplished; that the evil are cast into the hells, and the good elevated into heaven, and thus that all things are reduced into order, the spiritual equilibrium between good and evil, or between heaven and hell, being thence restored. It was granted me to see from beginning to end how the Last Judgment was accomplished; and also how Babylon was destroyed, also how those who are meant by "the dragon" were cast into the abyss, and how the New Heaven was formed, and the New Church instituted in the heavens, which is meant by "the New Jerusalem." It was granted me to see all these things with my own eyes, in order that I might be able to testify of them. This Last Judgment was commenced in the beginning of the year 1757, and was fully accomplished at the end of that year.

46. But it is to be known that the Last Judgment was effected upon those who had lived from the Lord's time to this day, but not upon those who had lived before. For a Last Judgment had twice before existed on this earth; one which is described in the Word by "the flood," the other was effected by the Lord Himself when He was in the world, which is also meant by the Lord's words:—

Now is the judgment of this world, now is the prince of this world cast out (*John* xii. 31);

and in another place:—

These things I have spoken unto you that in Me ye may have peace; be of good cheer, I have overcome the world (*John* xvi. 33);

and also by these words in *Isaiah:*—

Who is this that cometh from Edom, walking in the multitude of His strength, great to save? I have trodden the wine-press alone, therefore I have trodden them in My anger; whence their victory is sprinkled upon My garments, for the day of vengeance is in My heart, and the year of My redeemed has come; therefore He became a Saviour (*Isa.* lxiii. 1-8);

and in many other places. A Last Judgment has twice before existed on this earth, because every judgment exists at the end of a church, as shown above in an article for the purpose, and there have been two churches on this earth, one before the flood, and one after it. The church before the flood is described in the first chapters of *Genesis* by the new creation of the heaven and the earth, and by paradise; its end, by the eating of the tree of science, and the subsequent particulars; and its Last Judgment by the flood; the whole by mere correspondences, according to the style of the Word; in the internal or spiritual sense of which, by "the creation of the heaven and the earth," the institution of a new church is meant, see the first article; by "the paradise in Eden," its celestial wisdom; by "the tree of science," and by "the serpent," the scientific which destroyed it; and by "the flood," the Last Judgment upon the men of whom it consisted. But the other church, which was after the flood, is also described in certain passages in the Word (as in *Deut.* xxxii. 7-14), and elsewhere. This church was extended through much of the Asiatic world, and was continued with the posterity of Jacob. Its end was, when the Lord came into the world. A Last Judgment was then effected by Him upon all who belonged to that church from its first institution; and, at the same time, upon the residue from the first church. The Lord came into the world for that end, to reduce all things in the heavens into order, and through the heavens all things on earth, and at the same time to make His Human Divine; for if this had not been done, no one could have been saved. That there were two churches on this earth before the Lord's coming is shown in various passages in the *Arcana Cœlestia*, a collection of which may be seen below;[12] and that the Lord came into the world to reduce all things in the heavens into order, and through them all things on earth, and to make His Human Divine.[13] The third church on this

---

[12] The first and Most Ancient Church on this earth was that which is described in the first chapters of *Genesis*, and it was a celestial church, the chief of all the churches (n. 607, 895, 920, 1121-1124, 2896, 4493, 8891, 9942, 10,545). Their quality; they who were of that church are in heaven (n. 1114-1125). They are in the greatest light there (n. 1117). There were various churches after the flood, which are called in one word, the Ancient Church (n. 1125-1127, 1327, 10,355). Through what kingdoms of Asia the Ancient Church was extended (n. 1238, 2385). The quality of the men of the Ancient Church (n. 609, 895). The Ancient Church was a representative church (n. 519, 521, 2896). What the quality of the Ancient Church was, when it began to decline (n. 1128). The distinction between the Most Ancient and Ancient Church (n. 597, 607, 640, 641, 765, 784, 895, 4493). Of the church that commenced from Eber, which was called the Hebrew church (n. 1238, 1241, 1343, 4516, 4517). The distinction between the Ancient and the Hebrew church (n. 1343, 4874). Of the church instituted among the posterity of Jacob, or sons of Israel (n. 4281, 4288, 4310, 4500, 4899, 4912, 6304, 7048, 9320, 10,396, 10,-526, 10,535, 10,698). The statutes, judgments and laws, which were commanded among the sons of Israel, were in part like those which existed in the Ancient Church (n. 4449). In what manner the representative rites of the church which was instituted among the sons of Israel, differed from the representative rites of the Ancient Church (n. 4288, 10,149). In the Most Ancient Church there was immediate revelation from heaven; in the Ancient Church revelation by correspondences; in the church among the sons of Israel, by a living voice; and in the Christian church by the Word (n. 10,355). The Lord was the God of the Most Ancient Church, and also of the Ancient Church, and was called Jehovah (n. 1343, 6846).

[13] The Lord, when He was in the world, reduced all things in the heavens and in the hells into order (n. 4075, 4287, 9937). The Lord then freed the spiritual world from the antediluvians (n. 1266). Their quality (n. 310, 311, 560, 562, 563, 570, 581, 586, 607, 660, 805, 808, 1034, 1120, 1265-1272). The Lord by temptations and victories subjugated the hells, and reduced all things into order, and at the same time glorified His Human (n. 4287, 9937). The Lord effected this by Himself, or by His own Power (n. 1692, 9937). The Lord alone fought (n. 8273). Hence the Lord alone became righteousness and merit (n. 1813, 2025-2027, 9715, 9809, 10,019). Thus the Lord united His Human with the Divine (n. 1725, 1729, 1733, 1737, 3318, 3381, 3382, 4286). The passion of the cross was the last temptation, and plenary victory, by which He glorified Himself, that is, made His Human Divine, and subjugated the hells (n. 2776, 10,655, 10,659, 10,828). The Lord could not be tempted as to the Divine itself (n. 2795, 2803, 2813, 2814). Therefore He assumed a human from the mother, into which He admitted temptations (n. 1414, 1444, 1573, 5041, 5157, 7193, 9315). He expelled whatever was hereditary from the mother, and put off the human he received from her, even until He was her son no longer, and He put on the Human Divine (n. 2159, 2574, 2649, 3036, 10,830). The Lord saved men by the subjugation of the hells, and the glorification of His Human (n. 4180, 10,019, 10,152, 10,655, 10,659, 10,828).

earth is the Christian. Upon this church, and, at the same time, upon all those who had been in the first heaven since the Lord's time, the Last Judgment of which I now treat, was effected.

47. How this Last Judgment was effected cannot be described in all its details in this little work, for they are many, but shall be described in the *Explanation of the Apocalypse*. For the judgment was accomplished not only upon all the men of the Christian church, but also upon all who are called Mohammedans, and, moreover, upon all the Gentiles in the whole world. And it was effected in this order: first upon those of the Papal religion; then upon the Mohammedans; afterwards upon the Gentiles; and lastly upon the Reformed. The judgment upon those who were of the Papal religion shall be shown in the following article, on Babylon which has been destroyed; the judgment upon the Reformed in the article, on the first heaven which passed away; but something shall be said in this article, on the judgment upon the Mohammedans and Gentiles.

48. The following was seen to be the arrangement in the spiritual world of all the nations and people to be judged. Collected in the middle, appeared those who are called the Reformed, where they were also distinct according to their countries; the Germans there towards the north; the Swedes there towards the west; the Danes in the west; the Dutch towards the east and the south; the English in the centre. Surrounding this whole mid-region in which were the Reformed, appeared collected those of the Papal religion, the greater part of them in the western, some part in the southern quarter. Beyond them were the Mohammedans, also distinct according to their countries, who all appeared in the south-west. Beyond these, the Gentiles were congregated in vast numbers, constituting the very circumference. Beyond these appeared as it were a sea, which was the boundary. This arrangement of the nations in the various quarters, was an arrangement according to each nation's common faculty of receiving Divine truths; for in the spiritual world every one is known from the quarter, and the part of it, in which he dwells; and, moreover, in a society with many, he is known from his tarryings with reference to the quarters; concerning which, see the work on *Heaven and Hell*

(n. 148, 149). It is the same when he goes from place to place; all advance to the quarters is then effected according to the successive states of the thoughts from the affections which belong to his own life; in accordance with which all those who are spoken of in what follows were led to their own places. In a word, the ways in which every one walks in the spiritual world are actual determinations of the thoughts of the mind; whence it is, that "ways," "walking," and the like, in the spiritual sense of the Word, signify the determinations and progressions of spiritual life.

49. In the Word, the four quarters are called "the four winds," and a gathering is called "a gathering from the four winds"; as where the Last Judgment is the subject treated of in *Matthew:*—

He shall send His angels, and they shall gather together the elect from the four winds, from one end of the heavens to the other (xxiv. 31);

and elsewhere:—

All nations shall be gathered together before the Son of man, and He shall separate them one from another, as a shepherd separates the sheep from the goats, and He shall set the sheep on the right and the goats on the left (*Matt.* xxv. 31, 32).

This signifies that the Lord will then separate those who are in truths and at the same time in good, from those who are in truths and not in good; for in the spiritual sense of the Word, "the right" signifies good, and "the left" truth, and "sheep" and "goats" the same. The judgment was effected upon these alone; the evil who were in no truths being in the hells already; for all the evil in heart who have denied the Divine, and have rejected the truths of the church from their belief are cast thither after death, and therefore before the judgment. "The first heaven" which passed away, consisted of those who were in truths, and not in good, and "the new heaven" was formed of those who were in truths, and at the same time in good.

50. As regards the judgment upon the Mohammedans and Gentiles, which is treated of in this article, it was thus effected. The Mohammedans were led forth from their places, where they were gathered together in the south-west, by a way round the

Christians, from the west, through the north, to the east, as far as its southern boundary; and the good were separated from the evil in the way. The evil were cast into marshes and lakes, many too being scattered about in a certain far desert. But the good were led through the east to a land of great extent near the south, and habitations were there given them. They who were led thither had in the world acknowledged the Lord as the greatest Prophet, and as the Son of God, and had believed that He was sent by the Father to instruct the human race, and at the same time had lived a moral spiritual life according to their religious principles. Most of these, when instructed, receive faith in the Lord, and acknowledge Him to be one with the Father. Communication is also granted them with the Christian heaven, by influx from the Lord; but they are not commingled with it, because religion separates them. All of that religion, as soon as they come into the other life among their own, first seek Mohammed, yet he does not appear, but in his place there are two others, who call themselves Mohammeds, and who have obtained seats in the middle, under the Christian heaven, towards the left part of it. These two are in the place of Mohammed, because all after death, whatever be their religion, are first led to those they had worshiped in the world, for every one's religion adheres to him, but they recede on perceiving that these can render them no assistance. They are thus yielded up into their own religion at first, as the only possible means of effecting their withdrawal from it. Where Mohammed himself is, and what he is, and whence come those two who fill his place, shall be told in the book in which the *Apocalypse* is explained.

51. The judgment was effected upon the Gentiles in nearly the same manner as upon the Mohammedans; but they were not led like them in a circuit, but only a short way in the west, where the evil were separated from the good, the evil being there cast into two great gulfs, which stretched obliquely into the deep, but the good were conducted above the middle, where the Christians were, towards the land of the Mohammedans in the eastern quarter, and dwellings were given them behind, and beyond the Mohammedans, to a great extent in the southern quarter. But those of the Gentiles who in the world had worshiped God under the Human form, and had led lives of charity according to their religious principles, were conjoined with Christians in heaven, for they acknowledge and adore the Lord more than others; the most intelligent of them are from Africa. The multitude of the Gentiles and Mohammedans who appeared, was so great, that it could be numbered only by myriads. The judgment on this vast multitude was effected in a few days, for every one after being yielded up into his own love and into his own faith, is immediately assigned and carried to his like.

52. From all these particulars appears the truth of the Lord's prediction concerning the Last Judgment, that:—

They shall come from the east and west, and from the north and south, and shall sit down in the kingdom of God (*Luke* xiii. 29).

IX.

BABYLON AND ITS DESTRUCTION.

53. That all the things which are predicted in the *Apocalypse* are at this day fulfilled, may be seen above (n. 40–44); and that the Last Judgment has already been accomplished, may be seen in the preceding article; where it is also shown how the judgment was effected upon the Mohammedans and Gentiles. Now follows an account of the manner in which it was effected upon the Papists, who are meant by "Babylon," which is treated of in many parts of the *Apocalypse*, and its destruction especially in chapter xviii., where it is thus described:—

An angel cried vehemently with a great voice, Babylon hath fallen, hath fallen, and has become the habitation of demons, and the hold of every foul spirit, and the cage of every unclean and hateful bird (v. 2).

But before it is told how that destruction was effected, I shall premise,

I. *What is meant by "Babylon," and what its quality is.*
II. *The quality of those in the other life who are of Babylon.*
III. *Where their habitations have hitherto been.*
IV. *Why they were there tolerated until the day of the Last Judgment.*

V. *How they were destroyed, and their habitations made a desert.*

VI. *Those of them who were in the affection of truth from good were preserved.*

VII. *The state of those hereafter who come thence from the earth.*

54. I. *What is meant by Babylon, and what its quality is.* By Babylon are meant all who wish to have dominion by religion. To have dominion by religion, is to have dominion over men's souls, thus over their very spiritual life, and to use the Divine things, which are in their religion, as the means. All those who have dominion for an end, and religion for the means are in general Babylon. They are called Babylon because such dominion began in ancient times; but it was destroyed in its beginning. Its commencement is described by the city and the tower, the head of which was to be in heaven; and its destruction, by the confusion of lips, whence its name Babel was derived (*Gen.* xi. 1–9). What the particulars there related mean in the internal or spiritual sense of the Word, may be seen explained in the *Arcana Cœlestia* (n. 1283–1328). Moreover that this dominion began and was instituted in Babel, appears in *Daniel*, where it is said of Nebuchadnezzar, that he set up an image which all were to adore (chap. iii.). And it is also meant by Belshazzar and his peers drinking out of the golden and silver vessels, which Nebuchadnezzar had carried away from the temple of Jerusalem, at the same time they worshiped gods of gold, silver, copper, and iron; wherefore it was written on the wall:—

He hath numbered, he hath weighed, he hath divided; and on the same night the king himself was slain (chap. v.).

"The vessels of gold and silver" of the temple of Jerusalem, signify the goods and truths of the church; "drinking out of them," and at the same time worshiping gods of gold, silver, copper, and iron, signify profanation; and "the writing upon the wall," and "the death of the king" signify visitation, and destruction denounced against those who make use of Divine goods and truths as means. What their quality is who are called Babylon, is also described sometimes in the prophets; as in *Isaiah:*—

> Thou mayest take up this parable concerning the king of Babylonia. Jehovah hath broken the staff of the wicked, the sceptre of those having dominion; thou, Lucifer, hast fallen from heaven; thou art cut down even to the earth; thou hast said in thy mind, I will ascend into the heavens; I will exalt my throne over the stars of God, and I will sit on the mountain of the assembly, in the sides of the north, I will become like the Most High. Nevertheless thou shalt be cast down into hell, to the sides of the pit; I will cut off the name and residue of Babylon and will cause her to become an hereditary possession of the bittern (xiv. 4, 5, 12, 13, 14, 15, 22, 23).

And again it is said in the same:—

> The lion said, Babylon is fallen, is fallen, and all the graven images of her god are cast down (xxi. 9).

See also (xlvii. and xlviii. 14–20; and *Jer.* l. 1–3). From these passages it is now evident what Babylonia is. It should be known that the church becomes Babylonia, when charity and faith cease, and the love of self begins to rule in their place; for this love in proportion as it is unchecked, rushes on, aiming to dominate not merely over all whom it can subject to itself on earth, but even over heaven; nor does it rest there, but it climbs the very throne of God, and transfers to itself His Divine power. That it did this, even before the Lord's coming, appears from the passages of the Word adduced above. But that Babylonia was destroyed by the Lord when He was in the world, both by their becoming altogether idolatrous, and by the Last Judgment upon them in the spiritual world. This is meant by the prophetic sayings, that "Lucifer," who there is Babylon, was cast into hell, and that "Babylon has fallen"; and moreover by "the writing on the wall," and "the death of Belshazzar"; and also by "the stone, hewn from the rock," which destroyed the statue, of which Nebuchadnezzar dreamed.

55. But Babylon treated of in the *Apocalypse*, is the Babylon of this day, which arose after the Lord's coming, and is known to be with the Papists. This Babylon is more pernicious and more heinous than that which existed before the Lord's coming, because it profanes the interior goods and truths of the church, which the Lord revealed to the world, when He revealed Himself. How pernicious, how inwardly heinous it is, may appear from the following summary. They acknowledge and adore the Lord apart from all power of saving: they en-entirely separate His Divine from His Human, and transfer to themselves His Divine power, which belonged to His Human;[14] for they remit sins; they send to heaven; they cast into hell; they save whom they will; they sell salvation; thus they arrogate to themselves what belongs to the Divine power alone: and since they exercise this power, it follows that they make gods of themselves, each one according to his station, by transference from the highest of them, whom they call Christ's vicar, down to the lowest; thus they regard themselves as the Lord, and adore Him, not for His own sake, but for theirs. They not only adulterate and falsify the Word, but even take it away from the people, lest they should enter into the smallest light of truth; and not satisfied with this, they moreover annihilate it, acknowledging the Divine in the decrees of Rome, superior to the Divine in the Word; so that they exclude all from the way to heaven; for the acknowledgment of the Lord, faith in Him, and love to Him, are the way to heaven; and the Word is what teaches the way: whence it is, that without the Lord, by means of the Word, there is no salvation. They strive with all diligence to extinguish the light of heaven, which is from Divine truth, in order that ignorance may exist in the place of it, and the denser the ignorance, the more acceptable it is to them. They extinguish the light of heaven, by prohibiting the reading of the Word, and of books which contain doctrines from the Word; instituting worship by masses in a language not understood by the simple, and in which there is no Divine truth; and besides, they fill their world with falsities which are darkness itself, and which remove and dissipate the light. They likewise persuade the common people, that they have life in the faith of their priests, thus in the faith of another and not in their own. They also place all worship in a holy external, without the internal, making the internal empty, because it is without the knowledges of good and truth; and yet Divine worship is external, only so far as it is internal, since

---

[14] The attribution by the church, of two natures to the Lord, and thus the separation of His Divine from His Human, was effected in a council, for the sake of the Pope, that the Pope might be acknowledged as the Lord's vicar, disclosed from heaven in the *Arcana Cœlestia* (n. 4738).

the external proceeds from the internal. Besides this, they introduce idolatries of various kinds. They make and multiply saints; they see and tolerate the adoration of these saints, and even the prayers offered to them almost as to gods; they set up their idols everywhere; boast of the great abundance of miracles done by them; set them over cities, temples, and monasteries; their bones taken out of their tombs they account holy, which yet are most vile; thus turning the minds of all from the worship of God, to the worship of men. Moreover, they use much artful precaution lest any one should come out of that thick darkness into light, from idolatrous worship to Divine worship; for they multiply monasteries, from which they send out spies and guards in all directions; they extort the confessions of the heart, which are also confessions of the thoughts and intentions, and if any one will not confess, they threaten him with infernal fire and torments in purgatory; and those who dare to speak against the Papal throne, and their dominion, they shut up in a horrible prison, which is called the Inquisition. All these things they do for the sole end that they may possess the world and its treasures, and live in luxury and be the greatest, while the rest are slaves. But domination such as this, is not that of heaven over hell, but of hell over heaven, for as far as the love of having dominion is with man, especially with the man of the church, so far hell reigns. That this love reigns in hell, and makes hell, may be seen in the work on *Heaven and Hell* (n. 551–565). From this summary it may appear that they have no church there, but Babylon; for the church is where the Lord Himself is worshiped, and where the Word is read.

56. II. *The quality of those in the other life who are Babylon* can appear only to one to whom it has been given by the Lord to be together with those who are in the spiritual world. Since this has been granted to me, I am able to speak from experience, for I have seen them, I have heard them, and I have spoken with them. Every man after death is in a life similar to his life in the world; this cannot be changed, save only as regards the delights of the love, which are turned into correspondences, as may appear from the two articles in the work on *Heaven and Hell* (n. 470–484; and 485–490). It is the same with the life of those now treated of, which is altogether such as it was in the world, with this difference, that the hidden things of their hearts are there uncovered, for they are in the spirit, in which reside the interior things of the thoughts and intentions, which they had concealed in the world, and had covered over with a holy external. And since these hidden things were then laid open, it was perceived that more than half of those who had usurped the power of opening and shutting heaven, were altogether atheists; but since dominion resides in their minds as in the world, and is based on this principle, that all power was given by the Father to the Lord Himself, and that it was transferred to Peter, and by order of succession to the primates of the church, therefore an oral confession about the Lord remains adjoined to their atheism; but even this remains only so long as they enjoy some dominion by means of it. But the rest of them, who are not atheists, are so empty, as to be entirely ignorant of man's spiritual life, of the means of salvation, of the Divine truths which lead to heaven; and they know nothing at all of heavenly faith and love, believing that heaven may be granted of the Pope's favor to any one, whatever he be. Now since every one is in a life in the spiritual world, similar to his life in the natural world, without any difference, so long as he is neither in heaven nor in hell (as is shown, and may be seen in the work on *Heaven and Hell*, n. 453–480), and since the spiritual world, as regards its external appearance, is altogether like the natural world (n. 170–176), therefore they also live a similar moral and civil life, and above all have similar worship, for this is inrooted, and inheres to man in his inmost, nor can any one after death be withdrawn from it, except he be in good from truths, and in truths from good. But it is more difficult to withdraw the nation now treated of from its worship, than other nations, because it is not in good from truths, and still less in truths from good; for its truths are not from the Word, with the exception of some few, which they have falsified by applying them to dominion; and hence it has none other than spurious good, for such as the truths are, such does the good become. These things are said, in order that it may be known, that the worship of this nation, in the spiritual world, is altogether similar to its worship in the natural world. These things premised, I will now relate some particulars of the worship and life of the Papists in the spiritual world. They have a certain council, in place of the council or consistory at Rome, in which their primates meet, and consult on various matters of their religion, especially on the means of holding the common people in blind obedience, and of enlarging their dominion. This council is situated in the southern quarter, near the east; but no one who has been a Pope or a cardinal in the world dares to enter it, because the semblance of Divine authority possesses their minds, from their having in the world arrogated the Lord's power to themselves; wherefore, as soon as they present themselves there, they are carried out, and cast to their like in a desert. But those among them, who have been upright in mind, and have not from confirmed belief usurped such power, are in a certain obscure chamber behind this council. There is another assembly in the western quarter, near the north; the business there, is the intromission of the credulous common people into heaven. They there dispose around them a number of societies which live in various external delights; in some of the societies they play, in some they dance, in some they compose the face into the various expressions of hilarity and mirthfulness; in some they converse in a friendly manner; in some they discuss civil affairs, in others religious matters; in other societies again, they talk obscenities; and so on. They admit their dependents into one of these societies such as each may desire, and call it heaven; but all of them, after being there a few hours, are wearied and depart, because those joys are external, and not internal. In this way, moreover, many are withdrawn from a belief in their doctrinal concerning intromission into heaven. As regards their worship in particular, it is almost like their worship in the world; as in the world, it consists in masses, not performed in the common language of spirits, but in one composed of lofty-sounding words, which induce an external holiness and awe, and are utterly unintelligible. In like manner they adore saints, and expose idols to view; but their saints are nowhere to be seen, for all those who have sought to be worshiped as deities, are in hell; the rest who did not seek to be worshiped, are among common spirits. This their prelates know, for they seek and find them, and when found they despise them; yet they conceal it from the people, that the saints may still be worshiped as tutelar deities, but that the primates themselves, who are set over the people, may be worshiped as the lords of heaven. In like manner, moreover, they multiply temples and monasteries as they did in the world; they scrape together riches, and accumulate costly things, which they hide in cellars; for costly things exist in the spiritual, as well as in the natural world, and far more abundantly. In like manner they send forth monks, to allure the Gentiles to their religious persuasion, in order that they may subject them to their rule. They commonly have watch towers erected in the middle of their assemblies, from which they are enabled to enjoy an extended view into all the surrounding region. And moreover, by various means and arts they establish for themselves communications with persons far and near, joining in league with them, and drawing them over to their own party. Such is their state in general; but as to particulars, many prelates of that religion take away all power from the Lord, and claim it for themselves, and because they do this, they do not acknowledge any Divine. They still counterfeit holiness in externals; yet this holiness in itself is profane, because in their internals there is no acknowledgment of the Divine. Hence it is that they communicate with certain societies of the lowest heaven by a holy external, and with the hells by a profane internal, so that they are in both; on which account, moreover, they allure simple good spirits, and give them habitations near themselves, and also congregate wicked spirits, and dispose them around the society in all directions, by the simple good conjoining themselves with heaven, and by the wicked with hell. Hence they are enabled to accomplish heinous things which they perpetrate from hell. For the simple good who are in the lowest heavens look only to their holy external, and their very holy adoration of the Lord in externals, but they do not see their wickedness, and therefore they favor them, and this is their greatest protection; yet in process of time they all recede from their holy external, and then, being separated from heaven, they are cast into hell. From these things it may be known in some degree, what is the quality of those in the other life who are from Babylon. But I am aware that they who are in this world, and have no idea of man's state after death, of heaven, or of hell, but an inane and empty one, will wonder at the existence of such things in the spiritual world. But, that man is equally a man after death, that he lives in fellowships as he did in the world, that he dwells in houses, hears preaching in temples, discharges duties, and sees things in that world, similar to those in the former world he has left, may appear from all that has been said and shown of the things I have heard and seen, in the work on *Heaven and Hell*.

57. I have spoken with some from that nation, concerning the keys given to Peter; whether they believe that the power of the Lord over heaven and earth was transferred to him? and because this was the fundamental of their religion, they vehemently insisted on it, saying, that there was no doubt about it, because it was said manifestly. But when I asked them whether they knew that in each expression of the Word there is a spiritual sense, which is the sense of the Word in heaven, they said at first, that they did not know it, but afterwards they said they would inquire; and on inquiring, they were instructed that there is a spiritual sense within each expression of the Word, which differs from the sense of the letter, as the spiritual differs from the natural; and they were also instructed that no person named in the Word is named in heaven, but that some spiritual thing is there understood in place of him. Finally, they were informed, that instead of "Peter" in the Word is meant the truth of the faith of the church, from the good of charity, and that the same is meant by "a rock," which is there named with Peter, for it is said:—

Thou art Peter, and upon this rock will I build My church (*Matt.* xvi. 18, *seq.*).

By this is not meant that any power was given to Peter, but that it is given to truth from good, for in the heavens all power belongs to truth from good, or to good through truth; and since all good, and all truth, are from the Lord, and nothing from man, that all power is the Lord's. When they heard this they replied indignantly, that they wished to know whether there is a spiritual sense in those words, wherefore the Word which is in heaven was given them, in which Word there is not the natural sense, but the spiritual, because it is for the angels, who are spiritual; that there is such a Word in heaven, may be seen in the work on *Heaven and Hell* (n. 259–261). And when they read it, they saw manifestly that Peter is not named there, but truth from good, which is from the Lord, instead of him.[15] Seeing this they rejected it with anger, and would almost have torn it in pieces with their teeth, had it not at that moment been taken away. Hence they were convinced, although unwilling to be convinced, that the Lord alone has that power, and by no means can it belong to any man, because it is the Divine power.

58. III. *Where their habitations in the spiritual world have hitherto been.* It was said above (n. 48), that all the nations and peoples in the spiritual world were seen to be as follows: collected in the middle appeared those who are called the Reformed; around this middle, those of the Papal religion; the Mohammedans, beyond them; and lastly the various Gentiles. Hence it may appear that the Papists formed the nearest circumference around the Reformed in the centre. The reason of this is that they who are in the light of truth from the Word are in the centre, and they who are in the light of truth from the Word are also in the light of heaven, for the light of heaven is from the Divine truth, and the Word is that in which this is. That the light of heaven is from the Divine truth, may be seen in the work on *Heaven and Hell* (n. 126–140); and that it is the Divine truth (n. 303–310). Light, moreover, pro-

---

[15] The twelve disciples of the Lord represented the church as to the all of truth and good, or of faith and love, as in like manner did the twelve tribes of Israel (n. 2179, 3354, 3488, 3858, 6397). Peter, James, and John, represented faith, charity, and the goods of charity (n. 3750). Peter represented faith (n. 4738, 6000, 6073, 6344, 10,087, 10,580). The keys of the kingdom of heaven being given to Peter, signifies that all power is given to truth from good, or to faith from charity, proceeding from the Lord; thus that all power belongs to the Lord (n. 6344). "A key" signifies the power of opening and shutting (n. 9410). All power is in good by truths, or in truths from good, proceeding from the Lord (n. 3091, 3563, 6344, 6413, 6948, 8200, 8304, 9327, 9410, 9639, 9643, 10,019, 10,182). "A rock" in the Word signifies the Lord as to Divine truth (n. 8581, 10,580). All names of persons and places in the Word signify things and states (n. 768, 1888, 4310, 4442, 10,329). Their names do not enter heaven, but are turned into the things they signify, and they cannot be pronounced in heaven (n. 1878, 5225, 6516, 10,216, 10,282). How elegant is the internal sense of the Word, where mere names occur, is illustrated by examples (n. 1224, 1264, 1888).

ceeds from the centre towards the circumferences, and illuminates. Hence it is that the Papists proximately surround the centre, for they have the Word, and it is also read by those of the ecclesiastical order, though not by the people. This is the reason why the Papal nation in the spiritual world have obtained habitations around those who are in the light of truth from the Word. Their manner of dwelling, before their habitations were utterly destroyed, and made into a desert, shall now be told. The greatest part of them dwelt in the south and in the west; but some in the north and in the east. In the south dwelt those who had excelled others in talent in the world, and had confirmed themselves in their own religion. Great numbers of the nobility and the rich also dwelt there. They did not dwell upon the earth there, but under it, from dread of robbers, guards being placed at the entrances. In that quarter, moreover, there was a great city, extending nearly from east to west, and somewhat into the west, situated very near the centre where the Reformed were. Myriads of men or spirits tarried in that city. It was full of temples and monasteries. The ecclesiastics also carried into it all precious things which they were enabled by their various artifices to scrape together, and they hid them in its cells and subterranean crypts, which were so elaborately formed, that no one besides themselves could enter, for they were disposed around in the form of a labyrinth. On the treasures there amassed, in the full confidence that they could never be destroyed, they had set their hearts. When I saw those crypts I was amazed at the art displayed in constructing them, and enlarging them without end. The most of those who call themselves of the society of Jesus were there, and cultivated amicable relations with the rich who dwelt round about. Towards the east in that quarter was the council where they consulted on the enlargement of their dominion, and on the means of keeping the people in blind obedience (see above, n. 56). This concerning their habitations in the southern quarter. In the *north*, dwelt those who less excelled in ability, and had less confirmed themselves in their own religion, because they were in an obscure faculty of discerning and thence in blind faith. The multitude was not so great there as in the south. Most of them were in a great city, extending lengthwise from the angle of the east to the west, and also a little into the west. It also was full of temples and monasteries. On its outmost side which was near the east there were many of various religions, and also some of the Reformed. A few places, moreover, beyond the city in that quarter, were occupied by the Papists. In the *east* dwelt those who had been in the greatest delight of ruling in the world, and at the same time in somewhat of natural light. They appeared there on mountains, but only in the quarter which faces the north; there were none in the other part which faces the south. In the angle towards the north, there was a mountain, on the top of which they had placed a certain one of unsound mind, whom, by communications of the thoughts, which are known in the spiritual, but unknown in the natural world, they were enabled to inspire to command anything they chose. And they gave out that he was the very God of heaven, appearing under a human form, and thus paid him Divine worship. They did this, because the people were desirous of receding from their idolatrous worship, wherefore, they devised it as a means of keeping them in obedience. That mountain is meant in *Isaiah* (xiv. 13) by "the mountain of assembly in the sides of the north," and those on the mountains are there meant by "Lucifer" (ver. 12); for such of the Babylonish crew as dwelt in the east, were in greater light than others, which light also, they had prepared for themselves by artifice. There also appeared some who were building a tower, which should reach even to heaven where the angels are, but this was only representative of their machinations; for machinations are presented in the spiritual world, before the eyes of those who stand at a distance, by many things which yet do not exist actually with those who are in the machinations: this is a common thing there. By this appearance it was given me to know what was signified by:—

The tower whose head should be in heaven, whence the place was called Babel (*Gen.* xi. 1–10).

These things are concerning their habitations in the east. In the west, in front, dwelt those of that religion who lived in the dark ages, for the most part under-ground, one pos-

terity beneath another. The whole tract in front which
looked to the north, was, as it were, excavated, and filled with
monasteries. The entrances to them lay through caverns covered by roofs, through which they went out and in. They rarely
spoke with those who lived in the following ages, being of a
different disposition, and not so malicious; for as, in their times,
there was no contention with the Reformed, there was therefore less of the craft and malice from hatred and revenge. In
the western quarter beyond that tract, were many mountains,
on which dwelt the wickedest of that nation, who in heart denied the Divine and yet orally professed their belief in Him,
and adored Him with gestures more devoutly than others.
They who were there, devised nefarious arts to keep the common people under the yoke of their sway, and also to force others
to submit to that yoke: these arts it is not allowed to describe,
they are so heinous. In general they are such as are mentioned
in the work on *Heaven and Hell* (n. 580). The mountains on
which they dwelt, are meant in the *Apocalypse* by "the seven
mountains," and those who were there are described by the
woman sitting upon the scarlet beast:—

I saw a woman sitting upon a scarlet beast, full of names of blasphemy,
having seven heads, and ten horns: she had on the forehead a name written, mystery, Babylon the great, mother of the whoredoms and abominations of the earth: the seven heads are seven mountains, on which the
woman sitteth (*Apoc.* xvii. 3, 5, 9).

By "a woman" in the internal sense, is meant the church, here
in the opposite sense, a profane religion; by "the scarlet beast,"
the profanation of celestial love; by "the seven mountains," the
profane love of ruling. These are concerning their habitations
in the west. The reason why they dwell distinct according to
quarters is, because all in the spiritual world are carried into
that quarter, and into that part of it, which corresponds to their
affections and loves, and no one to any other place; concerning
which see the work on *Heaven and Hell*, where it treats of the
four quarters of heaven (n. 141–153). In general, all the consultations of the Babylonish race tend to this, that they may
dominate, not only over heaven, but over the whole earth, and
thus that they may possess heaven and earth, obtaining each
by means of the other. To effect this, they continually devise

and hatch new statutes and new doctrinals. They make the same endeavor also in the other life as they made in the world, for every one after death is such as he was in the world, especially as to his religion. It was granted me to hear certain of the primates consulting about a doctrine, which was to be a rule for the people: it consisted of many articles, but they all tended to this; that they might obtain dominion over the heavens, and the earth, and that they might have all power for themselves, and the Lord none. These doctrinals were afterwards read before the bystanders, and thereupon a voice was heard from heaven, declaring, that they were dictated from the deepest hell, though the hearers did not know it; which was further confirmed by this; that a crowd of devils from that hell, of the blackest and direst appearance, ascended, and tore those doctrinals from them, not with their hands, but with their teeth, and carried them down to their hell. The people who saw it were astounded.

59. IV. *Why they were there tolerated, until the day of the Last Judgment.* The reason was, because it is from Divine order that all who can be preserved, shall be preserved, even until they can no longer be among the good. Therefore all those are preserved, who can emulate spiritual life in externals, and present it in a moral life, as if it were therein, whatever they may be as to faith and love in internals; so also those are preserved who are in external holiness, though not in internal. Such were many of that nation, for they could speak piously with the common people, and adore the Lord in a holy manner to implant religion in their minds, and lead them to think of heaven and hell, and could hold them in doing goods by preaching works. Thus they were able to lead many to a life of good, and therefore into the way to heaven; on which account also, many of that religion were saved, although few of their leaders. For these are such as the Lord means by:—

False prophets, who come in sheep's clothing, but inwardly are ravening wolves (*Matt.* vii. 15).

By "prophets," in the internal sense of the Word, are meant those who teach truth, and by it lead to good; and by "false prophets," those who teach falsity, and seduce by it. They are also like the scribes and Pharisees, who are described by the Lord in these words:—

> They sit in Moses' seat; all things that they bid you observe, observe and do, but do not according to their works; for they say and do not; all their works they do to be seen of men; they shut up the kingdom of the heavens against men, but go not in themselves: they eat widows' houses, for a pretence pouring forth long prayers. Woe unto you, hypocrites, ye make clean the outside of the cup and platter, but within they are full of rapine and iniquity; cleanse first the inside of the cup and platter, that the outside may be clean also; ye are like whited sepulchres, which appear outwardly beautiful, but within are full of the bones of the dead: thus ye outwardly appear just before men, but within ye are full of hypocrisy and iniquity (*Matt.* xxiii. 1–34).

Another reason moreover why they were tolerated was, because every man after death retains his religious principles that he has acquired in the world; into which therefore he is introduced, when first he comes into the other life. Now with this nation, the religious principle was implanted by those who gave an oral preference to sanctity, and feigned holy gestures, and moreover, impressed the people with a belief that they could be saved through them; hence also they were removed, but were preserved among their own. But the principal reason was, that all are preserved from one judgment to another, who live a life similar to a spiritual life in externals, and emulate as it were a pious and holy internal; by whom the simple may receive instruction and guidance: for the simple in faith and heart look no farther than to see what is external, and apparent before the eyes. Hence all such were tolerated from the commencement of the Christian church, until the day of the judgment. That a Last Judgment has existed twice before, and now exists for the third time, was shown above. Of all these "the former heaven" consisted, and they are meant in the *Apocalypse* (xx. 5, 6) by "those who are not of the first resurrection." But since they were such as above described, that heaven was destroyed, and they of the second resurrection were cast out. But it ought to be known that they only were preserved who suffered themselves to be held in bonds by laws both civil and spiritual, they being capable of living together in society; nevertheless they who could not be held in bonds by those laws were not preserved, but were cast into hell long before the day of the Last Judgment: for societies are continually purified and purged from such. Hence, they who led a wicked life, who enticed the common people to do evils, and entered on abominable arts, such as exist among spirits in the hells (see the work on *Heaven and Hell*, n. 580), were cast out of societies, and this in their turns. In like manner also those who are interiorly good are removed from societies, lest they should be contaminated by those who are interiorly evil; for the good perceive the interiors, and therefore pay no regard to the exteriors, except just so far as they agree with the interiors; they are sent in their turns to places of instruction (concerning which see the work on *Heaven and Hell*, n. 512–520), and are carried thence into heaven; for "the new heaven" is formed of them, and they are meant by "those who are of the first resurrection." These things are said that it may be known, why so many of the Papal religion were tolerated and preserved until the day of the Last Judgment; but more will be said on the same subject in the following article, where "the first heaven" which passed away is to be treated of.

60. V. *How they were destroyed, and their habitations made a desert.* This I will here describe in a few words; more fully in the *Explanation of the Apocalypse*. That Babylonia there treated of has been destroyed, no one but he who saw it can know, and it was given me to see how the Last Judgment was brought about and accomplished upon all, especially upon those of Babylon. I, therefore, will describe it. This was granted me, principally, in order to reveal to the world, that all things predicted in the *Apocalypse* are Divinely inspired, and that the *Apocalypse* is a prophetic book of the Word. For if this were not revealed to the world, and at the same time the internal sense which is in each expression there, as in each expression of the Prophets of the Old Testament, that book might be rejected, on account of not being understood; which would produce such incredulity, that the things there said would not be held worthy of belief, nor that any such Last Judgment would come; in which unbelief those of the Babylon would confirm themselves more than others. Lest this should be, it pleased the Lord to make me an eye-witness. But all that I saw of the Last Judgment upon those of the Babylon, or of the destruction of Babylon, cannot be here adduced, being in itself sufficient to fill a volume. In this place I shall merely relate certain general things, reserving the particulars for the *Explanation of the Apocalypse*. Inasmuch as the Babylonish nation was settled in and extended over many tracts in the spiritual world, and had formed to itself societies in all the quarters there (as was shown above, n. 58), I will describe how they were destroyed separately in each quarter.

61. Destruction was effected after visitation, for visitation always precedes. The act of exploring what the men are, and moreover the separation of the good from the evil, is visitation; and the good are then removed, and the evil are left behind. This having been done, there were great earthquakes, from which they perceived that the Last Judgment was at hand, and trembling seized them all. Then those who dwelt in the *southern quarter*, and especially in the great city there (see n. 58), were seen running to and fro, some with the intention of betaking themselves to flight, some of hiding themselves in the crypts, others of hiding in the cells and caves where their treasures were, out of which others again carried anything they could lay their hands on. But after the earthquakes there burst up an ebullition from below, which overturned everything in the city and in the region round it. After this ebullition came a vehement wind from the east which laid bare, shook, and overthrew everything to its foundations, and then all who were there were led forth, from every part, and from all their hiding-places, and cast into a sea of black waters: those who were cast into it, were many myriads. Afterwards from that whole region a smoke ascended, as after a conflagration, and finally a thick dust, which was borne by the east wind to the sea, and strewn over it; for their treasures were turned into dust, with all those things they had called holy because they possessed them. This dust was strewn over the sea, because such dust signifies what is damned. At last there was seen as it were a blackness flying over that whole region, which when it was viewed narrowly appeared like a dragon; a sign that the whole of that great city and region was become a desert. This was seen, because "dragons" signify the falsities of such a religion, and "the abode of dragons" signifies the desert after their overthrow; as in *Jeremiah* (ix. 11; x. 22; xlix. 33; *Mal.* i. 3). It was also seen that some had as it were a millstone around the left arm, which was a representative of their having confirmed their abominable dogmas from the Word; a millstone signifies such things: hence it was plain what these words signify in the *Apocalypse:*—

> The angel took up a stone like a great millstone, and cast it into the sea, saying, thus with violence shall that great city Babylon be thrown down, and shall no more be found (*Apoc.* xviii. 21).

But they who were in the council, which also was in that region, but nearer to the east, in which they were consulting on the modes of enlarging their dominion, and of keeping the people in ignorance, and thence in blind obedience (see above, n. 58), were not cast into that black sea, but into a gulf which opened itself long and deep beneath and around them. Thus was the Last Judgment accomplished upon the Babylonians in the southern quarter. But the Last Judgment upon those *in front in the western quarter*, and upon those in the *northern quarter*, where the other great city stood, was thus effected. After great earthquakes, which rent everything in those quarters to the very foundations—these are the earthquakes which are meant in the Word (*Matt.* xxiv. 7; *Luke* xxi. 11; likewise *Apoc.* vi. 12; viii. 5; xi. 13; xvi. 18); and in the prophecies of the Old Testament, and not any earthquakes in this world—an east wind went forth from the south through the west into the north, and laid bare that whole region; first that part of it in front in the western quarter, where the people of the dark ages dwelt underground, and afterwards the great city, which extended from that quarter even through the north to the east, and from these regions thus laid bare, all things were exposed to view. But because there were not such great riches there, no ebullition, and no sulphurous fire consuming treasures were seen, but only overturn and destruction, and at length exhalation of the whole into smoke; for the east wind went forth, blowing to and fro; it overthrew and destroyed and also swept away. The monks and common people were led forth to the number of m. myriads; some were cast into the black sea, on that side of which faces the west; some into the great southern gulf, mentioned above; some into the western gulf, and some into the hells of the Gentiles, for a part of those who lived in the dark ages were idolaters like the Gentiles. A smoke also was seen to ascend from that region, and to proceed as far as the sea; over which it hovered, depositing a black crust there; for that part of the sea into which they were cast, was encrusted over with the dust and smoke, into which their dwellings and their riches were reduced; wherefore that sea has no longer a visible existence, but in its place is seen, as it were a black soil, under which is their hell. The Last Judgment upon those who dwelt upon the mountains in the *eastern quarter* (see n. 58), was thus accomplished. Their mountains were seen to subside into the deep, and all those who were upon them to be swallowed up; and he whom they had placed upon one of the mountains, and whom they proclaimed to be god, was seen to become first black, then fiery, and with them to be cast headlong into hell. For the monks of the various orders who were upon those mountains, said that he was God and that they were Christ, and wherever they went, they took with them the abominable persuasion that themselves were Christ. Finally, judgment was effected upon those who dwelt more remotely in the *western quarter*, upon the mountains there, and who are meant by "the woman sitting upon the scarlet beast who had seven heads which are seven mountains," of whom also something is related above (n. 58). Their mountains also were seen, some were open in the middle, where an immense chasm was made and whirled about in a spiral, into which those on the mountains were cast. Other mountains were torn up by their foundations and turned upside down, so that the summit became the base; those who were thence in the plains were inundated as with a deluge, and covered over, and those who were among them from other quarters were cast into gulfs. But the things now related are only a small part of all I saw; more will be given in the *Explanation of the Apocalypse.* They were effected and accomplished in the beginning of the year 1757. As regards the *gulfs* into which all were cast, except those who were cast into the black sea, they are many. Four of them were disclosed to me; one great gulf in the southern quarter, towards the east there; another in the western quarter, towards the south; a third in the western quarter, towards the north there; a fourth still further in the angle between the west and the north: the gulfs and the sea are their hells. These were seen, but in addition to these there are many more, which were not seen; for the hells of the Babylonish people are distinct according to the various profanations of spiritual things, which are of the good and truth of the church.

62. Thus now was the spiritual world freed from such spirits, and the angels rejoiced on account of its liberation from them, because they who were of Babylon infested and seduced all whomsoever they could, and there more than in the world; for their cunning is more malignant there, because they are spirits; for it is the spirit of each in which all his wickedness is hidden, since the spirit of the man is what thinks, wills, intends, and plots. Many of them were explored, and it was found that they believed nothing at all, and that the heinous lust of seducing, the rich for the sake of their riches, and the poor for the sake of dominion, was rooted in their minds, and that on account of that end they kept all in the densest ignorance, thus blocking up the way to light, thus to heaven: for the way to light and to heaven is obstructed, when the knowledges of spiritual things are overwhelmed by idolatries, and when the Word is adulterated, weakened, and taken away.

63. VI. *Those of them who were in the affection of truth from good were preserved.* Those of the Papal nation who lived piously, and were in good, although not in truths, and still from affection desired to know truths, were taken away and carried into a certain region, in front in the western quarter, near the north, and there habitations were given them, and societies of them were instituted, and then priests from the Reformed were sent to them, who instructed them from the Word, and as they are instructed, they are accepted in heaven.

64. *The state of those hereafter who come thence from the earth.* Since the Last Judgment has now been accomplished, and by means of it all things are reduced by the Lord into order, and since all who are interiorly good are taken into heaven, and all who are interiorly evil are cast into hell, it is not permitted them henceforth as heretofore, to form societies below heaven and above hell, nor to have anything in common with others, but as soon as they come thither, which is after the death of each, they are altogether separated, and after passing a certain time in the world of spirits, they are carried into their own places. They therefore who profane holy things, that is, who claim for themselves the power of opening and shutting heaven, and of remitting sins, which yet are powers belonging to the Lord alone, and who make Papal bulls equal to the Word, and have dominion for an end, are henceforth carried away immediately into that black sea, or into the gulfs, where the hells of profaners are. But it was said to me from heaven, that those of that religious persuasion who are such, do not look at all to the life after death, because they deny it in heart, but only to life in the world; and that hence they hold of no account this lot of theirs after death, which yet is to endure to eternity, but laugh at it, as a thing of nought.

X.

THE FORMER HEAVEN AND ITS ABOLISHMENT.

65. It is said in the *Apocalypse:*—

I saw a great throne, and One sitting upon it, from whose face the earth and the heaven fled away, and their place was not found (xx. 11).

And afterwards:—

I saw a new heaven and a new earth; the first heaven and the first earth had passed away (xxi. 1).

That by "a new heaven and a new earth," and by the passing away of the former heaven and the former earth is not meant the visible heaven and our habitable earth, but an angelic heaven and a church, was shown above in the first article, and also in those which follow it. For the Word in itself is spiritual, and therefore treats of spiritual things; and spiritual things are the things of heaven and the church; these are expressed by natural things in the sense of the letter, because natural things serve as a basis to spiritual things, and without such a basis the Word would not be a Divine work, because it would not be complete; for the natural, which is the ultimate in Divine order, completes and makes the interiors, which are spiritual and celestial, to subsist upon it, as a house upon its foundation. Now because man has thought of the things of the Word from the natural and not from the spiritual, therefore, by "the heaven and the earth" which are mentioned here and elsewhere, they have understood none other than the heaven and earth which exist in the world of nature; hence it is that everyone expects the passing away and destruction of these, and then also the creation of new ones. But lest they should expect this everlastingly, from age to age in vain, the spiritual sense of the Word is opened, that thus it may be known what is meant by many things in the Word, which, when thought of naturally, do not enter the understanding, and, at the same time, what is meant by "the heaven and the earth" which will pass away.

66. But before showing what is meant by "the first heaven and the first earth," it should be known, that by "the first heaven" is not meant the heaven formed of those who have become angels from the first creation of this world to the present time, for that heaven is abiding, and endures to eternity; for all who enter heaven are under the Lord's protection, and he who has once been received by the Lord, can never be plucked away from Him. But by "the first heaven" is meant that which was composed of others than those who have become angels, and for the most part of those who could not become angels. Who they were, and their quality, shall be told in the following pages. This heaven it is, of which it is said, that it "passed away." It was called heaven, because they who were in it dwelt on high, forming societies upon rocks and mountains, and living in delights similar to natural ones, but still not in any that were spiritual; for very many who come from the earth into the spiritual world, believe themselves to be in heaven, when they are on high, and in heavenly joy, when they are in delights such as they had in the world. Hence it was called heaven, but "the first heaven which passed away."

67. It is moreover to be known, that this heaven which is called "the first," did not consist of any who had lived before the Lord's coming into the world, but all were from those who lived after His coming, for as was shown above (n. 33–38) a Last Judgment is effected at the end of every church, and then the former heaven is abolished, and a new heaven is created or formed; for all who lived in an external moral life, and in external piety and sanctity, although not in any internal, were tolerated from the beginning to the end of the church, provided the internals which belong to the thoughts and intentions could be held in bonds by the laws of society, civil and moral; but at the end of the church their internals are disclosed, and the judgment is then effected upon them. Hence it is that a Last Judgment has been effected upon the inhabitants of this planet twice before, and now for the third time (see above, n. 46); thus also a heaven and an earth have twice passed away before, and a new heaven and a new earth have been created; for the heaven and the earth are the church in either world, as shown above (n. 1–5). Hence it is plain, that "the new heaven and the new earth," mentioned in the prophets of the Old Testament, are not that "new heaven and new earth" mentioned in the *Apocalypse*, but that the former existed from the Lord when He was in the world, and that the latter exist from Him now. Concerning those in the prophets of the Old Testament, it is thus written:—

Behold, I am about to create a new heaven and a new earth, neither shall the former be remembered (*Isa.* lxv. 17).

And in another place:—

I am about to make a new heaven and a new earth (*Isa.* lxvi. 22).

Besides what is said in *Daniel*.

68. Since the first heaven which passed away is the subject now treated of, and since no one knows anything concerning it, I will describe it in order.

I. *Of whom the first heaven consisted.*
II. *What its quality was.*
III. *How it passed away.*

69. I. *Of whom the first heaven consisted.* The first heaven was composed of all those upon whom the Last Judgment was effected, for it was not effected upon those in hell, nor upon those in heaven, nor upon those in the world of spirits, concerning which world see the work on *Heaven and Hell* (n. 421–520), nor upon any man yet living, but solely upon those who had made to themselves the likeness of a heaven, of whom the greater part were on mountains and rocks; these also were they whom the Lord meant by "the goats," which He placed on the left (*Matt.* xxv. 32, 33, *seq.*). Hence it may appear, that the first heaven existed, not merely from Christians, but also from Mohammedans and Gentiles, who had all formed to themselves such heavens in their own places. What their quality was shall be told in a few words. They were those who had lived in the world in external and not in internal holiness; who were just and sincere for the sake of civil and moral laws, but not for the sake of Divine laws, therefore who were external or natural and not internal or spiritual men; who also were in the doctrinals of the church, and were able to teach them, although they were not in a life according to them; and who filled various offices, and did uses, but not for the sake of uses. These, and all throughout the whole world who were like them, and who lived after the Lord's coming, constituted "the first heaven." This heaven therefore was such as the world and church is upon earth, among those who do good not because it is good, but because they fear the laws, and the loss of fame, honor, and gain; they who do good for no other origin, do not fear God, but men, nor do they have any conscience. In the first heaven of the Reformed, there was a large part of them, who believed that man is saved by faith alone, and had not lived the life of faith, which is charity; and who loved much to be seen of men. In all these, so long as they were associated together, the interiors were closed that they might not appear, but when the Last Judgment was at hand they were opened; and it was then found that inwardly they were obsessed by falsities and evils of every kind, and that they were against the Divine, and were actually in hell. For every one after death is immediately bound to his like, the good to their like in heaven, but the evil to their like in hell, yet they do not go to them before the interiors are disclosed; in the meantime they may be consociated with those who are like them in externals. But it is to be known that all who were interiorly good thus who were spiritual, were separated from them, and elevated into heaven, and that all who were exteriorly as well as interiorly evil, were also separated from them, and cast into hell; and this from the time immediately succeeding the Lord's advent, down to the last time, when the judgment was; and that those only were left, to form societies among themselves, who constituted the first heaven, and who were such as are described above.

70. There were many reasons why such societies, or such heavens were tolerated; the principal reason was, that by external holiness, and by external sincerity and justice, they were conjoined with the simple good, who were either in the lowest heaven, or were still in the world of spirits and not yet introduced into heaven. For in the spiritual world, there is a communication, and thence a conjunction, of all with their like; and the simple good, in the lowest heaven, and in the world of spirits, look principally to externals, yet are not interiorly evil; wherefore if these spirits had been forcibly removed from them before the appointed time, heaven would have suffered in its ultimates; and yet it is the ultimate, upon which the superior heaven subsists, as upon its own basis. That they were tolerated until the last time on this account, the Lord teaches in the following words:—

> The servants of the householder came and said unto him, Didst thou not sow good seed in thy field, whence then are the tares? And they said, Wilt thou then that we go and gather them up? But he said, Nay, lest, whilst ye gather up the tares, ye root up at the same time the wheat with them; let both therefore grow together until the harvest, and at the time of harvest I will say to the reapers, gather ye together first the tares, and bind them in bundles to burn; but gather the wheat into barns. He that hath sowed the good seed, is the Son of man; the field is the world; the good seed are the sons of the kingdom, the tares are the sons of evil; the harvest is the consummation of the age: as therefore the tares are gathered together, and burnt with fire, so shall it be in the consummation of the age (*Matt.* xiii. 27–30, 37–40).

"The consummation of this age," is the last time of the church; "the tares" are those who are interiorly evil; "the wheat" are those who are interiorly good; "the gathering the tares together, and binding them in bundles to burn," is the Last Judgment.[16] The like is meant in the same chapter by the Lord's parable of the fishes of every kind, which were gathered together, and the good placed in vessels, but the bad cast away; concerning which it is also said:—

So shall it be in the consummation of the age; the angels shall go forth, and separate the evil from the midst of the just (vers. 47–49).

They are compared to fishes, because "fishes" in the spiritual sense of the Word, signify natural and external men, both good and evil; what "the just" signify may be seen below.[17]

71. II. *What the quality of the first heaven was*, may be concluded from the things already said of it; as also from this, that they who are not spiritual by acknowledgment of the Divine, by a life of good, and by the affection of truth, and still appear as spiritual by external holiness, by discoursing on Divine things, and by sincerities for the sake of themselves and the world, rush into the abominations which agree with their lusts, when they are left to their own internals; for nothing withholds them, neither fear of God, nor faith, nor conscience. Hence it was, that as soon as they who were in the first heaven were let into their interiors, they appeared conjoined with the hells.

72. III. *How the first heaven passed away*, was described before, in describing the Last Judgment upon the Mohamme-

---

[16] "Bundles" in the Word signify the arrangement of the truths and falsities with man into series, thus also the arrangement of men in whom truths and falsities are (n. 4686, 4687, 5339, 5530, 7408, 10,303). "The Son of man" is the Lord as to Divine truths (n. 1729, 1733, 2159, 2628, 2803, 2813, 3373, 3704, 7499, 8897, 9807). "Sons" are the affections of truth from good (n. 489, 491, 533, 2623, 3373, 4257, 8649, 9807); therefore "the sons of the kingdom" are those who are in the affections of truth from good; and "the sons of evil," those who are in the affections of falsity from evil; whence the latter are called "tares," and the former "good seed," for "tares" signify falsity from evil, and "good seed," truth from good; "the seed of the field" is truth from good, in man, from the Lord (n. 1940, 3038, 3310, 3373, 10,248, 10,249). "Seed" in the opposite sense is falsity from evil (n. 10,249). "The seed of the field" is also the nutrition of the mind by Divine truth from the Word and "sowing" is instruction (n. 6158, 9272). "The consummation of the age" is the last time of the church (n. 4535, 10,622).

[17] "Fishes," in the spiritual sense of the Word, signify scientifics, which belong to the natural or external man, and hence also natural or external men, both evil and good (n. 40, 991). Animals of all kinds correspond with such things as are with man (n. 45, 46, 246, 714, 716, 719, 2179, 2180, 3519, 9280, 10,609). In the Word, they to whom the Lord's justice and merit are attributed, are called "just"; they to whom their own justice and merit are attributed, are called "unjust" (n. 3686, 5069, 9263).

dans and Gentiles (n. 50, 51); and upon the Papists (n. 61–63), since they also in their own places were constituents of the first heaven. It remains that something be said of the Last Judgment upon the Reformed, who are also called Protestants and Evangelical, or how the first heaven composed of them passed away; for, as was said above, judgment was effected upon those only of whom the first heaven consisted. After being visited, and let into their own interiors, they were separated from each other, and divided into classes according to evils and falsities therefrom, and according to falsities and evils therefrom, and were cast into hells corresponding to their loves. Their hells surrounded the middle region on all sides, for the Reformed were in the middle, the Papists around them, the Mohammedans around the Papists, and the Gentiles in the outmost circuit (see n. 48). Those who were not cast into hells, were cast out into deserts; but there were some sent down to the plains in the southern and northern quarters, there to form societies, and be instructed and prepared for heaven; these are they who were preserved. But how all these things were accomplished, cannot be described in particular in this place, for the judgment upon the Reformed was of longer continuance than upon others, and was effected by successive changes. Now since much that is worthy of mention was then heard and seen, I will present the particulars in their own order in the *Explanation of the Apocalypse.*

XI.

THE STATE OF THE WORLD AND OF THE CHURCH HEREAFTER.

73. The state of the world hereafter will be altogether similar to what it has been heretofore, for the great change which has taken place in the spiritual world, does not induce any change in the natural world as to the external form; so that after this there will be civil affairs as before, there will be peace, treaties, and wars as before, with all other things which belong to societies in general and in particular. The Lord said that:—

> In the last times there will be wars, and then nation will rise against nation, and kingdom against kingdom, and there will be famines, pestilences, and earthquakes in divers places (*Matt.* xxiv. 6, 7).

This does not signify that such things will exist in the natural world, but that the things corresponding with them will exist in the spiritual world: for the Word in its prophecies does not treat of the kingdoms on earth, nor of the nations there, thus neither concerning their wars, nor of famines, pestilences, and earthquakes there, but of such things as correspond to them in the spiritual world; what these things are, is explained in the *Arcana Cœlestia,* and a collection of passages on the subject may be seen below.[18] But as for the state of the church, this it is which will be dissimilar hereafter; it will be similar indeed as to the external appearance, but dissimilar as to the internal. As to the external appearance divided churches will exist as heretofore, their doctrines will be taught as heretofore; and the same religions as now will exist among the Gentiles. But henceforth the man of the church will be in a more free state of thinking on matters of faith, thus on the spiritual things which relate to heaven, because spiritual freedom has been restored to him. For all things in the heavens and in the hells are now reduced into order, and all thought concerning Divine things and against the Divine inflows from thence; from the heavens all thought which is in harmony with Divine things, and from the hells all which is against Divine things. But man does not observe this change of state in himself, because he does not reflect upon it, and because he knows nothing of spiritual freedom and of influx; nevertheless it is per-

---

[18] That "wars" in the Word signify spiritual combats (n. 1659, 1664, 8295, 10,-455). Hence all "the arms of war," as "the bow," "the sword," "the shield," signify something of spiritual combat (n. 1788, 2686). "Kingdoms" signify churches as to truths and as to falsities (n. 1672, 2546). "Nations" signify those in the church who are in goods and who are in evils (n. 1059, 1159, 1205, 1258, 1260, 1416, 1849, 4574, 6005, 6306, 6858, 8054, 8317, 9320, 9327). "Famine" signifies a defect of the knowledges of good and truth (n. 1460, 3364, 5277, 5279, 5281, 5300, 5360, 5376, 5893). It also signifies the desolation of the church (n. 5279, 5415, 5576, 6110, 6144, 7102). "Pestilence" signifies the vastation and consummation of good and truth (n. 7102, 7505, 7507, 7511). "Earthquakes" signify changes of the state of the church (n. 3355).

ceived in heaven, and also by man himself after his death. Because spiritual freedom has been restored to man, therefore the spiritual sense of the Word has now been disclosed, and by it interior Divine truths have been revealed; for man in his former state would not have understood them, and he who would have understood them, would have profaned them. That man has freedom by means of the equilibrium between heaven and hell, and, that man cannot be reformed except in freedom, may be seen in the work on *Heaven and Hell* (n. 597 at the end).

74. I have had various conversations with angels, concerning the state of the church hereafter. They said that they know not things to come, for the knowledge of things to come belongs to the Lord alone; but they know that the slavery and captivity in which the man of the church was formerly, has been taken away, and that now, from restored freedom, he can better perceive interior truths, if he wills to perceive them, and thus be made more internal, if he wills to become so; but that still they have slender hope of the men of the Christian church, but much of some nation far distant from the Christian world, and therefore removed from infesters, which nation is such that it is capable of receiving spiritual light, and of being made a celestial-spiritual man, and they said, that at this day interior Divine truths are revealed in that nation, and are also received in spiritual faith, that is, in life and heart, and that they adore the Lord.

THE END.

CONTINUATION

CONCERNING

THE LAST JUDGMENT

CONTINUATION

CONCERNING

The Last Judgment

AND CONCERNING

THE SPIRITUAL WORLD

FROM THE LATIN OF

EMANUEL SWEDENBORG

SERVANT OF THE LORD JESUS CHRIST

CONTENTS.

	Sections.
I. The Last Judgment has been accomplished	1–7
II. The state of the World and of the Church before the Last Judgment and after it	8–13
III. The Last Judgment on the Reformed	14–31
IV. The Spiritual World	32–38
V. The English in the Spiritual World	39–47
VI. The Dutch in the Spiritual World	48–55
VII. The Papists in the Spiritual World	56–60
VIII. The Popish Saints in the Spiritual World	61–67
IX. The Mohammedans in the Spiritual World	68–72
X. The Africans and the Gentiles in the Spiritual World	73–78
XI. The Jews in the Spiritual World	79–82
XII. The Quakers in the Spiritual World	83–85
XIII. The Moravians in the Spiritual World	86–90

CONTINUATION

CONCERNING

THE LAST JUDGMENT.

I.

THE LAST JUDGMENT HAS BEEN ACCOMPLISHED.

1. In the former small work on The Last Judgment, the following subjects were treated of: The day of the Last Judgment does not mean the destruction of the world (n. 1–5). The procreations of the human race will never cease (n. 6–13). Heaven and hell are from the human race (n. 14–22). All who have ever been born men from the beginning of creation, and are deceased, are either in heaven or in hell (n. 23–27). The Last Judgment must be where all are together; therefore in the spiritual world, and not on the earth (n. 28–32). The Last Judgment exists when the end of the church is; and the end of the church is when there is no faith, because there is no charity (n. 33–39). All the things which are predicted in the *Apocalypse* are at this day fulfilled (n. 40–44). The Last Judgment has been accomplished (n. 45–52). Babylon and its destruction (n. 53–64). The former heaven and its abolition (n. 65–72). The state of the world and of the church hereafter (n. 73–74).

2. The subject of the Last Judgment is continued, principally that it may be known what the state of the world and the church was before the Last Judgment, and what the state of the world and the church has become since; also, how the Last Judgment was accomplished upon the Reformed.

3. It is a common opinion in the Christian world, that the whole heaven we see, and the whole earth inhabited by men will perish at the day of the Last Judgment, and that a new heaven and a new earth will exist in their places; that the souls of men will then receive their bodies, and that man will thus again be man as before. This opinion has become a matter of faith, because the Word has not been understood otherwise than according to the sense of its letter; and it could not be understood otherwise, until its spiritual sense was disclosed, also, because by many the belief has been acquired that the soul is only a breath exhaled by man; and that spirits, as well as angels, are of the substance of wind. While there was such a deficiency of understanding concerning souls, and concerning spirits and angels, the Last Judgment could not be thought of in any other manner. But when it comes to be understood, that a man is a man after death, just as he was a man in the world, with the sole difference that then he is clothed with a spiritual body, and not as before with a natural body; and that the spiritual body appears before those who are spiritual, even as the natural body appears before those who are natural, it may then also be understood, that the Last Judgment will not be in the natural, but in the spiritual world; for all the men who were ever born and have died, are together there.

4. When this is understood, then may the paradoxes be dissipated, which man would otherwise think concerning the state of souls after death, and their reunion with putrid corpses, and concerning the destruction of the created universe, thus concerning the Last Judgment. The paradoxes concerning the state of souls after death that he would think are these: That man would then be like an exhalation, or like wind, or like ether; either that he would be floating in the air, or not abiding in any place, but in a somewhere, which they call Pu;* and that he would see nothing, because he had no eyes; hear nothing, because he had no ears; speak nothing, because he had no mouth; and would therefore be blind, deaf, and dumb; and continually in the expectation, which could not but be sad, of receiving again at the day of the Last Judgment, those functions of the soul from which all the delight of life proceeds. Also that the souls of all who have lived since the first creation, must be in

---

* From the Greek *pou* = where.

a like miserable state, and that the men who lived fifty or sixty centuries ago, were likewise still floating in the air, or remaining in Pu, and awaiting judgment; besides other lamentable things.

5. I pass over paradoxes, similar to, and equally numerous with these, which the man who does not know that he is a man after death as before, must think concerning the destruction of the universe. But when he knows that a man after death is not an exhalation or a wind, but a spirit, and if he has lived well, an angel in heaven, and that spirits and angels are men in a perfect form, can then think from his understanding concerning the state of man after death, and the Last Judgment, and not from faith separate from the understanding, from which mere traditions go forth: and he may also with certainty conclude from his understanding, that the Last Judgment, which is predicted in the Word, will not exist in the natural world, but in the spiritual world, where all are together: and furthermore, that whenever it does exist, it must be revealed, for the sake of belief in the Word.

6. Put away from you the idea that the soul is like an exhalation, and then think of your own state, or of the state of your friends, or of the state of your infants after death. Will you not think that you will live a man, and they likewise? And since there is no life which is life without the senses, you cannot think otherwise than that they also see, hear, and speak; thus also panegyrists write over the deceased, placing them in heaven among the angels, in white garments, and in paradises. But if afterwards you relapse into the idea, that the soul is an exhalation, and has no sensitive life until after the Last Judgment, can you help being distracted when you think, What and where shall I be in the meantime? Shall I float in the air, or remain in Pu? Yet the preacher teaches me that after death I shall come among the happy, if I have believed well and lived well. You may believe then, as the truth is, that you are a man after death as well as before it, with only the difference that there is between the natural and the spiritual. Thus also all those think who believe in eternal life, and know nothing of this hypothetical tradition concerning the soul.

7. From what has been said already, it may appear that the Last Judgment cannot exist in the natural world, but in the spiritual world. That it also has existed there, may be seen from the things related of it from sight, in the former small work on *The Last Judgment* (n. 45-72), and still further from the particulars about to be related from sight, of the Last Judgment upon the Reformed. He who attends may also see it from the new things which are now revealed concerning heaven, the Word, and the church. What man can draw such things from himself?

II.

THE STATE OF THE WORLD AND OF THE CHURCH BEFORE THE LAST JUDGMENT, AND AFTER IT.

8. That the Last Judgment has been accomplished in the spiritual world, may appear from what has just been said. Nevertheless, in order to know anything of the state of the world and the church before and after it, it is altogether necessary that the following things should be known:—

I. *What is meant by "the former heaven" and "the former earth" which passed away (Apoc. xxi. 1).*

II. *Who, and of what quality were those who were in the former heaven and in the former earth.*

III. *Before the Last Judgment was effected upon them much of the communication between heaven and the world, thus also between the Lord and the church, was intercepted.*

IV. *After the Last Judgment the communication was restored.*

V. *Hence it is, that after the Last Judgment, and not before, revelations were made for the New Church.*

VI. *The state of the world and of the church before the Last Judgment was like evening and night, but after it like morning and day.*

9. I. *What is meant by "the former heaven" and "the former earth" which passed away, mentioned in the Apocalypse* (xxi. 1). "The former heaven" and "the former earth" there mentioned, does not mean the heaven visible to the eyes of men in the world, nor the earth which is inhabited by men; nor the former heaven, in which all those are who have lived well since the first creation. But congregations of spirits are meant who had made seeming heavens between heaven and hell for themselves, and because all spirits and angels dwell upon lands, as well as men, therefore by "the former heaven" and "the former earth," these are meant. The passing away of that heaven and that earth was seen, and it has been described from sight in the work on *The Last Judgment* (n. 45–72).

10. II. *Who, and of what quality were those who were in "the former heaven," and "the former earth,"* was described in the small work on *The Last Judgment;* but because the understanding of what follows depends on the knowledge of who they were and their quality, something shall here be said concerning them. All those who gathered themselves together under heaven, and in various places formed seeming heavens for themselves, and also called them heavens, were conjoined with the angels of the lowest heaven, but only as to externals, not as to internals. For the most part they were the goats and those akin to them, who are named in *Matthew* (xxv. 41–46); who indeed, in the world had not done evils, for they had lived well morally; but they had not done goods from a good origin, for they had separated faith from charity, and hence had not regarded evils as sins. Because they had lived as Christians in externals, they were conjoined with the angels of the lowest heaven, who were like them in externals, but not like them in internals; they being "the sheep," and in faith, yet in the faith of charity. On account of this conjunction they were necessarily tolerated; for to separate them, before the Last Judgment, would have brought injury upon those who were in the lowest heaven, who would have been drawn into destruction with them. This is what the Lord foretold in *Matthew:*—

Jesus spake a parable; the kingdom of the heavens is like unto a man who sowed good seed in his field; but while men slept, his enemy came, and sowed tares, and went away; when the blade was sprung up, and brought forth fruit, then appeared the tares also; so the servants of the householder coming, said unto him, Lord, didst not thou sow good seed in thy field? Wilt thou then that we go and gather them up? But he said,

Nay, lest, while ye gather up the tares, ye root up at the same time the wheat with them: let both grow together until the harvest; and in the time of harvest I will say to the reapers, Gather ye together first the tares, and bind them in bundles to burn them; but gather the wheat into my barn. He who hath sown the good seed, is the Son of man; the field is the world; the seed are the sons of the kingdom; the tares are the sons of evil; the harvest is the consummation of the age; as therefore the tares are gathered together, and burned, so shall it be in the consummation of the age (xiii. 24–30, 37–40).

"The consummation of the age" is the last time of the church; "the tares" are those who are interiorly evil; "the wheat" are those who are interiorly good; "the gathering together in bundles to burn," is the Last Judgment upon them; that harm should not be done to the good by separation before the Last Judgment, is signified by "lest in gathering up the tares, ye root up at the same time the wheat with them: let both grow until the harvest."

11. III. *Before the Last Judgment was effected upon them, much of the communication between heaven and the world, thus between the Lord and the church, was intercepted.* All enlightenment comes to man from the Lord through heaven, and it enters by an internal way. So long as there were congregations of such spirits between heaven and the world, or between the Lord and the church, man could not be enlightened. It was as when a sunbeam is cut off by a black interposing cloud, or as when the sun is eclipsed, and its light arrested, by the interjacent moon. Wherefore, if anything had been then revealed by the Lord, either it would not have been understood, or if understood, still it would not have been received, or if received, still it would afterwards have been suffocated. Now since all these interposing congregations were dissipated by the Last Judgment, it is plain, IV. *That the communication between heaven and the world, or between the Lord and the church, has been restored.*

12. V. *Hence it is, that after the Last Judgment has been accomplished, and not before, revelations were made for the New Church.* For since communication has been restored by the Last Judgment, man can be enlightened and reformed; that is, can understand the Divine truth of the Word, receive it when understood, and retain it when received, for the interposing obstacles are removed; and therefore John, after the former heaven and the former earth passed away, said that:—

> He saw a New Heaven and a New Earth, and then, the holy city Jerusalem, descending from God out of heaven, prepared as a Bride before her Husband; and he heard the One sitting upon the throne, say, Behold, I make all things new (*Apoc.* xxi. 1, 2, 5).

That the church is meant by "Jerusalem" may be seen in *The Doctrine Concerning the Lord* (n. 62–64). Concerning its new things (see n. 65 there).

13. VI. *The state of the world and of the church before the Last Judgment was like evening and night, but after it, like morning and day.* When the light of truth does not appear, and truth is not received, there is a state of the church in the world like evening and night; that there was a state before the Last Judgment, may appear from what is said above (n. 11); but when the light of truth appears, and the truth is received, there is a state of the church in the world like morning and day. Hence it is, that these two states of the church are called "evening and morning" and "night and day," in the Word; as in the following passages:—

> The Holy One said unto me, Until the evening the morning two thousand three hundred; then shall the sanctuary be justified (*Dan.* viii. 14).
>
> The vision of the evening and the morning is truth (*Dan.* viii. 26).
>
> There shall be one day, which is known to Jehovah, neither day nor night, for about the time of evening there shall be light (*Zech.* xiv. 7).
>
> One crying unto me out of Seir, Watchman, what of the night? The watchman said, The morning cometh, and also the night (*Isa.* xxi. 11, 12).

Concerning the last time of the church, Jesus said:—

> Watch, for ye know not when the Lord of the house will come, whether at evening, at midnight, at cock-crowing, or in the morning (*Mark* xiii. 35).
>
> Jesus said, I must work while it is day; the night cometh, when no one can work (*John* ix. 4);

and elsewhere (as in *Isa.* xvii. 14; *Jer.* vi. 4, 5; *Ps.* xxx. 6; lxv. 9; xc. 6). Since such things are meant by "evening and night," therefore the Lord, in order to fulfil the Word, also was buried in the evening and afterward rose again in the morning.

III.

THE LAST JUDGMENT UPON THE REFORMED.

14. In the former small work on *The Last Judgment* it treated of the judgment upon those who are meant by Babylon; and something of the judgment upon the Mohammedans and upon the Gentiles; but not of the judgment upon the Reformed. It was said only, that the Reformed were in the middle, arranged there according to countries; the Papists around them; the Mohammedans around the Papists, and around these the Gentiles and peoples of various religions. The Reformed constituted the middle, or central region, because the Word is read by them and the Lord is worshiped, and hence with them there is the greatest light; and spiritual light, which is from the Lord as a sun, which in its essence is the Divine love, proceeds and extends itself on every side, and enlightens even those who are in the extreme circumferences, and opens the faculty of understanding truths, as far as from their religion they can receive them. For spiritual light in its essence is the Divine wisdom, and it enters the understanding in man, as far as, from knowledges received, he has the faculty of perceiving it; and it does not pass through spaces, like the light of the world, but through the affections and perceptions of truth, therefore, in an instant, to the last limits of the heavens. From these are the appearances of spaces in that world. Concerning these things more may be seen in *The Doctrine Concerning the Sacred Scripture* (n. 104–113).

15. The Last Judgment upon the Reformed shall be described in the following order.

I. *Upon whom of the Reformed the Last Judgment was effected.*
II. *The signs and visitations before the Last Judgment.*
III. *How the universal judgment was effected.*
IV. *The salvation of the sheep.*

16. I. *Upon whom among the Reformed the Last Judgment was effected.* The Last Judgment was effected upon those only of the Reformed, who in the world confessed God, read the

Word, heard preaching, partook of the sacrament of the Supper, and did not neglect the solemnities of the worship of the church; and yet thought that adulteries, various kinds of theft, lying, revenge, hatred, and the like, were allowable. These although they confessed God, still made no account of sins against Him; they read the Word, and still they made no account of the precepts of life in it; they heard preachings, and still they paid no attention to them; they went to the sacrament of the Supper, and still they did not desist from the evils of their former life; they did not neglect the solemnities of worship, and still they amended their lives in nothing. Thus they lived as if from religion, in their externals, yet in their internals they had nothing of it. These are they who are meant by "the dragon" in the *Apocalypse* (chap. xii.); for it is there said of the dragon, that it was seen in heaven, that it fought with Michael in heaven, and that it drew down the third part of the stars from heaven; which things are said, because these, by means of the confession of God, by reading the Word, and by external worship, communicated with heaven. The same are meant by "the goats" in *Matthew*, chap. xxv.; to whom it is not said that they did evils, but that they omitted to do goods; and all such omit to do goods which are goods, because they do not shun evils as sins, and although they do not do them, still they think them allowable, and thus do them in spirit, and also in body, when permitted.

17. Upon all these from the Reformed the Last Judgment was effected, but not upon those who did not believe in God, who contemned the Word, and rejected from their hearts the holy things of the church; for all these, when they came from the natural world into the spiritual world, were cast into hell.

18. All who lived like Christians in externals, and made no account of the Christian life, made one exteriorly with the heavens, but interiorly with the hells, and since they could not be torn away in a moment from their conjunction with heaven, they were detained in the world of spirits, which is midway between heaven and hell, and it was permitted them to form societies, and to live together as in the world; and there by arts unknown to the world, to cause splendid appearances, and by this means to persuade themselves and others, that they were in heaven; therefore, from that external appearance they called their societies heavens. The heavens and the earths upon which they dwelt, are meant by "the former heaven, and the former earth which passed away" (*Apoc.* xxi. 1).

19. Meanwhile, so long as they remained there, the interiors of their minds were closed, and the exteriors were opened; by which means, their evils, by which they made one with the hells, did not appear. But when the Last Judgment was at hand, their interiors were disclosed, and they then appeared before all such as they really were; and since they then acted in unity with the hells, they were no longer able to simulate the Christian life, but from delight rushed into evils and crimes of every kind, and were turned into devils, and, moreover, were seen as such, some black, some fiery, and some livid like corpses; those who were in the pride of their own intelligence, appearing black; those who were in the insane love of ruling over all, appearing fiery; and those who were in the neglect and contempt of truth, appearing livid like corpses. Thus were the scenes of those theatres changed.

20. The Reformed constitute the inmost or middle part of the world of spirits, which is midway between heaven and hell, and are there arranged according to countries. In the centre of this middle region are the English; towards the south and the east of it are the Dutch; towards the north, the Germans; towards the west and the north, the Swedes; and towards the west, the Danes. But those only who have lived the life of charity, and its faith, are in that middle region: many societies of them dwell there. Surrounding them are those of the Reformed, who have not lived the life of faith and charity: these are they who made as it were heavens to themselves. But there is a different arrangement of all in heaven, and also of all in hell. The reason why the Reformed constitute the middle there is, because with them the Word is read, and the Lord is also worshiped, from which the greatest light is there; and thence, as from a centre, this light is propagated to all the circumferences and enlightens. For the light in which spirits and angels are, proceeds from the Lord as a sun, and this sun, in its essence, is the Divine love, and the light which proceeds from it in its essence is the Divine wisdom: all the spiritual of that world is derived from it. Concerning the Lord as the sun in the spiritual world, and concerning the light and heat of that sun, see the work on *Heaven and Hell* (n. 116–140).

21. Every arrangement of the societies in that world, is an arrangement according to the differences of love; the reason of which is, that love is the life of man, and the Lord, who is Divine love itself, arranges them according to its reception; and the differences of loves are innumerable, which no one knows but the Lord alone. He so conjoins the societies, that they all lead as it were one life of man; the societies of the heavens one life of celestial and spiritual love; the societies of the hells, one life of diabolical and infernal love; He conjoins the heavens and the hells by oppositions. Because there is such an arrangement, every man after death goes into the society of his own love, nor can he go into any other, for his love opposes it. Hence it is that they who are in spiritual love are in heaven, but they who are in natural love only, are in hell. Spiritual love is implanted solely by the life of charity, and natural love remains natural, if the life of charity is omitted; and natural love, if it is not subjected to spiritual love, is opposed to it.

22. From these things it may appear, upon whom of the Reformed the Last Judgment was effected; that it was not upon those who were in the centre, but upon those who were around it; who from external morality, as was said, appeared exteriorly like Christians, but interiorly they were not Christians, because they had no spiritual life.

23. II. *The signs and visitations before the Last Judgment.* There was seen above those who had formed to themselves seeming heavens as it were a storm cloud, which appearance was from the presence of the Lord in the angelic heavens above them, especially from His presence in the lowest heaven, lest any of them on account of the conjunction should be carried away and perish with them. The higher heavens moreover were brought down nearer to them, by which the interiors of those upon whom the judgment was about to come were disclosed; on which disclosure, they appeared no longer like moral Christians, as before, but like demons. They were tumultuous and strove among themselves about God, the Lord, the Word, faith, and the church; and because their lusts for evils were then also set free, they rejected all these things with contempt and ridicule, and rushed into every kind of enormity. Thus the state of those heavenly inhabitants was changed. Then at the same time all their splendid appearances, which they had made for themselves by arts unknown in the world, vanished away; their palaces were turned into vile huts; their gardens into stagnant pools; their temples into heaps of rubbish; and the very hills upon which they dwelt, into gravel heaps, and into other similar things, which corresponded to their wicked minds and lusts. For all the visible things of the spiritual world are correspondences of the affections of spirits and angels. These were the signs of the coming judgment.

24. As the disclosure of the interiors increased, so the order among the inhabitants was changed and inverted. Those who were most powerful in reasonings against the holy things of the church, rushed into the middle, and assumed the dominion; and the rest, who were less powerful in reasonings, receded to the circumferences, and acknowledged those who were in the middle as their tutor-angels. Thus they collected themselves together into the form of hell.

25. These changes of their state were accompanied by various concussions of their dwellings and lands; which were followed by earthquakes, mighty according to their perversions. Here and there, too, chasms were made towards the hells which were under them, and a communication was thus opened with them. Exhalations were then seen ascending like smoke mingled with sparks of fire. These also were signs which preceded, which are also meant by the Lord's words concerning the consummation of the age, and then concerning the Last Judgment, in the *Evangelists:*—

Nation shall be stirred up against nation; there shall be great earthquakes in divers places; signs also from heaven, terrible and great. And there shall be distress of nations, the sea and the billows roaring (*Luke* xxi. 10, 11, 25; *Matt.* xxiv. 7; *Mark* xiii. 8).

26. *Visitations* also were made by angels; for before any ill conditioned society perishes, visitation always precedes. The angels exhorted them to desist, and denounced destruction upon them if they did not. Then they also sought out and separated any good spirits who were intermingled with them.

But the multitude, excited by their leaders, reviled the angels, and rushed in upon them, for the purpose of dragging them into the forum, and treating them in an abominable manner; just as was done in Sodom. Most of them were in faith separated from charity; and there were also some who professed charity, and yet lived shamefully.

27. III. *How the universal judgment was effected.* After the visitations and premonitory signs of the coming judgment could not turn their minds from criminal acts, and from seditious plottings against those who acknowledged the Lord as the God of heaven and earth, held the Word holy, and led a life of charity, the Last Judgment came upon them. It was thus effected.

28. The Lord was seen in a bright cloud with angels, and a sound as of trumpets was heard from it; which was a sign representative of the protection of the angels of heaven by the Lord, and of the gathering of the good from every side. For the Lord does not bring destruction upon any one, but only protects His own, and draws them away from communication with the evil; and when they are withdrawn, the evil come into their own lusts, and from them rush into every kind of abomination. Then all who were about to perish, were seen together like a great dragon, with its tail extended in a curve, and elevated towards heaven, bending itself about on high in various directions, as though it would destroy heaven, and draw it down. But the effort was vain, for the tail was cast down, and the dragon, which had also appeared elevated, sank down. It was granted me to see this representation, that I might know and make known who are meant by "the dragon" in the *Apocalypse;* namely, that "the dragon" means all who read the Word, hear preachings, and perform the holy things of the church, making no account of the lusts of evil by which they are enticed, and interiorly they meditate thefts and frauds, adulteries and obscenities, hatred and revenge, lies and blasphemies; and who thus live in spirit like devils, and in body like angels. These constituted the body of the dragon, but the tail was constituted of those who, when in the world, were in faith separated from charity, and were like the former as to thoughts and intentions.

29. Then I saw some of the rocks upon which they were, subsiding even to the lowest depths; some carried far away; some opening in the middle, and those who were on them cast down through the chasm; and some inundated as with a flood. And I saw many collected into companies, as into bundles, according to the genera and species of evil, and cast hither and thither into whirlpools, marshes, stagnant pools, and deserts, which were so many hells. The rest who were not on rocks, but scattered here and there, and who yet were in similar evils, fled amazed to the Papists, Mohammedans, and Gentiles, and professed their religions, which they could do without any disturbance of mind, because they had no religion; but still lest they should seduce these also, they were driven away, and thrust down to their companions in the hells. This is a general description of their destruction; the particulars which I saw, are more than can be here described.

30. *The salvation of the sheep.* After the Last Judgment was accomplished, there was then joy in heaven, and also light in the world of spirits, such as was not before. The joy in heaven and its quality, after the dragon was cast down, is described in the *Apocalypse* (xii. 10–12); and there was light in the world of spirits, because those infernal societies had been interposed like clouds which darken the earth. A similar light also then arose with men in the world, from which they had new enlightenment.

31. I then saw angelic spirits in great numbers rising from below, and elevated into heaven, who were the sheep, there reserved and guarded by the Lord for ages back, lest they should come into the malignant sphere flowing forth from dragonists, and their charity be suffocated. These are they, who are meant in the Word, by "those who went forth from the sepulchres"; also, by "the souls of those slain for the testimony of Jesus," who were watching; and by those "who are of the first resurrection."

CONTINUATION

CONCERNING

THE SPIRITUAL WORLD.

IV.

THE SPIRITUAL WORLD.

32. The spiritual world has been treated of in a special work on *Heaven and Hell*, in which many particulars of that world are described; and since every man enters that world after death, his state then is also described there. Who does not know that man will live after death, because he is born a man, and created in the image of God, and because the Lord, in His Word, teaches it? But what his future life will be has hitherto been unknown. It has been believed that he would then be a soul, of which no other idea was conceived than as of air or ether, in which some capacity of thought would reside, without such sight as belongs to the eye, without such hearing as belongs to the ear, and without speech such as belongs to the mouth. And yet man is equally a man after death; and such a man that he does not know otherwise than that he is still in the former world; he sees, hears, and speaks as in the former world; he walks, runs, and sits as in the former world; he eats and drinks as in the former world; he sleeps and wakes as in the former world; he enjoys conjugial delight as in the former world; in a word he is a man as to each and all things. From which it is plain, that death is but a continuation of life, and is only transition.

33. There are many causes why man has not known of this state of his after death; one of which is, that he could not be enlightened, so little faith had he in the immortality of the soul; as may appear from many even of the learned, who believe that they are like beasts, only more perfect than they, in being able to speak; and therefore in their heart they deny the life after death, although they profess it with the mouth. From this thought of theirs they have become so sensual, that they could not believe that a man is a man after death, because they do not see him with their eyes, for they say, how can a soul be such a man? It is otherwise with those who believe they will live after death; these think interiorly in themselves, that they will come into heaven, enjoy delights with the angels, see heavenly paradises, and stand before the Lord in white garments, besides other things. This is their interior thought; their exterior thought may wander from it, when they think of the soul from the hypothesis of the learned.

34. That a man is equally a man after death, although he does not appear before the eyes, may appear from the angels seen by Abraham, Gideon, Daniel, and other prophets; from the angels seen in the Lord's sepulchre, and afterwards, oftentimes, by John in the *Apocalypse;* especially from the Lord Himself, who showed His disciples that He was a Man, by touch, and by eating, and yet became invisible before their eyes. The reason why they saw Him was, because the eyes of their spirits were then opened; and when these are opened, the things in the spiritual world appear as clearly as the things in the natural world.

35. Because it has pleased the Lord to open for me the eyes of my spirit, and to keep them open now for nineteen years, it has been given me to see the things which are in the spiritual world, and also to describe them. I can affirm that they are not visions, but *things seen* in all wakefulness.

36. The difference between a man in the natural world, and a man in the spiritual world, is, that the one man is clothed with a spiritual body, but the other with a natural body; and the spiritual man sees the spiritual man, as clearly as the natural man sees the natural man; but the natural man cannot see the spiritual man, and the spiritual man cannot see the natural man, on account of the difference between the natural and the spiritual; what kind of difference this is, can be described, but not in a few words.

37. From the things seen during so many years, I am enabled to relate the following: that there are lands in the spiritual world, just as in the natural world; and that there are hills and mountains, plains and valleys, and also fountains and rivers, lakes and seas; there are paradises and gardens, groves and woods, and palaces and houses; also that there are writings and books, offices and trades; and that there are precious stones, gold and silver; in a word, there are each and all things that exist in the natural world, and they are infinitely more perfect in the heavens.

38. But the difference in general is this; that all things in the spiritual world are from a spiritual origin, and hence, as to their essence, are spiritual, they are from the sun there which is pure love; and all things in the natural world are from a natural origin, and hence as to their essence are natural, for they are from the sun there which is pure fire. Hence it is, that the spiritual man must be nourished with food from a spiritual origin, as the natural man is with food from a natural origin. More may be seen in the work on *Heaven and Hell*.

V.

THE ENGLISH IN THE SPIRITUAL WORLD.

39. There are two states of thought with man, an external and an internal state; man is in the external state in the natural world, in the internal state in the spiritual world: these states make one with the good, but not with the evil. What a man is as to his internal, is rarely manifest in the natural world, because from his infancy, he has wished to be moral, and has learned to seem so. But what he is, clearly appears in the spiritual world, for spiritual light discloses it, and also man is then a spirit, and the spirit is the internal man. Now, since it has been given me to be in that light, and from it, to see what the internal is in the men of various kingdoms, by an intercourse of many years with angels and spirits, it behooves me to manifest it, because of its importance. Here I will say something of the noble English nation only.

40. The more excellent of the English nation are in the centre of all Christians (see above, n. 20). The reason why they are in the centre is, because they have interior intellectual light. This is not apparent to any one in the natural world, but it is conspicuous in the spiritual world. This light they derive from the liberty of thinking, and thence of speaking and of writing, in which they are. With others, who are not in such liberty, intellectual light is darkened because it has no outlet. But this light is not active of itself, but is rendered active by others, especially by men of reputation and authority among them. As soon as anything is said by these men, or as soon as anything they approve is read, that light shines forth, and seldom before. On this account governors are placed over them in the spiritual world, and priests of great reputation for learning and distinguished ability are given them, whose commands and monitions, from this their natural disposition, they cheerfully obey.

41. They rarely go out of their own society, because they love it as in the world they love their country. There is also a similarity of minds among them, from which they contract intimacy with friends of their own country, and rarely with others. They also mutually aid each other; and they love sincerity.

42. There are two great cities similar to London, into which most of the English come after death; these cities it was given me to see, as well as to walk through. The middle of the one city answers to that part of the English London where there is a meeting of merchants, called the Exchange; there the governors dwell. Above that middle is the east; below it is the west; on the right side of it is the south; on the left side of it is the north. They who have led a life of charity more than the rest, dwell in the eastern quarter, where there are magnificent palaces. The wise, with whom there are many splendid things, dwell in the southern quarter. They who more than others love the liberty of speaking and of writing, dwell in the northern quarter. They who make profession of faith, dwell in the western quarter; to the right in this quarter, there is an entrance into the city, and an exit from it; they who live wickedly are there sent out of it. The presbyters, who are in the west, and who, as was said, profess faith, dare not enter the city through the broad streets, but only through the narrower ways, because they who are in the faith of charity, are the only inhabitants who are tolerated in the city. I have heard them complaining of the preachers in the west, that they prepare their discourses with such art and at the same time eloquence, interweaving justification by faith to them unknown, that they do not know whether good is to be done or not; they preach intrinsic good, and separate it from extrinsic good, which they sometimes call meritorious, and therefore not acceptable to God; yet still they call it good, because it is useful. But when those who dwell in the eastern and southern quarters of the city hear such mystical discourses, they walk out of the temples, and the preachers are afterwards deprived of the priesthood.

43. The other great city similar to London, is not in the Christian centre (of which n. 20), but lies beyond it in the north. They who are interiorly evil come into it after death. In the middle of it there is an open communication with hell, by which they are swallowed up in turn.

44. I once heard presbyters from England conversing together concerning faith alone, and I saw a certain image made by them which represented faith alone. It appeared in obscure light like a great giant, and in their eyes like a beautiful man; but when the light of heaven was let in, the upper part of it appeared like a monster, and the lower like a serpent, not unlike the description which is given of Dagon, the idol of the Philistines. When they saw this they left it, and the bystanders cast it into a stagnant pool.

45. It was perceived from those of the English who are in the spiritual world, that they have as it were a twofold theology, one from the doctrine of faith, and the other from the doctrine of life; from the doctrine of faith for those who are initiated into the priesthood: from the doctrine of life for those who are not initiated into the priesthood, and who are commonly called the laity. This doctrine of life is set forth in the exhortation which is read in the temples on any Sabbath day, to those who go to the Sacrament of the Supper; in which it is openly said that if they do not shun evils as sins, they cast themselves into eternal damnation, and that if they then approach the holy communion the devil will enter into them, as he entered into Judas. I have sometimes spoken with the priests concerning this doctrine of life, that it does not agree with their doctrine of faith. They made no reply, but thought what they did not dare to utter. You may see that exhortation in *The Doctrine of Life for the New Jerusalem* (n. 5–7).

46. I have often seen a certain Englishman, who became celebrated by a book he published some years ago, in which he attempted to establish the conjunction of faith and charity by an influx and interior operation of the Holy Spirit. He gave out that this influx affected man in an inexpressible manner, and without his being conscious of it, but did not touch, much less manifestly move his will or excite his thought to do anything as of himself, except permissively; the reason being, that nothing of the man might enter into the Divine Providence as one with it; also that thus evils might not appear before God. He thus excluded the external exercises of charity for the sake of any salvation, but favoring them for the sake of the public good. Since his arguments were ingenious, and the snake in the grass was not seen, his book was received as most orthodox. This author retained the same dogma after his departure from the world, nor could he recede from it, because it was confirmed in him. The angels spoke with him, and said that this was not the truth, but mere ingenuity with eloquence; and that the truth is, that man ought to shun evil and do good as from himself, yet with the acknowledgment that it is from the Lord, and that there is no faith before this, still less is that thought which he calls faith. And since this was opposed to his dogma, it was permitted him of his own sagacity to inquire further, whether such unknown influx and internal operation apart from the external operation of man is given. He was then seen to strain his mind, and to wander about in thought in various ways, always in the persuasion that man is no otherwise renewed and saved. But as often as he came to the end of his way, his eyes were opened, and he saw that he was wandering, and even confessed it to those who were present. I saw him wandering thus for two years, and in the end of his ways confessing that no such influx is given, unless evil in the external man be removed, which is effected by shunning evils as sins, as if from himself; and I heard him at length saying, that all who confirm themselves in that heresy, will be insane from the pride of their own intelligence.

47. I have spoken with Melancthon, and then asked him concerning his state; but he was not willing to reply. Wherefore I was informed of his lot by others, which is that he is alternately in a fretted stone chamber, and alternately in hell, and that in his chamber he appears clothed in a bear's skin on account of the cold, and because of the uncleanness there he does not admit newcomers from the world, who wish to visit him on account of the reputation of his name. He still speaks of faith alone, which in the world he established more than others.

VI.

THE DUTCH IN THE SPIRITUAL WORLD.

48. It was said above (n. 20), that Christians with whom the Word is read and the Lord is worshiped, are in the middle of the nations and people of the whole spiritual world, because the greatest spiritual light is with them, and the light is radiated thence as from a centre into all the circumference even to the last boundary; and it enlightens, according to what is said in *The Doctrine of the New Jerusalem Concerning the Sacred Scripture* (n. 104–113). In this middle, the Reformed Christians have places allotted to them according to their reception of spiritual light from the Lord; and since the English have that light stored up in the intellectual part, therefore they are in the inmost of that middle region; and because the Dutch keep that light more nearly conjoined to natural light, and hence there is no such brightness of light apparent among them, but in its place something not transparent which is receptive of rationality from spiritual light, and at the same time from spiritual heat, they, in the Christian middle region, have obtained dwellings in the east and south; in the east from the faculty of receiving spiritual heat, which in them is charity, and in the south from the faculty of receiving spiritual light, which in them is faith. That the quarters in the spiritual world are not like the quarters in the natural world, and that dwellings according to quarters, are dwellings according to the reception of faith and love, and that they who excel in love and charity, are in the east, and they who excel in intelligence and faith, are in the south, may be seen in the work on *Heaven and Hell* (n. 141–153). Another reason why they are in these quarters of the Christian middle region is, that trade is their final love, and money is the mediate subservient love, and that love is spiritual; but where money is the final love, and trade the mediate subservient love, the love is natural, and partakes of avarice. In the before-mentioned spiritual love, which regarded in itself is the common good, in which and from which is the good of the country, the Dutch excel others.

49. The Dutch adhere more firmly than others to the principles of their religion, nor are they drawn away from them; and if they are convinced that one or another of them is not in agreement, still they do not admit it, but turn themselves back, and remain unmoved. Thus they remove themselves from an interior intuition of truth, for they keep their rational under obedience, in spiritual things. Because they are such, when they enter the spiritual world after death, they are prepared for receiving the spiritual of heaven, which is Divine truth, quite differently from others. They are not taught, because they do not receive; but what heaven is, is described to them, and afterwards it is granted them to ascend there, and to see it; and then whatever agrees with their genius is infused into them, which being done, they are sent down, and return to their companions with a full desire for heaven. If then they do not receive this truth, that God is One in Person and in essence, and that this God is the Lord, and that in Him is the Trinity; and also this truth, that faith and charity as matters of knowledge and discourse, are of no avail apart from the life of faith and charity, and that faith and charity are given by the Lord when evils are shunned as sins; if when they are taught these truths, they turn themselves away, and still think of God as existing in three Persons, and of religion, merely that there is such a thing, they are reduced to misery, and their trade is taken away, until they are brought to the greatest extremities. And they are then led to those who have abundance of everything, and a flourishing trade, and when there, the thought is insinuated into them from heaven, whence it is that they are such, and at the same time to reflect on the faith of these persons concerning the Lord, and upon their life, in that they shun evils as sins. In a little time they make inquiries, and perceive an agreement with their own thought and reflection; this is done repeatedly. At length, they think of themselves, that in order to be relieved from their miseries, they must believe and do the same. Then, as they receive that faith, and live that life of charity, opulence and enjoyment of life are given them. In this manner, those of them who have led anything of a life of charity in the world, are amended by themselves, and not by others, and are prepared for heaven. They afterwards became more constant than others, so that they may be called constancies; and they do not allow themselves to be led away by any reasoning, fallacy, or obscurity brought on by sophistries, or by any preposterous view from confirmations alone.

50. The Dutch are easily distinguished from others in the spiritual world, because they appear in like garments as in the natural world, with the difference that those are in more shining ones who have received faith and that spiritual life. They appear in similar garments, because they remain constant in the principles of their religion; and in the spiritual world all are clothed according to their religious principles; whence it is, that they who are in Divine truths, have garments of white and of fine linen.

51. The cities in which the Dutch dwell, are guarded in a peculiar manner, all the streets in them are covered, and in the streets are gates, in order that they may not be viewed from the surrounding rocks and hills. This they do from their inherent prudence in concealing their designs, and not divulging their intentions; for these things in the spiritual world are brought forth by inspection. When any one enters a city with the purpose of exploring their state, when he is about to depart, he is led to the closed gates of the streets, back and forth to many, and this to extreme weariness, and he is then let out; this is done to the end that he may not return. Wives who claim dominion over their husbands, dwell on one side of the city, and only meet them by invitation, given formally; and the husbands then lead them to houses, where married pairs are living, without there being any dominion of the one over the other, and show them how neat and clean their houses are, and how delightful their life is, and that these are the results of mutual and conjugial love. Those who attend to, and are affected with these things, desist from dominion, and they live together, and they then obtain a dwelling nearer to the middle, and are called angels. The reason is, that conjugial love is a celestial love, which is without dominion.

53. In the days of the Last Judgment, I saw many thousands of that nation cast out of the cities there, and out of the villages and surrounding lands. They were those who when in the world had done nothing of good from any religion or conscience, but only on account of reputation, that they might appear sincere for the sake of gain; for such when the prospect of fame and gain is taken away, as is the case in the spiritual world, then rush into every abomination; and when they are in the fields, and outside the cities, they rob every one they encounter. I saw them cast into a fiery gulf stretching under the eastern tract, and into a dark cavern stretching under the southern tract. This casting out I saw on the 9th day of January, 1757. Those only were left, among whom there was religion, and a conscience from religion.

54. I have spoken, but only once, with Calvin; he was in a society of heaven, which appears in front, above the head; and he said that he did not agree with Luther and Melancthon about faith alone, because works are so often named in the Word, and the doing of them commanded, and that therefore, faith and works ought to be conjoined. I heard from one of the governors of that society, that Calvin was accepted in his society, because he was upright and made no disturbance.

55. What Luther's lot is, shall be told elsewhere, for I have often heard and seen him. Here, I shall only say, that he has often wished to recede from his faith alone, but in vain; and that therefore, he is still in the world of spirits, which is midway between heaven and hell; where he sometimes suffers hard things.

VII.

THE PAPISTS IN THE SPIRITUAL WORLD.

56. The Papists, and the Last Judgment upon them, were treated of in the small work on *The Last Judgment* (n. 53–64). The Papists in the spiritual world appear around the Reformed, and are separated from them by an interval, which they are not permitted to pass. Nevertheless, those who are of the order of Jesuits, by clandestine arts procure for themselves communications, and also send out emissaries, by unknown paths, for the purpose of seducing them. But they are discovered, and after being punished, they are either sent back to their companions, or are cast into hell.

57. After the Last Judgment, their state was so changed, that they were not allowed to gather together in companies, as before; but ways were appointed to every love, both good and evil, which those who come from the world immediately enter, and go to a society corresponding to their love. Thus the wicked are borne away to a society which is in conjunction with the hells, and the good to a society which is in conjunction with the heavens; thus precaution is taken that they may not form artificial heavens for themselves as before. Such societies in the world of spirits, which is midway between heaven and hell, are innumerable; being as many as there are genera and species of good and evil affections. And in the meantime, before spirits are either elevated into heaven, or cast down into hell, they are in spiritual conjunction with men in the world, because they too are in the midst between heaven and hell.

58. All those of the Papists, who have not been wholly idolaters, and who, from their religious persuasion, have done goods out of a sincere heart, and have also looked to the Lord, are led to societies which are instituted in the confines nearest to the Reformed, and are instructed there, the Word being read, and the Lord preached to them; and they who receive truths and apply them to life, are elevated into heaven and become angels. There are many such societies of them in every quarter, and they are guarded on all sides from the treacheries and cunning devices of the monks, and from the Babylonish leaven. Moreover, all their infants are in heaven, because, being educated by the angels under the guidance of the Lord, they know nothing of the falsities of the religion of their parents.

59. All who come from the earth into the spiritual world, are at first kept in the confession of faith, and in the religion of their country; and so therefore are the Papists. On this account, they always have some representative Pontiff set over them, whom they also adore with the same ceremony as in the world. Rarely does any Pope from the world act the Pontiff there; yet he who was Pope at Rome twenty years ago,* was appointed over the Papists, because he cherished in heart that the Word is more holy than is believed, and that the Lord ought to be worshiped. But, after filling the office of Pope for some years, he abdicated it, and betook himself to the Reformed Christians, among whom he still is, and enjoys a happy life. It was granted me to speak with him, and he said, that he adored the Lord alone, because He is God, who has power over heaven and earth, and that the invocations of saints, and also their masses, are trifles; and that when he was in the world, he intended to restore that church, but that for reasons, which he mentioned, he found it impossible to do so. When the great northern city of the Papists was destroyed, on the day of the Last Judgment, I saw him carried out of it on a couch, and taken to a place of safety. Quite a different thing happened to his successor.

60. Here I am allowed to add something memorable. It was granted me to speak with Louis XIV., grandfather of the reigning king of France, who while he was in the world, worshiped the Lord, read the Word, and acknowledged the Pope only as the highest one of the church; in consequence of which, he has great dignity in the spiritual world, and rules the best society of the French nation. Once I saw him as it were descending by ladders, and after he descended I heard him saying, that he seemed to himself as if at Versailles, and then

---

* This was published in 1763.

there was silence round about for half an hour; at the end of that time, he said, that he had spoken with the king of France, his grandson, concerning the Bull Unigenitus, advising him to desist from his former design, and not to accept it, because it was detrimental to the French nation, he said that he insinuated this into his thought profoundly. This took place in the year 1759, on the 13th day of December, about eight o'clock in the evening.

VIII.

THE POPISH SAINTS IN THE SPIRITUAL WORLD.

61. It is known that man has from his parents implanted or hereditary evil, but in what it consists is known to few. It consists in the love of ruling, which is such, that as far as the reins are given it, so far it bursts forth, until it even burns with the lust of ruling over all, and at length of wishing to be invoked and worshiped as God. This love is the serpent, which deceived Eve and Adam, for it said to the woman:—

God knows, that in the day ye eat of the fruit of the tree, your eyes shall be opened, and then ye shall be as God (*Gen.* iii. 4, 5).

As far therefore as man rushes with loosened reins into this love, so far he turns himself away from God, and turns towards himself, and becomes an atheist; and then the Divine truths which are of the Word, may serve as means, but because dominion is the end, the means are in the heart only as they serve him. This is the reason why those who are in the mediate and in the ultimate degree of the love of ruling, are all in hell, for that love is the devil there; and in hell there are some of such a nature, that they cannot bear to hear any one speaking of God.

62. Those of the Papal nation have this love who have had dominion from the frenzy of its delight, and have despised the Word, and preferred the dictates of the Pope to it. They are utterly devastated as to externals, until they no longer know anything of the church, and then they are cast down into hell and become devils. There is a certain separate hell for those who wish to be invoked as gods, where such is their fantasy, that they do not see what is, but what is not. Their delirium is such as affects persons in a malignant fever, who see things floating in the air and in the chamber, and on the covering of the bed, which do not exist. This worst of evils is meant by:—

The head of the serpent, which is bruised by the Seed of the woman, and which wounds His heel (*Gen.* iii. 15).

"The heel" of the Lord, who is "the Seed of the woman," is the Divine proceeding in ultimates, which is the Word in the sense of the letter.

63. Because man from heredity is such, that he wishes to rule, and as the reins are loosened, successively over more, and at length over all, and because the wish to be invoked and worshiped as God, is the inmost of this love of ruling, therefore all who have been made saints by the Papal bulls, are removed from the sight of others and hidden, and are deprived of all intercourse with their worshipers. This is done, lest that worst root of evils should be excited in them, and they should be hurried into such fantastic deliriums as prevail in the abovementioned hell. In such deliriums are those who, when they lived in the world, have eagerly sought to be made saints after death, for the purpose of being invoked.

64. Many of the Papal nation, especially the monks, when they come into the spiritual world, seek the saints, each the saint of his own order; yet they do not find them, and therefore they wonder. But afterwards they are instructed by others, that they are either intermingled with those who are in the heavens, or with those who are in the hells, every one according to his life in the world; and that in whichsoever they are, they know nothing of the worship and invocation of themselves; and that they who know it, and wished to be invoked, are in that separate and delirious hell. The worship of saints is such an abomination in heaven, that whenever they hear of it they are horrified, because as far as worship is paid to any man, in so far it is withheld from the Lord, for thus He alone cannot be worshiped; and if the Lord is not alone worshiped, a discrimination is made, which destroys communion, and the felicity of life which flows from it.

65. That I might know, for the sake of informing others, what kind of men the Popish saints are, as many as a hundred of them, who knew of their canonization, were brought up from the lower earth. The greater part ascended from behind, and only a few in front, and I spoke with one of them, who they said was Xavier. While he talked with me, he was quite foolish, yet he was able to tell me, that in his place, where he remains confined, he is not so; but that he becomes foolish as often as he thinks that he is a saint. I heard a like murmur from those who were behind.

66. It is otherwise with the so-called saints who are in heaven; they know nothing at all of what is doing upon earth, nor have I spoken with them, lest any idea of this should enter their minds. Only once Mary, the mother of the Lord, passed by, and appeared over head in white raiment, and then, stopping awhile, she said that she had been the mother of the Lord, and that He was indeed born of her, but that He became God, and put off all the human from her, and that therefore she now adores Him as her God, and is unwilling that any one should acknowledge Him as her Son, because in Him all is Divine.

67. I will here add this Relation. A certain woman in splendid raiment and with saint-like countenance, occasionally appears in a middle altitude, to the Parisians who are in a society in the spiritual world, and tells them she is Genevieve. But as soon as any of them begin to adore her, then instantly her countenance is changed, and her raiment too, and she becomes like an ordinary woman, and chides them for wishing to adore a woman, who, among her companions, is in no more repute than a maid servant; wondering that men in the world are caught by such trifles. The angels said that she appears for the purpose of separating those there who worship man from those who worship the Lord.

XI.

THE MOHAMMEDANS IN THE SPIRITUAL WORLD; AND MOHAMMED.

68. The Mohammedans in the spiritual world appear behind the Papists in the west, and form as it were a circle around them. The principal reason why they appear there is, because they acknowledge the Lord as the Greatest Prophet, the Son of God, the Wisest of all, who was sent into the world to teach men. Every one in that world dwells at a distance from the Christian centre where the Reformed are, according to his confession of the Lord and of one God; for that confession conjoins minds with heaven, and determines distance from the east, above which the Lord is. They who, from the life of evil, are not in that confession in heart, are in the hells beneath them.

69. Since religion makes man's inmost, and all the rest proceeds from the inmost, and since Mohammed is closely connected with their religion, therefore some Mohammed is always placed in their sight; and in order that they may turn their faces to the east, above which the Lord is, he is placed beneath in the Christian centre. It is not the Mohammed himself who wrote the Koran, but another who fills his office; nor is it always the same, but he is changed. Once it was one from Saxony, who had been taken by the Algerians, and became a Mohammedan; and who, having been also a Christian, was actuated to speak to them concerning the Lord, that He was not the Son of Joseph, as they believed in the world, but the Son of God Himself, by which he insinuated into them an idea of the unity of the Lord's Person and Essence with the Father. To this Mohammed, others afterwards succeeded, who were actuated to declare the same. By this means, many of them accede to a truly Christian faith concerning the Lord, and they who do so accede, are carried to a society nearer to the east, where communication is granted them from heaven, into which they are afterwards elevated. In the place where the seat of that Mohammed is, there appears a fire like a torch, that he may be known, but it is invisible to all but Mohammedans.

70. Mohammed himself, who wrote the Koran, is not to be seen at the present day. I was told, that in early times he presided over the Mohammedans, but because he wished to domineer over all things of their religion as a God, he was cast out of his seat which he held beneath the Papists, and was sent downwards, to the right side near the south. Once some societies of Mohammedans were excited by the malicious to acknowledge Mohammed as God. To quell the sedition, Mohammed was raised up from below and shown to them, and then I also saw him. He appeared like corporeal spirits, who have no interior perception, his face approaching to black; and I heard him saying these words only, "I am your Mohammed;" and soon sinking down, as it were, he returned to his place.

71. As regards their religion, it was permitted such as it is, because of its agreement with the genius of the Orientals, on which account, too, it was received in so many kingdoms; and because, at the same time, it made the precepts of the Decalogue a matter of religion, and it had something from the Word, and especially because it acknowledged the Lord as the Son of God, and the wisest of all. And besides it dissipated the idolatries of many nations. The reason why Mohammed was not made the means of opening to his followers a more interior religion, was on account of polygamy, which exhales uncleanness towards heaven; for the marriage of a husband with one wife, corresponds to the marriage of the Lord and the Church.

72. Many of them are receptive of truth, and they see justice in reasons, as I was enabled to observe from conversations with them in the spiritual world. I spoke with them concerning the One God, the resurrection, and marriage. Of *the One God* they said, that they do not comprehend the Christians when speaking of the Trinity, and saying that there are three Persons, and that each Person is God, and still saying that God is one. But I replied, that the angels in the heaven which is from Christians, do not speak thus, but say, that God is one in essence and in Person, and in whom is a Trine, and that men on earth call this Trine three Persons; and that this Trine is in the Lord. In confirmation, I read before them out of *Matthew* and *Luke*, all that is said there of the conception of the Lord from God the Father, as well as the passages in which He Himself teaches, that He and the Father are one. On hearing this they perceived it, saying that thus the Divine essence is in Him. Of the *Resurrection* they said, that they do not comprehend Christians when they speak of the state of man after death, making the soul like wind or air, and hence is deprived of all delight before its reunion with the body at the day of the Last Judgment. But I replied, that only some talk thus, but that they who are not of that class, believe they will come into heaven after death, will speak with the angels, and enter upon heavenly joy, which they do not conceive to be dissimilar to their joy in the world, although they do not describe it; and I told them, that at the present day, many particulars of the state after death are revealed to them, which they did not know before. Of *Marriage*, I have had many conversations with them, and have told them, among other things, that conjugial love is a celestial love, which can exist only between two, and that conjunction with many wives does not admit the celestial of that love. They heard my reasons, and perceived their justice; as also this, that polygamy was permitted them, because they are Orientals, who without this permission would have burned for foul adulteries more than Europeans, and would have perished.

X.

THE AFRICANS AND THE GENTILES IN THE SPIRITUAL WORLD.

73. The Gentiles who know nothing concerning the Lord, appear around those who know of Him; so that no others make the extreme circumferences but those who are altogether idolatrous, and have adored the sun and moon. But they who acknowledge one God, and make precepts like those of the Decalogue a part of religion and of life, are seen in a higher region, and thus communicate more immediately with the Christians in the centre; for thus the communication is not intercepted by the Mohammedans and Papists. The Gentiles are also distinguished according to their genius and faculty of receiving light through the heavens from the Lord; for there are some of them who are more interior, and some who are more exterior; and these diversities are not derived from their place of birth, but from their religion. The Africans are more interior than the rest.

74. All who acknowledge and worship one God, the Creator of the universe, have concerning Him the idea of Man: they say, that concerning God, no one can have any other idea. When they hear that many cherish the idea of Him as of a small cloud, they inquire where they are, and on being told that they are among Christians, they deny the possibility of it. But it is replied, that Christians have this idea, because God in the Word is called Spirit, and of a spirit, they are accustomed to think that it is like a particle of cloud, not knowing that every spirit and every angel is a man. Yet when they were explored, to discover whether their spiritual and natural ideas were alike, it was found that they were not alike with those who interiorly acknowledge the Lord as the God of heaven and earth. I heard a certain presbyter of the Christians saying, that no one can have an idea of the Divine Human; and I saw him led about to various Gentiles, in succession to those who were more and more interior, and from them to their heavens, and at length to the Christian heaven, and the interior perception of all concerning God was communicated to him, and he perceived that their idea of God was no other than the idea of Man, which is the same as the idea of the Divine Human.

75. There are many societies of Gentiles, especially from the Africans, who, on being instructed by the angels concerning the Lord, say that it cannot be otherwise than that God the Creator of the universe should appear in the world, because He created them and loves them; and that the appearance must be made before the very eyes in the Human form. When they are told, that He did not appear as the angels are wont to appear, but that He was born Man, and thus became visible, they hesitate awhile, and inquire whether He was born from a human father; and on hearing that He was conceived by the God of the universe, and born of a virgin, they say that thus

He has the Divine essence itself, which because it is infinite and life itself, He was not such a man as others are. They are afterwards informed by the angels, that in aspect He was like another man, but that when He was in the world, His Divine essence, which in itself is infinite and life itself, rejected the finite nature and its life from the mother, and thus made His Human, which was conceived and born in the world, Divine. The Africans comprehended and received these things, because they think more interiorly and spiritually than others.

76. Such being the character of the Africans even in the world, there is, at the present day, a revelation with them, which commencing in the centre, is communicated around, but does not reach the seas. They acknowledge our Lord as the God of heaven and earth, and laugh at the monks in those parts they visit, and at the Christians who talk of a three-fold Divinity, and of salvation by mere thinking, saying, that there is no man who has any worship, who does not live according to his religion, and that whosoever does not, must become stupid and wicked, because then he receives nothing from heaven. Ingenious wickedness they also call stupidity, because in it there is not life but death. I have heard the angels rejoicing over this revelation, because, by means of it, a communication is opened for them with the human rational, hitherto closed up by the blindness which has been drawn over the things of faith. It was told me from heaven, that the truths now published in *The Doctrine of the New Jerusalem Concerning the Lord, Concerning the Word*, and in *The Doctrine of Life for the New Jerusalem*, are orally dictated by angelic spirits to the inhabitants of that country.

77. When I spoke with the Africans in the spiritual world, they appeared in striped garments of linen: they said that such garments correspond to them, and that their women have striped garments of silk. Of their little children, they related, that they frequently ask their nurses for food, saying that they are hungry, and when food is set before them, they examine and taste whether it agrees with them, and eat but little; whence it is evident, that spiritual hunger, which is a desire of knowing genuine truths, produces this effect; for it is a correspondence. When the Africans wish to know their state as to the

affection and perception of truth, they draw their swords; and if these shine, they know that they are in genuine truths, in a degree according to the shining; this, too, is from correspondence. Of marriage they said, that it is indeed allowed them by law to have several wives, but that still they take but one, because love truly conjugial is not divided; and that if it is divided, its essence which is heavenly perishes, and it becomes external and thence lascivious, and in a short time grows vile, as its potency diminishes, and at length is loathed when the potency is lost; but love truly conjugial, which is internal, and derives nothing from lasciviousness, remains to eternity, and increases in potency, and in the same degree in delight.

78. Strangers from Europe they said, are not admitted, and when any penetrate into their country, especially monks, they ask them what they know, and when they relate any particulars of their religious persuasion, they call them trifles which offend their very ears, and they then send them out of the way to work, in order that they may do something useful; and if they refuse to work, they sell them for slaves, whom their law allows them to chastise at will; and if they cannot drive them to do anything useful, they are at last sold for a small sum to the lowest class.

XI.

THE JEWS IN THE SPIRITUAL WORLD.

79. Before the Last Judgment the Jews appeared in a valley in the spiritual world, at the left side of the Christian centre; but after it, they were transferred into the north, and forbidden to hold intercourse with Christians, except with those who wandered outside the cities. In that quarter, there are two great cities into which the Jews are led after death, and which before the judgment, were called Jerusalems, but after it by another name, because after the judgment by "Jerusalem" is meant the church in which the Lord alone is adored. In these cities, converted Jews are appointed over them, who admonish them not to speak scoffingly of Christ; and punish those who still do so. The streets of their cities are filled with mire up to the ankles, and their houses are full of uncleanness, from which they smell, so that they cannot be approached.

80. An angel sometimes appears to them in a middle altitude above them, with a rod in his hand, and gives them to believe that he is Moses, and exhorts them to desist from the madness of expecting the Messiah even there, because Christ, who governs them and all other men, is the Messiah: he says, that he knows it to be so, and also, that when he was in the world, he knew something concerning Him. On hearing this, they retire; the chief part of them forgetting, and only a few retaining it. They who do retain it are sent to synagogues, which are composed of the converted, and are there instructed; and if they receive instruction, they have new garments given them in place of their old tattered ones, and are presented with the Word neatly written, and with a dwelling in a not unsightly city. But they who do not receive, are cast down into the hells, beneath their great tract; many also are cast into forests and into deserts, where they commit robberies among themselves.

81. In that world, as in the former, they traffic in various things, especially in precious stones, which, by unknown ways, they procure for themselves from heaven, where there are precious stones in abundance. The reason of their trading in precious stones is, that they read the Word in its original language, and regard the sense of its letter as holy, and precious stones correspond to the sense of the letter of the Word. On the subject of this correspondence, see *The Doctrine of the New Jerusalem Concerning the Sacred Scripture* (n. 42–45). They sell their precious stones to the Gentiles who encircle them in the northern quarter. They also have the art of producing imitations, and of inducing the fancy that they are genuine; but they who do so are heavily fined by their governors.

82. The Jews are more ignorant than others as to their being in the spiritual world, believing that they are still in the natural world. The reason is, that they are wholly external men, and do not think at all of their religion from the interior. On this account also they speak of the Messiah just as they did before, as that He will come with David, and will go before them glittering with diadems, and introduce them into the land of Canaan; and that in the way, by lifting his rod, he will dry up the rivers which they will pass over; and that Christians, whom among themselves they call Gentiles, will then lay hold of the skirts of their garments, and humbly entreat to be allowed to accompany them, and that they will receive the rich according to their wealth, and that even the rich are to serve them. For they are unwilling to know, that "the land of Canaan" in the Word, means the church, and "Jerusalem," the church as to doctrine; and hence that "Jews" mean all those who will be of the Lord's church. That such is the meaning of "Jews" in the Word, may be seen in *The Doctrine Concerning the Sacred Scripture* (n. 51). When they are asked, whether they believe that they also are to enter the land of Canaan, they reply, that they will then descend into it. When it is said, that this land cannot possibly hold them all, they reply that it will then be enlarged. When it is said that they do not know where Bethlehem is nor who is of the stock of David, they say, that it is known to the Messiah who is to come. When asked, how the Messiah the Son of Jehovah, can dwell with those who are so evil, they reply that they are not evil. When it is said that still Moses describes them in his song (*Deut.* xxxii.) as the worst of nations, they answer, that Moses at that time was angry, because he was to die. But when they are told, that Moses wrote it by the command of Jehovah, they are silent, and go away to consult about the matter. When it is said, that they took their origin from a Canaanite, and from the whoredom of Judah with his daughter-in-law (*Gen.* xxxviii.), they are enraged, and say, that it suffices them to be descended from Abraham. When they are told that interiorly in the Word there is a spiritual sense, which treats of Christ alone, they reply, that it is not so, but that interiorly in the Word there is nothing but gold; besides many such things.

XII.

THE QUAKERS IN THE SPIRITUAL WORLD.

83. There are enthusiastic spirits, separated from all others, of such gross perception, that they believe themselves to be the Holy Spirit. When Quakerism commenced, these spirits, being drawn out as it were from encircling forests where they were wandering, obsessed many; infusing the persuasion that they were moved by the Holy Spirit; and because they perceived the influx sensibly, they became so completely filled with this kind of religious persuasion, that they believed themselves more enlightened and holier than the rest; therefore also they could not be withdrawn from their religious persuasion. They who have confirmed themselves therein, come into a similar enthusiasm after death, and are separated from the rest, and sent away to their like in forests, where, at a distance, they appear like wild swine. But they who have not confirmed themselves, being separated from the others, are remanded to a place like a desert, in the extreme borders of the southern quarter, where they have caves for their temples.

84. After the former enthusiastic spirits were removed from them, the trembling which from these spirits had seized their bodies ceased, and they now feel a motion in their left side. It was shown, that from the first time they have gone successively into worse things, and at length, by command of their holy spirit, into heinous things, which they divulge to no one. I conversed with the founder of their religious persuasion, and with Penn, who said that they had no part in such things. But they who have perpetrated such things, are sent down after death into a dark place, where they sit in corners, appearing like the dregs of oil.

85. Since they have rejected the two sacraments, Baptism and the Holy Supper, and still read the Word, and preach the Lord, and speak obsessed by enthusiastic spirits, and thus commix the holy things of the Word with truths profaned, therefore no society is formed of them in the spiritual world, but after being dissociated they wander hither and thither, and are dispersed, and gathered into the above mentioned desert

XIII.

THE MORAVIANS IN THE SPIRITUAL WORLD.

86. I have conversed much with the Moravians, who are also called Herrnhuters. They appeared, at first, in a valley not far from the Jews; but after being examined and detected, were conveyed away into uninhabited places. When they were being examined, they knew how with cunning to captivate minds, saying, that they were the remains of the Apostolic Church, and that therefore they salute each other as brethren, and those who receive their interior mysteries as mothers; also that they teach faith better than others and love the Lord because He suffered the cross, calling Him the Lamb, and the Throne of grace; with other like expressions, by which they induce the belief that the Christian church itself is with them. Those who are captivated by their smooth speeches and draw near to them, are examined by them to see whether they are such that they dare disclose to them their mysteries; if not they conceal them; if they can they reveal them; and then they warn and also threaten those who divulge their mystery concerning the Lord.

87. Since they did the same in the spiritual world, when yet it was perceived that interiorly they did not think so, in order that this might be disclosed, they were admitted into the lowest heaven; but they did not endure the sphere of the charity and faith of the angels there, and they fled away. Afterwards, because in the world they believed that they alone would be alive, and would enter the third heaven, they were also carried up into this heaven, but on perceiving the sphere of love to the Lord there, they were seized with anguish of heart, and began to suffer interior tortures, and to move convulsively, like those who are in the agony of death, therefore they cast themselves down headlong thence. In this manner it was first made manifest that inwardly they had cherished nothing of charity toward the neighbor, and nothing of love to the Lord. They were afterwards sent to those whose function it is to examine the interiors of the thoughts, and these said of them, that they hold the Lord in little estimation, that they reject the life of charity so as to abhor it, and that they make the Word of the Old Testament useless, and despise the Word of the *Evangelists;* only of their good pleasure selecting from Paul, where anything is said of faith alone; and that these are their mysteries, which they conceal from the world.

88. After it was made manifest that they acknowledge the Lord only as the Arians do, that they despise the Word of the *Prophets* and *Evangelists,* and hold a life of charity in hatred, when yet upon these three things as on pillars the whole heaven depends; then they who were in the knowledge and at the same time in the belief of their mysteries, were adjudged Anti-Christs, who reject the three essentials of the Christian church, namely, the Divine of the Lord, the Word, and charity, and were cast outside the Christian world into a desert, which is in the end of the southern quarter near the Quakers.

89. When Zinzendorf first came into the spiritual world after death, and was permitted to speak as before in the world, I heard him asserting, that he knew the mysteries of heaven, and that no one enters heaven who is not of his doctrine; and also, that they who do good works for the sake of salvation, are utterly damned, and that he would rather admit atheists into his congregation than them. The Lord, he said, was adopted by God the Father as His Son, because He endured the cross, and that still He was simply a man. When it was said to him, that the Lord was conceived by God the Father, he replied, that he thought of that matter as he chose, not daring to speak out as the Jews do. Moreover, I have perceived many scandals from his followers, when I have been reading the *Evangelists.*

90. They say, that they have a sensation, and thence an interior confirmation of their dogmas. But it was shown to them, that their sensation was from visionary spirits, who confirm a man in all his religious persuasions, and enter more closely with those, who like the Moravians, love their religious persuasion, and think much concerning it. These spirits also talked with them, and they mutually recognized each other.

THE END.